BUSINESS

and

GOVERNMENT

ISSUES OF PUBLIC POLICY

Marshall E. Dimock
New York University

FOURTH EDITION

HOLT, RINEHART AND WINSTON, INC.

New York

Library of Congress Catalog Card Number: 61-7854
21857-0511
Printed in the United States of America

PREFACE TO THE FOURTH EDITION

After four editions, covering a span of fifteen years, I have decided to telescope what was said in earlier prefaces and to state briefly what changes are to be found in this new edition. The users of the book are now familiar with its underlying philosophy and aims and hence an extended rationale is no longer needed.

Recently someone who has "taught" this book for several years wrote to me as follows: "So much has happened during the past five years, both in domestic and in foreign policy, that I cannot, in fairness to my students, use a book that is not up-to-date." Consider for a moment how right he is: important new labor legislation; two recessions; a turnover in Presidential and party leadership; a steady flow of vast sums into overseas military and assistance programs to the point where our gold reserves have been adversely affected; at the same time a considerable pick-up of Communist bloc expenditures on similar programs in uncommitted nations; revolutions and uprisings in many parts of the world, some of them close to home, and with this, a continual testing of the United Nations and of American foreign policy; successes and failures in our space program and in the domestic and international exploitation of atomic energy for peaceful purposes; continuing dissatisfaction with mounting agricultural surpluses and a reluctant admission that we still lack a successful farm policy; a mild upturn in anti-trust enforcement, but this accompanied by a gnawing doubt about the future of competition.

Nor is this all. The plight of the railroads has made it imperative that a new and possibly bold over-all transportation policy be adopted, and there is talk that the Kennedy Administration will tackle this problem head-on. Public-utility regulation and public power projects have been much in the news and new legislation has resulted: TVA, for example, has been authorized to sell bonds to the investing public. With the change of administration, it seems clear that the conservation of resources will come in for a hard scrutiny, for as other countries develop, they need more of their own primary resources and there is correspondingly less for export.

These and other problems dealt with in this edition have moved with startling speed during the past five years, so that almost every day brings a different problem to the center of the stage in public attention. What this underscores, of course, are the many basic problems of policy and of the business-government relationship that challenge our leadership as never before.

This book tries to take a sober and mature view of these problems and to advance alternative lines from which a constructive solution will likely emerge. The attempt is to get down to brass tacks, in the manner that a corporation official or a government official in the State Department or the Labor Department must. With the emphasis on solutions, certain things must be brought together:

First, much reliable and relevant fact. Theories alone will not serve our problems; they come *after* the facts and grow out of them. In this fourth edition I have tried to improve the factual content.

Secondly, the analysis of constructive alternatives for solving particular problems. The basic laws offer alternatives to which many fields of knowledge—especially economics, political science, and business administration—may contribute.

Finally, the suggestion of possible solutions—and here I have tried to be objective. I admit to generally liberal-democratic sympathies, however, and hence I favor competition, a balanced economy, and free-enterprise solutions.

The purpose of the course is to make students think; to arm them with facts; to encourage them to imagine that they are already policy officials; to make them realize that *both* business and government need to be effective if our values and our way of life are to endure. I try to give them the "feel" of institutions as I have experienced them, for quite deliberately my own experience has been in business, labor, agriculture, government, and international agencies such as the United Nations. Business and government, domestic and international affairs, economic and political policies—today these fields are so interrelated and mutually dependent that one can hardly profess any degree of competence in any of them without some knowledge of all, and especially of the *relationships* among them. Such is the objective of this book. I hope it will help to produce better policy-makers, decision-makers, and executives in both public and private affairs, because this is our urgent need today.

My acknowledgments go all the way back to the 1920s and I cannot repeat them here. Many of the most helpful hints have come from instructors using earlier editions, who not only call attention to errors of fact or interpretation but also make constructive suggestions for improving the book. My greatest debt is to my wife, Gladys Odgen Dimock, who diverted her attention from a book of her own and spent a solid year helping me with this revision. I should also like to thank many federal and business officials for responding to my pleas for information and assistance, and the staff of Baker Library at Dartmouth College where much of the reference work was done.

M.E.D.

Bethel, Vermont
January 10, 1961

CONTENTS

v

PART I

THE CONTRIVANCE OF PUBLIC POLICY

I
INSTITUTIONS AND PUBLIC POLICY

The study of business and government; issues of public policy: cause and effect of social change, belief systems, concept of the public interest; structure of the economy: varieties of control, economic functions of government, government as assistance; business-government relationship today.

The two most powerful institutions in society today are business and government. Where they meet on common ground—amicably or otherwise—together they determine public policy, both foreign and domestic, for the nation. Hence a study of business and government is a study of the dynamics of public policy formation. It tries to identify the problems arising in the business-government relationship, to explain the facts and the issues, to explore the institutional arrangements for settling them, and to suggest possible alternative arrangements.

The decisions of many people, businessmen and public officials alike, help to shape the course of public policy. Rapid social change, characteristic of the modern community, multiplies the issues and adds urgency to their solution. Hence the community needs men and women trained in the universities to understand why social change occurs in the first place, how it may be anticipated, how it is expressed, and how it may be directed so as to maintain an equilibrium—social, economic, and political—among the many interests and segments that constitute the national economy.

For this reason a study of business and government must also try to develop in the individual a judicious, unprejudiced approach to the subject. In the "Spectacular Sixties," as this new decade has already been called, a rational approach to public policy by leaders in business and government alike is the one most apt to prove advantageous for the nation.

The term "business" is used here in its broadest sense to mean the whole national economy. The so-called Big Three of business are the power blocs of industry, labor, and agriculture, all of them related and interdependent. In its broadest sense the term "government," on the other hand, is too broad to be useful in the present context, for it may be construed to cover every organized institution, public and private, in the nation. In common usage, however, the term "government" means the organized political state exercising legal authority over the people and the institutions coming within its jurisdiction.

Government is essentially like other institutions but differs in at least two respects: First, the organized political state is said to be sovereign in that it exercises a superior authority according to which all individuals and groups within its borders must obey it laws; and second, government is the only institution in which membership is not voluntary but imposed at birth on all within its domain; nor may the individual withdraw from the state without leaving the territory thereof. Since the Middle Ages when the church claimed and exercised a similar authority, no group except government has commanded such universal membership.

ISSUES OF PUBLIC POLICY

Some of the main issues to be examined in a study of business and government are (1) how to give pressure groups all the freedom they deserve and still find a way to protect the public interest through a balancing of claims; (2) how to strengthen the private competitive system and avoid monopoly; (3) how to assist segments of the economy without creating special privileges and unfair advantages; (4) how to settle labor disputes without giving government undue powers or without leading to retaliatory measures against management; (5) how to maintain the farm economy in sound health and still abide by the rules of free enterprise; (6) whether public utilities, being legalized monopolies, should be regulated, required to compete, or socialized; (7) what the social and political implications are of atomic energy; (8) how much government ownership should or can be countenanced in a free-enterprise system and how such ownership can be made efficient and held accountable; (9) what the role of government should be in stabilizing the economy through monetary, tax, social security, and other devices; (10) the degree to which economic planning is justified; (11) the problem of the conservation of basic natural resources; (12) the impact of war on the economy; (13) how to foster world trade; (14) what policy should guide assistance to underdeveloped nations; and (15) what policy should guide the new field of space explorations.

Although no one can become expert in any of these subjects in a single course, it is possible to develop not only an objective and realistic understanding of the issues of public policy but also an approach to their solution that will always be a useful tool whether one remains a private citizen, enters government service, or becomes a legislator. The most difficult problem confronting businessmen (and to this, add labor leaders and farmers), says Peter Drucker, is adjustment to change.[1] And that is a basic reason for studying public policy.

Public policy is what the guiding principle is or ought to be in various fields of national activity, such as foreign affairs, labor relations, agri-

---

[1] Peter Drucker, *The Practice of Management* (New York, 1954), Chap. 8.

cultural production, and the like. Public policy is the distillation of the policies of many *private* groups; their compromise and reconciliation at the point where official agencies have the power to decide, becomes the *public* policy on any subject. The result is usually a comprehensive public law such as the Sherman Antitrust Act in the field of industrial corporations or the Taft-Hartley Act regulating labor relations.

A study of public policy is also concerned with what that policy *should* be irrespective of what it is. Trade with foreign nations is restricted, for example, but should it not be free, and if so, to what extent? These are legitimate questions of public policy.

Finally, public policy is also a matter of *method,* in many ways the most rewarding aspect of the subject for our purpose. One studies public policy formation by finding out who wants what, and why; by discovering how each interest group in the nation gets what it wants; by learning how all parties of interest set about influencing public opinion and the constituted authorities of government, particularly the legislature; in other words, by studying the political process.[2] These steps are involved: First, what is the problem or the issue? Second, what are the facts? Third, what are the choices or alternative solutions? Fourth, which of these choices has been made and expressed in legislation? The final step is a critique of the attempted or proposed solution in the light of economic, political, social, or other relevant knowledge.

The Cause and Effect of Social Change

Rapid social change in recent years has made a study of public policy increasingly important. What is social change, what causes it, and what are its consequences? Some preliminary suggestions will be useful.

In general terms, social change accompanies the evolution of a community from the simple to the complex. The causes of such change are many but may be subsumed under the heading of challenge, or stress, either from within the community or from the outside. War and the threat of war are the principal challenges from the outside. Technological advances, congested populations in large urban centers, and the dislocations of economic depression are examples of stress stemming from the inside. Social change expresses itself as tensions, issues on which groups divide, and strongly felt wants that remain unsatisfied, all of which disturb the equilibrium of society. People's hopes and aspirations are still another source of unrest that stimulates change. So is education because as it enlarges people's understanding of the world they live in, it also increases their demands and their yearnings.

In whatever quarter social change occurs it generates currents that affect every other part of the community. An illustration is the familiar

[2] On these points, see Daniel Lerner and Harold D. Lasswell (eds.), *The Policy Sciences: Recent Developments in Scope and Method* (Palo Alto, Calif., 1952); and David B. Truman, *The Governmental Process* (New York, 1951).

spiral of wages and prices: labor demands and receives a wage boost; employers immediately raise their prices; thus farmers pay more for what they must buy, and those in the service trades or on fixed incomes (such as pensioners) begin to feel the "pinch" and are able to purchase less for what they have to spend. The purchasing power of money is somewhat reduced as a result; it may become harder to sell goods in foreign markets; and if the spiral is a serious and prolonged one, depositors may have less incentive to save or to invest. This is to say simply that a progressively complicated, mechanized, and urbanized society becomes increasingly interdependent, that sudden change in any part threatens the equilibrium of the whole, and that public policy must take into account all these reciprocating factors.

Belief Systems

Change and tension are also affected by people's economic, social, and political beliefs, what are sometimes called their ideologies or belief systems. The conservative, for example, is apt to resist change simply because it is change, or at least to slow it down and make it as orderly as possible, whereas the liberal is more receptive to innovations as long as they contribute to human satisfactions in the community. The conservative emphasizes property as a human value, thinks better of the past than of the future, respects authority and tradition, is inclined to pessimism about human nature, and is often self-centered regarding his own and his group's concerns. The liberal is much the opposite on each score. He is optimistic about human improvability, is more concerned with principles such as truth and justice than with the destinies of special groups including his own, inclines to distinguish between property and human rights (although respecting the former when it serves human ends), and is disposed to rely more on government and less on tradition to solve problems created by social innovation.

Professor Clinton Rossiter has identified seven shades in the political spectrum that influence men's views of the proper role of government in the community. These are: [3]

> 1. *Revolutionary radicalism,* a belief in replacing the past with sweeping social change brought about by violent methods, as under communism.
>
> 2. *Radicalism,* advocating fundamental change from the past but relying on peaceful methods and gradual progress.
>
> 3. *Liberalism,* a balanced view, appreciating the past but welcoming improvement by means of peaceful experiment and orderly change.
>
> 4. *Conservatism,* a discriminating defense of the social order against change or reform unless absolutely necessary.

[3] Clinton Rossiter, *Conservatism in America* (New York, 1955), pp. 11–15.

5. *"Standpattism,"* an indiscriminate attempt to prevent change in any direction for any purpose.

6. *Reaction,* an effort to return to an earlier period, by fairly radical means if necessary.

7. *Revolutionary reaction,* a return to the past but by the use of force and violence, as under fascism.

This political spectrum goes from left to right around the rim of a circle so that each category shades into its neighbors; thus one may speak of liberal conservatives and conservative liberals. The last category merges with the first across the bridge of violence.

For our purposes the differences between conservatives and liberals are reflected in their approach to what is desirable in the business-government relationship. Where the conservative believes that government should interfere in the economy as little as possible, the liberal justifies such interference if private methods fail to enforce competition, to solve a labor dispute, or to conserve natural resources since all these matters relate to human values that the liberal would preserve. Both conservatives and liberals, of course, believe government to have a necessary and legitimate role in the protection of liberty and property, which both groups espouse. Their difference usually lies in the methods by which they would instrument their common principles, the liberal being the more willing of the two to institute new or more sweeping procedures if the old ones become inadequate.

The Public Interest

Every category in the political spectrum claims to serve the public interest. But what is the public interest? In fact, this concept means different things to different people depending on their approach to issues of public policy and their political orientation. There are four main types of outlook, each stressing that which reflects the particular adherent's emphasis:

1. *Elitist:* the public interest is any policy serving the interest of the ruling group (also called the elite) on the theory that what is good for the group is good for the nation. There are many kinds of elite, based on class, birth, education, property ownership, or sheer power to dominate others.

2. *Nationalist:* the public interest is anything that contributes to the power of the nation-state, irrespective of the distribution of power and wealth within its borders.

√ 3. *Pluralistic:* the public interest is giving each major group in the community its "just" deserts and allowing none to take too much for fear of disturbing the equilibrium of society and causing serious tensions.

4. *Idealistic:* the public interest is any policy that fosters spiritual or absolute values such as truth, goodness, and beauty in such a way that

all classes and individuals are benefited in proportion to their ability and effort.

In practice, all four are often combined in varying proportions in any political system. To arrive at a satisfactory over-all definition of the public interest is difficult, but in a free economy where so much depends on common values and voluntary effort, this key concept is the touchstone of all public decision-making. For the individual such a definition must depend on what he considers important, what his values are. In our American democracy we usually say that the public interest is anything that makes all the people happier, freer, and stronger. This requires a constant regard for the question: Is the selfish interest of any group compatible with the equal rights of others and the welfare of all?

STRUCTURE OF THE ECONOMY

The main elements of the free-enterprise system are (1) the *private ownership* of property and of the means of production and distribution; (2) the acceptance of *profit-making* in business; (3) *freedom of choice* and entry to the market by employers, workers, and consumers; and (4) insistence on *competition.*

As to structure, the American economy is divided into a number of segments, each of a different type and under a different kind of control. Today, for example, five types predominate:

1. The *privately owned and controlled business concern* taking the form of an unincorporated firm or partnership, or of a small corporation whose ownership and management are in the same hands. To the extent that farms are privately owned and operated (which still applies to most of them), agriculture also comes under this heading.

2. The *semipublic corporation,* a giant enterprise with thousands or even hundreds of thousands of stockholders who own but do not manage the business. Generally speaking, this is the kind of organization whose shares are offered on a stock exchange, but large farming corporations also are included.

3. *Public utilities,* that are either privately or publicly owned but publicly regulated as legal monopolies with regard to prices, services, and the like.

4. *Cooperatives,* both consumer and producer, in which those who use the business own it and divide the net return, if any, among themselves.

5. *Governmental economic enterprise* where the government owns or operates an economic service, or does both, making use of either a regular administrative department of the government for that purpose, or a government corporation.

These five categories constitute the main classifications in our economy and determine its character as a mixed one. In the outline on page 10 they are arranged according to the type of control under which they normally operate.

Perhaps the most telling factor in the American economy, however, relates to the distribution of power and influence, for the course of the economy shifts according to the location of power, the methods by which it is acquired, the responsibility with which it is used, and the purpose for which it is employed. Numerically, the individual firm or partnership— of which there are more than 4 million in the United States—far exceeds any other form of business enterprise. That these units are small should not belie their importance since they are a bulwark of the free-enterprise system and collectively are not without influence.

Yet more than 700,000 semipublic corporations (especially the giants such as U. S. Steel and Dupont) have far more control over prices, mergers, competition, and demands for governmental assistance. M. A. Adelman reports that following World War II, the two hundred largest corporations held nearly one fourth of all income-yielding wealth and employed nearly one fifth of the total labor force outside of government.[4] For the same period, Adolf Berle found that large corporations grew nearly three times as fast as all others, except financial corporations like the big insurance companies, because they generate their own capital from funds that would otherwise be paid out to stockholders as dividends.[5] According to Adelman, 45 percent of all productive property in the United States was owned by 135 corporations in 1951.[6] In 1959, one half of one percent of all manufacturing corporations in the country had 57 percent of total sales.[7]

Varieties of Ownership, Operation, and Control

In every nation in the world today there is some admixture of both private and public ownership, operation, and control in the economy, with shadings from one to the other as in a spectrum. In the United States a considerable amount of collective action is combined with a vast amount of private responsibility, while at the other extreme, the USSR allows small areas of private ownership to remain in a system that is dominantly collective. Most other nations fall somewhere within this range of possibilities. In outline form the pattern is something like this:

[4] *The New York Times,* Dec. 2, 1951.

[5] U. S. House of Representatives, *Hearings* before the Subcommittee on Study of Monopoly Power (Cellar Committee) of the Committee on the Judiciary (81st Cong., 1st Sess., 1949), Serial No. 14, Pt. 1, p. 256.

[6] M. A. Adelman, "The Measurement of Industrial Concentration, *Review of Economics and Statistics* (Nov. 1951), p. 289.

[7] Reported in *The New York Times,* Feb. 3, 1959.

I. Ownership
　　1. Private
　　　　a. Small business or farm
　　　　b. A partnership arrangement
　　　　c. Semipublic corporation
　　　　d. Public utilities
　　2. Public, through a regular government department or a government corporation
　　3. Joint private-public, or mixed enterprise, backed by both public and private capital
　　4. Cooperative, producer or consumer, an enterprise owned by those whom it serves

II. Operation (sometimes separate from ownership)
　　1. Private ownership and operation
　　2. Public ownership and operation as in the case of public schools or the Tennessee Valley Authority
　　3. Private ownership and public operation where stock is subscribed by private enterprise and management is chosen by the government
　　4. Public ownership and private operation, as in public property leased to a private operator: timberland, for example
　　5. Cooperative ownership and operation

III. Control
　　1. Classified by *means* of control
　　　　a. Through public ownership, as by a government corporation
　　　　b. Through goverment regulation
　　2. Classified by *type* of control
　　　　a. Private control by
　　　　　　(1) Stockholders
　　　　　　(2) Owners-operators
　　　　　　(3) Other corporations
　　　　　　(4) Banks
　　　　b. Public control through
　　　　　　(1) Minor regulation
　　　　　　(2) Major regulation
　　　　　　(3) Public-utility regulation
　　　　　　(4) Government ownership and operation
　　　　　　(5) Wartime control
　　　　　　(6) National economic planning

Thus, when broken down into their components, the varieties of the public-private relationship appear in all their many forms. Instead of a mere twofold division as between private and public categories, there is a four- or fivefold classification at the very least. Today a mixed economy is the common pattern and terms such as capitalism, socialism, collectivism, and individualism, while still useful, are increasingly more academic than practical in their application.

The Four Economic Functions of Government

American government performs four principal functions relative to the economy, and in combination they constitute a greater or a lesser degree of control. First, government provides many forms of *assistance* such as research, the consular service, subsidies to shipping and agriculture, and the like. This assistance creates many problems of public policy, as illustrated in the disposal of surplus war plants after World War II.

Second, government *regulates* a large part of the economy, as in the work of the Interstate Commerce Commission relative to railroads, the Securities and Exchange Commission relative to investments, and state public-utility commissions relative to many kinds of public-utility enterprise such as electric power, natural gas, water supply, and telephones.

Third, government *operates* a certain number of economic services itself, including credit facilities for farmers, the power program of the Tennessee Valley Authority, municipal water systems, or a theater in the Panama Canal Zone.

Fourth and finally, in recent years government has undertaken a limited *planning and stabilization* function for the economy as a whole, as illustrated by the work of the National Resources Planning Board during the depression of the 1930s and the more recent work of the Council of Economic Advisers which is now an important part of our system.

All four functions of assistance, regulation, operation, and stabilization are closely related, and in practice no one of them can be pursued without reference to the others. Furthermore, all have been relatively constant in the role of government, although from time to time the degree of emphasis among them has varied rather widely. Herbert Hoover, for example, contended for "more business in government and less government in business," believing that the economic functions of government should be limited to protection coupled with as little regulation as possible. But his successor, Franklin D. Roosevelt, was prepared in the face of a serious economic dislocation to have the government undertake much broader economic responsibilities. In other words, the degree of emphasis at a particular time is as important as the classification itself. Theories are sometimes overwhelmed by the need to act.

Taken together, the control activities of government cut across all the broad categories of economic enterprise: entry into business, conduct of the enterprise, results, and relationships. First, government may determine the conditions under which persons or associations may *enter* certain lines of business as in the granting of a charter, a franchise, or a license, or permitting cattlemen, lumbermen, or oil companies, for example, to use public lands.

Second, government may regulate or assist the *conduct* of economic ventures of many kinds once they are under way. This is by far the largest area of public control and, generally speaking, may be classified into controls that merely lay down general standards and prohibitions and those that interfere with matters that may be considered managerial. The fixing of prices and wages during wartime and limitations on agricultural production are extreme examples of the control of the conduct of a private business enterprise.

Third, public control may extend to the *results* of business operations as in the limitation of public-utility profits, the recapture of railway earnings over a certain amount, and the imposition of excess-profits taxes on business generally.

Fourth and finally, government controls the *relationships* between the various segments of the economy, the purpose being to settle conflicts of interest or of legal right and to prevent an undue concentration of economic power in one place. Examples are the prohibition of interlocking directorates among corporations, the abolition of certain kinds of holding companies, and the regulation of labor relations. In many ways this last type of control calls for the highest kind of economic and political statesmanship, testing to the full the knowledge and insights of the nation's business leaders and government officials.

The Assistance Function

Of the four economic functions of government, assistance is relatively less emphasized in this study than the others because the regulatory and control functions have become so much more important. To keep our bearings, therefore, a brief consideration of assistance will be presented here.

Although on a comparative basis the function of assistance is less prominent than it used to be, it is still a large one. Thus, considering the whole of its activities, government does more to assist and to help develop industrial, labor, agricultural, and consumer interests than it does to regulate them. If this comes as a surprise, it is a measure of the degree to which we take for granted some of the most basic duties of a liberal-democratic government, and hence fail adequately to appreciate their value. These duties, among other things, provide basic services shared as a right by all citizens of a civilized and stable society: the legal system, the courts and police, the consular and diplomatic service, the postal system, laws regarding patents, incorporation, contracts, bankruptcy, and the like.

Assistance as such, however, usually means something more specific: First, government helps to *foster and promote* (language found in many federal statutes) a particular segment of the economy by creating a department or a bureau to look after its interests, granting such aids as tariff protection, favorable credit facilities, local tax exemption to new industries, and a vast amount of research and fact finding including crop reports, labor statistics, and foreign trade information. Second, government in certain areas grants a financial *subsidy*, as in outright cash paid to railways, motor carriers, the airlines, and offshore shipping; or it sells war plants to private companies at a fraction of the original cost.

Government assistance to industry and commerce started earlier and, until the onset of the depression of the 1930s, was larger than its corresponding service to agriculture and labor, but these two partners of industry have been catching up in recent years.[8] The consumer interest, although in terms of people the largest, is nevertheless inchoate and largely unorganized, and hence it is the hardest of all to serve. But here also advances are being made. The principle to remember is that in a pluralistic society such as ours government has a duty to promote all interests equally and fairly because equality of treatment is an essential of democracy and special favoritism a characteristic of minority rule.

In its responsibility to foster and promote industry and commerce, a brief list of government's activities includes the monetary system; the establishment of the Bureau of Standards; the collection and distribution of technical and trade information; the conduct of many kinds of research as in atomic energy; the maintenance of the channels of foreign trade; financial loans and guarantees; the policing of competition; subsidies to transportation and other industries; and tariff protection. Assistance to agriculture, which has greatly expanded since 1933, includes research and publication, counseling in all kinds of farm operation delivered to the farm by county agents, the sale and improvement of lands formerly part of the public domain, vast irrigation projects, the promotion of cooperatives, the provision of several kinds of credit facilities, rural electrification, crop insurance, the regulation of commodity and livestock exchanges, research and demonstration in home economics, and home and farm ownership programs. Finally, a sizable list of services also has been developed for the benefit of labor since the turn of the century, including labor statistics, wages and hours legislation, the protection of women and children, social security, workmen's compensation, free employment exchanges, laws guaranteeing the right to organize and to bargain collectively, facilities for helping settle labor disputes, and rules affecting fair employment practices. The subjects mentioned in these three lists constitute a large part of the discussion in the chapters that follow. Suppose, therefore, that we concentrate here on the matter of subsidies.

Subsidies. At one time or another government has made subsidy payments to nearly every major economic group in the nation, starting early in our history and continuing ever since. Although our national experience with subsidies is a long one, they remain a most difficult problem of public policy to those who must decide when to grant them, how much to grant, when to discontinue them, and how to reconcile them with the market-induced allocation of resources. In addition, there is a cause-and-

[8] For a brief but interesting historical resumé of this subject, see Merle Fainsod, Lincoln Gordon, and Joseph C. Palamountain, Jr., *Government and the American Economy* (New York, 3d ed., 1959), Chap. 5, "Promotion of Business Enterprise."

effect relationship between subsidy and regulation, the former tending to beget the latter. During the nineteenth century, for example, infant American railroads received public largess to the extent of some 183 million acres of public lands (some of it containing valuable timber and mineral resources) plus extensive tax exemptions, topped by cash contributions from various governmental agencies.[9] Improved transportation was accompanied by new towns, industries, and prosperity; free lands became valuable; the railroads soon became powerful and then abuses set in. At that point, labor and agriculture demanded that the railroads be regulated and their political power be checked. The railroads have been thoroughly regulated ever since and are only now trying to secure a relaxation of federal controls.

This story is repeated in the case of every new transportation industry that has been developed—waterways, motorways, shipping, aviation. Of these, shipping receives the most generous help today and hence is more dependent on the hand that feeds it than any other sector of the transportation industry. Subsidies are paid on both the building of ships and their operation in sums that amounted to an average of $17 million a year between 1937 and 1942, and $162 million annually during the postwar period from 1948 through 1953; in 1959 the figure stood at $257 million. The justification of such subsidies, of course, is national defense, with the economic fact of costs higher to American than to foreign shipbuilders as a supporting argument.

Building subsidies are usually one third the total cost but may run as high as one half or even more. When the huge liner *United States* was built, out of a total cost of $76.8 million, the American taxpayer contributed $43.9 million, or more than half, and three fourths of the remainder was secured on a loan from the federal government. In addition, the company was able to take advantage of the fact that taxes on subsidized shipping are waived as long as there is an agreement to build up reserves for new construction. In another example of government generosity, after World War I, 220 ships built at a cost of $516 million were sold to private companies for $41 million, and after World War II, 1950 ships built at a cost of $4.5 billion were sold for $1.7 billion.[10] In instances such as these the subsidy lies in the difference between the cost price to the government and the sale price to the private company.

It is not meant to imply by these illustrations that there is necessarily anything wrong with such policies. It is chiefly after a major war that criticism arises. At this time government is anxious to "get out of business," and its sales of surplus properties—usually to the biggest and most powerful companies—look suspiciously like "give-aways." In the case of

[9] The total for railways was $1.44 billion up to 1936. See Federal Coordinator of Transportation, *Public Aids to Transportation* (Washington, D.C., 1940), Vol. 1, p. 19.

[10] See Blair Bolles, *How to Get Rich in Washington* (New York, 1952), p. 112. On the larger issues, consult Truman C. Bigham and M. J. Roberts, *Transportation* (New York, 2d ed., 1952), Chap. 22.

iron and steel 116 plants costing $750 million (they were the newest and best of their kind) were sold at the end of World War II for $260 million, or at the rate of 35 cents on the dollar. When it is realized that $20 billion worth of plant and $40 billion worth of other materials had to be disposed of on a similar basis, the magnitude of the forces involved can be appreciated. So important did surplus disposal become after World War II that some writers have called it a major cause of economic concentration and a factor in the drift toward public control and socialism.[11]

To foster and promote industry through the work of the Department of Commerce is a necessary and proper function of government, but it is obviously improper when an interest is permitted to make raids on the public treasury with no pretense of a comparable return to the public interest. Between these two extremes are many vexing problems of public policy as interesting to the moral philosopher as they are to the professional economist.

THE BUSINESS-GOVERNMENT RELATIONSHIP TODAY

Although the business-government relationship has always existed in some degree since governments first appeared in the world, it has greatly changed in character as society has become complex. A simple society is generally an integrated one, and hence government and business are less likely to be considered as separate entities.[12] Indeed, during most of recorded history business and government have been so closely united as hardly to be distinguishable except as separate studies are made of them in retrospect. In western Europe they began to be considered separate institutions at about the end of the eighteenth century along with the rise of the first industrial revolution. Since then both have grown by enormous strides, pacing each other and becoming progressively separate but interdependent as well.

In the United States today we have concluded a second industrial revolution based on technology and have started a third, induced by the practical application of atomic energy in industry and of automation almost everywhere: the factory, the office, the farm, even the home. Our industrial development stems from physical invention having direct economic uses, plus a rapid growth of social invention, especially the giant association. In industry this association is the giant corporation, in labor it is the industrial union, in agriculture it is the big commercial farm plus farmer to retail-outlet control by a single corporation; and in government it is the large, consolidated agency such as the Housing and

---

[11] Walter Adams and Horace M. Gray, *Monopoly in America* (New York, 1955), Chap. 6, "Disposal of Surplus Property."

[12] See Margaret Mead (ed.), *Cooperation and Competition among Primitive Peoples* (New York, 1939), and Melville J. Herskovits, *The Economic Life of Primitive Peoples* (New York, 1940).

Home Finance Agency or the Defense Department. From all these developments the distillation is concentration of power, clashes of vigorous pressure groups, and gropings for a new balance between government and the economy.

To project future tendencies is harder than to summarize the past, but the attempt may prove useful. Despite periodic setbacks, there is more individual liberty today than there was three or four hundred years ago or even more recently. But in the context of economic and political institutions, individualism is giving way to the need for group action because as parts of a larger whole men no longer have so much right as formerly to act in an unpredictable fashion. Large corporations with hundreds of thousands of employees and stockholders facetiously refer to themselves as "socialisms," so complex and impersonal has become the organization of economic functions in their domains. Small units of business enterprise, like the individualism on which they are based, tend to give ground before the thrusts of giant competitors. Labor unions are becoming larger and more powerful under the expert guidance of experienced leaders, and the influence of labor in the political field is now a major one. Agriculture, with a long history of pressure-group and political activity, is generally effective in making its wants known at all levels of government. The character of the free-enterprise system and of private property is changing. Government concern for the economy in all its components has tended upward since the Civil War. Outside the United States various forms of collectivism have appeared that would be unwelcome in this country.

It is likely that all these tendencies will become more pronounced in the future. Here is additional reason, therefore, to study the meaning and implications of the business-government relationship in the modern economy, for in it are located the controls that can assure economic equilibrium, the essential freedoms, and orderly progress in an age dominated by large institutions.

Supplementary Reading

Lerner, Daniel, and Harold D. Lasswell (eds.), *The Policy Sciences: Recent Developments in Scope and Method* (Palo Alto, Calif., 1952). Methods of investigating public policy.

Steiner, George A., *Government's Role in Economic Life* (New York, 1953), Chaps. 3, 4, 7, 8. A longer account of the historical evolution of the business-government relationship.

Berle, A. A., Jr., *The 20th Century Capitalist Revolution* (New York, 1954). The growing power and political character of corporate life.

Boulding, Kenneth E., *The Organizational Revolution* (New York, 1953). Changing power relationships in society.

——, *Principles of Economic Policy* (Englewood Cliffs, N.J., 1958). Broad perspectives.

Orton, William, *The Economic Role of the State* (Chicago, 1950). The underlying theory of the economic functions of government.

Clark, John M., *Economic Institutions and Human Welfare* (New York, 1957).
Wisdom from one of the pioneers in this field of study.

MacIver, Robert M., *Democracy and the Economic Challenge* (New York, 2d
ed., 1952). Power relationships and equilibrium.

Dewhurst, J. Frederic, and Associates, *America's Needs and Resources* (New
York, Twentieth Century Fund, 1955). The basic facts; analyzes the postwar
American economy and the prospects for it during the ensuing decade.

Fainsod, Merle, Lincoln Gordon, and Joseph C. Palamountain, Jr., *Government
and the American Economy* (New York, 3d ed., 1959). Historical summary.

Lyon, Leverett S., Myron W. Watkins, and Victor Abramson, *Government and
Economic Life* (Washington, D.C., Brookings Institution, 1940), 2 vols. A
comprehensive work, somewhat old but still good.

Lane, Robert E., *The Regulation of Businessmen* (New Haven, Conn., 1954).
How the business community reacts to public control.

Council of Economic Advisers, *Business and Government, Fourth Annual Report
to the President* (Washington, D.C., 1940). An official pronouncement.

American Economic Association, *Readings in the Social Control of Business*
(Philadelphia, 1942). A symposium, with emphasis on the enforcement of
competition.

Means, Gardiner C., *The Structure of the American Economy* (U. S. National
Resources Committee, Washington, D.C., 1939, 1940). The most complete
study of its kind.

————, "The Distribution of Control and Responsibility in a Modern Economy," in B. E. Lippincott (ed.), *Government Control of the Economic Order*
(Minneapolis, 1935). The need for economics and political science to work
together.

Adams, Walter, *The Structure of American Industry* (New York, 2d ed., 1954).
Deals with size and power in the principal segments.

Watson, Donald S., *Economic Policy: Business and Government* (New York,
1960). The first five chapters, dealing systematically with public policy, are
especially recommended.

Smith, Howard R., *Government and Business: A Study of Economic Evolution*
(New York, 1958). The economic-history approach.

Dahl, Robert A., and Charles E. Lindblom, *Politics, Economics, and Welfare*
(New York, 1953). A theoretical analysis.

2
PRESSURE GROUPS AS CATALYSTS

Pressure groups, government, and the economy; the issues; lobbying; the Big Three—industry, labor, and agriculture; relationships to the executive branch; political parties; businessmen in politics; lobbying abuses and legislative control.

The free-enterprise economy of the United States is large, diverse, amorphous, and increasingly dependent on and hence concerned with the course of public policy at all levels of government from the federal to the local. In this apparent planlessness that characterizes the business-government relationship, pressure groups are the catalysts that coalesce and mobilize the demands of the many sectors of the economy so as to present them more or less intelligibly to voters, to legislatures, and to the executive branches of government.

Each pressure group works primarily for itself, or in a limited or temporary alliance with others. Hence governments on the receiving end of these representations must sort them out, judge them against the criterion of the public interest, honor some, and reject others so as to maintain a balance among them.

A *pressure group* is an association of individuals or groups whose interests are similar, organized and often liberally financed to try to influence elections, legislation, and administration. A *lobby* is the functioning arm of a particular pressure group and consists of one or more people whose job it is to work on government officials in every branch—not excluding the judiciary—to further the interests of the parent body.

Pressure groups exercise a greater influence in the United States than elsewhere, the reasons being that our political-party system is looser, the nation is industrially and institutionally more complex, and our attitude toward private enterprise and its servant, government, is different from that in most other nations. In addition, interest groups thrive best where there is the greatest amount of freedom, and the plethora of our interest groups may therefore be taken as evidence that we are free.

The activities of pressure groups are guarded under the first amendment to the Constitution which protects the right of petition. This right is not, however, wholly unrestricted, for legislatures have an equal right to outlaw certain abuses deemed contrary to the public interest, as in the case of bribery, extortion, and the like. Abuses by pressure groups may be carried to such lengths that, as Stuart Chase has said in his book *Democracy under Pressure,* interest groups and the "me-first" boys who run them are often "the despair of patriots" so selfish and narrow does their outlook sometimes become.[1] The problem is to prescribe ground rules that will preserve the right of group interests to be heard and at the same time prevent a haphazard struggle between them in matters of social action affecting the whole nation.

Pressure groups are part of the democratic process in that they provide continuous consultation between government and the governed, they supply political parties, legislatures, and administrators with highly technical and specialized advice, and they convey people's real feelings and opinions about a proposed policy or action. In other words, pressure groups are one of the means by which people participate in a democratic government. The other side of the picture is that not all interests are organized; among those that are, some are much stronger than others; and in some cases the leadership of a particular group does not faithfully reflect its attitudes and true desires.

The major issues of public policy created by pressure-group activity in the United States, therefore, are these: Can enough economic statesmanship be engendered within our competitive system and among its pressure groups to assure a balancing of power in the public interest? And can enough political statesmanship be developed on the part of legislators and government officials to recognize the just claims of pressure groups and to reject those that constitute special privilege or an undue concentration of power in one place?

Pressure groups are not so large as government or the economy, but they are more cohesive and more clear-cut in their objectives. Most, but not all, are organized for an economic purpose. They may or may not devote their full attention to influencing government; trade unions and trade associations, for example, perform a variety of functions of which pressure on government is only one, although frequently the main one. Pressure groups have members, an organization, paid officials, and often impressive financial resources. In 1950, for example, lobbyists in Washington reported spending an aggregate of $10.3 million, $1.3 million of which was by the American Medical Association alone. Since then, reported expenditures have fallen to less than half for reasons that will be discussed below, although registered lobbyists have sharply increased from 312 in 1950 to nearly 1000 in 1955. However, the figures for both registrants and expenditures are imperfect because of loopholes in the law requiring such information to be reported. Experts have estimated that in fact lobbying is a billion-dollar business, and those on the receiving end of such pressures have little doubt of it.[2]

---

[1] Stuart Chase, *Democracy under Pressure* (New York, 1945), pp. 6, 9.
[2] *The New York Times,* June 13, 1954.

So well do organized pressure groups perform their function as a link between the people and their government that increasingly they tend to eclipse political parties themselves. They influence parties in the formulation of policy and even in the choice of candidates. What is now sometimes called the Third House of Congress, meaning the pressure groups, is more than a figure of speech. In a publication of one of the most effective lobbies in Washington—the National Lumber Manufacturers' Association—it has been frankly observed that "It is largely true that an industry and its members get or do not get their due at Washington, as they are, or are not, well represented." [3] Pressure groups seem to have taken to heart a French proverb that "Those who are absent are always in the wrong" because few are ever absent when a subject of even remote importance to them is under consideration, at either the legislative or the administrative level.

HOW PRESSURE GROUPS OPERATE

Pressure groups converge on state capitals and municipal buildings as well as on Washington, so that each group of any importance has three or more levels of activity. Wherever laws are made and administered, there pressure groups will be found—assuming, of course, that their interests are at stake. Studies made in New York and New Jersey show that lobbying is relatively as great, if not in fact greater, at state capitals than in Washington.[4] Nationwide business concerns such as insurance companies, railroads, electric power companies, and the chain stores take pride in their national coverage and in some cases, notably the insurance companies, they operate a central clearing house of information concernnig legislative trends of interest to the group. Municipal lobbying is usually not so formal as that at state and federal capitals, but for that reason it is often more effective.

The two aspects of activity by a pressure group are (1) an attempt to prevent other interests, including the government, from affecting something that the group is against—this is the defensive aspect of its work—and (2) an attempt to "put over" on the government and on other interests the things the group favors, this being the aggressive aspect. The pressure-group listening post in Washington or at the state capitals is on the alert for danger signals and for chances to secure favorable action on any law or administrative action that affects the group's interests. The lobby staff may include a former government official or even a former Congressman, who has the advantage of being able to go onto the House and Senate floors and into the private cloakrooms because all former members of Congress are entitled to keep the "privilege of the floor" for life. The staff

---

[3] *Highlights of a Decade of Achievement of the National Lumber Manufacturers' Association* (1929), p. 54.

[4] Belle Zeller, *Pressure Politics in New York* (New York, 1937), and D. D. McKean, *Pressures on the Legislature of New Jersey* (New York, 1938).

may also include women lobbyists on the ground that they are more effective than men in the use of certain traditional techniques—those of a normally attractive woman, for example, if not exactly those of a Cleopatra or a Mata Hari. A research staff studies trends and arms the director with the ammunition he needs for both the defensive and the aggressive phases of the campaign. The director is also busy building up sentiment among his constituents and, as is the wont of oligarchy everywhere, impressing them with the dangers that beset them but for his good offices. This is usually done through a monthly publication of some kind giving inside information as far as it can be ascertained.

A pressure-group campaign usually includes long-term objectives aimed at influencing government and public opinion in favor of the viewpoint of the pressure group, together with short-range action programs to defeat or pass a particular law or influence an administrative order of an executive agency. Most of the money is spent on the long-range program, an activity euphemistically referred to as "education" but popularly called propaganda. This is the realm of ideology, attitudes, and emotional coloration. People have repeatedly been told, for example, that business is efficient and government wasteful; that bureaucratic officials eat holes in our liberties while businessmen release productive forces in the economy; that if labor becomes too powerful, it will take over the free-enterprise system; that any comprehensive national health program is necessarily socialistic. All these assertions, of course, are susceptible of objective study and any intelligent person may form a rational opinion on them. But the propagandist assumes that most people are too busy, too lethargic, or already too rigidly oriented to show any interest in so logical an inquiry, and often he is right. He wants to hook people and keep them hooked, a job that is seldom very difficult.

Methods Employed

Every medium of communication and influence is used by the pressure group to secure its ends. Paid advertising may result in favorable editorials; sponsored radio and television programs stress points of view along with plugs for particular products; endowed professorships have even been established, selected students offered scholarships, and universities given grants for special research purposes; canned stories and editorials are sent out to weekly and daily newspapers; news letters and "fact" sheets are circulated; lecturers are hired for women's clubs; sometimes Congressmen themselves are hired to write an article or to deliver a speech at an especially attractive fee; contributions are made to campaign funds; free books and research studies are distributed to economists, journalists, businessmen, and Congressmen; organizations with patriotic-sounding names sometimes serve as fronts for groups whose real intent is concealed so far as possible.

When government is about to act on a pending issue, other methods are added. The lobbyist appears along with his rivals at hearings before Congressional committees and writes speeches to be delivered by friendly Congressmen on the floor of the legislature; cocktail and dinner parties are given (the Reciprocity Treaty of 1854 was said to have been "floated through on waves of champagne"); organized delegations are called in from the hinterland to visit key members of Congress; more or less disguised bribes are sometimes paid for votes (formerly a more popular procedure than at present); pressure is stepped up on newspapers, radio, television, and magazines to run features that will help one side and hinder the other. Deals also are made with other pressure groups in which future support is promised for help on the issue at hand. In 1955, for instance, a lobbying organization trying to defeat the adoption of a measure affecting the Interstate Commerce Commission issued printed instructions for the release of a flood of mail to the members of the House and Senate Judiciary Committees considering the measure. "Do not be content with the activity of your own group in this important matter," it said in part. "There must be traffic, transportation, and shipper groups, chambers of commerce, trade associations, and other groups in your local area who will adopt appropriate resolutions." [5] With the rapid improvement of communication media, the battle is fought on all fronts, the heat is on most of the time, and the legislator finds himself in the center, pulled this way and that depending on the strength and persistence of the contestants.

When a number of lobbies converge on an important issue, the result may be confusing to the newcomer, but to the old hand it is like the command of the referee to shake hands at the start of a prize fight. In the spring of 1955, for example, the Senate was debating an extension of the Reciprocal Trade Agreements Act. Lined up against the bill was the so-called Nation-wide Committee of Industry, Agriculture, and Labor on Import-Export Policy, which had already spent many thousands of dollars in its campaign to defeat the measure outright and was prepared to spend a good many more. The Committee for a National Trade Policy, on the other hand, headed by the brother of the late Senator Robert A. Taft, was just as energetically in favor of the measure. The Independent Petroleum Association of America and the Foreign Oil Policy Committee, representing the small oil companies, opposed the bill on the score that it would permit the importation of "cheap, foreign oil," but at the same time an informal organization of six major oil companies was working to continue these imports.

According to *The New York Times*, these various lobbies dramatized, emphasized, publicized, and insisted on their various points of view, using all types of devices to air their views, including formal testimony presented by officers of the lobbies before committees of Congress, news releases and handouts, "information digests," and statistical tables tumbling in increasing volume from the capital's innumerable mimeograph machines. Con-

[5] *The New York Times*, Dec. 20, 1955.

gressmen were "buttonholed," invited to parties (organized to create an atmosphere of "jolly good will"), and subjected to the device of pressure by indirection according to which a lobbyist contacts a prominent community leader he knows in a Congressman's home district who in turn gets in touch with the Congressman. The powerful oil companies are especially successful with this kind of pressure and, because it is indirect rather than direct lobbying, none of the expense involved needs to be reported under the law. By experienced hands at the lobbyist game, reported *The New York Times*, "all these techniques are used with the smoothness of long practice." [6]

The effect of such techniques on individual Congressmen, however, may not always be as the lobbyist hopes; indeed, it may be exasperating to the point of intolerability. More than a hundred years ago, for instance, Senator Thomas Hart Benton of Missouri told a lobbyist that he would help to secure a ship subsidy only on condition that "when the vessels are finished they will be used to take all such damned rascals as you, sir, out of the country" [7]; and in more recent times Congressman John Steven McGroarty of California wrote to a constituent, "One of the countless drawbacks of being in Congress is that I am compelled to receive impertinent letters from a jackass like you in which you say I promised to have the Sierra Madre mountains reforested and I have been in Congress two months and haven't done it. Will you please take two running jumps and go to hell." [8]

WHO'S WHO AMONG PRESSURE GROUPS

The pressure interests fall into six principal groupings, the first of which is the Big Three of industry, labor, and agriculture. Then (2) there are the professional societies representing medicine, dentistry, accounting, law, education, and the like. (3) The organized forces of reform and religion such as the Roman Catholic Church and the National Council of Churches of Christ in the U.S.A., a Protestant group, form an important category as do (4) the various women's associations such as the League of Women Voters, the American Association of University Women, and the Daughters of the American Revolution. (5) Another subdivision includes patriotic and peace groups such as the Veterans of Foreign Wars, the National Council for the Prevention of War, and the like. And then (6) there are organizations for the preservation of civil rights, such as the American Civil Liberties Union and the National Association for the Advancement of Colored People.

Finally, in addition to these six categories, the administrative side of

[6] *Ibid.*, Apr. 26, 1955.

[7] John F. Kennedy, "To Keep the Lobbyist within Bounds," *The New York Times Magazine*, Feb. 19, 1956. p. 11.

[8] John F. Kennedy, "The Challenge of Political Courage," *The New York Times Magazine*, Dec. 18, 1955, p. 13.

government itself is often referred to as a pressure group, and in a sense the characterization is accurate. On the other hand, when a government agency undertakes to lobby for or against a particular piece of legislation it is more often than not in response to the demand of a private pressure group and in concert with it. In other words, government in a democracy does not have a separate will of its own because it must operate within the electorate's zone of acceptance. Strictly speaking, therefore, government does not constitute a separate category in the who's who of pressure groups, though its influence, of course, may count for a good deal under the right circumstances.

It is with the Big Three that this chapter is immediately concerned.

The Business Lobbies

The most powerful group of lobbies are those of organized employers. This category includes not only the two giants—the National Association of Manufacturers and the United States Chamber of Commerce—but also thousands of trade associations and public-utility organizations. In the industrial field the picture is of two great stars surrounded by a galaxy of satellites.

To what extent do these business lobbies present a common front? In recent years the number of separate business enterprises outside of agriculture has ranged from 3.2 million to 4.6 million, of which more than 4 million are classified as small business whose pressure-group quotient is practically nil. Like the consumer who is everybody, small business, who is nearly everybody in industry, is virtually unorganized as a single cohesive group.

As a general rule, employer pressure-group power is directly related to size, and the larger the corporation the greater the influence derived from pressure-group activity. The reason is that power incurs a social responsibility that often must be enforced through the means of government. Thus the smaller and less consequential an economic unit, the greater is its freedom from public interference, while big business is vulnerable to successful attack by those who demand closer regulation for their own protection. But again, the large unit is well able to lobby for the purpose, among other things, of avoiding regulation. A rapidly growing corporation acquiring a nation-wide coverage and gobbling up smaller competitors soon develops a political sixth sense akin to that of the professional politician; naturally it engages in pressure-group politics and also, as a rule, in party politics as well. The motive and the means are both inherent in size.

The National Association of Manufacturers is the older of the two main pressure houses of organized business, largely financed by a small group of powerful corporations and directed by a much smaller group within the main body. It was not always thus. For a long time after the NAM was founded in 1895 by 256 firms, its membership and direction were primarily controlled by small manufacturers. It now has 22,000 members and in recent years has increasingly become the spokesman for big business. Its policies are conservative.[9] The change occurred with the advent of the New Deal in 1933. Since then the NAM has largely concentrated its fire on organized labor, labor legislation, and "creeping socialism." At about the same time the NAM also started an ambitious campaign of "public education," making use of many media including billboards and enlarging its annual expenditures for this purpose by some 200 percent in three years. The NAM *News* once reported that "If all NAM-produced pamphlets ordered for distribution to employees, students, and community leaders in 1950 had been stacked one on top of the other, they would have reached nearly four miles into the sky—the height of 16 Empire State Buildings." Since the creation of the Literature Department of the NAM in 1946, more than 18.6 million pamphlets had been produced and distributed, the most popular type being the full-color comic-type booklet.

Larger than the NAM, the U. S. Chamber of Commerce is more representative of smaller (but not the smallest) units of business and is often more powerful both in Washington and in the state capitals. Created in 1912, the Chamber of Commerce is a federation of several thousand local chambers of commerce, trade associations, and the like, plus thousands of separate firm members. Unlike the NAM, it speaks more for groups than for individuals—an important point to remember when assessing its influence. Its policies are determined at annual meetings and by occasional polls of member associations on pending issues. The Chamber of Commerce also carries on an extensive research program and publishes *Nation's Business*.

Being a more accurate cross-section of American business than the NAM, the Chamber of Commerce is interested in a wider range of questions, and its views are usually less conservative. As much opposed to "government interference" as the NAM, the Chamber of Commerce nevertheless gives careful attention to improving the efficiency and responsibility of government. Though critical of government in time of prosperity, during a depression the Chamber of Commerce becomes more "cooperative." During the 1930s, for example, it approved several New Deal measures including the regulation of security issues, aid to agriculture, and certain forms of relief and public works programs that it considered constructive. But it also consistently favors self-government in business, resists unnecessary government interference, and unalterably opposes the government entering business itself in competition with private enterprise. Since 1957, worried over the political power of organized labor, it has taken a cue from the General Electric Company and spearheaded a drive to get businessmen to enter politics themselves.

Bolstering the NAM and the U. S. Chamber of Commerce are some

[9] On the attitude of the NAM, see V. O. Key, *Politics, Parties, and Pressure Groups* (New York, 4th ed., 1958).

8000 trade associations, roughly a quarter of which are national in scope. A trade association is a voluntary cooperative non-profit organization composed of members who are ordinarily competitors, engaged in a particular type of business enterprise such as the production of oil, the manufacture of bird seed, or the retail sale of drugs. In form, such an association may be corporate or noncorporate, is managed by a board of directors, and employs a staff that normally enjoys a great deal of discretion so that, as a class, trade-association executives are influential people.

Trade associations have greatly increased in the past few decades partly because on two occasions, at least, they were encouraged by the government itself. The first time was during the Hoover administration, described by one historian as a "government alliance with the great trade associations" or as Mr. Hoover himself put it, a "passing from a period of extreme individualistic action into a period of associated activities." The second occasion was in the early days of the New Deal when for a short time under the National Recovery Administration the national economy was run by a formal alliance between trade associations and the federal government.

Trade associations usually perform a variety of interrelated functions but all point toward influencing or restraining the government in ways that will help the industry in question. As a service agency for that industry, the trade association undertakes research, the gathering of statistics, and the promotion of trade in addition to lobbying. It also sometimes encourages monopoly by uniting corporations in a scheme of collective bargaining with regard to allocating markets, fixing prices, and adopting uniform procedures on such matters as bidding, freight rates, fair-trade practices, and the like.

The degree to which these associations are interwoven in the American economy is illustrated in the published hearings of the Temporary National Economic Committee. Referring to these hearings, at which business gave forth over a three-year period more economic information than government had ever before received, Lynch has remarked that "nowhere, it seems, could the story of the American economy be told without involving trade associations." One trade association after another complained to the committee of discriminations against it by other associations; but "While trade associations were thus making public complaints against barriers which have damaged their economic interests," added Lynch, "other associations were quietly working and lobbying to perpetuate these barriers and to erect others to assure themselves of the benefits such impediments create." [10]

One of the strongest trade associations operates in the field of insurance. In the TNEC hearings, for example, the insurance business was represented by two trade groups, the Association of Life

[10] David Lynch, *The Concentration of Economic Power* (New York, 1946), pp. 100–101.

Insurance Presidents and the Group Association. In testimony before the committee it was shown that the Association of Life Insurance Presidents disposed of an annual budget of nearly half a million dollars, that it had successfully lobbied against savings-bank insurance laws in New York, Pennsylvania, Rhode Island, Missouri, and elsewhere, and that while undertaking to defeat a tax measure in Florida it had prepared a complete card-index file of the members of the legislature, giving personal information and indicating the most effective approach in each case. In addition, the association admitted trying to gain control of the Georgia legislature by entertaining, contributing to campaign funds, attempting to elect legislators who "owe us something instead of our owing them," and "seeing that their wives and daughters were looked after properly." [11] The insurance lobby has long been recognized as one of the most effective in the nation.

In addition to these groups representing the business community, a more recent organization is the Committee for Economic Development. Founded in 1942 primarily in an effort to discover the means of converting from a wartime to a peacetime economy without excessive dislocations, this agency was reorganized on a permanent basis in 1946. Its board of trustees consists of 150 businessmen and educators and its goals are (1) high levels of employment, increasing productivity, high living standards, and greater economic stability in a dynamic free society, and (2) public understanding of these objectives and ways in which they can be reached. The CED is primarily a research organization, but because of its backing, its ample resources, and the fact that its publications are authoritative, it also constitutes an effective lobby when it wants to be heard.

In summary, the pressure groups of industry are the smallest of the Big Three as far as members are concerned, but they are the wealthiest. What management lacks in size, therefore, it makes up in financial power. The money power in politics, said William Bennett Munro in his book, *The Invisible Government,* is the power that rules; it may lose out temporarily from time to time but its staying power is greater than that of any other competitor for influence.

The Lobbies of Organized Labor

Labor organizations are not so numerous as those representing industry, but the aggregate of their members is greater. Out of a total of 71.3 million organizables in 1960, about 18 million (approximately one fourth) belong to unions, the majority affiliated with the merged American Federation of Labor and the Congress of Industrial Organizations. The four railroad brotherhoods, the United Mine Workers, and

---

[11] Temporary National Economic Committee, *Hearings,* Pt. 10 (1940), pp. 4153–4447.

a few smaller unions remain separate, and the International Brotherhood of Teamsters has been ejected. But the bulk of organized labor is now under a single roof for the first time since the CIO separated from the AFL in 1935.

With regard to internal organization the AFL was a loose arrangement of sovereign unions constituting a kind of confederation under which the separate unions enjoyed a good deal of autonomy. The CIO, on the other hand, assumed from the outset a greater responsibility for creating and maintaining its member unions and hence established a more centralized internal setup. Both labor organizations, however, operated through elected councils similar to the boards of directors of business corporations, and each was headed by a president and several vice presidents. According to the terms of the 1955 merger, President George Meany of the AFL became president of the new organization and Walter Reuther, head of the CIO, became one of twenty-seven vice presidents. Then, "in order to promote industrial unionism," a new department called the Council of Industrial Organizations was added to the existing AFL departments (Metal Trades, Building Trades, and the like), to be headed by Walter Reuther, and all CIO unions were expected to enroll. In addition, merger has brought the formerly independent AFL unions under closer control in the parent body.

The legal, public relations, and legislative divisions of the AFL-CIO are chiefly responsible for relations with Congress and the executive, but until the merger these were on an informal rather than a formal basis. Research departments were and are excellent—as good as any conducted by management groups—but labor's public relations programs were meager, poorly financed, run by skeleton staffs, with effectiveness only fair to poor. It was not until the passage of the Taft-Hartley Act of 1947 that organized labor apparently fully awakened to the importance of trying to influence public opinion.

Traditionally, organized labor in the United States has been nonpartisan in its politics, following the policy established by Samuel Gompers, founder of the AFL and for many years its president. Since the great depression, however, and especially since the passage of the Taft-Hartley Act, labor has become increasingly active in the political field.[12] Until the merger of December 1955 the CIO was consistently more political than the AFL, making no secret of supporting a particular party and candidate, but later the AFL also took a more positive stand.

The lobbying techniques of organized labor tend to change with the times. The traditional method of both the AFL and the CIO was to send a legislative representative to the Capitol where he would buttonhole friendly Congressmen and try to persuade those

[12] For a further discussion of labor and government, see Part III below.

on the fence to enter labor's camp. In this manner the channels of friendship and information were at least kept open. But more recently the method has been to call in delegations from the home state or district of the legislator being approached. This is in line with modern lobbying techniques and is effective because it confronts the lawmaker with his own constituents whose influence may sway hundreds or even thousands of votes and who must be reckoned with at the next election. The unions now also keep careful records of how individual Congressmen vote on measures affecting labor, and these records are circulated as widely as possible as campaign materials in the home district. This also is an effective weapon.

What labor primarily seeks are adequate wages, reasonable hours, and favorable working conditions. Underlying these is recognition of the right to organize and to bargain collectively with management. Labor also wants steady employment and a sense of security, and there is increasing progress toward a guaranteed annual wage. These are the immediate goals; others are of a more long-range character that include social legislation such as social security, public housing, and public health measures. Labor also wants industrial safety legislation, good public schools, and an equal voice in public affairs. Like its industrial rivals, of course, labor favors reform for the other fellow, including the regulation of legal monopolies. It also favors a progressive income-tax schedule to lighten the tax burden on low-income groups, restricted immigration, the regulation of prison industries so as to control cheap labor and its products, and the regulation of currency and prices if such measures will help prevent recurring depressions.

Although it works for progressive legislation, organized labor in the United States cannot truthfully be called radical. Indeed, public opinion polls have consistently shown that, by and large, labor is as conservative when it comes to the private ownership of property and the maintenance of the free-enterprise system as is a cross-section of employers themselves. An important difference, however, is that labor generally takes a favorable attitude toward government whereas business opinion is more often negative and becomes increasingly so as one ascends the business hierarchy.[13] What is the explanation of this difference and what does it portend? An attempt will be made to answer this question in a later chapter.

The Farm Lobbies

Although he was once the stanchest individualist in the nation, in the past generation the farmer has become one of the most politically active of men.[14] This is due largely to the seriousness of his

---

[13] National Opinion Research Center, *The Public Looks at Politics and Politicians,* Report No. 20 (Mar. 1944).

[14] For a further discussion of agriculture and government, see Part IV below.

economic situation and to the ready response for action of his three principal pressure groups: the National Grange, the American Farm Bureau Fededation, and the National Farmers Union. These organizations claim to have a combined membership of some 2.6 million out of about 5 million men and women who earn their living on the land. Percentagewise, therefore, agriculture's batting average on the score of organized membership is better than labor's. Furthermore, although the membership of the farm organizations is one seventh that of labor's forces, until recently the farmers were a political match for anyone and if they stood together, there was hardly anything they could not obtain from Congress and the state legislatures. In the last few years, however, for reasons that are discussed in a later chapter, the so-called farm bloc has lost some of its power.

The National Grange, the oldest of the farm organizations, was founded in 1867 and for twenty years or so thereafter had a reputation for radicalism. The Populist and Granger movements advocating the regulation of railways and trusts both stemmed from the National Grange. But today it occupies the right wing in its field.

The American Farm Bureau Federation also leans to the right in its policies and is politically close to the Republican party. Founded in 1920, it is now the largest of the organized farm groups. It usually supports the interests of the biggest and most prosperous farm operators and its main strength centers in the Middle West. The National Farmers Union, the newest of the three main groups, is less conservative than its rivals, tends to support the Democratic party, speaks for the "little fellow" among others, and in the last few years has been gaining in influence.

In addition, there are a number of what may be called trade associations among specialized farm operators such as dairymen, grazers, citrus growers, and the like. There have also been several attempts to organize labor unions among farmers. Among these, the strongest is the National Agricultural Workers Union, originally supported by the AFL and now part of the AFL-CIO. In its policies it is closer to the stand of the National Farmers Union than it is to that of the Grange or the Farm Bureau.

The advantage that the farm pressure groups have over both industry and labor is based on the geographical (instead of population) determination of representation in Congress and the state legislatures. Every state contains large areas that are agricultural, and even major industrial states like New York, Connecticut, and Illinois are also prosperous farm states. Although population is now predominantly urban, legislative representation continues, therefore, to be largely agricultural, especially in the Senate, where each state has only two Senators irrespective of the number of its citizens. Cities have long been handicapped by rural-controlled state legislatures which have blocked all attempts to secure reapportionment. Hence, although its influence is diminishing and the 1960 census will somewhat strengthen urban districts, organized agriculture still holds a strategic position.[15]

The pressure methods of agriculture differ in one important respect from those of either labor or business, and again the reason is the nation-wide coverage of agriculture and support of its pressure organizations. Because of this the head executive of the organization is a political force who must be respected, and it is usually he who does the lobbying, who wears out the shoe leather going from one office to the next and seeing legislators in person. The relationship is largely a personal one supported on the side of the lobbyist by a solid foundation of Granges, county agents, farmer committees of many kinds, state agricultural schools, and numerous action programs at the grass-roots level. Consequently, there is not the same need experienced by both industry and labor to "educate" the general public in order to create pressure from that quarter as well.

Farmers seek much the same things that labor and employers want: a sufficient income; high prices for their products and moderate prices for what they must buy; good roads and schools; governmental assistance in the form of soil conservation programs and fertilizers, but no restraints except those willingly agreed to. Organized agriculture also favors the regulation of industrial monopolies, the money markets, and manufacturers in order to support the real income of the farmer, and it wants organized labor regulated so that the city worker will not receive more than the farmer for the same expenditure of effort. The formula is always the same: make the other fellow toe the mark but leave me alone.

THE IMPACT OF PRESSURE GROUPS ON ADMINISTRATIVE AGENCIES

The attention of the Big Three is by no means confined to legislatures. The executive branch receives a continuing consideration. The growing magnitude of these three major interests has caused separate executive departments, devoted to their particular welfare, to be created in the federal government. The laws establishing the Departments of Commerce, Labor, and Agriculture use almost identical language in the words, "to foster and promote" the interests and welfare of the group in question.

The times at which these departments were created reflect in each case a period of pressure-group influence in American politics and correspond to the time at which each of the three main segments

[15] On this point, see Gordon E. Baker, *Rural versus Urban Political Power* (New York, Doubleday Short Studies in Political Science, 1955).

of the American economy became politically strong. Since our economy was almost wholly agriculture-oriented until the last quarter of the nineteenth century, for example, the Department of Agriculture, in 1862, was the first of the three to be set up. The Department of Commerce did not appear until 1903 and for the next ten years the affairs of labor were combined with it, but in 1913 organized labor had become sufficiently influential to secure its own federal department. The secretaries of these three agencies are members of the President's cabinet and are among his main advisers on economic and political policy relative to the Big Three.

The Department of Agriculture is not only the oldest of the three, it is also the largest and most influential. There are several reasons for Agriculture's predominance. Nearly every function relative to agriculture comes under the Department's jurisdiction, which is not true for industry and labor. The number of action programs conducted by the Department far surpasses those of the departments of Commerce and Labor, nor have the two smaller agencies ever undertaken the extensive subsidy and assistance operations of their senior brother. A similar situation exists in the executive branch of the state governments, where agriculture is always a prominent department. The agencies dealing with commerce and labor, except in the largest and most industrialized states, are either scattered among different administrative units or do not exist at all. As a result of these differences, the federal budget estimates for 1961, for example, showed for the Department of Agriculture the sum of $5.6 billion (including subsidies, of course), while the corresponding figure for the Department of Commerce and the Small Business Administration was only $455 million and for the Department of Labor and the NLRB combined it was $435 million.

In assessing the relative strength of the Big Three in the federal government, however, the fact that not all agencies benefiting each have necessarily been included within the formal units that represent them is an important item to be remembered. An accurate picture of the economic machinery of government is not so orderly. If, for example, all federal programs of special concern to labor or which organized labor had been chiefly responsible for getting started were combined in the Department of Labor, that agency would be several times its present size and would include many social security operations, the National Labor Relations Board, the several agencies relating to railway labor, and the various mediation, conciliation, and wage stabilization agencies that appear from time to time in one form or another. Even in the states, if a formal labor department is lacking, there is always a workmen's compensation board at the very least, and generally also other bureaus concerned with labor functions tucked away in the maze that usually characterizes a state executive branch.

Federal agencies dealing with business but located outside the Department of Commerce are even more numerous and important, including as they do the Interstate Commerce Commission, the Federal Trade Commission, the U. S. Tariff Commission, the Federal Communications Commission, and the Civil Aeronautics Board, among others.[16] In this field, however, the situation is a little different from that of labor because most of these agencies were created for regulatory purposes and Congress has preferred to keep them independent on the ground that regulatory functions, to be effective and fair, must stand alone and not be combined with departments chiefly responsible for policy.

Having been influential in the establishment of particular government agencies, pressure groups naturally take a personal interest in their activities. They regard the agencies with somewhat the same solicitous concern with which a parent contemplates his child, desiring among other things that it shall thrive physically and financially so as to be able, in case of need, to support its parent. Pressure groups play a determinative role, for example, in the many periodic attempts to reorganize government agencies in order to bring them up-to-date, to prune off obsolete functions, to round out jurisdictions, and generally to make them more efficient and responsive. When reorganizers appear with a critical attitude, they may be told by the fond guardian to keep their hands off, lest a change in the child lead it to disregard parental influence or to show less consideration in the future.

It is a mutual relationship, of course, because more often than not the officials of a threatened agency also resist innovation and are more than willing to call on pressure groups for help; indeed, it is often in this way that pressure groups are alerted to the threat of reorganization. Their subsequent activities may delay any change for a long time as was the case, for example, with the establishment of the newest federal department, the Department of Health, Education, and Welfare.

The line of approach to a government agency may be more effective from the pressure group than from the chief executive. Although the President and the state governors are theoretically responsible for directing the administration, in fact they may not have full legal or practical control. Certain agencies revolve in a self-contained sphere of their own; over-all public policy suffers from lack of coordination and plan; chief executives are reputed to be poor administrators; and government is accused of inefficiency. In such a situation it is the pressure group that must often bear the blame, and similarly it is through the pressure group that remedies may be most effectively initiated.

Akin to these matters is the question of what the future policy should be concerning the role of the executive departments represent-

---

[16] For a further discussion of these agencies, see Parts II, V, and VI below.

ing the Big Three. If the Departments of Commerce, Labor, and Agriculture regarded themselves only as special pleaders for special interests, then policies of broad national interest involving compromise and statesmanship would be largely neglected. In theory, the secretaries directing these three agencies are supposed to combine both emphases: to work for the economic group represented but to oppose it if its pressures threaten the national welfare. This is like balancing buckets of water on both shoulders at once; the success of the act depends on the ability of the secretary and the orientation of the administration in the White House. But in a free competitive economy and a free governmental system, is there any alternative?

Pressure Groups and Party Politics

The foregoing discussion leads directly into the question of the effect of pressure-group activity on party leadership and party responsibility. Political parties today constitute an aspect of our governmental system that was not contemplated by the framers of the Constitution. In theory, political parties are responsible for nominating candidates to public office, for formulating platforms so as to offer the voter a choice among alternative programs, for fostering new legislation, and, when they win an election, for taking over the reins of administration and assuming charge of the execution of public policy. The party system is also supposed to assure cooperation between the legislative and the executive branches of the government.

But in practice, do the parties really accomplish all these objectives? Reliable authorities say they do not. Political parties have become almost exclusively interested in winning elections and holding office.[17] The reason is partly that pressure groups have acquired so much power and influence that they dominate party functions, including the determination of public policy and increasingly even the selection of candidates.[18] Money talks, at election time as at others, and pressure groups have found that it costs less to elect Senators in the West than in the populous East, and each of their votes counts as much as that, say, of the Senator from New York.

Pressure groups have also undermined the political party in its relations with successful candidates once they have assumed office. An elected officeholder represents an area, say, the state of Michigan. But the pressure spokesman represents a solid interest, like the labor vote of Detroit. To whom is the lawmaker and administrator most likely to listen? A Congressman is normally elected by constituents representing many interests and lacking unity or a common platform, whereas a lobbyist speaks for a single interest that carries the weight of a con-

[17] E. E. Schattschneider, *Party Government* (New York, 1942), Chaps. 1–3.
[18] Peter Odegard and E. Allen Helms, *American Politics* (New York, rev. ed., 1947), and Key, *op. cit.*

centrated force behind it. If a state is predominantly agricultural, furthermore, the Congressman is likely to be of that group, in which case other interests, such as labor and business, will redouble their pressures on him in order to secure their share of his attention. In this process the officeholder may not with impunity forget his party loyalty, but his natural response will be to pressure interests. The pressure groups know this: "The representation of a territorial area or of a certain part of the population," it has been said, "often counts for less in point of influence than the industrial representation marshaled in a given cause." Officials, it is declared, prefer to have "the view of an industry, rather than to listen ad infinitum to the variant views of countless individuals." [19]

In addition to the activities of their pressure groups, individual businessmen are now being urged to assume an active personal role in politics at the party level, as distinct from the political role of their corporation. In 1956 General Electric and Gulf Oil led a movement that was taken up in force by the United States Chamber of Commerce. In 1957 "clinics on Congressional issues" were held under that sponsorship in a dozen cities all over the country. The main issues discussed were tax reform, federal aid to education, and labor reform. In the following year the president of the Chamber of Commerce urged businessmen to "get into politics" if they would match the political power of the labor unions. "Get to work at the precinct and ward levels," he said, "where political decisions are made and officeholders chosen." Businessmen should pay more attention to candidates for Congress, state legislatures, and local councils rather than trying to win over people "already elected and already committed to a political philosophy hostile to business." Employees should become "informed about issues and candidates and . . . make their opinion effective by voting." The company should use every available means in this process, including letters, bulletin boards, publications, meetings, and personal contacts, the objective being "to help establish a more favorable attitude toward business in the next Congress." [20]

Early in 1959 the president of the Chamber of Commerce again spoke out. Businessmen, he said, should stop complaining about the political activity of the unions. "We have been talking to ourselves instead of to Congress too long," he cautioned, and added, "Organized labor has recognized that the democratic process belongs to those who use it." To speed the use of the process in the business community the Chamber of Commerce organized a cross-country chartered-plane tour by a team of officials and specialists "to alert business to what is happening in Congress." In a series of informal discussions the subjects dealt with were how to cope with inflation, proposed solutions for curbing "labor monopolies," the need for adequate national security

[19] National Lumber Manufacturers' Association, *op. cit.*, p. 53.
[20] *The New York Times*, Sept. 20, 1958.

at reasonable cost, and suggestions for a new tax structure. Again, a dozen cities were on the circuit.[21]

A few months later the president of American Can entered the lists, announcing that the company would henceforth participate in politics right down to the ward and precinct levels. Business, he said, had become "too refined" and was "spending too much effort trying to find areas of agreement with organized labor and the government." The time had come to oppose "powerful forces which are seriously undermining our political and economic system." So the company was "testing" in some of its plants a nine-week course in practical politics as prepared by the United States Chamber of Commerce. It was expected that enrollees would be "sufficiently informed to exert a healthy and beneficial influence on politics in their precincts and wards." Everyone in management, from the front office to the shipping dock, would be "informed, equipped, and encouraged" to "speak out" on issues affecting the company and the country at large. Employees, their families, and their neighbors would receive "a continuous flow of facts and viewpoints," through face-to-face contact and in writing, in order to "round out understanding." Company managers were to "learn the art of practical politics." A team of 153 executives all over the country were to "act as official spokesmen" for the company "in direct relationship with the 153 Congressmen and 52 Senators" who represented states and Congressional districts in which the company had facilities.[22]

By 1960 the United States Chamber of Commerce had sold almost 50,000 sets of its instruction pamphlet, "Action Course in Practical Politics." Dozens of large corporations had used these or similar materials of their own, and at least one new consulting concern had appeared to offer advice on political-instruction programs. A majority of enrollees in these courses were from the ranks of middle management, and the Republican party was keeping lists and recruiting from them for party workers.

Not everyone who knew of these efforts was prepared to give them unqualified support, however. Thus, Charles P. Taft, brother of the late Senator, remarked that although politics is a legitimate activity of businessmen because "government regulation in the state or national capital makes a common front essential to an industry," the present movement is vulnerable on several counts. Taft criticized it for the large scale on which it was being undertaken and for its coloration as a public-relations operation. Based on self-interest, the motivation was narrow and might backfire. He also disliked the fact that it was aimed largely at organized labor which in his opinion is not politically so effective as is generally supposed.[23]

[21] *Ibid.*, Feb. 10, 1959.   [22] *Ibid.*, May 21, 1959.
[23] *The New York Times Magazine*, Aug. 31, 1959, p. 10.

THE REGULATION OF PRESSURE GROUPS AND LOBBIES

The legitimate aspects of lobbying are sometimes forgotten when abuses come to light, and in the heat of controversy abuses do occur. An example is the so-called Case exposé that led President Eisenhower to veto the natural gas bill in 1956 on the ground that although he approved of the contents of the measure, he deemed the efforts of some lobbyists to be "so arrogant and so much in defiance of acceptable standards of propriety as to risk creating doubt among the American people concerning the integrity of governmental processes." Senator Aiken of Vermont commented that he had never seen "such intensive, varied, and ingenious lobbying for a piece of legislation," and *The New York Times* reported that the Senate debate had been marked by some of the most intense lobbying in years by gas and oil interests that spent an estimated $1.5 million to push the bill and by consumer interests opposing it.[24] The climax came when Senator Case of South Dakota announced on the floor of the Senate that he had been inclined to vote for the bill but would oppose it because a man "interested" in its passage had delivered to his office twenty-five $100 bills in a plain white envelope as a "campaign contribution." To make matters worse, it was later brought out that the so-called contribution had been made *after* the donor had learned that Senator Case favored the bill and expected to vote for it; in other words, the Senator was not being bribed, he was being rewarded for being a good boy. As Arthur Krock of *The New York Times* remarked, furthermore, why was Case selected in the first place, since he was already on the "right" side and known to be a sensitive plant in politics? Was it stupidity on the part of the "interested" person, or was the "benevolence" merely one of many? [25]

Those who worry about such abuses and the increasing strength and influence of pressure groups have offered a number of plans for their control, the most extreme being to outlaw them altogether. It is argued that they are selfish and shortsighted, create irrepressible conflicts in our economic setup, and nullify the liberal American tradition that seeks rational compromise among competing interests in the broad public interest. But in addition to the fact that many pressure groups serve a useful and legitimate purpose, it is hard to see how they could be suppressed without depriving the nation of its essential freedoms.

[24] *The New York Times,* Feb. 12, 1956.
[25] *Ibid.,* Feb. 14, 1956. In this instance a Senate investigation identified the responsible parties, and a federal grand jury indicted two lawyers and a company on charges of conspiring to violate the Federal Lobby Act, and in addition, the two lawyers were charged with violating a section of the U. S. Criminal Code making it a crime to offer anything of value to a member of Congress to influence his vote on legislation.

The medicine would be worse than the disease. The rights of free assembly, petition, and press are guaranteed in the Constitution.

The alternative to suppression is the regulation of excessive pressure-group practices accompanied by publicity and public education, and this is the tack that has been followed. But with what results? So far they have been disappointing. Although many state governments have made some gesture in the direction of regulation, most of these laws lack teeth. Usually the state is content merely to register lobbyists, and many escape the requirement. Even drastic lobbying laws like those of Georgia, Alabama, and Louisiana are not really enforced, and laws denying lobbyists access to the floor of the legislature are openly disregarded. In Louisiana an interloper in 1955 voted three times from the desk of an absent representative before he was spotted and arrested.[26] Where signs of progress are found in the control of lobbying, it seems to stem more from the influence of public opinion than from the force of law.

When the Temporary National Economic Committee concluded its work in 1941 after nearly three years of study, its final report contained a section dealing with trade associations which recommended that those whose members are engaged in interstate commerce should be required to register with an appropriate federal agency and to file periodic reports of their activities. The committee also believed "that the time has come to make a clear legislative proscription of certain types of activity on the part of trade associations." [27]

Nevertheless, Congress passed no general law to regulate lobbies until 1946. Previously, the only groups required to register as legislative agents were utility lobbyists, shipping-company lobbyists, and the representatives of foreign interests. In 1946, however, Title III of the Legislative Reorganization Act of that year called for the registration of all persons and organizations employed "for the purpose of attempting to influence the passage or defeat of any legislation" by Congress. Every lobbyist was thereafter required to furnish Congress with information concerning the identity of his employer, the duration of his employment, the extent of his compensation including expense accounts, the purposes for which funds put at his disposal were spent, and the "proposed legislation he is employed to support or oppose."

During the first year of this law the number of registrations was considerably less than Congress had a right to expect, amounting to less than nine hundred, although subsequent action by the Justice Department brought in nearly two hundred more by 1948. By 1952 there were ten registered lobbyists for every Congressman in Washington. In that same year, however, the control program received a setback when a special three-judge court held the criminal penal-

---

[26] *Ibid.*, May 18, 1955.
[27] Temporary National Economic Committee, *Final Report and Recommendations* (Washington, D.C., 1941), p. 38

ties section of the new law to be unconstitutional on the ground that other sections were too vague to constitute an ascertainable standard of guilt. But in 1954 a second case,[28] this time contesting the requirement to make financial reports, went to the Supreme Court, and the Court upheld the constitutionality of the law by a 5 to 3 decision on the ground that to deny Congress the power to require disclosure of lobbying activities "would be to deny Congress in large measure the power of self-protection." The evil the lobbying statute was designed to prevent, said Chief Justice Warren, was to keep "the voice of the people" from being drowned out by "the voice of special interest groups seeking favored treatment while masquerading as proponents of the public weal."[29]

Nevertheless, despite this favorable decision by the Supreme Court, the interpretation was a narrow one, and the law as it stands is clearly inadequate. It now applies only to "direct" lobbying and not to "indirect" lobbying (causing pressure from the folks back home, for example), which has been developed to a fine point and actually constitutes the bulk of most pressure-group activity. In addition, many individuals and organizations leave blank the space provided for listing expenditures on the ground that nothing has been spent for "direct" lobbying, and some groups fail to register at all for the same reason. In connection with the Senate debate on the natural gas bill in 1955, for example, one group that failed to register was the Natural Gas and Oil Resources Committee formed in the previous year. It favored the bill and hired the New York public relations firm of Hill & Knowlton to publicize the industry and to "inform the public on the merits of a free . . . industry operating in a competitive economy." But when asked if the program included lobbying, a spokesman for the committee replied that he saw "no cause to answer such a question."[30] For reasons such as these the figures reported for pressure groups that are active and the money they spend do not show the true picture. In addition, because of the 1952 court decision voiding the criminal penalties section of the law, which was not reviewed in the 1954 decision, there is an almost total lack of enforcement. "The real remedy," commented *The New York Times*, "would be a complete rewrite of the act itself."[31]

Perhaps, as Stephen K. Bailey has said, it is impossible to write a lobby registration law that does not contain loopholes. The consequence has been "that a vast amount of lobbying has gone on under different names, and some of the largest and most frightening centers of private power in the American society have entirely escaped the registration net."[32] Even when registration takes place, there is no

---

[28] *United States* v. *Harriss* (347 U.S. 612, 1954).
[29] *The New York Times,* June 8, 1954.　　　[30] *Ibid.,* Feb. 7, 1956.
[31] *Ibid.,* June 13, 1954.
[32] Stephen K. Bailey. "Pressure Groups in the United States," *The Listener,* Vol. LIX, No. 1517 (London, April 24, 1958), p. 679.

adequate follow-up. The secretary of the Senate and the clerk of the House merely receive such reports from the lobbies as are submitted and file them for safekeeping. Although they are left open for inspection, they never receive sufficient scrutiny.

Following the Case incident of 1956, an eight-member bipartisan Senate investigating committee was created to study the twin subjects of lobbying and campaign expenditures. After fourteen months of desultory hearings with virtually no cooperation offered from any source, Senatorial or otherwise, the committee prepared a draft bill designed to tighten control on each subject of its study (in the case of lobbying it proposed that control be transferred to the General Accounting Office), returned more than half of its $350,000 appropriation to the Treasury, and disbanded.

Although the proposed new legislation got nowhere, one positive step did come from the committee's work. It had been learned that of nearly $2 million collected by the Natural Gas and Oil Resources Committee, $1.6 million had come from 26 big oil and gas companies which apparently then treated their contributions as business expenses and deducted them from their 1956 income tax returns. The Internal Revenue Service was informed of this development, which violated a rule in force since 1919 to the effect that "sums of money expended for lobbying purposes, the promotion or defeat of legislation, the exploitation of propaganda, including advertising other than trade advertising, and contributions for campaign expenses, are not deductible from gross income." This rule had been upheld in 1959 in a dual case before the Supreme Court,[33] which stated simply, "We think that the regulations must be construed to mean what they say. . . ." The Internal Revenue Service instituted a check and extended the original rule: tax deductions for *industry-wide* campaigns against legislation considered harmful to *a whole industry,* the new policy stated, are not properly deductible expenses.

The United States Chamber of Commerce called this action a "form of censorship by taxation," the American Newspaper Publishers Association feared it might cut down newspaper ads on public issues, the National Association of Manufacturers worried that it might outlaw the deduction of dues paid to trade associations (75 percent of whose work, it was said, was lobbying), and it was reported that the AFL-CIO also planned to issue a protest. Finally, in June 1960 a bill to permit full deductibility of lobbying expenses was favorably reported to the House by the Ways and Means Committee, so the issue is apparently still a live one.

In exploring the reasons for the failure of regulation one may well ask whether lobby control legislation is not perhaps in advance of what public opinion favors. The failure is no light matter, how-

---

[33] *Cammarano v. U.S., F. Strauss & Co., Inc., v. Commr. of Internal Revenue* (358 U.S. 498, 1959).

ever, because if mild measures are insufficient, more drastic ones may be tried. Legitimate groups engaged in legitimate work have no reason to shun publicity, and no other kind of pressure group should be supported. And finally, there is the point that the unbridled activities of lobbyists are likely to lead to an increase in economic planning on the part of government in order to reconcile the increasingly insistent demands of competing groups. Caught at the center of many pressures, government must find some way out of the dilemma in which negligent public attitudes have placed it.

Supplementary Reading

Blaisdell, Donald C., *Economic Power and Political Pressures*, Temporary National Economic Committee, Monograph 26 (Washington, D.C., 1941).
———, *American Democracy under Pressure* (New York, 1957). Reveals the extent of the challenge.
Chase, Stuart, *Democracy under Pressure—Special Interests vs. the Public Interest* (New York, 1945). A critical view.
Crawford, Kenneth C., *The Pressure Boys* (New York, 1939). A realistic study by a newspaperman.
Schriftgiesser, Karl, *The Lobbyists: The Art and Business of Influencing Lawmakers* (Boston, 1951). Both realistic and critical.
———, *Business Comes of Age* (New York, 1959). The story of the CED.
Childs, Harwood L., *Labor and Capital in National Politics* (Columbus, Ohio, 1930). A case study of industry and labor.
Garceau, Olivier, *Political Life of the American Medical Association* (Cambridge, Mass., 1941).
McCune, Wesley, *The Farm Bloc* (New York, 1943).
———, *Who's Behind Our Farm Policy?* (New York, 1956). Alliances that do not meet the eye.
Rutherford, Mary L., *The Influence of the American Bar Association on Public Opinion and Legislation* (Chicago, 1937).
Schattschneider, E. E., *Politics, Pressures and the Tariff* (New York, 1935).
Latham, Earl, *The Group Basis of Politics: A Study in Basing Point Legislation* (Ithaca, N.Y., 1952).
Bailey, Stephen K., *Congress Makes a Law: The Story Behind the Employment Act of 1946* (New York, 1950).
Gross, Bertram, *The Legislative Struggle* (New York, 1953). Both systematic and realistic.
Truman, David B., *The Governmental Process* (New York, 1951). How groups make "access" to government.
Hardin, C. M., *The Politics of Agriculture* (Glencoe, Ill., 1952). Traces the development of policy.
Lane, R. E., *The Regulation of Business Men* (New Haven, Conn., 1954). Basic attitudes toward control.
Kornhauser, A., et al., *When Labor Votes* (New York, 1956). A study of the auto workers.
Fells, R. S. F., *The Meaning of Modern Business* (New York, 1960).

Vose, Clement E., *Caucasians Only: The NAACP and the Restrictive Covenant Cases* (Berkeley, Calif., 1959).

Kelley, S., *Professional Public Relations and Political Power* (Baltimore, 1956).

Key, V. O., *Politics, Parties, and Pressure Groups* (New York, 4th ed., 1958). Relation between political parties and pressure groups.

Baker, Gordon E., *Rural versus Urban Political Power* (New York, 1955).

Horsky, Charles A., *The Washington Lawyer* (Boston, 1953).

3

THE CHALLENGE OF BIG GOVERNMENT

Principles of American government; the Constitution, economic provisions and growth; spread of federalism; growth of governmental powers: express, reserved, concurrent, implied, and resultant; commerce power; taxing power; police power, state and federal; separation of powers; judicial review; protection of private rights; administrative framework of the federal government; cost of government.

Is government a threat to free enterprise, as some businessmen contend? If it has a legitimate role in the economy, what is that role? How big is government and what is the reason for its size? To answer these questions one must know something of the powers of government and their effect on the business community.

Since the federal Constitution was adopted in 1789, American government has changed almost as much in its way as the structure of the economy has been modified by technological invention and new forms of organization. Nevertheless, the dominant characteristics and underlying principles of the governmental system may be readily stated, the more easily because a written constitution and a Supreme Court with power to interpret it have enforced a degree of consistency on governmental functioning.

The five great principles of the American governmental system are a *written constitution* prescribing expressly limited powers; a *federal form* of government in which authority is divided between a central government and the several states; the *separation of powers* into three branches—legislative, executive, and judicial—to prevent any one of them from acquiring too much power; *judicial review* of legislative and administrative acts to determine their conformity to the Constitution, accompanied by the power of the courts to declare laws unconstitutional (it is in this respect that American government differs most from similar governments of other nations); and finally the *Bill of Rights* setting forth the citizen's rights and immunities as found in the first ten amendments to the Constitution, in addition to which other private rights are provided for in the main body of that instrument.

Not all of these five principles are expressly stated in the Constitution. The first, a written constitution, is obvious in the nature of the document itself. The second, a federal system, is expressly set forth in the Tenth Amendment which provides that "The powers not delegated to the United States by the Constitution, nor prohibited by it to the States, are reserved to the States respectively, or to the people." The separation of powers is not spelled out in the form of a distributing clause as in some state constitutions, but the intent is clear from the arrangement of the first three articles. The power of the federal courts to declare unconstitutional acts of Congress, the state legislatures, and the executive branch is a matter of inference and not a specific provision. Finally, the Bill of Rights, or the first ten amendments, is an integral part of the Constitution itself because although adopted by the amending process, this occurred during the first Congress and had already been agreed on as a condition precedent to ratification by many of the states.

THE CONSTITUTION

The confluence of forces that produced the American Constitution provides a clear example of the close relationship that has always existed between economic and political institutions. The delegates to the Philadelphia Convention of 1787 were not authorized to draft a new instrument but merely to revise and possibly strengthen the Articles of Confederation; and yet a wholly new document was the outcome of their labors, largely because the economic provisions of the Articles of Confederation, drawn up during the stress of the Revolution, had proved so inadequate in practice. Among the problems confronting the delegates at Philadelphia was the basic necessity of improving the credit of the United States by strengthening the taxing, currency, and debt powers of the central government. There was also the matter of interstate commerce, several of the states having begun to impose tariffs and other financial burdens on commerce with their neighbors; consequently the delegates enacted the commerce power giving the federal government control in the foreign and interstate fields and confining the area of state regulation to commerce within their borders. Because the commerce power has been so broadly interpreted, for the purposes of the present study it exceeds in importance any other grant of power contained in the Constitution.

The delegates at Philadelphia also tried to protect property and to stabilize business relationships in other ways. Property was safeguarded by provisions covering the sanctity of contracts, regulating the right of eminent domain (the taking of private property for public use), and assuring equal protection of the laws and due process of law, all of which have since proved of the greatest significance to business interests. A careful reading of the Constitution will show how much it is an economic as well as a political document.

The nature of the American governmental system was determined at Philadelphia by men who were chiefly affiliated with business, financial, and other economic interests and who were deeply concerned that government should stabilize conditions but not interfere too much with property or business rights.[1] The result, says Macmahon, is a system that "has combined elements of vigor and feebleness verging on paralysis. This was the natural and indeed intentional outcome of the ideas and circumstances which shaped the Constitution. . . ."[2] What were these ideas and circumstances? A first principle was that safety, especially for property, "must be sought in the calculated balancing of diverse interests," in line with the prevailing view that government's legitimate role was to protect property but otherwise to let individualistic forces alone. French radicalism, influential at that time, emphasized confidence in men rather than in institutions, and resulted in this country in a suspicion of authority. In addition, as former colonists, Americans were experiencing a psychological reaction against authority, as a result of their recent ordeal in our own Revolution. To them, government meant not the people but king and royal governor, and hence was not looked on with favor. It is this attitude that was partly responsible for the system of checks and balances being written into the Constitution. According to this system each of the three branches of the federal government is to some extent checked by the other two, even though their powers remain separate.

Produced in so individualistic a milieu, the Constitution naturally emphasized the economic concepts of natural law and a balancing of forces, thus carrying economic thinking over into the field of government. The main features of the constitutional system of 1789, concludes Macmahon, were "limited government, federalism, and the scheme of separately chosen executives who share with bicameral legislatures the uncertain responsibilities of leadership."[3] The result might be called individualism and laissez faire in government. Once adopted and put to use, however, this early American governmental system immediately began to change, under the pressure of necessity, into something quite different in practice if not in principle, just as the laissez-faire theories of the classical economists also changed into something different from the original pattern and for the same compelling reasons.

As far as the Constitution is concerned, since the first Congress adopted the first ten amendments (collectively known as the Bill of Rights), change has been slow, only twenty-two amendments in all having been ratified by the states in the past century and a half. Of these amendments, the Fourteenth, one of the so-called Civil War amendments, contains phrases that have assumed the greatest importance in government's relation to business: ". . . nor shall any state deprive

[1] Charles A. Beard, *An Economic Interpretation of the Constitution* (New York, 1935).

[2] Arthur W. Macmahon, "Government, United States," *Encyclopedia of the Social Sciences*, Vol. VII, p. 15.

[3] *Ibid.,* p. 15.

any person of life, liberty, or property, without due process of law; nor deny to any person within its jurisdiction the equal protection of the laws." The due-process-of-law clause, especially, has been invoked in cases of conflict with the police power of the states, which is the reserved power of the states to regulate and restrict whenever the matter applies to the health, safety, morals, or welfare of its citizens. Such state laws may and often do affect the property and contract rights of private corporations, thus bringing the matter under federal jurisdiction. When the word "person" in the Fourteenth Amendment was judicially interpreted to apply to business corporations (artificial persons) the result was to create one of the principal legal dramas of the American scene. Frequent reference will be made to this judicial battleground, especially when it comes to a discussion of the regulation of public utilities. The Sixteenth Amendment also has great economic significance because it allows the federal government to impose an income tax, now the principal source of federal revenue and a direct means of using the taxing power for social as well as for revenue purposes.[4]

Although there have been relatively few amendments to the Constitution, there are other methods of changing a governmental system and all have been active. For one thing, as the powers conferred by a constitution are used, the constitution itself must be interpreted, a dynamic process in which the legislative and executive branches as well as the courts are involved, and it is by this method that our so-called living Constitution has repeatedly been adjusted to the altered circumstances of each new generation. The use particularly of the commerce, taxing, and police powers, has progressively opened up new areas of governmental activity, especially in the economic field, in an attempt to keep pace with new demands. Through interpretation, the courts have also invented the judicial theory of implied and resulting powers so as to free the federal government from the rigidities of fixed, express powers.

Constitutions are also altered by people's attitudes and their points of view, and these too have changed since 1789. As a result, new political machinery never imagined by the framers of the Constitution has been invented, the most notable being the function performed by political parties and pressure groups in giving vitality and direction to American public policy. Judicial review of legislative and administrative action also has added to the American governmental system, although

---

[4] Two other amendments, the Eighteenth and the Twenty-first, deal with the sale of intoxicating liquors, a subject of considerable social and economic import, but they have cancelled each other out. The other amendments, however, have been primarily concerned with governmental questions: the Eleventh with suits brought against the states, the Twelfth with the method of electing the President and Vice President, the Thirteenth, Fourteenth (in part), and the Fifteenth (all Civil War amendments) with the rights and privileges of the then recently freed slaves, the Seventeenth with the direct election of Senators, the Nineteenth with woman's suffrage, the Twentieth with the elimination of the so-called lame duck session of Congress, and the Twenty-second with the limitation of the President's term of office.

again, not specifically provided for in the Constitution. And finally, a constantly growing number of major executive departments and regulatory commissions, not to mention scores of government corporations, have become a large and prominent part of our governmental mechanism. Most of these agencies are concerned with economic matters, and none were specifically provided for in the Constitution as originally adopted. All of which proves that even the stipulations of a written instrument may be elastic and that government, like the structure of business itself, will surely take on new meaning when emerging forces are sufficiently powerful and persistent.

THE SPREAD OF FEDERALISM

Since the Civil War and especially since the last part of the nineteenth century when big business in America was hitting its stride, no shift of governmental power in this country compares with the steady drive toward federal centralization. One need not be an economic determinist to realize that big business and big government go hand in hand.

In the early years of the republic there was a sharp cleavage between federalist and anti-federalist sentiment. The anti-federalists were the majority, consisted of Southern planters, frontiersmen, farmers, and small businessmen—all champions of states' rights—and were dead set against the ratification of the Constitution if it meant giving the federal government and the larger states too much power. Business interests generally, on the other hand, although a minority, were more vocal than the majority and predominantly on the side of increasing the power and influence of the federal government in the hope of ensuring stable economic conditions. The major issues of the constitutional convention at Philadelphia—large industrial versus small agricultural states, the assumption of state debts by the federal government versus state responsibility, a single versus a plural executive—all revolved around this central problem of balancing federal and state powers. Alexander Hamilton, avowed spokesman for the business community, even advocated a national plan of manufactures by which the government could encourage rapid business expansion. He and his followers favored protective tariffs, aid to infant industries, the federal ownership and exploitation of western lands—all the things that were destined later to expand federal authority at the expense of the states. It was the Federalists, too, who promoted a strong federal judiciary. They believed, as in time proved to be the case, that it would constitute a chief means of establishing federal supremacy, maintaining the rule of law, eliminating state restrictions and particularisms, and encouraging a nation-wide economy. In the clash of interests at Philadelphia and afterward during the fight for the ratification of the Constitution, the Federalist minority proved stronger than its more diffused opponents.

This early trend toward federal centralization was stimulated by the victory of the north in the Civil War, a conflict that again involved the issue of states' rights as against a strong federal union. The Northern states were already the center of industry and finance, and the war opened up possibilities in the West which had never before been appreciated. With the building of transcontinental railways shortly after the close of the war, business, as is its wont, followed the routes of improved transportation and soon became national in scope.

Following the lead of business, government also began to expand. A continental area had to be administered. As the more powerful business interests became even stronger, complaints were heard from farmers, small businessmen, workers, and consumers about the growing domination of large corporations. At first these weaker groups sought regulatory legislation at their state capitals, but soon they were hammering on the doors of Congress for railroad and antitrust legislation, arguing that only the federal government was sufficiently strong to engage such formidable adversaries and that it alone possessed the nation-wide jurisdiction necessary to deal with the national problems that the big corporations were beginning to create. Thus a government already expanding to cover a continental area was required still further to increase its scope by adding new functions, ironically enough, demanded by the same interests that had opposed a strong federal government in the first place.

The federal government continued to expand at a fair pace until the first part of the twentieth century. Then came World War I, followed ten years later by the great depression of the 1930s, and in yet another decade by World War II. When the Constitution was adopted, the annual expenditure of the federal government totaled some $6 million. At the outset of the Civil War it was $60 million, but during that conflict it rose to $683 million. By 1915 expenditures were averaging $720 million a year, but with World War I they went up to more than $8 billion, a figure that was not again reached until the latter years of the depression of the 1930s. The highest point of all was attained during World War II, when some $98 billion was spent in 1945. The estimate for 1961 was $79.3 billion.

Inevitably the concentration of power in Washington has quickly accelerated with each emergency of war or depression. Businessmen who had been the first to champion federal centralization now for the most part went over to the other side of the political fence, arguing that too much federal authority threatens the free-enterprise system from two quarters: excessive regulation on the one hand and competition from government itself on the other. Now also, those who once stood against the trend toward federalism, found themselves on the opposite side of the issue: Farmers wanted governmental assistance for themselves and tighter regulation for Wall Street and the trusts. Labor wanted social security, public housing, stabilized employment, increased bargaining power legally guaranteed, and more effective control of abuses by employers. And businessmen, although usually favoring a relaxation of regulations on themselves, just as often urged stricter controls over organized labor, the adoption of higher tariffs and subsidies, and government-supported export prices to stimulate the sale of agricultural and manufactured surpluses abroad, thus keeping domestic prices at a high level.

The shift of governmental authority from state and local centers to Washington has been most pronounced in the field of major economic regulation, where federal agencies have almost wholly supplanted state agencies in the control of transportation, water power, banking and credit, security issues, holding companies, major industrial disputes, and antitrust prosecutions. One of the newest fields that the federal government has entered and which it now dominates is public welfare, as illustrated by far-flung social security programs and the extensive federal relief and work relief operations of the 1930s. A third large area is that of agriculture, once the stronghold of individualism but where in recent years, as a Washington columnist once remarked, farm organizations have been literally wedded to the federal government and until lately could get from it anything short of good growing weather.

How have these shifts of power from the periphery to the center been accomplished? First, of course, under pressure, Congress has passed legislation authorizing the government to enter new fields or to extend old ones. Then the Supreme Court, making use of the concepts of implied and other powers as developed in the early part of the nineteenth century by Chief Justice John Marshall, has upheld the assertion of federal authority in these new or expanded areas. Behind such increases of power, it should be remembered, stands the will of the people who have not only favored such extensions but have worked hard through their pressure groups to achieve them.

Another method by which the authority of the central government has been broadened is through the now familiar device of federal aid to the states, a system whereby the federal government matches dollars with state and local agencies to undertake a particular public program such as highway construction, vocational education, the support of state militias, and the like. The fields occupied by federal aid and the sums annually expended enormously increased during the depression of the 1930s and have not contracted since. It was during the depression also that the federal government became direct banker to many large cities, supplying their financial needs for relief and public works programs and extending credits through agencies such as the Reconstruction Finance Corporation and the Commodity Credit Corporation, two of the largest corporations ever operated by the federal government.

With its greater financial resources and armed with the support of favorable Supreme Court decisions, the government at Washington now enjoys an authority hardly to be recognized in the light of what the Founding Fathers thought they had achieved at Philadelphia in 1787.

They believed they had restricted the central government to an expressly defined sphere of activity and had assured expansive jurisdictions to the state and local governments. The way things have worked out, both the federal and the state governments have extended their powers, but the federal government relatively much more than the states. There are now few areas where state and local governments exercise a jurisdiction from which the federal government is wholly excluded. Moreover, in a contest of authority, the outcome is almost always in favor of the federal government.

THE GROWTH OF GOVERNMENTAL POWERS

The growth of governmental powers has proceeded according to a familiar formula. First appears the need for governmental action in a specific area. Pressure is then exerted through political parties and interest groups, resulting in the passage of legislation. Someone can always be relied on to contest the law, the case is brought to trial, and if important constitutional issues are involved, eventually it is heard and decided by the Supreme Court of the United States. The more prominent of these decisions have enunciated principles or rules defining a power of the federal government not expressly stated in the Constitution, or extending the scope of powers that are.

Powers Express, Reserved, Concurrent, Implied, and Resultant

The American system of government is based in part on the principle of *express* federal powers specifically set forth in the Constitution, with those remaining—the *reserved* powers—to be exercised by the states (unless prohibited by the Constitution) or retained by the people. These reserve powers, however, have gradually been whittled away and in practice many are now *concurrent*—that is, they may be exercised by both the states and the federal government, neither having exclusive sway. In addition, the Constitution stipulates that certain federal powers shall be exercised only by the federal government in accordance with express prohibitions against concurrent action; these include foreign affairs, defense, coining money, issuing currency, foreign and interstate commerce, post offices and post roads, bankruptcy, patents and copyrights, weights and measures, naturalization, and territories, all of which have economic significance.

Added to the express powers of the federal government, Supreme Court interpretations have created another area of exclusive federal control of surpassing interest in this study: This is the commerce power which, although express, has been judicially expanded by means of the doctrine of *implied* powers. As Macmahon has graphically pointed out, the courts have given a negative turn to the clause empowering Congress "to regulate commerce with foreign nations, and among the several states." The rule that the states cannot interfere with such commerce, says Macmahon, "has nationalized the treatment of business. An incidental result has been to embarrass effective state control of economic matters unless attended by complementary national action. A large proportion of the regulatory enactments of Congress can be traced to this predicament." [5] With the federal government enjoying such exclusive preserves one might almost say that American federalism has reversed itself. It is more constructive, however, to emphasize the concurrency of authority between the central government and the states than the competitive angle.

The doctrine of implied powers by which the commerce power, among others, has been expanded has played an outstanding role in the evolution of business-government relations and has an interesting history. At the end of the section in the Constitution listing the express powers of Congress there is the so-called elastic clause stating that "The Congress shall have the power . . . to make all laws which shall be necessary and proper for carrying into execution the foregoing powers, and all other powers vested by this Constitution in the government of the United States, or in any department or officer thereof." When the Supreme Court decided the famous case of *McCulloch* v. *Maryland* [6] in 1819, Chief Justice John Marshall used the wording of this necessary-and-proper clause to open the door to federal expansion. The immediate issue was the authority of the federal government to charter a national bank, a basic economic matter. Although nowhere in the Constitution is it expressly stated that the United States may create such an institution, and despite the opposition of the adherents of states' rights who saw in it a potential threat to local business and the encouragement of big business, Congress did create a national bank. The point in controversy before the Court was whether the state of Maryland might levy a tax on federal bank notes, an impost which the federal attorneys argued was excessive and discriminatory. In considering the case the Court was also called upon to determine whether the federal government possessed the power in the first place to create such a national banking institution. The decision on both issues upheld the federal government and resulted in the twin doctrines of implied powers and the supremacy of the federal over state authority.

How was this doctrine of implied powers arrived at? The Court admitted that the Constitution provides no express authority to create a national bank, but held that there exists an implied power which is a power that may reasonably and necessarily be deduced from an express power. "Let the end be legitimate," said the Court, "let it be within the scope of the Constitution, and all means which are appropriate, . . .

[5] Macmahon, *op. cit.*, p. 18.   [6] (4 Wheaton 316. 1819).

which are not prohibited, but consistent with the letter and spirit of the Constitution, are constitutional." And then this impressive statement:

> . . . The sword and the purse, all the external relations, and no in-considerable portion of the industry of the nation, are entrusted to its government. It can never be pretended that these vast powers draw after them others of inferior importance, merely because they are inferior. . . . But it may, with great reason, be contended that a gov-ernment, intrusted with such ample powers, on the execution of which the happiness and prosperity of the nation so vitally depends, must also be intrusted with ample means for their execution.

From what express power is this implied power deducible? From one or from several: the express powers to lay and collect taxes, to borrow money, to regulate commerce, to declare and conduct war, to raise and support armies and navies.

It was not long before the doctrine of implied powers was enlarged to include the doctrine of *resultant* power, defined as the power deriv-ing from two or more express powers. What does this mean? As an ex-periment, read carefully the case of *McCulloch* v. *Maryland* and then answer two questions: First, if you grant Chief Justice Marshall's premises (and one can hardly take issue with an opponent who rests his argument on the "nature of the case"), how can you deny that resultant powers are admissible? And second, if the opinion means what it says, is there any limit to the extension of federal power under the Constitution as long as the Court considers such action "necessary and proper"?

The second point involved, the doctrine of federal supremacy, is of almost equal significance as the basis of many recent decisions allowing federal agencies to occupy fields formerly controlled by the states. Article VI of the Constitution states that:

> This Constitution, and the laws of the United States which shall be made in pursuance thereof; and all treaties made, or which shall be made, under the authority of the United States, shall be the supreme law of the land; and the Judges in every State shall be bound thereby, anything in the Constitution or laws of any State to the contrary not-withstanding.

The Constitution was adopted by the people and not by the states, said the Court in the case of *McCulloch* v. *Maryland*, and it follows that the Constitution is superior to the states and operates on them as on the federal government. And then this clincher: "The government of the United States . . . though limited in its powers, is supreme; and its laws, when made in pursuance of the Constitution, form the supreme law of the land." Such an interpretation raises an interesting question: When the Constitution was adopted, the states were considered as sov-ereign, but after this decision was rendered, were they still sovereign? Can there be such a thing as dual sovereignty? Or doesn't it matter? To the economy, at least, it makes some difference whether regulation, for example, is on a nation-wide basis or piecemeal on a state basis.

The Commerce Power and Interstate Commerce

As already noted, the commerce clause in the Constitution is probably the most popular vehicle of federal expansion, with the taxing power running a close second. The commerce clause sounds simple enough: the federal government is to regulate foreign and interstate commerce, the states to retain jurisdiction over commerce within their respective borders. But as Macmahon has said, "Limited government, especially when federal, invites conflicting groups to couch their grim struggles as questions in the meaning of words." [7] Here the key words are "commerce" and "interstate." [8]

What is meant by commerce? Again it was Chief Justice Marshall, in *Gibbons* v. *Ogden*,[9] who opened the way to a broad construction capable of covering future technological developments no matter how revolutionary their effect. Commerce, said the Court, includes traffic and intercourse, but as a concept it cannot be confined by words. Taking their cue from this decision federal justices have since rarely found any difficulty in extending the commerce category. Commerce now means all forms of transportation and facilities related thereto; encompasses all kinds of communication including telephone, radio, and television; and covers all goods and commodities moving across state lines. It need not invariably involve the making of money because it has in some cases even been made to cover a pleasure jaunt across state lines.

Nor is commerce necessarily limited to tangibles. Since 1944 even the insurance business has been considered a part of interstate commerce and subject to federal regulation. This was the outcome of the case of *United States* v. *South-Eastern Underwriters* [10] which reversed the decision seventy-five years earlier in the case of *Paul* v. *Virginia*,[11] in which the insurance business was considered so intangible as not to fall within the commerce category. The concept of commerce also includes the products of child labor: the products themselves are tangible enough but how can one tell by looking at them whether they have been made by the hands of adults or of minors? This doubt led the Supreme Court in the case of *Hammer* v. *Dagenhart* [12] to invalidate an act of Congress barring the products of child labor from interstate commerce. But thirty-three years later in *United States* v. *Darby Lumber Company* [13]

[7] Macmahon, *op. cit.*, p. 18.

[8] No particular problem arises with the concept of commerce with foreign nations (or with the Indian tribes which are mentioned in the same clause) since the states rarely have occasion to concern themselves with such matters.

[9] (9 Wheaton 1. 1824).

[10] (322 U.S. 533. 1944).

[11] (8 Wallace 168. 1869).

[12] (247 U.S. 251. 1918).

[13] (312 U.S. 100. 1941).

the earlier decision was expressly overruled and child labor was, in effect, held to be a tangible.

In the matter of jurisdiction over commerce which is interstate and that which is not, the courts have repeatedly held that the control of Congress over interstate commerce is plenary—that is, full, complete, and exclusive—and hence the states may not invade the field. This interpretation grew out of the case of *Gibbons* v. *Ogden,* which involved the granting of an exclusive navigation franchise by the state of New York, thus creating a monopoly held to be in conflict with the right of the United States government to grant licenses for interstate navigation. (Parenthetically, it will be noted that this case also illustrates an early antipathy toward monopoly.) In its realm, said the Court, the power of Congress over interstate commerce is complete and exclusive, and the states may not exercise coordinate or concurrent power when Congress has acted.

But the principle does not work the other way: because of the doctrine of federal supremacy, the states are not protected against federal interference. When state and federal policy conflict, state policy must be made to conform since otherwise there would be an obstruction of interstate commerce. A leading case in this field is *Houston, E. & W. Texas R. Co.* v. *United States,*[14] known as the *Shreveport* case. Here a freight rate established by the Interstate Commerce Commission was higher than a rate set by the Texas railway commission between points in Texas and Louisiana that were in competition. As a result of the decision, the Texas railway commission was required to raise its rates to accord with the federal pattern. Rendered in 1914, this decision marked a turning point in federal-state relations relative to railway regulation, and since then federal control has almost wholly displaced state control in this area of the economy.

The trend of Supreme Court decisions is toward obliterating the line between interstate and intrastate commerce. Increasingly it seems, commerce is regarded as a continuous process from the conversion of raw materials to the distribution of the finished product. Thus the former distinction between production as a matter for state control and distribution among the states as a matter of federal control tends to give way. This trend was temporarily checked in the decision in the so-called NRA case of *Schechter* v. *United States,*[15] in which the Supreme Court declared the National Industrial Recovery Act to be unconstitutional on the grounds, first, that the regulation of the wholesale distribution of poultry in New York City was a matter properly reserved to the state, and second, that the act attempted to delegate legislative authority to the President in violation of the separation-of-powers principle. Two years later, however, the earlier tendency was renewed when the National Labor Relations Act was upheld in the case of *NLRB* v.

[14] (234 U.S. 342. 1914).   [15] (295 U.S. 495. 1935).

Jones & Laughlin Steel Corp.[16] and again in 1939 when the constitutionality of the second Agricultural Adjustment Act was sustained in *Mulford* v. *Smith.*[17]

In summary it may be said that despite an occasional turning back toward states' rights, the main thrust of Supreme Court decisions is toward increasing centralization under the commerce power. For the first hundred years after the Constitution was adopted this power, which now occupies first place in importance, was scarcely ever used in an affirmative manner because the reasons for doing so did not yet exist. Modern conditions have changed the picture, and the new period of extension of federal authority through the commerce power was ushered in with the passage of the Interstate Commerce Commission Act of 1887 followed by the Sherman Antitrust Act in 1890. Since then Congress has rapidly occupied the commerce field, made plenary use of its power, and has even encroached on the province of the states.

The Taxing Power

The taxing power in the Constitution states that Congress shall have the power "To lay and collect taxes, duties, imposts, and excises, to pay the debts and provide for the common defense and general welfare of the United States." [18] Taxes are an increasingly large item in business finances. They may be used by government to discourage or to stimulate financial and business concentrations, and imposts may be employed to increase governmental regulations and interferences. The burden may fall so heavily on the lower and middle income groups as to cause purchasing power to shrink, and in the form of tariffs, taxes may encourage or restrict international trade. These and many other reasons make fiscal policy a principal tool by which government may try to regulate the economy. According to the tax employed, for example, the range between the highest and the lowest incomes may be narrowed, the sale of a product, as was formerly the case with oleomargarine, may be restricted and that of a dangerous product virtually eliminated.

The taxing power carries these wide implications partly because tied to it is the "general welfare" clause of the Constitution which opens up vistas of government activity almost as limitless as those permitted under the "elastic" clause. Theoretically, the words "general welfare" give Congress no more actual power than it would otherwise possess because, again theoretically, the federal government is one of limited powers. But in practice the right to appropriate money under the Constitution, for whatever purpose, seems to be virtually without bounds. As already indicated, what Congress cannot do directly may be managed indirectly by devices such as federal aid to the states. The states are not circumscribed as to what they may do, nor is the federal govern-

---

[16] (301 U.S. 1. 1937). [17] (307 U.S. 38. 1939).
[18] For a further discussion of the taxing power, see the last section in this chapter.

ment limited in what it may assist them to do, whether the object be relief, public works, social security, education, or something else. This has been made clear in court decisions, as in the cases of *Massachusetts v. Mellon* [19] and *Frothingham v. Mellon*.[20] Like the doctrine of implied powers, therefore, or the expansive interpretation of the commerce power, the taxing power and the authority to appropriate money have created a vast field of federal activity, the limits of which no one can accurately gauge. Like the phrase "necessary and proper," the term "general welfare" depends for its meaning on what content those in authority choose to give to it.

Because revenues must be supplied to government at the federal, state, and local levels, the authority to tax also occurs at three different levels, and dual and even triple taxation is apparently unavoidable. When the financial requirements of the federal government during the Civil War increased to the point where existing sources of revenue were insufficient, Congress levied an income tax, the constitutionality of which was upheld by the Supreme Court in 1890.[21] But five years later the decision was reversed,[22] and it required the Sixteenth Amendment to bring the issue to a close in 1913. Since then Congress has had the power "to lay and collect taxes on incomes, from whatever source derived, without apportionment among the several states, and without regard to any census or enumeration."

The principal rules applying to the financial powers of the federal government are these:

1. All *direct taxes* (such as property taxes) must be apportioned among the states on the basis of population, but a tax of this kind is hard to administer and not widely used.

2. All *indirect taxes* (such as excise taxes on tobacco and liquor) must be uniform, that is, the same rate must apply everywhere without reference to state apportionment and hence it is an easy tax to administer.

3. All *export taxes* are expressly forbidden in that "no tax or duty shall be laid on articles exported from any state."

4. All *bills for raising revenue* must originate in the House of Representatives.

5. In tax matters, as in legislation generally, Congress is responsible for policy but the executive branch must execute it and decide sublegislative issues relative thereto. It was on this basis, for example, that the Supreme Court upheld the flexible tariff law of 1922 which authorized the President to raise or lower rates within limits set by Congress.[23]

The financial powers of the states derive partly from the federal

---

[19] (262 U.S. 447. 1923).   [20] (262 U.S. 447. 1923).
[21] *Springer* v. *United States* (102 U.S. 586. 1890).
[22] *Pollock* v. *Farmer's Loan & Trust* (157 U.S. 429; 158 U.S. 601. 1895).
[23] *Hampton & Co.* v. *United States* (276 U.S. 406. 1928).

Constitution and partly from their own constitutions. The main rules judicially constructed from these two sources are these:

1. A state must have jurisdiction and thus cannot tax tangibles, and as a rule intangibles, outside of its own borders.

2. The supremacy of federal laws and treaties must be respected.

3. Federal powers and instrumentalities may not be interfered with.[24]

4. Taxes on interstate and foreign commerce are not allowed.[25]

5. Articles to be taxed must be classified and treated alike so as to conform to the equal-protection-of-the-laws provision of the Fourteenth Amendment.

6. The products of citizens of other states may not be discriminated against.

7. Funds may be appropriated only for a public purpose and not for a private one.[26]

At the next lower level, counties, cities, and other subdivisions of the states derive their power to tax wholly from state legislatures. Occasionally, especially where there is home rule, the local taxing power is granted under the state constitution, but in that case it is usually subject to repeal or to change by the legislature. The localities are also bound by whatever regulations may be issued by the state legislatures with regard to the manner of levying and collecting taxes, and limits have been set on certain local tax rates in nearly every state.

The Police Power of the States

The police power, now one of the last bastions of states' rights, also is vague and undefined in precise terms, but in general terms it has come to mean the powers reserved to the states to legislate concerning the safety, health, morals, and welfare of its citizens. Apparently to John Marshall goes the credit for giving the concept its importance in American constitutional law. In the famous case of *Brown* v. *Maryland* decided in 1827, the issue involved the authority of a state to tax merchandise coming across its borders. In his decision, Chief Justice Marshall used the terms *original package* and *police power,* establishing the rule that as long as goods remain in the original package they are still subject to the control of Congress over interstate commerce, but that once broken open or sold, they came under the police power of the states.

The term was slow to gain currency until the case, ten years later, of *Charles River Bridge* v. *Warren Bridge*.[27] In this famous controversy involving the contract clause of the Constitution, Chief Justice Taney used the words "police power" to signify the power of the states "to

---

[24] *McCulloch* v. *Maryland* (4 Wheaton 419. 1827).

[25] *Brown* v. *Maryland* (12 Wheaton 316. 1819).

[26] The leading case on this point is *Loan Association* v. *Topeka* (20 Wallace 655. 1874).

[27] (11 Peters 420. 1837).

promote the happiness and prosperity of the community." But it was not until nearly twenty years later that the concept came to be an established one. A celebrated case arising during the 1850s was *Cooley* v. *Board of Wardens of Port of Philadelphia* [28] wherein the Supreme Court held that a state might regulate pilotage on the ground that Congress had failed to pre-empt the field; the state might therefore be allowed to exercise its police power over a matter indirectly affecting foreign commerce. Thereafter rather extensive use of the state police power was permitted by the courts in matters relating to safety of transportation, but when Congress made affirmative use of its own power in this field by passing the Interstate Commerce Act in 1887, the states were eliminated. In other fields, also, the question of the police power of the states was a little more settled after the Fourteenth Amendment to the Constitution was adopted following the Civil War; thereafter the state police power was regarded as "a power excepted and reserved to the states," a power that "remains in them in full and unimpaired sovereignty," the reserved authority of the state legislatures to pass "all manner of wholesome and reasonable laws which shall be for the good and welfare of the commonwealth." [29]

Although court decisions following the passage of the Fourteenth Amendment did help to clarify the question, they also brought into sharper relief instances in which claims arising under the state police power conflicted with the private rights and immunities protected by the due-process-of-law wording in the amendment itself. Thus, decisions in scores of celebrated cases involving vital economic issues have depended on the judges' choice between these rival concepts. Hamilton and Rodee have observed that:

> If the abridgement of individual right loomed larger in the judicial mind, the statute [being questioned] was condemned; if the act seemed to the justices to serve such ends as public safety, public health, public morals or occasionally even an indefinite public welfare, it was approved. . . . "Public benefit" is measured against "private sacrifice" and victory goes with the concept which is weighted with the more compelling values.[30]

To define such broad terms as *life, liberty,* and *property* as contained in the Fourteenth Amendment is equally difficult and often subjective. Property, for example, has been held to involve the right to make a fair profit or one that is not "confiscatory." And the term *liberty* today occasions more judicial controversy than any of the three because it has been held to mean liberty of contract which involves the whole question of wage agreements and industrial relations.

---

[28] (12 Howard 299. 1852).

[29] Walton H. Hamilton and Carlton C. Rodee, "Police Power," *Encyclopedia of the Social Sciences,* Vol. XII, p. 190.

[30] Hamilton and Rodee, *op. cit.,* p. 192.

The Federal Police Power

If the police power is a power reserved to the states, how could there also be a federal police power? Logically, of course, it would be impossible, but in practice the concept now has currency even in decisions by "jurists who are caught off guard or who consciously give exact names to current realities." [31] The federal police power is the use of federal powers, especially the commerce, taxing, and postal powers, for the same general purposes and intent for which the state police power is used.

Under the federal police power Congress has legislated in a number of fields affecting the morals, safety, health, and welfare of society which, in many instances, directly or indirectly affect business. Thus, the Postmaster General has been authorized to keep obscene and seditious matter from the mails, action that periodically creates celebrated controversies as in the case of *Lady Chatterley's Lover*. Lottery tickets were early excluded from the mails on the ground that gambling is injurious to public morality. Under the commerce power the white-slave traffic across state lines was made a federal offense. Under the legal fiction that revenue was involved (but actually to discourage their use), narcotic drugs have been so heavily taxed as to limit their sale. In the industrial field the products of child labor have been barred from interstate commerce and employers' liability for industrial accidents has been established. The use of federal powers for police purposes tends to grow rather than to diminish.

A good example in judicial history of the use of the federal police power is the so-called *Oleomargarine* case. In *McCray* v. *United States* [32] Congress, under pressure from the dairy lobby, imposed so high a tax on substitutes colored to look like butter that the effect was to protect the butter market and discourage the wide use of oleomargarine. When the act was challenged, the Supreme Court upheld it on the ground that if revenue could be derived from the tax, it was not the province of the Court to examine any additional or ulterior motive on the part of Congress. [33] But the Court has looked into motive in other cases, on the basis of which it then declared Congressional police-power legislation to be void. To refer to child labor once more, when Congress tried for the second time to tax the products of child labor in interstate commerce the Court decided, in the case of *Bailey* v. *Drexel Furniture Co.*, [34] that the tax constituted a penalty rather than a bona fide tax and voided the act; but in 1941 child labor was again restricted under the commerce power, and this time it was upheld.

[31] *Ibid.*, p. 192.   [32] (195 U.S. 27. 1904).

[33] Pressure from consumer groups caused Congress to repeal this tax in 1950, and many of the states, except for some where the dairy interests are strong, followed that example.

[34] (259 U.S. 20, 1922).

THE SEPARATION OF POWERS DOCTRINE

By now it should be clear that the powers of government are not always as they seem, and this is also true of the separation-of-powers doctrine. Actually, of course, it is not that powers have been completely separated because under the Constitution they were deliberately admixed in order to create a system of checks and balances. The President, for example, in effect shares in the legislative power when he recommends or vetoes bills; Congress in effect exercises administrative authority when it creates or abolishes departments and agencies; the courts are responsible for something akin to legislation when they decide public policy in areas such as the police power and due process. Checks and balances are as much a part of our governmental system as the separation of powers, but logically the two doctrines are contradictory.

In so far as a separation occurs, therefore, it is one of instrumentalities—the legislative, executive, and judicial institutions within the government—and not a division of powers as such. The principal purpose of the doctrine is to prevent the dominance of any one branch and to make sure that the general lines of authority are respected. This was emphasized in the leading case of *Kilbourn* v. *Thompson*,[35] where the issue concerned the power of Congress to punish for contempt, this being an action more judicial than legislative. Said the Court, "It is essential to the successful working of this system [separation of powers] that the persons entrusted with power in any one of these branches shall not be permitted to encroach upon the powers conferred upon the others, but that each shall by the law of its creation be limited to the powers appropriate to its own department." Doubt may and does arise, of course, as to what is "appropriate" in every instance. As Mr. Justice Holmes observed in another case also involving the separation of powers, legislation, execution, and adjudication are not fields of black and white; there are many shaded areas where judgment and discretion must be exercised.[36]

With the passing of time the separation-of-powers doctrine has become increasingly flexible. In the NRA case already referred to, for example, a principle developed by the courts is that legislative power may not be delegated. But if a law succeeds in establishing a norm, a standard, a basic policy, then on that authority the executive branch may promulgate rules having all the effect of discretionary legislation. This occurred under the so-called flexible tariff law of the Hoover administration which allowed the President to alter duties 50 percent in either direction on the basis of findings by the U. S. Tariff Commission. The principal reason for the modification of the separation-of-powers theory is economic in origin. This is primarily an outgrowth of the ap-

---

[35] (103 U.S. 168. 1881).
[36] *Springer* v. *Government of Philippine Islands* (277 U.S. 189. 1928).

pearance of powerful regulatory commissions created within the framework of the federal government in response to public demand for the regulation of major economic activities.

JUDICIAL REVIEW

The power of the courts to invalidate statutes is a prime consideration for the nation's economy. Whenever a government extends public assistance, regulation, or ownership and operation in some sector of the economy, the action may be questioned in the law courts, and it is then the responsibility of the courts—and especially the Supreme Court which has final authority—to decide the issue on constitutional grounds. Judicial review is not an automatic procedure. The question of constitutionality arises only when an individual or a group affected by a particular law brings suit to test its validity, alleging that rights or immunities have been violated or that the action complained of is in excess of legislative or administrative authority. The motives for such action may be obscure, but there must be a bona fide case, because the courts will not give advisory opinions as to constitutionality. Once the matter is tried before a court, however, and a law has been held to be null and void, it becomes inoperative in all similar cases.

The power of the courts to invalidate legislation, therefore, has far-reaching consequences. A prominent area is the effect of such power on the regulation of various sectors of the economy by independent commissions. For public utilities in particular a stream of legal battles over valuations, rates, and the like constitutes a burden on the financial and personnel resources of the regulating agency.[37] The right of the courts to the final word in the interpretation of both legislative and administrative action offers a form of protection to private property and private rights that tends to make society more conservative. Legislatures tread cautiously or even avoid social experimentation altogether if it seems likely that a law will be voided. As for the judiciary itself, very often it is faced with the responsibility for deciding difficult questions of public policy such as would strain the wisdom of a Solomon. When a decision is widely unpopular, the courts become involved in criticism and political controversy in a manner that ordinarily, in other kinds of cases, they are spared.

Why is the United States singular in this matter of judicial review? Because in most other nations the legislature is supreme and its action is final. The reason may be lack of a written constitution as in Great Britain, or that the legislature has constitutionally been designated the final authority on all matters of public policy. In Great Britain, for example, any form of government including socialism may be legislated into existence without the courts having any right to determine the

[37] See Chap. 17.

propriety of the action. In most nations, however—Great Britain in-cluded—the courts do have the power to determine whether an *adminis-trative* action is in excess of authority, but this is quite different from determining whether the law itself is in excess of authority.

Like other features of the American constitutional system that have been examined in this chapter, judicial review (or the American doctrine of judicial supremacy, as Charles G. Haines called it in his book of that title) has grown into something considerably more prominent than was originally intended. There is no question that the framers of the Con-stitution gave to the Supreme Court the power to determine whether state laws conform to the Constitution. This is provided by inescapable im-plication in the articles defining the jurisdiction of the Supreme Court and the "supreme law of the land." But there is still some question whether it was ever intended that the Supreme Court should have the right to invalidate the laws of Congress. Legally, this doubt was resolved as early as 1803 in the case of *Marbury* v. *Madison*.[38] A federal law was involved which provided among other things that the Supreme Court should issue the writ of mandamus (an order to a lower court or to an administrative agency to take a specified action) as a part of its original jurisdiction. The decision, which was written by Chief Justice Marshall, held that Congress could not so legislate because the authority to issue such a writ was not included in the original jurisdiction of the Supreme Court as fixed by the Constitution and the authority of the Constitution is superior to that of Congress. The general proposition was then stated that any federal law not in conformity with the Constitution is null and void. Judicial review has built on this foundation ever since.

Paralleling the early history of the use of the commerce clause, the power of judicial review of legislation was not used again for some time —not, indeed, until more than fifty years later in the case of *Dred Scott* v. *Sanford*[39] in which the Missouri Compromise was invalidated. Since the Civil War, however, judicial review has been of primary importance, first, because it has been invoked in scores of cases involving the due-process-of-law clause of the Fourteenth Amendment—an area affecting the authority of the states to legislate on economic and social issues— and, second, because the power has been exercised on acts of Congress involving the use of the commerce, taxing, and other powers in highly controversial matters such as the regulation of the profits of public utili-ties and problems of industrial relations.

Perhaps the most famous public contest over judicial review occurred during the New Deal administration of Franklin D. Roosevelt when, in the four years between 1933 and 1937, the Supreme Court invalidated no less than thirteen federal and fifty-three state statutes. Some of the federal legislation involved was considered the backbone of the New Deal social and economic program, and the resulting frustration led the

[38] (1 Cranch 137. 1803).   [39] (19 Howard 393. 1857).

administration to engage in the so-called court-packing dispute and raised an outcry against the Nine Old Men. Actually, judicial review has been a controversial subject almost continuously since the decision in *Marbury* v. *Madison*. Each political party has accused the other of appointing justices to the Supreme Court who were known to share a particular political viewpoint, Franklin D. Roosevelt—who during his more than three terms in office was finally able to appoint a whole new Court—being no exception. Consequently, many proposals seek periodically to diminish or to limit the power of judicial review, the most common being the requirement of a two thirds instead of a mere majority vote by the members of the Court, the limitation of the Court's jurisdiction by Constitutional amendment, an increase in the number of justices, and the possible overriding of judicial vetoes by Congress, also, presumably, by Constitutional amendment.

THE PROTECTION OF PRIVATE RIGHTS

Some of the many references in the Constitution to the private rights and immunities of citizens and groups have already been noted. The protection of such rights stems from the first ten amendments collectively known as the Bill of Rights; the due-process-of-law clauses of the Fifth and Fourteenth amendments, the former applying to the federal government and the latter to the states; the equal-protection-of-the-laws provision of the Fourteenth Amendment; stipulations regarding the nonviolability of contracts; and safeguards surrounding the right of eminent domain. Although this discussion of private rights will be taken up again at intervals throughout the book, a few comments here will round out the picture of the guarantees afforded the individual (it will be recalled that corporations are held to be "individuals") against unduly aggressive governmental action.

The courts have decided that all Constitutional guarantees found in the first ten amendments were intended as restrictions on the federal government only, and hence do not apply to the states. But since most state constitutions contain these same provisions, often in addition to others of the same nature, the citizen is protected at both levels. Most provisions of the federal Bill of Rights guard the rights of the individual in civil and criminal court proceedings, while others guarantee freedom of speech, religion, press, petition, and assembly. Additional clauses contained in the main body of the Constitution are equally significant and apply at all levels of government. Thus Article IV states that "Full faith and credit shall be given in each State to the public acts, records, and judicial proceedings of every other State. . . . The citizens of each state shall be entitled to all privileges and immunities of citizens in the several States." These principles make us one people with equal rights and free from most state discriminations. They also encourage equality of treatment in business relations.

A further list of rights and immunities is contained in Article I, Section 9 of the Constitution, and these also apply at all levels of government. It is stipulated that no tax or duty shall be laid on articles exported from any state; no bill of attainder or ex post facto (retroactive) law shall be passed; "the privilege of the writ of habeas corpus [testing the right to hold a person in custody] shall not be suspended, unless when in cases of rebellion or invasion the public safety may require it"; no preference shall be given to the ports of one state over those of another; no state shall enter into any treaty, alliance, or confederation; no state shall pass any law impairing the obligation of contracts, or, except with the consent of Congress, lay any imposts or duties on imports or exports.

At the administrative level in the executive branch of the government these express Constitutional protections to private rights have been supplemented—again by the courts—so that gradually a body of principles has been evolved applicable to due process of law in administrative proceedings. This development is to be underscored because most governmental action affecting business stems from administrative execution of the law. The principal rules in this area are:

1. An administrative agency must possess *jurisdiction* conferred by law, or its actions will be considered *ultra vires* (literally, in excess of power).

2. The hearing officer in an administrative agency in a proceeding affecting property or material interests must be an *impartial* arbitrator without any disqualifying personal connection with the matter before him.

3. Those affected by administrative rules having the force of law must receive suitable advance *notice* of the action and, in case of need, must be offered an opportunity for a fair *hearing* to learn the charges against them and the findings of fact involved in the case.

4. Findings in administrative hearings must be supported by degrees of *evidence* ranging from "some" to "substantial."

5. Ordinarily, the courts will not take jurisdiction of a case until the complainant has exhausted his *remedies* before an administrative agency having the proper jurisdiction. When the courts do review administrative decisions, they usually confine themselves to questions of law, leaving matters of fact to the administrative agency involved, although, as will be seen later, questions of fact are sometimes disguised as questions of law.

For one of the Supreme Court's leading disquisitions on this whole question of administrative due process, see the case of *Morgan* v. *United States* [40] dealing with the regulatory powers of the Secretary of Agriculture.

[40] (304 U.S. 1. 1938).

THE ADMINISTRATIVE FRAMEWORK OF GOVERNMENT

In the course of this study there will be constant reference to the work of federal departments, bureaus, regulatory agencies, and corporations, and consequently an over-all view of the structure of the executive branch may be helpful. Even to the Hoover Commission, "It is almost impossible to comprehend the organization and management problems of the Federal Government unless one has some concept of its hugeness and complexity. The sheer size, complexity and geographical dispersion of its operations almost stagger the imagination. . . . The Federal Government has become the largest enterprise on earth." [41] Let us see if we can make the structure a little more intelligible.

The official organization chart of the federal government for 1959-1960 (shown in Fig. 1 on page 67) includes all three branches, and although it lists only the more important agencies of the executive branch, this is enough for present purposes. It takes only a brief glance at this picture to see the extent to which the agencies of the Executive Office of the President, the ten major departments, and the scores of independent offices and establishments deal with economic matters affecting all parts of the economy.

Thus, the Executive Office of the President, which has greatly expanded in recent years, includes the Bureau of the Budget, the Council of Economic Advisers, the National Aeronautics and Space Council, the National Security Council, the Office of Civil and Defense Mobilization, and the President's Advisory Committee on Government Organization. Budgetary planning, economic stabilization, the space program, national defense, and administrative adjustment to change are therefore at the apex of the federal administrative structure. In addition, the Civil Service Commission, responsible for personnel administration, and the General Services Administration, the federal housekeeping agency and the biggest purchasing organization in the world, have a close working relationship with the President's office.

Of the ten major departments, which in fact resemble holding companies, it has already been noted that those relating to the Big Three of commerce, labor, and agriculture were established "to foster and promote" the interests of these sectors of the economy. Like other departments and independent establishments, they also possess important regulatory and control functions. The Treasury Department administers the income tax and helps formulate financial policy. The Interior Department, among other functions, is involved in conservation and the administration and control of public lands and national parks, mining, and

[41] Commission on Organization of the Executive Branch of the Government, *Concluding Report*, May 1949 (Washington, D.C., 1949), pp. 3-4.

various forms of fuel and power. The Post Office Department operates a service that is indispensable in a modern economy. The Defense Department, consisting of Army, Navy, and Air Force, is one of the nation's largest employers and buyers. The Justice Department includes, among other agencies, the Antitrust Division. The State Department administers the Foreign Service and the foreign-aid programs. The Department of Health, Education, and Welfare encompasses the whole of the social security program (except unemployment compensation) plus education and many of the government's medical services.

The independent offices and establishments of the federal government are so many that they almost have to be classified to be understood. For our purposes, the headings of regulatory commissions, government corporations, and agencies having action or administrative duties will serve. Only the more important ones are included; there are many more smaller ones.

REGULATORY AGENCIES (the first seven are the major regulatory commissions)

> Interstate Commerce Commission
> Federal Trade Commission
> Federal Power Commission
> Federal Communications Commission
> National Labor Relations Board
> Securities and Exchange Commission
> Civil Aeronautics Board
> Federal Reserve System, Board of Governors
> National Mediation Board

GOVERNMENT CORPORATIONS

> In the Department of Agriculture:
>   Commodity Credit Corporation
>   Commodity Exchange Authority
>   Federal Crop Insurance Corporation
> Farm Credit Administration, with 50 subsidiary corporations
> Export-Import Bank of Washington
> Federal Deposit Insurance Corporation
> Federal Home Loan Bank Board, comprising 11 banking subsidiaries, including the Federal Savings and Loan Insurance Corporation
> Federal National Mortgage Association
> Development Loan Fund
> National Capital Housing Authority
> Tennessee Valley Authority
> Saint Lawrence Seaway Development Corporation
> Virgin Islands Corporation

Fig. 1. The Government of the United States

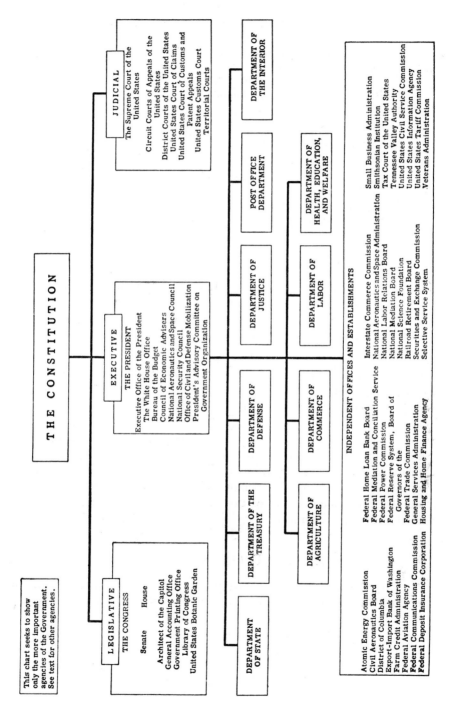

This chart seeks to show only the more important agencies of the Government. See text for other agencies.

THE CONSTITUTION

LEGISLATIVE

THE CONGRESS

Senate   House

Architect of the Capitol
General Accounting Office
Government Printing Office
Library of Congress
United States Botanic Garden

EXECUTIVE

THE PRESIDENT

Executive Office of the President
The White House Office
Bureau of the Budget
Council of Economic Advisers
National Aeronautics and Space Council
National Security Council
Office of Civil and Defense Mobilization
President's Advisory Committee on
Government Organization

JUDICIAL

The Supreme Court of the
United States

Circuit Courts of Appeals of the
United States
District Courts of the United States
United States Court of Claims
United States Court of Customs and
Patent Appeals
United States Customs Court
Territorial Courts

DEPARTMENT OF STATE

DEPARTMENT OF THE TREASURY

DEPARTMENT OF DEFENSE

DEPARTMENT OF JUSTICE

POST OFFICE DEPARTMENT

DEPARTMENT OF THE INTERIOR

DEPARTMENT OF AGRICULTURE

DEPARTMENT OF COMMERCE

DEPARTMENT OF LABOR

DEPARTMENT OF HEALTH, EDUCATION, AND WELFARE

INDEPENDENT OFFICES AND ESTABLISHMENTS

Atomic Energy Commission
Civil Aeronautics Board
District of Columbia
Export-Import Bank of Washington
Farm Credit Administration
Federal Aviation Agency
Federal Communications Commission
Federal Deposit Insurance Corporation

Federal Home Loan Bank Board
Federal Mediation and Conciliation Service
Federal Power Commission
Federal Reserve System, Board of
Governors of the
Federal Trade Commission
General Services Administration
Housing and Home Finance Agency

Interstate Commerce Commission
National Aeronautics and Space Administration
National Labor Relations Board
National Mediation Board
National Science Foundation
Railroad Retirement Board
Securities and Exchange Commission
Selective Service System

Small Business Administration
Smithsonian Institution
Tax Court of the United States
Tennessee Valley Authority
United States Civil Service Commission
United States Information Agency
United States Tariff Commission
Veterans Administration

SOURCE: *U. S. Government Organization Manual*

Panama Canal Company
Federal Prison Industries, Inc., in the Justice Department

ADMINISTRATIVE OR ACTION PROGRAMS

Atomic Energy Commission
United States Information Agency
United States Tariff Commission
Selective Service System
Veterans Administration
Housing and Home Finance Agency
Small Business Administration
Federal Aviation Agency
Federal Mediation and Conciliation Service
Railroad Retirement Board
National Science Foundation
Civil Service Commission
General Services Administration
Attached to the legislative rather than to the executive branch, but
   having administrative or operating functions:
   General Accounting Office
   Government Printing Office

In general outline the organization of the executive branch in state governments follows the federal pattern in that it is variegated and not
closely integrated with the office of the chief executive. The executive
branch is, of course, much smaller in the states except for the larger
and more industrialized ones. The governor is usually surrounded by
staff, coordinating, and advisory units supplemented by regular departments in the more important areas, plus regulatory commissions and government corporations. As a matter of fact, in many states the relative
number and independence of this "fourth branch" is even greater than
in the federal government.

THE COST OF GOVERNMENT

Even if the functions of government were limited to taxation, government would remain an object of major interest to business because
of the huge size of our national debt, the direct result of war and depression. Interest and principal must be paid out of the annual income of the
economy, and interest on the federal debt alone now amounts to $9.5
billion each year [42]—almost three times the cost of operating the federal
government prior to 1930. When the depression started in 1929, the
federal debt stood at $17 billion; when this nation entered World

---

[42] The corresponding figure for state and local government in 1958 was $1.5 billion.

War II in 1941, the national debt had risen to almost $49 billion; and at the end of the war in 1945, the total was well over $258 billion. Similarly, the total net expenditures of the federal government were $3.29 billion in 1929, $13.26 billion in 1941, and $98.4 billion in 1945. By 1948 expenditures had dropped to $33.1 billion but this was still more than ten times the 1929 rate and more than double the 1941 rate. Expenditures were expected to level off in 1948 but the Korean war sent them up to $74.3 billion by 1953 and the national debt went to $228 billion. By 1960 expenditures stood at $78.3 billion,[43] the national debt at $284.7 billion, and the temporary legal debt ceiling at $295 billion. Figure 2 shows how the gross public debt of the United States rose between 1916 and 1958.

FIG. 2. GROSS PUBLIC DEBT OF THE UNITED STATES, 1916–1958

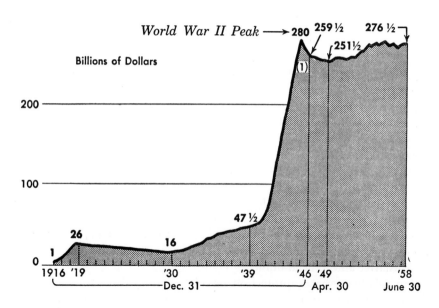

[1] Excluding Victory Loan proceeds used to repay debt in 1946.

SOURCE: U. S. Treasury Department

Where the money goes is equally interesting, for it shows the high ratio of past, present, and future military expenditures (including interest on the national debt) to peacetime needs (see Fig. 3). A comparison with figures for 1952 shows that the *ratio* of expenditures is down for major national security (from 67 percent to 57 percent of the total budget) and veterans services and benefits; is up for labor, welfare, and agriculture; and is little changed for international affairs and finance,

[43] By 1958 state and local expenditures aggregated more than $53 billion a year.

natural resources, commerce and housing, the cost of general government, and interest.

Table 1 on this page shows what a large part of federal peacetime expenditures goes to programs having a business-government relationship. Substantial increases have occurred since 1952 in national security, veterans services and benefits, labor and welfare, and agriculture and agricultural resources, among others; whereas the only shrinkage has been in the field of international affairs and finance.

TABLE 1

Budget Expenditures by Function
(in millions)

	1952	1957	1961 (estimated)
Major national security, including also atomic energy and military assistance	$43,976	$43,270	$45,568
International affairs and finance	2,826	1,973	2,242
Veterans services and benefits	4,863	4,793	5,471
Labor and welfare, including also public health, education, research, and penal institutions	2,168	3,022	4,569
Agriculture and agricultural resources	1,045	4,525	5,623
Natural resources, also recreation	1,366	1,297	1,938
Commerce and housing, including also space exploration, postal service, and civil and defense mobilization	2,624	1,455	2,709
General government, including also the legislative and judicial branches, civilian weather services, protection services, and alien control	1,463	1,790	1,911
Interest	5,934	7,308	9,585
Total expenditures	$66,265	$69,433	$79,616

Source: U.S. Bureau of the Budget

Finally, there is the question of what the national debt means in terms of each individual's share of it. At the end of World War I that share was $228; by the end of World War II it was $1905; thereafter it declined until the outbreak of the Korean war, after which the upward trend was resumed and by 1958 it stood at $1588, to which some $336 may be added for the individual's share of debts at the state and local levels. At the same time, per capita expenditures were $409 for the federal government and $259 for state and local governments.

FIG. 3. THE BUDGET DOLLAR: WHERE IT GOES
TOTAL—$79.8 BILLION
(FISCAL YEAR 1961, ESTIMATED)

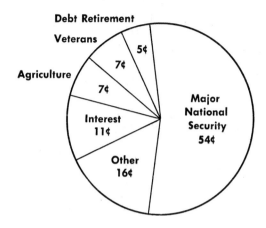

SOURCE: U. S. Bureau of the Budget

The Committee on National Debt Policy, an organization of business-men and economists, for several years tried to formulate constructive policies for long-range fiscal management. The following guidelines in one of its studies of public policy, among others, are worth re-emphasiz-ing: [44]

1. A vigorous, dynamic economy is essential to carrying the debt burden.

2. Excessive government spending makes it harder to reduce debt and to reduce taxes, which curb economic activity, because high taxes reduce profits and inhibit risk funds.

3. A debt-retirement plan geared to national income should be adopted and readjusted as needed.

4. The vast size of government makes imperative its more effective operation; thus capable people must be attracted to and retained in the government service.

Sources of Tax Revenues

Except for tariffs, the states may draw on the same sources of revenue as the federal government, but the problem differs for the two because in terms of scope and a first claim on sources, the task of the federal government is easier than that of the states and localities. Indeed, this is

[44] Committee on Public Debt Policy, National Debt Series, *Our National Debt and the Budget* (pamphlet, New York, 1937), p. 20.

one reason that federal centralization has occurred to the extent that it has at the expense of the states.

For the federal government, the income tax collected from individuals and from business enterprises is now the principal source of revenue. Figure 4, for example, shows that some 80 percent of the total budget receipts come from this combined source alone. Tariff receipts, once a substantial source of revenue, are now useful only as an instrument of policy affecting international trade. In 1940, for example, customs receipts produced only $349 million; in 1960 they were still only $1.1 billion. Excise taxes, which are internal taxes on commodities such as tobacco, liquor, luxuries, and the like, have increased more slowly than the income tax but nevertheless constitute some 11 percent of all federal revenue.

Fig. 4. The Budget Dollar: Where It Comes From
Total—$84 Billion
(Fiscal Year 1961, Estimated)

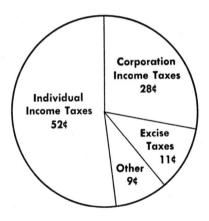

SOURCE: U. S. Bureau of the Budget

At the state level, although the states are virtually unrestricted in what they may tax, the trend has been toward gasoline, sales, and income taxes and away from real-estate and personal property taxes. The latter are now the principal sources of city and local revenue, along with license fees, fines, and the like. Also, many cities have adopted a municipal income tax and the plan is spreading, especially in the Middle West, as municipal budgets continue to expand. Approximately two thirds of the states have passed income tax laws and three fourths of them have adopted the sales tax. The composite picture, therefore, includes income taxes at the federal level; gasoline, income, and sales taxes at the state level; and property taxes at the local level.

Because government financial policy is so important in the area of taxation, the Committee for Economic Development conducted a careful study of what policy should be and suggests that the first of the three broad objectives of a proper tax system be that it

> . . . must impose the least possible restriction upon an expansion of production and employment. Particular care should be taken not to discourage the launching of new enterprises and the natural urge of every business man to try to make his business grow. By the continuous starting of new businesses, and the steady growth of old ones, more jobs get created and more wages get paid. Care must also be taken that personal income taxation does not penalize unusual abilities, or undermine thrift, ambition and hard work by unduly limiting the rewards. This general objective means, also, that taxes should cut as little as possible into the buying power of consumers; for the more buying power each one has, the broader is the market for all goods and services.[45]

From this principle it is concluded that corporate income taxes should be reduced in order to create a stronger profit incentive—a recommendation with which not everyone, by any means, would agree. The two remaining objectives of the CED's proper tax system are to apportion the tax burden fairly and to provide adequate revenues for government.

Has government become too large? Government provides many services to the economy and to its citizens: schools, courts, roads, sanitary systems. Should the number and quality of these services be reduced, or should they only be made more efficient? Government has also developed an enormous apparatus for regulating, encouraging, stabilizing, and otherwise controlling the various parts of the economy, and for this the pressure groups themselves are responsible. A study of business and government should try to find the answer to the question, What are the *essential* economic functions of government—those that will perform the job that needs to be done without curtailing our liberties or allowing an unbridled bureaucracy to secure the kind of control that should remain in the hands of the private citizen?

Supplementary Reading

Appleby, Paul H., *Big Democracy* (New York, 1945). The why and how of governmental expansion.

———, *Policy and Administration* (University, Ala., 1949).

MacIver, Robert M., *The Web of Government* (New York, 1947). Governmental power and why it grows.

Commission on Organization of the Executive Branch of the Government, *Concluding Report; Regulatory Commissions; Federal Business Enterprises; Revolving Funds and Business Enterprises of the Government; General Man-*

---

[45] Committee for Economic Development, "A Postwar Federal Tax Plan for High Employment" (Washington, D.C., 1944), p. 7.

agement of the Executive Branch; all either Commission or Task Force reports (Washington, D.C., 1949).

Hyneman, Charles S., *Bureaucracy in a Democracy* (New York, 1950). Stresses the regulatory commissions.

Herring, Pendleton, *Public Administration and the Public Interest* (New York, 1936). Deals primarily with the regulatory commissions.

Holcombe, Arthur N., *Our More Perfect Union* (Cambridge, Mass., 1950). Principles of the American system of government.

Bernstein, M. H., *Regulating Business by Independent Commission* (Princeton, N.J., 1955). The single largest area of public control.

Sutton, F. X., and others, *The American Business Creed* (Cambridge, Mass., 1956). Attitudes toward control.

Benson L., *Merchants, Farmers, and Railroads* (Cambridge, Mass., 1955). Regulation in general.

Vasey, Wayne, *Government and Social Welfare* (New York, 1958). An important area of expansion.

Key, V. O., *Politics, Parties, and Pressure Groups* (New York, 4th ed., 1958).

Fabricant, Solomon, *The Rising Trend of Government Employment* (New York, National Bureau of Economic Research, 1949).

———, *The Trend of Governmental Activity in the United States since 1900* (New York, National Bureau of Economic Research, 1952).

Swisher, Carl B., *American Constitutional Development* (Boston, 1954). A convenient reference book.

Pritchett, C. Herman, *The Roosevelt Court: A Study in Judicial Politics and Values* (New York, 1948). Judicial review during a crucial period.

Carr, Robert K., *The Supreme Court and Judicial Review* (New York, 1942). The role of the judiciary.

Corwin, Edward S., *The Constitution and What It Means Today* (Princeton, N.J., 1947). Popularly written and reliable.

Wheare, Kenneth C., *Federal Government* (New York, 3d ed., 1953). Views the subject broadly.

U. S. Commission on Intergovernmental Relations, *Report* (Washington, D.C., 1955). In addition to this volume, 15 separate studies were issued.

Anderson, William, *The Nation and the States, Rivals or Partners?* (Minneapolis, Minn., 1955). The latest and best treatment of the subject.

Redford, Emmette S., *Administration of National Economic Control* (New York, 1952). Administrative aspects of economic problems.

Davis, Kenneth C., *Administrative Law* (St. Paul, Minn., 1951). Judicial control of legislation.

Steiner, George A., *Government's Role in Economic Life* (New York, 1953). Chap. 13, "The Administrative Machinery of Government."

Groves, Harold M., *Financing Government* (New York, 1945). One of the best authorities on public finance.

Blough, Roy, *The Federal Taxing Process* (New York, 1952). By one who has been close to government.

Paul, Randolph E., *Taxation in the United States* (Boston, 1954). By a former U. S. Treasury official, writing on the history, the law, and the economics of taxation.

Bureau of the Budget, *The Federal Budget in Brief*, fiscal year 1961 (Washington, D.C., 1960). A small publication giving the highlights of the budget.

PART II

COMPETITION
AND
FREE
ENTERPRISE

4

THE MONOPOLY ISSUE

The issues; key terms defined; growth of monopoly; over-all picture of economic concentration: effect of war and reconversion, mergers, size and financial power; where competition remains; intent of antitrust laws; administered prices.

The greatest issue of American domestic policy is whether the private-enterprise system, based on competition and freedom of choice, will gradually give way to monopoly of either the private or the public kind, or a combination of both. There are many laws and policies on which the outcome of this issue eventually depends, but the central one is whether the antitrust laws can keep the economy sufficiently competitive, or whether they are a weak reed and some other remedy must be found. Judging from the experience of other countries, if the antitrust laws do fail then the main alternatives are either limited government monopolies in the form of government ownership and operation, or mixed enterprises, both of which resemble private monopoly more than they do private competition.

What are the areas of agreement on this issue? To begin with, most influential labor leaders, farm leaders, and professional leaders as well as most businessmen agree that the *objectives* of our economic system are sound: a chance for everyone to compete in his own field, to own property, to earn a sufficient profit, and to choose employment and patronage in a free market. Furthermore, lip service, at least, is paid to the idea that supply and demand and a self-regulating market are the best assurance to producers and consumers that they will get what they want with maximum efficiency and freedom of choice.

If most people agree on these propositions, however, they often disagree as to the *institutional arrangements* needed to achieve them. The basic antitrust law, the Sherman Act of 1890, for example, is no longer so popular or so widely supported as it once was, although nearly everyone would admit that without it there would be far less competition and individual ownership today than is actually the case.

In several areas of the economy there are now typically a few large competitors who dominate the field, a condition known as oligopoly or monopolistic competition. Is this as satisfactory an arrangement for the economy as when many small firms competed with one another? How much competition must there be to ensure that prices will be market-induced instead of administratively determined, and that men and women with ability and access to capital will be allowed to enter an industry at will? Conversely, how much economic concentration can a nation stand before the transition point to socialism is reached? Although this is a long-range question, the issue may not be so remote as is generally supposed.

In the international field, America's competition is with nations where public monopoly and thorough economic planning are indigenous. Does this fact justify a relaxation of our monopoly laws and a greater tolerance of competition-reducing industrial giantism? Or does the strength of our system still lie in many competitors operating at a higher degree of efficiency than is possible under great size? Technology tends to produce large plant and large corporations, a kind of growth that is said to be justified by greater efficiency of production. But is the kind of growth justified that is merely profit-induced, that aims chiefly to control assets and markets through what Louis Brandeis used to call "banker control"? Are there both good and bad trusts, as Woodrow Wilson used to say? And if so, by what criteria are they to be differentiated?

Those who would justify bigness and economic concentration make much of the point that the vast powers exercised by modern managers and labor leaders should cause no public concern because these leaders would not abuse their power even if they had the chance. But this is not what history teaches; are we so very different? How shall we dispose of the unpleasant fact that power, long continued, seems inevitably to result in abuses and declining abilities, whereas competition keeps power in check and stimulates ability?

Industry is not the only area in which competition has suffered: there are similar tendencies in the fields of labor and agriculture. Is it possible to control the growth of monopoly in one field without controlling it in others? And if concentration in industry were reduced, could it also be reduced in labor and agriculture? If industrial corporations have created the condition of monopoly, must they not also contribute to its solution? In other words, in terms of government policy, where is a start to be made?

The government's methods of discouraging monopoly and prosecuting it when it appears leave much to be desired, partly because too little attention is given to prevention and partly because authority is divided between the Antitrust Division of the Justice Department and the Federal Trade Commission. Could these problems be solved through proper legislation and better administration? And would public opinion support such improvements? Why are labor and farm leaders seemingly less concerned about monopoly than they were a generation or so ago? Will the public remain largely lethargic to monopoly so long as prosperity prevails?

Finally, if bigness and monopoly are as inevitable as death and taxes, as some people among both conservatives and radicals are heard to say, then what are the possibilities of reaching the problem from the other end: by strengthening small business and encouraging it to be more aggressive and more united in its approach to government? Or is this also a visionary notion? These are some of the issues. What are the facts?

Key Terms and Concepts Defined

Old words change their meaning and new ones are invented almost as fast as industrial organizations invent new ways to evade the antitrust laws. In a complex and shifting field, therefore, word usages must be tied down as securely as possible. In this discussion the term *monopoly* has been used as virtually interchangeable with the term *economic concentration,* which is the modern preference. The terms *competition* and *monopoly* are usually regarded as opposites, and so they are, but neither has much significance when employed in an absolute sense. Theoretically, there may be pure or perfect competition and complete monopoly, but such instances are rare. From a practical standpoint, therefore, the concern here is with degrees of competition and degrees of monopoly, which is why the neutral term, *economic concentration,* serves a useful purpose.

The term *competition* has been defined as a form of rivalry in the acquisition of profit. Competition may be perfect, imperfect, pure, fair, unfair, monopolistic, nonprice, oligopolistic, cutthroat, predatory, discriminatory, potential, effective, or workable.[1] There are also several implications of the term *monopoly*.[2] It may, for example, be *general,* in which case monopoly is the power to augment one's profit either by fixing the selling price and thus indirectly determining the quantity to be sold, or by fixing the quantity and thus indirectly determining the selling price. When a single seller controls the entire supply of a commodity (which rarely happens), then monopoly is said to be *generic.* It becomes *absolute* when the monopolist can fix the price and the quantity of his produce without regard to the effect on consumers, competitors, or the government; he can do this, of course, only when consumers and potential competitors have no recourse and it is certain that the state will not intervene. A variation of this form of monopoly is when a *number* of sellers acting in unison through formal or tacit agreement, control the entire supply of a commodity. An extreme use of the word makes it mean anything that is not perfect competition, but this has little value. And finally, monopoly may be *legal,* as in the case of a regulated public utility.

For practical purposes, therefore, *monopoly may be said to exist*

---

[1] Clair Wilcox, *Competition and Monopoly in American Industry,* Temporary National Economic Committee, Monograph No. 21 (Washington, D.C., 1941), pp. 2–9.

[2] *Ibid.,* pp. 9–11.

whenever a seller or a group of sellers (or buyers), acting in unison, gain a sufficient control of the market for a broadly defined commodity to enable them to augment their profit by limiting output and raising price; the application of the restraint may be either actual or potential.

Complete monopoly is as nonexistent as pure competition, both concepts, according to Hamilton and Till, belonging to picture books rather than to everyday activity. "Everywhere, departures blur the simple lines of black and white into a motley outline streaked with many colors." [3] Actual situations range all the way from a high degree of competition to 90 percent or more of monopolistic control. Degrees of economic concentration are capable of measurement and verification. The factors are the effects of such concentration on competitors in the same line as well as on suppliers and on labor, the relative size of the business, its percentage of output in the industry, and evidences of conspiracy to limit competition. Businessmen and their trade associations sometimes contend that monopoly cannot properly be said to exist unless brought about by deliberate agreement, but more realistically, the ultimate test of monopoly is the *possession* of sufficient economic power that may be used at will to restrict output and affect price by administrative decision. When the *degree of power* is the criterion, then it does not matter that all the evils attributable to monopoly fail to appear at a given time. The point is that monopoly power is able to indulge in as many or as few objectionable practices as it chooses.

The problem of monopoly is complicated by the fact that the ways of the monopolist are constantly changing, being apparently as fluid as society itself. Devices in restraint of trade at the time the Sherman Antitrust Act was passed are now for the most part obsolete, while new and more effective ones have appeared. In the past, control of raw materials was an important tool of monopoly, but today there are only a few industries in which monopolistic control of limited natural resources is the real problem. At present such factors as the control of technology through patents, of research, and of know-how are far more likely to constitute the basis of monopoly power. When these fail, a whole array of ingenious devices may be used to curtail the free play of competition: markets are allotted, fields of production are allocated among a privileged few, quotas are placed on output, prices are artificially fixed and enforced through marketing agreements, price leadership is imposed, patent pools are set up, interlocking directorates and financial interests are arranged, trade-association activities are subsidized, gentlemen's understandings discriminate against particular buyers and sellers who have failed to cooperate, and in some cases, by taking advantage of already entrenched positions, monopoly groups make use of their power over credit to squeeze small industries and lesser rivals out of the market. [4]

---

[3] Walton Hamilton and Irene Till, *Antitrust in Action,* Temporary National Economic Committee, Monograph No. 16 (Washington, D.C., 1941), p. 3.

[4] Wendell Berge, "Monopoly and the South," speech delivered Nov. 22, 1946.

THE GROWTH OF MONOPOLY

Monopoly became a major economic problem in the United States when business became nation-wide following the Civil War. By the end of the nineteenth century the Grangers and the little fellows in business had become sufficiently exercised over the growing power of the railroads and trusts to secure passage of the Interstate Commerce Act of 1887 and the Sherman Act of 1890, the first two major landmarks in the federal control of business. Although coming three years after the Interstate Commerce Act relating to the railways, the Sherman Act deserves the title of basic legislation for the regulation of American industry because it applies to any kind of business from the manufacture of locomotives to the sale of peanuts, and hence straddles the entire economy. Thus the Sherman Act differs from other public-control legislation applying to special categories such as public utilities or transportation.

Called a charter of freedom for American industry,[5] the Sherman Act was passed in order to keep the free-enterprise system free and competitive, to prevent monopolies and price fixing, and to protect thousands of entrepreneurs against the dominance of the few. Accordingly, the act announced as the basic principle of American business that "Every contract, combination in the form of trust or otherwise, or conspiracy, in restraint of trade or commerce . . . is hereby declared illegal." There were no "if's," "and's," or "but's" about it. In the eyes of the common law and in the consciences of Victorian Americans, monopolies in restraint of trade were devilish and, like sin, should be abolished.

But public opinion and Congress had overlooked several pertinent facts. No law is self-enforcing, but requires adequate sanctions and machinery. Words enunciating laws are virtually meaningless until judicially defined, when they may come to permit something quite different from the apparent original intent. An industrial society is complex and rests on delicate balances that cannot be dealt with by clumsy methods. Brilliant corporation lawyers can seemingly outsmart almost any restrictive statute or at least delay the final reckoning, and public opinion, though convinced of the sin of monopoly, is a weak support when it comes to adequate financial resources for antitrust prosecutions. Experience has shown that "to make monopoly in all its forms as odious at law as morally it was outrageous" was not a sufficient defense against the schemings of the ingenious few.[6]

The Sherman Act, basic defense of the free-enterprise system, has remained virtually unchanged by Congress since it was passed at the time when big business was hitting its stride. A part of it was weakened by the Miller-Tydings amendment of 1937—sneaked through as a rider to an appropriation bill—which eased the way for the manufacturer who

[5] Mr. Chief Justice Hughes, *Appalachian Coals* v. *United States* (228 U.S. 344, at 359. 1933).
[6] Hamilton and Till, *op. cit.*, p. 6.

would fix a set price for a trade-marked product. The Sherman Act was supplemented in 1914 by the Clayton Act and the creation of the Federal Trade Commission for its administration, but the machinery for the enforcement of both statutes is kept in separate agencies of the federal government and hence there is not, even today, a unified attack on the problem of monopoly.

The move toward industrial concentration that began in the 1880s, gained force in the 1890s, and soon after the turn of the century had achieved a size which, although formidable at the time, is nevertheless dwarfed by present-day magnitudes. By 1904 the trusts, as they were then called, controlled 40 percent of all manufacturing capital in the United States. In addition, twenty-six trusts controlled 80 percent or more of production in their respective fields, and there were at least eight giants, some of which are still household names, that dominated 90 percent or more of the output of some or all of their respective products. These giants were the American Can Company, the American Sugar Refining Company, the American Tobacco Company, the Corn Products Refining Company, the Standard Oil Company, and the United Shoe Machinery Company. Concerning the impact of early twentieth-century concentrations on the economy, Wilcox has observed that "In this group one finds firms that succeeded in attaining a monopoly position sufficiently complete and sufficiently enduring to insure to their owners something well in excess of a competitive return."[7]

The course of antitrust enforcement history since 1904 is a fairly familiar story. President Theodore Roosevelt made trust-busting and the big stick symbols of his domestic policy, but generally with more heat than effect. President Woodrow Wilson continued and even somewhat intensified the attack on the trust problem, and the Clayton and Federal Trade Commission Acts were passed in 1914. Three years later, however, when the United States entered World War I, Wilson's domestic program including monopoly control, although well under way, was unavoidably pushed into second place. Then during the prosperous 1920s the antitrust laws were soft-pedaled and "the corporation was evolved into an intricate and evasive structure, and merger, amalgamation, integration, and holding company was the order of the day."[8] This was followed by the New Deal era from 1933 until the United States entered World II in 1941. During the early part of this period under the National Recovery Administration a moratorium was declared on the enforcement of the antitrust laws and generally resulted in monopoly tendencies, but after the NRA was ruled unconstitutional in 1935, more money and manpower was devoted to the attack on monopoly than in any previous period in our history, with some notable victories but with an over-all continuation of the trend toward concentration. Since World War II the antitrust program has been actively pushed but without enough financial or administrative support to produce the results that are needed.

[7] Wilcox, *op. cit.*, p. 65.   [8] Hamilton and Till, *op. cit.*, p. 23.

OVER-ALL PICTURE OF ECONOMIC CONCENTRATION

As already suggested, monopoly is largely a matter of degree and of trends, so if we are to predict and to control, we must have as accurate a picture of the problem as possible. Fortunately, the subject of industrial concentration has been rather thoroughly investigated in recent years.[9] The following considerations stand out:

Industrial Concentration Stimulated by War and Reconversion

To meet the requirements of the armed services during World War II for goods of every description, the government turned to the largest business corporations because they possessed advantages in capital, patents, and experience, and were also in a position to furnish wartime personnel to the government. By 1941, fifty-six firms—less than one half of 1 percent of all manufacturing firms in the nation—had been awarded 75 percent of all contracts and of these, six corporations held almost one third.[10] Even during the Korean war, by 1951 General Motors alone had received 15 percent of all federal contracts up to that time. Thus the larger part of the government's war contracts was awarded to the big companies which tended to become bigger, while the small companies, despite efforts through subcontracting arrangements and otherwise, lost ground.

Then under reconversion, in the two years between 1945 and 1947, the federal government sold 70 percent of all publicly owned war plant to 250 large manfacturing firms already controlling more than 66 percent of all industrial facilities in the United States, while the remaining 30 percent of war plant was thinly spread out among some of 262,000 smaller firms controlling only 33 percent of all facilities. One of these plants alone—the steel plant at Geneva, Utah—had cost the government $200 million and was sold to U.S. Steel, the colossus of the industry, for $45.5 million, making it the biggest producer of steel in the West as well as elsewhere.[11] As a result of such policies, by 1952 a few corporations having more than $100 million assets each, owned 51 percent of all the assets in the manufacturing field. At the end of 1955 this figure had risen to 57 percent and by 1956 it was 59 percent. By 1960 it was estimated that one half of 1 percent of all manufacturing corporations in the nation had 57 percent of total sales, leaving only 43 percent for the many thousands of

---

[9] See, for example, George W. Stocking and Myron W. Watkins, *Monopoly and Free Enterprise* (New York, 1951).

[10] *Business Week* (Aug. 1941), p. 32. See also James E. Murray, "Has Small Business a Future?" *Vital Speeches*, Vol. IX (May 15, 1943), pp. 473–477.

[11] Robert S. Allen, "Arsenal of Monopoly," *The New Republic* (Apr. 21, 1947), p. 19.

smaller enterprises.[12] Furthermore, profits per dollar of sales also increase with size. Thus in 1958 profits after federal income tax ranged from 0.5¢ for corporations with assets of less than $1 million, to 7.1¢ for those in the asset class of $100 million or more.

From the standpoint of employment, between 1938 and 1942 the total number of workers employed by 95 percent of the nation's corporations (the smallest concerns) declined by 23 percent, while those employed by the largest 5 percent increased by 22 percent.[13] By 1956, 22 percent of all commercial and industrial firms (except the railroads) had fewer than 20 employees or none at all and accounted for only a quarter of all wage and salaried workers in the category; while nearly one sixth of all workers were in the 200 big firms employing 10,000 workers or more.[14]

Concentration Promoted through Mergers

The merger movement in the United States got its start in the 1880s and 1890s and, despite legislative attempts to curb it through the Sherman and Clayton acts, the trend toward combinations has flourished. By 1929 some 7000 mergers had been consummated in that decade, and they embraced not only competing firms (so-called horizontal mergers), but also firms in a related line of business (vertical mergers), such as a chain grocery concern taking on a bakery. Mergers were also conglomerate (the acquisition of an unrelated business, such as the International Telephone and Telegraph Company purchase of a refrigerator company). This practice is now justified under the heading of "diversification" and is becoming increasingly popular.

Mergers are more common during periods of prosperity than during a depression and they also seem to follow the trend of the stock market. The rapid rate of mergers during the 1920s slackened off during the depression of the 1930s (there were only 101 in 1934), but picked up again during World War II. Between 1940 and 1946 more than 2450 manufacturing and mining firms, with assets constituting some 5.5 percent of the total assets of all manufacturing companies, were absorbed by other corporations.[15] By 1948 the 200 largest manufacturing corporations had an aggregate of 4722 subsidiaries and affiliates (62 percent of all such subsidiaries), and the 500 largest had 6281, or 82 percent of all such subsidiaries.[16]

By 1955, nearly 8000 mergers had been effected since World War II despite the passage of the Celler-Kefauver amendment of 1950 to the

[12] Reported in *The New York Times*, Feb. 3, 1959.

[13] Howard R. Bowen, "The Impact of the War upon Smaller Manufacturing Plants," *Survey of Current Business*, Vol. XXIII (July and Sept. 1943), pp. 19ff.

[14] *Statistical Abstract of the United States*, 1959, Table 616, p. 487.

[15] Federal Trade Commission, *Report on the Merger Movement* (Washington, D.C., 1948), p. 17.

[16] Federal Trade Commission. *A List of 1000 Large Manufacturing Companies, Their Subsidiaries and Affiliates, 1949* (Washington, D.C., 1951).

Clayton Act prohibiting a company from acquiring the assets of another (formerly the prohibition applied only to stock) where the effect "may be substantially to lessen competition . . . or tend to create a monopoly." This wording, however, has been somewhat diluted by a prior Supreme Court ruling that a merger may be permitted if one of the parties to the deal is so unprofitable as to be on the point of failure.[17] In addition, the Federal Trade Commission, which has partial jurisdiction over mergers, has ruled that the antitrust laws are not *necessarily* violated by the merger of two companies that together control even as much as half of the market for a particular product. As a corollary, the commission also holds that a

FIG. 5. NUMBER OF MERGERS AND ACQUISITIONS IN MANUFACTURING AND MINING, 1919–1958

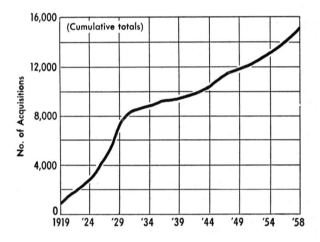

SOURCE: U. S. Federal Trade Commission

merger affecting only a small part of the market is not *necessarily* pure. Other factors to be considered include the general competitive situation, the number of competitors, and the degree of concentration in the industry.

The mergers that reached a record number in 1959 are increasingly conglomerate in character and also in other ways differ from the earlier variety. Where formerly a merger was most often engineered as an aspect of financial manipulation, today the reasons are broader: to cut costs, as when two independent automobile manfacturers combined in 1954; to offer a wider range of products, as in the joining of two home-appliance firms; or to invade new markets, as when two concerns command markets in different parts of the country and join to gain a wider coverage. Other

[17] The leading case on this point is *International Shoe Co. v. Federal Trade Commission* (280 U.S. 291. 1930).

advantages of merger today may be summarized as additional capacity, product diversification, backward integration (acquiring a source of raw materials), forward integration (acquiring distribution outlets), additional capacity through new markets, surplus cash available to the acquiring company, lack of financial resources needed for expansion (it is often cheaper to buy than to build), and tax savings resulting from buying out a distressed concern.[18]

For these economic reasons some recent mergers have been among smaller firms, a trend that does not, however, diminish the simultaneous effort of the giants to absorb their weaker rivals, also for economic reasons. In 1958, two thirds of the acquisitions in the manufacturing field were by corporations having assets of $10 million or more.[19] In terms of volume of production and value of goods sold it seems that concentration rather than competition is now characteristic of great areas of the American economy. There are still thousands of small firms and some areas of enterprise where competition still prevails, but Walter Lippmann's quip that "competition is something of which producers have only as much as they cannot eliminate" is a fair description.[20]

In large areas of the economy what competition there is exists among giants, involving the unlikely juxtaposition of those two incongruous words, monopolistic competition. It is sometimes suggested that as long as two or more firms remain in a particular field, competition is preserved. This might be true if monopoly were simply control by a single firm. Definitions of competition and monopoly assumed in recent Supreme Court decisions, however, show monopoly to mean much more than this. There is an antithesis between monopoly and competition and not even a legal ceremony can make a happy marriage of the two. A competitive system is one in which there are enough business enterprises involved in every sector of the economy so that no one corporation can artificially restrict output, fix prices, or acquire the power to do so if it chooses. Otherwise competition has no meaning in the respective definitions of capitalism and socialism.

Suppose, for example, that the railroad system of a socialistic nation were divided into several operating units and the records of each were periodically compared as to expenses, profits, and efficiency. It would then be possible to determine which unit was superior to the others, and this might be (and in socialist nations often is) called competition. In fact, it is only a facsimile. Certain giant monopolistic corporations in the United States already use this device to spur a better performance by employees in the branches of the enterprise. If public opinion will accept this substitute and if it can be made to believe that real competition is possible among industrial giants as well as among smaller and more nu-

[18] Federal Trade Commission, *Report on Corporate Mergers and Acquisitions* (Washington, D.C., May 1955).

[19] *Statistical Abstract of the United States*, 1959, Table 638, p. 501.

[20] Temporary National Economic Committee, *Hearings*, Pt. 25, p. 13,085.

merous companies, then the way will be open to some type of collectivism, whether of the public or the private variety, and neither is much more acceptable than the other.

Size and Financial Power Show the Extent of Giantism

Americans are said to worship bigness. If this were true, the state of the American economy would be a matter for congratulation. A few comparisons will reveal how very big our giant firms have become.

At hearings before the Temporary National Economic Committee in 1938, Dr. Willard Thorp defined a large corporation as one possessing assets of $5 million or more, but today the figure of $50 million is a more realistic dividing line between the great and the small among corporations. According to this standard, even in 1938 there were 1373 manufacturing corporations exceeding the $50-million-asset mark, and in 1956 there were 1976, constituting .2 of 1 percent of the total and holding 60 percent of all assets reported. By 1955, nearly 70 corporations had assets of more than $1 *billion* each, of which 33 were nonfinancial institutions, 18 were banks (a figure later reduced to 17 when two billionaire banks combined), and 15 were insurance and finance companies. With assets of $17.6 billion in 1958, American Telephone and Telegraph Company is the biggest corporation in the United States. Three times in 1959 the net quarterly earnings of his giant were more than $1 billion; the only other American corporation ever to match that record was General Motors for one quarter in 1955. In 1958 also, AT&T had 1,700,000 shareholders, which was more than the combined total for the next three largest corporations: Ford Motor, General Electric, and Standard Oil of New Jersey. After AT&T, the next largest corporation is Metropolitan Life with assets in 1959 of $17.1 billion and $90 billion of life insurance in force covering 42.3 million persons.

The situation with regard to size according to assets in various industrial groups and the increases that have occurred in the five years between 1951 and 1956 are shown in Table 2.

The automobile industry is a prime example of how concentration grows from small beginnings in one industry after another until a few corporate giants dominate the fields in which they operate. Thus, in the 60-year history of the automobile down to 1956, something like 2600 different makes of car had come and mostly gone on the American market, so that by 1953 only 17 remained and these were produced by only nine corporations. Three years later the number of makes had dropped to 15 produced by five industrial giants. But of these, the so-called Big Three of General Motors, Ford, and Chrysler accounted for more than 95 percent of all production in 1955. Indeed, General Motors alone produced almost half of all the cars on the American market.[21]

[21] Hubert W. Kelley, Jr., "Mutiny of the Car Dealers," *Harper's Magazine* (Aug. 1956), pp. 69–75.

Some sidelights on concentration were brought out at the hearings of the Celler Committee of the House of Representatives in a study of monopoly power in 1949. The representative of a small cereal business, for example, the Van Brode Milling Company of Clinton, Massachusetts, told of the difficulties of a small firm getting started in a line dominated by large competitors. The Van Brode business was set up in 1940, and because of favorable conditions during World War II it was able to get a better start than it might have under more normal circumstances. In 1949 it was the only small firm left in the breakfast-cereal field, all the

TABLE 2

ASSETS OF LARGE CORPORATIONS, BY INDUSTRIAL GROUPS, 1951 AND 1956

	Number		Assets (in millions)	
	1951	*1956*	*1951*	*1956*
All industrial groups	596,385	827,916	$647,524	$948,951
All industrial groups, corporations with assets of $50 million and over	1,373	1,976	380,128	576,672
Manufacturing	373	501	87,954	133,139
Trade	68	83	10,494	14,087
Construction	3	5	185	425
Finance, insurance, real estate, and lessors of real property	640	1,067	203,440	321,963
Agriculture, forestry, and fishery	1	1	363	386
Mining and quarrying	34	46	4,928	6,462
Public utilities	244	257	71,359	98,102
Services	10	16	1,406	2,078

SOURCE: *Statistical Abstract of the United States, 1955,* Table 583, and *1956,* Table 621.

others having either failed or been absorbed by Kellogg or General Foods. Van Brode could not afford to advertise on the scale of its large competitors and so did not advertise at all. Consequently, its overhead costs were relatively low and it sold mainly to federal, state, and other tax-free institutions where advertising is not a factor in a sales campaign. Because the government is the largest client in the cereal field, the big companies started a price war, cutting their regular commercial prices in half except on raisin bran flakes which the small firm did not make. It was estimated that if Van Brode failed, the government would have to pay some $2 million more for its cereals annually because the big companies would then charge the regular commercial rate for all their products.[22]

Competition Still Strong in Some Areas

In 1949 it was found by the Celler Committee that in the shoe, ladies' garment, and furniture industries—or "wherever there is style"—price leadership in particular is lacking unless there is "a trade association that is able to act very effectively without getting caught by the Attorney General." [23] Ten years earlier for the TNEC Wilcox drew up the following list of industries where concentration was generally absent and competition largely survived: [24]

Agriculture—"In agriculture as a whole and in each of its branches, production units are numerous, the typical unit is small, and the degree of concentration is low." Nevertheless, as shown in later chapters, the picture is changing and "an evolving agricultural policy has seriously compromised the rule of competition" in this field also.[25]

Lumber—"The lumber industry has a large number of enterprises, most of them small in size, a large reserve of productive capacity, and a low degree of concentration."

Bituminous coal—Here "production units are numerous, most of them are small, and no one of them controls a significant fraction of the annual output."

Fisheries—A low degree of concentration except in New England.

Cotton textiles, woolen and worsted goods, silk, and rayon—There are areas of relative concentration but in general "producers are numerous, small, and widely scattered. . . ." By 1954, however, this was no longer quite accurate because the trend toward synthetic fabrics blended with wool had resulted in a series of mergers—"the battle of the fibers," so-called—that had all but eliminated the giants in the wool textile industry; as a result of the shift the giants are now the manufacturers of rayon, dacron, orlon, and the like.[26]

Knitted goods—Degree of concentration relatively low.

Men's clothing—High degree of competition.

Women's apparel—Least concentration of all.

Leather—Relatively competitive.

Service trades—Small and competitive.

This is not an exhaustive list but it does offer a sample. Some characterizations are hard to make: both the tire and tube industry and the food

[22] U. S. House of Representatives, *Hearings* before the Subcommittee on Study of Monopoly Power of the Committee on the Judiciary (81st Cong., 1st Sess. Washington, D.C., 1949), Serial No. 14, Pt. 2-A, pp. 230–239.

[23] *Ibid.*, Pt. 1, p. 124. [24] Wilcox, *op. cit.*, pp. 21–22, 31.

[25] Hamilton and Till, *op. cit.*, p. 117. [26] *The New York Times*, July 25, 1954.

products industry, for example, are highly concentrated but they are also marked by active competition between individual products.

The area of the economy where competition remains, therefore, is still a considerable one; nevertheless, the very factors that have caused these industries to remain competitive have also been the reason for many informal agreements whereby the rigors of competition may be tempered. Moreover, in a volatile and changing society such as ours, the picture alters quickly. The milk industry, for example, joins the procession toward concentration at the point of distribution, although it is originally classified in the category of agriculture where concentration is still relatively low; and textiles, listed as largely competitive in the 1930s, no longer are. In considering the prospects of competition and monopoly, therefore, this dynamic aspect of the economy should be given due weight. As Hamilton and Till point out:

> Industries are moving at various tempos in various directions. If some move toward increased concentration, others are moving toward a bigger and better competition; still others shuttle back and forth in response to the stimuli which constantly beat upon them. A shift in technology, a deal in high finance, the appearance of a substitute, the loss of a foreign market, the development of a by-product—and the fabric of trade practice reveals new lines. An over-competition, with its induced demand for security, may breed conspiracy. A restraint itself, through some weakness in its armament, often invites a return to competition.[27]

But it is the long-run trend that decides the outcome, and the current is strongly set in the direction of concentration.

Kefauver Investigation of Administered Prices

The hearings and reports of the Senate Subcommittee on Antitrust and Monopoly, lasting over a three-year period from 1957 to 1960, constitute the most extensive survey of economic concentration since the notable study of the Temporary National Economic Committee immediately preceding World War II. The Kefauver inquiry related to industrial prices and practices, especially automobiles and steel. Senator O'Mahoney, in transmitting the four volumes of hearings and the long reports and supporting data, claimed that the study "incorporates the most comprehensive body of factual data" on this subject "ever prepared." [28] Among those who testified were E. G. Nourse, J. K. Galbraith, Gardiner Means, and Jules Backman.

Are administered prices, as contrasted with market-induced prices,

---

[27] Hamilton and Till, *op. cit.*, p. 118.

[28] Reports: *Concentration in American Industry* (July 12, 1957, 85th Cong., 1st Sess.); *Administered Prices: Steel* (March 13, 1958, 85th Cong., 2d Sess.); *Administered Prices: Automobiles* (Nov. 1, 1958, 85th Cong., 2d Sess.). Hearings: *Administered Prices: Hearings*, 4 parts, 85th Cong., 1st Sess. (July–Nov. 1957).

realistic and distinctive? Professional opinion was divided. Do such prices signify monopolistic control? The majority of the committee thought that they do and that after further study the antitrust laws should be amended to cope with the problem. And finally, are certain industrial corporations using their monopoly power to exact "unreasonably" high administered prices? The majority of the committee concluded that they were; the minority placed the blame on labor's bargaining power, thought that competition is still effective, or contented themselves with the statement that corporations exist to make profits.

Professional opinion on this issue of so-called sticky prices is sharply divided. Professor Donald Dewey, reviewing the hearings, remarked that "the net effect . . . is to make one depressed with the state of economics as a profession," [29] whereas Gardiner Means, who has studied administered prices more than any other economist, believes that "this phenomenon requires the rebuilding of practically all economic theory except that of perfect competition." [30] Whether mature judgment concerning administered prices will also entail drastic revisions of the antitrust laws remains to be seen.

THE INTENT OF THE ANTITRUST LAWS

Before going on to the next three chapters where the various antitrust laws, the methods of their enforcement, and an evaluation of their effectiveness are examined, it may be helpful to set down the main purposes and provisions of these laws as developed between 1890 when the Sherman Act was passed and 1950 when the Celler-Kefauver Amendment plugged the loophole in the Clayton Act:

The *Sherman Act* absolutely prohibits:
Entering into a contract, combination, or conspiracy in restraint of trade (Section 1)
Monopolizing, attempting to monopolize, or combining and conspiring to monopolize trade (Section 2)
The *Clayton Act* of 1914 prohibits, where the effect is substantially to lessen competition or tends to promote monopoly:
Acquiring the stock of competing corporations (Section 7)
Acquiring the assets of competing corporations (Section 7, as amended by the Celler-Kefauver Amendment of 1950)
Entering into exclusive or tying contracts (Section 3)
Discriminating unfairly among purchasers (Section 2, as amended by the Robinson-Patman Act of 1936)
The *Clayton* and *Federal Trade Commission Acts* of 1914, and the *Robinson-Patman Act* of 1936 prohibit:

[29] *American Economic Review*, Vol. XLIX, No. 1 (March 1959), p. 198.
[30] *American Economic Review, Papers and Proceedings*, Vol. XLIX, No. 2 (May 1959), p. 451.

Engaging in particular forms of price discrimination (Robinson-Patman Act, Sections 1 and 3)

Serving as a director of a competing corporation (Clayton Act, Section 8)

Using unfair methods of competition (FTC Act, Section 5)

Employing unfair or deceptive acts or practices (FTC Act, Section 5, as amended by the Wheeler-Lea Act, Section 3)

We still pay lip service to the antitrust laws and condemn the evils of monopoly even when we are not quite sure what they are, but this is about all we do about it; and today we seem not very certain about disliking monopoly even in principle. We call it inevitable, or an unfortunate but irrevocable aspect of human nature, or we turn our back on it to shop in a chain store where prices on some items are lower than elsewhere. Though politically poles apart, the monopolist and the socialist, each for his own reasons, agree that competition is injurious, that it creates an unnecessary duplication of commodities and services, and that giant monopolies are the wave of the future. The monopolist differs from his radical friend only in thinking that his own position is secure because the public will never become sufficiently aroused to do anything about the situation that private monopoly helps to create.

In the minds of many businessmen, say Hamilton and Till, "the belief in antitrust belongs to one world and the actualities of business conduct to quite another." The Sherman Act throughout the political community

> . . . is held in least favor where power and influence are greatest. A rather instinctive suspicion of Antitrust prevails in high industrial quarters. As a symbol the Sherman Act is grand. It sets down a lofty profession of economic faith; it proclaims industry to be the instrument of the common good; it preaches the philosophy which makes the market the rightful agency of business control. The statute holds enough of the raw material of thought, out of which the creed of *laissez faire* was formulated, to have high ceremonial value in financial circles. It serves its function best, however, as a generality, left in Olympian aloofness, unsullied by contact with mundane affairs. As a control which might do active duty in his own industry, the ordinary man of affairs views it as suspect. As a scheme of regulation it moves toward diffusion of power and runs directly against the trend toward concentration.

One thing that is certain, conclude these authors, is that "the halo about the law serves the practical purpose of forestalling any substitute measure for the control of industry." [31]

Supplementary Reading

Adams, Walter, and Horace M. Gray, *Monopoly in America* (New York, 1955). A comprehensive and forthright analysis, stressing mistakes in public policy.

[31] *Ibid.,* pp. 4, 26.

————, and ————, (eds.), *The Structure of American Industry* (New York, 1950). A number of case studies, by industry.

Stocking, George W., and Myron W. Watkins, *Monopoly and Free Enterprise* (New York, 1951). The most complete study of this subject ever undertaken.

Lilienthal, David E., *Big Business: A New Era* (New York, 1953). The justification for big business.

Fisher, Burton R., and Stephen B. Withey, *Big Business as the People See It* (Ann Arbor, Mich., Survey Research Center, 1951). The best study of public opinion in this area.

Chamberlain, Edward, *The Theory of Monopolistic Competition* (Cambridge, Mass., 1938). A good theoretical analysis.

Fellner, W. J., *Competition among the Few* (New York, 1949).

Latham, Earl, *Political Theories of Monopoly Power* (College Park, Md., Bureau of Governmental Research, 1957).

Kirsch, William, *Monopoly and Social Control* (Washington, D.C., 1952).

Lindblom, C. E., *Unions and Capitalism* (New Haven, Conn., 1949).

Dewey, Donald, *Monopoly in Economics and Law* (Chicago, 1959).

Ackley, Gardner, *et al.*, "Administered Prices Reconsidered," *American Economic Review, Papers and Proceedings,* Vol. XLIX, No. 2 (May 1959).

United States Congress, Subcommittee on Antitrust and Monopoly, *Hearings, Administered Prices,* 4 vols. (85th Cong., 1st Sess., 1957). Testimony by E. G. Nourse, J. K. Galbraith, G. C. Means, and others.

Burns, Arthur R., *The Decline of Competition* (New York, 1936). A good theoretical analysis with proposed remedies.

Machlup, Fritz, *The Political Economy of Monopoly: Business, Labor, and Government Policies* (Baltimore, Md., 1952). One of the most systematic studies ever undertaken.

Berle, Adolf A., Jr., *The 20th Century Capitalist Revolution* (New York, 1954). Stresses the power and institutional implications of monopoly trends.

Edwards, Corwin, *Maintaining Competition: Requisites of a Government Policy* (New York, 1949). Constructive as well as factual and analytical.

Wilcox, Clair, *Competition and Monopoly in American Industry,* Temporary National Economic Committee, Monograph No. 21 (Washington, D.C., 1941). One of the first realistic analyses.

————, *Public Policies toward Business* (Chicago, 1955). The book revolves about the theme of competition.

Galbraith, J. K., *American Capitalism* (Boston, 1952). The theory of countervailing power to offset monopoly.

Purdy, H. L., N. L. Lindahl, and W. A. Carter, *Corporate Concentration and Public Policy* (New York, 2d ed., 1950). Stresses policy questions.

Quinn, T. K., *Giant Business: Threat to Democracy* (New York, 1953). A critical appraisal.

Weston, J. Fred, *The Role of Mergers in the Growth of Large Firms* (Berkeley, Calif., 1953). Factual and theoretical.

Adelman, M. A., "Business Size and Public Policy," *The Journal of Business of the University of Chicago,* Vol. XXIV, No. 4 (Oct. 1951), pp. 269–279. Results of a factual study.

5
PROBLEMS OF ANTITRUST ENFORCEMENT

---

*The issues; Sherman Act; methods of monopoly: the trust,
price leadership, basing-point system, patent pools; how an
antitrust case is handled; shortage of funds and personnel;
sanctions and enforcement; results.*

Antitrust enforcement in the United States goes back almost three quarters of a century, and yet the problem of monopoly is still very much present. The record of enforcement is one of ups and downs. The increased size of corporations is clear, but economists dispute whether there has been a corresponding increase in *concentration*. Unqualified statements are unsafe and yet it is generally agreed that in antitrust enforcement, much remains to be done. Would it help to make the monopoly laws more specific, or does compliance depend rather on the favorable attitude of businessmen themselves? If so, how might cooperation be stimulated? Could additional restrictions and sanctions be enacted by Congress without unduly limiting free enterprise? Assuming that the laws might be tightened, could Congress be induced to make larger appropriations to the Antitrust Division of the Department of Justice so as to expand its staff and make enforcement more effective? And finally, what are the chances of securing a united enforcement effort through a united agency instead of two separate ones?

THE SHERMAN ACT

The three basic antimonopoly laws are the Sherman Act, on the one hand, primarily concerned with the form and structure of alleged combinations and conspiracies in restraint of trade, and the Clayton and Federal Trade Commission acts on the other, aimed chiefly at the practices of alleged monopolists. The Sherman Act would break up combinations in restraint of trade, while the other two are directed at prevention and are concerned also with practices that impair the effectiveness of competition even though they do not necessarily result in monopoly. The

Sherman Act is enforced by the Antitrust Division of the Department of Justice and the other two by an independent regulatory commission, the Federal Trade Commission. The Sherman Act, being administered by the nation's legal department, utilizes the services of federal attorneys, economic analysts, and the investigators of the Federal Bureau of Investigation, while the Federal Trade Commission is an independent administrative establishment and makes use of the administrative process in a quasi-judicial manner. *But both agencies rely on the courts for final enforcement, the rendering of judicial decisions, and the imposition of sanctions and penalties.*

The passage of the Sherman Act in 1890 followed several attempts among the states to limit the spread of monopoly. Thirteen states had passed antitrust legislation prior to 1890 and others had either forbidden monopolies or had at least declared them "contrary to the genius of a free people" in their constitutions. Since the problem was national in scope, however, such measures were of little effect, and pressure for federal action resulted in the passage of the Sherman Act.

The circumstances surrounding the passage of the act provide many clues as to why enforcement has been so difficult.[1] Among the many limiting factors, the following stand out:

1. *The wording of the law is ambiguous.* Section I enjoined *"Every"* contract, combination, or conspiracy in restraint of trade, but it did not set up adequate standards for determining what constitutes monopolistic behavior. This created an uncertainty on the part of the business community as well as among enforcement officials that resulted in the transfer of this unpopular task to the courts.

2. *It was assumed that common-law rules applicable to restraints of trade—and particularly the law of conspiracy—would apply, but these also were vague, uncertain, and variable.* Generally speaking, the common law did not *forbid* making or entering into an agreement to restrain trade, it merely refused to *recognize* the validity and enforceability of such an agreement when the question came before a court. "The element of novelty," say Hamilton and Till, "was the public character of the act."[2]

3. *Inadequate provision was made for enforcement.* Federal experience with the major regulation of industry was new. The federal government had used a regulatory tribunal for the first time only three years

---

[1] For a good brief treatment, see Walton Hamilton and Irene Till, *Antitrust in Action*, Temporary National Economic Committee, Monograph No. 16 (Washington, D.C., 1941). For a more extended discussion, see A. H. Walker, *History of the Sherman Law* (New York, 1910), Chaps. I–II, or Hans Thorelli, *The Federal Antitrust Policy* (Baltimore, Md., 1954).

[2] "The older rule against restraints had been largely an affair of private law. Contracts in restraint would not be enforced in the courts; the person injured might have his damages; he was entitled to relief from a collusion against him. It was only when the combination smacked of a criminal conspiracy that the offense clearly took on a public character."—Hamilton and Till, *op. cit.*, p. 9.

previously, when the Interstate Commerce Commission was created. Congress apparently assumed—naively, it now appears—that the Sherman law would be virtually self-enforcing.

4. *Adequate funds were not supplied and have never been forthcoming.* This fatal omission is probably the greatest weakness of all, because without adequate funds for enforcement, no program can realize its full potentialities.

Despite these evidences of groping and inexperience, however, the Sherman Act went considerably beyond the monopoly laws of the states. For one thing, it provided that offenses might be proceeded against criminally as well as civilly, and it authorized the seemingly stiff penalties of corporate dissolution and triple damages. It is, in fact, a tough law, and by no means all its faults are attributable to the circumstances of its enactment. At any time during the past half century or so its wording and intent could have been more clearly defined, its administration strengthened, and its financial resources made adequate. What has been lacking is a climate of opinion favorable to more vigorous enforcement.

METHODS OF RESTRAINING TRADE

To the institutional factors impeding antitrust enforcement must be added the difficulty of keeping pace with the methods of the monopolist, which are limitless and constantly changing. In the early years of the Sherman Act the nation's attention was focused on trusts, mergers, and pools—devices that now, except for mergers, seem simple and unsophisticated. In the trust, stock voting power is assigned to a small board of directors wielding monopolistic power; in the merger there is an actual absorption of previously separate and competing units; while the pool involves an agreement to fix prices, allocate markets, and divide income and profits according to a fixed ratio. These early methods of concentration were structural and hence easier to detect and prosecute than the newer practices more common today, which are both legion and subtle.

One of the first and most effective of the trusts, organized by the Rockefeller family and Standard Oil, was in the petroleum field and offers a good example of the methods then used to limit competition. In 1870 the Standard Oil Company of Ohio was formed, replacing partnership arrangements with a new corporate structure. At that time the company had 250 competitors and controlled only 10 percent of the national output of oil products. Less than ten years later, the company had increased its control of the industry to 95 percent, a result achieved by mergers, the control of sources and pipe lines, railroad rebates, and cutthroat competition.

In the early 1890s, however, by action of the state of Ohio, this oil trust was broken up in a state supreme court case, following which a holding company was organized around the Standard Oil Company of New Jersey, involving thirty-seven subsidiary corporations and covering the entire range of the petroleum industry from production to refining, pipe lines, and retailing. Competition was eliminated and profits increased by the simple expedient of giving the holding company's board of directors control of the stock of the subsidiary corporations, centrally fixing prices and profits, and dividing the business and the profits of each participating unit on a pro rata basis. This combination was not prosecuted under the Sherman Act until 1906, and it was only in 1911 that the Supreme Court finally ordered dissolution following decision in the case of *Standard Oil Co.* v. *United States.*[3] The Court held that combining the stocks of the various subsidiary corporations in the hands of Standard Oil of New Jersey constituted a combination in restraint of trade, as well as an attempt to monopolize the interstate trade in petroleum. The decree enjoined the subsidiaries from paying dividends to the holding company, which was forbidden to exert any other form of control over them; all concerned were enjoined from entering into or carrying into effect any other or similar combination which would violate the decree; and all parties were forbidden to engage in interstate commerce as long as the illegal combination remained in existence. Today every part of the nation still has its Standard Oil Company, but such units are no longer in the objectionable form of a trust or holding company.

It was in this case also that the Supreme Court formulated, in an *obiter dictum* (literally, something over and above what is actually necessary to decide a case), the so-called rule of reason: the Court held that the Sherman Act forbade only contracts and combinations that *unreasonably* restrain interstate commerce, but not those that promote efficiency and progress.

John D. Rockefeller, founder of the Standard Oil empire, was entirely candid and convinced of the rightness of what he had achieved. Because his words exemplify a common attitude toward combination, they bear quoting in part:

> Every refiner in the country was invited to become a member of the Standard Oil Company, and to participate in every benefit which this most aggressive competitor could secure. That had never happened before in the old system of competitive struggle. The weakest competitors were contemplating stepping down and out; it was only a question of days or weeks; they well knew that their obligations at the banks could not be met. Their anxiety was very great. The Standard Oil Company turned to them with confidence and said: "We will take your burdens, we will utilize your ability, we will give you representation; we will all unite together and build a substantial structure on the basis of cooperation."[4]

When men can be so satisfied that what they are doing is morally right, it is little wonder that they resent a criminal or even a civil prosecution

---

[3] (221 U.S. 1. 1911).

[4] Quoted in Charles C. Rohlfing, Edward W. Carter, Bradford W. West, and John G. Hervey, *Business and Government* (Chicago, 4th ed., 1941), p. 123.

for restraining trade. To Rockefeller, it was obvious that competition and cooperation had come to mean the same thing.

Today, the merger is more popular than ever, accomplished with a certain degree of control by the Antitrust Division and the Federal Trade Commission, but other devices have been invented that are often hard to uncover and even harder to convict. "Current restraints," comment Hamilton and Till, "bear the stamp of their industrial culture. The overt, the blatant, the outrageous is gone, or dwells on the fringes of polite society. The agent of common accord may be independent of all the participating firms. . . . Men may move in lockstep, not by agreement among themselves but in automatic response to identical stimuli." [5]

For example, nine major oil companies at one time relied for their prices on market reports published in a single journal; in a big city the four largest building contractors depended for their estimates on an agency with which technically they had no connection; a large manufacturer of brass products converts his views of "market prospects" into price and the little fellows in the trade automatically follow suit; a price is published in a metropolitan newspaper and a given group of corporations instantly adjusts to this figure, not by "conspiracy" but by prearranged signal; an engineer develops a "cost formula" for canvas goods and the trade comes out with a common price; and cheese prices are set at a "kept" auction at Plymouth, Wisconsin, which has been nationally agreed upon as the most reliable indicator.[6] Even though most people would agree that such methods constitute illegal restraint, it must still be proved to a court that insists on evidence meeting the technical requirements of the law.

This follow-the-leader method of setting prices is a common one among monopolists today, and the trade association is ideally suited to carrying it out. Every important firm in a particular industry belongs to such an association and all are disposed to cooperate. The following communication from a trade association to its members shows how the technique is employed in a manner to avoid prosecution for conspiracy:

> By this time you should be in a position to select your "market leader" who has the courage and those qualities of leadership that others recognize and will follow. After he is selected, give him your wholehearted support. Remember not to agree upon a price, but each individual has the right to determine what he wants to do and to announce it, thus avoiding any conspiracy. Your "market leader" can set a price and the organizations can send out a notice.[7]

So long as firms "cooperate," all should make money and there will be "harmony" in the industry; and if any firm refuses, then the industry can apply a kind of concerted squeeze play by narrowing the margin between the cost of materials and the selling price of the product, and then

---

[5] Hamilton and Till, *op. cit.*, pp. 14–15.   [6] *Ibid.*, pp. 13–14.
[7] Temporary National Economic Committee, *Hearings*, Pt. 16, p. 9,040.

holding this vise in position until the recalcitrant firm either fails or capitulates. Furthermore, the price-leadership game is a safe one because collusion is not apparent in the form of meetings held and agreements recorded, however obvious concerted action may be. Of the many devices for eliminating competition and controlling output and prices, therefore, price leadership stands high and is widespread, especially where there is a giant in the industry, and usually there is. The petroleum and steel industries have demonstrated the skill that may be developed in making price leadership work.

Another method of achieving price uniformity is the basing-point system, which also operates according to an automatic formula, is devoid of open collusion, and is hard to prosecute. The device was held unlawful in the case of *Federal Trade Commission* v. *The Cement Institute*,[8] and a subsequent attempt by the cement and steel industries to get Congress to legalize the practice was vetoed by the President in 1950. Nevertheless, the practice had become widespread and the forces behind it are still so strong that the issue remains a live one.

Under the basing-point system there is uniformity of price on a delivered basis irrespective of the point of origin or the point of delivery of the product. There is involved a basic price, set high enough to enable all producers to ship over a wide area, plus the freight charge from the basing point (of which there may be one or several throughout the nation) to destination. No f.o.b. sales are permitted, and since each producer knows the price at the buyer's location, the computation is simple and automatic. If no mistake in arithmetic is made, the delivered price should come out the same even to decimal points for every member of the industry.

Like price leadership, the basing-point system was popular and constituted a most effective method of price control. Among the industries making use of it at the time of the hearings before the Temporary National Economic Committee were lumber, iron and steel, pig iron, cement, lime, brick, asphalt shingles and roofing, window glass, white lead, metal lath, building tile, floor tile, gypsum plaster, bolts, nuts and rivets, cast-iron soil pipe, range boilers, valves and fittings, sewer pipe, paper and paper products, salt, sugar, corn derivatives, industrial alcohol, linseed oil, fertilizers, chemicals, transportation equipment, and power cable.[9] The multiple basing-point system, one of the several variations of the device, received considerable impetus when it was written into codes drawn up by the National Recovery Administration as a means of establishing price control for numerous industries during the early days of the New Deal.

By permitting producers to sell in each others' markets, the basing-point system took the curse off price fixing, which was its major objective.

[8] (333 U.S. 683. 1948).
[9] Temporary National Economic Committee, *Final Report and Recommendations,* p. 33.

Again, self-government in the industry effectively disciplined those who did not cooperate. Any firm attempting to cut prices within its own area became a "chiseler" or a "price cutter" and was subject to retaliation.

Certain other methods of restraining trade are more direct and more open than pricing systems, patent pools being the principal case in point. In an uncautious moment one manufacturer wrote to a colleague that "the patents upon which we pay royalties are of dubious validity, but they provide a device by which the industry may maintain a collective security, and for such a defense against the chaos of competition the price is small." A patent pool may be controlled by a corporation, a group of corporations, a trade association, or some similar arrangement within the industry; it may cover all patents within the industry or only some; and their use may be permitted free or on a royalty basis. There are many variations. Consequently patents have both a social and an antisocial use depending on who controls them and for what purpose. The federal Constitution seeks "to promote the progress of Science and the useful Arts," and in pursuance of this laudable objective Congress has legislated to give an inventor the "exclusive" right to his novelty for a period of seventeen years. Today, however, many inventions originate in corporations and the patents on them go not to the individual inventor but to the corporation.

The Hartford-Empire Company, the great bottle trust, is a classic example of how competition may be virtually eliminated for decades on the basis of patent monopolies and licensing agreements. Prior to being forced into temporary receivership in 1945 by order of the Supreme Court in an antitrust proceeding, Hartford-Empire had controlled all but a small part of the bottle industry since the combination was formed in 1922. As a holding company, it ran a patent pool—euphemistically called the Hartford umbrella—and licensed users; it operated a research laboratory and secured new patents; and it built machines and leased them to companies allowed to come under the "umbrella." Territory was divided, products were doled out, and independents who tried to buck the trust were soon forced, generally by means of patent-infringement proceedings, to come in under the umbrella or quit. The Supreme Court decision forced Hartford-Empire to sell machines outright and allowed independents to buy from other manufacturers as long as they paid a "reasonable" royalty to Hartford-Empire.[10]

Shoe machinery was another tight patent combine in which a single company manufactured, leased, and serviced all the machinery employed in the industry. In the fashioning of optical lenses, the product and its price were controlled by means of closely held patents through all the various stages of manufacturing, wholesaling, and retailing.

The TNEC investigated the matter of patent pools in 1939 and exposed monopolistic abuses so flagrant that the whole patent system

---

[10] *Hartford-Empire Co.* v. *United States* (323 U.S. 386. 1945).

threatened to fall into disrepute. The committee recommended amendatory patent legislation but it was not until the Patent Act of 1952, under which the patent laws were revised and codified, that Congress showed any real evidence of wanting to remedy the situation. In 1955 a subcommittee of the Senate Judiciary Committee studied the matter again and instituted a number of reports by experts. Among other findings was the fact that in most cases a patent goes to the corporation who hired the inventor instead of to the inventor himself; in the period from 1939 to 1955, 176 corporations had obtained more than 121,000 patents, or better than 20 percent of the total issued. General Electric led the field with nearly 11,000 patents and AT&T was second with better than 8000.

Several antitrust actions have concentrated on the matter of patents. Thus in 1949, AT&T was charged with, among other things, suppressing improvements and withholding patents from competing companies, and under the consent decree which settled the case in 1956, was ordered to make existing patents available to the industry free and new ones at reasonable rates.

Other devices of the monopolist are interlocking directorates, creating an intricate web of relationships among corporations and their financial interests; price agreements, market sharing, noncompetitive prices among dominant firms, group boycotts, and market dominance; cartels in domestic and foreign markets; regulations under the police power of the federal government or the states in matters affecting health and sanitation such as the pasteurization of raw milk; holding-company control in utilities and related fields; legally created monopolies such as public utilities and transportation; and the legalized restraint of competition, as in the bituminous coal industry.

Although some of these restrictions are legal as a matter of public policy, they may serve private ends. Thus Hamilton and Till state:

> In fact all regulatory measures, however righteous their intent, run the risk of becoming legal defenses for private restraints. When business takes to politics, the police power becomes a counter in an acquisitive game. All over the country the use of a legal sanction as a defense against authority is widespread. Such instances do not prove that sheer contact with a regulatory measure creates an immunity. But it does allow privilege to dig in behind a fortified line and calls for enforcement to look well to its strategy.[11]

In most devices of monopoly, a main tool is the trade association. "The real core of the trade association movement," says Whitney, "has lain in its attack on free competition." [12] The influence of these agencies on concentration and restraint of trade is greater today than that of

[11] Hamilton and Till, *op. cit.*, p. 18.
[12] Simon N. Whitney, *Trade Associations and Industrial Control* (New York, 1934), p. 38.

the trust in its prime. In testimony before the TNEC it was brought out that in most cases before the Federal Trade Commission involving unlawful restraint a trade association was the prime mover,[13] especially where price leadership and the basing-point system were concerned. The work of the associations perfectly equips them for such a role, including as it does the preparation of market surveys, cost-reporting devices, common cost-accounting methods, the collection and dissemination of statistics, agreement on uniform terms of sale, and other standardized procedures. The executive committee of a trade association or even its paid executive acting alone may raise or lower prices for an industry, and as long as no record of the proceedings is kept and no other incriminating evidence can be found, illegal collusion in violation of the Sherman Act is hard to prove.

HOW THE ANTITRUST DIVISION HANDLES A CASE

Against the sophisticated manipulations of trade associations and industrial giants, how do the procedures of the Antitrust Division of the Justice Department measure up? Any antitrust enforcement agency, of course, has a complicated task because conspiracy is so easily avoided in a technical sense, but the Antitrust Division must face other problems as well.

The four main steps in the handling of an antitrust case by the Antitrust Division are receipt of the complaint, investigation and preparation of the suit, trial, and sanctions. Prior to the filing of the suit, however, a case may be settled by negotiations in which the party who might be a defendant in a *civil* antitrust action is notified and invited to discuss the matter with Justice Department officials. If an understanding is reached, and often it is, then illegal practices are discontinued by the offender and costly litigation is avoided.

A case may also be settled prior to trial by consent decree. The process is for the defendant and the Antitrust Division to discuss a settlement, agree on its provisions, and submit the decree to a court for formal entry as a court judgment binding on the defendant and the Justice Department alike. However, unless extraordinary reasons can be shown to a court, a consent decree is permanent and blocks any further action in that area by the Antitrust Division. Nor may a consent decree be used in any further private antitrust suits for damages against the same defendant.

Finally, an antitrust case may also be terminated by a consent judgment, which is settlement by negotiation after the matter goes to court

---

[13] Quoted in Hamilton and Till, *op. cit.,* p. 16. See also Walton Hamilton, *Patents and Free Enterprise,* Temporary National Economic Committee, Monograph No. 31 (Washington, D.C., 1941).

but before the trial is concluded, in which event the court itself is party to the agreement.

Most complaints against alleged monopolists come from other businessmen, usually small competitors adversely affected by the concentrated power of the aggressors. Most complaints are in the form of letters, but some are presented in person, some through an attorney, and some through appeal to a Congressman. There would be more if many small businessmen did not fear retaliation. The Justice Department has been keeping records since 1932 of the number of complaints received, as shown in Table 3. The increase of more than 300 percent between 1932 and 1940 was partly due to a quicker trend toward monopoly by industry and hence there was more to complain of, and partly due to more determined efforts by the Antitrust Division. It should be noted, of course, that many complaints produce no clues worth a major investigation.

TABLE 3

COMPLAINTS RECEIVED BY ANTITRUST DIVISION

Year	Number	Year	Number
1932	356	1946	669
1933	499	1947	1,031
1934 *	1,020	1948	1,341
1935 *	1,451	1949	1,355
1936	730	1950	1,163
1937	581	1951	813
1938	923	1952	788
1939	1,375	1953	787
1940	1,993	1954	1,056
1941 †	2,032	1955	1,264
1942 †	3,674	1956	1,246
1943 †	3,070	1957	1,229
1944	1,069	1958	1,136
1945	520	1959	1,232

* Unusually high because of alleged violations of NRA codes.

† Complaints arising under War Statutes are consolidated with complaints arising under the antitrust laws for these years.

SOURCE: Records of the Antitrust Division, Justice Department.

This method of learning about violations of the antimonopoly laws is far too rickety a foundation for a program of enforcement, and yet because industry is vastly complex, it is hard to learn inside information, and the Antitrust Division's budget is chronically low, complaints of this kind must be heavily relied on.

After complaints have been sifted, or when independent research shows the need for investigation, a case is assigned to a staff attorney. Most investigations are thereafter conducted in cooperation with the Federal Bureau of Investigation, a coordinate division in the Justice Department. Its employees are not especially trained for this kind of work, but they are well grounded in investigation techniques in general and the coverage of the FBI is nation-wide. Furthermore, the Antitrust Division itself has neither the funds nor the personnel for the job except in unusual cases when topflight lawyers may be assigned. As the material flows in, the attorney in charge prepares the case for trial. Beginning about 1932, economists were added to the division's staff to advise on policy and investigations; in 1953 there were a peak of 30 economists in addition to 249 attorneys, but the number of economists has since declined.

In the prosecution of an antitrust suit the difficulty of obtaining proof is a main obstacle. Because witnesses are often loath to talk, possibly for fear of retaliation, a case is sometimes made to originate with a grand jury where information under oath may be secured. The Antitrust Division does not have the power to subpoena incriminating documents from the files of the accused, but a grand jury does and this factor weighs in choosing the grand-jury device which precedes and does not replace the court trial. It is a blunt instrument, however, employed by the Division only for lack of a better one. It involves the continuous session of twenty-three citizen grand jurors assisted by government lawyers and FBI investigators, with a judge in the offing, and constitutes an extravagant method of investigation and indictment.

As to the type of suit instituted, under the Sherman Act the government may make use of either a *criminal* action or a plea in *equity*. Prior to 1938 the policy was to bring most antitrust cases on the civil side of the docket, but few were litigated and when consent decrees were entered, they were often violated and the violators were not punished. Then came a swing to criminal indictments, either followed through in the courts or used as a "big stick" to force a civil settlement. The shock of indictment, quite apart from the criminal penalties attached, was at least a partial deterrent to continued violations. In a criminal proceeding the offending corporation is charged with a misdemeanor, and if the verdict is unfavorable, a jail sentence is possible—though unlikely—and a fine may be imposed. The maximum possible fine was increased by Congress in 1955 from $5000 to $50,000.

Under equity proceedings agreements in restraint of trade can be declared null and void and court injunctions issued forbidding recurrences. There is no reason why both the criminal and equity types of action may not be brought against the same defendant, of course, and in some instances they have been, despite the added time and expense to the government.

In yet other cases, huge corporations may be broken up and partially dissolved, but this is not generally done except where concentration is virtually complete as in the case of the Standard Oil trust in 1911. Concerning the problem here, Hamilton and Till have commented:

> A major difficulty is that in most industries a trickle of rivalry is preserved to becloud the issue for the courts. And the blatant monopoly is often safeguarded by rights of patent which can be pleaded in extenuation. *Not one line in the Sherman Act proclaims the exact norm to which competitive practice must conform or lists the requisites which make up proof of violation.* The confused industrial picture and the lack of definite criteria make the courts hesitate; they are loath to sanction extreme remedies, and retreat into requirements of proof which spell ultimate defeat for the government.[14]

The trial of an antitrust case is usually slow and costly, the average expense per case running to something like $50,000 annually and often extending over a period of more than a year. In a suit against the American Medical Association,[15] for example, it was eighteen months after action was begun before the court of last resort removed the ultimate legal difficulty and the matter could even go to trial. In the years between 1936 and 1939, the Antitrust Division spent $150,000 on a single suit, the *Madison Oil* case,[16] which the government ultimately won. By 1952 a dozen or so cases had been dragging along for ten years or more and at least one dated from the 1920s. On a major case the staff will consist of from six to eight attorneys and a couple of technical consultants, but on less complicated ones the drain on personnel is not so great.

In addition to criminal prosecutions and proceedings in equity, two other suits are possible under the Sherman Act, but neither is widely used. Any individual may sue privately for triple damages but then he, and not the government, must prepare, finance, and prove the case. In practice this device has been important mainly to the federal government since 1955 when a prior judicial ruling that it was not a "person" and hence could not sue for damages was remedied by legislation. In 1959, furthermore, the right of an individual to sue for damages was strengthened when the Supreme Court unanimously reversed a lower court and ruled that a small businessman was entitled to bring a private antitrust suit without necessarily proving that his case would have a particular effect on the public at large. An appliance store had sued a neighboring department store and ten national manufactures of appliances and their distributors alleging that they had conspired to keep it from

[14] Hamilton and Till, *op. cit.*, p. 75 (italics added).
[15] *United States v. American Medical Association* (317 U.S. 519. 1943).
[16] *United States v. Socony-Vacuum Oil Co.* (310 U.S. 150. 1940).

obtaining merchandise except on unfavorable terms or at discriminatory prices. The defendants argued that the public's ability to buy their appliances could not be affected by what happened to the plaintiff because there were hundreds of other appliance dealers, some of them within a few blocks of the plaintiff, selling the same goods. The lower court, presided over by a former head of the Antitrust Division, accepted this view, but the Supreme Court noted that under it, if customers were still able to buy in a competitive market, a group of powerful businessmen might act in concert to put a single merchant out of business. This practice is called "group boycott," which is a concerted refusal to deal. Such a conspiracy, said Justice Black, "is not to be tolerated merely because the victim is just one merchant whose business is so small that his destruction makes little difference to the economy." [17]

In addition to this type of suit, yet another course is a libel action against a good or a ware, a device that has been used only seldom in the history of antitrust and in each instance the issue was decided out of court.

THE RECORD OF ANTITRUST ENFORCEMENT

In the first seventy years of antitrust enforcement 687 civil cases were instituted and of those that were tried, about two thirds were won by the government. The record in criminal cases is to a similar effect: during the same seventy-year period, 671 criminal actions were instituted and penal sentences were imposed in more than half. Of these, some involved trade unions, two were not strict antitrust cases, and a number involved racketeering practices. Table 4 shows the number of antitrust cases of both kinds instituted by ten-year periods.

A comparison of Table 4 with Table 3 on page 103, which gives the number of complaints received annually by the Antitrust Division, shows that the chances of action on an antitrust complaint seem rather slight. Nevertheless, although the 63 new cases filed by the division in 1959 were less than the 70 filed in the peak year of 1942, just before World War II stopped the antitrust drive of the New Deal, 10 of the 1959 suits were against mergers. This was more than double the figure for mergers for 1958 and was the greatest number of such suits since the passage of the Clayton Act in 1914. Of the cases closed in 1959, which also amounted to 63, all but two of the criminal cases and three of the civil cases ended in judgments or consent decrees claimed as victories by the government.

As of 1952, prison sentences had been imposed on 110 individuals but only eight had ever served their term. As of the same year, fines imposed in criminal cases affected 20,000 defendants and totaled nearly $13

---

[17] *Klor's, Inc.* v. *Broadway-Hale Stores, Inc., Admiral Corp., Admiral Distributors, Inc., et al.* (359 U.S. 207. 1959).

million, an average of some $205,000 a year. Since 1952 the sum collected in fines has increased each year until by 1959 it had passed $914,-000. But because so many individuals and corporations have been involved as defendants, the average fine has been relatively small and hardly constitutes a realistic deterrent to misbehavior. Since the maximum fine was raised from $5000 to $50,000, however, fines may become a more effective weapon. Actually, a larger sum has been collected out of court than in suits that went to judgment; as in the case of traffic violators, corporations would often rather pay their fine than confront a judge.

TABLE 4

CASES INSTITUTED, ANTITRUST DIVISION
BY TEN-YEAR PERIODS

Period	Number of Cases
1890-1900	17
1901-1910	56
1911-1920	141
1921-1930	160
1931-1940	154
1941-1950	493
1951-1960	413

SOURCE: Antitrust Division, Department of Justice.

A major difficulty in antitrust enforcement is a traditional reluctance by Congress to provide the funds needed to give enforcement real effect. "A statute lives by appropriations—and from the first the demands of Antitrust have fallen upon the deaf ear of Congress." [18] When the Antitrust Division became part of the Justice Department in 1903, its annual appropriation was $100,000 and in 1933 it was only a little more than three times as much; indeed, it was not until 1940, when the Sherman Act had been in existence for fifty years, that as much as a million dollars was provided for enforcement purposes. "Billions for military defense," said David Cushman Coyle, "but only 2½ cents per capita for defense of free business." [19] In 1950 the division's appropriation was some $3.8 million but thereafter a decline set in and by 1955 it was only $3.1 million. By 1960 it had risen again to the $3.8-million level.

The larger appropriations since the 1930s have had their effect. By 1955 antitrust cases were being filed at the rate of about 40 a year and being determined somewhat faster than that as stubborn old cases were

[18] Hamilton and Till, op. cit., p. 23.
[19] David Cushman Coyle, "The Big Cannot Be Free," The Atlantic Monthly (June 1947), p. 77.

taken down from the shelves, dusted off, and presented to a new head of the Antitrust Division, with what must have been malicious curiosity on the part of veteran staff members who had seen more than one head of the Antitrust Division become frustrated by the toughness of this backlog. By 1954, eight of the dozen oldest cases had been closed. Of the 51 cases terminated in 1955, 28 were by consent decree or consent judgment and some of the others were dismissed for lack of evidence. The rate of filing after 1955 averaged about 55 cases a year.

Those who claim that all the Antitrust Division needs is sufficient funds and staff seem to have a strong talking point. When it is realized that it costs as much as $50,000 a year to prosecute the average antitrust case, that some large corporations have legal staffs equal in number to the entire legal staff of the Antitrust Division, and that the financial resources of such corporations are far greater, the conclusion seems justified that the real efficiency of the antitrust laws has never adequately been tested. Hamilton and Till call it "Big Act, Little Stick."

Since it is impossible for financial reasons to provide an adequate follow-up once a court decision has been rendered, it is hard to say just how effective antitrust judgments have been. Thus, in the case of equity decrees,

> The law presumes innocence even after a party has been formally accused. It must, therefore, be presumed, for want of evidence to the contrary, that the companies named have lived up to the decrees. But to assume that they have foresworn the objectives toward which the forbidden practices moved would be either to disparage their zeal in the pursuit of gain or to reflect upon the competence of their legal counsel.[20]

An injunction is no real deterrent because it is directed only to the defending party. It applies only to specific acts and not to future acts that may have the same effect, and has little force in inducing a wider compliance with the law. There is little means of policing the order because although the court may punish for contempt, the Antitrust Division lacks sufficient time, funds, and personnel to follow up on a decision rendered. Consequently, the task of policing an injunction falls mainly to the industry itself and to the force of public opinion where this is informed in the first place and able and willing to make itself felt in the second. Thus:

> A victory for the government has its effect, not as a command to be obeyed, but as an incitement to "the fear of God." Its impact is emotional rather than legislative; its urge is toward inducing businessmen to scrutinize their operations and to abandon practices exposed to legal attack. But where restraint means enhanced profits or greater industrial security, a mere sermon from the bench is not enough.[21]

[20] *Ibid.*, p. 78.   [21] *Ibid.*, p. 76.

The antitrust policy of the administration that took office in 1953 included an attempt to improve the policing of antitrust decisions. Until then only twelve contempt enforcement proceedings to compel compliance with court decrees had ever been instituted, but in the two years that followed, eight such proceedings were begun. Future action of this kind will depend in part, at least, on the degree to which the Antitrust Division receives adequate support, both financial from Congress and moral from the administration in office.

Indeed, a major difficulty in antitrust enforcement is that the attempt has not been consistently pushed and there have been marked ups and downs of effort and conviction. This can be traced partially to the effect of war and depression, both of which have encouraged concentration, but it is also due to differences in the political objectives of the political parties and leaders who happened to be in power. In the earliest period of enforcement, from 1890 to 1902, antitrust activities were directed mainly against the railroads, a limitation stemming largely from the 1895 Supreme Court decision in the *Sugar Trust* case [22] to the effect that manufacturing was not interstate commerce and hence not subject to regulation by Congress. Nevertheless, some progress was made with respect to the railroads and in addition, in the case of *United States* v. *Trans-Missouri Freight Association* [23] price-fixing agreements were declared unlawful.

In the second enforcement period, from 1902 to 1920, the ruling in the *Sugar Trust* case was superseded by the decision in the *Swift* case [24] written by Mr. Justice Holmes, and thereafter a number of important cases were effectively prosecuted. In 1920, however, in a case against U. S. Steel [25] the Supreme Court held that size, and the power that accompanies it, did not constitute a violation of the Sherman Act unless it could be shown that the power was exercised.

Antitrust prosecutions fell off to such an extent between 1920 and 1936 that a New York industrial engineer who was himself indicted under the Sherman Act was led to observe that:

> Practically, under the Harding, Coolidge, and Hoover administrations, industry enjoyed to all intents and purposes, a moratorium from the Sherman Act, and, through the more or less effective trade associations which were developed in most of our industries, competition was, to a very considerable extent, controlled. The Department of Justice acted with great restraint and intelligence and only enforced the Sherman Act against those industries who violated the laws in a flagrant and unreasonable manner.[26]

---

[22] *United States* v. *E. C. Knight Co.* (156 U.S. 1. 1895).   [23] (166 U.S. 290. 1897)

[24] *Swift & Co.* v. *United States* (196 U.S. 375. 1905).

[25] *United States* v. *U. S Steel* (251 U.S. 417. 1920).

[26] Charles A. Stevenson, in a speech entitled, "Price Control and Allotment of Business," June 26, 1934.

By 1933, because of limited appropriations and staff, the Antitrust Division was never able to press more than five major suits at one time, and then no staff was available for developing new cases. Violations of the Sherman Act were so much an accepted procedure in business practice as to create an assumption that the antitrust laws were merely symbols of a good but impractical economic theory. Under such policies concentrations of economic power were not seriously impeded and grew rapidly.

The fourth period of enforcement started in 1936. By that time the depression had had its effect and government-sponsored cartelization under the NRA had been tried and found wanting. Public opinion seemed ready to favor a return to competition and the Supreme Court showed a willingness to interpret the Sherman Act to meet the necessities of the times.

Prior to this time, furthermore, cases brought by the Antitrust Division were largely concerned with developing occasional new points of law, testing to determine whether a particular practice of a particular business concern violated the Sherman Act. This policy is still pursued, of course, where necessary. In 1950, for example, the Clayton Act was amended in regard to mergers and five years later the Antitrust Division was still feeling its way in enforcement because there had been no court decisions to interpret the new language. To obtain such a judicial appraisal the division instituted suits to test the five facets of the problem that needed it.

But test cases alone constitute a fragmentary kind of enforcement and make no fundamental change in the economic structure of the nation or in the methods of doing business, with the result that in former years when this practice predominated, antitrust cases were of interest mainly to lawyers as a legal game. The impact of a decision favorable to the government was scarcely felt by the public and even the defendant company itself was little affected because a new device could be quickly instituted to replace the activity condemned. Consequently, having recovered from the NRA experience, in 1938 the Antitrust Division changed its policy of trying to pick firms off one by one and started using the antitrust laws in a frontal attack on an entire industry, including every restraint from producer through processor, jobber, carrier, and retailer. In so doing the division expanded its operations to cover a wide variety of industries including medical practice, newspaper associations, insurance, railroads, and labor unions among others. The government instituted and won a number of important cases and Congress was more generous with its financial support.

Favorable judicial decisions had been anticipated by the ruling in *United States* v. *Trenton Potteries* [27] wherein price fixing by a trade association was held to be illegal even though the prices themselves are

---

[27] (251 U.S. 417. 1927).

reasonable. In *United States* v. *Socony-Vacuum Oil Co.*,[28] decided in 1940, price fixing was again declared to be illegal per se. To the same effect was the decision in *Interstate Circuit* v. *United States*,[29] a case involving monopoly in the motion-picture industry.

Further, the case of *United States* v. *Hartford-Empire Co.*[30] dissolved a monopoly based on patent holdings. The Supreme Court apparently returned to the original meaning and interpretation of the Sherman Act, taking the view that monopoly *as such* is forbidden, as against the earlier belief that only the *abuses* of monopoly are affected. Looking increasingly at the economics of the monopoly problem, the Court is realistically concerned with the possession of power and not merely the proving of abuses growing out of that power. The effect of these cases was to ban price fixing, irrespective of whether it is accomplished by collusion among competitors or by monopoly power. Size in itself, at least in the dicta of the Court, is now an offense. Monopoly power cannot reasonably be reconciled with the objectives of the Sherman Act because the mere existence of power makes it possible for corporations or groups of corporations to fix prices, exclude competitors, and otherwise control a market in the interests of the few.

Nowhere has this position been better stated than in the opinion of Justice Hand in the *Alcoa* case,[31] in which it was held that size in and of itself is objectionable. Even if there were no illegal tactics or evidence of wrong intentions, said the court, the fact of 90 percent control of an industry is in itself a violation of the antitrust laws. Size which gives power to control an industry is per se an offense. Bigness may now be a crime whenever the courts say it looks too big. Other cases bearing on this point are *American Tobacco Co.* v. *United States*,[32] *International Salt Co.* v. *United States*,[33] and *United States* v. *Pullman Co.*[34] In the *International Salt* opinion, for example, the Court ruled for the first time that other practices than price fixing may be unreasonable and hence illegal; that, in the words of the Court, "it is unreasonable per se to foreclose competitors from any substantial market."

Finally there is the decision in the *Cement* case [35] which invalidated the basing-point system. In a 22,000-word majority opinion based on a three-year hearing by the Federal Trade Commission, in which the trial examiner assembled 49,000 pages of evidence and 50,000 pages of exhibits, supported by lawyers' briefs and appendices aggregating 4000 pages more, the Supreme Court ruled that uniform prices throughout the country, resulting from the basing-point system, overlook differences in transportation and other costs and are an illegal mask for monopoly and restraint of trade. Hope was expressed that the decision

---

[28] (310 U.S. 150. 1940), the so-called *Madison* case.   [29] (306 U.S. 208. 1939).

[30] (324 U.S. 570. 1944).

[31] *United States* v. *Aluminum Co. of America* (322 U.S. 716. 1945).

[32] (328 U.S. 781. 1946).   [33] (332 U.S. 392. 1947).   [34] (330 U.S. 806. 1946).

[35] *Federal Trade Commission* v. *Cement Institute* (333 U.S. 683. 1948).

would help the little fellow and make possible some degree of industrial decentralization. The government's case had been in process for eleven years and when finally it was settled it was regarded in Washington as the single greatest victory in the history of federal antitrust enforcement.

But in the same year, 1948, the Court seemed to backslide in its progress toward realistic economic decisions when it settled the case of *United States* v. *Columbia Steel Co.*[36] In a 5 to 4 decision it was held not to be "unreasonable" for U. S. Steel, through a subsidiary, to acquire Consolidated Steel, the largest independent fabricator on the West Coast, even though this purchase, following that of the government steel plant at Geneva, Utah, after World War II, would give Big Steel virtual control of the industry in the Far West. The majority of the Court upheld the merger on the ground that no "unreasonable restraint" had been proved by the government, but in so doing seemed to overlook the regional implications of its decision. The minority opinion in this case, written by Mr. Justice Douglas, is a strong defense of antitrust and will probably be considered a legal, economic, and political classic.

In 1953 another policy of antitrust received impetus when the then head of the Antitrust Division, a former judge, set out to avoid formal court proceedings where possible in civil cases. Instead, he stressed pretrial negotiations and consent decrees except where a point of law needed clarification. The result was to expedite cases, reduce expenses, lighten court calendars, neutralize the natural antagonism of the business community, and educate businessmen whose transgressions were based in part, at least, on ignorance. Unhappily, the consent-decree policy came under criticism in 1959 when a long-standing suit against American Telephone and Telegraph Company was settled by that short-cut method. In theory, a consent decree should achieve approximately the same results as a successful law suit but without the same wear and tear on all the parties to it. In the case of AT&T, however, much less was achieved when the Antitrust Division backed down on its original demand that the corporation divest itself of its manufacturing subsidiary, Western Electric, and buy its supplies competitively from independent concerns. There were several other cases settled by consent decree that also aroused criticism and the House Antitrust subcommittee decided to look into the matter.

A consent decree is ordinarily secretly negotiated and then presented with only a brief explanation to a judge who, if he is not familiar with the matter, may fail to recognize all of its implications. Such a procedure can lead to mistakes and in the case of AT&T it was reported that, privately, nearly everyone in the Justice Department believed the decision was in error. The House subcommittee made three major recommendations: (1) the consent-decree device should be avoided

[36] (334 U.S. 495, 1948).

in cases where novel issues demand judicial resolution; (2) notice should be given to the public of the terms of a consent decree before it becomes final; and (3) judges should be free, at their discretion, to permit the use of a consent decree as evidence in a later private antitrust suit for damages against the same defendant.[37]

In 1958 the Antitrust Division again broadened its approach to enforcement when it began to police industries regulated by other federal agencies. It is sometimes charged that administrative agencies get too close to the industries under their jurisdiction, a view shared by the Antitrust Division. The natural-gas industry, for example, is regulated by the Federal Power Commission but the Antitrust Division secured an indictment charging existing suppliers in a Midwestern area with trying to keep out a new supplier, and the division also instituted a civil suit to block a proposed merger by two gas pipeline companies. This action accorded with yet another broad approach by the division during the 1950s: to proceed against mergers whenever possible so as to forestall the development of a monopoly situation that would be much harder and costlier to unravel once it had hardened. Again, in the field of television, the Antitrust Division advised the Federal Communications Commission to proceed against certain networks for practices which were violations of the antitrust laws, and at the same time had before the Supreme Court a precedent-setting move to undo on antitrust grounds a transfer of television stations already approved by the FCC.[38]

Two major tests of government strength in antitrust enforcement —the Dupont and the steel-merger cases—have recently occurred. The case against Dupont was brought under the Clayton Act in 1949. Dupont owned 63 million shares, constituting 23 percent, of General Motor's outstanding stock, making it the largest single shareholder in GM. The government charged that through this arrangement, Dupont secured the inside track in the sale of finishes and fabrics to General Motors, to the detriment of other competitors. In 1957 the Supreme Court overturned a lower court ruling that the government had failed to prove its contention and ordered the case back to the lower court for determination of "the equitable relief necessary."[39] The government urged that Dupont be required to sell its General Motors stock, and Dupont asked to be allowed to retain its stock but surrender its voting rights. On the ground that the government's demand was "unnecessarily harsh and punitive" and might have a "serious impact" on the market value of the stock of both companies, the judge ruled in favor of Dupont. Early in 1960 the Antitrust Division filed notice of appeal to the Supreme Court.

The steel-merger case arose when Bethlehem Steel Corporation, the second largest producer of steel in the industry, and Youngstown Sheet & Tube Company, the sixth largest, announced in 1954 that they were considering a plan to merge and asked the government to decide whether

[37] Anthony Lewis in *The New York Times*, May 26, 1959.   [38] *Ibid.*, June 8, 1958.
[39] *U.S. v. E. I. DuPont de Nemours & Co.* (177 F. Supp. 1. 1959).

the action would violate the Clayton Act. The Antitrust Division said it would. Two years later the two companies moved to force the government's decision to a court test and signed a tentative merger agreement. The next day the Antitrust Division filed an antitrust suit in the Federal District Court of New York. It was the largest antimerger suit ever filed under the Clayton Act and the merger, if allowed, would have been one of the largest in history.

The case went to trial in 1958 after the court had denied a government move for a summary judgment to enjoin the merger. At the end of the proceedings Judge Edward Weinfeld ruled against the steel companies. The government, he said, "is not required to establish the certitude that competition in fact will be substantially lessened"; only "reasonable probability" is necessary. Furthermore, the defendants' contention that the proposed merger would bring certain economic benefits in better competition with the giant in the field, U. S. Steel, and greater productive capacity in the Chicago area was met with the statement by the court that Congress has never made a distinction "between good mergers and bad mergers." If the merger "offends the statute in any relevant market, the good motives and even demonstrable benefits are irrelevant and afford no defense." [40]

This decision was likely to have far-reaching effects on antitrust enforcement. For one thing, it made it possible to try suits quickly under the Clayton Act instead of interminably under the Sherman Act. In addition, it helped to prevent an evil before it had time to develop. In such cases, furthermore, the defendants are on notice from the beginning that the government is investigating them and hence they cannot charge unfairness if the government upsets established business situations.

Although the foregoing summary does not include all the leading cases, it is enough to show the highlights of antitrust enforcement as far as the courts are concerned. No consistent pattern appears, but the trend seems to be in the direction of a more realistic application of the antitrust laws than in the past. In the Antitrust Division, the trend in recent years seems more hopeful than otherwise. After more than seventy years the antitrust laws begin to show signs of some effectiveness. One wonders, however, whether this improvement will continue or whether giantism is now so firmly embedded in the American economy that nothing useful can be done about it.

Supplementary Reading

Hamilton, Walton, *Patents and Free Enterprise,* Temporary National Economic Committee, Monograph No. 31 (Washington, D.C., 1941). Shows how procedures under the patent laws may lead to restraints of trade.

[40] *U.S.* v. *Bethlehem Steel Corp.* (168 F. Supp. 576. 1958).

———, and Irene Till, *Antitrust in Action,* Temporary National Economic Committee, Monograph No. 16 (Washington, D.C., 1941). The most valuable single source.

Wheeler, John T., *Competition and Its Regulation* (New York, 1954). Recent and reliable.

Edwards, Corwin D., *Maintaining Competition* (New York, 1949). The final chapter deals with administration.

Wilcox, Clair, *Competition and Monopoly in American Industry,* Temporary National Economic Committee, Monograph No. 21 (Washington, D.C., 1941). The latter part deals with methods of strengthening antitrust enforcement.

Dirlam, Joel B., and Alfred E. Kahn, *Fair Competition: The Law and Economics of Antitrust Policy* (Ithaca, N.Y., 1954). Brief, readable, constructive.

American Economic Association, *Readings in the Social Control of Industry* (Philadelphia, 1942). A symposium, with emphasis on antitrust.

Latham, Earl, *The Group Basis of Politics—A Study in Basing-point Legislation* (Ithaca, N.Y., 1952). A case study.

Adams, Walter, "The Aluminum Case," *American Economic Review,* Vol. XLI (Dec. 1951), pp. 915–922.

Commerce Clearing House, *A New Look at Antitrust Enforcement Trends, Antitrust Law Symposium* (New York, 1950).

Adelman, M. A., "Business Size and Public Policy," *Journal of Business,* Vol. XXIV (Oct. 1951). Size is not necessarily objectionable.

Clark, John M., "The Law and Economics of Basing Points: Appraisals and Proposals," *American Economic Review,* Vol. XXXIX (Mar. 1949), pp. 430–447.

———, "The Orientation of Antitrust Policy," *American Economic Review, Papers and Proceedings,* Vol. XL (1950).

Department of Justice, *Report of the Attorney General's National Committee to Study the Antitrust Laws* (Washington, D.C., 1955). A mirror of opinion, with few constructive proposals.

Stocking, George W., "The Attorney General's Committee's Report: The Businessman's Guide through Antitrust," *Georgetown Law Journal,* Vol. XLIV (Nov. 1955). A critical appraisal.

Kaplan, A. D. H., *Big Enterprise in Our Competitive System* (Washington, D.C., Brookings Institution, 1954). A sympathetic view of bigness.

6

THE WORK OF THE FEDERAL TRADE COMMISSION

The issues; Sherman, Clayton, and Federal Trade Commission acts; legislation administered by the FTC; programs and functions; how the FTC handles a case; investigation, trial, stipulation; compliance; accomplishment by periods; accomplishment by area of jurisdiction; state and federal fair-trade legislation; evaluation of the FTC.

After the Sherman Act, the next legislative landmarks in monopoly control were the Clayton and Federal Trade Commission acts, passed by Congress in the early part of the Wilson administration. Up to that time, the sole approach to antitrust enforcement had been through long and often bitter litigation in the courts. Thereafter, regulation was simultaneously pursued by an administrative tribunal which, however, also relied on the courts. No more in this second major opportunity than in the first did Congress specifically define such key words as "monopoly," "restraint of trade," "unfair competition," or "substantial," and hence it was for the courts to decide these issues when cases came before them.

There were plenty of other issues, though few of them were recognized at the time. Thus, was an administrative tribunal better than a regular executive department of the government for preventing and prosecuting monopolies? Was it an advantage or a disadvantage to have two agencies doing the work that might be done by one? To what extent would fact-finding and prevention be emphasized? With so much of the Clayton and Trade Commission acts relating to unethical or unfair practices, would not the FTC tend to play around with these problems and neglect the basic monopoly issue?

Again, to what extent would overlapping terms for commissioners protect the FTC from sudden fluctuations in political sentiment toward the trust problem? And would Congress support this new agency any better than it had the Antitrust Division, or would there now be anemia in both? It is easier, of course, to see these problems in retrospect than it was when the legislation was drafted and enacted and before new developments in the business community had arisen to complicate the situation.

The Clayton and Federal Trade Commission acts were the result of a confluence of powerful political forces with different objectives but the same legislative intent: the business community wanted a clearer definition than the Sherman Act offered of what constitutes monopoly; [1] the liberal forces backing Wilson also sought clarity but were even more concerned with putting teeth into antitrust enforcement; organized labor, backing Wilson, demanded an express immunity from the antitrust laws and thought to obtain it by this means; and finally, the programs of all three political parties—Republicans under Taft, Democrats under Wilson himself, and Bull Moosers under Theodore Roosevelt—were pledged to antitrust reform. Without delay, therefore, the twin laws were passed through the legislative mill and signed by the President. Instead of a single federal antitrust statute there were now three; instead of a single enforcement agency there were two.

The Clayton and FTC laws supplemented and strengthened the Sherman Act, but strictly speaking they were not amendments to it, being independent statutes. The Clayton Act, clearer and more concrete than the Sherman Act, specifically condemns certain practices as unlawful and in restraint of trade. The FTC Act created the Federal Trade Commission itself to enforce both the Clayton and the FTC acts and to investigate corporate policies, management, and particular practices if these seemed to run counter to the law. The commission was to forestall restrictive practices by "pitiless publicity" and quasi-judicial proceedings supported by the authority of the courts.

It should be noted that the FTC was to be a study or research agency as well as a prosecuting or action agency. It also took over the work carried on since 1903 by the Bureau of Corporations, a useful but undistinguished agency primarily interested in research—a move that was perhaps a greater mistake than is generally realized. When a newly created public agency absorbs an older one, it inevitably takes on some of the atmosphere and tempo of its predecessor along with its personnel with all their set habits and ways of doing things, and this fact may help explain the direction taken by the FTC almost from the outset.

Although added at the last moment as a kind of compromise, Section 5 of the FTC act nevertheless comes close to being the heart of the act, providing as it does that the FTC shall conduct investigations, hold hearings, and enter cease-and-desist orders in cases of proved violation. Former Commissioner Abram F. Myers, who had had firsthand knowledge

[1] "Business men, trade associations, and commercial and industrial interests to whom the uncertainty of the law had become exasperating . . . took the view . . . that after nearly a quarter of a century of experience with the anti-trust law, it should be possible for the statesmen in Washington to make up their minds just what conduct they wished to forbid. and to describe it in language which the citizen could understand."—G. C. Henderson, *The Federal Trade Commission* (New Haven, 1924), p. 14.

of the origins of the act, has said that "It was thought that this catch-all provision would embrace all monopolistic practices not specifically enumerated in the Clayton Act, including minor abuses not worthy of the attention of the courts in the first instance." [2]

When the Clayton and FTC bills were in final form, it was the consensus that they would deal broadly with the prevention and prosecution of monopoly and not merely apply to lesser evils and minor practices. "Apparently," says Herring, "Congress expected the Commission to deal with the prevention of monopoly rather than the punishment of fraudulent practices. . . ." [3] For the first few years the commission adhered to this objective, but over the longer course, and with important exceptions in the 1940s and again more recently, it has concentrated on defining fair and prosecuting alleged unfair trade practices.

THE FRAMEWORK AND FUNCTIONS OF THE FTC

The Federal Trade Commission has five commissioners appointed by the President by and with the consent of the Senate; terms are for seven years and not more than three commissioners may be of the same political party. The commission elects its own chairman and the position rotates so that every member serves as chairman at least once during his term of office. Instead of each commissioner sharing in the administration of the FTC as was done formerly, since 1950 administrative responsibility has been vested in the chairman, assisted by an executive director, with the commission as a whole handling policy questions, complaints, and case decisions. Four bureaus deal with litigation, consultation (including voluntary compliance), economics (chiefly preparing information for the commission and Congress), and investigation, to which nine field offices are attached. There is also an administrative office and a comptroller reporting to the executive director, a secretary to the commission, a unit of hearing examiners, and a general counsel. This organization is better than the former one and there is somewhat more continuity in administration and in theory, at least, the commissioners can spend more time on cases and issues of policy than was formerly possible.

Like the Antitrust Division, the jurisdiction of the FTC has been added to several times so that it now includes several acts instead of the original two. The *Federal Trade Commission Act* of 1914 not only set up the commission but also provides for substantive regulations of industry. Section 5 states that "unfair methods of competition in commerce, *and unfair or deceptive acts or practices in commerce,* are hereby declared unlawful." The italicized portion was added by amendment by the *Wheeler-Lea Act* of 1938 (which prohibits fraudulent advertising) and re-

[2] Abram F. Myers, address at the Institute of Public Affairs, University of Virginia, July 9, 1932.

[3] Pendleton Herring, *Public Administration and the Public Interest* (New York, 1936), p. 111.

flects the commission's growing preoccupation with unfair and fraudulent trade practices as contrasted with the original emphasis on the prevention of monopoly. This broadened jurisdiction permits the commission to deal with false advertising in food, drugs, cosmetics, and other commodities and devices concerning which the public is easily deluded.

Research and investigatory work is provided for in Section 6 of the FTC Act, which authorizes the commission to "gather and compile information concerning, and to investigate from time to time the organization, business, conduct, practices, and management of any corporation engaged in commerce, excepting banks and common carriers. . . ."

As a companion law to the FTC Act, the *Clayton Act* of 1914 was passed "to supplement" existing statutes "against unlawful restraints and monopolies," and expressly mentions price discriminations, tying contracts, stock acquisitions, and interlocking directorates as examples of actions the commission is expected to prevent or to prosecute. The *Robinson-Patman Act* of 1936, known as the antichain-store act, enlarged the commission's jurisdiction by trying more clearly to define the price and other discriminations referred to in the Clayton Act. Among other provisions, it is now illegal for manufacturers to quote different prices to their retailer-customers except where actual economies might result from larger purchases; thus large customers, such as chain stores, may not exact price concessions from manufacturers that might reduce competition. The *Lanham Act* of 1946 permits the FTC to ask the Patent Office to cancel a trade-mark that has been used to create an illegal monopoly.

Constituting an exception to the Clayton Act, the *Webb-Pomerene Act* of 1918 authorizes the organization and operation of American export associations under the supervision of the FTC as long as domestic trade and competition are not damaged thereby. The *Wool Products Labeling Act* of 1940, the *Fur Products Labeling Act* of 1952, the *Flammable Fabrics Act* of 1953, and the *Textile Fibers Products Identification Act* of 1958, as the names imply, require the content labeling of the products in question and create penalties for misbranding. These statutes are further evidence of the commission's concern for the protection of consumers and competitors from various forms of hazard, unfairness, misrepresentation, and fraud.

All these laws constituting the jurisdiction of the FTC relate to a central purpose, and none is extraneous to the purpose of antitrust enforcement, which cannot be said of the many statutes administered by the Antitrust Division that have no integral connection with monopoly. It will be appreciated, however, that when product labeling, the misuse of trade-marks, and the supervision of certain classes of prices and export activities become a large part of the commission's concern, basic antitrust activities are likely to be somewhat neglected.

From an administrative standpoint there are three points to remember. The first is that the functions of the FTC are both administrative and quasi-judicial in that procedures similar to those of a court action are employed. The second is that internally, the work of the commission is divided into three major functions: administrative in the ordinary sense; legal, especially with regard to litigation; and economic, stressing research and also statistics and accounting. The third point is that the commission's law-enforcement work falls into two general categories: enforcement through formal hearings called trials and leading to mandatory orders against offenders; and enforcement by securing the voluntary cooperation of the business community. Voluntary compliance may be by way of the trade-practice conference designed to educate businessmen as to what they may and may not do under the law, it may be through a stipulation-agreement under which a company agrees formally to stop the practice complained of, or it may be simply by means of an administrative correction of a minor infraction. As in the case of the Antitrust Division, the most recent policy of the FTC is to stress voluntary compliance wherever possible, partly in order to conserve time, funds, and personnel, which are always limited, and partly to maintain friendly relations with the business community, the assumption being that most businessmen are willing to obey the law if they know what it means.

HOW THE FTC HANDLES A CASE

The same four steps in the procedure of the Antitrust Division also apply in handling cases coming before the FTC. They include receipt of a complaint, investigation, and hearing, followed by decision and enforcement. A basic difference, however, is that the FTC, as a quasi-judicial tribunal, has the power to subpoena witnesses.

A complaint may originate before the FTC by the informal action of an injured competitor or consumer (he may simply write a letter setting forth the facts), by a request from Congress or the President, or by action of the commission itself based on its own inquiry into a particular situation. When an individual or a corporation files an application for complaint, it is always the public (the government) and never the informant who brings the action—this is the first important rule to remember. Another is that before a case will be docketed it must satisfy three jurisdictional requirements: it must deal with interstate rather than intrastate matters; it must come within the commission's legal jurisdiction; and the situation complained of must affect a public interest and not merely the private interest of an individual. This last rule, found in Section 5 of the FTC Act, was meant to avoid purely private controversies.

If upon receipt of an application for complaint the question of jurisdiction is favorably settled, then the case is docketed for investigation and assigned to attorney-examiners for the purpose of developing all the facts. One or more of the field offices of the commission's Bureau of Investigation may be called on, the party complained of is interviewed, as are competitors, consumers, and members of the general public where necessary. Thus, unlike the Antitrust Division that must rely on the FBI for its investigations, the FTC makes its own.

When the investigation is completed, the record is summarized both as to fact and law, and a final report is prepared containing a recommendation for the issuance of a formal complaint, the negotiation of a stipulation-agreement, or the closing of the case. This report goes before the commission, and subsequent action depends on which recommendation the commission adopts.

If a formal complaint is issued, it identifies the respondent, alleges violation of the law, and states the charges. The original complainant is not a party to the proceeding. The respondent may file an answer and under certain conditions may offer to settle the matter. In case of contest, a hearing is held before a hearing examiner. The respondent appears in his own behalf or through an attorney, and he may present evidence and cross-examine witnesses. Counsel for the complainant has the general burden of proof. The hearing examiner then prepares an "initial decision" which becomes the commission's decision in thirty days unless there is appeal to the commission or it reviews the case on its own initiative. If the initial decision is upheld on appeal, then an order is issued requiring the respondent to cease and desist from the practice declared illegal.

If, instead of by litigation, the case is to be settled by stipulation-agreement, the procedure is an informal one but there are formal safeguards. The respondent admits his guilt and promises to reform. He signs a written statement setting forth the facts and the acts complained of, promises to "cease and desist forever," and agrees that in case of failure to conform, the facts as set forth in his signed statement may be used against him in a formal hearing. The commission then stipulates that the case shall be closed on condition that the respondent keeps his promise.

Stipulation-agreement was introduced in 1925 and has been widely used, over 3000 cases having been disposed of in this manner during the first ten years. In 1959, more than 1000 respondents were willing to settle their cases by this voluntary method. It has been subject to criticism, however, on the ground that it forsakes Wilson's admonition to give "pitiless publicity" to offenders, that it is "too soft," and that it is used in some major cases of chronic violation that should go to formal hearing. The FTC favors the stipulation-agreement, however, as an economical and amicable method of achieving its ends and holds that the sanctions involved are at least as satisfactory as those resulting from litigation.

In the matter of enforcement and compliance, the procedures and authority of the FTC are superior to those of the Antitrust Division. The rules are these:

In cases coming under the Clayton Act:

1. Within sixty days the respondent must report how he is carrying out the cease-and-desist order.
2. In case of noncompliance, the FTC applies to the appropriate federal court of appeals to affirm the commission's order.

3. Where affirmation is accompanied by a decree of enforcement, contempt proceedings may thereafter be brought by the commission in the court of appeals.

Until 1938 this same procedure also applied in cases coming under the Federal Trade Commission Act, but in that year the Wheeler-Lea Act extended the commission's enforcement authority so that now the procedure is somewhat different:

In cases coming under the FTC Act and other statutes administered by the FTC:

1. A cease-and-desist order becomes final sixty days after the decision has been served on the respondent, unless in the meantime the respondent petitions a court of appeals to review the order.
2. In case of such review, the order of the commission becomes final after affirmation by the court of appeals, or by the Supreme Court, if it reaches that body on certiorari.[4]
3. For each violation thereafter, a fine not exceeding $5000 may be imposed by a court if the commission brings suit for that purpose.

In any case, of course, the respondent may petition for an appeal from the decision of the FTC, presumably on a question of law rather than of fact, to the appropriate court of appeals and to the Supreme Court if that body is willing to review the matter.

Having secured a court order, however, compliance is something else again. In 1953, for example, the chairman of the FTC admitted that "with respect to most of its orders the commission does not know with any degree of certainty" whether they are being complied with.[5] Since then, however, there has been set up in the Office of the General Counsel a Division of Compliance which supervises and directs compliance with orders to cease and desist. If voluntary compliance is lacking, the division prepares complaints and assists in the trial in the federal district courts of civil penalty suits relative to FTC act orders, and also assists in proceedings for contempt in violation of court decrees of enforcement relative to Clayton Act orders.

THE RECORD OF ACCOMPLISHMENT BY PERIODS

It is one thing to become familiar with the formal structure, rules, and procedure of a regulatory commission and another to understand what kind of forces press in on it from all sides, internally as well as externally, making it either more effective or less so than the laws them-

---

[4] Certiorari allows the Supreme Court to exercise discretion as to the cases over which it will take appellate jurisdiction.

[5] *The New York Times,* Sept. 22, 1953.

selves would lead one to expect. Fortunately some thorough studies have been made showing the play of these vital forces.[6] In the case of the FTC the analysis may be dealt with in four periods:

The Formative Years, 1914-1920

Like any new public agency, the FTC took some time to get started and hence was not fully under way until the United States entered World War I in 1917. Despite the disrupting effect of a wartime economy, in that year President Wilson asked the FTC to make a major investigation of the food industry, which soon led to a knock-down-and-drag-out battle with the packing industry. It was apparent that the FTC, not content to limit itself to minor matters of business ethics, meant to make a frontal attack on the twin giants of monopoly and restraint of trade.

The FTC thereafter recommended vital changes in the organization of the food industry and public ownership for some of its branches. Conspiracy in restraint of trade was charged against the big five packers, Swift, Armour, Cudahy, Morris, and Wilson. "The sweeping character of this investigation and the bold changes suggested," says Herring, "caused a political backfire almost fatal to the commission." Some Congressmen called for an investigation of the commission, alleging that it must be infested with socialists, while others stoutly defended its courage. Suspected employees were exonerated but later dropped.[7] The cost of the advertising campaign of Swift & Company alone amounted by 1919 to nearly six times the total annual appropriation of the FTC. Then the Antitrust Division stepped into the picture, the case was settled out of court by consent decree, and the packers succeeded in having Congress transfer jurisdiction over stockyards from the FTC to the Department of Agriculture. The FTC learned in this rugged fashion that pressure groups and their Congressional supporters can play rough when they want to. The episode left a lasting impression on the FTC.

1920-1925

The painful experience of the packing-industry investigation was followed in 1920 by an adverse Supreme Court decision in the case of *Federal Trade Commission* v. *Gratz*,[8] in which it was held that in defining its jurisdiction the FTC was not free to interpret the vague wording of the 1914 legislation. Other limiting court decisions followed, and thus a second obstacle blocked the path of the liberal members of the commission when they sought a bold attack on monopoly. Nevertheless, as late

---

[6] The best brief one, perhaps, is that of Herring, *op. cit.*, Chaps. VII and VIII; see also Thomas C. Blaisdell, *The Federal Trade Commission* (New York, 1932); Henderson, *op. cit.*; and Lowell Mason, *The Language of Dissent* (New York, 1959), a former member of the FTC.

[7] Herring, *op. cit.*, p. 119.   [8] (253 U.S. 421. 1920).

as 1924, at least one expert "saw no reason why the Federal Trade Commission should not realize the promise of the legislation of 1914." [9] Though bleeding from many wounds, the FTC was still interested in major issues concerning monopoly rather than in minor ones concerning trade practices.

1925-1933

After 1925, however, it is generally agreed by students of its history that the FTC rapidly became quiescent. The let-business-alone policy of President Coolidge was reflected in the kind of appointments he made and the FTC did not escape. "We justify the greater and greater accumulations of capital," said Coolidge, "because we believe that therefrom flows the support of all science, art, learning, and the charities which minister to the humanities of life, all carrying their beneficent effects to the people as a whole." [10] In the FTC, the conservative reaction was spearheaded by Commissioner William E. Humphrey who came to dominate the agency.

The objectives, policies, and procedures of the FTC rapidly conformed. "Under the old policy of litigation," said Humphrey, "it became an instrument of oppression and disturbance instead of a help to business." [11] A majority of the commission were of a like mind with the courts and this twin conservatism would have hindered a vigorous enforcement policy even if one had been intended. Indeed, adverse court decisions were fewer during this period because the commission's policy was to avoid litigation.

Inevitably, therefore, the emphasis of the FTC shifted from major assaults on monopoly to research and to minor prosecutions of unfair practices indulged in by a minority of industry. Chief innovations were the wide use of the trade-practice conference and the stipulation-agreement. Increasingly the work of the commission was assigned by Congressmen who wanted studies made of this or that subject. One of these, however—the public-utilities investigation of 1928—proved a bonanza. Conducted over a four-year period with Judge Healy of Vermont at the head, it produced one hundred volumes of hearings and reports and laid the foundation for the Public Utility Act of 1935, Title I of which is the Public Utility Holding Company Act.

1933 to Date

When the Franklin D. Roosevelt administration came to office there was an attempt to change the personnel of the FTC so as to shift its emphasis back to the trustbusting of an earlier period. Commissioner Hum-

---

[9] Henderson, *op. cit.*, p. 342   [10] *The Boston Herald*, Nov. 28, 1920.
[11] Address of W. E. Humphrey at the Institute of Statesmanship, Winter Park, Florida, Jan. 6, 1931.

phrey's resignation was requested: "I do not feel," wrote the President, "that your mind and mine go along together on either the policies or the administering of the Federal Trade Commission and, frankly, I think it best for the people of this country that I should have a full confidence." Obviously regarding the FTC as part of the executive branch of the government, the President felt that its policies should be in accord with his. But in the Supreme Court case of *Humphrey's Executor* v. *United States* [12] in which the President's authority to remove Humphrey was tested, the nation learned otherwise. The Court held that members of quasi-judicial tribunals, appointed for a definite term of office, can be removed only for cause and hence are independent of Presidential policy and direction. Thus the President lost the first round in his determination to reorient the FTC.

During the NRA period, antitrust went into an eclipse, to be revived, however, at the end of that ill-fated experiment. Since then three trends may be observed: First, stress in the FTC continues to be primarily on unfair practices rather than on major prosecutions, although there are a growing number of the latter as exemplified by the eleven-year investigation leading to the *Cement* case banning the basing-point system. Second, although the jurisdiction of the commission has been considerably broadened, except for the Robinson-Patman Act of 1936 and the Celler-Kefauver Amendment of 1950 to the Clayton Act relating to mergers the added power has served merely to increase the emphasis on fraudulent and unfair practices rather than to stimulate a return to monopoly prosecutions per se. And finally, despite its limited view, the FTC has nevertheless been generally revitalized as compared with its earlier quiescent state.

By 1960 the commission had outstanding some 164 sets of trade-practice rules, 9255 stipulation-agreements, and 5735 formal orders to cease and desist, covering almost every segment of American business. They ranged from baby chicks to steel and steel products, from liver pills and cancer cures to printing, insecticides, the products of mines and oil wells, lumber, wood products, automobiles, foodstuffs, and building materials. Also by 1960, more than 1000 investigations were being completed each year as against only four or five hundred a year in the early 1950s. The commission issues annually an average of 254 complaints against alleged deceptive practices, and 72 against alleged restraints of trade.

As in the case of the Antitrust Division, however, an obstacle also faced by the FTC is lack of financial backing by Congress. When the commission was set up in 1915 the number of business concerns in the United States was a little more than 2 million, and by 1959 it was nearer 4.6 million. In the year of its organization the FTC was required to police advertising on which American business spent $200 million annually, and by 1959 the figure was above $10 billion. And yet in the latter year the

[12] (295 U.S. 602. 1935).

staff of the commission totaled only 724 employees, only 35 more than it had in 1918. Friends of the commission feel that it should have an annual appropriation of from $10 million to $15 million, but in 1960 it was only $6.8 million. A Princeton economist once remarked that Congress provides no more money to run the FTC than it does for the Battle Monuments Commission, and that the budget for the FTC division responsible for combating monopolistic mergers is about the same size as the amount Congress provides for postage for its own members.[13]

THE RECORD OF ACCOMPLISHMENT BY AREA OF JURISDICTION

A summary of what the FTC has accomplished in its almost fifty years of existence, classified according to area of jurisdiction, shows a rather spotty picture. As far as *monopoly and restraint of trade* are concerned, Herring concludes that the FTC has played an "insignificant part in curbing the trusts." [14] After reviewing the commission's experiences with the oil, steel, and meat-packing industries, Blaisdell agrees that attempts to restore competition have been of very little effect.[15] Abram Myers, a former commissioner, says with some obvious exaggeration that the chief function of the FTC today is to prevent "false and misleading advertising in reference to hair restorers, anti-fat remedies, etc.—a somewhat inglorious end to a noble experiment." [16] Nevertheless, the situation is considerably better than it was during the 1920s.

Since cases growing out of Sections 2, 3, 7, and 8 of the Clayton Act are numerous and contradictory in some instances, the most that can be done is to cite some of the leading ones as indicative of trends. Thus the effect of Section 2 was sharpened when amended by the Robinson-Patman Act of 1936. This section prohibits price discriminations not justified by savings in cost nor otherwise permissible under the act, when the effect would be substantially to lessen competition. The Robinson-Patman Act was passed partly because a Supreme Court decision [17] allowed manufacturers to quote lower prices to chain stores than to clubs of retailers purchasing through a common agent, although an FTC study had shown that it cost no more to sell to one group than to the other. "The determining factor," said the Court, "is the quantity consumed. . . . Effective competition requires that merchants have freedom of action in conducting their own affairs." In other words, instead of discouraging bigness, the Court was actually encouraging it; the Robinson-Patman Act was a partial remedy.

The Robinson-Patman Act is implicit recognition of the fact that al-

---

[13] Jesse Markham in testimony before the Senate Antitrust and Monopoly Subcommittee, reported in *The New York Times,* Aug. 24, 1955.

[14] Herring, *op. cit.,* p. 115.   [15] Blaisdell, *op. cit.,* p. 255.

[16] Quoted in Herring, *op. cit.,* p. 115.

[17] In *Federal Trade Commission* v. *National Biscuit Co.* (266 U.S. 613. 1924).

though the antitrust laws have not been outstandingly effective, there may still be some hope of preventing further restrictions in distribution, if small firms can be protected from discriminations that benefit giant distributors. It was hoped that by controlling price differentials on the selling side of the market, competition might be maintained on the buying side. The discriminations affected now are those that the FTC and the courts, in interpreting the provisions of the statute, hold to be unreasonably restrictive and conducive to monopoly. Thus under certain circumstances, price differentials are permitted between the prices of goods of different quality, of a different quantity, or where there are bona fide differences in the cost of selling. There may also be differentials to "meet competition," to allow changes of price to reflect new conditions and differentials in services or allowances.

Such a program requires extensive government controls of price differentials, with all the difficulties of interpretation and enforcement that accompany this kind of operation. Concerning differentials as to quantity, for example, the law says that when the FTC finds that "available purchasers of greater quantities" of particular commodities "are so few as to render differentials on account thereof unjustly discriminatory or promotive of monopoly in any line of commerce," the commission may, "after due investigation and hearing of all interested parties, fix and establish quantity limits and revise the same as it finds necessary." Here effectiveness of administration clearly depends on the skill with which meaning is given to such vague terms as "promotive of monopoly."

Section 3 of the Clayton Act prohibits tying contracts, a device that the courts have generally frowned on. It is now a criminal offense to fix a price, a rebate, or a discount, or to sell or lease goods on condition that the purchaser (or lessee) refrain from using or offering for sale the goods of a competitor. A leading case [18] involves an arrangement under which a company had contracted with 20,000 distributors not to handle competing products, an action that was declared unlawful. The effect of this and similar decisions, however, is to cause corporations increasingly to resort to dealers and agents of their own, so that where something was gained by the FTC on the one hand it was lost on the other.

Section 7 of the Clayton Act, which could become of major importance to antitrust enforcement, makes it unlawful for a corporation to acquire the stock of another where the effect would be substantially to lessen competition, restrain commerce, or create a monopoly. But among the 547 mergers consummated between 1929 and 1936, the FTC found that 54 percent had been brought about through the acquisition not of the stock but of the assets of a competitor. Adverse decisions of the Supreme Court were largely responsible for opening this loophole that made such mergers possible.[19] Moreover, in the *Thatcher* and *Swift*

---

[18] *Butterick* v. *Federal Trade Commission* (4 F. [2d] 910. 1925).

[19] An example being *Arrow-Hart & Hegeman Co.* v. *Federal Trade Commission* (291 U.S. 587. 1934).

cases [20] in 1926 and 1928, the Supreme Court decreed by a majority of one that the FTC could not order a company that had effected a merger to divest itself of the assets of its merged competitor while the proceeding was pending, by voting stock it had unlawfully acquired, although the opinion recognized that the acquisition of such stock was in violation of Section 7. The so-called Celler-Kefauver amendment passed in 1950 after a considerable battle with the lobbies was intended to close this loophole by prohibiting the acquisition of assets as well as of stock, but with a few individual exceptions, ten years later the effect of this language did not seem to have slowed the wave of mergers that was then in full swing.

Surprisingly little use has been made of Section 8 of the Clayton Act, which provides that no *director* may sit on the board of two or more corporations if the effect is to eliminate competition between the two companies and to violate "any of the provisions of any of the antitrust laws." This section, however, is seemingly a flexible one. Thus it has been found possible to achieve the results of an interlock by the indirect method of assigning the directors of competing corporations to sit jointly on the board of a third corporation; and it has also been found possible to assign *officers* instead of directors to the board of a competitor. Consequently, as of 1951, for example, General Motors was interlocked with ten of the largest corporations in the country, American Telephone and Telegraph and Chase National Bank with nine of the largest twenty-five, and Mutual Life and Metropolitan Life with eight.

One reason for the commission's inaction with regard to interlocking directorships is that the scope of Section 8 has been limited by Congress and still further restricted by the courts.[21] In 1948 the FTC issued a *Report on the Merger Movement* showing that many interlocking directorates in 1000 of the nation's largest manufacturing corporations are legal because of the evasions used, and probably should be forbidden in the interests of competition. The FTC then undertook to prepare the necessary legislation and an amendment was actually introduced in Congress in 1951, but nothing came of it.

Turning now to the Federal Trade Commission Act, Section 7 provides that in suits brought by the Antitrust Division in equity proceedings, the FTC may be asked to act as master in chancery and to report an appropriate form of decree.[22] The device has been little used and in any case is merely advisory, since the court may adopt or reject any part or the whole of such a report if it chooses. Another cooperative arrangement with the Department of Justice, provided by law, also sounds well on paper: the Attorney General may call on the FTC to study and make

[20] *Thatcher Manufacturing Co.* v. *Federal Trade Commission* (272 U.S. 554. 1926); *Swift & Co.* v. *Federal Trade Commission* (276 U.S. 311. 1928).

[21] Clair Wilcox, *Competition and Monopoly in American Industry*, Temporary National Economic Committee, Monograph No. 21 (Washington, D.C., 1941), p. 190.

[22] A master in chancery is a party designated by a court to hear a case in the court's behalf, thus saving the court's time or supplying it with expert assistance.

recommendations "for the readjustment of the business of any corporation alleged to be violating the antitrust acts in order that the corporation may thereafter maintain its organization, management, and conduct of business in accordance with law." Such an authority opens up interesting possibilities but has seldom been invoked.

With regard to *unfair trade practices,* a study of the cases dealing with false and misleading advertising, fraud, deceit, misrepresentation, and the like shows a record that both administratively and judicially is more favorable to the apparent intent of the statutes than is the case with antitrust enforcement. The quasi-judicial work of the FTC is centered in this area and thousands of cases of a bewildering variety have been handled. In the *Winsted Hosiery Company* case,[23] for example, the commission was upheld on a ruling that false and misleading trade names constitute unfair competition. Other cases deal with the circulation of false statements concerning competitors, false and misleading advertising, exaggerated medical claims, misbranding, fraudulent claims of official approval, and unethical tactics employed to embarrass or harass competitors. In one case a New York silverware firm advertised regular $19.98 stainless steel flatware for only $9.98 and the commission found that the $19.98 price was strictly fictitious. In another a hosiery firm said its product had received an academy award but the commission could not find the academy. In yet another the fine print in the contract of a so-called charm school committed the students to lessons for an indefinite period, even if they failed to find the secret of charm and wanted to leave, and the commission made the school change its enrollment cards. Other situations have given rise to amusing questions. For instance, is the public misled into dreaming of impossible resiliency by looking at a trade mark showing the hugely swelling contents of an unfinished mattress? [24] And is it an unfair trade practice for a local chamber of commerce to fight mail-order houses by encouraging local residents to turn in mail-order catalogues at local theaters, thus increasing the expenses of the company? [25]

As the courts have repeatedly observed, there is always in any industry a small minority that will use deceit, fraud, and other forms of dishonesty. To protect the law-abiding majority, therefore, the courts will usually support a reasonable assertion of authority by the FTC. Such activity not only protects the innocent and helpless public but also buttresses the self-government of industry. The task of policing advertising in newspapers and over the radio and television that annually aggregates billions of dollars is a colossal undertaking that cannot help but leave the FTC but little time or energy for major prosecutions of monopoly. This is yet

[23] *Federal Trade Commission* v. *Winsted Hosiery Co.* (258 U.S. 483. 1921).

[24] *Ostermoor & Co.* v. *Federal Trade Commission* (16 F. [2d] 962. 1927).

[25] *Federal Trade Commission* v. *Chamber of Commerce of Missoula* (5 F.T.C. 451. 1923).

another reason that the FTC, which set out to deal primarily with business restraints and monopoly, is now chiefly concerned with the enforcement of business ethics.

Turning now to *export associations* and the Webb-Pomerene Act, the subject is of increasing importance to the United States because of the growth of powerful international cartels combining financial and business interests over a network of nations. Such cartels have become a dominant feature of the international economy and the monopoly problem involved is now more than a strictly domestic issue. Cartels possess domestic as well as international ramifications and their forms and permutations assume great complexity and evidence remarkable ingenuity.[26] They first became strong in Germany during the 1870s and are now a feature of most national economies.

Prior to 1918 cartels of any kind in the United States were unqualifiedly prohibited under the Sherman Act. In that year, however, the Webb-Pomerene Export Act exempted export associations—a form of cartel—from the provisions of the Sherman Act on the ground that such associations would help to develop foreign trade in exportable surpluses in areas where other nations also used concerted action of this kind. The Webb-Pomerene Act stipulates that the association must be organized for the sole purpose of engaging in export trade, that it will do nothing substantially (that word again!) to lessen competition in the domestic market, that it register with and report to the FTC and, if found to be restricting trade, that the Antitrust Division be requested to bring action against it. Thus, one agency has supervision and a second one applies the sanctions. By 1940, 118 export associations were registered and their maximum share of American foreign trade was 17 percent. By 1960 there were only 37 associations but they did more than $1 billion worth of export business. Some of these associations have participated in international cartels, outstanding cases being copper and oil.

As to the effect of such associations on the domestic economy, an informed consensus supports the conclusion of the Temporary National Economic Committee that although Webb-Pomerene associations are presumed by law to impose no controls, in practice "they implement measures designed both directly and indirectly to restrain competition within the home economy and serve as media for the development of informal programs of restraint." [27] It must be obvious that when quotas are assigned and prices fixed in the foreign markets, prices in the domestic market also are influenced; nor can firms combine for sales abroad without abandoning competition at home. Thus "collective decisions governing the volume of exports must inevitably affect the volume of domestic sales, or the volume and cost of production, and thus the prices which

---

[26] For a general classification and treatment, see Wilcox, *op. cit.*, pp. 218–224.

[27] David Lynch, *The Concentration of Economic Power* (New York, 1946), p. 238. See also his discussion of the international steel cartel and the part played in it by U. S. Steel, pp. 235–237.

domestic consumers are required to pay." [28] Supporters of antitrust enforcement believe the Webb-Pomerene policy to have been a mistaken one and that it should be abandoned.

Trade-practice conferences and aids to small business are an aspect of the FTC program that is popular with the business community. Not provided for by law, in operation the trade-practice conference is a form of business self-government under official sponsorship. Commenced in 1919, it was greatly expanded after 1925, was de-emphasized during the 1930s and 1940s, and then considerably revived in the 1950s as part of the policy of cooperation with businessmen ushered in by President Eisenhower. Under the informal conference procedure, an industry or the commission itself may initiate a meeting at which the members of a trade or industry formulate rules of fair and unfair practice. The conferees work under the general guidance of a special division of the FTC located in the Bureau of Consultation, and when their draft is complete, it is submitted for approval to the commission as a whole.

The rules and standards thus formulated fall into two groups: those which the commission "affirmatively approves" and those which it accepts as "expressions of the trade." The principal advantages of the conference device are that what constitutes fair and unfair practice is usually concretely defined, so that no subsequent violation can be exonerated on the ground that the law was uncertain, and the government is not estopped from proceeding later against members of the industry if new forms of restraint and unfair practice arise. The disadvantages are that in some cases, instead of being clearly identified, particular practices are merely described in glittering generalities. Sometimes also the Antitrust Division has complained that practices approved by the FTC have seemed inconsistent with the antitrust laws. In 1930, for example, the head of the Antitrust Division pointed to "unhealthy" price fixing through so-called codes of ethics,[29] and in 1953 a member of the FTC itself remarked that the codes were of doubtful value.[30]

Since the conference procedure was initiated in 1919, there has been an average of ten trade-practice conferences and hearings a year and by 1960 some 164 codes were in effect, so that in time the ethics of most of American industry may well have been codified. Irrespective of justifiable criticism, this must be accounted a considerable accomplishment.

Also located in the Bureau of Consultation is a Division of Small Business whose function is to foster opportunities for the successful operation of small independent business, tell the little fellow what his rights are under the law, tell him how to institute a complaint against an unfair competitor, and keep him informed of the progress of investigations in which he has an interest.

Since knowledge is power, antitrust enforcement must first have the facts. A proud claim of the FTC is that its *general investigations and*

[28] Wilcox, *op. cit.*, p. 221. [29] Herring, *op. cit.*, p. 132.
[30] Lowell E. Mason, reported in *The New York Times*, Feb. 2, 1953.

economic studies have analyzed the structure and practices of industry with telling effect. Of all the federal agencies assisting the work of the TNEC, for example, the FTC undertook and completed the largest number of research assignments. It prepared monographs on the trade-practice conference, on the relative efficiency of large, medium-sized, and small business,[31] on monopolistic practices, and on the liquor, milk, and poultry industries. The public-utility investigation of 1928 has already been mentioned. Another, dealing with chain stores, was also started in 1928 and ran to thirty-three volumes when completed four years later.

The FTC has completed approximately 154 studies since 1914, many of which are of the basic type mentioned above, in areas useful to the Antitrust Division and to Congressional committees and research experts, as well as to the commission's own staff.

THE FAIR-TRADE LAWS

Among the several reasons that enforcement of the federal antitrust laws has been handicapped is that so-called fair-trade laws in the states encouraged rather than discouraged the growth of monopoly. A fair-trade law permits a manufacturer to fix and enforce minimum retail prices on his product. Though much has been said on both sides of this controversial issue—which appears to become more controversial all the time —the consensus seems to be that such laws do in fact stimulate monopoly. As long ago as 1938 a leading economist minced no words in testifying on the fair-trade issue before the TNEC when he said, "We have been witnessing the latest attempt of monopoly, under the deceptive slogan of fair competition, to restrict economic freedom and to further narrow the remaining frontier of industrial opportunity." [32]

How a pressure campaign was organized and put across in behalf of fair-trade laws was described in the TNEC hearings and makes interesting reading. The term *fair-trade law* itself was a clever piece of propaganda because it elicits a favorable response. The second part of the formula was equally astute: resale-price maintenance, as it was called, was sold to legislators on the basis that it would help the retailer and the small independent merchant; the fact that it also gave the manufacturer the power to fix prices to the consumer was conveniently glossed over. A prominent organ of business tipped its hat to the achievement in these words concerning the principal pressure group involved:

> Most importantly, it set up the National Association of Retail Druggists as a power which in three short years was to roll up a record of accomplishment unmatched by any other pressure group in the country's

---

[31] Temporary National Economic Committee, *Control of Unfair Competitive Practices through Trade Practice Procedure of the Federal Trade Commission*, Monograph No. 34 (Washington, D.C., 1941), and *Relative Efficiency of Large, Medium-sized, and Small Business*, Monograph No. 13 (Washington, D.C., 1941).

[32] Temporary National Economic Committee, *Hearings*, Pt. 5, p. 1,676.

history. . . . Having won the resale-price maintenance fight in the face of the most overwhelming obstacles, the National Association of Retail Druggists is entitled to take rank as the nation's most powerful trade association today.[33]

The association in question could scarcely fail to win when "the whole undertaking demonstrates how legislators will yield to pressure when no counterbalancing influence is at hand to assist the lawmaker to maintain his equilibrium or to hold his ground." [34]

Traditionally, the states have stood consistently with the federal government on antitrust policy; indeed, state antitrust laws antedated the Sherman Act by some years. Why, then, did the states reverse their direction? Pressures as described above, disillusionment with antitrust enforcement, and the influence of the NRA were among the leading reasons. California was the first to turn back on its former position on monopoly when in 1931 it passed a fair-trade law that was a thin mask for restraint. The snowball began to roll following the NRA and by 1937, 41 states had enacted fair-trade legislation.

These laws—applying only to goods sold within state borders, of course—exempted certain contracts between manufacturer and retailer from the state antitrust laws. A manufacturer was permitted, if he wished, to set the minimum resale price of his product to the consumer even after he had relinquished possession of it to the jobber, the wholesaler, and the retailer, provided, however, that the product bore the trade-mark, brand, or name of the producer and was in competition with similar products manufactured by others. The laws usually stipulated, furthermore, that when a manufacturer and a retailer entered into a resale-price contract, no other retailer who had notice of it might sell below the contract figure. In other words, monopoly prices were protected through the sanctity of contract, and by means of the so-called "nonsigner" clause in the law the terms of the contract could even be imposed on retailers who were not party to it. Henceforth, manufacturers were in a position to coerce all retailers to support a monopoly price and to foreswear competition with regard to those products.

Since state fair-trade laws could not apply in interstate commerce, in 1937 Congress passed the Miller-Tydings Act "enabling" any state legislature that so desired to authorize resale-price agreements between manufacturers located outside its jurisdiction and retailers within the state. By 1951 every state except Vermont, Texas, Missouri, and the District of Columbia had taken advantage of this act. In that year, however, the Supreme Court found that the Miller-Tydings Act did not protect the "nonsigner" clause in interstate commerce and nullified a section of the fair-trade law of Louisiana,[35] thus affecting every similar clause in every state law. Within a matter of days, big New York department stores and

---

[33] *Business Week*, Aug. 28, 1937.　　[34] Lynch, *op. cit.*, p. 145.
[35] *Schwegmann Bros. et al. v Calvert Distillers Corp.* (341 U.S. 384. 1951).

other stores throughout the country, loaded as they were with inventories resulting from scare buying after the outbreak of the Korean war, began a price war on name-brand articles that became front-page news as drastic reductions were made on thousands of items. Manufacturers met the situation by refusing to deliver goods to stores involved and after the first rush, the movement subsided.

A new drive on Congress was then started by organized manufacturers, wholesalers, and retailers (again led by the powerful drug lobby) and opposed by organized labor, farm, and consumer groups. The result was that in July 1952 Congress passed the McGuire Act permitting (but not requiring) private price fixing in interstate commerce by manufacturers of name-brand and trade-marked products in cases where fair-trade laws were in existence, and applying equally to sellers not party to the contract. Thus the "nonsigner" clause was apparently reinstated.

Nevertheless, a number of state fair-trade laws were tested in state courts and found to be unconstitutional, chiefly on the ground of the "nonsigner" clause, and in at least two states the laws were thrown out altogether. Retailers opposed to fair trade continued to violate the laws and consumers were glad to go along with them. The only method of enforcement was for a manufacturer to send out bogus shoppers to spot violators and then to secure a court injunction against them under as severe a contempt penalty as could be obtained—a costly and time-consuming procedure. The corporation that gave it a thorough trial was General Electric, which by 1958 was reported to be spending $1 million a year to enforce its minimum prices and to have filed some 3000 petitions for injunctions against price cutters in the preceding six years.[36] An association of retail jewelers once actually requested the FTC to help enforce a state fair-trade law, to which the commission replied that it could not enforce a federal law against price-fixing agreements and simultaneously enforce state laws requiring price maintenance. The commission took the occasion to tell retailers, furthermore, that they could "with impunity" ignore state fair-trade laws where they were not being diligently enforced.[37] Many retailers welcomed this advice and took advantage of it.

Several Congressmen finally came out against the fair-trade laws as unenforceable in the same manner that prohibition was unenforceable. The Attorney General's Committee to Study the Antitrust Laws, a body of 61 experts that reported in 1955, condemned fair trade as an arm of monopoly. A price survey by the Justice Department in 1956 in eight cities not covered by fair-trade laws and involving 132 common drug, housewear, appliance, and similar articles showed that, on the average, prices were 19 percent below the fair-trade prices fixed in other areas. Consumers became increasingly aware of this price gap and discount houses flourished. Then in 1957 the Supreme Court refused to review a

---

[36] *The New York Times*, Feb. 26, 1958.   [37] *Ibid.*, Feb. 21, 1955.

lower court decision permitting a mail-order company in the District of Columbia to advertise and sell goods by mail in states where fair-trade laws were still valid.[38]

By 1955 public opinion had become so aroused and enforcement so difficult that Westinghouse announced the end of its fair-trade arrangements in the sale of its small appliances; so did Schaeffer Pen, so did McGraw Electric with regard to its Toastmasters, and so did General Electric in Michigan and Indiana, two states where the situation had become more than usually confused as the result of court decisions on the fair-trade issue.

Early in 1958 the National Association of Retail Druggists and its Bureau of Education on Fair Trade again took up the attack. The association claimed to have 37,000 members and to speak for more than one million retailers and wholesalers in many fields. Under the association's urging, a bill was introduced in the House as an amendment to the FTC Act to apply to all trade-marked products in interstate commerce and permitting a manufacturer, if he wished to do so, to fix the retail price of his product throughout the nation—provided a substantial part of it crossed state lines—simply by giving the distributors notice. The bill started through Congress but almost at once General Electric was forced unwillingly to announce that it had abandoned fair trade for its small appliances. Again, other companies followed suit and another price war broke out, then subsided again.

Supporters of the federal fair-trade bill included Senator Hubert Humphrey, who introduced a measure of his own in the Senate; the American Fair Trade Council, which claimed to represent some 2000 "fair-trade manufacturers"; and many other trade associations. The opposition was headed by the Consumer Information Bureau, an organization of small businessmen and educators who defended the right of a retailer to charge any price he liked. Also in opposition were the departments of Justice, Commerce, and Agriculture, the Bureau of the Budget, the FTC, the farm organizations, and the AFL-CIO. The bill was defeated. Had it been passed, in the opinion of lawyers and economists the effect would have been to wipe out discount houses, and retail price competition unless a store was going out of business or goods were damaged, and increase the cost of living.

Fair-trade bills were again introduced in 1958 and their supporters were more determined than ever to secure passage. By this time only 29 states still had fair-trade laws and these were in some degree unenforceable. Before a Senate Commerce subcommittee the acting head of the Antitrust Division testified that in effect, "fair trade seems akin to a federal subsidy." The amount of the subsidy would be fixed by private manufacturers or processors and would be paid, almost like a sales tax, by the consumer. Furthermore, a federal fair-trade law would be almost

---

[38] *General Electric Co.* v. *Masters Mail Order Co.* (355 U.S. 220. 1957).

impossible to enforce. For one thing, the big chain stores and mail-order houses had merely to put out products under their own private brand names and then undersell retailers handling nationally advertised brand products. It would take an army of federal enforcement agents to prevent discount houses from underselling retailers whose prices were fixed by manufacturers.[39]

As in 1958, in 1959 and 1960 also, fair-trade bills were tabled or defeated. At the same time the drug industry, in hearings before the Senate Antimonopoly subcommittee, came under sharp criticism for pricing policies that in some cases included a tremendous markup over costs. The inquiry gave added ammunition to the opponents of federal fair-trade legislation. Meanwhile, a case reached the Supreme Court, involving an attempted fair-trade practice in states that do not have fair-trade laws or where such laws have been declared unconstitutional. Under a doctrine established in 1919 in the case of *United States* v. *Colgate,*[40] the court had held that the Sherman Act left manufacturers free to choose their customers, thus leaving a manufacturer unilaterally free to announce retail prices and then refuse to sell to dealers who did not abide by them. The later case, decided in 1960, in effect, reversed this ruling.[41]

The opponents of fair trade concede that should the laws be abolished, it would probably mean the end of marginal retail operations that have been kept in business solely through price protection. And in addition, no one can guess how many efficient but small operations may be put out of business by cutthroat competition from the big stores that are in a position to cut retail prices very sharply and still make a profit. On the other hand, as the then acting head of the Antitrust Division pointed out in 1959, a federal fair-trade law would not help small businessmen, but would work rather to the advantage of their chief competitors: discount houses and mass retailers with private brands.[42] Furthermore, in the opinion of the Antitrust Division, price fixing is price fixing, under whatever name.

EVALUATION OF THE FTC

On occasions in its history the Federal Trade Commission has justified the optimism expressed at the time of its creation. In recent years it seems to have become more alert, more responsive to public criticism. Thus, when inquiry into the television scandals of the fall of 1959 revealed not only the rigging of quiz programs but also the existence of a system called payola, under which record companies quietly paid disk jockeys to promote particular records, the FTC moved in quickly on the

[39] Testimony by Robert A. Bicks, acting head of the Antitrust Division, before a Senate Commerce subcommittee, reported in *The New York Times*, June 17, 1959.
[40] *U.S.* v. *Colgate* (250 U.S. 300. 1919).
[41] *U.S.* v. *Park, Davis & Co.* (4 L. Ed. 2d 505. 1960).
[42] *The New York Times*, June 17, 1959.

ground that the system deceived the public and restricted competition. Indeed, the commission moved faster than many officials could recall, assigned 40 staff members to the investigation, and only four weeks later issued a complaint charging deceptive and unfair trade practices against the record companies.

Shortly afterwards, as though to take advantage of an opportunity to stimulate additional good will on the part of the public, the commission held a two-day conference attended by the representatives of 47 major civic, professional, and welfare organizations to explore ways of making the American consumer a more "educated buyer." The subjects discussed were practices such as fictitious pricing, bait advertising, tricks in direct selling, false advertising, inadequate labeling of fabrics and furs, spurious offers of self-betterment opportunities, phony correspondence schools, make-money-at-home schemes, and vending-machine frauds.

The FTC has also shown that the administrative process can often accomplish certain results more acceptably than the judicial process, which is longer, more formal, more expensive, and more complicated. Moreover, the commission has scored an occasional judicial triumph, as in the Alcoa case.

In addition, the FTC studies the economy broadly for evidence of concentration and hence is in a better position than the Antitrust Division to exercise prediction and control. In 1958, for example, the commission launched an investigation of grocery chains and their suppliers to determine the degree of concentration of power at the retail level. According to the National Association of Retail Grocers, a wave of mergers since 1955 in the retail-food-distribution industry involved more than 2000 community food shops with a combined annual sales of more than $2 billion.[43] The FTC then created a task force to discover violaters of the Robinson-Patman Act, which stipulates that sellers must provide equally proportionate terms to all buyers. Unfair practices said to be common in the industry included hidden discounts, rebates, secret allowances, and discriminatory pressures on suppliers to get preferred treatment. By 1959, under the Robinson-Patman Act the commission was conducting 125 restraint-of-trade investigations in the food industry, 12 cases of alleged deceptive practices, and 260 antimonopoly investigations. The National Association of Retail Grocers called this action significant, if not unusual, creative vigor.[44]

But the FTC also suffers from severe disabilities: it is the prey of political forces that would clip its wings or force it in directions it would rather avoid; its method does not have the definitiveness of the work of the Antitrust Division; and it sometimes dissipates its energies over too wide an area when already it is undermanned and undernourished. The questions of public policy that remain are, How can the FTC be improved; and should it not, perhaps, be combined with another federal

---

[43] *The New York Times*, Nov. 16, 1958.   [44] *Ibid.*, Nov. 10, 1959.

agency for more effectiveness? Both questions require more careful study than they have so far received.

Supplementary Reading

Commission on Organization of the Executive Branch of the Government, *Task Force Report on Regulatory Commissions, Appendix N* (Washington, D.C., 1949). Evaluation of the administrative tribunal.

———, *Regulatory Commissions* (Washington, D.C., 1949). Deals in part with the Federal Trade Commission.

Herring, Pendleton, *Public Administration and the Public Interest* (New York, 1936). Chapters 7 and 8 deal with the Federal Trade Commission; recommended for historical aspect and pressure-group influences.

George Washington University, *The Federal Trade Commission, George Washington Law Review* (Silver Anniversary Number, Jan.–Feb. 1940). An excellent symposium.

Thorelli, Hans B., *The Federal Antitrust Policy* (Baltimore, Md., 1955). Historical and analytical.

Edwards, Corwin D., *The Price Discrimination Law* (Washington, D.C., Brookings Institution, 1959). The definitive study of the Robinson-Patman Act.

Kaysen, Carl, and Donald F. Turner, *Antitrust Policy* (Cambridge, Mass., 1959). An economic and legal analysis.

Palamountain, J. C., *The Politics of Distribution* (Cambridge, Mass., 1955). Toward a realistic approach.

Watkins, Myron W., *Public Regulation of Competitive Practices in Business Enterprise* (New York, 1940). By one of the best authorities in the field.

Wallace, Robert A., and Paul H. Douglas, "Antitrust Policies and the New Attack on the Federal Trade Commission," *University of Chicago Law Review,* Vol. 19 (summer 1952).

Loevinger, Lee, *The Law of Free Enterprise* (New York, 1949).

Wilcox, Clair, *Public Policies toward Business* (Chicago, 1955). Chapters 7 and 8 deal with some of the technical problems confronting the FTC.

Lynch, David, *The Concentration of Economic Power* (New York, 1946). Summarizes fair-trade legislation and TNEC recommendations relative to the FTC.

United States Congress, Select Committee on Small Business of the House of Representatives, *Fair Trade: The Problem and the Issues* (82d Cong., 2d Sess., H. Rep. 1292, 1952). The best brief presentation.

Grether, Ewald T., *Price Control under Fair Trade Legislation* (New York, 1939). A first-rate study.

Federal Trade Commission. *Control of Unfair Competitive Practices through Trade Practice Procedure of the Federal Trade Commission,* Temporary National Economic Committee, Monograph No. 34 (Washington, D.C., 1941).

Mason, Edward S., *Controlling World Trade* (New York, 1946). The role of cartels.

Miller, J. P., *Unfair Competition* (Cambridge, Mass., 1941).

Adams, Walter, "The Aluminum Case: Legal Victory—Economic Defeat," *American Economic Review,* Vol. 41 (1951), pp. 913–923. Relates to what is perhaps the most important case in recent years.

Nicholls, William H., "The Tobacco Case of 1946," *American Economic Review*, Vol. 39 (1949), pp. 284–297. Tacit, nonaggressive oligopoly brought within reach of the conspiracy provisions of the Sherman Act.

United States Congress, Select Committee on Small Business of the House of Representatives, *Antitrust Law Enforcement by the Federal Trade Commission and the Antitrust Division*. Department of Justice (81st Cong., 2d Sess., H. Rep. 3236, 1951). One of the best critical appraisals.

Case books: Milton Handler, *Cases on Trade Regulation* (Chicago, 1937), and *Supplement to Cases and Other Materials on Trade Regulation* (Brooklyn, 1947); G. O. Dykstra and L. G. Dykstra, *Selected Cases on Government and Business* (Chicago, 1937); S. C. Oppenheim, *Cases on Federal Antitrust Laws* (St. Paul, Minn., 1948), and *Recent Cases on Federal Antitrust Laws* (St. Paul, Minn., 1951); Louis B. Schwartz, *Free Enterprise and Economic Organization* (Brooklyn, 1952).

7

REVITALIZING ANTITRUST
ENFORCEMENT

The importance of competition; effects of monopoly; role of public opinion; strengthening the Sherman Act and the Antitrust Division; federal incorporation; strengthening the Federal Trade Commission; Attorney General's Committee to Study the Antitrust Laws; size and efficiency; the tax weapon; encouragement of small business; essentials of a program; revisions of statutes and structure; commerce courts.

In the late 1950s antitrust enforcement improved somewhat over former years. If there were some bad mistakes, as when the suit against AT&T was settled by consent decree, there were also some notable achievements as when the proposed merger of two huge steel companies was prevented by court decision. Nevertheless, antitrust enforcement has lagged behind the rapid pace of merger and conglomeration. Judged by control of markets and prices, administered prices are a greater problem than ever and concentration is becoming accepted as the inevitable concomitant of progress.

The free-enterprise system rests on competition. But what is meant by competition and how much is indispensable to freedom in business enterprise? Since pure competition and pure monopoly are both impossible, the issue is largely one of degree and effect. A public policy aimed at eliminating every device of monopoly, says a modern economist, would face a task of impossible scope and complexity; further, *it is by no means clear that "the preservation of all the competitive elements would be in the public interest,"* or *that* every aspect of market control by an individual corporation is necessarily bad.[1]

The monopoly problem is more a matter of an excess of power than an excess of control, of power that is potential as well as power that has

[1] Edward S. Mason, "Monopoly in Law and Economics," *Readings in the Social Control of Industry* (Philadelphia, 1942), p. 44 (italics added).

already been used in objectionable ways. Monopoly power, says Corwin Edwards, is power over a particular product or group of products, but also it is vastly more than that:

> Today great business enterprises obtain much of their power from their over-all size as measured by assets or income and from structural characteristics such as vertical integration, which permits them to squeeze competitors who must look to them for supplies or markets, and horizontal diversification, which permits them to remain indifferent to their profits and losses in any one market and thus to follow tactics which may destroy less diversified competitors.[2]

Although the concept of monopoly has been broadened in recent years, concludes Edwards, it must be still further broadened and redefined.

Monopoly results in fewer owners and operators of small individually owned businesses, adds to the degree of power wielded by a few owners and managers of big corporations, reduces the number of those possessing any economic power at all, and squeezes the little fellow, the worker, and the consumer; as a consequence, monopoly throws economic and political systems out of balance. The tests of monopoly, therefore, are *potential* power and *potential* results.

There are three main viewpoints with reference to antitrust enforcement. First, there are those who say that the antitrust laws are basically sound and enforcement possible, but that improvements must be made; most groups of small businessmen, for example, hold to this opinion. Second, others contend that the laws should be repealed or greatly relaxed, the U. S. Chamber of Commerce having at various times taken this stand. And finally, there are those who say that the objective of antitrust is sound but that enforcement must reluctantly be acknowledged unsatisfactory and thus additional methods of control must be devised, an attitude that both farm and labor groups are inclined to take.

In terms of realistic politics, a better antitrust enforcement program depends on the support it receives as compared with the force of those who oppose it. Unfortunately, as Hamilton and Till have shown, "the cause of antitrust lacks that massed support which causes congressional purse strings to loosen. Its appeal is greatest to the man on the outside who wants to barge in on a trade and needs its help in making his way. It is least to persons who, already established, are wary of interference." The general public is sympathetic, say these authorities, but "the pressure of the many" is hard to muster and what counts is the pressure of the sophisticated few who know their way around.[3]

An inquiry in 1951 by the Survey Research Center at the University of Michigan found that although most people favor big business as a

---

[2] Corwin D. Edwards, *Papers and Proceedings, American Economic Review,* Vol. XXXVIII (May 1948), p. 204.

[3] Walton Hamilton and Irene Till, *Antitrust in Action,* Temporary National Economic Committee, Monograph No. 16 (Washington, D.C., 1941), pp. 25–26.

highly productive, employment-creating machine, many also recognize its power over prices, the availability of goods, wages, and the level of employment. Indeed, the power of the big corporation was found to be a major concern in public thinking and was generally regarded with misgiving. When asked if they thought the good things about big business outweighed the bad, most people said they did; but in some areas, more people felt that the bad effects predominated. In power over small business and the influence of big business over labor-management relations, for example, more people felt that the bad effects were uppermost.[4] Four years later the Opinion Research Corporation of Princeton conducted a poll in 83 communities throughout the nation, sampling the opinion of a statistically accurate profile of the voting population. In answer to the question of whether they thought big business had been a good thing for the country, 80 percent said they did and only 8 percent took the negative view. On the other hand, at a conference sponsored in 1959 by the National Industrial Conference Board, when a member cited another survey by the Opinion Research Corporation to show how big business was highly rated in public opinion, Professor Andrew Hacker of Cornell replied that he did not trust that kind of study. "The American people can say one thing and mean something else," he said, and added, "I think the American people down deep distrust corporate activity."[5]

If Professor Hacker is right, then on balance there may be enough opinion favorable to the control of big business in the public interest to support a stronger line of antitrust enforcement.

PROPOSALS TO STRENGTHEN THE ANTITRUST DIVISION

Many of the methods suggested for strengthening the Sherman Act and the Antitrust Division have been anticipated in this study. Chief among them are these:

1. Congress should define offenses as clearly as possible.

2. Congress should increase appropriations for enforcement purposes.

3. Adequate personnel should be made available, especially at the first and final stages covering investigation and the policing of decisions.

4. Loopholes in the laws should be plugged.

5. The Antitrust Division should be relieved of the administration of laws having nothing to do with antitrust. In 1929, for example, the division provided legal services with regard to four other acts; in 1952 this number had increased to thirty-four, all outside the field of antitrust proper. As funds for the division have increased, so also have its extraneous duties.

A main suggestion for better antitrust enforcement is to streamline

---

[4] Burton R. Fisher and Stephen B. Withey, *Big Business as the People See It* (Ann Arbor, Mich., Survey Research Center, 1951).

[5] Reported in the New York *Herald Tribune*, Nov. 25, 1959.

the administration of the Sherman Act, and Hamilton and Till have offered a six-point plan to this end. "If litigation must continue to be the instrument of public policy," they say, "it will enjoy an easier, speedier, more certain process, less freighted with procedures, less confused by the irrelevancies of legalism," if such a plan is adopted. Litigation, they add, "needs to borrow a bit of directness and dispatch from the world of business within which it must operate." [6] But how? The six points include adequate funds and more personnel for the Antitrust Division, which should also have the power to issue subpoenas; the substitution of civil procedure for the criminal process and the imposition of a fine amounting to twice the total of net income accruing during the period of wrongdoing; power to the Antitrust Division to sue both agent and principal in cases of violation; and endowing the consumer with authority to bring suit in monopoly cases.

Realizing that such changes alone might not be fully effective, these authors then outline an administrative procedure to take the place of the present judicial procedure of enforcement. Briefly, the plan would (1) encourage the Antitrust Division to render advisory opinions when business men are in doubt—advance clearance, so to speak; this policy has been adopted and, with the consent decree, shows the value of nonjudicial settlements. It is also proposed (2) that the Antitrust Division have the facts of industrial organization, prices, and practices always current and at hand; (3) that it exercise constant supervision over industry, thus becoming an instrument of industrial self-government; and finally (4) that from the decisions of the Antitrust Division there be appeal to a special industrial court of five or seven members who would be expert in the field of antitrust. [7] Reorganized in this fashion, the Antitrust Division might somewhat resemble the Federal Trade Commission in its powers and procedures but not, it is to be hoped, in its rather uncertain record of enforcement.

The Temporary National Economic Committee also sought to cure some of the evils of monopoly and to this end urged decentralization of industry, outlawry of the basing-point system (which in fact was accomplished in 1948), adequate funds for a vigorous enforcement of the antitrust laws, repeal of the Miller-Tydings law allowing resale-price maintenance (it was neutralized by the Supreme Court in 1951 but the McGuire Act took its place in 1952); adoption by Congress of national standards for national corporations, amendment of the patent laws to permit a patent's use by anyone willing to pay a fair price for the privilege, and the registration of trade associations and the regulation of their activities that encourage monopoly.

Senator Joseph C. O'Mahoney, chairman of the TNEC, has long championed compulsory federal incorporation for all concerns desiring to do business on a nation-wide scale. He argues that since a corporation

---

[6] Hamilton and Till, op. cit., p. 105. [7] Ibid., p. 112.

gets its power from the government that charters it, nation-wide corporations should get their charters from the federal government. Monopolistic and other antisocial practices, he believes, have increased in part because governments are negligent in awarding charters and in failing to supervise the use made of them. General Motors, said O'Mahoney in 1955, is the largest manufacturing company in the world, an economic state that influences every community in the nation. But it is actually governed or capable of being governed by the 50 largest stockholders out of a total of more than 540,000.[8] Under federal incorporation, federal charters would set forth in plain words the powers, duties, and responsibilities of such giants and two desirable purposes would be served: the establishment of monopolies would be checked, and action against them would be more effective. Although the logic is irrefutable, the weight of opposition to the plan has so far outbalanced that of support for it.

Senator O'Mahoney has also suggested that where corporation officials are convicted as individual defendants in criminal antitrust cases, the courts should impose the same fines as on the corporation—the maximum now being $50,000. Yet another proposal comes from Theodore K. Quinn, a former vice-president of General Electric who resigned from that corporation when he learned that he was slated to become president, because he had come to believe that giantism in industry is harmful. Before a Senate committee in 1955, Quinn suggested that corporations with $250 million or more of assets, or which did more than 10 percent of the business in any major line, should be declared affected with a public interest, in which case at least one new director named by the President and confirmed by the Senate should be appointed to sit on the board of such a corporation.

"The only practical remedy for preserving competition," says another authority, is to apply dissolution and divestment proceedings under Section 4 of the Sherman Act.[9] Dissolution means to put out of business an illegal combination or trade association; and divestiture and divorcement are something less than this, meaning the disposal of particular plants, securities, or other assets by a particular company so as to allow competing firms to enter the field. The power to order a dissolution has seldom been invoked and the question is, Could it be used more often and more effectively? Two obstacles are first, that the courts have generally adopted inadequate and incomplete concepts of monopoly and competition, and second, there is an unwillingness to disturb property relationships unless flagrant and overt abuses are shown.[10] But the future of the monopoly laws would seem to turn on the use of the power to dissolve and divest more than on any other power now on the books, and it will be interesting to follow future developments, if any, in this area.

---

[8] *The New York Times,* Dec. 11, 1955.

[9] Vernon A. Mund, *Government and Business* (New York, 1950), p. 182.

[10] E. S. Corwin, *The Constitution and What It Means Today* (Princeton, N.J., 1947), p. viii.

PROPOSALS TO STRENGTHEN THE FEDERAL TRADE COMMISSION

From many and diverse sources come proposals to retool the Federal Trade Commission. Fundamental weaknesses have been brought to light by experts who have studied the record. Considering the vagueness of the legislation, the inherent irresponsibility of a five-man commission, and the fact that objectives and policies have constantly fluctuated, Herring expresses doubt as to whether "an independent commission is an administrative device properly suited to meet present demands for the regulation and guidance of industry and commerce." He adds that "conflicting personalities and widely divergent viewpoints among the commissioners must be put down as a basic cause of weakness in the Federal Trade Commission." [11]

Congress intended that the FTC should concentrate on the prevention and prosecution of monopolies, not the policing of unfair trade practices—of much less consequence to the economy. But it is partly due to the interference of Congressmen themselves and of politicians that the original objective has been largely lost to sight. For that and other reasons that have been mentioned, along about 1925 the FTC got off the main track and has been perambulating rather than concentrating much of the time ever since. Fundamental reforms of jurisdiction, motivation, and personnel would probably be necessary to change the direction of the commission now.

As in the case of the Antitrust Division, financial support for the FTC is basic to increased usefulness. This was the main recommendation of the TNEC which strongly urged "the absolute necessity of providing funds for these agencies [Antitrust Division and FTC] adequate to the task which confronts them." Other TNEC recommendations related to the statutes enforced by the FTC: Section 7 of the Clayton Act should be made to cover the assets as well as the stock of other corporations (this was accomplished in 1950); trade associations should be registered (this also has been provided for) and their restrictive practices prosecuted; wider use should be made of the FTC as master in chancery to relieve the courts and speed antitrust suits; and a general overhauling of the antitrust laws should be undertaken "in order that the struggle against monopoly and the uneconomic concentration of economic power in private hands may be carried on with better effect than heretofore." [12]

As the third great merger movement in the history of American business swung into full stride in the mid-1950s, proposals to control such combinations were heard from many quarters, including Congress, and the FTC named a thirteen-member task force to spotlight any corpora-

---

[11] Pendleton Herring, *Public Administration and the Public Interest* (New York, 1936), pp. 110, 133.

[12] Temporary National Economic Committee, *Final Report and Recommendations,* pp. 9, 35–36.

tion mergers that might have an adverse effect on the national economy.
Proposed remedies were also outlined by the head of the Antitrust Division and repeated in the President's Economic Report in 1956: First, all
firms "of significant size" engaging in interstate commerce and planning
to merge should be required to give advance notice to the antitrust agencies and to supply the information needed to assess the probable impact
of such a merger on competition. Legislation pending at the time in
Congress sought to define this "significant size" as meaning capital, surplus, and undivided profits aggregating more than $10 million, and the
head of the Antitrust Division wanted the advance notice to be ninety
days. Second, federal regulation should extend to all bank mergers, since
the 1950 amendment to the Clayton Act did not cover banks. (The Antitrust Division has succeeded in partially closing that loophole.) Third,
federal approval should be required for the acquisition of banks by
holding companies. (The Bank Holding Company Act of 1956 has partially met this need.) And fourth, the Clayton Act should further be
amended to make cease-and-desist orders of the FTC final when issued,
unless appealed to the courts.

Then in 1955 came the Report of the Attorney General's Committee
to Study the Antitrust Laws, which was widely heralded as "the most
comprehensive study of the antitrust laws that has been undertaken in
decades." [13] The committee, consisting of some sixty lawyers and economists, was instructed "to evaluate the antitrust laws in their fundamental
aspects." It labored over a period of a year and a half, and then rendered
a 393-page study accompanied by several sharp dissents, especially from
economist members. The main subjects dealt with were undue limitations
on competitive conditions; trade or commerce with foreign nations;
mergers; distribution; patent problems; exemptions from antitrust coverage; economic indicia of competition and monopoly; and antitrust administration and enforcement. The subjects were good ones but few recommendations resulted beyond one to extend to the so-called rule of reason
to the enforcement procedures of the FTC. And it can hardly be said
that the research was "fundamental"; indeed, the procedure was that of
a study group and not a fact-finding group. Furthermore, observes Stocking, "it made surprisingly little use of available studies relevant to preserving free enterprise, and it manifested no curiosity about the inade-
quately explored areas of business behavior and structural relationships
that, if illuminated, might aid greatly in shaping sound policy toward
business. . . . The committee's report . . . is not a study of the fundamental aspects of the antitrust problem but a profession of faith in the
industrial status quo—a confessional of a group of dedicated men who
have made peace with their environment." [14]

---

[13] *The New York Times,* Jan. 3, 1955.
[14] George W. Stocking, "The Attorney General's Committee's Report: The Businessman's Guide through Antitrust," *The Georgetown Law Journal,* Vol. 44 (Nov. 1955),
pp. 56–57.

There have been many other proposals. Some experts believe that much of the difficulty lies in the type of men who often come to rest in a commission post: a run of lame ducks and deserving politicians who could not get their first choice of plums. "Without partisanship," commented Anthony Lewis in 1959, "it is fair to say that President Eisenhower has not had the quality of advice on agency appointments that he has had from the Justice Department on judicial nominations." Nor was there the atmosphere of excitement in government that might attract able young college graduates to jobs in the commissions.[15] As a remedy to at least part of the difficulty it has been suggested that the office of commissioner be upgraded and commissioners themselves given longer tenure —perhaps even life tenure—in the hope that they would thus become immune to influence-peddling. The objection to this scheme is that it would still further reduce flexibility in agencies that, more than most, must keep abreast of new developments in the business community in order to forestall those which may become monopolistic.

Another suggestion, similar to a recommendation once made by the Hoover Commission, is to transfer the adjudicative functions of the regulatory commissions to administrative courts and their regulatory functions to the executive departments of the government. This, it is said, might make regulation more responsive to the political leadership of the administration in office and would also substitute the more direct methods of the executive branch for the cautious procedures of the commission. But the price would be a weakening of the nonpartisan attitude toward regulation that seems indispensable if competing private interests are to be balanced against one another in the public interest.

When Louis J. Hector resigned from the Civil Aeronautics Board in 1959, he sent a 72-page memorandum to the White House giving his views on regulatory commissions in general and the CAB in particular.[16] Of general application was his belief that commission regulation is the least effective of government functions today because so much of a commissioner's time is taken up with the trivia of his job, and from the administrative standpoint, confusion and inefficiency are the rule. "If private business tried to conduct its affairs this way," he commented, "it would go broke." Regulatory agencies fail to develop general policies, he said, because to devise clear, workable general policies is much harder than to make specific decisions in individual cases on the basis of reports crammed with statistics that are more often scanned than read. Furthermore, commissioners do not generally give the reasons for their vote on a case, which is just as well since "many policies actually followed by the regulatory agencies in practice probably could not stand the light of clear public expression." [17] The picture is one of bored commissioners fum-

---

[15] Anthony Lewis, "To Regulate the Regulators," *The New York Times Magazine*, Feb. 22, 1959. p. 13.

[16] Louis J. Hector, "Memorandum to the President: Problems of the CAB and The Independent Regulatory Commissions," (mimeographed), Sept. 10, 1959.

[17] Reported by Richard E. Mooney in *The New York Times*, Sept. 21, 1959.

bling among piles of individual cases, and looking over but seldom studying stacks of reports prepared by bureaucratic subordinates. The result
of this unhappy situation is a rapid turnover of personnel because "no
competent executive—government, military, or business—can tolerate for
long the inefficiency and the confused administration" in a system which,
partly for these reasons, "invites improper influence."

Mr. Hector offered as a possible solution a plan to separate the functions of commissions, transferring adjudication to administrative courts,
investigation and prosecution to the Justice Department, and everything
else including policy determination to the regular departments of the
executive branch. This suggestion is similar to that of the Hoover Commission and others, and it remains to be seen what further study will
bring forth.

In much of the criticism of regulatory commissions, a major point
seems to be that of all the factors involved—business interest, political
desirability, administrative management, and public policy—it is this
last one that receives the short end of the stick. Harvey J. Levin points
out that the three most common standards by which monopoly power is
judged are (1) market structure, which stresses such elements as number
and size of companies, product differentiation, and entrance to the industry; (2) business conduct, which is the action of business leaders themselves; and (3) market performance, which is sometimes the basis for
allowing action that would otherwise be condemned. Mr. Levin suggests
that a fourth and more useful standard might be that of the public interest itself. Thus, the structure of business and its behavior, including its
tendency to concentration, should be judged in terms of the nation's basic
economic policies and national security. It would be necessary, first, to
know much more than we do about business practices and to identify
those that actually do obstruct national policy. When these are clear, says
Mr. Levin, then "the public might give more constant support to an
effort to curb the private power in the market place." [18]

It is one thing to formulate recommendations, however, and another
to get them converted into legislation, and still another to administer
them effectively with scant funds and limited personnel. For example,
when the Clayton Act was amended in 1950, the White House requested
$500,000 for enforcement. The sum was reduced one third by the House
appropriations committee; an amendment from the House floor cut it
out altogether; the Senate appropriations committee voted $250,000; and
this was reduced to $225,000 by a general 10-percent cut in all appropria-
tions under the Independent Offices Act.

THE FUTURE OF THE ANTIMONOPOLY LAWS

In any final evaluation of antitrust enforcement we come back to the
fact that public opinion is the determining element. If the statutes are to

[18] Harvey J. Levin, "Afterthoughts on Antitrust," *Challenge* (Jan. 1959) pp. 48–52.

be made to work, it will be because effective public opinion and well-organized pressure groups make them work. All other factors, though important, depend on the motivation and control at these focal points in government—the rest is merely machinery and technique. If available evidence points to a gradual weakening of people's interest and faith in the antitrust laws, then the laws will eventually be relaxed, repealed, or superseded.

Ever since the demise of NRA, businessmen and their associations have been calling on state and federal governments alike for formulas based on the self-government of industry, a partnership in which industry and government, it is held, would work harmoniously together instead of in conflict. Official business, speaking through the U. S. Chamber of Commerce, once proposed that

> The anti-trust laws shall be modified so as to make clear that the laws permit agreements increasing the possibilities of keeping production related to consumption. . . . Businesses desiring to combine should have opportunity to ascertain from a suitable government authority whether or not the proposed combination will be in violation of the anti-trust laws. Each industry shall be permitted to formulate and to put into effect rules of fair competition which receive governmental approval. . . . Rules of fair competition formulated by a clearly preponderant part of an industry as suitable for the whole country, with due consideration for small units and approved by the governmental agency, should be enforceable against all concerned in the industry.[19]

Efficiency and Size

There are those who extol the virtues of bigness. David E. Lilienthal, former chairman of the Tennessee Valley Authority and the Atomic Energy Commission, approves of bigness in all of its manifestations, an attitude that comes, one may assume, from working with big things. Lilienthal argues that the United States, with only a small portion of the earth's population and natural resources, is nevertheless its greatest industrial producer because our business is big. He admits the dangers of concentration and centralization but believes them to be under control. Hence our antitrust policy should be relaxed in order to foster even greater production. There is no real hazard in big business because labor also is big, government is a more effective regulator than formerly, business leadership shows a sense of public responsibility, and decentralization can be effective.[20]

Public opinion appears to be increasingly favorable to giantism and monopoly because large units of standardized production are assumed to be efficient and hence potentially able to provide lower prices to the consumer. One authority, for example, has remarked that mail-order houses

---

[19] Resolution adopted by the U. S. Chamber of Commerce in 1936.
[20] *Collier's* (May 31, June 7, 21, and 28, 1952).

and chain stores (and also producer and consumer cooperatives) are advantageous to the farmer because efficiency due to large size makes possible lower prices for what the farmer buys than independent merchants are able to offer.[21] Those sympathetic to bigness naturally cultivate this opinion of their innate competence.

This supposed relation between size and efficiency, however, leads into a difficult terrain where the guidance of tested principles is needed. To begin with, the optimum size of a corporation depends on a number of factors including the nature of its business and the nature of its market; there is no such thing as an ideal size for every undertaking. Second, giant corporations may enjoy advantages denied to smaller ones, in access to patents, funds, research facilities, expert staff advice, first-rate public relations programs, and the recruitment of superior executive personnel—but none of these things is *necessarily* true for the giants except as compared with very small competitors. Third, large markets, large volume, full use of plant, and standardized methods will lower unit costs *up to a certain point,* but beyond that point, and depending on the type of business, inefficiencies from another quarter soon offset further gains. According to David Cushman Coyle, a noted engineer and economist,

> All through the nineteenth century and down to date, science and invention have been piling up examples of the value of big machines, big factories, and mass production. . . . In some lines of production . . . larger operations turned out more goods for less money, compared with the smaller productive units that they displaced. . . . How could the public ever guess that *the big plant is only sometimes more efficient, or that in most industries the middlesized plant works better than either the small or the big.*[22]

A conclusion that seems justified is that optimum size varies with the industry and the type of product, that there is a limit beyond which additional growth generates inefficiencies in supervision and operation due to the rigidities of creeping bureaucracy, and that in general the most efficient unit is the medium-sized one. It is possible that a business today may be too small to realize the economies implicit in modern technology, but another may be too large for competent management. Between these extremes lies the optimum which, of course, will change with the development of new machinery, new processes, and new management techniques. But it is an increasingly recognized fallacy that the largest concern in any industry will invariably have the lowest costs or produce the highest profits.

A variation of the efficiency theme holds that if economic giants are not actually more efficient in a managerial comparison, at least they are

---

[21] Albert L. Meyers, *Agriculture and the National Economy,* Temporary National Economic Committee, Monograph No. 23 (Washington, D.C., 1940).

[22] David Cushman Coyle, "The Big Cannot Be Free," *Atlantic Monthly,* Vol. 179 (June 1947), p. 74 (italics added).

more efficient in a broad social sense because they are able to withstand depression better than smaller units with slimmer resources; they can adjust themselves more effectively to changing economic conditions and trends and hence they are not driven helplessly by forces outside their control. Obviously all this is true if for no other reason than that large financial reserves make it possible for a big firm to absorb losses for a longer period than a small competitor is able to handle. But this is not the whole of the matter because the more significant comparison is between financial reserves and relative efficiency. Thus the chances of survival of a small or medium-sized firm are as good or better than those of a giant, if the financial resources of the smaller firm are *relatively* as great as those of the larger one and if they are properly managed. Lacking these qualifications, both the giant and the smaller firm may be expected to suffer or even to fail in time of depression.

Nevertheless, in the aggregate, the giants are in fact entitled to their reputation for greater stability and staying power, compared with the hundreds of thousands of small firms that make up the economy. This may be one reason that public opinion seems more tolerant toward giantism and monopoly than it once was. Critics of this complacency, however, make two telling points: monopolies are themselves a contributing factor to depression because they throw the natural forces of the economy out of balance; and if power and stability are so easily achieved, why not make monopoly complete and adopt state socialism?

If monopolies are not entitled to the claim of greater institutional efficiency as their social justification, what else may be said in their behalf? One of their arguments, says Coyle, is "liberty," the right to be left alone. Hence it is that more is *said* about free enterprise by monopolists than by smaller and more competitive concerns. Coyle shows how false this claim of unrestricted freedom really is when he points out that "According to American mythology all men have an 'inalienable' right to liberty (except when convicted of a crime). The fact is that the right to liberty makes sense only for small and unimportant people. *The big cannot be free, or in the end they will destroy all freedom.* . . . In the face of the theory of inalienable liberty, we have had to recognize that 'free' competition works reasonably well only so long as none of the competitors gets too big." [23] The more one ponders this proposition the more convinced one becomes of the essential rightness of the argument. The converse of the principle is that the larger and more powerful an individual or a corporation becomes, the greater is his social responsibility and hence, if the need appears, the more his conduct may be circumscribed.

The Tax Weapon

A method of supplementing the antitrust laws that has received a good deal of attention in recent years is the provision of favorable credit

[23] *Ibid.,* p. 73 (italics added).

facilities and the correction of tax inequities as applied to independent businessmen, or, alternatively, using the tax weapon to discourage the growth of nation-wide chains. Although the former method is more fair than the latter, actually most of the effort so far has been in the direction of punitive taxation.

The first case in which the Supreme Court ruled on the regulatory chain-store tax issue occurred in 1931.[24] The Indiana legislature had passed a graduated tax making the levy higher for each unit in a chain, and the issue was whether this violated the equal protection of the laws provision of the Fourteenth Amendment. The Court held that it did not. There is a reasonable classification between types of stores, said the Court, and so long as the classification is in fact reasonable, there is no depriva-tion of equal protection.[25] Since taxes are necessary to the operation of government, the courts have been slow to interfere with legislative discre-tion and will seldom review substantive legislation arising under the police power and the commerce clause to determine constitutionality. In consequence, the taxing power as an instrument of regulation has been largely free of judicial restraint.

In another case the Supreme Court upheld a Florida chain-store tax imposed on stock on hand and in storage—although the rate for chains was twice as high as for independent merchants—but refused to counte-nance higher license fees for chains when no basis for a reasonable dis-crimination could be found.[26] An even more telling victory for the inde-pendent merchant occurred when the Louisiana legislature imposed rates graduated according to the total number of stores operated by a chain, *including those in other states,* and the Supreme Court upheld the law.[27]

Allied to the use of taxation as a main line of attack on monopoly is the need to encourage small and medium-sized businesses. The greatest problems of small enterprise, says a report of the Committee for Eco-nomic Development,[28] lie in the areas of management (more failures are due to unskillful management than to any other single cause), financing and taxation, and competitive opportunity. The CED opposed subsidies, direct loans, or unrestricted guarantees on commercial loans for small business except in periods of grave emergency, but it did recommend an independent review of the antitrust laws, the provision of management-consulting services, special attention to the problems of small business by bankers and universities, and reforms in taxation. These last included

---

[24] *Tax Commissioners of Indiana* v. *Jackson* (283 U.S. 527. 1931).

[25] The Court quoted with approval its dictum in an earlier decision: "A very wide discretion must be conceded to the legislative power of the state in the classifica-tion of trades, callings, businesses, or occupations which may be subjected to special forms of regulation or taxation through an excise or license tax. If the selection is neither capricious nor arbitrary, and rests upon some reasonable consideration of differ-ence or policy, there is no denial of the equal protection of the law."

[26] *Liggett* v. *Lee* (288 U.S. 517. 1933).

[27] *Great A & P Tea Co.* v *Grosjean* (301 U.S. 412. 1937).

[28] Committee for Economic Development, *Meeting the Special Problems of Small Business* (New York, 1947).

reduction of both business and personal income taxes; the right to carry forward losses to apply against later earnings for a period of six years; the averaging of income taxes over a period of five years when income is irregular; more favorable allowances for depreciation; and the elimination of double taxation on corporate income.

Although progress in the direction of these proposals has been slow and largely disappointing, there can be no doubt that they constitute a constructive approach to the problems of small business. Nevertheless such an approach is merely an aid and no substitute for government control of monopoly because after power reaches a certain stage of concentration it can overwhelm all small-scale competition at will, irrespective of how efficient it may be.

Essentials of a Constructive Program

In a broad, statesmanlike attempt to rebuild antitrust enforcement, there are several factors that might be considered:

1. *Should the antitrust laws be fundamentally overhauled, brought within the framework of one statute, and simplified and clarified in the process?* It would be a big job but possibly it is worth the effort. Belatedly rather than never, it might be better to admit that clarity of law is essential to effectiveness of administration. The law should specifically state what size a licensee may attain before it becomes a monopoly, what percentage of the trade may be controlled by a single company, how corporations shall be created and under what circumstances they may merge, the extent to which interlocking directorates may be permitted, and the positive rules of fair and unfair competition.

2. *Should the dual jurisdiction between the Antitrust Division of the Justice Department and the Federal Trade Commission be restudied and possibly abolished?* The present arrangement is neither so logical nor so effective as it might be made. Both programs need a common arm for research and investigation as well as a common instrument of enforcement and follow-up. The Justice Department should, of course, as part of its normal function, prosecute the government's case in the courts; but should it try to do more? What seems to be needed is a single streamlined administrative agency with access to facts and the authority to compel testimony and to police decisions. Such an agency should be free of any extraneous duties having no direct connection with antitrust enforcement.

3. *Should greater emphasis be placed on the prevention of monopolistic restraints, possibly by registration and publicity?* Prevention is usually easier than cure. Once monopolies take form it is almost impossible to undo them. The Swedish government has perhaps pointed the way to effective prevention in its "Public Law Concerning the Supervision of Restrictive Practices in the National Economy," passed in 1937 and providing for advance registration of all agreements that might restrict com-

petition. In addition, full publicity is required: when a license is approved it is announced, and when restraints of trade are found this also is made public. As explained in a Swedish publication, "It is believed that one of the principal means of checking restrictive practices is to spread the knowledge of them. . . . The pressure of public opinion could be mobilized against monopolistic abuses." On the other hand, says another commentary, "a balance should be struck between the legitimate interest of the public and of business at large to know facts—a knowledge which probably will tend to lessen monopolistic excesses—and the interests of firms in protection of their business secrets." [29] These aspects are safeguarded under the Swedish law.

This plan somewhat resembles Senator O'Mahoney's proposal of compulsory federal incorporation, or the use of advisory opinions and trade-practice conferences, devices based on the assumption that it is better to stop an evil before it gets started than to try to halt a massive force once it is in motion. It is easier and more effective to write necessary public controls *into* corporate authority at the time it is granted than to try to impose such controls from the *outside* after the enterprise begins to wander from the straight and narrow path.

4. Finally, *should a special commerce court dealing with restraints of trade be established to give expertness and consistency to court decisions under the antitrust laws?* Such a proposal would assure litigants the right to a judicial appeal handled by competent lawyers in a court staffed with judges who are equally expert. Such a tribunal would be part of the constitutional court system of the nation with ultimate appellate jurisdiction vested in the Supreme Court of the United States. The plan would not detract, therefore, from the authority of the judiciary; rather, it would add to the effectiveness of the courts and relieve them of a specialized burden for which they sometimes have no adequate qualification. Industrial courts have been widely used abroad and the formula has been advocated by leading students of the problem in the United States.

All these proposals have merit but it seems clear, from the experience of the past seventy years or more, that none will be successful without the conscious backing of the public, including the business community. It has been argued that the objective to be gained by a proper antitrust enforcement is so blurred and popular interest in competition so dulled that talk of reviving the antitrust laws is futile. According to one able and thoughtful economist, "The free enterprise system, as a system, is on its way out, and the most that we can expect from antitrust laws is that they will make the transition less painful." After reaffirming that he favors better antitrust laws better enforced, Professor Lewis is constrained to say that no revision of the statutes, no amount of additional antitrust appropriations, and "no extra shots of zeal" in enforcement will prove capable, in his opinion, of "bolstering competition sufficiently to warrant perma-

---

[29] Pamphlet, *Industriens Utredningstitut* (Stockholm, 1946).

nent reliance upon it as the central organizing and regulating force in our economic system." The way, he says, is effectively and permanently blocked by large-scale industrial, marketing, and labor units and he sees no way of reducing their size in any significant measure. Ultimately he expects to see "rational design and collective responsibility substituted for the automatic forces of the market and a free enterprise system that is now weakened and vanishing." [30]

As early as 1935 when the *Encyclopedia of the Social Sciences* was published, Professor Myron W. Watkins saw the gradual abandonment of competition and the antitrust laws by the business community, noting that "the diversion of the thrust of administrative regulatory policy from unfairness to trade competitors to unfairness to trade customers reflects the general shift in public opinion from the trust busting sentiment of a previous generation to resignation to the inevitableness of economic concentration and to the endeavor to find such protection as may be had in the exercise of public control rather than in restoration of free competition." In the light of the historical record, says this authority, it seems entirely fatuous to suppose that protection to small and medium-sized enterprise will be afforded by "the self-government of a privileged class in whose hands economic power is already largely centered." [31]

With minor measures and mere tinkering there is no possibility of regaining the ground that has been lost. Strong public opinion favoring an antitrust program focused on a unified and clarified statutory base, supported by an integrated and effective administration, emphasizing prevention as well as cure, and entrusted to a specialized industrial court for appeal purposes, may have a chance of success. Strong and able personnel, it goes without saying, is essential.

Obviously there are many "ifs" in such a program. According to the trend thesis of predictability, antitrust enforcement is perhaps at a turning point. But many a seeming trend has been known to reverse or to redirect itself. There may be further relaxations of the antitrust laws, accompanied by some kind of NRA arrangement. The erstwhile supporters of antitrust may relinquish hope of halting concentration and turn to other methods of public control in which public ownership predominates. Underlying all these possibilities are the questions: Can competition be enforced? Do businessmen really favor competition or do they merely say they do? Are monopolies something we must learn to live with?

Supplementary Reading

Attorney General's Committee to Study the Antitrust Laws, *Report* (Washington, D.C., Mar. 31, 1955).

[30] Ben W. Lewis, *American Economic Review, Papers and Proceedings,* Vol. XXXVIII (May 1948), pp. 212, 214.
[31] Myron W. Watkins, "Unfair Competition," *Encyclopedia of the Social Sciences,* Vol. XV, pp. 177–178.

Stocking, George W., "The Attorney General's Committee's Report: The Businessman's Guide Through Antitrust," *Georgetown Law Journal,* Vol. 44 (Nov. 1955).

———, and Myron W. Watkins, *Monopoly and Free Enterprise* (New York, 1951). The final chapter summarizes proposed remedies.

Chamberlin, E. D. (ed.), *Monopoly and Competition and Their Regulation* (New York, 1954). Deals comparatively with the subject, showing how other countries cope with the problem of monopoly.

Edwards, Corwin D., *Maintaining Competition* (New York, 1949). The final chapter makes suggestions for better antitrust enforcement.

Keezer, Dexter M. (ed.), "The Antitrust Laws: A Symposium," *American Economic Review,* Vol. XXXIX (June 1949).

Lilienthal, David E., *Big Business, A New Era* (New York, 1953).

———, "Our Anti-Trust Laws Are Crippling America," *Collier's* (May 31, 1952). A defense of bigness.

Mason, Edward S., *Economic Concentration and the Monopoly Problem* (Cambridge, Mass., 1957).

Kaysen, Carl, "The Social Significance of the Modern Corporation," *American Economic Review, Papers and Proceedings,* Vol. XLVII (May 1957).

Wilcox, Clair, *Public Policies toward Business* (Homewood, Ill., 1955). Chapter 9, "Enforcement of Antitrust."

Mund, Vernon, *Government and Business* (New York, 1950). Chapter 12, "The Administration of the Sherman Act."

Handler, M., *Antitrust in Perspective: The Complementary Roles of Rule and Discretion* (New York, 1957).

Whitney, S. N., *Antitrust Policies* (New York, Twentieth Century Fund, 2 vols., 1958).

Brandeis, L. D., *The Curse of Bigness: Miscellaneous Papers* (New York, 1935), Parts II and III.

Mason, Edward S. (ed.), *The Corporation in Modern Society* (Cambridge, Mass., 1959).

United States Congress, *United States versus Economic Concentration and Monopoly,* Staff Report to the Monopoly Subcommittee of the Committee on Small Business, House of Representatives, 1946.

Adelman, M. A., "Effective Competition and the Anti-Trust Laws," *Harvard Law Review,* Vol. LXI (Sept. 1948).

Anshen, Melvin, and F. D. Wormuth, *Private Enterprise and Public Policy* (New York, 1954). Chapter 5, "Trade Regulation: Special Problems."

Kaplan, A. D. H., *Small Business: Its Place and Problems* (New York, 1948). What can be done to improve its competitive position.

———, *Big Enterprise in a Competitive Economy* (Washington, D.C., 1954). The introduction and Chapters 1 and 2 deal with public opinion.

Maurer, Herrymon, *Great Enterprise: Growth and Behavior of the Big Corporation* (New York, 1955). A four-year study of 50 top corporations.

Committee for Economic Development, *Meeting the Special Problems of Small Business* (New York, 1947).

PART III

ORGANIZED
LABOR
AND
GOVERNMENT

8
LABOR AS AN ECONOMIC AND POLITICAL FORCE

Characteristics of American labor movement; growing size and financial power of unions; effect of economic concentration on labor; what labor wants; labor legislation since 1930; Wagner Act and the NLRB; Taft-Hartley Act; Landrum-Griffin Act; wage-hour legislation; court decisions; child and other low-paid labor; public-employment offices; workmen's compensation, health, and safety; FEPC laws; labor and antitrust; labor as a political force.

A major reason for government's growing concern for the economy, especially during the past generation or so, has been the emergence of labor as an organized movement possessed of great economic and political as well as social significance. Since the passage of the Wagner Act of 1935 the right of labor to organize and to bargain collectively has been recognized, so that this aspect of labor-union activity (a basic one, to be sure) is no longer a matter of sharp issue in national policy. But in other respects the relations of government and labor involve more and deeper issues than ever before.

In many respects the issues resemble those just dealt with in the chapters on trade and commerce, involving the twin questions of power and responsibility. How much power should organized labor have, and for what purposes? What danger is there that labor might use its newfound power to limit production, or to create areas of price inflexibility (as a result of wage controls) that might weaken the free-market system? If labor should become increasingly concerned with political organization and pressure to the point of founding a full-fledged political party, would that be a desirable or an undesirable development for the nation? And what should be the attitude of organized labor to automation, the effects of which are not yet fully understood?

Only a little over a century ago the population of the United States was 85-percent rural. Of a total working force of 7.7 million, 64 percent were rural. Today, our population is 60-percent urban and, of a working force of 71.3 million, 86 percent are urban. Furthermore, of the working

force today, approximately one fourth—some 18 million—belong to labor
unions. The total popular vote in the Presidential election of 1956 was
more than 61.6 million. Not every member of the working force is eligible
to vote, of course, either because he is underage or because of residence
and registration requirements; but the majority may vote, and consequently it takes only a little exercise in arithmetic to show how real an
influence organized labor could exert on the political life of the nation
if it chose to do so.

FIG. 6. GROWTH OF LABOR UNIONS IN THE UNITED STATES

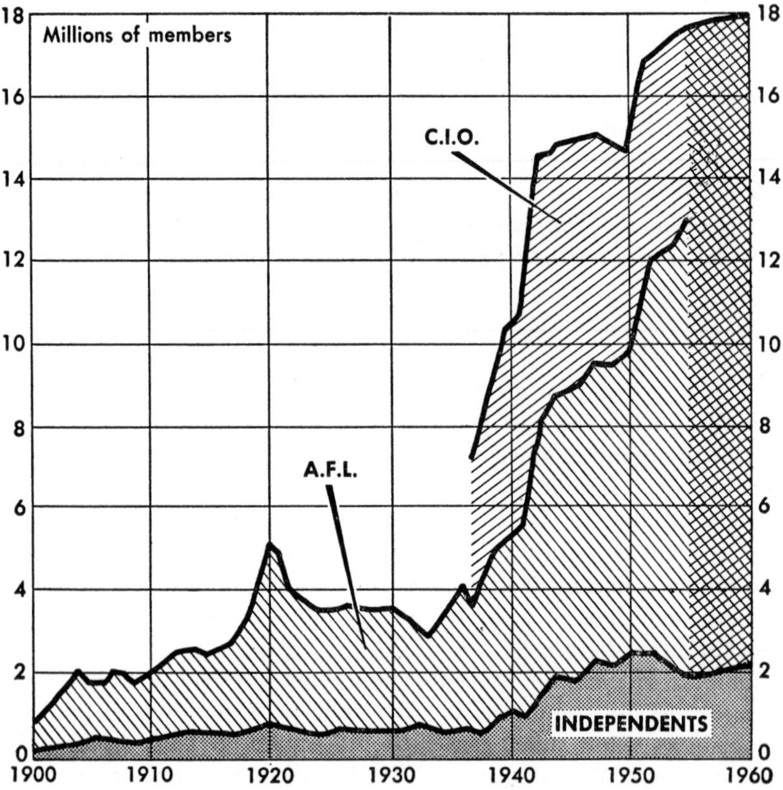

SOURCE: *Statistical Abstract of the United States, 1959*, p. 203.

So far, however, organized labor in this country has not chosen to
exert all the influence of a labor movement in Europe, for example, because its character is different from that of unions in most other countries, Great Britain included. Whereas labor organizations abroad have
tended strongly toward political action and a program of socialism, in
the United States political emphasis has traditionally been de-emphasized
by labor leaders and there is no pronounced tendency toward socialism.
The failure of Marxist philosophy to take hold in this country is partly
explained by the circumstances of the American scene: a nation where the
opportunity to make money has created millionaires out of immigrants;

where the level of real wages by 1955 was twice as high as in Great Britain and three or four times as high as in France or Italy; where social equality is taken for granted; where most people consider themselves middle class and the term *proletariat* is little understood.

Under such conditions, organized labor in the past has been content to emphasize economic rather than political influence. Union leaders have assumed that as long as labor was allowed to organize and to bargain collectively with employers, its economic power was enough to secure to labor its just share of the benefits of our machine technology. Even at the end of the depression of the 1930s, the American Institute of Public Opinion found that of every sixteen Americans, one thinks of himself as lower class, one as upper class, while the remaining fourteen, or 87.5 percent, regard themselves as middle class. This is the more interesting because in 1939 when the survey was made, 54 percent of the nation's families had annual incomes of $1200 or less.[1]

Traditionally, American labor has constituted a cross-section of American political opinion, being middle-of-the-road or conservative rather than radical. "Over a long period," says V. O. Key, "the policies of the American Federation of Labor regarding the role of government were astonishingly similar to those of business. Labor insisted as vociferously as business that the true doctrine was that of *laissez faire;* let the state leave labor alone; it could take care of itself through organization, collective bargaining, and the strike." [2] Labor is still nonradical, but if the amount of legislation passed by Congress at the behest of labor is any indicator, labor's attitude toward government has changed almost as much as the farmer's attitude has changed in the years since 1930. Although we are still too close to the events of the past generation fully to appreciate their meaning, it seems clear that organized labor has entered a new phase of its career, becoming less conservative, more political, and more convinced of the necessity of playing power politics in order to compete with other interest groups using similar devices. William Green, for many years president of the AFL, remarked as early as 1939 that the labor movement had had to adapt itself to changed conditions. "For many years its chief emphasis," said Green, "was on the use of its economic power, the united efforts of the workers, to add to the sum of human happiness. But as we observed the changed conditions of industry our philosophy broadened. We now seek benefit for the workers and all our fellow men by the use of either direct economic strength or legislation as the situation demands." [3] Like organized agriculture, organized labor has had to concern itself with basic economic and political analysis. Why do depressions occur? How can workers be made more secure? Is the annual wage the answer? What is the effect of automation? To solve these questions, labor organizations today employ research staffs and economic

---

[1] Joel Seidman, "Organized Labor in Political Campaigns," *Public Opinion Quarterly,* Vol. III (1939), p. 650.

[2] V. O. Key, *Politics, Parties, and Pressure Groups* (New York, 1942), p. 79.

[3] William Green, *Labor and Democracy* (Princeton, N.J., 1939), p. 67.

and political analysts equal in ability to the best the employers' groups can offer.

Nor do the similarities with employers' groups stop here, because in many ways organized labor today is itself a giant business. Thus in a survey published in 1957, the National Industrial Conference Board reported that a total of 191 unions in the United States and Canada, with a combined membership of 18.3 million, received a combined income of more than $620 million a year, solely from dues. Because of more members and higher dues, this was larger by $162 million than the figure for 1955.[4] Some $254 million went to the international union treasuries, leaving the locals with $366 million for their own needs. Of the unions in the group, only about a million members were located in Canada. Although some unions are increasingly investing their funds in stocks and at least one by 1955 had nearly doubled its assets since World War II through market transactions, most unions prefer to invest in government bonds, partly to play it safe, partly to have quick access to funds in time of need (as in the case of a strike), and partly to avoid any criticism that an attempt is being made to influence labor-management relations by a form of blackmail. The International Brotherhood of Electrical Workers, for example, in order to guard against any hint of union intrusion in company affairs, has all its stock held in the name of its financial adviser (a bank, which even votes the proxies) and not even the union's members know what companies are represented in the portfolio.

Such sums, however, are a small part of union financing, the major part today being the accumulation of pension and welfare funds into reserves that in 1959 were estimated to exceed all the reserves of mutual savings banks in the nation: more than $40 billion, $16 billion of which was invested in corporate bonds and stocks. These welfare-fund reserves were growing rapidly, furthermore, and already covered some 30 percent of all nongovernmental and nonagricultural workers.[5] Union trustees share in the control of welfare funds but in most basic industries, funds are managed by employers or banks designated by them and investments are conservative.

With the accumulation of such sums there is some speculation that the unions may be tempted to use them to influence the labor policy of management or even to buy control of the industries in which their members work. But labor's official policy is dead set against any such move except in a few cases where the unions have stepped in to prevent a failing concern from going out of business.[6] George Meany, president of the combined AFL-CIO, has made it clear that in his opinion the objectives of organized labor are not to "amass great power" and "pile up great

[4] *The New York Times,* Dec. 17, 1957.

[5] "Labor's Money in Wall Street," *Industrial Bulletin,* New York State Labor Department (July 1959).

[6] A. H. Raskin, "New Issue: Labor as Big Business," *The New York Times Magazine,* Feb. 22, 1959.

treasuries" but rather to "build up the standards of living of people in any particular industry." As labor grows, says Meany, "it must realize it has responsibilities to the people as a whole and it must discharge these responsibilities in a way to reflect credit upon itself." [7]

Nevertheless, it was perhaps inevitable that the accumulation of vast welfare-fund reserves—in part, at least, under union control—should lead to abuses ranging from sloppy bookkeeping to actual embezzlement, and these instances have attracted much public notice. Although some of the largest and most powerful unions have been wholly free from a suspicion of financial wrongdoing, a few union leaders have dipped freely into union funds for their own purposes. When such cases are discovered, they are bound to have an unfavorable effect on public thinking about the unions. Hence, as Raskin points out, perspective is needed in this area lest Congress be tempted to use a meat axe instead of a broom to correct the situation. "The fact is," says Raskin, "that corruption is no more the norm in labor than it is in industry or politics. What makes it more disturbing than wrongdoing elsewhere in our society is the lack of adequate internal or external curbs to prevent misuse of power." [8] In retrospect, comments Loftus, what has happened to labor was inevitable: labor has grown up in the image of business because the mass of employees have accepted the business of private enterprise as a way of life. Hence labor is making the same mistakes that business made only a generation or two ago. "In business," says Loftus, "we had the accumulation of wealth and power, conspicuous consumption, corruption, abuses of rights and privileges, and a public-be-damned attitude. Regulation followed." [9]

The Taft-Hartley Act of 1947 was designed in part to guarantee full responsibility in the administration of union finances but, in practice, proved inadequate to the task. A two-year study by a committee of Congress headed by Senator Paul Douglas criticized not only the unions but also employers and the insurance industry, and proposed legislative checks. The result was the Welfare and Pension Plans Disclosure Act of 1958, which requires that descriptions of pension plans and reports on their operation be filed with the Department of Labor. The unions were also doing their part. After the AFL-CIO merger of 1955, the combined leadership of the new organization set about cleaning house and several unions were expelled. In 1956 a jointly financed labor-management research foundation, The Foundation on Collectively Bargained Health and Welfare Plans, was set up to develop plans for the broadest possible range of health and welfare benefits within the framework of union-employer contracts, to show how to make these benefits available at minimum cost,

[7] *The New York Times*, Mar. 28, 1956.

[8] A. H. Rankin, "Labor's Agonizing Reappraisal," *Challenge* (June–July 1957), pp. 8–12.

[9] Joseph Loftus, "The McClellan Committee Hearings and Labor," *Michigan Business Review* (July 1958), pp. 8–12.

and to devise efficient methods of operation free of any taint of improper practice. A year later the foundation reported that aside from abuses then under Congressional investigation by the McClellan committee, "well-intentioned ineptitude" on the part of honest trustees had caused the loss of millions of dollars in welfare funds. The trustees were simply not sufficiently expert in the intricacies of insurance. The report then offered suggestions for cutting down costs and guaranteeing tighter administrative control.[10]

Then in 1957 there were a number of important developments. A Congressional committee (improbably called the Senate Select Committee on Improper Activities in the Labor or Management Field), headed by Senator John L. McClellan, set out to study labor-union abuses, investigated among others the International Brotherhood of Teamsters and found that its president, Dave Beck, had apparently confused union funds with those of his own purse to a shocking degree. The AFL-CIO suspended Beck as a vice president of the national body, suspended the Teamsters as a member union, and then expelled them altogether. Meanwhile the AFL-CIO also drew up a code of ethics and set a deadline for compliance with it by the individual unions. Organized labor quietly supported the work of the McClellan committee with only an occasional pro forma blast to remind union members of labor's basic independence in such matters, and privately, some labor leaders were willing to admit that without the help of the McClellan committee, organized labor could not have moved as fast as eventually it did to expel corrupt unions.[11]

Just to make sure of the situation, in 1959 Congress passed the Labor Management Reporting and Disclosure Act, known also as the Landrum-Griffin Act. As far as welfare funds are concerned, this law is directed toward obtaining information on the organization of labor unions and their officers and their interests in welfare plans; in addition it provides penalties whenever fraudulent practices are revealed. Pension plans now also benefit from another law, the Life Insurance Company Income Tax Act of 1959, under which insurance companies are granted tax benefits on their pension-fund reserves (those of the unions included) which make possible lower premium costs on group contracts.

Many of the difficulties that beset organized labor stem from technology, the same forces, indeed, that affect industry. Productivity per worker has increased steadily in the past two hundred years and, with automation, the pace has accelerated. For workers as for others, some of the consequences are disturbing. The temporary displacement of human labor by machines has always created difficulties and to these must now be added even more serious social consequences: the worker receives less on-the-job satisfaction from his employment, and the concentration of economic power is intensified as control over production passes to continually larger industrial giants.

[10] *The New York Times*, June 3, 1956, and May 20, 1957.
[11] Loftus, *op. cit.*, p. 10.

A key to the difficulty is the fact that mass-production industries require less skill on the part of workers and hence, on a skill basis alone, workers have less bargaining power than formerly unless they belong to an organized union. Edsel Ford once testified that in the automobile industry only about 10 percent of the workers need be skilled [12] and in 1955 another expert applied this same figure to the whole working force of the nation.[13] In the same year the Secretary of Labor declared that the level of labor skills had deteriorated so dangerously that our survival as a nation could be imperiled.[14] Automation requires few but highly skilled workers, along with another group of workers who need have no skills at all. By 1959 jobs in the service-producing industries and white-collar occupations were increasing, the number of new jobseekers coming into the job market was increasing, and the educational and training requirements for jobs also were increasing. At the same time, jobs in the goods-producing industries were slowing down as automation, mechanization, and new production techniques boosted productivity to the point where fewer and fewer workers were able to produce more and more goods.[15]

The more these conditions prevail in the goods-producing industries, again, the more numerous are the social consequences. The chance to rise on the economic ladder is restricted, class groups take form, group bargaining is substituted for individual bargaining, standardization of both worker and process is encouraged, the worker is pressed into a mold of deadening uniformity from which he naturally rebels, and conflicts with employers become more frequent with government called in to settle disputes when matters get out of hand. Thus individualism fights a last-ditch battle on the industrial-relations as on other economic fronts. One may perhaps take some courage from a statement by Isador Lubin that by the time automation dominates American industry (and he did not say when), a half to a third of the nation's labor force will have to be skilled in order to handle the new processes.[16]

The psychological approach to the solution of social problems is first to discover what people want and then to determine whether, and to what extent, these wants can be satisfied. A few years ago Elmo Roper took a poll and concluded that "In describing what labor wants, perhaps I have been describing what everyone, everywhere, wants." [17] The Roper study also confirmed what others have found, that labor desires economic security, the opportunity to rise, human treatment, and a chance to be recognized and to feel important. This is good American doctrine as well as good psychological theory. In more concrete terms, in 1949 Philip Murray, head of the CIO, outlined labor's wants in these terms:

[12] Temporary National Economic Committee, *Hearings,* Pt. 30, pp. 16,221–16,234.
[13] Isador Lubin, *The New York Times,* June 2, 1955.
[14] *The New York Times,* Mar. 8, 1955
[15] Seymour L. Wolfbein, "The Future Job Market," *Challenge* (Oct. 1959).
[16] *The New York Times,* June 2, 1955. [17] *American Mercury* (Feb. 1944).

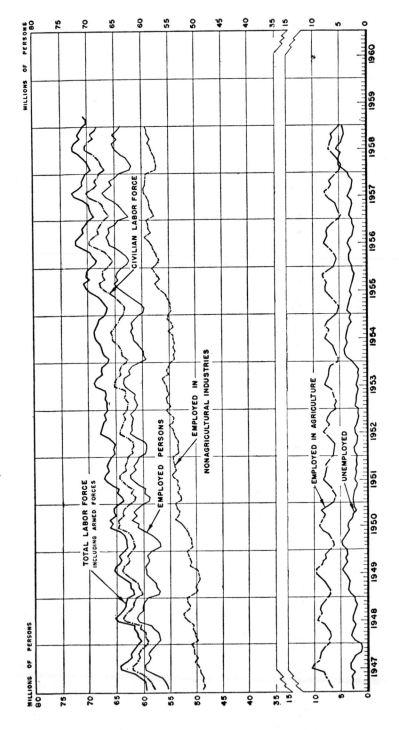

FIG. 7. TRENDS IN THE LABOR FORCE, 1947-1958

SOURCE: U. S. Department of Commerce, Bureau of the Census

Obviously millions of workers and their families are interested in improving their standard of living, of achieving security—not only from unemployment, but from the crises of illness and accident and from the financial burdens that so tragically haunt the lives of millions of our older citizens. They are insisting upon a strengthened structure of civil rights and democratic liberties. They seek the abundant life which America can produce for all of us, and they are determined to use their unions and their government to achieve it. They want an intelligent, constructive militance from their unions; they want a government devoted wholeheartedly to a . . . program that will act in the general welfare; and they are interested in the creation of political-action mechanisms which will ensure the election of legislative bodies capable of overcoming the stand-pat complexes of entrenched minorities.[18]

What labor wants, therefore, can be stated under two broad headings, the industrial and the political. In the industrial area, workers want the right to organize under unions of their own choice; the right to collective bargaining with employers; higher real wages reflecting increased productivity; minimum hours of work assuring time for leisure and recreation; and safe and congenial working conditions. To these may be added others that are more debatable, such as the closed shop, the check-off system of union-dues maintenance, and labor-management committees to give labor a voice in management. In the political area, labor wants an equal voice in popular government; social security and other benefits against unemployment, old age, illness, accidents, and the like; protection of civil rights; prevention of monopoly prices and conditions; antidepression measures aimed at securing steady employment; and protection against cheap labor by restrictions on immigration, child labor, imported labor, prison labor, and the like. There is nothing final or static about these wants, of course. Indeed, because labor's demands increase each year, many employers fear there may be no limit to what organized labor will insist on if its economic and political influence is not curtailed. Accordingly the validity of such a fear becomes a central issue of labor relations.

Although some positive statements have been made here, it must be remembered that generalizations about labor are as precarious as they are about management or any other aspect of society. Not all labor is organized and even among the part that is, there are alternative positions on most issues. A growing number of labor leaders, for example, apparently think that labor must become more political if its gains are to endure, but whether this view will prevail generally depends, as already suggested, on a number of variables. It cannot be said too often that labor is not something apart from the rest of the community; labor is intrinsic in the complex of society and of social pressures and changes.

[18] "What Union Labor Wants," *The New Republic* (Mar. 27, 1950), pp. 12–16.

LABOR IN THE NEW DEAL AND POST-WORLD WAR II PERIODS

During the depression of the 1930s labor was a prominent object of legislation designed to stimulate economic recovery. During the late 1940s the concern of Congress with labor continued, but with a changed emphasis. The earlier period saw the high level of labor legislation, just as it saw the peak of social and economic legislation of all kinds. Some of these landmarks are dealt with in the present chapter and others in the one that follows on industrial relations, but to gain a perspective, all the statutes are listed here:

The right to organize and to bargain collectively:
Section 7A of the National Industrial Recovery Act of 1933
National Labor Relations Act (Wagner Act) of 1935
Bituminous Coal Act of 1937
Labor Management Relations Act (Taft-Hartley) of 1947
Welfare and Pension Plans Disclosure Act of 1958
Labor Management Reporting and Disclosure Act (Landrum-Griffin) of 1959
Minimum wages and maximum hours:
Walsh-Healey Act of 1936 relating to public contracts
Fair Labor Standards Act of 1938 covering wages and hours
Employment opportunities:
Wagner-Peyser Act of 1933 creating the U. S. Employment Service
Child labor:
A section of the Fair Labor Standards Act of 1938
Social security:
Social Security Act of 1935 and subsequent amendments
Railroad Labor Act of 1934
Railroad Retirement Act of 1937

Labor has sponsored laws on public housing, education, and health but they need not concern us here. Most of the legislation listed above deals with wages, hours, conditions of employment, and the right to organize and to bargain collectively.

Labor's Magna Carta, the Wagner Act of 1935

The Wagner Act of 1935, creating the National Labor Relations Board and assuring the right to collective bargaining, is rightly considered the outstanding piece of labor legislation of the New Deal era. The foundation of the Wagner Act was laid two years earlier in Section 7A of the National Industrial Recovery Act. Prior to this time, collective bargaining had been limited and optional, with collective labor agreements binding only on the signatories and enforceable only through private suits for contract violation. After Section 7A, however, collective agreements, when negotiated by the industry and approved by the President of the United States, acquired all the force of the other provisions of NRA codes and accordingly were not only applicable throughout the industry in question but enforceable by the government. It need hardly be said that this represented a major step forward for American labor unions.

The enforcement of Section 7A was first vested in a National Labor Board, created for that purpose by Executive Order and later superseded by a National Labor Relations Board established by Public Resolution of Congress. The function of these agencies was to settle complaints and disagreements arising under NRA provisions and independently of them. Neither agency is to be confused with the National Labor Relations Board, later brought into existence by the Wagner Act.[19] Initial experience with these first two boards and with labor relations boards set up under some of the NRA codes contributed much to later success in the field.

The heart of the Wagner Act is the provision that employees "shall have the right to self-organization, to form, join, or assist labor organizations, to bargain collectively through representatives of their own choosing, and to engage in concerted activities, for the purpose of collective bargaining or other mutual aid or protection." This did not automatically put all workers into unions irrespective of their wishes, but it did provide for a number of procedures and protections: a free election might be held under federal supervision to determine whether the employees of a particular concern wanted to organize at all; if they did, the union so established was to be of the members' own choice and not a company union; management was forbidden to attempt to influence the employees in their election; and once the union was set up, it enjoyed the right to bargain collectively with the employer for wage and other agreements. Clearly, public opinion was much changed from the time when, a hundred years before, a labor union was regarded as an unlawful conspiracy and thus illegal per se.

To carry out the provisions of the Wagner Act, a National Labor Relations Board of three members (later increased to five by the Taft-Hartley Act) was created, superseding the agency originally set up under Section 7A of the NIRA. With the consent of the Senate, the President appoints the members of the board for terms of five years each and, since the Taft-Hartley amendments, the general counsel of the board for a term of four years. It is important to note here that unlike the practice in most governmental agencies where the general counsel is not particularly important, in the NLRB he is an independent official accountable to no one in the agency. His authority in the matter of com-

[19] Leverett S. Lyon, and others, *The National Recovery Administration: An Analysis and Appraisal* (Washington, D.C., 1935), Chap. XVII, and Lewis Lorwin and Arthur Wubnig, *Labor Relations Boards* (Washington, D.C., 1935).

plaints is final except on judicial appeal. When the office of general counsel is vacant, the work of the board comes virtually to a halt. Fortunately, a recent law now makes an interim appointment possible.

The two main functions of the NLRB are first, to supervise plant elections when so requested, to determine whether a union shall be installed and if so, which one (if there are several), and then to certify the collective-bargaining agent so determined; and second, to hear and decide complaints of unfair labor practices committed by either management or labor and prohibited under the labor laws. Under the Wagner Act only employers were forbidden certain types of practice but the Taft-Hartley Act and the more recent Landrum-Griffin Act have also outlawed certain practices on the part of the unions. Within certain limits, the NLRB could determine its own jurisdiction which it rather drastically narrowed in 1953 to exclude many cases where the number of workers involved was small. Since the states were barred from handling these rejected petitions, they fell into a kind of no-man's land. In 1958, however, two cases arose in which an individual sued a union for damages in a state court. The defendant unions contended that only the NLRB had jurisdiction, but on appeal, the Supreme Court allowed the decisions of the state courts to stand.[20] A few months later the NLRB tried to reduce the area of the no-man's land and brought many small companies within its jurisdiction. Then in 1959 the Landrum-Griffin Act prohibited the board from declining to assert jurisdiction over any labor dispute in which it would have acted under the standards prevailing on August 1, 1959. The same law made it clear that the state courts might assert jurisdiction over any labor dispute in which the NLRB declined to act.

For all its powers, however, the NLRB may not intrude itself into a labor dispute nor may it even suggest a settlement until a formal complaint is filed. Judicial appeal from its decisions may be taken on questions of jurisdiction, legal interpretation, or administrative due process. For enforcement, the board must rely on the courts, and it may also petition the courts for injunctions against unfair practices. The constitutionality of the Wagner Act was upheld by the Supreme Court in the case of *NLRB* v. *Jones & Laughlin Steel Corp.* in 1937.[21]

For more than fifteen years the Wagner Act was under attack by management, speaking for the most part through the National Association of Manufacturers, the U. S. Chamber of Commerce, and the American Bar Association. Indeed, the act was regarded as so serious a threat by some business interests that its repeal constituted a principal emphasis of the NAM program after 1935 and was given credit for the legal and administrative reorganization of that agency.[22] Chiefly because of its

[20] *International Union, etc.* v. *Russell* (356 U.S. 634, 1958); *International Assn. of Machinists* v. *Gonzales* (356 U.S. 617. 1958).

[21] (301 U.S. 1. 1937).

[22] Donald C. Blaisdell, *Economic Power and Political Pressures*, Temporary National Economic Committee, Monograph No. 26 (Washington, D.C., 1941), pp. 94–96.

long-standing opposition to the closed shop, the NAM has worked continuously either to repeal the Wagner Act or drastically to modify it, and deserves much credit for the passage of the Taft-Hartley law in 1947. While not so heated on the subject, the U. S. Chamber of Commerce also played a prominent part in lobbying for the Taft-Hartley law and in securing its passage over a Presidential veto. Since the enactment of Taft-Hartley, however, and especially after the Republican administration assumed office in 1953, the NLRB has shifted its attitudes and policies to the point where management seems less critical than formerly.

The Taft-Hartley Act of 1947

The passage of the Taft-Hartley Act (officially known as the Labor-Management Relations Act of 1947) over the veto of President Truman was packed with drama. Feeling ran high for and against, in Congress, in the press, and among the public. Lobbies worked overtime all over the country, with Washington the focal point of effort. Although the President himself had at one time proposed drastic changes in the labor laws of the nation, when the Taft-Hartley bill was presented for his signature he thought it went too far. His veto was quickly overridden by a Republican-Democratic coalition with six votes to spare.

As amended in 1951, the chief policy changes brought about by the Taft-Hartley Act were: (1) the closed shop, in which an employee must be a union member to obtain a job, was outlawed; and (2), the union shop, in which a nonunion employee may be hired on condition that he either join the union or resign after a trial period, was hedged about with certain restrictions but was not prohibited. These two provisions alone, it is estimated, affected some 7 million workers at the time the act was passed. Other provisions compel the registration by the unions, with the NLRB, of certain financial, organizational, and personnel data; deprive unions with Communist officers of their right to the facilities of the NLRB; regulate the stability of union funds; and impose restrictions on union welfare funds and the check-off system (whereby union dues are deducted by management from a member's wages).

In an effort to impose duties on labor as well as on management, another group of provisions outlaws six designated "unfair" labor practices by unions: they may not restrain or coerce employers in the choice of a bargaining agency; persuade employers to discriminate against an employee in limited union-shop actions; issue ultimata in collective-bargaining proceedings; charge "excessive" initiation fees; or attempt to force employers to pay for services "which are not performed," a practice termed *featherbedding*.

A hotly debated provision of the law and one that immediately aroused the charge that labor was being deprived of its fundamental liberties was the restriction on its political activities. Title III of Taft-Hartley amends the Federal Corrupt Practices Act (relating to permissible expenditures in political campaigns) to include labor unions. Under the law, the unions are now forbidden to make a "contribution" or an "expenditure" from union funds "in connection with" any election to any political office. This was intended to prohibit a union from officially working against or supporting a candidate, if the money for it is from union funds. If such activity is supported by individual subscriptions, however, the ban did not hold. Title III also declares that any federal government employee who goes on strike shall be immediately discharged.

Other provisions of the Taft-Hartley Act may be postponed for later consideration, with but passing mention at this point: The U. S. Conciliation Service of the Department of Labor was replaced by a new federal statutory mediation service; emergency machinery was set up for handling "national paralysis" disputes or strikes which "imperil the national health or safety"; and a joint Congressional committee was established to study labor-management relations and to observe the workings of the new law. Other changes related to the organization and management of labor unions, the political activities of unions, and the whole area of industrial relations, which is the subject of the chapter that follows.

When the shouting had died down and the new law duly enrolled, it was judged the most detailed and extensive regulation of labor unions and of industrial relations that the nation had ever seen. Would the new situation foster industrial peace or, as union leaders had argued at the hearings, would it alienate and embitter organized labor? Time would give the answer. One thing, at least, was clear: the National Association of Manufacturers and the U. S. Chamber of Commerce did secure most of what they had fought for from 1935 to 1947. To some observers, however, there was an irony in this because, as an authority on pressure groups has pointed out,

> According to the NAM there is no place in the American system for control, or even regulation, of industrial relations by the Federal Government. That right belongs to individuals, and the preservation of individual liberty depends upon its protection against alienation by government. Attempts to regulate employment relations, production, hours, wages, and working conditions hamper and destroy the freedom of individual enterprise which the NAM regards as synonymous with individual freedom. The NAM feels that the Constitution does not authorize the Federal Government to legislate in this field.[23]

What does Taft-Hartley do to this concept of laissez faire? And when organized labor observes organized employers making extensive use of federal power to its own ends, is it not human to expect that labor also will try to secure further governmental regulation and control of industry if it sees the chance? Not only labor, but the whole country, had learned

[23] *Ibid.*, p. 93.

an instructive lesson in the dynamics of the business-government relationship.

Organized labor has several times tried to tone down the Taft-Hartley Act, and so did President Eisenhower in fulfillment of a campaign pledge, but without success. The courts also have been involved, in cases testing various aspects of the act, and so far the obvious intents of the statute have been upheld. As already suggested, until 1959 most changes had been made by the NLRB itself under new policies inaugurated in 1953. For example, where formerly an employer was forbidden to question a worker concerning his union affiliation, a vote by the board in 1954 sanctioned such action on the ground that it did not "in itself imply any threat." Again, where formerly an employer who broadcast antiunion speeches during working hours prior to a union-representation election was obliged to provide the union with time for a rebuttal, since 1955 there is no such obligation. And where formerly it was considered illegal coercion for an employer to threaten to move his plant if the union should win an election, such action was later reclassified as "prophecy" and hence legal.

When it came to new legislation, far from softening the provisions of Taft-Hartley, a successful attempt was made instead to impose further restrictions on the unions in the name of union reform. The abuses brought to light by the investigations of the McClellan committee in 1957 stimulated a demand for tighter union regulation. A stringent bill offered by the administration was countered by a more liberal one in the Senate, and in the maneuvering that followed, the initiative was taken by Congressmen Phil Landrum and Robert Griffin who secured the passage of the Labor-Management Reporting and Disclosure Act of 1959 as an amendment to the Wagner and Taft-Hartley laws. This measure went considerably beyond what even the White House had requested. Reports by the unions regarding finances, organization, procedures, and internal controls are required to be filed in great detail with the Department of Labor. Union officers are required to meet certain conditions and are made subject to the accountability laws covering trustees so as to protect union funds. Union members are protected against leadership abuses through a so-called bill of rights guaranteeing freedom of speech, periodic secret elections, and the like, and criminal penalties are provided in case of violations. The respective jurisdictions of the NLRB and the state courts were clarified. The Taft-Hartley requirement of a non-Communist affidavit as a condition of NLRB assistance was struck out, but Communists, former Communists, and persons convicted of certain crimes are excluded from union office for stated periods of time. Other provisions cover secondary boycotts and picketing and are discussed in the following chapter.

President Eisenhower declared himself well pleased with this law but as in the case of Taft-Hartley, the unions expressed their fear that the effects would be harmful to them. Among impartial observers the consensus seemed to be that the small unions would indeed suffer but that since they were not making much progress anyway, the result would be largely academic; whereas the strong unions, including the Teamsters at whom the law was chiefly aimed, would be only mildly affected by it. Since it was passed in the year preceding a Presidential election, it seemed that its main effects would be more political than otherwise.

Although a few states have so-called little Wagner Acts, one effect of Taft-Hartley was to open the way for the enactment of so-called right-to-work laws forbidding the closed shop, the union shop, and any other form of compulsory union membership. By 1960, nineteen states had such laws on their books. With Landrum-Griffin, the unions feared that the way would be opened still further for this kind of restrictive state legislation. As one lawyer put it, "This bill is as running over with states rights as the constitution of the Confederacy." [24] Employer organizations contend that these laws merely protect the individual's right to choose between joining or not joining a union, while preserving his right to work, but the unions regard them as potentially dangerous, fear they might be used or misused sometime in the future, especially during a depression, to weaken the unions and even to destroy them. Both groups have concentrated their lobbying activities at the state capitols where the battle at that level is at least as hotly fought as the battles in Washington were fought over Taft-Hartley and Landrum-Griffin. It is to labor's credit, no doubt, that although right-to-work legislation was a ballot issue in six states in 1958, the voters of only one state approved such a law.

In a ten-year study of right-to-work laws, however, Professor Frederick Meyers found that their effect had not been great. In a report published by The Fund for the Republic, Meyers commented, among other things, that "In the traditional areas of the closed shop the law has been generally disregarded and the practices that have continued are illegal under federal as well as state legislation." [25]

The Wage-Hour Law of 1938

Prior to the passage of the Fair Labor Standards Act of 1938, especially in times of economic depression but also during relative national prosperity, many American families received annual incomes so low as to permit a very small purchasing power above a subsistence level. Although part of the act relates to the employment of children in industry, the main object of the wage-hour law is to offer a partial solution to the problem of low incomes. The method adopted was legally to

---

[24] Quoted by A. H. Raskin in *The New York Times,* Sept. 6, 1959.
[25] Frederick Meyers, *The Right to Work in Practice* (New York, Fund for the Republic, 1959).

fix minimum wages and overtime pay so as to increase mass purchasing power, and to set maximum hours (the figure stands at forty a week) so as to provide an opportunity for more workers to secure employment.

To carry out these provisions, the Wage-Hour Division was set up in the U. S. Department of Labor where, under an administrator and a staff of inspectors and hearing officers operating through ten regional and two territorial offices, investigations are made, complaints heard, and quasi-judicial orders handed down. Eventually combined with this agency, in 1942, was the Public Contracts Division created under the Walsh-Healey Act in 1936, also located in the Labor Department and discharging functions similar to the wage-hour law but in the more limited field of public contracts.

Three problems arising under the provisions of these two acts deserve special mention. The first is the difficulty of establishing by law wages applicable to the whole nation sufficiently flexible to follow changes in the cost of living index. The original minimum hourly wage was 25 cents, with time and a half for overtime, but six years later it was revised by Congress to 40 cents. With the increase of prices during and after World War II this base soon became obsolete and in 1949 it was raised to 75 cents. In 1955, with the cost of living 13 percent above the 1950 level, the President proposed an increase to 90 cents, many Congressmen favored $1.25, and a compromise was reached at $1.00. Opposition normally comes from Southern Democrats and the NAM, which favors outright repeal of both the wage-hour and the public contracts laws. When the new level became effective in March 1956, approximately 24 million workers were covered by the wage-hour statute but more than half the work force of the nation was not protected by it. The cost of living index continued to rise and by the end of 1959 stood at 125.5 compared with a base of 100 for 1947. Bills were offered in Congress to increase the minimum-wage rate ($1.25 was generally favored) and also to extend the coverage of the law to include six or seven million more workers, but by early 1961 no change had as yet been made. Those not covered are workers in the retail trades, the service industries, the construction industries, and agriculture. The average hours and gross earnings (including overtime), both hourly and weekly, in manufacturing from 1923 through the early part of 1959 are shown in Table 5, along with figures for the consumer price index for the same years, for purposes of comparison.

The second problem is to determine what constitutes "prevailing minimum wages" under the Walsh-Healey Act relating to public contracts. This law, passed in 1936, provides that in every government supply contract exceeding $10,000, a stipulation shall guarantee the payment of "prevailing minimum wages as determined by the Secretary of Labor." Any violation may cause the cancellation of the contract and the offending party may not thereafter receive government contracts for a period of three years. Although the problem is by no means insuperable,

TABLE 5

AVERAGE HOURS AND GROSS EARNINGS OF PRODUCTION WORKERS IN
MANUFACTURING: 1923-1959

Year	Gross average hourly earnings	Average weekly hours	Gross average weekly earnings	Consumer price index †
1923	$0.52	45.6	$23.82	72.9
1924	.55	43.7	23.93	73.1
1925	.55	44.5	24.37	75.0
1926	.55	45.0	24.65	75.6
1927	.55	45.0	24.74	74.2
1928	.56	44.4	24.97	73.3
1929	.57	44.2	25.03	73.3
1930	.55	42.1	23.25	71.4
1931	.51	40.5	20.87	65.0
1932	.45	38.3	17.05	58.4
1933	.44	38.1	16.73	55.3
1934	.53	34.6	18.40	57.2
1935	.55	36.6	20.13	58.7
1936	.56	39.2	21.78	59.3
1937	.62	38.6	24.05	61.4
1938	.63	35.6	22.30	60.3
1939	.63	37.7	23.86	59.4
1940	.66	38.1	25.20	59.9
1941	.73	40.6	29.58	62.9
1942	.85	42.9	36.65	69.7
1943	.96	44.9	43.14	74.0
1944	1.02	45.2	46.08	75.2
1945	1.02	43.4	44.39	76.9
1946	1.08	40.4	43.74	83.4
1947	1.24	40.4	49.97	95.5
1948	1.35	40.1	54.14	102.8
1949	1.40	39.2	54.92	101.8
1950	1.47	40.5	59.33	102.8
1951	1.59	40.7	64.71	111.0
1952	1.67	40.7	67.97	113.5
1953	1.77	40.5	71.69	114.4
1954	1.81	39.7	71.86	114.8
1955	1.88	40.7	76.52	114.5
1956	1.98	40.4	79.99	116.2
1957	2.07	39.8	82.39	120.2
1958	2.13	39.2	83.50	123.6
1959 *	2.21	40.1	88.62	123.7

* Through March only.   † 1947 = 100.

SOURCE: Department of Labor, Bureau of Labor Statistics.

nevertheless when wage rates and prices vary widely in different parts of the country, decision as to just what constitutes the prevailing rate is sometimes hard to make.

The third and final problem concerns the enforcement of these two related laws. Obviously it would be impossible for federal inspectors to police the entire low-income area of the economy to make sure that minimum or prevailing wage rates are not violated. Fortunately, employees themselves can usually be relied upon to report infringements of the law and to ask for investigations. This method has worked reasonably well despite the fact that low-paid employees are generally less familiar with their rights than more skilled ones. Nevertheless, the Administrator of the Fair Labor Standards Act reported in 1956 that more than half the businesses checked in the preceding year were found violating the law, as a result of which back wages due employees came to $12 million and affected some 130,000 employees. Although the majority of these violations were unintentional, they had the same effect as a willful violation in denying employees the wages due them under the law.[26] Some of the more difficult problems of enforcement have arisen among seasonal or itinerant workers hired by marginal businesses and having no established abodes. As for sanctions, the maximum fine for the violation of any provision of the wage-hour law is $10,000.

In 1947 an hour's work by the average worker would buy at least four times the goods and services a worker earned in an hour a hundred years earlier. In 1953, when the wage-hour law had been in operation for some fifteen years (but not solely for that reason, of course) the American wage-worker was reported to be earning more money, to be more fully employed, and to be enjoying a higher standard of living than ever before in the history of the nation.[27] And by 1955, as a class, only farmers worked excessively long hours: farmers and farm managers worked 57.2 hours a week and farm laborers 50 hours. By comparison, the average work week in other occupations was for professional and technical male workers, 54.1 hours; men clerical workers, 40.8; women clerical workers, 37.6; men sales workers, 42; women sales workers, 33.3; men machine operators, 42.6; women household workers, 30.1; and ordinary laborers, excluding farm and mine workers, a group where there was no figure for women, 37.8 hours.[28]

The unions have continued their efforts to improve wages and hours, of course, one of their goals being the so-called GAW, meaning a guaranteed annual wage or, more accurately, a guaranteed employment plan. What the unions want, ultimately, is to be treated like white-collar workers in so far as stability of income is concerned. Because of the cost and the seasonal nature of production in some industries, management has opposed GAW except in a few cases, notably the Wrigley chewing-gum company and a Southern railroad that have had a variation of the

[26] *The New York Times,* Feb. 27, 1956.   [27] *Ibid.,* Sept. 8, 1953.
[28] *Ibid.,* Jan. 19, 1956.

plan in successful operation for twenty years or so. Nevertheless, in the spring of 1955 the United Automobile Workers secured a modified GAW plan from Ford, Chrysler, and General Motors. These companies agreed to supplement state unemployment benefits to laid-off workers up to 60–65 percent of their take-home pay for periods up to six months. About a year later some 200,000 workers in the automobile industry were laid off and the so-called SUB plan went into effect for approximately a third of them.

Another wage procedure is the so-called escalator clause which ties wage changes to the consumer price index. This clause was first offered by General Motors in 1948 in return for a long-term contract with UAW. Most unions feared that if the price index fell, it would take wages along with it, but several years of rising prices were reassuring and the plan was increasingly adopted in the decade that followed. Adjustments under an escalator clause vary but until recently wage rates were raised or lowered by a penny an hour every time the price index rose or fell by half a point. In the steel settlement of 1960, however, the escalator clause was modified by the imposition of a top limit on possible increases in one year, and also by being tied to the cost of insurance paid by the company as a fringe benefit on behalf of its workers: if the cost of insurance goes up, the increase can be taken out of the cost-of-living wage raises the workers would otherwise receive under the terms of their contract.

The constitutionality of the wage-hour law and of the child labor provisions that are part of it was upheld in the celebrated case of *United States* v. *Darby Lumber Co.*[29] in 1941, a dispute involving a firm in Georgia shipping lumber to other states. In this case the Supreme Court reversed an earlier decision [30] and held that Congress does possess the constitutional power to prohibit the shipment in interstate commerce of goods manufactured by employees whose wages are less than a prescribed minimum or whose weekly hours of labor at that wage are greater than a prescribed maximum; further, that Congress also has the power to prohibit the employment of workmen in the production of goods for interstate commerce at other than prescribed wages and hours.[31]

The Court also took this occasion to re-emphasize the plenary character of the jurisdiction of Congress over interstate commerce. Thus, "While manufacture is not of itself interstate commerce, the shipment of manufactured goods interstate is such commerce and the prohibition of such shipment by Congress is indubitably a regulation of the commerce."

---

[29] (312 U.S. 100. 1941).   [30] *Hammer* v. *Dagenhart* (247 U.S. 251. 1918).

[31] Cases particularly cited were *B. & O. R. Co.* v. *Interstate Commerce Commission* (221 U.S. 612, 1911), sustaining the Hours of Service Act; the *Second Employers' Liability case* (223 U.S. 1. 1912), upholding the Federal Employers' Liability Act of 1908; *Champion* v. *Ames* (188 U.S. 321. 1903), which is the so-called *Lottery* case; and *Kentucky Whip & Collar Co.* v. *Illinois C. R. Co.* (299 U.S. 334. 1937), regulating prison-made goods.

Further, the power of Congress over interstate commerce "is complete in itself, may be exercised to its utmost extent, and acknowledges no limitations other than are prescribed in the Constitution." In short, the jurisdiction of Congress over interstate commerce in matters affecting child labor, minimum wages, maximum hours, and the wages and hours of men and women alike now rests on a secure legal foundation.

From an economic standpoint the idea of raising purchasing power is an acceptable one although there are honest differences of opinion, of course, as to whether the government should try to impose these standards by law or whether they can be secured through the operation of market forces. A good deal of recent evidence seems to indicate that natural forces alone do not accomplish the desired result. As already noted, a difficulty is how to alter minimum wage rates according to price trends, and as long as Congress retains control of this matter instead of delegating it to an administrative agency, the problem will remain a vexing one because Congress is hardly organized for such a function.

Some authorities fear that the wage-hour law will hamper rather than benefit similar laws in the states. Well over half the states now have minimum wage legislation, and in some of the largest industrial states the base rate is higher than that of the federal government. The danger is that the federal law will depress standards in the more prosperous states. Unless one is unalterably opposed to governmental intervention in the field of wage rates, however, it is generally concluded that the wage-hour law will have a salutary effect on the economy if it is intelligently and efficiently administered.

The Regulation of Child and Other Low-paid Labor

Organized labor tried for years to secure the passage of an amendment to the Constitution outlawing child labor, but has never succeeded. First, because powerful business pressures opposed it, and then because the partial success of the Fair Labor Standards Act of 1938 diluted the drive, the amendment still lacks a few state ratifications. Several states have tried to prohibit child labor since shortly after the Civil War and some now have such statutes in force; but to succeed, the move must be universal. Child labor is cheap labor and if businesses in different states are to compete on equal terms, they must have uniform laws on this subject, among others. Thus the argument in favor of the amendment rests on economic as well as on health, cultural, and social grounds.

A partial prohibition of child labor was written into the Fair Labor Standards Act of 1938, a section of which prohibits directly the employment of children under 16 years of age (under 18 years of age in certain hazardous occupations) in interstate commerce or the production of goods for interstate commerce. It also bars from interstate commerce goods produced in places where such "oppressive child labor" is employed. Specific exemptions apply to the employment of children by their parents, except in mining and manufacturing. In other fields, the Labor Department may grant children under 16 permission to work as long as their health, schooling, and general well-being are not impaired.

Compliance, however, is something else. It has been reported for example, that "nearly 10 percent" of the 33,000 establishments investigated in 1951 were employing minors in violation of the federal law.[32] By the time the law was twenty years old, in 1958, more than 11,000 boys and girls were found to be illegally employed, nearly two thirds of them on nonfarm jobs. Of those on the farms, one fifth were under ten and half under fourteen. In addition, more than 2000 minors were working at hazardous jobs ranging from truck driving and logging to operating dangerous woodworking and papermaking machinery.[33]

Other types of workers considered by organized labor as a threat to American working standards are convict labor, contract labor brought in from foreign countries—as from Mexico, for example—and persons admitted to the country under the immigration laws. All these matters are now fully regulated and controlled by the federal government, largely at the behest of organized labor's pressures on Congress.

The U. S. Employment Service

An outstanding gain of the past generation has been the widespread organization of free employment offices, now virtually blanketing the nation. In 1932, under an obsolete system, there were only 250 free employment offices in the United States, whereas eight years later, as a result of the Wagner-Peyser Act of 1933 which created the United States Employment Service, there were 1500. At various times in the intervening years the number had been much greater when the USES made referrals to the federal works program, including WPA, which provided jobs for millions of unemployed men and women during the early and mid-1930s. By 1945, USES placements were averaging better than 10 million a year and by 1958 the figure was 15 million, a third of which were repeat placements for people already registered with the service; more than a million were veterans, and 250,000 were handicapped persons. More than 1.5 million counseling interviews also were held.

A nation-wide network of free public-employment offices offers several outstanding advantages to the economy. As a partial means of securing full employment the USES is a useful tool because in a complex society men and job opportunities must be brought together deliberately rather than by chance. The USES was also a key unit of wartime mobilization. In addition, because of the high standards set, it helps to improve conditions and standards in private employment agencies as well. Thus the

---

[32] Reported by the National Child Labor Committee in *The New York Times,* Nov. 27, 1952.

[33] Reported by the Secretary of Labor in *The New York Times,* May 3, 1959.

USES is an aid to the working man, the employer, organized labor, and the government.

When Congress passed the Wagner-Peyser Act in 1933, it was decided to make the system predominantly a state rather than a federal program. At the federal level the system headed up in the U. S. Employment Service (in the Labor Department) which, through annual appropriations, matched state with federal funds on a contractual basis that permitted the federal government to determine placement procedures and civil service personnel standards. If the states failed to conform, the money was withheld. By the end of the 1930s the system was well established, but with the onset of World War II the demands on it were such that in order to secure greater uniformity and efficiency, the whole program was integrated under federal administration. When the war was over state political pressures forced Congress, over President Truman's veto, to order a return to the former grant-in-aid procedure.

Two issues will help determine the future of the public-employment-office program. The first has already been alluded to: Would not a unified federal system, such as existed during World War II, be more efficient than the joint ownership and management arrangement now in effect? The answer is that probably it would, but states' rights sentiment is opposed; and in fact, there is no serious reason why a state-administered program should not be effectively conducted under federal supervision. The second issue is the potential threat of free public-employment offices to labor unions which, in a very real sense, are employment offices themselves, some even operating hiring halls of their own. From the standpoint of organized labor, a public employment office is no rival so long as the government recognizes labor's rights and interests; but if government were to favor interests hostile to the unions, a real crisis might arise. The issue has already appeared over the question of whether public-employment offices would certify men to companies whose employees are out on strike, which in labor's view would be strikebreaking, pure and simple. The policy so far has been that where a union has a contract with an employer, the public-employment office will take no action that might constitute strikebreaking.

Workmen's Compensation, Health, and Safety

The foregoing discussion of employment may be completed with a brief consideration of working conditions. Beginning about 1910, the states started passing workmen's compensation laws and coverage is now universal. Thus, the cost of hundreds of thousands of accidents that occur each year in employment is spread over the whole economy so as not to fall solely on the injured worker and his employer. Formerly, damages could be had only through a suit against the employer proving negligence, a system obviously too cumbersome in an industrial economy. Furthermore, coverage is constantly being widened and increases made in

injury, medical, hospital, disability, death, burial, and survivor benefits. By 1957, $1 billion, or approximately 9 percent of all social insur-
ance payments, came under the heading of workmen's compensation.

On the preventive side, state and federal safety and health laws have
made considerable progress in recent years. Labor-union insistence, employer concern, and public demand share the credit but considerable improvement is still possible, especially in dangerous employments. In the
principal industrial states, the inspection of factories and workshops is
now conducted by full-time administrative agencies. Matters commonly
covered are ventilation, fire hazards, sanitation, safety devices, and sweat-
shops. At the federal level, authority relates primarily to transportation,
covering such matters as air brakes, automatic couplers, and locomotive
boiler inspection on the railroads.

Fair Employment Practices Legislation

One of the most controversial issues of recent years is so-called FEPC
legislation aimed at the compulsory elimination of discriminatory employment practices due to race, color, and creed. The main issue is
whether such policies should be enacted into law and provided with enforcement machinery, or whether public opinion should be allowed to
solve the problem more gradually. The matter came to a head during
World War II when, between 1941 and 1946, the Committee on Fair
Employment Practice tried to promote the fullest use of available manpower and eliminate discriminatory employment practices. At the end
of the war there was a determined effort in Congress to make the FEPC
a permanent organization of the federal government, but after a bitter
fight the policy failed to pass.[34] Nevertheless, nearly a quarter of the
states, including most of the highly industrialized ones, have passed
state and municipal FEPC legislation so that a third of the nation's population and an eighth of the nation's nonwhites are covered by such
laws.[35] In addition, several states have passed laws aimed at avoiding
discrimination in particular fields such as public works, defense work,
public utilities, and the like. Moreover, the Supreme Court has upheld
the right of a state to prohibit discrimination by labor unions against
Negroes.[36]

In states that have passed FEPC laws, the pattern of enforcement is
generally by an independent board or commission following the federal
model of 1941-1946. One state entrusts the duty to its labor department,
another to its education department. Whether the results of these laws

[34] It is described by Louis Kesselman in *The Social Politics of FEPC, A Study in
Reform Pressure Movements* (Chapel Hill, N.C., 1948).

[35] Eleven states and 25 municipalities, as of 1953, with New Jersey, New York,
Massachusetts, and Connecticut taking the lead. See Mary Bedell, "Employment and
Income of Negro Workers—1940-52," *Monthly Labor Review,* Vol. 76 (June 1953), pp.
596–601.

[36] *Railway Mail Association* v. *Corsi* (326 U.S. 88. 1945).

have been any better than the degree of public opinion behind them is a matter on which reliable information is still lacking.

Those who advocate FEPC laws point out that equality of economic opportunity for those with equal skills is a basic right, that if it is not voluntarily accorded it should be enforced, and that it would be an economic benefit both domestically and internationally. Those who oppose FEPC legislation, on the other hand, contend that only education and public opinion can solve the problem, that employers should not be required to accept employees against their will, that discriminations due to differences in ability are likely to be restricted, and that the ill will engendered by compulsion is not worth the alleged gains. An economic factor is that the controversy boils when labor is plentiful and cools off when labor is scarce. Considering the strength and persistence of the pressure groups involved, however, the conclusion cannot fairly be avoided that FEPC will remain an issue for some time.

LABOR AND THE ANTITRUST LAWS

With the merging of the AFL and the CIO in 1955, many people asked, Does this mean that labor has become a monopoly? By which they meant, of course, would all unions now become a single federation of unions? And of course they have not. Nevertheless, in terms of the antitrust laws, the question of whether labor might constitute an illegal combination, either in its organization or its behavior, has been to the fore almost since the beginnings of the English common law and certainly since the passage of the Sherman Act of 1890.

Between 1890 and 1914, labor was several times held to have violated the Sherman Act, despite labor's contention that it was the intent of that statute to exempt labor unions. Then, in the drafting and passage of the Clayton Act, President Wilson and his legislative leaders thought they had inserted language into the bill that would leave no doubt that the antitrust laws were not to apply to labor unions. But soon afterward the courts ruled that the language employed removed the unions and their activities from the jurisdiction of the Sherman Act only in so far as the unions were "lawfully carrying out their legitimate objects." As it turned out, therefore, labor sustained more unfavorable court decisions, fines, and imprisonments after the passage of the Clayton Act than before it.

A new period for organized labor and antitrust commenced in the early 1940s with the Supreme Court decision in the case of *United States* v. *Hutcheson* [37] wherein the rule was laid down that unions are immune from the antitrust laws except where they combine or conspire with nonunion groups, such as employers or their associations, to restrain trade. In other words, if the behavior of an employer is in violation of the antitrust laws, the collusion of a labor union draws it also into the

[37] (312 U.S. 219. 1940).

situation. Thus labor organization and collective bargaining, per se, are no longer subject to antitrust prosecution except in so far as the unions undertake certain kinds of action in concert with employers. There have been several cases of this kind in recent years, an example being that of *United States* v. *Employing Plasterers' Association et al.*[38] It would take a highly partisan individual to extend antitrust immunity to a union acting in collusion with an employer because this kind of conspiracy is several times more harmful to the public than a conspiracy by either group acting alone.

There is talk, especially since the investigations of 1957, of bringing the unions under the antitrust laws. It is argued that employment, which is an indispensable means of performance, is no longer controlled by competition among workers but by strong unions that in practice have achieved a monopoly. Hence the immunitites that organized labor has won should be removed and the unions treated as any large business enterprise is treated. So far, however, nothing has come of such proposals.

LABOR AS A POLITICAL FORCE

The two principal methods by which organized labor may work to secure its interests are economic and political. Both involve the use of pressure, in the former case on the employer and in the latter on government. Foreign experts have made much of the fact that organized labor in this country has been politically backward and even downright opposed to a close involvement in governmental affairs. The traditional emphasis of labor is voluntarism, corresponding to laissez faire in industry.

Many good reasons have been advanced to explain this laissez-faire attitude: If labor tied itself too closely to government, it was argued, labor would lose its independence of action; the methods of the trade union are better than those of the politician who, in former days at least, relied on a kind of blackmail to secure more than he gave. Furthermore, it was reasoned, if labor acted as a concerted force in politics, the great middle class might become suspicious of its motives and act to restrain it. And finally, in the minds of most American labor leaders, concerted political action was associated with the more radical labor movements abroad and hence it was concluded—in line with the early American view that government is a necessary evil—that as unions (but not necessarily as individuals), the less contact labor had with politics the better it would be for labor.

The relatively nonpolitical character of the American labor movement, therefore, until fairly recently has been considered one of its outstanding points of difference with labor movements elsewhere. But all

---

[38] (347 U.S. 186. 1953).

this is now considerably changed. Organized agriculture and organized industry have intensified their political activity, and labor also now considers it necessary to protect itself from governmental restraints that it believes against its best interests. Belatedly, therefore, and rather grudgingly, organized labor has adopted a positive political program of its own.

The new political orientation is shown in the words of William Green, for years president of the American Federation of Labor, the stronghold of organized labor's laissez-faire policies toward government: "We now seek benefit for the workers and all our fellow men by the use of either direct economic strength or legislation as the situation demands."[39] The changed attitude was even more trenchantly expressed by John L. Lewis, who led his United Mine Workers out of the AFL in 1935 to form the CIO partly because he was dissatisfied with the political quiescence of the parent organization. Speaking in 1937 he remarked that

> Time was, before the depression, when the representative labor leader would have said: "Guarantee labor the right to organize and we shall do the rest." Now he knows that modern, mass-production industry— not only natural resources industries, but the manufacturing and mechanical industries as well—are uncoordinated, uncorrelated, and overcapacitated. With the guarantee of "the right to organize," such industries may be unionized, but, on the other hand, better living standards, shorter working hours, and improved employment conditions for their members cannot be hoped for unless legislative and other provision be made for economic planning and for price, production, and profit controls. Because of these fundamental conditions, it is obvious to industrial workers that the labor movement *must organize and exert itself not only in the economic field, but also in the political arena.*[40]

The second stage in labor's political mobilization was a direct and apparently, to Congress, an unforeseen result of the Taft-Hartley labor law of 1947. Although a part of this legislation attempted to regulate labor's political activities, the effect seemed rather to intensify than to diminish labor's use of this medium. A provision of the act, it will be recalled, prohibited the use of union funds, contributions, or expenditures in connection with any election to any political office. But it did not prohibit the unions from setting up separate organizations to carry on their political activities, and this is what happened. Six months after the enactment of the Taft-Hartley law, the labor unions were fairly well organized into political action groups of their own making.

The AFL organized Labor's League for Political Education as a permanent agency, a step said to be "unprecedented" for the Federation, "as its political set-up has hitherto been limited to the temporary re-

---

[39] William Green, *op. cit.*, p. 67.
[40] John L. Lewis in *Public Opinion Quarterly*, Vol. I (Oct. 1937), p. 27 (italics added).

vival of non-partisan committees at election time which became moribund after election."[41] The AFL also called on its president to establish "cooperation and joint action with all labor and bona fide liberal forces" toward the election of a progressive Congress.[42] The CIO already had its Political Action Committee (PAC) and by 1944 it was a fully organized and going concern. "This organization," said a Washington correspondent, "is pledged to a doorbell-ringing crusade as the final act in its educational campaign calling on the voters to cast their ballots only for those sympathetic with the labor viewpoint, which they identify as that of most of the population."[43]

When the AFL and CIO combined, the new organization created a Committee on Political Education, known as COPE, as the political arm of the united labor movement. In addition, many unions and union groups maintain their own political committees and most of them cooperate with COPE. In the 1954 Congressional campaign, forty-one labor committees reported spending something more than $2 million, which was an average of less than 14 cents a member. In 1956, following the merger, the AFL-CIO hoped to collect $1 from each member, which would have netted some $15 million, but only $3 million was anticipated and less than $1 million received.

The political effectiveness of the labor unions, however, is not to be measured in such financial terms. In 1954, for example, the AFL scored every member of Congress on his voting record, prepared a "black list" of sixty-one names, and circulated it along with its interpretation of the record to ten million AFL members, along with the recommendation to register and vote in the Congressional elections of that year. So many followed this advice that several candidates objectionable to labor were in fact defeated. At the same time, both the AFL and the CIO political arms appointed a woman leader to show working women and the wives of workingmen that undertaking an active part in politics is a way to achieve a better way of life, and again, the immediate focus was on the pending Congressional elections. By 1956 the combined AFL-CIO was holding monthly legislative conferences attended by representatives of affiliated unions, the purpose being to exchange information, compare notes, and map strategy; these conferences do not determine policy, since responsibility in that area lies elsewhere in the union organization. When Congress adjourned in 1956 and every year since then, COPE has distributed 15 million copies of the members' voting records as guides to endorsement by state and district political committees. Action such as this may be very effective indeed. In the 1958 elections, for example, after endorsing certain House, Senate, and gubernatorial candidates, COPE's "batting average" was .700.

With a ten-year record of a substantial degree of success at the polls, after the 1958 elections there was some fear that labor might gain a

---

[41] *The New York Times,* Dec. 7, 1947.
[43] *Ibid.,* Dec. 7, 1947.
[42] *Ibid.,* June 24, 1947.

dominant position in politics and that it might even take control of the Democratic party. Postmaster General Arthur E. Summerfield, for example, appeared to be in a state of near panic when he told a convention of the NAM,

> Americans will watch with fascinated interest these next two years as the minions of this rampaging political combine move to reward their masters. I know of no time in our country's history when the forces of intelligent conservatism have been in greater danger of obliteration.[44]

There was also the fear in some quarters that the merged AFL-CIO might even form a new political party of its own. There had once been an American Labor party, founded in New York in 1936 to give labor and liberals a chance to vote the Democratic ticket without becoming supporters of Tammany. For a few years the party was locally effective but when Communists began to take it over in the early 1940s, its labor members pulled out and in 1956 the ALP quietly died an unlamented death from political anemia. On the question of whether labor would try to set up a national party of its own, "Nothing," said President Meany of the AFL-CIO, "could be further from the truth," and he added that as far as such a party was concerned, he did not know of a single responsible trade-union leader who favored such a step. "Our main objective," he said on another occasion, "is to elect strong, liberal majorities to Congress." [45]

As it turns out, far from the fears of 1958 having been realized, the political influence of organized labor seems instead to have remained merely one of many. Thus, labor did not secure the election of a democratic candidate to the Presidency in 1952 or in 1956 despite official endorsement of him. It did not secure the repeal or even the favorable amendment of the Taft-Hartley Act, it could not prevent the passage of an even more stringent labor law (the Landrum-Griffin Act of 1959) than Taft-Hartley, nor by 1960 had it secured an increase in the minimum-wage rate even though this objective had been high on labor's priority list for two or three years. Politics is a complicated game and labor is still in process of learning it. Early in 1959, for example—a full year ahead of time—it started the very delicate operation of trying to get the "right" candidates nominated by Democratic organizations in each Senate and House contest without offending rivals who might turn out to be the party's nominees. It had sometimes turned out that a successful candidate in Congress, having been endorsed by labor, had nevertheless voted against it in the pinch because he remembered that he had not been labor's first choice for the party nomination.[46]

Labor's right to discuss politics on a regular weekly telecast during an election campaign was challenged under the Corrupt Practices Act

---

[44] *The New York Times*, Dec. 6, 1958.   [45] *Ibid.*, Sept. 6, 1955, and Nov. 21, 1955.
[46] Joseph A. Loftus, *The New York Times*, May 17, 1959.

which prohibits any "contribution" or "expenditure" by a corporation or a union "in connection with" federal primaries, conventions, or elections. Programs sponsored by the United Automobile Workers during the 1954 primaries were in question. The union argued that Congress had not intended to prevent such programs and that if it did, then the law violated the First Amendment to the Constitution guaranteeing freedom of speech. The case went to the Supreme Court and then back to the lower federal court for a retrial.[47] In 1957 the union was acquitted of having violated the law, but the constitutionality of the law itself was not brought into question.

Supplementary Reading

Metz, Harold W., *Labor Policy of the Federal Government* (Washington, D.C., 1945).
———, and Meyer Jacobstein, *A National Labor Policy* (Washington, D.C., 1947).
Millis, Harry A., and Royal E. Montgomery, *Organized Labor* (New York, 1945), Vol. III of the comprehensive work, *The Economics of Labor.*
———, and Emily Brown, *From the Wagner Act to Taft-Hartley* (Chicago, 1950).
Dulles, F. R., *Labor in America* (New York, 1955).
Calkins, Fay, *CIO and the Democratic Party* (Chicago, 1952).
Kornhauser, A., *et al., When Labor Votes* (New York, 1956).
Leiserson, William M., *American Trade Union Democracy* (New York, 1959).
Sufrin, S. C., and Robert C. Sedgwick, *Labor Economics and Problems at Mid-Century* (New York, 1956).
Harrington, Michael (ed.), *Labor in a Free Society* (Berkeley, Calif., 1959). Arden House Conference.
Reder, Melvin W., *Labor in a Growing Economy* (New York, 1957).
Kuhn, Alfred, *Labor Institutions and Economics* (New York, 1956).
Petro, Sylvester, *The Labor Policy of the Free Society* (New York, 1957).
Galenson, Walter, *The C.I.O. Challenge to the A.F.L.* (Cambridge, Mass., 1960). A history of the American labor movement from 1935 to 1941.
Hartley, Fred A., *Our New National Labor Policy* (New York, 1948).
Whitney, Fred, *Government and Collective Bargaining* (Philadelphia, 1951).
Taylor, Albion G., *Labor Problems and Labor Law* (New York, 1950).
Perlman, Selig, *A Theory of the Labor Movement* (New York, 1928). Invaluable for background, forces, and traditions.
Miller, Glenn W., *American Labor and the Government* (New York, 1948). A broad conspectus.
U. S. Department of Labor, *The American Workers' Fact Book* (Washington, D.C., 1956). Labor and the economy.
Seidman, Joel, *American Labor from Defense to Reconversion* (Chicago, 1953). By a distinguished labor historian.
Lindblom, Charles, *Unions and Capitalism* (New Haven, Conn., 1949). Stresses the economic aspects.

---

[47] *U.S. v. United Automobile Workers* (352 U.S. 567. 1957).

Commons, J. R., and J. B. Andrews, *Principles of Labor Legislation* (New York, 4th ed., 1936). Still the basic book in this area.

Bernstein, Irving, *The New Deal Collective Bargaining Policy* (Berkeley, Calif., 1950).

Brooks, R. R. R., *When Labor Organizes* (New Haven, Conn., 1938).

————, *Unions of Their Own Choosing* (New Haven, Conn., 1939). Both these books are realistic and stress the political aspects.

Peterson, Florence, *Survey of Labor Economics* (New York, 1951). By one who has had first-hand experience.

————, *American Labor Unions* (New York, 1945).

Kaplan, A. D. H., *The Guarantee of Annual Wages* (Washington, D.C., 1947).

Stigler, George, "The Economics of Minimum Wage Legislation," *American Economic Review*, Vol. XXXVI (June 1946).

Woytinsky, W. S., and associates, *Employment and Wages in the United States* (New York, 1953). A monumental study.

Leek, John H., *Government and Labor in the United States* (New York, 1952). A general survey.

Berman, Edward, *Labor and the Sherman Act* (New York, 1930). The monopoly issue.

Ruchames, Louis, *Race, Jobs and Politics: The Story of the FEPC* (New York, 1953).

9

LABOR DISPUTES AND PUBLIC POLICY

---

*Employer assumptions and industrial disputes; combative-
ness as a stage in institutional development; labor's share of
the national income; common types of industrial disputes;
vocabulary of industrial relations; the right to strike; picketing; alternate solutions; conciliation, mediation, and arbitration; mediation by the federal government; statesmanship and responsibility.*

When a group of workers first announced to an employer, "We
won't work for that rate of pay," the foundation was laid for collective
bargaining; but when they first said, "We'll strike if you don't pay
more," it was the beginning of industrial disputes. The difference between these two attitudes distinguishes the emphasis of this chapter and
the last one. Although the difference is real, the areas of collective bargaining and industrial disputes are united by mutual problems and
other connective tissue. Failure of collective-bargaining negotiations, for
example, is the chief cause of industrial disputes, while underlying the
whole field are common difficulties, relating to wages, hours, working
conditions, union recognition, charges of broken agreements, and so on.

> In a broad sense, the term industrial dispute . . . implies a definite
> employer-employee relation which still exists, although in more or less
> strained form, or which has only recently been broken. It may involve
> an employer and some or all of his employees, a group of employers
> in the same or related trades and their employees, or, in rate cases such
> as that of the general strike in England in 1926, all employers and
> the employees over a wide economic or geographical area regardless of
> industrial boundaries.[1]

The methods used to prevent or settle industrial disputes belong to the
comparatively modern field of industrial relations, and they are new because only when employers and workers are both free—which has not
so long been the case with workers—can such a development as industrial

[1] John A. Fitch, "Labor Disputes," *Encyclopedia of the Social Sciences*, Vol. VIII,
p. 633.

relations take place in any real sense. The issues involved are these: How much should government interfere between employer and employee? As a general rule, should labor and management be relied on to work out their own differences without direct governmental intervention? When government does step in, should it be primarily to offer its good offices, or to provide sanctions? How much industrial discord can be tolerated under modern industrial conditions? And finally, when are court injunctions in labor disputes justified?

The American worker, says one authority, has joined the middle class—not only in income but also in outlook. Within the framework of general pay increases, greater job security, broader social insurance, and shorter working hours, labor finds an opportunity to satisfy its urge for status. A tidy home, a new car, a television set, a son or daughter in college—these are the measures of the good life for millions of families in the mass-production industries. Their unfulfilled goals are largely summed up in the words, "more of the same." [2]

The partnership aspiration—a status of equality with management and the right of greater participation for the worker—also has become prominent. Thus, as early as 1941,

> The worker is held to have as much stake in his trade or industry as the manager or stockholder. He is a partner in production, and as such is entitled to an equal voice in shaping industrial policies. If the worker is to exercise his right of partnership, his right to be a free man must be recognized. Individual dignity and self-respect are possible only when the "boss" admits and respects the worker's independent and economic rights. [3]

Further insights into social motivation come from Herbert Harris:

> A man joins a union to improve his income, true enough. But that is not his only motive. He joins to avoid being pushed around, to assert his own dignity as an inhabitant of the United States, and to enjoy a sense of fraternity with others like him, even if it's only playing poker with the boys at the union hall. As an American he has inherited a tradition of independence and, however threadbare it may be in practice, it is still alluring to him as an ideal; and it is something that he as a rule can move toward only by acting within the framework of his own group. Otherwise he has virtually neither voice nor vote in the conduct of his job. [4]

MANAGEMENT-LABOR DISPUTES

The differences that arise between management and labor are due partly to concrete conditions complained of and partly to a different

[2] A. H. Raskin, "Industry and Labor: A New Era?," *The New York Times Magazine*, Aug. 7, 1955.

[3] Donald C. Blaisdell, *Economic Power and Political Pressures*, Temporary National Economic Committee, Monograph No. 26 (Washington, D.C., 1941), p. 93.

[4] Herbert Harris, *Labor's Civil War* (New York, 1940), pp. 10–11.

way of looking at a series of concepts that enter into the equation. To take the concepts first, these are private property, profits, dominance, and undivided managerial responsibility. The quarrel, it should be noted, is not so much with the concepts themselves—since both parties believe in the American system of free enterprise and democratic government—as with some of the implications growing out of them.

Private property, for example, is something that a moral person can be selfish about: it belongs only to him. But when this possessive attitude is carried over into the field of large-scale industry, then many people, including enlightened employers, think the concept of private property should be qualified. A corporation owned by thousands of stockholders and hiring thousands of employees is no longer a strictly personal matter, for there is now a joint ownership and a joint responsibility. Consequently, instead of acting as rugged individualists serving a single interest, the managers of big business should more properly assume the role of trustee of all interests connected with the enterprise, labor included. Others argue, however, that this would weaken the profit motive and corporate efficiency—that self-restraint in profit making distorts the whole free-enterprise process.

Another assumption, akin to the selfish view of private property, holds that *profits* may legitimately be as large as can be earned, even at the expense of depressed wages and irrespective of the wider social effect. Fortunately, here also the trusteeship principle is gaining ground, partly because of a wider recognition of the fact that with economic strength goes a social responsibility, but even more because of the practical need to sustain purchasing power and to maintain economic stability. An initial difficulty—in time of prosperity not so perplexing—is how to carry out this policy without first securing an agreement to concerted action. The wave of prosperity that swept over the nation in the 1950s made it possible for labor to demand and to receive progressively higher wages, creating a progressively higher standard of purchasing power, and concerted action was the practical if not the premeditated result. It seems fair to say, however, that organized labor deserves much of the credit for achieving such action, although prosperity was the condition precedent thereto.

A third element in the folklore of employers derives from the principle of *dominance* in the economy, traditionally and widely approved as socially desirable. In the field of industrial relations, however, an uncritical application of this concept causes employers to treat labor leaders with superiority and suspicion, as a result of which management gives up only so much as it is forced to. The social consequence is a feeling of resentment and distrust on both sides, instead of an attitude of cooperation and mutual understanding which is an indispensable condition of industrial accord. But this situation also is changing as both sides become more aware of their common interests and as labor leaders demonstrate not only their strength but also their statesmanship.

The fourth and final factor is a cardinal assumption of employers, not only in business but in all kinds of activity, that they must have *undivided responsibility* in order to succeed in any managerial undertaking. From this entirely valid principle of scientific management, however, is deduced the theory that no union or labor-management group should ever be allowed a degree of authority that will detract from the unity of executive responsibility. The theory is a sound one but the determination of where the dividing line shall fall causes much labor-management disagreement.[5] An executive naturally demands supreme loyalty to the enterprise he heads and believes that competing loyalties, as to a trade union, must not be allowed to interfere. But this assumption, of course, is likely to conflict with labor's claim, mentioned by Blaisdell, to "an equal voice in shaping industrial policies."

A characteristic common to both management and labor-union leadership now deserves special mention. Owing to the circumstances of American pioneering, not only on land but also in industrial development, this nation in the past has produced ruthless robber barons as industrial leaders and equally ruthless labor bosses as union organizers. This is not to say that all business executives and labor officials fell into these familiar categories, but many did. To one with a sense of historical movement, the emergence of this type of leader is recognized as a stage of institutional development, perhaps even a necessary and inevitable one. But being merely a stage, it gradually passes away as times and conditions demand a different type of leadership.

Those who know John L. Lewis and have seen him in action have often remarked that hard-hitting businessmen generally admire him even when their interests are opposed to his aims. The explanation is that Lewis, the labor leader, closely resembles them in his ruthless, energetic thrust for power. Labor leaders who in the past were most feared and respected were, for the most part, very much like the rugged individualists who sat across from them on the management side of the bargaining table. But just as robber barons in industry are less numerous today than fifty years ago, so also the headstrong type of labor leader has largely given way to a new kind. Now that the time has arrived when natural resources must be conserved instead of exploited and labor's basic claims to independent organization and collective bargaining are legally established and normally accepted by the business community, the administrator will increasingly prevail in both management and labor circles, combining qualities of social sensitivity, powers of economic and political analysis, and an ability to work with other people in a give-and-take effort to serve the common interest.

The factors of institutional development also explain another aspect of labor relations, now also largely in the past. Leaders in both business and labor sought to gain stature and prestige as they achieved reputations

[5] See James D. Mooney and Alan C. Reiley, *The Principles of Organization* (New York, 1939), Chaps. II–VII.

for being good fighters. Consequently they sometimes welcomed conflicts, at times even manufactured them. Minor grievances were blown up out of all proportion to their importance. Such behavior is normal and human, but fortunately today both labor and management have for the most part learned the folly of crying wolf. Rather, in both business and union circles, trained industrial-relations experts are being moved to the forefront to replace exhibitionist leaders on both sides.

Important as these institutional factors are, however, they can never quite dispose of the major reason for competition between labor and management: How is the "take" to be divided? The unions naturally want to get as much income for their members as they can, and just as naturally, the managers and owners of industry would earn as much profit as possible, at the expense of wages if they can get away with it, not only at the bargaining table but economically as well. The problem exists in every kind of economic system, whether socialist, cooperative, or of the private-enterprise type. Apparently, therefore, this point of controversy can never be wholly eliminated. A good statement of the basic difficulty was formulated by a group of German trade unions following World War I and, with some rewording, applies remarkably well to the situation in our own nation today. The suggested rewording has been inserted in the text:

> So long as private enterprise exists, it will produce economic classes [groups] which will struggle against [compete with] each other to decide their respective shares of the proceeds of industry. We hold this struggle to be unavoidable, because an impartial scientific agreement on this question is not [entirely] possible. But without prejudice to this view we also believe that, for the solution of various economic, financial, social and political problems, a joint effort by all parties is worth while. . . .[6]

How is labor's share of the national income to be determined? The theory of wages opens up a field far beyond the range of the present study. The main point to be made here is that wage theory, like economic theory generally, is frequently challenged as labor unions gain power and government takes a positive role with regard to industrial relations. Labor unions demand and get minimum wages and maximum hours by legal right and fixed by government instead of by the forces of supply and demand. Labor also demands a growing percentage of the total national income as a right justified by considerations of national economic policy. Thus in this field as in others, power, pressure-group, and governmental influences become more important as the so-called automatic forces of the market, though still basic and significant, are increasingly supplemented.

The strategy of industrial relations is to discover the point where,

---

[6] Quoted by J. B. S. Hardman in "Labor-Capital Cooperation," *Encyclopedia of the Social Sciences*, Vol. VIII, p. 626.

labor's demands having been largely met, the unions commence to cooperate with business in joint programs instead of fighting and obstructing. A condition precedent is that labor take a positive rather than a negative view of management, and that management be willing to accept labor unions as permanent, legitimate instruments in the operation of the economy. The fact is, of course, that neither management nor labor can be wholly independent of each other or of other elements in the community.

So much for certain concepts and assumptions that help determine industrial relations. Their importance is that they are the matrix from which concrete issues emerge. The first are the cause, the second are the manifestation that must so often be dealt with so long as the first remain unchanged. It may help to clarify the picture if some of the more common occasions of industrial disputes are listed. But no list, of course, can be final because the situations out of which disputes arise are complicated and changing.

COMMON CAUSES OF INDUSTRIAL DISPUTES

1. Dissatisfaction over wages
2. Attempts by labor to reduce hours or secure fringe benefits
3. Complaints concerning working conditions—comfort, safety, health
4. Charges of labor agreement violation
5. Inability to reach agreement when labor contracts expire
6. Failure of one side or the other to confer or to communicate
7. Discharge of a labor representative on the alleged ground of anti-labor bias
8. Dismissal of labor members having no official office or position
9. Jurisdictional or sympathy strikes
10. Primary (and formerly also secondary) boycotts
11. Resistance to laws or governmental policies, or dissatisfaction over alleged deprival of political rights as in the use of court injunctions in labor disputes
12. Violation of the union's sense of justice, including such things as discourtesy, thoughtless remarks, failure to give credit where due, and the like
13. Alleged discrimination as to race, religion, sex, the foreign-born, and so on
14. Resistance to speed-up methods, automation, and other technological advances

Two other grounds for dispute, namely, restrictions on the right to organize independently and to bargain collectively, are of much less importance today than before the passage of the Wagner Act of 1935 which set these two rights on a firm legal base. To prolong the list would mean including many singular situations such as refusal of an employer to allow his employees to attend the funeral of a fellow-worker or refusal to work with a person involved in a family squabble. Labor's reasons for causing a disturbance are by no means always basic and rational, any more than are many employer actions and attitudes. But minor irritations are less likely to cause trouble if attitudes on both sides are cooperative and the more basic complaints have been eliminated.

Although the relative importance of the items on the foregoing list varies considerably, in the long run the most common grievance is over wages and hours. Such disputes have been the chief cause of work stoppages in the United States, except for the years 1928-1929 and again from 1934 through 1941 when disputes over union organization were in the forefront. The relative importance of other factors varies with the provocation: workers are more likely to accept longer hours when wages and fringe benefits are high. Therefore, the policies of management, and secondarily of government, go far to determine how numerous and recurrent will be the causes of industrial disputes.

THE VOCABULARY OF INDUSTRIAL RELATIONS

A *labor contract* is "an agreement, express or implied, between an individual worker and an employer under which the former agrees to work in return for compensation." [7] As labor unions have become the main bargaining agents, however, the labor contract is now increasingly an agreement between a union and the management of a plant or even of a whole industry. Such a contract is for a specified term of a year or more, and at expiration it must be renegotiated. Such contracts are now more commonly termed *collective agreements* because in fact they do not possess all the characteristics of a contract in ordinary legal usage. Under the Taft-Hartley Act of 1947, neither unions nor employees may cancel an agreement without a sixty-day notice, providing a cooling-off period during which a strike or a lockout is barred.

Collective bargaining is the means by which a labor agreement or contract is negotiated, having for its purpose "the democratic establishment of the terms of the employment relations." The bargaining takes place between employers, acting singly or in groups, and union representatives, "thus bringing about negotiations between two parties or sets of parties whose economic strength has some approximation of equality." If successful, this process results in a controlling agreement which in form may range from an informal understanding to a written contract enforceable at law. The collective agreement is not a contract of individual employment, of course, and of itself puts no one to work. What it

---

[7] Ralph F. Fuchs, "Labor Contract," *Encyclopedia of the Social Sciences*, Vol. VIII, p. 629.

does is to bind the parties to introduce its terms into contracts of individual employment in circumstances to which it applies.[8]

A *labor injunction* is a court order secured by an employer in anticipation of a strike, during a strike, or at other times commanding a union or other workers to do a particular act or to refrain from taking action that would injure the personal or property rights of the employer. Labor injunctions were used rather freely from the time of the famous Debs case,[9] decided in 1895 and followed by *Loewe v. Lawlor* in 1908.[10] As a result, organized labor secured a section in the Clayton Act of 1914 relating to antitrust, which provided that "no restraining order or injunction shall be granted . . . in any case between an employer and employee, or between persons employed and persons seeking employment, involving or growing out of, a dispute concerning terms or conditions of employment. . . ." But despite this apparently clear language the courts took a narrow view of the matter in the case of *Duplex Printing Company* v. *Deering*,[11] decided in 1921, in which an injunction against a union was upheld on the ground that the issue involved a secondary boycott. It took the Norris-LaGuardia Anti-Injunction Act of 1932 to correct the situation by setting forth in detail the activities of workers undertaken "singly or in concert" which may not be enjoined "in any case growing out of any labor dispute." These provisions are far-reaching and include such matters as (1) ceasing or refusing to perform any work or to remain in any relation to employment; (2) becoming or remaining a member of any labor organization; (3) assembling peaceably to act or to organize to act in promotion of workers' interests in a labor dispute; and (4) agreeing to do or not to do any of the things set forth elsewhere in the statute. Although the effect of this law was to restrict rather than entirely to remove from the courts the authority to issue an injunction in labor disputes, the act represents one of labor's principal legislative triumphs. Under Taft-Hartley, however, injunctions are permitted under certain conditions, and they are mandatory in the case of secondary boycotts pending a hearing on the validity of the charges.

The Norris-LaGuardia Act also outlaws so-called *yellow-dog* or *anti-union contracts,* which up to that time had been one of labor's principal sources of complaint. Under a yellow-dog contract, management might require as a condition of hiring a worker that as long as he remained employed, he would not join a union. A leading case on this question is *Hitchman Coal and Coke Co.* v. *Mitchell,*[12] decided in 1917 and involving the United Mine Workers. Section 3 of the Norris-LaGuardia Act declares that yellow-dog contracts are "contrary to the public policy of the United States, shall not be enforceable in any court of the United States, and shall not afford any basis for the granting of legal or equitable relief by any such court."

[8] Fuchs, *op. cit.,* p. 631.   [9] *In re Debs* (158 U.S. 564. 1895).
[10] (208 U.S. 274. 1908).   [11] (254 U.S. 443. 1921).
[12] (245 U.S. 229. 1917).

A *strike* is a work stoppage ordered by employees in an attempt to secure or enforce their demands on management. A *jurisdictional strike* is one called to settle a dispute where two or more unions claim workers in borderline occupations employed in a plant covered by their agreements. Should the drivers for a brewery, for example, belong to the Brewery Workers' Union or the Teamsters' Union? The problem is more likely to arise, of course, between craft unions comprising specialized workers than between industrial unions where the membership is drawn from an entire industry. For many years the question of jurisdictional disputes constituted a major difficulty in the government of the AFL. Such strikes are now forbidden by the Taft-Hartley Act as an unfair labor practice and the National Labor Relations Board may obtain temporary injunctions against their use.

The management equivalent of a strike is the *lockout,* by which management shuts the workers out of its plant and refuses to open it until conditions have been met or a compromise arranged.

A *boycott* is a concerted action by a union which refuses to buy or to handle the product of a particular employer and urges others to do likewise so as to bring pressure to bear on him to achieve a certain end. When the action is by the employer's own workers, it is a *primary boycott* and when other unions join in, it is a *secondary boycott.* Taft-Hartley prohibits a secondary boycott but left loopholes. One of them related to the handling of cargoes to and from firms involved in labor disputes (so-called hot cargoes) and another concerned the purchase of materials by one firm from another that refused to hire union labor. With exemptions relating to the garment and the construction industries, both of these loopholes were closed by the Landrum-Griffin Act of 1959.

In addition, Taft-Hartley forbids employers to deduct union dues (called the *dues checkoff*) from the pay checks of employees unless so authorized in writing by the employee. Another practice, termed *maintenance of membership,* formerly required an employer to discharge a worker who lost his union membership, but Taft-Hartley allows expulsion from a union only for failure to pay dues or initiation fees. Formerly also, *welfare funds* negotiated as part of a wage agreement and to which management contributed were often administered by the unions, but Taft-Hartley outlawed existing union-administered funds and required that management participate in the administration of new ones. It must now also be established that the use of a welfare fund is confined to death, sickness, accident, retirement, medical, and unemployment benefits.

THE RIGHT TO STRIKE

Since labor's principal coercive weapon is the right to strike, any attempted legal restriction on its use is vigorously combated. Under modern industrial conditions business has so much money tied up in plant and equipment that a work stoppage for any cause may be a costly

TABLE 6

Work Stoppages: 1933 to 1958

YEAR	WORK STOPPAGES BEGINNING IN YEAR		WORKERS INVOLVED		MAN-DAYS IDLE		
	Number	Average duration (calendar days)	Number (thousands) *	Percent of total employed †	Number (thousands)	Percent of estimated working time ‡	Per worker involved
1933	1,695	16.9	1,170	6.3	16,900	0.36	14.4
1935	2,014	23.8	1,120	5.2	15,500	0.29	13.8
1936	2,172	23.3	789	3.1	13,900	0.21	17.6
1937	4,740	20.3	1,860	7.2	28,400	0.43	15.3
1938	2,772	23.6	688	2.8	9,150	0.15	13.3
1939	2,613	23.4	1,170	4.7	17,800	0.28	15.2
1940	2,508	20.9	577	2.3	6,700	0.10	11.6
1941	4,288	18.3	2,360	8.4	23,000	0.32	9.8
1942	2,968	11.7	840	2.8	4,180	0.05	5.0
1943	3,752	5.0	1,980	6.9	13,500	0.15	6.8
1944	4,956	5.6	2,120	7.0	8,720	0.09	4.1
1945	4,750	9.9	3,470	12.2	38,000	0.47	11.0
1946	4,985	24.2	4,600	14.5	116,000	1.43	25.2
1947	3,693	25.6	2,170	6.5	34,600	0.41	15.9
1948	3,419	21.8	1,960	5.5	34,100	0.37	17.4
1949	3,606	22.5	3,030	9.0	50,500	0.59	16.7
1950	4,843	19.2	2,410	6.9	38,800	0.44	16.1
1951	4,737	17.4	2,220	5.5	22,900	0.23	10.3
1952	5,117	19.6	3,540	8.8	59,100	0.57	16.7
1953	5,091	20.3	2,400	5.6	28,300	0.26	11.8
1954	3,468	22.5	1,530	3.7	22,600	0.21	14.7
1955	4,320	18.5	2,650	6.2	28,200	0.26	10.7
1956	3,825	18.9	1,900	4.3	33,100	0.29	17.4
1957	3,673	19.2	1,390	3.1	16,500	0.14	11.4
1958	3,694	19.7	2,060	4.8	23,900	0.22	11.6

* Workers counted more than once if involved in more than one stoppage during year.

† Total employed workers for 1933-1950 refers to all workers except those in occupations and professions in which there is little if any union organization or in which stoppages rarely, if ever, occur. In 1951, the concept was changed to coincide with the bureau's figures for nonagricultural employment, excluding government but including workers in all occupational groups. Tests show that percentage of total idleness computed on basis of these new figures usually differs by less than one tenth of a point while percentage of workers idle differs by about 0.5 or 0.6 of a point.

‡ Estimated working time computed by multiplying average number of employed workers by number of days worked by most employees.

SOURCE: Department of Labor, Bureau of Labor Statistics; *Handbook of Labor Statistics* and records. Basic data are currently published in the May issues of *Monthly Labor Review*.

affair and hence the strike weapon is usually an effective one. On the other hand, it is also costly to workers and unions because it cuts off workers' pay checks and also depletes union funds. When the Ford Motor Company granted the United Automobile Workers a form of the guaranteed annual wage in 1955, for example, it avoided a strike that would have cost the company $20 million a day in lost production, its suppliers $12.4 million in lost business, and the workers $2.7 million in wages, making a total of something like $35 million for every day the strike lasted. In addition to the cost, if public opinion is adverse to the purpose of a strike or the public is seriously inconvenienced by it, labor pays another heavy cost in alienated public support. As a weapon, therefore, the strike is two-edged. And yet in a free economy it is a necessary one because a test of a free as against a regimented economy includes the liberty of workers to enforce their legitimate demands.

Basically, the right to strike is the right to refuse to work, something that is strongly entrenched in American law. The Thirteenth Amendment to the Constitution, for example, stipulates that "Neither slavery nor involuntary servitude, except as punishment for crime whereof the party shall have been duly convicted, shall exist within the United States, or any place subject to their jurisdiction." If men and women were not free to accept employment or to quit as they choose, obviously there is involuntary servitude. And yet this right, as will be seen, has had to be somewhat qualified because when workers act in concert, a new factor is introduced into the situation.

"In most strikes," say Commons and Andrews, "something more than quitting work is involved. There is an antecedent agreement to quit, there are demands upon the employer, and there is a 'threat' that unless he yields, a strike will be called." [13] During both world wars labor voluntarily agreed to a no-strike pledge. Strikes are also less likely to occur during periods of depression when work is scarce, as well as during times of high prosperity when wage demands are more readily granted than at others. But during an era of rapid social change when economic forces are out of balance, strikes are likely to abound, as shown in Table 6's list of work stoppages from 1933 to 1958. Historically, strikes in the United States have been regulated primarily by judicial decisions and precedents, but more recently, and especially since Taft-Hartley, there has been a pronounced tendency to surround the right to strike by legal restrictions at both the federal and the state levels.

Judicial decisions tend to divide the question of strikes into two parts, the end and the means. If both are lawful, there is no difficulty, but if either is considered unlawful, then there may be judicial restraint. At one time or another American courts have followed three principal doctrines regarding the legality of strikes: (1) the *conspiracy* theory, derived from Britain; (2) the *malice* theory, which looks into motive and inquires

[13] John R. Commons and J. B. Andrews, *Principles of Labor Legislation* (New York, 4th ed., 1936), p. 112.

whether it is malicious; and (3) the *just-purpose* doctrine, which assumes that both employers and employees have the right to operate in a free market and that if either interferes "unlawfully" with the other's privilege, the purpose is not just.

Of all the reasons for which strikes may be called, the clearest presumption of just purpose is when the action is to secure wage increases, union recognition, or improved working hours and conditions. The purposes least likely to be sustained are where a burden or obstruction is imposed on interstate commerce, where dangerous conditions will result to the innocent public, and where it is held that such coercion unlawfully invades the discretionary area reserved to management, as illustrated by the firing of an employee for incompetence or the introduction of a labor-saving device.

The *sit-down strikes* that prevailed in 1937-1938, where employees refused either to work or to leave their places of employment, were declared unlawful by the Supreme Court in the case of *National Labor Relations Board* v. *Fansteel Metallurgical Corp.*,[14] decided in 1939. Such strikes, said the Court, constitute "a high-handed proceeding without shadow of legal right," invade the property rights of others, and make use of force and violence. Accordingly the NLRB was denied the right to order the reinstatement of sit-down strikers.

In some ways the most drastic provision of the Taft-Hartley law has to do with so-called *paralysis strikes,* which are strikes in major industries such as coal, steel, and the railroads. The law permits the government to obtain an eighty-day injunction against a strike that endangers the national health and safety. This provision was invoked sixteen times before it went, in the case of the long steel strike of 1959, to the Supreme Court for a decision as to constitutionality. Labor argued that "health and safety" should be narrowly construed and that the provision brought the courts into the administrative process, which was unconstitutional. But the court decided otherwise and upheld the law.[15]

Another provision of Taft-Hartley relates to *strikes against the government* and stipulates that federal workers who go out on strike face discharge, forfeit their civil service status, and for three years will be ineligible for re-employment by the government. Yet another proviso covers *damage suits* and permits employers to sue unions for breach of contract and for damages resulting from jurisdictional strikes and secondary boycotts.

Picketing is one of the principal means by which strikes are made effective. Picketing is the posting of a person or persons by a labor union at the entrance of a place or business affected by a strike in order to identify employees going to and from work, to persuade them to join the strike, and to discourage customers from entering. Strikes may succeed without picketing but they are more effective when picketing is permitted.

[14] (306 U.S. 240. 1939).
[15] *United Steel Workers of America* v. *U.S.* (80 S.Ct. 1. 1959).

"Picketing is a form of free speech—the working man's method of giving publicity to the facts of industrial life," said Justice William Douglas in a dissenting opinion in 1952. "As such, it is entitled to constitutional protection. . . . It is entitled to that protection though it incites to action. For it is the aim of most ideas to shape conduct." [16]

The question of picketing is a complex one because the courts of almost every state have adopted different rules relating to its various aspects. Generally speaking, however, there is a distinction between picketing which is peaceful and hence lawful and that which is nonpeaceful and therefore held to be unlawful. Nonpeaceful picketing includes the use of violence, intimidation, and threats while peaceful picketing, relying on "requests" and "persuasion," is usually upheld. A second question relates to how many pickets may be used and how they are deployed. In some jurisdictions only one picket may be stationed at each factory gate, and in others mass picketing is lawful as long as it is peaceful. In some cases picketers may not "parade" and in others they may.

A section of the Landrum-Griffin Act of 1959 limits picketing where the object of the action is to organize employees and coerce an employer to recognize a union, but allows picketing "for the purpose of truthfully advising the public (including customers) that an employer does not employ" union members. A condition, however, is that deliveries and services to the picketed establishment shall not be interrupted and hence the hours of picketing must be restricted.

A main purpose of picketing, of course, is to prevent the employer from using *strikebreakers,* or scabs as they are also called, in order to break a strike before an agreement is reached. Violence is most likely to occur under such circumstances. Believing that labor and management should try to work out peaceful settlements instead of complicating their future relations by resort to strikebreaking, Congress passed the Byrnes Act in 1936 (amended in 1938), making it unlawful to transport or cause to be transported in interstate or foreign commerce any person employed as a strikebreaker. This law is aimed not only at nation-wide strikebreaking organizations but also at employers who used them. The penalty imposed, as for a felony, indicates how important it was considered that such practices be discouraged.

ALTERNATIVE SOLUTIONS TO LABOR DISPUTES

In the alleviation of labor-management difficulties, four broad alternatives have all been used at one time or another. They include (1) repressive measures by employers; (2) benevolent policies by employers; (3) joint attacks on joint problems by means of collective bargaining,

[16] *United Assn. of Journeymen Plumbers & Steamfitters et al. v. O. J. Graham* (345 U.S. 192. 1952).

union-management committees, and the like; and (4) the settlement of disputes by government intervention, including some kind of mediation. Since some of these methods have already been discussed the treatment here will be brief.

Repressive measures include demotion, dismissal, and use of a black list (a list of workers or union officials maintained by the employer for discriminatory purposes). Although not usually approved by progressively minded employers, such procedures may appear to succeed "when labor is plentiful or when artificial barriers to labor mobility exist, as in isolated centers or in one-industry towns." [17] Although the then chairman of the Senate Civil Liberties Committee reported just prior to World War II that repressive measures were still in extensive use,[18] today they are much less evident, as the rights of organized labor become increasingly accepted and labor itself, with occasional exceptions, becomes more responsible.

The second approach, emphasizing benevolent or philanthropic measures by the employer, also was once more common than it is today. When industry is small, relationships in a business concern are personal and human, but when it is large and complex, they become impersonal and power-motivated. Employers were once often actuated by a spirit of *noblesse oblige* which included "looking out for the men." There is still need of such a spirit in industrial relations but it must be divorced from any trace of patronizing and uplift. As Fitch has remarked, "When offered as a form of philanthropy . . . such methods sometimes create rather than allay dissatisfaction. Intelligently managed personnel departments, on the other hand, organized on a frankly business basis and devoid of pseudo-philanthropic motives, may do much to lessen unrest and to create an atmosphere of understanding and good will." [19]

The third alternative, a joint labor-management approach to difficulties by means of collective bargaining, has already been discussed. In the long run this is the most rewarding policy because it is based on the psychological principle that people more readily accept and support what they have had some part in determining. The reverse also is true, that people generally resist what they feel is being imposed on them from the outside, either by another group or by the government.

The fourth approach is the use of government as umpire in settling industrial disputes. The role of government in this field, especially at the state and federal levels, has increased rapidly in the last fifty years. Where formerly the judiciary was the principal and almost the only agency of government to deal with industrial disputes, however, two developments have made the role of the courts relatively less prominent. First, legislation such as the Norris-LaGuardia Anti-Injunction Act has

---

[17] Fitch, *op. cit.*, p. 635.

[18] Senator Robert M. LaFollette, Jr., in Senate Report No. 6, 76th Cong., 1st Sess., (1944) Pt. 6.

[19] Fitch, *op. cit.*, p. 635.

limited or defined the courts' jurisdiction (although Taft-Hartley broadened it again); and second, the legislative and executive branches have increasingly entered the field, setting up permanent administrative machinery such as the Wage-Hour Division of the Labor Department, the National Labor Relations Board, and agencies of mediation, conciliation, and arbitration. Of these two institutional developments, the latter is chiefly responsible for the shifts of method that have occurred in government's role in this area.

Mediation, conciliation, and arbitration have in common the fact that a third party is asked to help in settling a dispute. In each case the method is generally more efficacious during the preliminary stage of the difficulty when the government or some other neutral party can aid in negotiations that are still pending. Once a break in the employment relationship has occurred and the two sides are at war in the form of a strike or a lockout, then a settlement is harder to secure, although the same agencies used in the preventive stage may still be employed.

In *mediation,* a designated neutral third party suggests a form of settlement which, however, the parties to the dispute are not obliged to accept. *Conciliation* is the action of a neutral third party who tries to bring about a friendly feeling between the disputants. In either case the procedure is informal, there is no prior agreement to submit the issue, and neither side is bound in advance to abide by the suggestions made.

Arbitration, on the other hand, is a quasi-judicial procedure by which the parties to a controversy agree in advance to submit the issues in the case for decision and to be bound by the finding of an arbitral tribunal; the award is then enforceable by an action at law. Arbitration may be either private or governmental, voluntary or compulsory. Private arbitration voluntarily agreed to is now a major aspect of industrial self-government. Some 4000 organizations and corporations in the United States, for example, have labor contracts containing an arbitration clause, and the American Arbitration Association maintains panels of arbitrators in some 1600 cities throughout the nation. One of the most expensive arbitrations in history involved the Southern Bell Telephone Company, cost the union something like $1 million, and the company a similar amount. In private arbitration there may be only a single arbitrator, but in the public variety there is usually a tribunal of three or more persons.

Both mediation and conciliation are entirely voluntary, but arbitration may be either voluntary or compulsory, except that once arbitration has been agreed to, compliance is compulsory. The terms *mediation* and *conciliation* are virtually interchangeable, the main difference being that mediation connotes a go-between where the parties will not agree to meet, whereas conciliation infers a conference between persons willing to talk things over. The theory underlying both mediation and conciliation is that disputes are less likely to recur if the parties settle their own differences by learning to work together, and that the exercise of free will is more likely to make decision palatable to both sides, whereas compulsion generally leaves one side—or even both—disappointed and may result in fresh difficulties.

Emphasis at both the state and federal levels, therefore, has been more on mediation than on arbitration. Machinery of some kind for settling industrial disputes has been set up in most state governments and, as in the case of the federal government, voluntary methods have generally been the rule. Not all states have created labor departments but where they have, a division of conciliation is usually included; where they have not, some other bureau generally has authority to make investigations and to attempt to conciliate a dispute. In some cases, as in Pennsylvania for example, provision is made for voluntary arbitration when other methods fail.

Some industrial states can claim a longer continuous record of industrial relations machinery than the federal government. In New York and Massachusetts, specialized agencies for mediation and conciliation were established as early as 1886. Kansas and Colorado are notable in that compulsory arbitration has long been required in disputes occurring in industries "affected with a public interest," that is, public utilities. In Kansas the Industrial Court was set up in 1920 and led to the leading Supreme Court cases of *Wolff Packing Co.* v. *Industrial Court* and *Dorchy* v. *Kansas,*[20] the effect of which was to hold parts of the Kansas act unconstitutional. In Colorado, strikes have long been forbidden during the time that the state Industrial Commission is investigating the issue. Since the passage of Taft-Hartley, federal policy has veered in the direction of these two state precedents.

Mediation is also a function of city government, especially in the larger industrial cities. In New York, for example, so zealous were the mediators in one case—the settlement of a milk strike in 1953—that a group of federal, state, and city mediators cooled its heels outside the conference room for a week waiting to be called in and were criticized by the conferees as adding more muddle than light to an already confused situation. "If mediators are going to do any good in future negotiations," commented one of the key negotiators, "someone will have to settle this jurisdictional dispute among all the government units that want to horn in on a situation like this. . . . There ought to be some coordination so that one expert mediator acts for all the agencies and we do not have a bunch of prima donnas whose main interest is in being in the middle of the picture when the agreement is signed." [21] Although the complaint here was doubtless unjustified because the strike affected the food supply of the city and every available resource was called in to help settle it, the language used may perhaps be excused on the ground that negotiations had been going on around the clock for a week and both industry and

---

[20] (262 U.S. 522. 1923) and (272 U.S. 306. 1926), respectively.
[21] *The New York Times,* Nov. 2, 1953.

union conferees were so exhausted that even minor differences became insuperable obstacles to compromise. This marathon procedure is not regarded with favor by experienced mediators, who have found that a good night's rest often makes possible a quicker solution to troublesome disputes than endless hours of captivity around the conference table.

In another industrial city, Philadelphia, a novel procedure for handling dockside disputes, inaugurated in 1952, was said a year later to be working very well. The major difficulty was to determine the hardship of certain kinds of stevedoring so that wage rates could be set accordingly, a problem that had caused many short strikes with attendant expense, loss of time, and recrimination. Finally a Jesuit priest having unlimited authority to act for both sides was appointed as job-site arbitrator. Within two hours of the receipt of a complaint this arbitrator, accompanied by a representative of each side to the dispute, would be on the scene, the condition of work was studied at once, complaints heard, and a settlement made that was prompt, final, and binding. As a result work stoppages virtually ceased and in the quieter atmosphere created, many other disputes could be settled by the regular union-management grievance machinery without the aid of arbitration. In addition, complaints of gangster control and of petty pilfering fell rather markedly, and it was anticipated that the improving reputation of the port would increase its business.

In some countries, more stringent methods are used, including compulsory arbitration, special labor courts, or a combination of the two. In Australia, since 1956 there has been a conciliation and arbitration commission composed of four judges, eight nonlawyers, and two conciliators. This body tries to settle interstate industrial disputes by conciliation and when that fails, resorts to compulsory arbiration, the terms of which are binding. There is also a three-man federal industrial court which acts if one of the parties to the dispute refuses to accept the commission's terms. Appeal from the court's decisions may be had only on a question of law. In New Zealand, a similar procedure has been used since 1894. In Sweden, by contrast, an official arbitration court from which there is no appeal may be set up to settle complex labor disputes, but this machinery has never been used. Only twice has the government considered such a step and each time the threat was enough to cause the parties to the dispute to come to an agreement by themselves. Labor relations in Sweden are regulated by a "main treaty" between employers' and employees' organizations which governs peaceful relations as well as conflicts and strikes and is generally agreed to work well.

In the United States there have been repeated suggestions for setting up a separate labor tribunal to handle industrial disputes. Thus in 1955 the Hoover Commission favored the separation of the functions of regulatory commissions by transferring their adjudicative duties to separate administrative courts. The National Labor Relations Board was included in this group and hence a separate labor court would have resulted. The

American Bar Association supported this proposal. More recently, Senator George A. Smathers has proposed the establishment of what he would call the United States Court of Labor-Management Relations, consisting of five judges, having jurisdiction over all national industry and to be resorted to when collective bargaining breaks down.[22] Opponents of the plan, however, contend that such a court would be open to political pressures which would merely serve still further to complicate the area of industrial disputes, and that in addition settlement by such means would inevitably raise the question of wages, whence it is only a short step to prices and then to price fixing which, except in time of war, is repugnant to the American pattern of free enterprise.

Conciliation and Mediation by the Federal Government

Prior to the Taft-Hartley Act of 1947, the principal means of settling industrial disputes at the federal level was the U. S. Conciliation Service of the Labor Department, a service which Taft-Hartley abolished. When the Labor Department was created in 1913, the organic statute empowered it "to act as mediator and to appoint commissioners of conciliation in labor disputes whenever in his [the Secretary of Labor's] judgment the interests of industrial peace require it to be done."

The record established by the Conciliation Service was impressive. Between 1913 and 1946, some 100,000 disputes were dealt with, involving minor and major industrial disagreements. In 1945 alone, the service handled 25,907 cases involving 14,506,121 workers. And in those controversies that reached the service before a work stoppage occurred, more than 95 percent were settled without any break in production.[23] Nevertheless, the agency was considered inadequate under modern conditions and hence was superseded when Title II of the Taft-Hartley Act created the Federal Mediation and Conciliation Service as an independent establishment of the federal government.

By placing this new agency on a specific statutory basis (the superseded one was created by legislation that was general and permissory) Congress hoped to raise it to a level of importance equal to that of the National Labor Relations Board. Another explanation is that the new service was created *de novo* and its duties were taken from the Department of Labor because of the insistence by industry that the Conciliation Service was "partial" to labor, a charge denied by the older organization. The new service was deliberately modeled after provisions in the Railway Labor Act of 1926. In industries that are interstate, each party must give the other a sixty-day notice of a proposed termination or modification of a contract; thirty days before the expiration of a contract the Federal Mediation and Conciliation Service must be notified; and then the status quo must be maintained until the end of the sixty-day cooling-off period

[22] Reported in *The New York Times*, Nov. 8, 1959.
[23] Edgar L. Warren, "The Case for Conciliation," *Mill and Factory* (Jan. 1946).

except in cases involving unfair labor practices by employers.[24] The service may also extend its good offices, either on request by one of the disputants or on its own motion after receiving official notice of a dispute, in any controversy affecting interstate commerce in all industries except railroads and airlines.

For railroads and airlines the procedure is a little different. Before a series of major disputes beginning in 1947 poured cold water on the assumption, the railway industry had been thought of as a model of labor-management relations for other industries because it had had a long history of joint settlement of disputes in a field that is solidly unionized and hence was considered "stabilized." Nevertheless, despite occasional lapses, the railway industry's reputation for successful labor-management relations is well merited.

The basic modern legislation, the Railway Labor Act of 1934, was amended in 1936 to bring the airlines under the same jurisdiction. The duty of the National Mediation Board, created in 1934, is to mediate differences between the railroads, the express and Pullman companies, and the airlines and their employees on rates of pay, rules, and working conditions. The board is also charged with determining representation disputes among employees, being empowered to make investigations and to hold elections to determine the proper employees' representative and to certify it to the parties and to the carrier. Disputes growing out of grievances or out of the interpretation or application of agreements concerning rates of pay, rules, or working conditions are referred to the National Railroad Adjustment Board. This agency consists of four divisions and represents equally the carriers and the unions. In case of deadlock the National Mediation Board may appoint a referee for the purpose of making an award. In a case where arbitration has been accepted in principle but the parties are unable to agree on who the neutral arbitrator shall be, the board may make the appointment. Despite this elaborate machinery, a major strike in 1950 caused the federal government to take over and operate the railroads until a settlement was reached nearly two years later, making this the longest railroad labor dispute in the United States.

A TIME FOR STATESMANLIKE MEASURES

A survey of the history of industrial relations in the United States reveals faltering steps and a perilous lack of ability to identify difficulties before they become aggravated. The publication of a carefully prepared plan, therefore, which appears to be both practical and visionary, is a major event. Such are the virtues of a report entitled, *Trends in Collective Bargaining*, published in 1945 by the Labor Committee of the Twen-

---

[24] *Mastro Plastics Corp. et al.* v. *National Labor Relations Board* (350 U.S. 270. 1956).

tieth Century Fund.[25] Among the highlights of this report, two deserve special mention here: The ultimate aim of collective bargaining is to summon forth the utmost use of the nation's resources. Consequently, management and labor "should keep in the front of their minds that their arrangements will influence the price of the product which must be sold to a third party, the consumer." In other words, the consumer must not be priced out of the market. The second point is that successful bargaining must rest on the recognition that managements and unions are mutually indispensable and functionally equal to each other; furthermore, both sides must recognize that to serve themselves best, they must serve the common prosperity most.

Ten years after this report was published, an official of the merged AFL-CIO remarked that labor had no ambition to take over the prerogatives of management or to mount the barricades in a struggle for control of the economic system. "We want the employers with whom we deal to be successful and to make plenty of money," he said. "We do not begrudge ownership its profits for we realize full well that the success of industrial enterprise is necessary for our own success in achieving substantial economic gains for our members. I would suggest," he added, "that it is high time that more people in the ranks of management begin to recognize that the converse is also true—that these gains achieved by trade unions for their members are also necessary to the long-run success of industrial enterprise in America." [26]

Every increase of power brings an increase of responsibility, a lesson that business organizations and labor unions are constantly learning. Organized labor has matured very rapidly in the last few years due in part, perhaps—and ironically enough—to the challenge presented to it by Taft-Hartley. During an earlier, more turbulent period, when the labor movement seemed to lack self-discipline and self-control, a good deal of thought was given to the possibility of forcing the unions to incorporate so as to make them susceptible to suit in the courts, end racketeering, and promote responsibility. In 1922, as a result of the Coronado coal strike that led to the Supreme Court decision of *United Mine Workers* v. *Coronado Coal Co.*[27]—the first of a pair of decisions on the subject—the Supreme Court modified the rule with regard to incorporation by holding that labor unions are entities that may be sued in federal courts, and since then a similar rule has been adopted in over half of the states. An unforeseen result of union suability, however, as far as employers are concerned, is that if unions may be sued, they may also sue.

As far as actual incorporation is concerned, one authority has commented that "Of all the proposals to 'regulate' unions, incorporation is

[25] S. T. Williamson, Herbert Harris, *et al.*, *Trends in Collective Bargaining* (New York, 1945), p. 210. A study of this report will repay the reader. For a summary of recommendations, see pp. 230–250.

[26] William F. Schnitzler, reported in *The New York Times*, Oct. 12, 1955.

[27] (259 U.S. 344. 1922).

perhaps the most unjust and absurd; and yet by sheer force of iteration on the part of antiunion employers, it has assumed—even in the minds of people who should know better—a certain metaphysical merit." [28] Business organizations are not *required* to incorporate, and when they do, it is to limit rather than to increase liability. Furthermore, racketeering is no more prevalent in labor unions than in other walks of life, business included.[29] The conclusion reached by a subcommittee on labor unions of the New York City Club is probably nearest the truth, that incorporation "could place no serious obstacle in the path of racketeering." On the contrary, paper corporations and dummy officers might easily lend themselves to the extension of racketeering activity, which "may be prosecuted under various federal laws, among them the anti-racketeering statute of 1933, the antitrust laws, and indirectly the Federal Income Tax Law." [30]

In the past few years the demand for union incorporation has subsided, partly because the unions themselves have less frequently provoked it. Labor has gained much in real wages, pensions, hours, and favorable working conditions, and industry is more prosperous than ever before in this nation. Injunctions, plant seizures, and other forms of government intervention in industrial disputes have been used sparingly in recent years. A new understanding between former sometimes bitter antagonists has developed, to the point where in some cases unions are joining with management to improve an employer's financial position by loaning him money, purchasing his stock to prevent a merger, and agreeing to reduced wages and employment. Unions have even advertised an employer's wares, eliminated waste in the distribution of his product, studied his customers' habits to determine salability, and promoted his efficiency through the introduction of labor-saving machinery.[31] In addition, employer-financed pension and welfare funds as well as stock-purchase plans have increased the workers' identification with, and loyalty to, the companies they work for.

A new pattern is also discernible in collective bargaining. "In a sense," comments one who knows, "it is unrealistic to talk of labor-management relations at all." More accurately, negotiations are now often between "the management of labor and the management of industry —the administrators of organizations that have had to grow more bureaucratic as they grew in size, wealth, and power." [32] Especially in some of the largest industries, the real bargaining is done by one or two men on each side who have become so understanding of one another's problems that instead of a controversy, there is a search for a formula that will enable each group to look good in the eyes of its principals, the union rank and file on the one hand and the owners of the business on the other.

But when management and labor evidence such close cooperation,

---

[28] Harris, *op. cit.*, p. 265.   [29] *Ibid.*, pp. 265–268.   [30] *Ibid.*, p. 267.
[31] All these examples are cited in Raskin, *op. cit.*   [32] *Ibid.*

what of the interests of the consumer? The fact is that in this tripartite relationship, prices to the consumer, as long as he will continue to pay them, are the last and the least item considered in a collective-bargaining session. Furthermore, cooperation may evolve into collusion—as it has in some instances—and even into corruption, and here again the consumer holds the bag. The discrimination against him is not deliberate, of course; it is simply that the consumer, being everybody, is unorganized and unrepresented, not only at the bargaining table but almost everywhere else as well. What is needed, therefore, says A. H. Raskin, is "a thorough-going acceptance by all the power forces in our economy of the idea that the benefits of rising productivity must be equitably shared among consumers, workers, and employers, not monopolized by those who command the greatest strength." [33]

Keeping Unions Democratic

In the minds of many people an issue that transcends all others is whether the rank and file of labor unions can succeed in keeping the unions democratic, or whether "the iron law of oligarchy" must inevitably result in dictatorship, either benevolent or evil. The Taft-Hartley law and the 1959 legislation relating to racketeering (Landrum-Griffin Act) were much concerned with this issue and it is likely to become increasingly prominent.

The paradox of the matter is that the more society legislates and regulates organized labor, the greater is the danger that dictatorship will occur in the unions. Not in all of them, of course, because many—perhaps most—have never had any serious trouble with democratic control. Hence it is only a small minority, but a much-discussed one, that creates the impression of narrow dictatorship.

But why the paradox? An experienced expert on labor, William Leiserson, analyzes the dilemma in this manner: [34] Organized labor strives for "industrial democracy" above all else; in its relations with employers it seeks a government of laws and not of men; it realizes that modern corporations and modern trade unions have both become governments in a very real sense; it also realizes that the democratic spirit is likely to be lost in the process, involving concentration and power, by which labor seeks its goals. Hence, why substitute the autocratic power of the union official for the erstwhile autocratic power of the business manager?

Leiserson admits that labor "tsars" sometimes exist. Such officials close the books on new members; as the union grows in size, the relations between officers and rank and file become strained and distant; the leader is accorded dictatorial powers including the authority to discipline or eliminate troublemakers and to make unrestricted appointments; there

---

[33] *Ibid.*

[34] William Leiserson, *American Trade Union Democracy* (New York, 1959). See especially Chap. 4, "Labor Democracy."

comes to be little or no review of top-brass action. Finally the top union official is virtually a law unto himself.

The explanation is partly the difficulty of making democracy work, of keeping interest and participation strong. In this sense, the problem is no different from that of formal government or the modern corporation. But there is also a special circumstance which applies to organized labor. The rank and file admire and feel the need for strong leadership because the movement lives in an atmosphere of fight and struggle. Almost everyone, but especially the managerial class and the public laws supporting it, is assumed to be lying in wait for a chance to weaken the unions. This fear of attack from the outside encourages the rank and file to give union leaders almost unlimited powers, even forcing such powers on their leaders in the face of a reluctance to assume them. The conclusion, therefore, is that unfriendly legislation feeds the fears of the rank and file and strengthens the tendency toward dictatorial powers in union management. The solution? More education of everyone—rank and file, employers, lawmakers. Better trained labor leaders. And finally, a clear recognition of these psychological and institutional factors when labor legislation is being considered.

Supplementary Reading

Witte, E. E., *The Government in Labor Disputes* (New York, 1932). By a leading authority in this field.

Reynolds, Lloyd G., *Labor Economics and Labor Relations* (New York, 3d ed., 1959). An outstanding treatment of the subject.

Slichter, Sumner H., *Union Policies and Industrial Management* (Washington, D.C., 1941). Stresses the administrative relationship.

Fitch, J. A., *Social Responsibilities of Organized Labor* (New York, 1957).

Taft, P., *The Structure and Government of Labor Unions* (Cambridge, Mass., 1954).

Derber, M., and E. Young (eds.), *Labor and the New Deal* (Madison, Wis., 1957).

Harbrecht, Paul P., *Pension Funds and Economic Power* (New York, Twentieth Century Fund, 1959). Social legislation adds to banker control.

Nossiter, Bernard D., "The Hidden Affair between Big Business and Big Labor," *Harper's Magazine* (July 1959).

Cochran, Bert (ed.), *American Labor in Midpassage* (New York, 1959).

Bell, Daniel, "The Supervision of Collective Bargaining," *Commentary*, Vol. 29, No. 3 (Mar. 1960).

Lester, R. A., *Labor and Industrial Relations* (New York, 1951).

——, *As Unions Mature* (Princeton, N.J., 1958).

Lens, Sidney, *The Crises of American Labor* (New York, 1959).

Taylor, Albion G., *Labor and the Supreme Court* (Ann Arbor, Mich., 1957).

Braun, Kurt, *Labor Disputes and Their Settlement* (Baltimore, Md., 1955).

Daugherty, Carroll R., *Labor Problems in American Industry* (Boston, 1948). By an outstanding authority.

Bloom, G. F., and H. R. Northrup, *Economics of Industrial Relations* (Philadelphia, rev. ed., 1954).

Bowman, D. O., *Public Control of Labor Relations* (New York, 1942). The best study to date of the National Labor Relations Board.

Gregory, C. H., *Labor and the Law* (New York, rev. ed., 1958). The best book on the legal aspects.

Twentieth Century Fund, *Labor and the Government* (New York, 1935). Well suited to this course.

————, *Trends in Collective Bargaining* (New York, 1945). A constructive program.

Blaisdell, Donald C., *Economic Power and Political Pressures,* Temporary National Economic Committee, Monograph No. 26 (Washington, D.C., 1941). Some good sections on what labor wants and on industrial relations.

Frankfurter, Felix, and N. Greene, *The Labor Injunction* (New York, 1930). Still the best treatise on the historical development.

Golden, Clinton S., and Harold S. Ruttenberg, *The Dynamics of Industrial Democracy* (New York, 1942). By two outstanding leaders of the labor movement.

Kaltenborn, Howard S., *Governmental Adjustment of Labor Disputes* (Chicago, 1943).

Berger, Monroe, *Equality by Statute: Legal Controls over Group Discrimination* (New York, 1952).

Kornhauser, A., R. Dubin, and A. M. Ross (eds.), *Industrial Conflict* (New York, 1954). Forty essays by psychologists, sociologists, and economists.

Casselman, P. H., *Labor Dictionary* (New York, 1949). An encyclopedia of labor information.

PART IV

AGRICULTURE
AND
GOVERNMENT

10

THE FARM PROBLEM

Revolution in agriculture; concern of government; evidences of instability; main issues; economic problems: land, population, number, kind, and size of farms, industrialized farms, employment, income, costs, indebtedness, parity, surpluses; concentration of control in marketing and processing; contract farming; brand-name advertising; proposed remedies: plans of CED and CEP.

Farms and farmers are fewer than they once were but farms and farm machinery are bigger and more efficient, and hence despite a booming population increase, food and fiber are produced in the United States to embarrassing levels. The revolution in industry in the nineteenth century was followed in the twentieth by a revolution in agriculture, and in both cases physical and social invention created a trail of maladjustments in the wake of prodigious progress. As in industry, the convulsion in agriculture was technologically induced, with mechanical power substituted for animal and human power, and easy transportation and communication bringing the farmer right into the city as far as his way of life, his markets, and the range of his social, economic, and political interests are concerned.

Among the innovations of the agricultural revolution, the corporation has been applied to farming, making possible the use of vastly expensive equipment to thousands of acres of land in a manner that no single farmer could afford; farm tenancy in some areas has created new ownership, social, and political relationships; producer cooperatives among farmers and contract farming have been developed as economic bulwarks; and, as in the case of business and labor, pressure groups have been organized for economic and political purposes.

The concern of government with agriculture was crystallized in 1862 when the U. S. Department of Agriculture was created. At that time the main objective was to increase the productivity and efficiency of agriculture, and here the record has been outstanding. Indeed, improved methods have created so high a level of production with so much less manpower than formerly that instability in the farm economy is now a vexing problem. Consequently, instead of leveling off, government's economic role in agriculture has been growing with a speed that called forth the remark as early as 1942 that "Farmers as a class have gotten themselves married to government and there is no possibility of divorce or separation." [1]

Instability in the agricultural economy is evidenced by overproduction in the case of some crops, notably wheat and cotton; by a piling up of agricultural surpluses in government bins; by farm incomes consistently lower than the national average even in good times; by growing farm indebtedness; by fewer farms and fewer farmers and a trend toward large corporation operations, so that family farms and farming as a way of life are jeopardized as never before. Such dislocations are hazardous to the American tradition. They threaten to stimulate the onset of depression, encourage price fixing by government and a weakening of the free-enterprise system, and have international repercussions in foreign trade. The main issues are these:

Should agricultural price supports on basic crops be continued in order to bolster farm incomes or withdrawn in the interest of a freer economy? Should surpluses be allowed to accumulate until they rot or can be dumped abroad, or can some better way be devised either to avoid them or to use them? Should government encourage an additional migration from farms to cities so as to reduce the burden on farm family income? Should some kind of relief be organized in behalf of seriously substandard farm families, of which the proportion is greater than in other segments of the economy? Should industrialized farming be encouraged in the interests of efficiency or curtailed in order to preserve farming as a way of life? Should a long-range, coherent agricultural program be formulated so as to increase farm living standards, widen markets, and stabilize the agricultural segment of the economy, or would such a program prove too costly in money, increased government responsibility, and a socialistic type of economic planning? And finally, as in the case of industry and labor, should farmers as a group become even more political than they are, for the sake of their own welfare and that of the economy?

Whatever answers may be given to these questions, three things seem clear: First, for good or ill, and with grass-roots participation, government is now the initiator and administrator of major policies and programs affecting agriculture; second, any successful farm program will be expensive to the taxpayer; and third, the problems of the farmer can only be solved within the broad framework of policies affecting the whole of the business-government relationship.

THE ECONOMIC PROBLEMS OF AGRICULTURE

The total land area of the nation is nearly 2 billion acres, of which about 20 percent is cropland and 50 percent is available for grazing.

---

[1] W. M. Kiplinger, *Washington Is Like That* (New York, 1942), p. 190.

Farming is nation-wide except for certain heavily industrialized areas, the desert, and the high mountains. In a dominantly agricultural economy, nine out of ten Americans lived on farms as late as 1800, but in 1958 only one out of eight was classified as rural. Consequently, instead of 90 percent of the total, our rural population is now only 12 percent, or less than 21 million individuals, many of whom do only part-time or no farming at all. During the depression of the 1930s and again after World War II there was a temporary increase in rural population as former farm people unemployed in the city or recently discharged from the armed forces returned to the family homestead for a period of readjustment; but the long-term trend is in the other direction. The striking fact is that although the farm population has dwindled by 4.2 million since 1950 and by 8.4 million since 1940, the rate of decrease is still too slow to match the loss of farm job opportunities as the use of machinery increases, even on small farms. It is also true that farming communities have the highest birth rate in the nation and cities must rely on them for population growth and maintenance.

The number of farms in the United States also has declined, being 6.5 million in 1920 and only 4.7 million in 1958. Of these, many are really only commuter or week-end homes having little rural economic significance, and more than a third are less than 50 acres in size, producing only a small percentage of the national farm output, and benefiting little from government farm programs. The bulk of farm products that move in commerce is produced by roughly 2.1 million commercial family farms ranging in size up to 1000 acres. At the top of the scale, less than 2 percent of the nation's farms—large farm factories often corporate-owned—produce 26 percent of all commercial food products and collect very high price-support payments from the government. A marked trend in farm economy has been toward fewer and larger farms, holdings of 500 to 1000 acres or more. About half of all farms are between 50 and 260 acres in size, but 10 percent are under 10 acres and some 6 percent are over 500 acres, with the tendency for size to increase.

A technological factor stimulating large size is the continual invention of new types of farm machinery. Thus a plow has been perfected that will work 14 acres an hour; the machine itself is 60 feet wide, cuts a swath of 42 feet, can be operated twenty-four hours a day, and is pulled by a 17-ton caterpillar tractor. Tractors, trucks, automobiles, planters of all kinds, harvesting combines, corn and cotton pickers, hay dryers, barn cleaners, manure loaders and spreaders, and milking machines have reduced the need for animal and manpower. Nor is this all: "Thanks to technology," reads a newspaper headline, "one third of U. S. farms are needed no more," [2] the reason being that in addition to new farm machinery, our knowledge of soils is constantly increasing, atomic research is on the verge of opening up vast new possibilities, better ways have been found to preserve foods, and we know more about plant innovations and

---

[2] *The Minneapolis Tribune*, Mar. 27, 1955.

plant breeding, as well as about the control of pests and diseases. The combined result of these developments is shown in Figure 8 on page 225.

The heavy capital investment needed for large land holdings, new kinds of equipment, and better methods has invited the corporation to enter the field of agriculture, and such ownership is increasing. One should not, of course, exaggerate the size of these corporations compared with those in the field of industry. For example, the *gross* annual sales of some 103,000 of our largest farms in 1949 averaged only $56,058 for each, which was hardly more than a week's volume of business in a large supermarket. Nevertheless, compared with the family-size farm and also from the standpoint of influence in the community, the difference is striking. By 1948 there were more than 7000 farm corporations. Six years later corporations held 5 percent of all farm land; four years more and the figure had risen to 8 percent of all farm land on an acreage basis but only 2 percent on a value basis. Such figures often come as a surprise to the average urbanite who buys his food and fiber with little understanding of the economics involved in their production. Often enough he still thinks of the farmer as "the man with the hoe."

In the matter of employment, following the pattern of a reduced farm population it was possible to say as early as 1940 that "We have reached the practical limits for employment of labor in agriculture." [3] Again, the reason is technological. In Oklahoma, for example, the combine harvester reduced employment during harvest from 11,000 in 1921 to 165 a decade later; in the state of Washington, "We no longer raise wheat . . . we manufacture it." [4] Also in the state of Washington, seven tractors pulling three drill sections each and following one another in a kind of surrealist combat formation seeded a strip 252 feet wide on each round of a 500-acre grain field. In 1880 a farm worker was barely able to harvest 21 acres; by 1950 he could handle more than twice as many. In 1921 a farm worker produced enough to feed and clothe eight people; today he can do the same for 19 people. With the index for farm output at a base of 100 for 1950, the annual total rose from 72 in 1930 to 123 in 1958. With the index for output per man hour at a base of 100 for 1947-1949, the total rose from 54 to 154 over the same period. Consequently, although over-all population and employment are rising sharply, farm employment goes down—by 50 percent since 1921. Agricultural labor was 9.6 percent of the total labor force of the nation in 1954; in six years it was down to 6.6 percent.

Income, Costs, and Indebtedness

Although the farmer is becoming more efficient, his share of the national income is and always has been disproportionately low. "For the

[3] Albert L. Meyers, *Agriculture and the National Economy,* Temporary National Economic Committee, Monograph No. 23 (Washington, D.C., 1940), p. 4.

[4] Temporary National Economic Committee, *Hearings,* Pt. 20, pp. 17,049-17,053.

past year," reported *The New York Times* in 1955, "every quarterly report of the President's Council of Economic Advisers has shown U. S. business and labor eating higher and higher on the hog. It has also shown the farmer getting less and less for his hogs." [5] In 1939, although farmers constituted nearly a quarter of the population, agricultural income was only a sixteenth of the total national income. Except for slight peaks during war years, this has been typical. Even in the so-called prosperous year of 1929 the average *gross* income of farmers was only $600 a year, and total farm income was only $5.6 billion. By 1932 total farm income had dropped to $2.3 billion, after which there was a gradual increase to a peak of $17 billion in 1948. But by 1954 it was back to $11.9 billion, which was less than 4 percent of the national income (a lower ratio than in 1933), making it some 10 percent short of what it should have been on a population basis.

By 1958, farm income was lower than at any time since 1943, the total realized income of farm operators having slipped 30 percent between 1951 (a postwar high point) and 1957, while farm costs rose by 24 percent during the same period. The 1953 average net income for all farm *families* was $3459, whereas for nonfarm families it was almost twice as much. And on an *individual* basis, in 1958 average per capita net farm income was only $569 (*down* 33 percent in three years), which was less than a quarter the figure for the nonfarm population. The fact is that despite a high rate of off-farm employment for many farmers, farm income has declined since 1951 at just about twice the rate that the total national income has risen. Nor do price-support payments solve the problem because, as shown, the chief beneficiaries of such payments have been the 2 million farmers who sell 88 percent of all farm products—in other words, those who get such payments need them least as far as income is concerned.

The decline in farm income is due to the fact that farm prices have declined as the cost of processing and marketing agricultural products goes up at the expense of the farmer's share of the retail food dollar. In 1946 this share stood at 52 cents, but ten years later it was only 42 cents, of which 30 cents went to purchase items such as feed, machinery, hired help, and the like, leaving only 12 cents for family use. Farm families once made much of what they needed in the home and made do without most of the luxuries available to city people. Today farm families want the same things their city neighbors have as a matter of course, including electrical equipment, television, clothes, new automobiles, bicycles and music lessons for the children, trips to town, and so on. Especially since the end of World War II the prices of such things have been going up along with the total national income and the income of most other groups in the economy—except farmers. For them, the gap between prices paid for what they need and prices received for what they raise is widening all

[5] Oct. 23, 1955.

the time. As might be expected, therefore, farm indebtedness also has risen since the relatively prosperous war years. Thus, farm mortgage debt increased from $4.9 billion in 1945 to $11.2 billion in 1959, and nonmortgage farm debt went up from $3.4 billion to $11.4 billion during the same period.

Outside of taxes, mortgage payments, interest, and insurance, most of what a farmer spends is for supplies and equipment needed in his business. It has been estimated, for example, that he buys about 8 percent of the total output of the chemical industry, largely for fertilizer, and about 7 percent of the total output of the food-processing industry, largely for commercial feed. In yearly averages, he buys more finished steel than is used for a year's output of passenger cars, enough rubber to replace tires on 6 million cars, and more crude petroleum than is used by any other industry.[6]

A major item in farm costs is farm implements and machinery, which the American inventive genius has developed to the point where nearly every important farm operation may now be done with the help of some kind of mechanical process. Although such machinery is often the factor on which efficient and hence profitable production depends, it is expensive to buy and maintain, and here concentration plays its usual role. A few manufacturing firms, including International Harvester and Deere & Company, dominate both manufacture and sales in the field of farm implements, and in practice the prices they set constitute the price level that all other manufacturers observe. For example, during the depression of the 1930s when farm prices fell by some 63 percent, the fall in the price of farm implements was held to only 6 percent.[7]

Parity and Surpluses

The purpose of government price-support programs is to establish farmers on a basis of economic equality with other groups in the economy, such as industry and labor. The formula is designed to enable a farmer to purchase at current prices as much as he was able to purchase at a relatively normal and stable period in the past. It is perhaps significant that when the formula was adopted for the first time in 1934, in order to find such a happy period it was necessary to go all the way back to 1910-1914 for a span of years during which the farm economy had been on a more or less even keel. The farm price index for these years was set at 100, a fairly arbitrarily established par designed to describe the ratio of the farmer's prices to his costs, including such items as taxes, mortgage interest, the purchase of machinery, hired help, insurance, and the like. The parity concept was not formally written into law, however, until it was made to apply to certain crops in the Agricultural Act of 1938.

---

[6] Conference on Economic Progress, *Full Prosperity for Agriculture* (Washington, D.C., 1955), p. 49.

[7] Meyers, *op. cit.*, p. 29.

In 1949 the parity formula was modified to take account of newer production and marketing methods and conditions, the revised base being the ten years immediately preceding the year in which price supports were to be applied. But the former base also was retained for purposes of long-range comparison, among others. Later adjustments in the parity formula were made when the Republican administration came to office in 1953, the idea being to abandon parity altogether as soon as Congress and the farmers could be persuaded that the concept was outmoded. In 1958 the American Farm Bureau Federation itself recommended that the base for support payments be calculated according to the average market prices of the preceding three crop years, a formula said to eliminate artificial incentives to production and to avoid price fixing by the government. Against it is the fact that it contains a built-in time lag between changes in market conditions and adjustments in price-support payments. The Department of Agriculture adopted it for payments on corn in 1958, and in his 1960 farm message the President recommended that it be extended to all other crops under government control as a substitute for the parity concept.

Although the intent of parity and price-support payments is to provide equality of income for farmers with other economic groups in the nation, the record shows a wide discrepancy between intent and results, the reason being that there is a sharp difference between parity of prices which the formula covers and parity of income which it ignores. Thus, even when prices are at 100 percent of parity, farmers still receive a good deal less than their share of the national income. Full parity prices coupled with few sales produce a low income, whereas lower prices and a greater volume of sales would do the opposite. So far, such factors have not been included in any support payment formula.

The ratio of prices received for farm products to prices paid by the farmer for what he must buy averaged around 80 during the late 1930s, rose to 105 after the start of World War II, and hovered around 110 from 1943 until the end of the war; then rose to 115 in 1947, a level attained only twice before since 1910 (in 1917 and 1918). By 1949 the ratio had declined to 100 which meant that in theory, at least, the farmers were getting an even break, although total farm income represented only 6 percent of total national income while farmers themselves constituted some 15 percent of the total population. The parity ratio went up to 107 in 1951 as a result of the Korean conflict, since when there has been a more or less steady decline. By 1958 it was down to 85 and farm income represented only 3.2 percent of the national income.

Thus the objective of economic equality for agriculture has not been attained, and in addition, the distribution of price support payments themselves have even further distorted agricultural income by favoring the larger, more prosperous farm operators. In 1953, for example, the top 9 percent of all farmers received half of all support payments from the government, while the remaining 91 percent shared thinly in the other half.[8] By 1959 many large operators (most of them corporations) were receiving $1 million or more annually for not growing certain farm crops, and Congress moved to impose a top limit on such payments.

A major aspect of the government's efforts to secure parity for agriculture is the attempt to limit production, the object being to raise the price of farm products and keep surpluses to a minimum. Unfortunately, a combination of increasing technology, more intensive use of the land that remains in cultivation, and guaranteed prices for legally grown crops has stimulated production to the point where enormous surpluses have piled up in government warehouses. These include everything from granaries and other private facilities (for which the government often pays a premium rent) to abandoned industrial plants, moth-balled liberty ships, and decommissioned tankers. To dispose of such unwelcome commodities, they have been donated to free school-lunch programs, donated to relieve disaster distress in friendly nations, bartered for strategic materials, and, under so-called Public Law 480 (passed in 1954), sold abroad for local curriencies which are then largely reinvested in developmental projects within the purchasing country. Nevertheless, by 1959, despite all efforts to prevent or to unload surpluses, they had reached a total worth of $10 billion—a rise of $3 billion in three years—and it was costing the government more than $700 million a year to store them.

CONCENTRATION OF CONTROL IN MARKETING AND PROCESSING

Having contended with mud in the sowing season and drought in the growing season, with balky machinery, numerous pests, the blazing sun of the harvest weeks and the sometimes reluctant assistance of his sons, in order to produce his crops, the farmer must then market them at as favorable a price as he can get. Furthermore, he must sell them at once or pay storage costs in the hope of a better price later on—if, indeed, his crops are the kind that bear storage without rotting. In this picture, the question of concentration of control—this time over markets and processing—again enters the situation as yet another obstacle. Of all segments of the economy, only agriculture is relatively free from bigness and the bargaining power that goes with it, whereas those who handle his product on the way to the consumer are often giants indeed. Consequently even if the average farmer recognizes his own advantage, which is by no means certain, he is generally unable to assure it.

Marketing agricultural products is far more complicated than most people realize. Eggs in the Boston market, for example, may pass through as many as four sets of handlers between the farm and the consumer. If a farmer must depend on a single wholesaler in the open market, fur-

---

[8] Conference on Economic Progress, *op. cit.*, p. 97.

thermore, the bargaining power is heavily on the side of the wholesaler who, in addition, is in a position to misrepresent grades, markets, and prices, and to enter into collusive agreements with other wholesalers to keep prices down if he wants to. Yet another difficulty arises when a farmer borrows in advance of the harvest from buyers, processors, or distributors in return for a contract to sell his crops to the lender. Where this system covers only part of a crop, outside buyers hesitate to enter the market because of the small volume remaining over what is under contract, and hence all farmers in the area suffer a loss of bargaining power. In the light of such disadvantages, the credit operations of the Farm Credit Administration assume importance because no selling strings are tied to its production and marketing loans.

FIG. 8. INDEXES OF FARM LABOR PRODUCTIVITY, 1910-1957

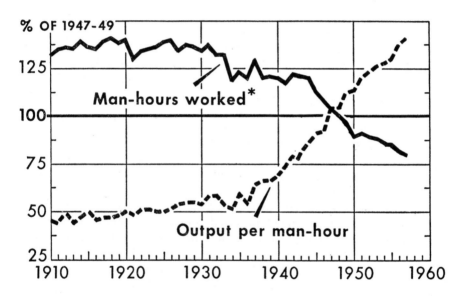

* In terms of time used by adult males

SOURCE: U. S. Department of Agriculture, Agricultural Research Service

Nevertheless, contract farming, or vertical integration as it is also called, has greatly increased in the last decade or so and promises to be still further taken up as a means of bringing a measure of financial security to the farm operator even at the expense of the independence of his operation and the choice of his market. Contracting has been common for some time in the production of hatching eggs, fruits and vegetables for canning and freezing, sugar beets, and some other specialty crops. The procedure, similar to one often used in industry, is based on contracts entered into between farmers and business concerns including chain stores, or between farmers and their producer cooperatives. It is in the broiler industry, however, that vertical integration has gone farthest and fastest, until by 1958 something like 90 percent of all broilers were produced under this method. A poultry processor, for example, or a feed dealer, owns the birds from embryo to sales package. He supplies the eggs, the feed, and in some cases the housing as well, specifying right down to the type of pullet to be raised and the make of cage and ventilator to be installed. He spells out bird-management procedures, the daily feeding and watering schedule, and even the type of litter to be used on the floors. Then on the appointed day he collects the birds and disposes of them either through his own processing plant or that of another wholesaler. All the farmer does is to house and feed the birds according to the terms of the contract. This procedure turns out a uniform product, reduces the life cycle of the broiler industry from 15 to 9 weeks, cuts the amount of feed needed to raise a three-pounder from 12 to 8 pounds, raised production more than 300 percent in ten years, increased the per capita consumption of chickens from about 18 to more than 25 pounds over the same period, makes broilers available to the housewife in every season of the year, and reduces the farm operator to the status of piece-wage worker on his own farm.[9] But vertical integration also provides him with a degree of financial security that would otherwise be lacking in an occupation where marketing is an uncertain variable and chickens continue to eat if they are not sold.

Indeed, small-time commercial farming today is so uncertain and the advantages of integration so appealing despite obvious drawbacks of a personal nature to men and women whose traditional independence is a part of the folklore of the American culture, that the new method is rapidly being extended to other areas of farm production. In the raising of hogs, for example, under the usual contract the producer delivers a specified number of hogs at a specified time to the contracting packer, who agrees to buy those of the highest grade at the delivery day's average market price plus a premium. The premium is made possible because the producer follows breeding, feeding, and housing procedures specified in the contract and the result is a higher, more uniform, and leaner grade of pork better able to compete at the retail meat counter with beef and poultry. A similar system is being applied to the commercial feeding of cattle in great mechanized feeding lots operated by the processors of sugar beets, grain, or cotton, the by-products of which constitute the feed. Similar arrangements are being developed in the production of lamb and mutton, and presumably in time, other areas also will be covered. The supporters of this system look forward to the day when even the great staple crops of wheat and corn will be handled under the contract procedure and government support programs will no longer be necessary.

[9] Reported by William M. Blair, *The New York Times*, Mar. 2, 1958.

The contract system is still too new for all of its consequences to have become clear but some of them may already be seen. In addition to more efficient production, a degree of financial security to the farmer, and the loss of his independence, it seems likely that a good many small operators will be forced out of business. If the plan were pushed far enough, it might come to the point where most commercial farmers will grow chiefly to fill specific orders under long-term contracts with giant retailing organizations. Such foodstuffs might bypass middlemen and the national-brand food manufacturers altogether, going instead directly to private brand labels controlled by the retail chains. Indeed, in 1958 it was predicted that by 1960, more than 90 percent of all meat and groceries would be sold by food chains powerful enough to make their own pricing structure for the products they sell.[10]

Another result of vertical integration is that even conservative farm leaders feel the need for "negotiation" and "collective bargaining" with the buyers of farm products, and in 1959 the Farm Bureau created the National Marketing Association to help organize state and regional groups for this purpose. Producer cooperatives and "trade" associations of specialized producers may also become more common. If the farmers are to retain their independence, they must have some control over the disposition of their product through the terms of their contracts with buyers. The census of agriculture taken in the fall of 1959 included a sample survey of the terms of such contracts and asked questions such as whether a contract was exclusive, whether a feed dealer supplied all feed and other necessary materials, and what the profit margins were under such arrangements. The machine has long been established on the American farm, notes one reporter, but "the new changes springing from integration are the results less of machines than of the administrative character of the Industrial Revolution; the effects nonetheless may mean the final industrialization of the farm." [11]

Aside from vertical integration, concentration of control is also apparent in food processing. The trend was noted by the Temporary National Economic Committee in 1940 when it was most pronounced in the preparation of breakfast cereals and the manufacture of soda crackers; in the case of these products also, the spread between farm and retail prices was greatest—and it still is. As might be expected, the profits of these industries were correspondingly high, National Biscuit Company reporting profits of 13.3 percent of net sales and Corn Products Refining Company 18.3 percent of net sales.

Except where contracting is in use, concentration as such is less common in the freezing and canning of fruits and vegetables, but because the market is locally restricted, the farmer is still at a disadvantage. These processing companies cannot afford to locate too closely together

---

[10] Dr. George Mehren, reported by Dick Bruner, "Administered Farms," *Challenge* (Nov. 1958) pp. 35–38.

[11] In *ibid.*, p. 38.

lest they run short of a continuous supply. Hence whether he sells under
the terms of a contract or in the open market, in both cases the farmer
is deprived of the benefits of competition. In the canning industry, furthermore, there is a monopoly factor in the manufacture of cans. Thus,
it is possible "that the profits of can and tinplate manufacturers are a
more important element in the spread between farmer and consumer than
the profits of the canning companies themselves." [12] The profits of
the two largest can manufacturers in 1939 were both in excess of 9 percent of sales, and it was estimated that one fourth of the price of a can
of tomatoes was the cost of the can. As early as 1935, three giant can firms
controlled 90 percent of the industry.

The dairy industry is particularly susceptible to concentration of
control in processing and distribution, and rapid advances have not
failed to appear. Again, the cause is chiefly technological. In the interests of public health, large cities have passed ordinances requiring
that all milk be pasteurized. The owner of a pasteurization plant therefore controls a gateway in the industry enabling him to drive a hard
bargain with the farmer. Improved transportation has made possible
the creation of large milk sheds around metropolitan areas, extending
sometimes through several states. Such milk sheds are carefully controlled
as to sanitation, quantity, quality, and price, and the producer who wishes
to sell outside has little choice. He might just as well comply with the
regulations, accept the price that is offered him, and ship through the
pasteurization plants, however much he may dislike the restrictions on
his freedom and on his bargaining power.

But more serious than controls imposed for public health reasons is
the fact that three giant dairy-products companies now dominate the
national scene in the dairy industry: the National Dairy Products Corporation, the Borden Company, and a relative newcomer, Foremost
Dairies, Inc. As early as 1932, National and Borden had assets of nearly
$500 million and annual gross sales of more than $550 million, they
controlled the product of more than 3 million dairy farms; and they
dominated the milk supply of large cities all over the country. Even in
the leading dairy state of Wisconsin, 84 percent of the fluid milk distribution in Milwaukee in 1930 was controlled by these two combines, and
in Baltimore subsidiaries of National alone controlled 85 percent of the
total milk distribution. In the case of Foremost, net income in 1954 was
$3 million compared with less than $2 million in the previous year; most
of the increase in sales and earnings reflected the "successful integration
of acquisitions," including dairy companies in California, Western Texas,
and Connecticut.[13]

In 1923 the dairy farmer received 52 cents of the consumer's milk
dollar and the distributor got 48 cents, but ten years later the farmer re-

[12] Meyers, *op. cit.*, pp. 22–23.
[13] *The New York Times*, Apr. 4, 1954.

ceived only 35 cents and the distributor's share had gone up to 65 cents. During this period, although general retail food prices dropped 20 percent, the price paid to the farmer for milk dropped 50 percent. Nevertheless, as so often happens when concentration occurs, delivered milk prices to consumers were relatively steady even during the depression. Thus during the years 1930 to 1932, when most of industry was taking a loss, National Dairy averaged 13 percent profit on its invested capital. Higher executive salaries were paid in the milk processing industry than in tobacco, flour, cotton, meat, bakeries, and tanneries.[14] In the decade preceding 1958 the farm price of milk declined by 16 percent but the retail price declined by only 3 percent.

In addition to the costs of processing, another factor that reduces the farmer's share of the retail dollar is the cost of advertising brand names. Since consumers seem to prefer to buy widely advertised brands even at prices above those of nonadvertising competitors of equal or superior quality, it pays the processor to advertise his wares as widely as possible. From the standpoint of the farmer, the consumer, and economic analysis, however, the tendency to substitute brand names for quality and price works primarily to the advantage of the processor. It is nearly impossible to determine what percentage of the price of widely advertised brand products is justly attributable to advertising expenses because such costs are almost always lumped with others, but Meyers was able to arrive at some rough estimates. National Biscuit Company, for example, which sells mostly to retailers, reported "selling, general, and administrative expenses" amounting to 35 percent of sales. General Mills, which sells primarily to wholesalers, reported similar expenses totaling 17.6 percent. And Ward Baking Company, the largest bread and baking company in the nation selling mostly to retailers, reported "delivery and selling and advertising expenses" amounting to 29 percent of sales.[15]

It seems as though our economy were rapidly becoming one of advertisers rather than one of price and quality competition. Even though production in volume yields economies in the manufacture of goods, these savings may be partly absorbed by the selling and advertising costs needed to push a particular brand. There can be no objection to large volume achieved by selling at low prices, unless they are lowered merely temporarily in order to force competitors out of the field. But large volume accompanied by large selling costs and high prices is of no benefit to the consumer and harms the farmer by reducing his share of the consumer dollar. The fact is that both consumer and farmer would be better served by a larger number of smaller firms with higher production costs but actively competing on a price basis.

[14] Temporary National Economic Committee, *Hearings*, Pt. 7, pp. 2,806–2,807.
[15] Meyers, *op. cit.*, p. 25.

WHAT REMEDIES?

This, then, is the problem: A dwindling group of traditionally independent people on fewer but larger farms producing with the help of complicated and costly machinery more food and fiber than the American people is willing or able to purchase at a price that is profitable to the farmer. Is it any wonder that the farmer has sought relief by whatever means he can, including the organization of producer cooperatives to increase bargaining power and reduce marketing costs, and by strengthening pressure groups in order to induce government to come to his aid?

But before taking a look in the following chapter at what government has tried to do for the farmer, let us first attempt to identify some kind of norm by which to judge these programs. John Fischer, editor-in-chief of *Harper's Magazine,* summarized the need rather well in a few lines when he wrote that we should have a farm program designed to (1) produce the kinds and amounts of farm products the country needs, and no more; (2) encourage family-operated farms of the necessary size and efficiency to survive without perpetual subsidy; (3) divert about a million unneeded farm workers to productive occupations, and restore about 40 million acres to grass and timber; (4) conserve the soil—our most valuable, and fastest-wasting asset; and (5) eliminate excessive subsidies to factory-type farms and overblown plantations.[16]

Many groups of experts have studied the farm problem in the past decade or so—the National Planning Association, the Twentieth Century Fund, the Food and Agriculture Organization of the United Nations (farming in a world setting), the Conference on Economic Progress, the Committee for Economic Development, and various committees of Congress that periodically try to find a solution to this major problem of public policy. Although there is general agreement that government price-support programs have not helped either the farmer or the taxpayer and have even been harmful to both, and that too much land is devoted by too many farmers to the growing of too many crops to be currently used by the American consumer, there is a good deal of fuzziness and manifest frustration in the suggested remedies. The recommendations of the National Planning Association, for example, are diverse to the point of confusion and loaded with dissenting footnotes by members of the group that prepared them.[17] The report of the Twentieth Century Fund approaches the farmer as an economic entity and ignores him as a man, which is surely a one-sided view. The Food and Agriculture Organization calls for a closer cooperation between farming and industry since each group depends on the other for its

[16] John Fischer, "A Radically New Farm Program," *The New Republic* (Jan. 30, 1956), p. 7.
[17] National Planning Association, *A Joint Statement on Farm Policy* (Washington, D.C., 1955).

market,[18] a proposition that most people would consider to be self-evident.

The CEP Plan

The Conference on Economic Progress was more specific. A research organization of liberal agricultural, labor, and business leaders, it offered a long-range program for agriculture in a report entitled *Full Prosperity for Agriculture* (1955).[19] This group denies that there is overproduction except in certain crops and stresses effective demand for farm products. Thus:

1. If the 8 million multiple and single-person families in the United States with annual incomes under $2000 before taxes were raised to a moderate standard of diet and nutrition, the additional annual consumption of farm products would approach the average annual size of what is now called surplus production.

2. In order to meet the growth of population, plus changes in domestic incomes and tastes and in world conditions, total farm production in this country should be *increased* by about 22 percent.

3. A goal of national policy should be to raise the annual income of farmers as a class by some $10 billion above the 1955 level of about $11 billion.

4. The low-income, low-producing farms should be reduced by about a million and the better family-type farms increased by about 450,000; at the same time the trend toward giant or corporate farming should be checked.

5. Some 750,000 farm-family workers and hired workers, comprising with their families about 2 million people, should have a chance to work outside of farming in order better to attain to the American standard of employment and living.

6. Agricultural welfare programs such as those of the Farmers' Home Administration should be expanded.

7. Export consumption should be sharply and immediately lifted by measures to enlarge trade and by some expansion in American financial aid to underdeveloped nations.

8. Adequate programs of land conservation and food reserves should be established.

9. The traditional methods of protecting farm incomes should be improved but with the continued use of price supports. As part of this plan, some 8.5 million acres of farm land should be taken out of production.

10. The family-type farm should be further strengthened by improved credit facilities and the encouragement of farm cooperatives.

[18] United Nations, Food and Agriculture Organization, *Agriculture and the World Economy* (Nov. 1955).
[19] Conference on Economic Progress, *op. cit.*

This plan would call for an annual outlay of some $2 billion in direct assistance to farmers and several billions more for programs of indirect assistance such as an expanded public-employment service, improved educational opportunities, and more financial aid for underdeveloped nations. At the time that this report was published, however, it was calculated that the cost would amount to only about 4 or 5 percent of the total federal budget, which "is not high when measured against the need."

Throughout this report, furthermore, the CEP stresses specific goals for production, income, standard of living, and the like, raising the question of how much national economic planning would be entailed if Congress were to give effect to these policy recommendations. Also, certain basic questions are only lightly touched on, such as how consumer demand on the part of substandard families is to be increased, and how world trade in farm products is to be furthered when most of the so-called underdeveloped countries are stressing their own agricultural economies as the mainstay of their domestic programs.

The CED Plan

The Committee for Economic Development, which is an organization of liberal businessmen, has studied the farm problem on a more or less continuing basis and in 1956 published a report on *Economic Policy for American Agriculture*.[20] As the title implies, emphasis was on the economics of the situation rather than on political practicality, but the proposals met with a wide approval. The plan stressed permanent solutions consistent with the free-enterprise system, even if the remedies proved costly. A successor report in 1957 entitled *Toward a Realistic Farm Program*,[21] went into the question more thoroughly.

The basic difficulty, said the CED, is that in trying to underwrite farm prices and income, the present farm policy of the federal government merely perpetuates an unreal price structure which encourages overproduction of farm crops and keeps too many people in farming, resulting in mounting surpluses. This imprisons the farmer ever more hopelessly "in his own basket of plenty" while taxing the public for the purpose of keeping its own food and fiber bills artificially high. It is senseless to keep people and material resources at work to produce farm surpluses while the nation strains to foster economic growth and national security. "Such a policy makes no sense, from the standpoint of the farmer, of the public at large (including the farmer), or of the national well-being."

As a remedy offered after much study, the CED proposed a series of

[20] Committee for Economic Development, *Economic Policy for American Agriculture* (New York, 1956).

[21] Committee for Economic Development, *Toward a Realistic Farm Program* (New York, 1957).

interlocking programs designed to increase the farmer's proportional share in the national prosperity, to rescue him from the preposterous position of "beggaring himself by an excess of industry," and to restore his "command over his own economic condition." By the use of efficient production methods the farmer should be able to achieve the buying power he needs as a consumer of all kinds of goods: machinery, fertilizer, feed, home appliances, and many more. The farmer's capacity to produce must be brought into line with what the market will absorb at prices acceptable to farmer and consumer alike. This means reducing production and allowing prices to reach levels at which the entire supply can be sold in the commercial market without government assistance.

From the standpoint of the farmer, overproduction is accompanied by wide swings of income for reasons beyond his control, such as the condition of the weather during the growing season and changes in consumer demand according to the economic state of the nation. In addition, many farmers lack the productive resources to earn a proper living from farming without some sort of public subsidy. Nevertheless, the farm problem boils down to a compound of too much farm production by too many people on the basis of artificial prices, and hence the CED made the following recommendations:

1. The gradual removal—but on a definite time schedule—of price and income supports except for temporary emergency situations; a voluntary land-retirement program through the better use of the present soil-bank plan, in order to reduce resources, both human and land, devoted to agriculture; and the disposal of present surpluses by continuing present efforts but also by temporarily reducing production below demand so that surpluses will be drawn off through normal market channels.

2. Gradual removal of acreage allotments and marketing controls, and restoration of the farmer's freedom to manage his own enterprise.

3. Stand-by authority for the temporary use of price-support loans and other emergency measures as needed.

4. Special programs to help the farmer who cannot make a reasonable living from farming without public subsidy find a better living in other industries.

5. The establishment of an advisory agricultural board, responsible to Congress, to work with the Secretary of Agriculture in gearing agricultural programs and policy to the over-all national economy. The advice of this board, however, should not be "fumbled into procedural limbo" or ignored. Instead, its recommendations should receive formal standing, and the Secretary of Agriculture should be required to report to Congress on the action taken on them, to explain his stand if it is different from them, and to ask for new legislation if it is needed to put them into effect.

As to costs, the CED expected that even in the short run they would be less than present government outlays for agriculture, and that in the long run they would be considerably less. The specific means of putting such a plan into effect would have to be carefully studied, and here the proposed advisory agricultural board should play a major role.

Although they differ on several points as well as on ways and means, these programs of the CEP and the CED are together on certain matters that are basic. Both agree, for example, that land should be conserved, that some should be taken out of cultivation, that a good many farm families should be encouraged to leave the land in order to make a better living in the city, and that whatever policy is adopted, it will be costly but not quite as costly as present programs. It is time now to go behind the scenes and see what is actually being done by government on behalf of agriculture.

Supplementary Reading

Committee for Economic Development, *Economic Policy for American Agriculture* (New York, 1956). A statement on national policy by the Research and Policy Committee.

Conference on Economic Progress, *Full Prosperity for Agriculture* (Washington, D.C., 1955). Goals for a farm policy.

McConnell, G., *The Decline of Agrarian Democracy* (Berkeley, Calif., 1953). Provides perspective.

Hickman, C. A., *Our Farm Program and Foreign Trade* (New York, Council on Foreign Relations, 1949). A conflict of national policies.

Schickele, R., *Agricultural Policy* (New York, 1954).

Peterson, William H., *The Great Farm Problem* (Chicago, 1959). The politico-economics of American agriculture.

Blaisdell, Donald C., *Government and Agriculture* (New York, 1940). By the author of *Economic Power and Political Pressures*.

Hardin, Charles M., *Politics of Agriculture* (Glencoe, Ill., 1952). Competition for policy and power.

Schultz, Theodore W., *Agriculture in an Unstable Economy* (New York, 1945).
———, *Production and Welfare of Agriculture* (New York, 1949).
———, *Redirecting Farm Policy* (New York, 1943). These three volumes are by one of America's outstanding agricultural economists.

Davis, J. S., *On Agricultural Policy, 1926-1938* (Palo Alto, Calif., 1939). By an outstanding authority on agricultural economics.

Black, John D., *Agricultural Reform in the United States* (New York, 1929). For the early period.

U. S. Department of Agriculture, *Farmers in a Changing World: 1940 Yearbook of Agriculture* (Washington, D.C., 1940). Integrates the social sciences in so far as agriculture is concerned.

Benedict, M. R., *Farm Policies of the United States, 1790-1950* (New York, 1953). A Twentieth Century Fund study.
———, *Can We Solve the Farm Problem?* (New York, 1955). Also a Twentieth Century Fund study.

Halcrow, Harold G., *Agricultural Policy of the United States* (New York, 1952). An excellent survey.

II
GOVERNMENT PROGRAMS FOR FARMERS

Farmer pressure groups and political attitudes; price support programs: AAA, Brannan Plan, soil bank; other government farm programs; farm credit agencies.

Because farmers are practical people, they have sometimes adopted remedies that theoretically they do not favor. But group action has replaced individual action in industry and in labor, and so farmers also have banded themselves together: in cooperatives, in pressure groups, and as voters in order to defend their economic position in society. Farmers see distributors reaching back to control production, produce buyers and processors attempting to control prices by the offer of loans to growers with strings attached, commission merchants taking advantage of agriculture's inferior bargaining position, transportation companies charging high rates at the expense of the producer, racketeers controlling key commodities in metropolitan centers, a few large corporations securing a giant grip on the manufacture of farm machinery, and processors profiting from the high-powered advertising of brand names at the expense of the farmer's share of the retail food dollar.

And so the farmer becomes a restrictionist himself. He tries to match the power of milk combines, for example, with cooperative producer units of his own. He calls for the regulation and prosecution of monopoly, seeks agricultural credit from government agencies, and supports the abolition of trade barriers and the regulation of transportation. He buys from the catalogue or from the chain grocery store when he goes to town, although theoretically he is opposed to big, nation-wide, monopolistic enterprise. Or he joins his local consumer's cooperative and goes into a variety of businesses himself. He supports his farm pressure group because it gives him some protection against the programs of Big Business and Big Labor that are harmful to the farm economy. And all the while, of course, he continues to think of himself as an individualistic, conservative citizen believing in unrestricted competition and laissez faire—an attitude that does not differ materially, of course, from that of his brother businessman or brother worker.

More than any other economic group in the nation, farmers have been close to government and once had a reputation for being able to get from Congress anything they cared to work for through the pressure groups that represent them: the National Grange, the American Farm Bureau Federation, and the National Farmers Union. For a number of reasons, however, circumstances have changed. Basic to all other aspects of the matter is the simple arithmetic fact that there are increasingly fewer farmers in the country and hence their combined influence, so far as it has remained combined, is shrinking. Unfortunately for the farmer, what was once a strong alliance between the cotton and tobacco growers of the South and the corn and wheat growers of the Middle West has been weakened, in part by government price-support programs. The producer of each specialized crop has specialized interests that may conflict with those of the producer of another crop, as in the case of the producer of corn on the one hand and of livestock on the other. This diversity of viewpoint is reflected in the farmers' pressure organizations which sometimes now work at cross-purposes where formerly they would have been united in a common effort.

Moreover, higher production per farm plus the fact that more than a third of all farmers derive part or most of their income from nonfarm employment, have caused farmers themselves to become important consumers of nonfarm products, and hence their orientation is becoming partially urbanized. These many factors are brought together when Congress considers a farm program in which a variety of goals must be reconciled.

AGRICULTURAL PRICE-SUPPORT PROGRAMS

When the Roosevelt administration came to office in 1933, the agricultural economy was so depressed, along with that of most of the rest of the economy, that it hardly paid many farmers to market their crops. To cite only the example of meat, the retail price of hamburg was 7 cents a pound in Detroit, and a shipment of cattle or hogs to the Chicago stockyards might not bring in enough to pay the transportation charges. A national policy of curbing output to raise prices seemed indicated. The last thing the farmer himself cares for is an artificial restriction of output, and yet in 1933 his very survival seemed to depend on it. A nation-wide referendum—one of the most ambitious polls in American history—was arranged to determine the farmers' attitude on a program of planned restriction and the verdict was overwhelmingly in favor of such a course.

This policy of restriction and control, originally based on expediency, soon developed into a philosophy: rather than unlimited price increases, the farmer sought a "just" or parity price that would bring his income in line with the income of other groups in the economy. Later there was added the idea of the so-called ever-normal granary, in effect a cushion between production and consumption based on the per capita consumption of food during the 1920s, plus the normal carry-over of crops from the one season to the next, plus estimated exports. In other words, the objective of this policy was to plan agricultural production and then take part of the supply out of the competitive domestic market so that what remained would bring a profitable price to the farmer. Obviously such a scheme involves a high degree of planning and control through the central instrumentality of the federal government.

The New Deal agricultural program removed cotton, corn, rice, wheat, and tobacco—the great staples—from the competitive market. In addition, other crops were bought up and held under the Food Stamp Plan (a scheme to get surplus food into the hands of needy persons without interfering with normal retail food sales); various marketing agreements, as in milk, were entered into under governmental auspices so as to control production and prices; various surpluses, such as butter, were purchased by specially created government corporations and held in warehouses until better prices could be secured; other government corporations—notably the Farm Credit Administration and the Commodity Credit Corporation—helped to finance farmers at low interest rates or paid out subsidies to them; distressed farmers were assisted by the Farm Security Administration which helped to set them back on their feet either by small loans or direct payments; cheap power was brought to a million farmers (now over 4.6 million) by the Rural Electrification Administration; a nation-wide program of soil conservation was launched; and the government tried to control the profits of middlemen and some of their practices.

But as wide an area as this list covers, it merely touches the high points. Indeed, so comprehensive was the agricultural program of the 1930s that, as Stuart Chase has pointed out, it may justly be said that "agriculture was in effect collectivized—lifted clean out of the free market and put in a market where prices, or production, or both, were controlled." [1]

The Two AAAs

The most spectacular part of the New Deal farm program was the Agricultural Adjustment Administration, often characterized as the most "radical" social experiment ever undertaken in the United States. There were, in fact, two AAA programs. The first, enacted in 1933, was declared unconstitutional in 1936.[2] An interim program was then set up, emphasizing soil conservation, until the second AAA was enacted in 1938. This one was upheld in *Mulford* v. *Smith*,[3] decided in 1939 after the composition of the Supreme Court had changed in consequence of new appointments.

Although the AAA programs may have been radical in their effect on the competitive system and the free market, their administration was remarkably democratic. To begin with, as already indicated, the pro-

---

[1] Stuart Chase, *Democracy under Pressure* (New York, 1945), p. 92.
[2] *United States* v. *Butler* (297 U.S. 1. 1933).   [3] (307 U.S. 38. 1939).

gram was adopted only after a nation-wide poll of farmer sentiment. And when the plan was finally in operation, a large part of it was administered by the farmers themselves acting through some 2500 county boards in addition to local committees.

In simple terms, the AAA program worked as follows: First, officials of the federal Department of Agriculture, with the active assistance of farm organizations, determined how much production, under depression conditions, could be sold at a satisfactory price. A national quota was arrived at for every staple crop. This total was then prorated for each crop on a national basis. With the help of the 2500 farmer committees the state quotas were then broken down on a county basis and finally in terms of what each farm would produce. Any farmer would be paid a government subsidy for not raising more than agreed. The AAA also sought to encourage farm exports at a price that the world market could sustain: if that price were low, then the government made up the difference in a subsidy to the farmer. In other words, the AAA program was like national economic planning in reverse: the machinery was the same but the purpose was to limit rather than to increase production.

When the first AAA was voided on the ground that Congress had exceeded its power in controlling production and that the accompanying processing tax with earmarked revenues was discriminatory, the interim program provided for payments to farmers who adopted soil conservation measures such as planting tilled land with soil- and moisture-holding crops like clover instead of market crops (usually soil depleting) like corn, tobacco, or cotton. This procedure had the obvious advantage of conserving farm resources for future generations even if its primary objective was to reduce production. The second AAA program enacted in 1938 restored much of the voided program of 1933 but employed different methods. Thereafter—and indeed, ever since—the system has worked like this: At harvest time, if the market price is below the support price, a farmer who has planted within the acreage allotment set by the government can get a government loan on his crop at the support level. If the market price rises above the support price, he can sell his crop and repay the loan. But if the market price does not rise sufficiently by the time the loan comes due—usually a year—then he keeps the loan and the government takes the crop.

Unlike industry and labor, agricultural production largely depends on the uncertainties of weather, but this factor also was taken into account in the AAA program. If the weather was unusually good and crops were larger than forecast, the government took over and held the surpluses; but if on the other hand the weather was poor and results were less than expected, the farmer was insured against loss in the area of particular staples through the Federal Crop Insurance Corporation, the cost being defrayed partly through premiums and partly by absorbing deficits.

As already indicated, the farmer's economic well-being and his relative share of the national income rose steadily during the early life of the AAA programs from 1933 until 1939, when the national defense program created a large overseas market for agricultural produce. At that point the price-support program went into high gear but in order to stimulate production rather than curtail it, and price-support payments were made to farmers up to 90 percent of parity. By 1947 prosperity on the farms had reached such a peak (a nearly unprecedented parity index of 115) that many farmers were becoming nervous and began to worry about a crash. Their fears were justified to the extent that by 1949 the parity index was down to 100 and was due to go even lower except for a brief period during the Korean conflict. In addition, surpluses began to accumulate at an accelerating rate. Some new farm policy was needed and the so-called Brannan Plan (named after President Truman's Secretary of Agriculture) was offered and at once became a matter of controversy until its defeat in Congress in 1949.

The Brannan Plan

Under the Brannan Plan, price-support subsidies would be paid for major crops such as corn, wheat, tobacco, and the like, but not on perishable crops such as fresh milk, eggs, cheese, meat, and vegetables, which constitute something like 75 percent of all farm output. These perishable crops would move into a free market in the retail stores, and prices would rise and fall according to supply and demand. Since the supply is abundant, this means generally low prices. The government would then pay the farmer the difference between the average low market price and the parity price guaranteed by the Department of Agriculture.

The plan was held to benefit not only farmers, who would be assured of a profitable price to themselves, but also city dwellers to whom prices would be lower. Consequently, the political effect of the proposal was to enlist the support of labor. The Farm Bureau, on the other hand, and those who successfully opposed the measure, charged that it was "socialistic" in that it merely robbed Peter to pay Paul, that no one could tell how much it might cost the taxpayer, that it was motivated by political considerations, and that in spreading subsidies to new areas it would still further undermine the free price system. Both major political parties were apparently squarely behind price supports; the question raised by the Brannan Plan was whether city dwellers also could be helped under the price-support formula.

Flexible or Rigid Price Supports?

Instead of the Brannan Plan, in 1948 Congress passed legislation providing that rigid 90 percent of parity price supports be replaced by flexible supports ranging from 75 to 90 percent of parity depending on whether it was desired to encourage or to discourage the production of particular crops. The new system was not to go into effect, however, until 1950, and the date was twice postponed for the basic crops. Finally in 1955 flexible rates were applied to all commodities except tobacco, and the list included all the basic crops, dairy products, certain designated nonbasic crops such as oats and barley (at the discretion of the Secretary of Agriculture), and wool. But despite these efforts, surpluses continued to mount above needed reserves, and many ways were used to dispose of them, including giveaways both at home and abroad. The constant threat was impending spoilage, even in the case of a grain like wheat which cannot be held more than two years without serious deterioration to the point of total loss.

Again a new farm policy was needed. In the face of falling farm income and a Presidential election, Congress sought to restore the former rigid price-support plan. The President vetoed it and asked for something more constructive, and in May 1956 Congress responded with the so-called soil bank. Under the short-term acreage reserve part of this plan, farmers received government payments for voluntarily withdrawing cropland from production. In practice, however, they withdrew their poorest land, stepped up production on what remained, and the result was record crops that piled up even greater surpluses than before. Consequently, in 1958 this part of the soil bank was abandoned and the second part, the conservation reserve, was stressed. Under it, farmers may contract with the government to withdraw land, even whole farms, from production on a long-term basis (up to ten years) in return for a rental per acre plus financial assistance in carrying out certain conservation practices designed to improve the soil, grow trees, conserve water, and attract wildlife. During the 1956-1959 period, 245,000 farmers placed more than 22.5 million acres in the conservation reserve and more than half of the total acreage was whole farms. In 1960 the President asked that the program be extended for another three years and that the goal of the program be raised from 28 million to 60 million acres.

OTHER GOVERNMENT PROGRAMS FOR FARMERS

The administration of federal price supports is only part of the work of the U. S. Department of Agriculture, created in 1862 largely as a research agency but now also responsible for many action programs. Aside from price supports, much emphasis is on methods of production, but distribution and farm welfare are gaining in importance. Perhaps because it has grown very rapidly, especially since 1933, the department has been subject to internal reorganization more than any other department in Washington. By 1960 its responsibilities came under four main headings and looked something like this:

Federal-state Relations

Under federal-state relations come a double-pronged soil conservation program and the Forest Service, to be discussed in a later chapter. In addition, the Agricultural Research Service covers all kinds of research of interest to farmers: plants, crops, farm and land management, agricultural engineering, new uses for agricultural products, livestock of all kinds, human nutrition, and home economics. This branch of the USDA is also responsible for certain regulatory programs relative to plant pest control, plant quarantine, animal disease eradication, animal inspection and quarantine, and meat inspection.

The regulation of the meat industry is of special interest to the present study as a particular business-government relationship. The function was created under the Meat Inspection Act of 1906 and constitutes one of the department's largest regulatory duties. Many types of inspection ensure the wholesomeness of meat and meat products, and sanitation in accordance with advanced principles of meat hygiene is required in the slaughtering and processing of cattle, sheep, swine, goats, horses, and their derivative products. The act of 1906 differed from earlier legislation in that its provisions are mandatory and the inspection service covers small establishments not previously affected by federal government regulation.

In addition, jurisdiction over the packing industry was transferred from the Federal Trade Commission to the USDA by the Packers and Stockyards Act of 1921, which directs the Secretary of Agriculture to approve all schedules of rates and charges exacted by stockyards companies, commission men, and dealers, and if necessary, to prescribe reasonable rates. All yards must be registered with, and all operators on the market must be licensed by the USDA. Under this legislation also, packers found guilty of attempting to monopolize business, manipulate prices, or discriminate unjustly against any person are subject to severe penalties. The authority of the Secretary of Agriculture under this law gave rise to the celebrated case of *Morgan* v. *United States*,[4] decided in 1938, in which the elements and procedures of a fair administrative hearing are set forth.

In addition to conservation, research, and regulation, in this first grouping of agencies within the USDA there is also a Farmer Cooperative Service (discussed in a later chapter in this section) and the Federal Extension Service created in 1914 as liaison between the USDA and a host of other agencies at the state and county levels, among them the land-grant colleges, county agricultural agents, home-demonstration agents, and 4-H Club agents located in nearly every county in the United States outside the large cities.

[4] (304 U.S. 1. 1938).

Marketing and Foreign Agriculture

The Agricultural Marketing Service in the USDA is interested in every aspect of the distribution of farm products, coordinates all statistical work in the department, issues reports on market conditions and prices, regulates market practices to prevent fraud, and helps distribute surpluses accumulated under the price-support program. The Commodity Exchange Authority regulates the operations of commodity exchanges that determine by competitive bidding the prices for major foodstuffs such as grain. These agencies are similar to stock exchanges except that they deal in commodity futures instead of industrial stocks and bonds; following World War II they were severely criticized as contributing to the inflationary spiral. Thus the Commodity Exchange Authority was given a broad jurisdiction over such matters as price manipulation and corners on the market, the dissemination of false and misleading information, the regulation of manipulative and dishonest practices, and the provision of information to the public. It must also "insure the benefits of membership privileges to cooperative associations of producers," the farmer's co-ops.

The third agency under this heading is the Foreign Agricultural Service, primarily responsible for developing foreign markets for United States farm products. It gathers information in this area through agricultural attachés stationed in all principal countries, as well as through agricultural marketing specialists sent abroad to make special investigations.

Agricultural Stabilization

In this third group of agencies the Commodity Credit Corporation is chiefly responsible for the *financing and control* of the price-support program to farmers and the storage of crop surpluses. The Commodity Stabilization Service then *administers* the price-support program as well as the acreage allotment and farm-marketing quotas that accompany it. It is also responsible for several other commodity programs including foreign purchase, sugar, international wheat agreements, storage and shipping, and the like. Finally, the Federal Crop Insurance Corporation assists the farmer to insure certain basic crops against loss from causes beyond his control such as weather, insects, and disease, but does not, of course, protect his profit or cover avoidable losses.

Agricultural Credit

Under this heading comes the Farmers Home Administration, lineal descendant of the New Deal's Resettlement Administration by way of the Farm Security Administration. This agency makes loans to farmers who cannot get credit elsewhere at reasonable rates and terms, and such credit is supplemented where necessary by assistance to borrowers in planning and adopting sound farm and home practices that will help them to succeed. Loans are made to help in the purchase of a farm, for operating purposes to buy such items as seed, feed, and fertilizer, to buy livestock, to conserve the soil, and for certain emergency purposes. Special assistance is offered veterans on a preferential basis, and tenant farmers who would buy the land they cultivate. In 1958, some 111,900 farmers in the United States borrowed an aggregate of more than $330 million, the largest amount loaned in any one year by the Farmers Home Administration or its predecessor agencies.

The Rural Electrification Administration was created in the USDA under the New Deal to make loans to farm groups and to bring central-station electric service and telephone service to rural areas where it was lacking or inadequate. This agency is more fully discussed in a later chapter.

From this brief summary of the functions of the USDA it can readily be seen that the department runs the gamut of functions in the servicing of a particular interest group. It carries on research and planning over a wide area of the economy, provides an enormous amount of assistance in many forms including billions of dollars in cash subsidy payments; regulates many aspects of the growing and distribution of food; and operates several economic services itself, most of them having to do with insurance and credit.

THE FARM CREDIT ADMINISTRATION

Agricultural credit on a nation-wide basis, as will readily be appreciated, is an indispensable adjunct to crop production and distribution, and the purpose is well served by the Farm Credit Administration, now one of the principal banking institutions in the United States. Although it has been in the making since 1916 when the first authorization on which it relies was enacted by Congress, the development of the FCA has been more rapid and significant since the passage of the Farm Credit Act of 1933.

The Farm Credit Administration itself is merely a coordinating agency for several separate banking associations, most of them government corporations run by and for farmers. Originally an independent establishment, the FCA was attached to the Department of Agriculture in 1939, became a part of the Food Production Administration of the USDA in 1942, and a year later was once more made a separate agency in the USDA where it reported directly to the Secretary of Agriculture. In 1953, however, it was returned to its original status as an independent agency as part of a plan gradually to convert the FCA from a public to a private institution and to give the farmer-users more control over it. At the time of the reorganization, however, the government had $290 million invested in the FCA and sponsors of the change conceded that it might be some time before all federal funds were removed from the system.

The FCA supervises and coordinates a cooperative credit system for agriculture, providing long- and short-term loans to farmers and their cooperative marketing, purchasing, and business service organizations. A thirteen-member Federal Farm Credit Board was set up in 1953 as a part-time policy-making body. The board members are nominated by farmer organizations and appointed by the President with Senate approval; and they in turn select the Governor of the FCA who is also the chief executive officer of the board.

For administrative purposes the country is divided into twelve districts heading up to the central organization in Washington. In each district there is (1) a federal land bank owned by a number of local farm loan associations, which in turn are owned by the farmers who use them; (2) a federal intermediate credit bank owned by local production credit associations, most of which are now also owned by the farmers who use them; (3) a bank for cooperatives; and (4) a local coordinating farm credit board. All of these institutions were created by the federal government with federal money and have been gradually but in recent years rapidly transferred to the ownership of the farmers who use them. Ultimate control, however, remains with the FCA, which enjoys a reputation for conservatism and sound business methods.

This complex but coordinated arrangement offers the farmer a complete long- and short-range credit system for production and distribution purposes and encourages farmer's cooperatives. Interest rates are set as low as is consistent with prudent business practice but in recent years they have risen steadily as a result of the tight money policy of the administration in office; in late 1959 the median rate stood at about 6½ percent but individual rates went as high as 8½ percent in some areas.

Some idea of the magnitude of the FCA program is gained from the financial summary for the year ending December 31, 1958, during which farmers and their cooperative associations made use of approximately $3.4 billion in credit. Of this total, the production credit associations did a volume of business amounting to $2.2 billion. During the same year the banks for cooperatives loaned $559 million, and by January 1, 1959, some $2.1 billion was loaned out in land-bank mortgage credit.

FARM PROGRAMS IN PERSPECTIVE

Taken together, the programs offered by government for the benefit of the farmer cover a wide area, from credit through production and distribution. It is true that not all farmers benefit from these programs in the same degree, especially in the case of price-support programs, and that the income of farmers as a group is lower than that of the national average. The economic situation of the farmer improved somewhat under the AAA programs but what part is fairly attributable to those programs and what part resulted from such factors as the general business revival following the depression of the 1930s cannot be wholly determined.

Nevertheless, some results are clear: Agricultural processes are now planned as no other part of the economy is planned; the free-market system in agriculture has gone into a not-so-temporary eclipse; consumers have been forced to pay more for farm products than they would have if the sale of surplus production had been allowed to continue; and both farmers and government executives have learned a great deal about planning and administration. Indeed, government's role in agriculture has become so central that two Pennsylvania farmers were constrained to say —reluctantly, no doubt—that "if the government should step out of the picture today, American farming would collapse." [5]

From a theoretical standpoint it is easy to demolish crop restrictions and the control of basic agricultural prices which underlie government price-support programs. If it is assumed that market forces are to be chiefly relied on, then the deliberate limitation of farm production, the payment of production and restriction subsidies, government purchase and disposal of farm surpluses, administered rates of interest on farm loans, and price fixing generally are inconsistent with the natural equilibrium theory and tend to undermine it. Moreover, the thoroughness with which the agricultural part of the economy is organized and controlled is bound to affect other parts of the economy and to dispose them to similar controls if the system as a whole is to remain in balance.[6] The agricultural problem can be *studied* as though it were a separate matter, but it can never be *solved* that way.

Supplementary Reading

Hardin, Charles M., *The Politics of Agriculture* (Glencoe, Ill., 1952). The major programs that farm organizations have fostered.

Chase, Stuart, *Democracy under Pressure* (New York, 1945). The New Deal and farm pressures are dealt with in Chapter IX.

Gaus, John M., and L. O. Woolcott, *Public Administration and the Department of Agriculture* (Chicago, 1941). The best institutional study.

Nourse, E. G., *et al.*, *Three Years of the Agricultural Adjustment Administration* (Washington, D.C., Brookings Institution, 1937).

Sparks, E. S., *History and Theory of Agricultural Credit in the United States* (New York, 1932). Good for the early period.

Hoffman, A. C., *Large Scale Organization in the Food Industries*, Temporary National Economic Committee, Monograph No. 35 (Washington, D.C., 1940). Deals with the processing and distributive aspects.

[5] P. Alston Waring and Walter Magnes Teller, *Roots of the Earth* (New York, 1943).

[6] These economic arguments have been marshaled by Leverett S. Lyon, Myron W. Watkins, and Victor Abramson, *Government and Economic Life* (Washington, D.C., The Brookings Institution, 1939), Vol. II, pp. 938–947.

Lynch, David, *The Concentration of Economic Power* (New York, 1946). See sections on monopolistic developments in the milk industry.

Kile, O. M., *The Farm Bureau Movement* (New York, 1921). Early pressure-group activity.

Baker, Gladys, *The County Agent* (Chicago, 1939). How farmers operate at the grass roots.

McCune, Wesley, *The Farm Bloc* (New York, 1943). One of the best studies of farm pressure groups.

Ackerman, Joseph, and Marshall Harris (eds.), *Family Farm Policy* (Chicago, 1947). The social program in agriculture.

McConnell, Grant, *The Decline of Agrarian Democracy* (Berkeley, Calif., 1953). The political movements of farm organizations.

Commission on Organization of the Executive Branch of the Government (first Hoover Commission), *Department of Agriculture* (Washington, D.C., 1949).

———, *Task Force Report on Agriculture Activities* (Washington, D.C., 1949).

Baker, Gordon E., *Rural versus Urban Political Power* (New York, 1955). The nature and consequences of unbalanced legislative representation.

Fite, Gilbert C., *George N. Peek and the Fight for Farm Parity* (Norman, Okla., 1954). Biography of the man largely responsible for the adoption of parity.

12

PROTECTING THE CONSUMER INTEREST

---

*The consumer and the market place; debt, costs, and ad-
vertising; the cooperative movement: definition and kinds;
principles and practices; legislative landmarks; issues of
public policy: effect on monopoly, relation to profit-making,
political action, taxation; consumer protection: foods, drugs,
and other.*

The farmer's problems as a producer are matched only by his problems as a consumer. Although he may raise some of his own food, he cannot raise all of it, and in the past he was wont to do without what he
considered luxuries or he bought them sparingly and with due consideration. But today he is exposed to pressures to consume, brought to bear as
much on him as on city dwellers by the many refinements of the various
advertising media, and hence what were once luxuries on the farm are
now regarded as needs. To some extent, food and clothing may be less
emphasized by the farm family than by the city family, but where home
appliances and automobiles are concerned, there is little difference. In
addition, the farmer must buy great quantities of things the city dweller
does not need: expensively complicated machinery for barn, field, and
road use; a constant supply of livestock feed, wire fencing, baling twine,
fertilizer, and gasoline and oil for his equipment; plus medical care for
his livestock, maintenance for barns as well as dwelling, taxes on land
and in some cases on personal property as well, and insurance for everything.

Hence, more than most people the farmer has become consumer conscious, as evidenced by the fact, among others, that the cooperative movement in the United States, both producer and consumer, receives more
support from agriculture than from industry or labor. Moreover, the
farmer has done much, along with the urban housewife, to secure government protection in areas of concentration where most of the consumer
dollar is spent. Although this chapter continues to discuss the farmer, the
subject is broadened to include cooperatives and the consumer problem
generally.

THE CONSUMER AND THE MARKET PLACE

In the wake of depression and war, the past generation has seen strik-ing changes in the market place and in consumer spending habits and living standards.[1] Prices, of course, are higher by a good deal: the con-sumer price index rose from 59 in 1936 to 125.6 in early 1960—in other words, it more than doubled. Nevertheless, partly because salaries and wages are higher but also because more women are working today than formerly and more farmers are taking up off-farm employment, family income is up and the consumer has about 50 percent more real purchasing power than he had twenty-five years ago. As late as 1936 it used to be taken for granted that a working wife was typically found in the lower income brackets, but by 1956 it was estimated that in the bracket begin-ning at $5000 a year and up to $10,000, probably some 60 percent of American families achieved their income status through the salaries of more than one earner. Per capita personal income rose by 188 percent between 1929 and 1957 but the consumer price index rose by only 44 percent; and within this span, the increase between 1950 and 1957 was 36 percent for per capita income and only 14 percent for consumer prices.

So far as this increased income is spent on food (about 25 percent of disposable income, or $440 per capita, in 1957), much of it goes out through the supermarket. Twenty years ago such markets found that they could profitably reduce distribution costs from 30 percent of retail prices to 12 percent. Since then the supermarket has been glamorized, the markup is 20 percent instead of 12 percent, and although price bargains are featured in their advertising, it is the so-called impulsive buyer on whom the supermarket counts. Consequently, emphasis is on gadgets, light reading matter, toys, drugs, eye-catching displays, unusual adver-tising, and novelty packaging.

But even in the city, the increased purchasing power of the con-sumer goes out less for food than for durable goods, especially automo-biles and television, but also, because many housewives work, for home appliances and glamorized kitchens sold under the guise of efficiency. Furthermore, where formerly such items were sold with a "lifetime" guarantee, today many are offered with a concealed but nonetheless effective "built-in obsolescence," a condition deliberately planned to encourage the housewife to change the model of her kitchen and her household equipment as often as her husband changes the model of the family car.[2] In 1930, for example, there were 20 different electrical home

[1] For an interesting summary, see Consumers Union of the U.S., Inc., "Twenty Years in Review, 1936–1956," *Consumer Reports* (May 1956), pp. 252–256.

[2] "We have already established the point that the consumer will today accept the philosophy and the fact of planned obsolescence. He no longer expects, nor indeed cares for, a guarantee for 'lifetime' service. He will readily purchase an appliance, say, to serve him for no more than two or three or five years, to be replaced at that time by a newer, and presumably better model."—from *Electrical Manufacturing* (Apr. 1956), quoted in Consumers' Union of the U.S., Inc., *Consumer Reports* (July 1956), p. 358.

appliances available to the consumer and by 1959 there were more than 100, all of them available on credit and each model sure to be superseded by a "better" one the following year.

More families, including farm families, own their homes today than a generation ago (for nonfarm families, 60 percent as against 40 percent), and total mortgage debt is enormously higher, having gone up from only $15.4 billion worth for urban family dwellings in 1936 to $118.2 billion worth in 1958. Today, however, mortgages are amortized over a much longer period and hence annual payments as a percentage of real income have not greatly increased. New homes are larger than those built ten years ago—or at least they contain more rooms even if some of these are smaller—partly because families are larger. In the decade ending in 1958, for example, the number of families with one child or none fell by 11 percent, while the number with four children or more increased by 28 percent. This fact alone has had a revolutionary effect on the American economy and the American way of life. There has been such a concerted move to the suburbs—largely because of the children—that these are rapidly becoming cities in their own right. Another flow of population is from the farms, where the birth rate is high, to the cities, and some of these people also find their way to the suburbs.

Higher incomes, larger families, better homes, and the impact of mass advertising have encouraged more families to go into debt than formerly, with the result that short-term consumer debt—installment buying, small loans, and charge accounts—have increased more than sevenfold since 1936 to a total outstanding in 1958 of $45 billion. Although most installment buying is still for automobiles, today it also covers nearly every consumer item except food, but including even such nontangibles as airplane travel. The only parts of consumer demand that have not kept pace with the stepped-up consumer trend to buy more are clothing and the services of beauty shops. Here the controlling factors are informality of dress, synthetic fibers that make fewer clothes go further, automatic washers that make them wearable again sooner, and the home permanent (or no permanent at all) that has reduced the need for professional services.

Outside of the home itself, the largest single expense in most families is the car—or cars—made indispensable by increased suburban living but pushed onto the consumer also by high-pressure sales techniques, the expense of which, of course, is passed along to the consumer. The car itself is bigger (except for the compacts), brighter, faster, less durable, and more expensive to buy and to maintain than it used to be. In this case as in others, advertising is a major factor impinging on the consumer in sound, in print, and in pictures in every medium of communication. Total advertising expenditures amounted to less than $2 billion in 1936 but by 1958 they had gone beyond $10 billion, of which nearly a third was for space in the daily press. Advertising expenditures gained speed quickly after 1950, the increase in television alone amounting to

695 percent between that year and 1958, at which time it accounted for more than 13 percent of all expenditures for advertising. Since by then 83 out of every 100 American families had one television set or more, the impact of this medium can hardly be exaggerated. Fortunately, when it was found that television made possible an advertising technique called subliminal, in which the viewer is unaware of persuasive messages emanating from the screen, public reaction against it caused plans to use it apparently to be abandoned.

As a result of the trend to bigger and better advertising, promotional competition has tended to replace price competition, passing the heavy expense onto the consumer. In addition, the emphasis on advertised brand names is such that the package often seems more important than its contents, creating confusion for the consumer who has no real knowledge of the true quality of a particular product or brand. An unhappy result for both manufacturer and retailer is that discount houses are now able to sell advertised brand-name products at rates as much as 20 to 30 percent below the so-called fair-trade prices, and the consumer is not slow to take advantage of them.

In a market that depends on heavy advertising plus easy credit to stimulate sales, the big manufacturer has the advantage, and this in turn is a factor in the greatest merger movement in our national history. A few years ago there were 35 companies producing home laundry equipment but in 1956 there were only 17; in the automobile business, only three manufacturers accounted for 95 percent of the total sales in 1956; in 1935 there were 725 breweries but by 1955 there were only 254. Meanwhile, the small manufacturers' share of total sales declined from 19 percent in 1947 to 14 percent in 1953 despite the greatly increased volume of business.

"They were not calling the consumer king back in 1936 as they are today," remarked *Consumer Reports* in 1956, but it added, "If the consumer is indeed king today, he is a somewhat harassed monarch."[3] He has a higher income, but also more debt than he has ever had before; what were formerly luxuries are now regarded as needs; the pressures to make him spend an ever larger part of his income are increasing every day; and the market where he buys his goods has taken on the characteristics of a "carnival."

THE COOPERATIVE MOVEMENT

Cooperatives are one means of reducing the price spread between producer and consumer, which is perhaps why the cooperative movement in the United States is strongest among farmers. A cooperative is an association formed to provide an economic service owned by those who use it and whose incentive is not profits but savings. In this country

[3] Consumers' Union of the U.S., Inc., *op. cit.* (May 1956), pp. 252, 256.

cooperatives are usually organized under the nonprofit-making provisions of state laws, thus differing from ordinary business concerns normally chartered as profit-making enterprises.

The cooperative movement, now world-wide, was started in 1828 in Rochdale, England, by Robert Owen, an outstanding social theorist and reformer. The four principles of a Rochdale cooperative are:

1. Membership open to all without regard to creed, color, class, or conviction.

2. Democratic control: each member has only one vote no matter how many shares of stock he holds.

3. Members may purchase shares of stock in a co-op for a fair but limited return, usually around 4 percent a year.

4. All net earnings are distributed in proportion to patronage; that is, on the basis of use rather than stock ownership.

In addition, there are four basic practices that cooperatives are supposed to follow, and most of them do:

1. Business for cash only.

2. Sales at going market prices.

3. Constant expansion of the business.

4. Continuous education of members and the public in the principles and methods of cooperation.

A cooperative is usually run by a board elected at a membership meeting and by a paid manager. The pattern is similar to that of the usual business corporation except that the membership takes a more active role and important policy decisions are made at membership meetings instead of by the board.

The two principal types of cooperatives are producer and consumer. In a producer cooperative the production of a particular group of people is pooled and sold through common distribution outlets, an outstanding example being in the dairy industry. In a consumer cooperative, on the other hand, a group of consumers owns and uses a retail business to eliminate profits at that level for their own benefit, a type of association strongest in the retail grocery field. Most farmers now belong to one or several cooperative groups but the movement also appears to some degree —and sometimes a large one—in nearly every kind of business including insurance, banking, credit unions, health services, undertaking services, apartment and housing developments, restaurants, grocery stores, student stores in college communities, electrical and telephone services, appliances, and many more; even the Associated Press is a cooperative. Perhaps the most spectacular cooperative in the United States is Nationwide Insurance, a combination of auto, fire, and life insurance companies operating under the dynamic leadership of Murray Lincoln. The auto company is the second largest mutual auto insurer in the country and the fourth largest of all types of auto insurers (stock, mutual, reciprocal, etc.). The life insurance company had more than $391 million worth of insurance in force in 1956 and expected soon to pass the billion-dollar mark. By 1960 the four Nationwide companies had more than 3.2 million policies in force, assets of more than $300 million, and owned or had a substantial interest in more than a dozen enterprises in the fields of insurance, investments, finance, real estate, building, banking, broadcasting, and manufacturing. The cooperative movement is also strong in the field of credit, with 18,000 credit unions having a total of 10 million members in 1957. It is estimated that one quarter of all American families belong to one or more cooperatives which, in money terms, however, still do only 2 or 3 percent of all business in the nation.

In the United States, farmers' cooperatives started in the Middle West and are now in the ranks of big business in some instances, owning mills, insurance companies, refineries, dairies, supermarkets, filling stations, and many other businesses. Most important, perhaps, from the standpoint of the farmer who holds the short end of the bargaining stick when it comes to disposing of his crop to a single handler, cooperative marketing seems to be the only way to obtain enough volume for low-cost operation and at the same time to avoid exploitation by the handler.

Legislative Landmarks

Government support of farmers' cooperatives has a long history, with these legislative landmarks:

The *Capper-Volstead Act* of 1922 provided that "persons engaged in the production of agricultural products as farmers, planters, ranchmen, dairymen, nut or fruit growers, may act together in associations . . . in collectively processing, preparing for market, handling, and marketing in interstate and foreign commerce, such products of persons so engaged." Farmers' cooperatives may enter into any and all agreements necessary to effectuate their purposes and may have marketing agencies in common. *Thus the antitrust laws were made expressly inoperative,* except that the Secretary of Agriculture shall police this provision and if, after investigation, he finds evidence of unduly rising prices, "he shall issue and cause to be served upon the association an order reciting the facts found by him, directing such association to cease and desist from monopolization or restraint of trade." In case of noncompliance with such an order, the Secretary may apply for intervention by the courts. In 1952, for example, the California Fruit Growers Exchange (Sunkist), a citrus-marketing cooperative, was sued under the antitrust laws by an independent fruit-processing company for $2.4 million, and four years later a verdict of $500,000 was rendered against the cooperative.

A wide range of services to cooperatives was provided for in the *Cooperative Marketing Act* of 1926. A division now called the Farmer

Cooperative Service was set up in the Department of Agriculture to supply producers' cooperatives with assistance relating to organization, management, processing, warehousing, manufacturing, storage, the cooperative purchasing of farm supplies, credit financing, insurance, and the like. The service, with three program sections relating to marketing, purchasing, and management, also consults with officials of farmers' cooperatives and works with educational agencies to spread information on cooperative principles and practices. The staff members of the service are expert in analyzing the problems of farmers' cooperatives and the problems of business administration they encounter, the purpose being to help farmers improve their enterprises. Both the *Agricultural Adjustment Act* of 1933 and the *Soil Conservation and Domestic Allotment Act* of 1936 also encouraged cooperative enterprise.

Under the *Farm Credit Act* of 1933 a Central Bank for Cooperatives and twelve district banks were organized to provide a permanent source of credit on a sound business basis to farmers' cooperatives; in effect they also supply a sort of regulatory control. The Central Bank for Cooperatives serves the district banks by making direct loans and by participating in loans that exceed the local banks' respective lending limits. The clients of the local banks must consist of farmers acting together in marketing farm products, purchasing farm supplies, or furnishing farm business services. The three types of loan are commodity, operating capital, and facility loans. This particular banking activity of the federal government is larger than most people realize: in 1958, more than 2500 farmer cooperatives used the credit facilities of these banks to the extent of $559 million.

The Farm Credit Act also authorized the organization of production credit associations which now largely own the Federal Intermediate Credit Banks. In 1958, 496 of these production credit associations had a total membership of 492,000 farmers, and by early 1959 all but a few associations had retired all government capital and were wholly owned by their members. The *Federal Farm Loan Act* of 1916 established twelve federal land banks, a cooperative system the stock of which is owned by some 1100 local national farm loan associations, which in turn are owned by their borrower-members. In 1958, farmers and ranchers borrowed $429 million from the cooperative land-bank system, which was somewhat less than in previous years, and were using some $2.1 billion of land-bank mortgage credit by the end of the year.

The *Federal Credit Unions Act* of 1934 authorized a federal credit-union system which, after many moves, is now part of the Social Security Administration in the Department of Health, Education, and Welfare. A federal credit union is a cooperative association organized to promote thrift among its members and as a source of credit for savings and for productive purposes. The Bureau of Federal Credit Unions grants charters to local groups applying for them, assists in various ways, and examines and supervises operations. Each credit union is confined to a group of persons having a common bond of association, occupation, or residence within an established neighborhood, community, or rural district. From the members' savings, the fund provides installment loans of limited size at rates of interest not to exceed 1 percent a month on the unpaid balance. As already indicated, the growth of credit unions has been very rapid.

The *Rural Electrification Act* of 1936 gave statutory base to a program created in the previous year under emergency legislation and authorized loans to bring electric power to rural areas where it was lacking; in 1949 the authorization was extended to cover rural telephones as well. Loans to meet the entire cost of a project are made for a term up to thirty-five years at a flat 2-percent interest to facilitate construction in more thinly settled areas; preference is given to public bodies, cooperatives, and nonprofit or limited-dividend associations. In practice, farmers' cooperatives are the most numerous clients of the REA. By 1959, loans totaling more than $3.8 billion had been made to 1081 borrowers to construct nearly 1.5 million miles of line to serve more than 5.1 million farms and rural dwellings that had formerly been without central-station electric service. Fifty-four percent of all rural users were supplied by systems financed by the REA. The REA is also alert to developments in the atomic field. In 1956 it approved the first loan (to a rural cooperative power association in Minnesota) to build facilities for the distribution of power made by atomic energy.

Cooperative housing legislation is of New Deal vintage, having been included in the *National Housing Act* of 1934 which authorizes the issuance of mortgages on cooperative housing projects. Such mortgages are provided and insured for any nonprofit cooperative housing corporation in whose dwellings permanent occupancy is restricted to members, or for nonprofit corporations organized to build homes for members. The Federal Housing Administration also furnishes technical advice and assistance in organizing housing cooperatives and in the planning, development, construction, and operation of their housing projects.

THE COOPERATIVE MOVEMENT AND ISSUES OF PUBLIC POLICY

A number of major issues arising out of the cooperative movement may be briefly suggested: First, is there any chance, as is sometimes claimed, that cooperatives can help check the growth of monopolies? Second, is the cooperative principle consistent with, or opposed to, individual ownership and the profit system? Third, are cooperatives really nonpolitical or are they associated with socialism? And finally, is their competition with other forms of business fair, or, as is sometimes charged, do they enjoy unfair tax advantages?

Cooperatives and Monopoly

Judged by the fact that the merger movement among industrial corporations has been proceeding faster than the growth of cooperatives, it seems that in the United States, at least, cooperatives cannot offer much of a counterbalance to monopoly. But the situation might be different if enough people saw in them the same possibilities for trust-busting that the Swedes, among others, have seen. The policy of cooperatives, says one co-op official, has been a practical one: to take up the fight against local monopolies and international cartels wherever harmful effects become apparent. In the history of cooperation, he continues,

> there are numerous examples of cooperative organizations successfully combating powerful combinations of a monopolistic character, compelling them to readjust their prices to the new conditions of competition, and gaining valuable concessions from them in the public interest. Thus in Sweden, where the consumers' cooperative movement has successfully acted against powerful industries in the margarine, flour milling, rubber and electric bulb cartels, it has been proved that the results of the extensive price reductions on the general market which the movement has thereby enforced have been most beneficial to the national household.[4]

The method is to go into the monopolized field as a competitor and then reduce prices low enough and long enough so that the rest of the industry must follow suit or go out of business. In Sweden, it is claimed, the results of cooperation have been to increase purchasing power, production, and volume of employment, to speed the turnover of commodities, strengthen private enterprises in the monopoly ring, and still to retain normal opportunities for profit.

An advantage enjoyed by cooperatives in the United States when competing with monopolistic combinations is that Congress has expressly exempted cooperatives from the provisions of the antitrust laws. In addition, in 1922 the Capper-Volstead Act expressly permitted farmers to act together in producer associations; and finally, cooperatives were excepted from the operation of the Patman Price Discrimination Act aimed at the chain stores. To be sure, these exemptions, having been granted, could always be withdrawn and restrictions imposed, but the farm vote is still strong enough to make such a move unlikely. Restriction is a possibility that officials of cooperatives always take into account, as seen in a statement by Murray Lincoln to the effect that ". . . cooperative world trade will have to grow to a point where it can figure as a substantial alternative to private or government directed cartels. There are no obstacles to this except the limits of our own initiative and the possibility of government regulations being forced upon us."

[4] Thorsten Ohde, *The Place of Cooperation in World Economy* (pamphlet; London, International Cooperative Alliance, June 1947), p. 16.

Nevertheless, despite the record in other countries on the monopoly issue and the growing strength of cooperatives in this country, the movement has a long way to go before it poses a serious threat to chain food stores and to monopoly in general.

Cooperatives and Profits

Are cooperatives consistent with or antithetical to the profit-making system? The answer depends on whose views are being considered. If by the profit-making system is meant an aggregation of individually owned businesses, then cooperatives are antithetical; but under this definition all stock corporations owned by more than one person also must be ruled out of the free-enterprise system. Moreover, no cooperative is content merely to break even: it always tries to earn patronage refunds for its members, interest on capital stock, and even surplus funds for corporate expansion. According to this test, therefore, cooperatives are profit-making institutions. Where they differ from the ordinary business is in the distribution of earnings to all users of the enterprise on the basis of the amount of patronage rather than the number of shares of stock held by each individual. Sometimes also, cooperatives try to eliminate the middleman or a whole series of middlemen and hence here too go contrary to the usual way of doing business. But in final analysis, unless one takes a narrow view of what is involved in the profit-making system, cooperatives do not appear to be inconsistent with it.

On the other hand, in the propaganda of many cooperative leaders—but by no means all—much is made of the need to replace the present so-called private profit system with one cooperatively inspired and controlled. Some spokesmen of socialist persuasion favor complete abolition, while others of more moderate view would merely check what they consider excesses in the private profit system. Nevertheless, "The practice of charging current local prices and then returning profits to consumers on the basis of their purchases . . ." says one authority on the subject, "might be cited as an example of the way in which the ordinary profit-making mechanism can be used for the abolition of profit." [5] This, of course, is what the opponents of cooperation suspect because many consumers are satisfied with much less in the way of rebates than an individual owner of a grocery store, for example, expects to receive in profits.

The calculated motive of replacing the private profit system, therefore, seems to vary with the economic and political viewpoint of the cooperative group in question. In this country it seems safe to assume that most members of cooperatives are more interested in economic benefits than in economic reform, but this would not be true in all cases and certainly is not in some other nations. Murray Lincoln reports that in Sweden cooperators are investing the surplus funds of cooperatives in

[5] Fred Hall, "Cooperation. British Empire," *Encyclopedia of the Social Sciences,* Vol. IV, p. 364.

private businesses with the idea of gradually securing common stock control of them. He notes that this is "something new" in the cooperative movement and points out that one advantage is that "with a voice in management, you can place a few of your own technical people in the plant and let them pick up experience in operations which some day you may want to try for yourself." [6] Cooperators may be on the side of the angels but some of them, apparently, have read Machiavelli and have also learned a lesson or two from hard-boiled businessmen in private enterprise.

The urge to expand the cooperative movement makes the earning of investable surplus funds a strong motive in many cases, casting additional doubt on whether it is the profit system, literally interpreted, that is under attack or only the excessive earnings of the few. Thus in an article entitled "Nickels Built the Factories," [7] the headnote was, "The U. S. Cooperative Movement, which was started with worn nickels in 1921, has mushroomed into scores of industries from coast to coast. Now it talks in millions with the biggest of Big Business." The gist of the piece is that on a day in 1943 a group of farmer cooperators handed over a check for $5 million to purchase the Globe Refinery at McPherson, Kansas, and that this was just one of a series of deals in which the same group took over twelve refineries and went out to look for more. Ordinary dirt farmers, concluded the author, often make good businessmen and apparently can hold their own in fast company. In 1951 a grape-growers' cooperative in New York State, using the Swedish method of gradual acquisition, arranged to buy the Welch Grape Juice Company for $15 million, and took control gradually until the full price of $28.6 million was paid in 1956. Instances such as these seem to indicate that profit-making, taking only partly the form of patronage rebates, is in fact a powerful incentive in the cooperative movement.

Cooperatives and Political Action

A matter almost as important as the cooperatives' attitude toward the profit system is that of political neutrality versus political action. Theoretically, of course, there is no problem because political neutrality is a tenet of the Rochdale statement of principles, and in the matter of ideologies, cooperatives in the United States adhere to this principle. In some other countries, however, the demands of ideologies are more urgent and it would not be surprising if, in line with the experience of other nations, the matter were to become a live one here.

On this question, Murray Lincoln, president of Nationwide Insurance and former president of the Cooperative League of the U.S.A., has declared himself with characteristic frankness:

[6] Murray D. Lincoln, "Cooperatives, Government, and World Trade," *Free World* (Dec. 1946).

[7] Bertram Fowler, "Nickels Built the Factories," *Collier's* (an undated reprint).

Strictly speaking, a Socialist cooperative is as impossible as a Catholic bicycle or a Republican grapefruit. Where cooperatives have espoused political views or have limited membership to certain groups, they have withered. . . . In a country where a majority of the people is Socialist, the cooperatives obviously will reflect Socialist views to some extent, and where, as in the United States, the majority is conservative, coops will be conservative. Nevertheless, a coop is not a chameleon; by its very nature it makes certain demands on its environment. . . . This implies an environment friendly, in some degree, to democracy.[8]

Of the two main aspects of politics—elections and legislation—the cooperative movement in the United States has not hesitated to sponsor legislation advantageous to itself and to resist what is obnoxious—behaving, in other words, in a manner characteristic of all interest groups. The enactments favoring cooperatives that the farm lobbies have secured have been mentioned; in addition, two thirds of the state legislatures have granted special legal status to the cooperatives and other privileges and exemptions. Attempts by the federal government to tax the "profits" of cooperatives have so far failed. Indeed, so long as farmers have a stake in the cooperative movement, politics will be a part of it, at least so far as legislation is concerned.

The Tax Issue

The attitude of business toward cooperatives falls into three main categories. First, those who enjoy a substantial business with cooperatives, like the tire companies, are favorable. Second, those who know little or nothing about cooperatives and are not in competition with them (the largest group of the three) have no definite opinions. And finally, those who are in competition with cooperatives, especially in the retail grocery field, oppose the movement. In this last group the two main complaints are that cooperatives tend to undermine the profit economy by their policies and their chain-store methods, and that they constitute unfair competition because they are exempted from taxes on "profits" to which their competitors are liable. On this last point the critics are joined by the National Tax Equality Association and a variety of trade associations.

In recent years the tax issue has generated a good deal of heat and not a little misunderstanding as to the issues really involved. For example, an article in *The New York Times* in 1946 observed, "It is generally agreed that the federal income-tax law and regulations which permit tax exemptions of cooperatives engaged in a variety of activities should be amended so as to remove the present inequalities of taxation between cooperative corporations and ordinary corporations." [9] This statement misleadingly conveys the impression that producers' and consumers' cooperatives are tax free, and such is not the case. Under the federal income-

---

[8] Lincoln, *op. cit.*   [9] *The New York Times*, Dec. 15, 1946.

tax law the internal revenue code sets up certain standards for tax exemptions, and whenever a corporation—cooperative or otherwise—receives funds that must be returned to its patrons, it may claim exemption in those amounts. The objective of the cooperatives is not to make money but to save it, and taxwise the difference is crucial. On the other hand, cooperatives are liable for and actually do pay federal corporation income taxes on all money not currently distributed to members, such as reserves; federal corporation income taxes on interest paid on shares held by members (shareholders also pay income taxes on this interest); and all state and local taxes in the same manner as any other business enterprise. In 1954, for example, the Eastern States Farmers Exchange paid out more than $600,000 in real estate, property, social security, and motor car taxes, and in licenses and registrations.

The real issue here is the attempt of the opponents of the cooperatives to tax patronage dividends, which are sizable in view of the fact that the total goods cooperatively bought and sold by farmers alone in 1957 amounted to around $13.5 billion (a figure up by some $4 billion in four years), of which more than $10 billion was for produce marketed. Cooperative corporations do not pay taxes on rebates growing from this business, although those who receive them do, just as they pay on any other kind of personal income whether from a cooperative, capital stock, interest, or royalties.

There are many kinds of cooperatives, but the issue arising over patronage dividends and taxation is substantially the same everywhere. For example, one type of marketing cooperative deducts a commission charge and then distributes the proceeds of each sale to its members as quickly as possible, and at the end of the year what money remains after expenses is returned to patrons in the form of a patronage refund. Thus the Sun Maid Raisin Growers' Cooperative in California advanced its patron-growers more than $5 million in 1935-1936, received from them more than $11 million in the form of produce, and returned to them as patronage dividends the difference between these two sums, or nearly $6 million. Was this last sum properly classified as patronage refunds and thus never actually the property of the cooperative, or was it, as the opposition claimed, profit to the cooperative? The cooperative regards these funds as money that at all times belongs to its members in the form of income temporarily withheld.

The campaign to revise federal and state tax laws applicable to cooperatives began in 1943 when the National Tax Equality Association was organized in Chicago. Two years later its propaganda had attracted so much attention that the Small Business Committee of the House of Representatives investigated the whole question. Legislation aimed at withdrawing the income-tax exemption for cooperatives was introduced, but when the farm organizations took up the defense the proposal was dropped. In 1951, however, Congress did pass legislation stipulating that cooperatives must pay corporation taxes on amounts retained for surplus or reserve, but not on amounts refunded as patronage dividends. The present situation regarding corporate earnings, therefore, is parallel to that of ordinary private corporations.

CONSUMER PROTECTION AND THE GOVERNMENT

Governments respond to organized pressure, and of all the major groups in the economy, the consumer is least organized of any. Industry, labor, and agriculture are well represented by interest groups that speak for them to legislators and public administrators, but the consumer, who is everybody, has only a small voice. He does have certain indirect protections as when deceptive and misleading advertising and improper labeling are checked by the Federal Trade Commission in the interests of fair competition, or prices are regulated during wartime to retard inflation, or certain standards are identified and maintained by the National Bureau of Standards for the benefit of industry, or minimum purchasing power is encouraged by the economic policy written into the Employment Act of 1946. Meat-inspection and pure food and drug legislation have been passed chiefly for health reasons, but they also offer a measure of protection to the consumer as such.

Pure Food and Drug Control

Since meat inspection has already been dealt with in the preceding chapter, something may be said here about the regulation of foods and drugs, a function established in the federal government by the Food and Drugs Act of 1906 and several times enlarged since then. Fifty years later, says *Consumer Reports,* "impure, contaminated, adulterated, and dangerous foods and drugs are still being sold," but we nevertheless have good reason to celebrate the golden anniversary of this pioneering law.[10]

The Food and Drug Administration, originally located in the Department of Agriculture, is now part of the complex that makes up the Department of Health, Education, and Welfare. The legislation enforced by the FDA covers foods, drugs, cosmetics, tea, imported milk, filled milk, and caustic poisons, and its activities are directed mainly toward promoting the purity, standard potency, and truthful and informative labeling of the commodities covered. The FDA has seventeen regional offices and thirty-six inspection stations, manned with chemists and inspectors and equipped with testing laboratories. Nevertheless, with all possible good will, for many years enforcement by the FDA was hampered by a chronic lack of funds: only $5.5 million in 1955, for example, compared with more than $14 million for meat inspection and $18 million for the eradication

---

[10] Consumers' Union of the U.S., Inc., "Fifty Years of the Food and Drug Act," *Consumer Reports* (July 1956), p. 359.

of plant and animal diseases in the same year. At a time when Canada was spending nearly 10 cents per person to administer its food and drug act, in the United States the corresponding figure was only $3\frac{1}{2}$ cents. In the early 1950s the FDA was forced to reduce its personnel, put up with obsolete laboratory equipment, curtail field travel by inspectors, abandon a projected educational program to promote cooperation by industry, cut reports to consumers, and allow a backlog of legal actions to pile up.[11]

Meanwhile, technology has been revolutionizing many aspects of the food and drug industries and both have grown at a spectacular rate since World War II. Frozen-food production multiplied six times in the decade preceding 1957; more than a third of current grocery sales involve items that did not exist ten years ago; the average food store carried only about 1000 items in 1939 and today they stock close to 6000. The cosmetics industry grew in volume of business from around $412 million before the war to more than $1 billion in 1955. Approximately 55,000 retail drug outlets in 1955 had a total sales of more than $4.5 billion, including new drugs that were sometimes insufficiently tested, new tranquilizers, stimulators, and sleep inducers. Today there are nearly 80,000 establishments doing business in foods, drugs, and cosmetics that are subject to inspection and regulation by the FDA, whose problem is even further complicated by high-pressure advertising and deteriorating standards in some areas.

In addition, there are hazards due to the increased handling of foodstuffs, the fact that many of them must be transported long distances and temporarily stored until they reach the consumer, the fact that mass production has occurred in such fields as poultry raising, and new kinds of processed and frozen foods are constantly being devised, some of them already partially or wholly cooked. These technological developments have been accompanied by the widespread use of so-called food additives: flavorings, sweeteners, emulsifiers, preservatives, anti-caking agents, stabilizers, and many more used to make food more attractive, or more stable, or to gain a competitive advantage. Some of these additives are harmless, some are harmless in small quantities, some are dangerous in repeated doses over a period of time, and some are dangerous in any case. Under an amendment to the Food, Drug, and Cosmetic Act passed in 1938, drug manufacturers were required to prove the safety of their product before it could be marketed, but no such provision applied to the manufacturers of foods. By 1959 there were something like 700 specific chemicals regularly employed in the food industry and the safety of at least 150 of them was unknown.

Congress finally recognized the potential danger of the situation and made additives the subject of another amendment to the Food, Drug, and Cosmetic Act, to take effect in March 1960. Under this law, manufacturers must pretest proposed food additives and submit data to the FDA showing

[11] *Ibid.*, p. 364.

that the chemicals will be safe in the amounts and under the conditions of their intended use; otherwise such products will not be permitted on the market. The law also empowers the FDA to approve the use in foods of safe amounts of some substances that are toxic in larger doses. In 1959 Congress moved to place the use of artificial colors in foods and drugs under this same type of control by the FDA.

The passage of the food-additive amendment gave new life to the FDA because in taking this notice of the agency Congress was moved to become more generous as well. Appropriations were increased up to $13.8 million in 1959; consequently the FDA's staff also grew, from 250 inspectors and scientists only a few years before to 1533.

As to procedure, FDA tests samples of products, some of which are sent to it by suspicious buyers, but more often acquired by the agency's own inspectors from plants, warehouses, shipments in transit, or purchased over the counter in retail stores. In 1959, for example, more than 40,000 samples were picked up for evaluation. When a questionable item is found, there are three possible corrective courses: (1) the FDA may issue a public warning (as in the case of tainted cranberries in 1959) and ask the producers and sellers of the product to halt sales until safety can be assured; (2) under a federal court order, the FDA may seize an entire stock of a questionable product and prevent its movement in interstate commerce; and (3) a manufacturer or shipper who refuses to cooperate in these proceedings may be prosecuted in the federal courts. Under the new law, a manufacturer adversely affected by an order relative to the use of a food additive may file objections to the order and ask for a public hearing, after which the FDA will again issue an order based on a fair evaluation of the whole record. In the event of further controversy, the second order is subject to judicial review in the U. S. Circuit Court of Appeals. These rules are in line with the provisions of the Administrative Procedure Act of 1946 governing hearings and decision-making procedures before the regulatory agencies of the federal government.

In 1959, the Senate subcommittee on antitrust and monopoly, under the chairmanship of Senator Estes Kefauver, extended its study of administered prices to include the drug industry. In the hearings, the industry was accused of maintaining unreasonably high prices, of monopolistic practices with regard to pricing and marketing, of excessively high-pressure advertising, and of profiteering at the expense of the consumer. In addition, the Food and Drug Administration was said to be unable to supervise the drug industry effectively—partly because of lack of funds and personnel—and to have allowed too much fraternization between officials of the FDA and representatives of the drug companies.

Among the remedies proposed during these hearings, the most drastic was to place the drug industry under public regulation as a public utility, with reference to performance as well as to prices. Instead, Senator Kefauver introduced a bill that he hoped would help to correct special aspects of the situation, especially with regard to pricing. Meanwhile, the

Secretary of the Department of Health, Education, and Welfare made an investigation of his own and drafted a bill that went further than the Kefauver measure. It would provide the FDA with a larger budget; authorize inspectors to determine in the factory if a product is faulty and if so, to stop its production before it gets on the market; authorize the FDA to certify the purity of all antibiotics; make it possible to exercise some control on promotional material put out by the drug companies; require the drug companies to keep records of adverse reactions to new drugs; and brand as adulterated any drugs not prepared or packed under adequate controls.

With the resources at its command the Food and Drug Administration nevertheless does a conscientious job. Shorthanded and pressed for funds as it is, a few years ago, for example, it seized 32 untested, mislabeled, low-potency, or decomposed drugs, 2544 tons of filthy or decomposed food, and some 150 tons of food tainted with poisonous or harmful materials. The degree of its conscientiousness is evidenced by the fact that one of its inspectors penetrated even to a small stone-burr grist mill tucked in among the folds of the Green Mountains of Vermont which occasionally shipped a few pounds of flour in interstate commerce as far away as New Hampshire. The FDA inspector from the Boston office made his visit and only a week later was able to report that the samples of floor sweepings and webbing collected at the mill had been examined "to ascertain whether they consisted in whole or in part of any filthy, putrid, or decomposed substances or were otherwise unfit for food." The analysis showed "no insect filth detected" and only one "live confused flour beetle larva found" in a quart of floor sweepings taken from the area around the grindstone, and that "webbing collected from window and walls of grinding room contained one live spider and fly parts enmeshed" in it.

At the other end of the magnitude scale, by 1959 the FDA was investigating stilbesterol as a fattening agent in poultry and beef, pesticides, penicillin used against mastitis and subsequently appearing in milk, strontium 90 in milk, and radiation in river water (from industrial wastes) and in vegetables.

Consumer Counsels in the Government

A brief look at the federal government's attempts, largely under the leadership of the New Deal, to establish agencies directly concerned with consumer interests shows the degree to which such activities are handicapped by lack of organization on the part of the consumer himself, lack of interest and attention within the government, and an apparent lack of coherent policy. The result is largely a study in futility. Among the federal agencies that have been created to look after consumer interests, shunted around, and finally abandoned, the following may be mentioned:

In the early days of the New Deal, consumer units and advisory bodies were set up in several of the new emergency agencies, later consolidated in a Consumers' Division of the National Recovery Administration, and still later transferred to the Department of Labor when the NRA was declared unconstitutional. Three years after that the files, records, and property of the Consumers' Division were again transferred, this time to the Division of Consumers' Counsel of the Agricultural Adjustment Administration in the Department of Agriculture, where the work went forward as a work-relief project known as the Consumer Standards Project. In 1941 some functions of the counsel were abandoned and the remainder again transferred, this time to the Agricultural Marketing Administration, which subsequently became the War Food Administration. In 1945 this agency was terminated and its remaining functions transferred to the Secretary of Agriculture; somewhere along the way the work of the Division of Consumers' Counsel simply vanished.

Meanwhile, in 1935 a Consumers' Counsel had been created in the National Bituminous Coal Commission and charged with representing consumer interests in any proceeding before the commission. But in 1939 the counsel was abolished and its functions transferred to the Office of the Solicitor in the Department of the Interior, to be known thereafter as the Consumers' Counsel Division. A second transfer in 1941 placed the functions of the division in the Office of the Bituminous Coal Consumers' Counsel, and two years after that they were abandoned. Whatever the total of these programs adds up to, it is a small one for the consumer.

In other countries, notably Great Britain, consumers have enjoyed much greater representation in government and in industry than they have in the United States, and it is possible that we might learn something from their experience. In Great Britain, for example, the main impetus to consumer representation came after 1945 when the Labor party undertook its program of socialization. The cooperative movement being strong in that country and the Labor party being sympathetic to it, cooperatives were given representation on the party's executive committee. The government also undertook to give consumers a voice in policy and management by setting up consumers' councils in the nationalized industries. The necessary provisions were written into the legislation and stipulated not only that there should be national consumer boards but also in some cases regional and local boards as well, paralleling the structure of the industry in question. Precedents had already been set in the case of broadcasting, harbor administration, electricity development, road transport, and even forestry. When basic industries such as coal, steel, railroads, and civil aviation were nationalized and hence monopolized, the need to protect consumer interests increased proportionately.

So far, experience indicates that able people will often serve on these consumer councils; that managements may be kept alert and made to defend and justify such actions as rate increases; and that consumers themselves and their legislative and local governmental representatives become much more sensitive to considerations of efficiency and price than would otherwise be the case. On the other hand, there is an adverse side to the picture: consumer councils, if not carefully chosen, may harass and unjustifiably interfere with management, thus becoming a good deal of a nuisance; or, if the consumer representatives are too compliant, they may become a cat's paw for management and the more able consumer members will come to feel that their efforts are not worth the small accomplishment.

Although it is perhaps too early for a final verdict, experience in Great Britain, in the Scandinavian countries, and in others where there is a well-developed sense of democratic control and civic responsibility, seems to warrant the prediction that consumer representation in government will expand and will become increasingly influential, a trend that may still develop in the United States.

Supplementary Reading

University of Minnesota, Center for Continuation Study, *Consumer Problems* (pamphlet; Univ. of Minn., 1956). A good comprehensive survey.

Consumers' Union of the U.S., Inc., *Consumer Reports* (Mount Vernon, N.Y., monthly).

American Academy of Political and Social Science, *The Annals,* "The Ultimate Consumer" (May 1934); "Consumer Cooperation" (May 1937); "Consumer Credit" (May 1938); "Marketing in Our American Economy" (May 1940).

Kyrk, Hazel, *The Family in the American Economy* (Chicago, Ill., 1953). A picture of family buying, spending, and saving, illustrated in their relationship to national wealth, the standard of living, social security, and consumer production.

Hoyt, Elizabeth E., Margaret G. Reid, Joseph M. McConnell, and Janet M. Hooks, *American Income and Its Use* (New York, 1954). A study of income distribution, standards and costs of living, etc., sponsored by the Federal Council of Churches.

Fowler, Bertram B., *The Cooperative Challenge* (Boston, 1947). Showing that cooperatives are big business.

Bowen, E. R., *A Cooperative Economic Democracy* (New York, 1936).

————, *The Cooperative Road to Abundance: The Alternative to Monopolism and Communism* (New York, 1953). A comprehensive social theory.

Ohde, Thorsten, *The Place of Cooperation in World Economy* (pamphlet; London, International Cooperative Alliance, June 1947). One of the best publications on the international aspects.

Stewart, Maxwell S., *Cooperatives in the United States—A Balance Sheet,* Public Affairs Pamphlet No. 32 (New York, 1944). A good brief treatment.

Greer, Paul, *Cooperatives: The British Achievement* (New York, 1955). Concrete; deals also with developments in Asia.

————, *Credit Unions, The People's Banks,* Public Affairs Pamphlet No. 50, (New York, 1942). An important phase of the cooperative movement.

Voorhis, Jerry, *The Cooperatives Look Ahead,* Public Affairs Pamphlet No. 32, (New York, 1952). Perhaps the best short discussion.

Turner, H. H., *Case Studies of Consumers' Cooperatives* (New York, 1941). An offset to too much theory.

Cole, G. D. H., *A Century of Cooperation* (London, 1945). A broad survey by a distinguished British social scientist.

Casselman, P. H., *The Cooperative Movement and Some of Its Problems* (New York, 1952). A realistic treatment.

Cooperative League of the U.S.A., *Yearbook,* and other publications, by the foremost cooperative agency in the United States.

United Nations, *Rural Progress through Cooperatives* (New York, 1954). The place of cooperative associations in agricultural development on a world basis.

Colombain, Maurice, *Co-operatives and Fundamental Education* (Paris, UNESCO, 1950). Also a world-wide survey.

Robson, William A. (ed.), *Problems of Nationalized Industry* (New York, 1952). Chapter 7, "The Consumer's Interest."

Campbell, P., *Consumer Representation in the New Deal* (New York, 1940). The official channels.

13

THE CONSERVATION OF
NATURAL RESOURCES

Importance and issues; resources: land, water, forests, oil and natural gas, minerals; growth of conservation movement; legislative landmarks; federal conservation agencies; regional conservation; TVA; other possible regional developments.

The conservation of natural resources is the wise use and management of natural assets to prevent depletion, to increase yield where possible, and to maintain a balance in nature. As such, conservation goes beyond the negative idea of saving to include the positive idea of improvement, as in the case of timber, for example, and planned use, as in the case of nonrenewable minerals.

The great dust storms of the 1930s brought conservation to the forefront of public attention as farmers from Arkansas and Oklahoma abandoned their impoverished land and headed west to become migrant workers in a depression market that needed only a few of them only part of the time. The people (also a natural resource) endured great hardships and the dust was spectacular: New Yorkers saw in the air concrete evidence of the Dust Bowl 2000 miles to the west; a Nebraska farmer sitting on his doorstep intently watching a dust storm, when asked what he was looking at, replied, "I'm counting the Kansas farms as they go by." Nor does conservation apply only to land. During World War II some of the nation's basic mineral resources, like petroleum, natural gas, copper, and zinc were found to be running low, and these are irreplaceable. As deep geologic waters are increasingly tapped and depleted in the arid Western states, that resource also is becoming short and cannot be replaced.

RESOURCES

Malthus predicted in 1798 that population growth would some day create an unendurable pressure on the world's resources. By 1957 world population was estimated at 2.7 billion and increasing at the rate of 1.5

percent, or 40 million a year [1]; two years later the United Nations put world population at 2.8 billion and predicted a total of 6.2 billion by the year 2000. In the United States, population reached 180 million in 1960. And yet we have been mining our fields, forest, and water resources at a suicidal rate. Indeed, the pinch has been felt for some time and those who realize its import are deeply concerned. The problem is no longer vaguely in the future. Already by 1952 the President's Materials Policy Committee reported that we had outgrown our raw-materials supply; that since World War I we had consumed more of most metals and mineral fuels than had been consumed by all nations in all of human history; that since 1940 we had had a deficit of raw materials; and that of seventy-four strategic and critical materials listed by the Munitions Board, we import our whole supply of more than forty and part of all the rest.[2] With 7 percent of the world population and 8 percent of the land area, we were using almost half of the free world's raw materials.

Other issues in the area of conservation are these: Should grazing on public lands be unlimited or regulated to prevent depletion? Should private operators be allowed to skin off timber resources, or should a program of planned use be enforced everywhere? To what extent should the oil and natural-gas industries be regulated so as to conserve these resources? Should soil conservation be encouraged on a regional basis or restricted on a narrow state basis? Are regional programs emphasizing many kinds of conservation, such as TVA, "creeping socialism" or an efficient and legitimate means of furthering the national economy?

Such a listing is only a sampling. To it might be added the development of irrigation and land-use programs in the arid West, the conversion of sea water into fresh water for industrial and domestic use, the quest in private and governmental laboratories for effective substitutes for basic raw materials, the development of atomic energy for industrial uses, the improvement of harbors and inland waterways, the control of pollution in rivers and in the air, the development of recreation areas, the preservation of the natural beauties of the nation, the protection of wildlife, and many more.

The Land Resource

The story of what has happened to our land heritage is told in a few simple figures. There are 1.9 billion acres of land surface in the United States, approximately 1.1 billion of which is in farms. But less than half of this, or 409 million acres, is available for crops; of this, as of 1950, only 345 million acres or about 84 percent of all farm acreage was profitable land; yet even so, less than 100 million acres are completely safe from soil erosion.

[1] Warren H. Leonard, "World Population in Relation to Potential Food Supply," *The Scientific Monthly* (Sept. 1957), pp. 113–124.
[2] Reported in *The New Republic* (July 7, 1952), p. 10.

The demand for food during World War I was such that "the plow that broke the plains" did its work and the food was produced, but at the expense of the land. After the war the market for farm products declined; the plains, normally dry, were difficult to recover with grass; the land lay unused; and by the mid-1930s the winds were whipping up the dust in what was to become known as the Dust Bowl, an area taking in parts of five states from Wyoming to Texas. Conservation practices under federal sponsorship, including the planting of trees in the so-called Shelter Belt, helped hold the land in place and were beginning to pay dividends when the food needs of World War II undid much of the work; again there was overstocking, overgrazing, and overplowing, and by February 1954 a combination of drought and high winds produced the worst dust storm in twenty years from Nebraska to the Mexican border. For most of a week visibility was cut to zero, schools closed, traffic slowed, dust piled up in the streets and sifted through dwellings. Traces of dust were found as far east as Pennsylvania and Georgia. The winter-wheat crop was threatened, hay and feed stacked for cattle were ruined, and the farmers of the area appealed to Washington for help. The winds continued and a month later, of the 25 million acres in the southern Great Plains, some 11 million were blowing in some degree, another 5 million insufficiently covered were in danger of blowing, and the total damage had surpassed the peak of damage of the mid-1930s. By now the wheat crop was definitely lost as the wind blew the soil from around the seedlings and whipped them out of the ground; on land that had been overgrazed, the sparse grasses also were being uprooted; even properly treated land was being smothered by the top soil from neighboring fields. The only remedy was to go deep into the subsoil with list or chisel plows capable of pulling damp clods up onto the surface; but the relief was only temporary because the clods dried out and became dust in their turn, taking what little moisture the land still had along with it. Nevertheless, as an emergency measure the deep plowing was pushed with the help of some $8 million federal funds to be paid out under the heading of conservation practices. But the program was hampered by the size of the average farm in that area (1200 acres) and the fact that many were owned by absentee landlords too busy elsewhere to give their attention to the soil.[3] By April, 16 million acres had been damaged, the worst areas being in Colorado, Kansas, the Oklahoma Panhandle, Texas, and New Mexico.

Under prolonged drought, first the crops go, then the soil is blown away, then the livestock must be sold, and finally the farmer himself must leave to make his living elsewhere. In 1956, judged by the growth rings on trees, the drought was the worst in 700 years. It covered most of seven states and parts of eight more, in some areas it had lasted for ten years, oak trees estimated to be 300 to 400 years old died from lack of moisture, even the hardy mesquite died by the thousands of acres, and

[3] Seth King in *The New York Times,* Apr. 9, 1954.

rivers and springs failed for the first time in recorded history. By the end of the year nearly 3 million acres of land had been blown out and 30 million more were ripe for blowing. Pressure was put on the federal government to turn back to private ownership some 5.5 million acres of blown-out land acquired during the great Dust Bowl disaster of the 1930s, but the fear was that this land also, on which a grass cover had gradually been restored, would be damaged by improper human management. Congress studied relief measures and finally provided that under the soil-bank program farmers could be paid a rental fee for keeping livestock from grazing on certain land. In addition, a Great Plains conservation program administered by the Soil Conservation Service was to meet part of the cost of restoring blown out land. It took a year to develop this program. Operations on the farms started in 1958.

By early 1957 the winter winds were less than normal, there was some precipitation, and finally the rains came. But it takes a lot of rain to repair drought damage, especially when it is combined with man-made damage from overcultivation and overgrazing. Two years later the dust was up again, to the point of blurring the skyline along the lakefront of Chicago. There was drought again on the plains that summer and by early 1960 severe dust storms were again anticipated.

The Water Resource

But overplowing, overgrazing, drought, and winds are not the only wreckers of the land. There are also the floods, which, however, are related to the central problem because when the land is properly used it retains rainfall and floods do not ordinarily occur. Along the Mississippi, for example, sediment at floodtime increases to *4.5 billion tons a day*, equal to a six-inch layer of top soil from forty-six 100-acre farms. Although water resources are abundant and generally replenishable in nonarid areas, there remains the problem of holding the water in the ground or impounding it for future use. Further, there are sources of water now in use, notably in southern California, that cannot be replenished because they are geologic waters held in so-called aquilifers— underground deposits of rain water which, through the course of ages, has seeped through the soil and porous stone until it is trapped by an impervious layer of rock. Once tapped, these wells can seldom be replenished and must be abandoned.

The problem of water resources is aggravated by the fact that the need for them is so much greater than formerly and the rate of need is increasing all the time. By 1958, withdrawals of water amounted to 240 billion gallons a day, of which roughly 10 percent was for home use and the rest was divided more or less equally between farms and factories. Sixty years ago the average household use was only 90 gallons of water a day, but with modern bathrooms, dishwashers, washing machines, air conditioners, and automatic lawn sprinklers—to say nothing of the family car to wash—water consumption in the home has risen to 148 gallons a day and in some hot dry areas it may run as high as 600 gallons a day. Outside of the home, the reason for increased consumption in the nation as a whole is partly that the farmer uses more, especially for irrigation purposes, but even more that industry also is using much greater quantities of water: 110 billion gallons a day which is eleven times as much as was used in 1900 and almost twice as much as in 1952.[4] Not only is water used in manufacturing processes (it takes five gallons of water to produce one gallon of milk and 65,000 gallons of water to produce a ton of steel) but water is also increasingly required for the production of hydroelectric power as the supply of other fuels declines. On top of that, enormous quantities of water are needed to operate atomic installations. And the problem of the industrial pollution of our streams and rivers, of course, follows in the wake of such uses to the point where what was once a river is now merely a drain.

In addition to industrial pollution, there is also sewage pollution. According to one finding, the sewage of 40 million persons in the United States "is discharged without any treatment into inland streams, lakes, or tidal waters."[5] In 1952 the Missouri River was called the longest open sewer in the nation, although at the same time it was also the source of water supply for many communities along its banks.[6]

Great as is our use of water today, however, it is estimated that by 1975, 227 million Americans will need at least 50 percent more water than is now available. It was partly for this reason that in 1952 Congress passed the Saline Water Act and provided for an Office of Saline Water in the Department of the Interior to direct research, both public and private, in this area. The work has been going forward and by 1960 several pilot plants were in operation using different methods of purifying salt water on a trial basis. One difficulty is that there are twenty-five different federal agencies each dealing with some aspect of the water problem: flood control, reclamation, navigation, pollution, and the like, but no agency is concerned with water policy as a whole.

The Forest Resource

Of the nearly 2 billion acres of land surface in the United States, forests once covered about one half; today they cover less than a third. Some 75 percent of our present forest land is classified as commercial in that it is capable of growing, or is actually growing, marketable timber, and what remains is useful for watershed, range, or other purposes. Unfortunately not all commercial forest land is producing as it should

[4] Robert and Leona Rienow, "The Day the Taps Run Dry," *Harper's Magazine* (Oct. 1958), pp. 74–78.
[5] Bernard Frank and Anthony Netboy, *Water, Land, and People* (New York, 1950), p. 150.
[6] Glenn J. Hopkins, officer of the U. S. Public Health Service in charge of the Missouri Drainage Basin, reported in *The New York Times,* Dec. 3, 1952.

because of having been denuded or poorly stocked with seedlings. World War II and the housing boom that followed created an enormous demand for saw timber and the supply by 1949 was short by some 3 billion board feet a year. Cooperation between Forest Service and the lumber industry improved the situation until by 1955 regrowth in forest areas was in balance with its use for the first time in 60 years; but the demand for timber and pulp is constantly increasing.

Oil and Natural Gas

America's once-rich petroleum resources are in a condition of diminishing production from diminishing reserves that can never be replenished. Competitive drilling has caused severe losses through premature encroachment of salt water and failure fully to capture gases for commercial use. Supplies are running out despite deeper drilling, the exploitation of offshore sources, and continuing prospecting and research. Meanwhile the demand for oil and natural gas has outstripped coal as a source of energy, especially on the railroads and for home heating. By 1955, half the oil and gas ever used in the United States was consumed in the preceding fifteen years. Production in this country has not met demand since 1947. Ten years later we were consuming 3 billion barrels of oil a year, 15 percent of which was imported, and the demand was increasing not only here but even faster in other nations. The estimated use of oil and natural gas in the United States by 1975 will be twice what it was in 1950.[7]

Other Mineral Wealth

Like the topsoil, mineral deposits are nonreplaceable and, like the land in this country, they are also in a generally unpromising condition. Half of all the coal ever used in the United States has been used since 1920. Fortunately, however, our reserves of coal are large; though the demand has dropped except in a few industries like steel, new processes for extracting energy from this mineral are being found and increasingly put to use. This may help supplement dwindling reserves of petroleum and natural gas.

In the case of other minerals and metals the picture is less favorable. The United States has less than 10 percent of its need for highgrade manganese, has less than 1 percent of the world supply of nickel but consumes about 50 percent; produces almost no chromium but uses about a third of the world supply; has exhausted its high-grade bauxite from which aluminum is derived (although low-grade ores are still available); is increasingly dependent on foreign imports for copper, lead, and zinc; uses about half of the world supply of tin, all of which is imported; and

---

[7] Charles A. Scarlott, "Changing Energy Scene," *The Scientific Monthly* (May 1957), pp. 221–228.

produces sulphur at increasing cost because of the low-grade ore. Only with regard to tungsten, molybdenum, vanadium, boron, magnesium, and titanium are we still in a favorable position so far as sources of supply are concerned.[8]

GROWTH OF THE CONSERVATION MOVEMENT

With a public domain amounting to 1.5 billion acres, the United States government was once the greatest landowner in the world. During the course of our national history, however, the larger part of this vast estate has either been sold or given away until by 1958 the public domain amounted to only 410 million acres, of which 24 million acres was in national parks and another 180 million acres in national forests. Until the turn of the century public policy concentrated on getting the public lands into the hands of private owners as quickly as possible, and to expedite this objective federal surveys were organized to make known the potentialities of the public domain. In retrospect, it now seems that many of the wastes of the past and the conservation problems of the present stem back to the speed and recklessness with which the public domain was disposed of.

It is no coincidence, therefore, that the beginning of the conservation movement in the United States appeared with the closing of the frontier. In general, from a commercial standpoint, the public domain today outside of forest reserves is marginal, producing comparatively small amounts of the raw materials of industry. The principal tangible accomplishment of the conservation movement of the past half century has been the wise husbandry of that small fraction of land resources still under federal control and its protection against unwise incursions by private interests.

Such threats to the public domain continue, of course, a major one in recent years being an attempt by some 17,000 ranchers holding grazing permits in the national forests to secure the right to deed such permits to their heirs or to sell them at will. At stake were some 200 million acres of lands in fourteen states, but only 3½ percent of all Western stockmen would have benefited from the proposed legislation. The late Bernard De Voto carried on a running campaign with the stockmen's association, and the stockmen were defeated.[9]

Although the public domain has been largely protected by the efforts of conservationists, some of their objectives have not been successfully attained because the movement came too late to do much good. Thus

---

[8] J. Frederic Dewhurst and Associates, *America's Needs and Resources, A New Survey* (New York, Twentieth Century Fund, 1955), pp. 767–772.

[9] Bernard De Voto, "Sacred Cows and Public Lands," *Harper's Magazine* (July 1948), p. 44; and "The Easy Chair," *ibid.*, for the issues of June 1947, p. 544; July 1948, p. 108; March 1951, p. 48; October 1952, p. 65; and February 1953, p. 53.

the reckless waste of soil, timber, water, and mineral resources was already an accomplished fact before Gifford Pinchot, Theodore Roosevelt, and other progressive leaders had developed the idea of conservation to the point where it was capable of making a real impact.

The principal legislative and other landmarks in this field of conservation are:

1871—Office of Commissioner of Fish and Fisheries created

1885—Bureau of Biological Survey created

1888—An irrigation division set up in the U. S. Geological Survey, later became the Bureau of Reclamation

1891—The first federal forest preserve established

1902—Reclamation Act created the Bureau of Reclamation

1906—The Forest Service created

1906—Alaskan fisheries protected

1910—Bureau of Mines created

1911—The Weeks Act created additional forest preserves

1916—National Park Service created

1920—The Mineral Leasing Act placed certain minerals under the jurisdiction of the Department of the Interior

1920—Hydroelectric developments on navigable streams vested in the Federal Power Commission

1929—Certain oil and mineral deposits reserved for defense

1933—Tennessee Valley Authority created

1933—Civilian Conservation Corps established

1934—Passage of the Taylor Grazing Act to regulate grazing, retard soil erosion, and control floods

1935—Legislation to conserve petroleum and coal

1935—Soil Conservation Service created

1936—A comprehensive flood-control act passed

1938—Natural Gas Act passed

1938—First Flood Control Act passed

1940—Fish and Wildlife Service created by merger of the Bureau of Fisheries and the Biological Survey

1944—Second Flood Control Act passed

1946—Third Flood Control Act passed

1946—Bureau of Land Management created by merger of the General Land Office and the Bureau of Grazing

1946—Fish and Wildlife Coordination Act passed, amended in 1958 to give fish and wild life agencies a voice in future water-resource developments

1950—Defense Production Act authorized conservation of strategic metals, minerals, and solid fuels

1952—Saline Water Act passed to encourage research in this area

1954—Watershed Protection and Flood Control Act authorized the

Soil Conservation Service to cooperate with local organizations
in small watersheds

1956—Great Plains conservation program authorized

1956—Small Reclamation Projects Act passed

1957—Study of effect of pesticides on wild life authorized

1958—Outdoor Recreation Resources Review Commission established,
to study requirements and coordination in this area

1958—Program for the discovery of mineral resources, including organic fuels, established

Though incomplete, this list shows the emphases of conservation policy
and that the greatest effort occurred in the early days, again during the
New Deal, and now more recently. In the great depression of the 1930s
people became actively interested in conservation. At that time Stuart
Chase could report that the federal government alone was spending almost
$1 billion a year on such projects, that they offered work to a million peo-
ple, and that the Secretary of the Interior was proposing to call his
agency the Department of Public Works and Conservation and had
adopted the revolutionary policy of matching land brought into cultivation as the result of reclamation or drainage by the retirement of sub-
marginal land of equivalent productive capacity and turning it back to
the public domain or the national forests.[10] In early 1960, two important
issues were unresolved: the passage of the National Wilderness Preservation bill to protect the remnant of publicly owned primeval land that is
the natural heritage of the nation; and a bill to further the control of
billboards on the federal interstate highway system.

FEDERAL CONSERVATION AGENCIES

Especially during the New Deal period, however, when so much
conservation work was in course, the federal government's program was
handicapped by poor planning and inadequate administrative arrangements. The Department of the Interior, for example, would be bringing
new areas of irrigated lands into production while at the same time the
Department of Agriculture was trying to reduce acreage and production,
not only on marginal lands but on others as well. On one occasion Congress appropriated funds to one government agency to utilize a certain
swampy area as a migratory bird refuge and a little later voted funds to
another agency to drain the same area for agricultural purposes. This was
no new situation; it only seemed worse than usual because more was being done and new programs were being inaugurated.

The difficulty is that the conservation work of the federal government
is scattered throughout a dozen or more public agencies, with concentra-

[10] Stuart Chase, *Rich Land, Poor Land* (New York, 1936).

tions, however, in the departments of Interior and Agriculture. What is the solution to the administrative problem in this area? Should a full-fledged federal department of conservation be created? It is doubtful that the plan could be made to work because conservation is a pervasive subject that cuts across many boundaries and it would require a series of major amputations to round up each segment of it into a single unit.

If consistent planning and programming cannot be successfully carried on at the operating level, then the problem may be partially solved at least by coordination, and that is precisely what at one time was done. A National Resources Board was created in 1934 and soon began to turn out some fundamental analyses of conservation problems and their possible handling. The board's first annual report will repay the reader.[11] It was not long before all forty-eight states and some two thousand counties had created planning commissions to work with the National Resources Planning Board, as it was later called, but the agency was allowed to go out of existence during World War II (Congress refused to appropriate the necessary funds for its work) and has never been reinstated. Its research and planning materials, however, are of great permanent worth.

Although conservation is the responsibility of many government agencies, some of the more important ones are these:

The National Park Service

The Department of the Interior, which for over a century has been housekeeper for the federal government, is now also one of its principal custodians of natural resources. The department's four assistant secretaries deal, respectively, with fish and wildlife, mineral resources, public-land management, and water and power development, with an aggregate jurisdiction over some 750 million acres of land. In this complex the National Park Service was established by Congress in 1916 "to conserve the scenery and the natural and historic objects and the wild life therein" and to make them available for the public to enjoy without impairing them for the enjoyment of future generations. The jurisdiction of the service covers a total of 183 military, historical, memorial, battlefield, and capital parks, national monuments, cemeteries, recreation areas, and parkways.

The popularity of the national parks has steadily grown and by 1959 nearly 63 million visitors were going through them each year. The result was to create a severe strain on the National Park Service, traditionally short of funds. Public pressure, in which the late Bernard De Voto played a leading part,[12] finally got a study made of the situation and in 1956 a ten-year improvement plan, called Mission 66, was

[11] National Resources Board, *Annual Report*, 1934 (Washington, D.C., 1934).
[12] See Bernard DeVoto in "The Easy Chair," "Let's Close the National Parks," *Harper's Magazine* (Oct. 1953), pp. 49–52.

inaugurated to bring the parks up to a point where they can take care of an anticipated 80 million visitors a year. Congress has given its blessing in the form of appropriations.

Bureau of Land Management

Also located in the Interior Department, the Bureau of Land Management is the result of a merger in 1946 of the General Land Office and the Grazing Service. Among other duties, today the bureau manages the land and mineral resources of some 475 million acres still in federal ownership as well as the publicly owned mineral resources on about 58 million acres of privately owned lands. The bureau's objective is to use these resources in every way consistent with the public interest. It identifies, classifies, uses, and disposes of public lands as needed and stresses the development, conservation, and proper utilization of the natural resources involved. The bureau also prepares maps, grants grazing permits and leases, rehabilitates deteriorated range lands, and manages the forests on its own lands as to cutting, protection from fire and disease, and the provision of recreational areas.

Fish and Wildlife Service

This agency of the Interior Department is also the result of a fairly recent merger. Its objective is to promote the conservation of birds, mammals, fishes, and other forms of wildlife, both for their recreational (chiefly hunting) and economic values. Among other duties, the service operates some 275 sanctuaries for wild fowl and game, regulates commercial fishing in some areas, conducts a fishery research program, promotes inland fisheries, controls injurious species of mammals such as rabid foxes, coyotes, and wolves, administers a grant-in-aid program to the states for the restoration of fish and wildlife areas, and studies river basins from the conservation standpoint.

Bureau of Reclamation

This agency of the Interior Department has played an outstanding role in the development and conservation of water resources in the Rocky Mountain states, the arid Southwest, and the Pacific coast states. As might be expected, therefore, its principal interest-group support comes from those areas. The bureau constructs reservoirs to irrigate arid and semiarid land so as to increase the productivity of surrounding farms. Irrigated acreage doubled in the fourteen years prior to 1953 and the value of crops in those areas multiplied seven times. In connection with some of the dams (but not all), power stations are built to be operated either by the bureau itself or by private companies. Flood runoff is controlled, rivers are regulated as to flow and pollution, navigation is improved, water is provided for nonfarm use, fish and wildlife are protected, and recreational facilities are created. By 1960 some of the great dams constructed by the Bureau of Reclamation included Hoover (formerly Boulder), Shasta, Hungry Horse, and Grand Coulee. The bureau also carries on extensive research.

The Bureau of Reclamation is not alone in its field. As a matter of fact, the policy and organizational struggles between it and the Army Corps of Engineers offer a classic example of bureaucratic and pressure-group infighting. Public versus private power is one of the issues; single-purpose versus multiple-purpose projects is another. Such splintered jurisdictions constitute an obstacle to developments such as TVA.

The Forest Service

Let us turn now to the Department of Agriculture. There the Forest Service has enjoyed a long reputation as one of the best administered programs in Washington, with outstanding personnel and a high level of managerial proficiency. The service promotes the conservation and best use of the nation's 150 national forests covering an aggregate of 180 million acres, a task that excites the imagination.

Created under President Theodore Roosevelt's administration in 1906, the Forest Service has grown from a handful of crusading conservationists to a great land-management, research, and educational agency with more than 6700 regular employees and twice that number at the height of danger during the forest-fire season. Under scientific management, the national forests now supply more than 6 billion board feet of lumber annually, and the harvest is growing. The forests also furnish seasonal grazing for millions of cattle and sheep and supply recreation for millions of citizens who use the camp sites and other facilities. In addition, a program of cooperation with the states for the management of state and private lands covers fire, pest, and flood protection and the distribution of young trees for planting woodlands, windbreaks, and shelterbelts.

Soil Conservation Service

Land use experts have warned that unless we check the waste of topsoil and restore its fertility, the United States will one day lose its title as breadbasket of the world and future generations will have to put up with a greatly lowered standard of living. Nor is this danger so remote as some would like to think. Floods and windstorms each year take a heavy toll of lands that have been stripped of their protection of trees and grasses and that should never have been cultivated in the first place. Generations of farmers have taken more out of the soil than they put back in the form of nutriment. It is a disturbing fact that our national wealth is being dissipated at the rate of hundreds of millions of tons of topsoil and organic and mineral nutriment each year.

Thus the work of the Soil Conservation Service assumes an immediate and far-reaching importance. Created in 1935 and several times strengthened by supplementary legislation, the service has developed a nation-wide program of conservation and economical land use, in which more than fifty land-improvement practices are introduced by trained agronomists to individual farmers, who are then assisted in many ways in putting them into use. Among the more common of these practices are contour plowing and cultivation, strip cropping, terracing, drainage and irrigation, fertilization, reforestation, crop rotation, and the management of range, woodland, and wildlife.

The program of the service is organized on a district basis in the states in accordance with state enabling legislation, and the districts are managed by the farmers themselves. As of 1959, 2829 districts covered nearly 1.64 billion acres and included 4.56 million farms in the United States and its territories, which is more than 96 percent of all farms in the continental United States. Participation in the program is voluntary and anyone may apply. The farmer signs a contract with the service in which each agrees to do certain things in a long-range program with a quota of accomplishment each year, and thereafter the farmer works directly with the service's technicians in making his plans. These technicians render many forms of assistance: they analyze the soil as to types and uses, work out drainage and irrigation projects, help in reforestation and cutting operations, draw contour lines, and provide the use of special equipment such as bulldozers and dump trucks on a rental basis. The objective is to make the best possible use of resources and to conserve and enrich them instead of wasting them. The technical advice and supervision are free, but the farmer pays for the actual work done for him or he does it himself, and hence the program is not an expensive one to the taxpayer.

Table 7 shows crop increases due to soil conservation measures after the service had been in operation for less than ten years. Percentage increase is based on the per-acre crop yields from conservation-treated farms for the three crop years of 1941 through 1943, as compared with yields during the three-year period before these same farms were treated. Increases are measured in units of produce—pounds of meat or cotton or bushels of wheat—instead of in dollars, the value of which has changed.

It is interesting to compare the data from this study with the percent increases in annual yields per acre of the seventeen major crops for all farms in the United States, which in the years 1941 through 1943 was only 9.7 percent over per-acre yields in the three preceding years.

Special problems handled by the Soil Conservation Service are the Dust Bowl and the planting of the so-called Shelter Belt. In the Dust

Bowl, cover crops instead of open cultivation are stressed, along with better management. The Shelter Belt, started with Dust Bowl operations in the 1930s, is a series of discontinuous plantings to afford protection against drying winds and drifting soil over an area extending some 1000 miles north and south, from North Dakota into the Texas Panhandle, and 200 miles east and west. The plantings were from five to ten rows of trees located where they would do the farmer the most good. Some 18,600 linear miles containing 217 million trees were set out on more than 30,000 farms. Although the work was stopped in 1942, the resurgence of dust storms since 1954 caused the work to be resumed under the Great Plains conservation program with even greater vigor than before.

TABLE 7

INCREASE IN YIELDS FROM CROPS AFTER JOINING SOIL CONSERVATION PROGRAM

(Crop years 1941, 1942, 1943)

Distribution	Number of farms	Acreage	Percent increase, all crops
Northeast	360	61,106	28.9
Southeast	1,469	379,290	33.8
Corn Belt	2,011	340,214	26.2
South Central	3,792	1,363,033	44.0
Northern Plains	1,162	1,402,950	37.8
Southwest	153	186,080	33.8
Far West	401	239,500	12.3
Total	9,348	3,972,173	35.7

SOURCE: Subcommittee of the Committee on Appropriations, House of Representatives, *Hearings on Agriculture Department Appropriation Bill for 1947* (79th Cong., 2d Sess.), p. 1010.

Yet another soil-conservation program in the Agriculture Department is the so-called ACP: the Agricultural Conservation Program, a form of financial relief to farmers which stresses conservation practices, thus in a sense killing two birds with one stone. At the local level the program operates through agricultural stabilization and conservation committees in cooperation with representatives of land-grant colleges, the Forest Service, the Soil Conservation Service, and others. Payments are made to farmers for practices such as planting temporary cover as well as permanent grasses, water conservation, temporary protection from wind and water erosion (deep plowing in the Dust Bowl comes under this heading), and the purchase and spreading of commercial fertilizer. The payments are designed to cover about half the cost of each practice. Congress puts $250 million a year at the disposal of the ACP.

REGIONAL CONSERVATION AND THE TVA

Problems of conservation seldom respect the man-drawn boundaries of governments, and the confines of a state are often too limited for the proper handling of land-use planning, flood control, irrigation, or reforestation programs. But equally, the total area of the nation may be too large and variegated for most administrative purposes. Conservation agencies, therefore, have sometimes made use of regional rather than state or national areas because the region may be drawn to suit the limits of the problem in question. The outstanding example of the regional device today is the Tennessee Valley Authority, created in 1933.

The conservation of natural resources is simple business and engineering logic, as becomes clear from a consideration of some of the common-sense factors involved. In order to determine the proper area for resource planning and administration, for example, the problem itself must first be delimited so that problem and area may be coterminous. Next, planning *with* nature makes more sense than planning *against* nature or with some of the factors missing. Then, because it would be impractical to create a planning and operational unit for each separate problem in the total situation, the technique of the regionalist is to look for a pattern: Where a number of social, economic, and physical problems overlap, a configuration appears around which one draws a line that roughly determines the boundaries of the region that is needed.

A river valley is a convenient natural area for the development of a regional conservation program because every aspect of a watershed is related: soil, water, and vegetation. If floods are washing away the soil, the forests must be attended to, farming practices reconsidered, and dams built to store the flash runoff of water. Large bodies of stored water offer possibilities for navigation and for the development of hydroelectric power. Alongside an improved agriculture, therefore, may be built a new and variegated industry, thus providing the balance of agriculture and industry most conducive to human welfare. This cause-and-effect thinking is the basis of the program of the TVA and that of other regional valley programs either already in existence or advocated.

Thus TVA is interesting for at least two reasons quite aside from the question of whether it constitutes a form of socialism, creeping or otherwise: First, TVA makes geography the basis of human planning and contrivance; and second, it makes use of the region, which is the middle choice between the extremes of federal centralization and a limited local jurisdiction. The regional device helps to check the march toward federal centralization and at the same time avoids the anarchy that sometimes results when local authorities try to solve piecemeal problems that transcend local boundaries.

Because it is a kind of pilot project that has largely justified the hopes of its sponsors, the generation-long record of TVA receives world-wide attention. Thousands of interested foreign visitors, among them government leaders, engineers, scientists, and writers, have looked at TVA with an eye to adapting some phase of it to their own countries. By 1960, TVA-type projects were under consideration or actually under construction, among others, in India, Pakistan, Afghanistan, Turkey, Israel, Jordan, Egypt, Tunisia, Rhodesia, Nyasaland, Peru, Puerto Rico, Mexico, Brazil, Colombia, Portugal, and France. At the same time, river-valley authorities modeled after TVA have been proposed in at least seven other areas in the United States.

TVA is a multipurpose development, meaning, in this case, that in an area covering more than 40,000 square miles in parts of seven states and inhabited by 3.5 million people, the project combines all the factors essential to cooperation with nature. These are flood control, improved navigation, better agricultural methods, soil and mineral conservation, reforestation, and the development of power resources and new industries, most of which depend on building dams. In addition, an elastic clause in the TVA legislation testifies to the interest of its framers in people as well as in other natural resources, for the authority was to consider "the economic and social well-being of the people living in said river basin." The Tennessee River valley is potentially one of the richest natural areas in the nation and statistics show that since 1933 it has moved toward the full use of its capacities more rapidly than any other section of the nation.

TVA is a nonstock corporation created and owned by the federal government. The corporate form was used to allow the agency more business freedom than is customarily found in old-style government departments, at the same time assuring its accountability to Congress. A board of directors of three full-time officials is appointed by the President with Senatorial approval and is authorized to exercise all the powers of the corporation; the board then appoints a general manager responsible for supervising the administration of the agency. The program operates along functional lines and with a high degree of efficiency.

The strategy of TVA has been to rely on existing state and local governments as far as possible and to keep its own administrative functions at a minimum. This procedure encourages grass-roots democracy and allows TVA to concentrate on its main task of planning and construction. Thus the authority builds the dams and generates the power but it does not sell electricity directly to individual consumers; rather, the private power companies, municipalities, cooperative associations, and large private industries buy the power wholesale from TVA and either use it themselves or distribute and sell it through their own systems. Likewise, with regard to conservation, TVA provides the funds with which to operate demonstration farms, but committees of local farmers actually administer the programs.[13] Centralized planning and decentralized administration is generally a sound policy, but on the other side of the coin, administration by one segment of a locality, may, and sometimes has, produced unsound results.

Private business began to flourish in the Tennessee Valley when the region's natural resources began to be properly developed and conserved. Cheap power attracted new industries that made available new jobs that boosted purchasing power that created a market for durable goods such as refrigerators and electric stoves and also stimulated retail sales and bank deposits. Prior to TVA's coming the Tennessee Valley had the lowest per capita use of electricity of any part of the nation; only ten years later it was second highest and the rate of increase was twice that of the national average. Electrified farms rose from 3 percent of the total in the area in 1933 to 95 percent in 1959. In the first six years, bank deposits increased 268 percent, compared with 112 percent for the nation, and retail sales expanded more than 400 percent while the national average rose by only 300 percent. Electric appliances worth $1.5 billion were sold in the valley from outside manufacturers in the eight years prior to 1954. And finally, during World War II the availability of cheap power attracted defense installations to the area, including Alcoa and the Atomic Energy Commission projects at Oak Ridge and Paducah.

The long-range plan of TVA, calling for nine major dams on the Tennessee River and a score of smaller ones on its tributaries, was almost complete ten years after the project was launched. By 1945 the authority had become the single largest producer of electricity in the nation. Today, generating capacity is more than 10.5 billion kilowatts and the power generated in one year is 40 times greater than in 1933. Two thirds of total generating capacity is in steam plants, which produce about 70 percent of output. The assets of TVA are more than $2 billion, mostly in land, structures, and equipment. The present output of power, however, is a quarter less than will be needed in the years immediately ahead. Some idea of the importance of this is conveyed by the fact that 51 percent of TVA's kilowatt hours are absorbed by federal government defense installations and industries with defense contracts.

In the long run, however, the power program of TVA means less to the people of the region, as to the nation, than the coordinated land-use plan of conservation. By 1958, some 72,000 test-demonstration farms had used TVA-produced fertilizers (the production of fertilizer being a permanent part of the total program), in 37 states under the guidance of the land-grant colleges. In other words, TVA not only illustrates what conservation can do for a vast region; it may even provide the soil-

[13] These theories are spelled out by David Lilienthal, *TVA: Democracy on the March* (New York, 1944).

building materials for use in other parts of the country. In addition, the TVA forestry program has helped bring some 90 percent of the valley's timberlands under some form of organized fire protection and has provided 265 million seedlings to farmers for reforestation and soil-erosion control. And the dam system has created many lakes that sustain fishing, boating, and camping enterprises. So much is heard about the TVA power program, largely because of the attacks of the private-power interests, that one is likely to overlook the fact that power is only one of the many activities carried on to conserve the natural and human resources in the watershed of the Tennessee River.

As far as flood control is concerned, TVA estimates that the city of Chattanooga was spared $23 million worth of flood damages in the four years between 1943 and 1947, and that the reduction of flood levels by 2 feet along certain parts of the Ohio and Mississippi rivers was the effect of TVA dams and is worth $200 million in flood-control protection to those parts of the country. In addition, TVA dams have provided a navigation channel 9 feet deep and 630 miles long; connected with the Gulf of Mexico and the Ohio River, it forms part of a 10,000-mile inland waterways system.

There is nothing in the federal Constitution relating to regional planning or to multipurpose conservation programs. Nevertheless, when it came time to test the validity of TVA, the Supreme Court of the United States easily deduced implied powers from the express powers set forth in the Constitution. Principal reliance was on the authority of Congress to improve the navigability of streams, but there are also the war powers, the postal power, the commerce power, and the power to spend money for the general welfare, if they should be needed. The first leading case was *Ashwander* v. *TVA* [14] which relied on the decision in *Arizona* v. *California*.[15] The Court held that the authority to develop and sell power is deducible from the express authority to improve navigation. "The fact that purposes other than navigation will also be served," said the Court in the *Arizona* case, "could not invalidate the exercise of the authority conferred, even if those other purposes would alone have justified an exercise of Congressional power. . . . The possible abuse of the power to regulate navigation is not an argument against its existence." All of which caused Stuart Chase to remark that "We start with navigation and end with a comprehensive program of regional planning. As a matter of fact—and I trust the Supreme Court is safely asleep as I whisper it—navigation is probably the least important aspect of the cycle, from the point of view of the well-being of the people of the valley." [16] Following the *Ashwander* case, the Supreme Court again upheld TVA in *Tennessee Electric Power Co.* v. *TVA*,[17] thus reinforcing the earlier decision.

[14] (297 U.S. 288. 1936).   [15] (283 U.S. 423. 1931).   [16] Chase, *op. cit.*, p. 272.
[17] (360 U.S. 118. 1939).

Other Plans of Regional Development

In a monumental study conducted by the Twentieth Century Fund entitled *America's Needs and Resources*,[18] it is estimated that approximately $80 billion would be required to improve the river valleys of the nation from the standpoint of navigation and port development, flood control, the development of hydroelectric power, irrigation, pollution abatement, water supply, and conservation and recreation. The minimum financial requirements are presented in Table 8:

TABLE 8

Estimated Cost and Time Required for River Valley
Development Programs
(Dollar figures in millions, 1950 prices)

Type of program	Total cost	Years required	Annual cost
Waterways and port development	$ 7,500	50–75	$ 125
Flood control	15,000	50–75	250
Irrigation	10,000	50–75	160
Hydroelectric power	30,000	50–75	480
Domestic and industrial water supply	6,250	25	250
Pollution abatement	10,000	25	400
Fish and wildlife conservation and recreation	1,250	50–75	20
Total	$80,000		$1,685 *

* For only first 25 years.

Source: J. Frederic Dewhurst and Associates, *America's Needs and Resources, A New Survey* (New York, Twentieth Century Fund, 1955), p. 572.

Illustrative of the type of scheme proposed are ten regional conservation programs which, although generally more limited than TVA, are nevertheless partly inspired by that model. There are possibilities for such programs in all of the 160 separate river basins in the country, with some more important than others, especially the Great Lakes–St. Lawrence region, the Connecticut and Merrimack valleys, the Ohio Valley, the lower Mississippi, the Arkansas River, the Missouri Valley, the Pacific Northwest, the Central Valley of California, and the Colorado Valley.

If in addition to these developments in the river valleys, other conservation projects covering rural and forest areas were also undertaken, this part of the program might take up to fifty years and cost some $25

[18] Dewhurst and Associates, *op. cit.*

billion. But there is little doubt that it would be a good investment because, broadly considered, economic gain is rooted on a continuing supply of natural resources. Floods are becoming more frequent and more destructive, as witness the enormous damage done in Connecticut in the summer of 1955. Each year billions of tons of solid material are washed out of the fields and pastures of the nation by erosion—topsoil that contains 40 million tons of phosphorus, potassium, and nitrogen. As Stuart Chase points out, "Plant food can be restored to soil that has been worn lean by cropping, but when water takes the soil itself—minerals, humus, microscopic organisms, everything—only nature can restore fertility to that land, and her rate under primeval conditions . . . is one inch in 500 years." [19] No one running a private business would hesitate to spend what is needed on repairs and maintenance for fear of eventually losing the business itself. Morris L. Cooke, an engineer by profession, in the mid-1930s stated his belief "that at our present rate of soil erosion, this country of ours has left to it less than a century of virile existence. . . . We have two decades at the most to plan our campaign." [20] It is worth noting that those two decades are now up.

Supplementary Reading

Twentieth Century Fund, *America's Needs and Resources, A New Survey* (New York, 1955). Chapter 17 is entitled "Land and Water Conservation and Development."

President's Materials Policy Commission, *Resources for Freedom* (Washington, D.C., 1952) 6 vols. The most complete up-to-date analysis of material resources.

Commission on Organization of the Executive Branch of the Government (first Hoover Commission), *Department of the Interior* (Washington, D.C., 1949).

———, *Task Force Report on Natural Resources* (Washington, D.C., 1949). A proposal to stress resource conservation.

Wengert, Norman, *Natural Resources and the Political Struggle* (New York, 1955). The role of pressure groups.

National Resources Planning Board, *Regional Factors in National Planning and Development* (Washington, D.C., 1935). One of the first comprehensive treatments of regionalism.

———, *General Report of the National Resources Board, Dec. 1, 1934* (Washington, D.C., 1934). This 445-page study is destined to become a classic.

Vogt, William, *The Road to Survival* (New York, 1948). Pressure of population on shrinking resources.

Russell, Sir E. John, *World Population and World Food Supplies* (London, 1954). The condition of food production.

Bennett, M. K., *The World's Food* (New York, 1954). A study of the interrelations of world populations, national diets, and food potentials.

Woytinsky, W. S., and E. S. Woytinsky, *World Population and Production* (New

---

[19] Chase, *op. cit.*, p. 38.   [20] Quoted in *ibid.*, p. 99.

York, Twentieth Century Fund, 1953). World resources, past, present, and future.

Pinchot, Gifford, *Breaking New Ground* (New York, 1947). By the pioneer in conservation.

Jarrett, Henry (ed.), *The Nation Looks at Its Resources* (Washington, D.C., 1954). Report of a mid-century conference.

Straus, Michael W., *Why Not Survive?* (New York, 1955). Emphasizes the proper use of resources.

Ciriacy-Wantrup, S. V., *Resource Conservation: Economics and Policies* (Berkeley, Calif., 1952). Examines basic principles.

Pritchett, C. Herman, *The Tennessee Valley Authority* (Chapel Hill, N.C., 1943). Stresses the governmental aspect.

Lilienthal, David E., *TVA: Democracy on the March* (New York, 1944). The best short treatment.

Selznick, David, *TVA and the Grass Roots* (Chicago, 1950). Stresses adjustment to environment.

Clapp, Gordon R., *The TVA: An Approach to the Development of a Region* (Chicago, 1955). By a man who spent twenty-one years with TVA.

McKinley, Charles, *Uncle Sam in the Pacific Northwest* (Berkeley, Calif., 1952). The impact of federal resource activity in a growing region.

Greene, L. S., and others, *Rescued Earth* (Knoxville, Tenn., 1948). A study of the public administration of natural resources in Tennessee.

Ayres, Eugene, and Charles Scarlott, *Energy Sources* (New York, 1952). The world's energy sources and our own dwindling supply of coal and oil.

Baumhoff, Richard G., *The Dammed Missouri Valley* (New York, 1951). Subtitled "One Sixth of Our Nation."

Hoyt, William G., and Walter M. Langbein, *Those Angry Waters* (Princeton, N.J., 1955). The cause and cure of floods in the United States.

Peterson, Elmer T., *Big Dam Foolishness* (New York, 1954). The fallacies of large storage dams.

Maass, Arthur, *Muddy Waters* (Cambridge, Mass., 1951). Government rivalries in water resource developments.

Leuchtenburg, William E., *Flood Control Politics: The Connecticut River Valley Problem* (Cambridge, Mass., 1953). The negotiation of a flood-control pact among New England states.

Stein, Harold (ed.), *Public Administration and Policy Development: A Case Book* (New York, 1952). Case entitled "The Kings River Project" is a study of pressure-group conflict; a good assignment for a class report.

Clawson, M., and B. Held, *The Federal Lands: Their Use and Management* (Baltimore, Md., 1957).

Coyle, David C., *Conservation: An American Story of Conflict and Accomplishment* (New Brunswick, N.J., 1957).

Renshaw, E. F., *Toward Responsible Government: An Economic Appraisal of Federal Investment in Water Resource Programs* (Chicago, 1957).

Lyons, B., *Tomorrow's Birthright: A Political and Economic Interpretation of Our Natural Resources* (New York, 1955).

PART V

FOREIGN ECONOMIC POLICY

14

TECHNICAL ASSISTANCE AND
THE PREVENTION OF WAR

Economic and political strategy: UNRRA, Truman Doc-
trine, Marshall Plan, NATO, the common market; Latin
America, the Far East; Point Four and the UN technical
assistance program; international finance institutions and
economic development.

National security is the protection of a land, a people, and a way of life from aggression and the threat of aggression. To achieve this goal requires a high strategy that must of necessity be primarily entrusted to government. In such a strategy, the military depends on the economy, both are largely influenced by the morale of the nation, and the successful and integrated employment of all three elements rests on principles and procedures operating through the nation's political structure.

Following World War II the United States was confronted with a situation different from any previous postwar condition when disarmament and what was once referred to as a "return to normalcy" were the next clear steps. World War II ended in 1945 and demobilization and economic decontrol quickly followed, but by 1947 it was clear that the Soviet Union had expansionist designs and that our traditional allies, although successful in war, were so reduced in economic and military strength as to be of little use to themselves, much less to us, in case of emergency. It was obvious that the United States would have to ally herself with a group of Western nations if aggression were to be curbed. In addition, developments in military technology had made the United States vulnerable to a surprise military attack, as a result of which distance from an aggressor no longer afforded the protection it once had. The weakness of our allies made the time factor increasingly determinative. Consequently, the United States adopted a policy of "peace through strength," which became even more urgent when fighting broke out in Korea and this nation led a police action there for the United Nations.

Based on what turned out to be an accurate calculation that the

Soviet Union would develop nuclear weapons by the early 1950s, two related aims of high policy in the United States were to increase the strength of the Western nations, hoping in the meantime that outstanding issues might be peacefully settled; and second, if this hope failed, to try to acquire enough strength to wage a successful war of defense if it came to that. If peaceful settlements and precautionary military strength were to be attained, three courses were indicated: First, to prepare against an atomic war through civil and military defense measures for ourselves and our allies; second, to prevent piecemeal military aggressions calling for a "fire brigade" kind of control, such as occurred in Greece and Korea; and third, to promote healthy economies in the free world through economic assistance, to which was added a program of technical assistance for the benefit of underdeveloped nations that might be receptive to Communist doctrine if they remained economically backward.[1]

The financial cost of such a world-wide program was recognized as colossal, especially if it should have to be maintained for any length of time. Some American strategists thought Soviet designs were calculated to weaken the Western world by calling out expensive police actions in which she was not directly engaged, to create dissent among the Western nations and then take advantage of their mistakes, and to bring about a quick global capitulation without primary resort to military decsion. Thus it seemed clear that timing and speed of preparation were as essential to national security as potential military strength.

But the questions arise, Can public opinion in a democracy respond fast enough to support what needs to be done? Can the American governmental machine be geared to function with the necessary speed and efficiency? Can the twin evils of inflation and depression be avoided? Can essential civilian and social services be maintained? And are the people willing to authorize enough taxes to bear the current load of expenditure without resorting to an inflationary policy of deficit spending?

On paper, America's resources seem adequate. But statistics are dangerous when primarily relied on in a power situation because they represent only *mass*—not *time, place,* and *form.* They cannot describe psychological motivation, institutional functioning, or cooperation among groups. In a power situation as in logistics, success depends on the right amount of every vital element being available in the right place, at the right time, in the right manner, and with the right organization and motivation. In 1949 Colin Clark, the Australian economist, estimated that production in the United States was eight and a half times that of Soviet Russia. By 1960 the United States still topped the USSR in basic

---

[1] This interpretation is largely based on G. A. Lincoln, W. S. Stone, and T. H. Harvey, *Economics of National Security* (New York, 1950). Although disclaiming official status, this study was written by those close to policy centers. Chap. XII is entitled, "The Outlook for the Future." See also U. S. Department of State, *Strengthening the Forces of Freedom, Selected Speeches and Statements of Secretary of State Acheson* (Washington, D.C., 1950).

production, but their production was increasing at a faster rate than ours. In the field of investment their progress overtook and surpassed the most developed capitalist countries in a relatively short time.[2] Since 1928, steel production in the USSR had multiplied ten times, coal more than ten times, petroleum six times, and electric power thirty-four times. By 1960 the USSR was boasting that its nuclear and other weapons of war were superior to ours.

In 1959 Soviet leaders were claiming that the national income of the USSR could be made to increase each year by more than 6 percent and furthermore that this rate of development would be made a permanent feature of the Soviet economy. The normal pace of expansion in the Western nations, on the other hand, has seldom gone much beyond 3 or 4 percent and at times in certain nations it has stopped altogether. Barbara Ward points out that the challenge to the West lies in the fact that not only is it likely that the USSR will make good on its claim, but will do so under a system in which the government is the chief planner, designer, and controller of the economy.[3] It is true, of course, that not all nations need the same rapid pace of economic expansion since some of them, including the United States, have already achieved a high standard of living. There are, however, gaps in the achievement of most nations and to be satisfied with an expansion rate of 3 percent may be a mistake. In four areas especially, a continuing expansion is badly needed if the Soviet challenge is to be met.

The first of these areas is national security. "There is not much use in proclaiming the superiority of the Western way of life," comments Miss Ward, "if its essential foundation—national security—is in danger." During the last decade in the United States we have given priority to a balanced budget, popular consumption, and domestic investment, leaving for defense only as much of the national income as we could "afford." It now seems that this is too little. The fact is that great as the expenditures of all governments are in the United States—and they doubled in the decade between 1949 and 1959—they were 15 percent of the gross national product in 1949 and only 20 percent ten years later.

The second area that would benefit from an expanded economy is education. While the United States is chronically short of schools, teachers, and proper standards of accomplishment, the USSR has given priority to education and now graduates each year more scientists, engineers, and technicians than any nation in the West. Similarly, in the area of research, the USSR is outstripping the West on a broader scientific front. And finally in the matter of foreign aid, the USSR entered the field only in 1955 but shows every sign of pushing its efforts to the point where it will mean increasing economic competition for the West. Added to these

[2] Reported by a committee of the United Nations studying investment, savings, and accumulation of capital in the western European economic systems in *The New York Times,* Feb. 23, 1956.

[3] Barbara Ward, "Now the Challenge of an Economic Sputnik," *The New York Times Magazine,* Feb. 8, 1959.

challenges, the United States has a rapidly rising birth rate and needs to expand local facilities of all kinds—housing, transportation, streets and roads, water supply, power, sewage disposal, education, health, social welfare, recreation—to meet the needs of an expanding population. There were 180 million Americans in 1960 and there will be an estimated 227 million in 1975. Under these combined conditions of competition with the USSR and expanding domestic requirements, concludes Miss Ward, a growth rate in the economy of 3 to 4 percent is too low, and hence "the first decision of domestic policy in the Atlantic world should be to increase the rate to, say, a steady 5 percent."

Many recent studies in the United States alone confirm this view.[4] Higher taxation, less emphasis on personal consumption, and more attention to national security, education, research, and aid to underdeveloped nations is the pattern that emerges from most of them. Such a policy of realism, says Helen Hill Miller, "is the price of progress and security—and it is the people who must pay the bill." No one can know how the people will react to such a course until the appeal is made, but it cannot be assured in advance "that the electorate will reject the argument that its current level of spending on immediate, short-term personal satisfactions must be curtailed in the interest of the kind of national agenda whose main items" have been analyzed in clear terms.[5] Gross national product in the United States reached $480 billion in 1959. If the rate of increase were stepped up from the less than 2.5 percent that prevailed in the late 1950s to 4.5 percent, then by 1965 the gross national product would yield $625 billion and in 1975 it would be $971 billion, or twice the figure for 1959.

Now just suppose, says Miss Ward, that these issues could be resolved and that decade after decade the West continued to grow under the institutions of freedom. Then Soviet Russia's last argument that tyranny and abundance must combine would be demolished, along with the greatest obstacle to the spread of Western institutions back into Russia itself. "These are the stakes," she concludes. "Can anyone doubt they are worth a supreme effort in the West?"

[4] Among these are National Planning Association, *Long Range Projections for Economic Growth: The American Economy in 1970* (Washington, D.C., 1959); Committee for Economic Development, *Trends in Public Expenditures in the Next Decades* (New York, 1959), and *The Problem of National Security: Some Economic and Administrative Aspects* (New York, 1958); Conference on Economic Progress, *The Federal Budget and the General Welfare* (New York, 1960); The Population Council, Inc., *Population: An International Dilemma* (Princeton, N.J., 1958); Committee for International Economic Growth, *One Hundred Countries; One and One-Quarter Billion People*, prepared by Paul G. Hoffman (Washington, D.C., 1960); Washington Center of Foreign Policy Research, Johns Hopkins University, *Developments in Military Technology and Their Impact on US Strategy and Foreign Policy* (Washington, D.C., 1959); The Rockefeller Report, *International Security—The Military Aspect* (New York, 1958); The President's Committee to Study the U. S. Military Assistance Program, headed by William H. Draper, Jr., *Report* (Washington, D.C., 1959).

[5] Helen Hill Miller, "What America Can Afford—A Review of National Needs in the 60's," *The New Republic* (Mar. 7, 1960).

ECONOMIC AND POLITICAL STRATEGY

Consistent with the requirements of a cold-war situation, in the years following World War II the United States undertook, somewhat disjointedly, a succession of economic programs designed to:

1. Provide temporary aid to war-devastated nations so as to achieve a subsistence standard of living until rehabilitation could be attained.

2. Promote economic recovery so as to enable the United States to stop relief programs, generate a standard of living sufficient to resist internal Communist influence, and re-establish international trade.

3. Develop enough industrial and military strength to enable the nations of the free world to resist military aggression.

In the words of former Secretary of State Dean Acheson, "It is hardly possible any longer to draw a sharp dividing line between economic affairs and political affairs. They are related and interacting." [6]

In the ten years following 1945, programs directed at the three foregoing objectives cost the United States $51.3 billion, of which $14.6 billion was for military purposes and $36.7 billion for economic development and technical assistance and other mutual security programs. Expenditures were almost wholly for economic aid until 1950 when military funds were increased to reach a peak in 1953 of more than $4 billion. Since then, expenditures in both categories have declined and the appropriation for all foreign-aid purposes in 1959 was $3.2 billion.

UNRRA

The first foreign assistance program was the United Nations Rehabilitation and Relief Administration (UNRRA), inaugurated by the United States in cooperation with the United Nations in 1943. It emphasized relief more than rehabilitation, however, operated until 1946 and cost more than $3.5 billion. The United States provided more than 73 percent of the total cost plus an additional $300 million for further relief after UNRRA was liquidated. UNRRA had little economic effect but as a temporary measure it did offer some relief at a time when it was badly needed by millions of destitute people.

The Truman Doctrine and the Marshall Plan

The next development, in 1947, was the enunciation of the so-called Truman Doctrine. As the first postwar foreign-aid program with national security as its main objective, this doctrine sought actively to contain communism, not only by economic but also by military assistance to foreign nations. The plan was implemented by a $400 million Con-

---

[6] Address before the National Convention of the U. S. Chamber of Commerce, Washington, D.C., May 3, 1949.

gressional appropriation to help bolster the economies and defenses of Greece and Turkey.

At about the same time, in the spring of 1947, it became clear that economic rehabilitation was lagging in Europe. In an address at Harvard University, Secretary of State George C. Marshall gave it as his opinion that

> Before the U. S. government can proceed much further in its efforts to alleviate the situation and help start the European world on its way to recovery, there must be some agreement among the countries of Europe as to the requirements of the situation and the part these countries themselves will take. . . . The initiative must come from Europe. The role of this country should be friendly aid in the drafting of a European program and later support of such a program as far as it may be practical for us to do so.

Nations in need of assistance were quick to accept the invitation and, spurred by the fall of Czechoslovakia to the Communists in 1948, Congress created the Economic Cooperation Administration (ECA) with an initial appropriation of some $5 billion. The plan itself became known as the Marshall Plan, or the European Recovery Plan (ERP). The European center of the project was the Organization for European Economic Cooperation (OEEC), supported by sixteen nations but boycotted by the USSR.

The formula of ERP had important economic and political implications. Based on the principle that each nation would assume responsibility and initiative, the plan was designed to return international trade to a state of normalcy. If the goods needed could be supplied within the OEEC area, the United States would not offer them. The funds were allocated to importers in each country who then made their purchases through private-enterprise channels, thereby reducing the role of government and fostering individual enterprise. Taking agricultural or other surplus products from the United States was de-emphasized in favor of items specifically needed for European recovery. There was a deliberate attempt to avoid an impression of coercion or charity, and hence the effect on European public and political opinion was generally favorable. In a sense, the program was a continuation of the Truman Doctrine, but based on self-help, accompanied by cooperative political and economic planning, and buttressed by accelerated international trade.

Actually not all the "ifs" in the Marshall Plan were realized, but by the target date of 1951 a good deal had been accomplished. International trade had increased, military strength had progressed, Communist influence was weaker in the ERP nations than in 1948, the Schuman Plan for economic cooperation in coal and steel had been established for western Europe, and there seemed to be some inclination toward a United States of Europe, although it was recognized that this last achievement would take some time to bring about.

On the financial side, nearly all ERP funds were provided on an outright grant basis. When it is considered, however, that a year before the act was due to expire industrial production in ERP countries had risen to a level 40 percent higher and total production 15 percent higher than *before* World War II, and that the standard of living had increased at least to the prewar level, the $13 billion invested by the United States seems to have been justified. Furthermore, even after ERP ended in 1952, the OEEC was retained and its function extended in the area of world trade and other economic matters, including inflation and the development of atomic energy for peacetime uses.

The Brussels Pact and NATO

On the military side, by the spring of 1948 the threat of atomic war had increased to the point where further joint action among the Western powers seemed necessary. Consequently, Great Britain, France, the Netherlands, Belgium, and Luxembourg negotiated and signed the Brussels Pact to provide for mutual military aid against aggression for a period of fifty years. A year later, at the instigation of the United States, the original five signatories, joined by Canada, Denmark, Iceland, Italy, Norway, Portugal, and the United States, signed the North Atlantic Treaty by which each agreed to keep up its military defenses by means of "continuous and effective self-help and mutual aid." Mutual aid was defined as the contribution by each party of such aid "as it reasonably can, consistent with its geographical location and resources and with due regard to the requirements of basic economic health." From the United States this meant, among other things, the supply of raw materials for armaments to be manufactured in the member nations. The signatories also specifically agreed to come to each others' military assistance in case of attack.

To further the objectives of this pact, in 1949 Congress passed the Mutual Defense Assistance Act which consolidated all grants-of-arms aid by the United States into one program, a plan that became known as the Mutual Defense Assistance Program (MDAP), the European branch of which is called the North Atlantic Treaty Organization (NATO). It was not originally anticipated that this new undertaking would mean the establishment of a joint command in the time of peace or that troops would have to be sent to Europe to help form a peacetime barrier. But the explosion of an atomic bomb in the USSR and the outbreak of the war in Korea set these developments in motion. In addition, in 1954 NATO was expanded to include Greece and Turkey.

Meanwhile, in 1952 came the first attempt to bring Germany into the western European defense system when the European Defense Community Treaty (EDC) was signed by six European nations. EDC would have created a joint European army under a kind of supranational authority responsible for the procurement of arms and the establishment of an arms pool, the whole to work in cooperation with NATO and both under the direction of SHAPE (Supreme Headquarters Allied Powers Europe), located in Paris. But after two years of struggle EDC died a rather lingering death when the French parliament finally refused to ratify the treaty. A substitute was quickly worked out when Great Britain committed herself to continental defense, something she had withheld under the abortive EDC. The Brussels Pact was expanded to include the Federal Republic of Germany and Italy, the whole was renamed Western European Union (WEU), and West Germany was permitted and agreed to rearm and was invited to join NATO, which she did in 1955. Under this rather complex arrangement WEU was to set the ceilings on armed forces and armaments contributed by its members to NATO and no increases would be permitted without the unanimous consent of its seven members. WEU is also to make sure that European—and especially West German—arms are manufactured only within agreed limits. Then to counteract the effect on some nations (especially France) of German rearmament, the high command of NATO was given increased powers over all continental armies, including their placement, logistic arrangements, and supplies.

By 1956, the fourteen nations of NATO (excluding West Germany) had spent for defense purposes a total of $312 billion. Of this, the share of the United States was $252 billion (about 81 percent), some of which, of course, went to fulfill large commitments in the Far East that had nothing directly to do with NATO. If there should be any question that these foreign military arrangements are germane to a discussion of the business-government relationship, the size of these sums, spent over a period of only seven years for a single purpose, should settle it. The other thirteen nations in NATO (again not counting West Germany) had spent an aggregate of $59.7 billion.

EUROPEAN ECONOMIC COOPERATION

Along with postwar political and military adjustments and economic rehabilitation in Europe, there was also an effort to bring about some kind of economic rationality among the nations of that continent. For this reason, and backed among others by the supporters of a closer political union, the European Coal and Steel Community (the so-called Schuman Plan) came into being in 1952, joined by France, the Federal Republic of Germany, Belgium, Italy, the Netherlands, and Luxembourg. Objectives were to remove tariffs, lower costs (especially transportation costs), stimulate consumption, and encourage economic activity. The plan worked well. After only five years, the 1958 production of coal and steel was 43 percent greater and shipments 50 percent greater than 1952 levels. By 1955, therefore, plans were made to formulate a second agreement to cover a wider market and a third to make possible the joint development of atomic energy. The common market was to abolish trade barriers within its confines gradually over a period of twelve to seventeen years and present a united front in trade matters to outside nations.

Through the OEEC (descendant of the Marshall Plan), overtures were made to other European nations with special attention to Great Britain, but for various reasons no other nation was able to or cared to join the plan. The Scandinavian nations were planning to set up a common market of their own; Switzerland could see no economic advantage to herself; Austria was restrained by the USSR. Great Britain objected to giving up her freedom of action in dealings with other nations in the British Commonwealth and worked instead for a free-trade-area arrangement under which trade barriers would be reduced among its members but freedom of action with outside nations would be retained. French opposition killed this plan, however, and Britain stayed outside of the common market. Hence when the European Economic Community, as it is officially known, came into being along with Euratom in January 1958, it included only six members (the Inner Six), each of which surrendered a portion of its national sovereignty to a supranational body consisting of a court, an advisory parliament, and a secretariat, for the sake of a clear economic advantage. In addition to reducing tariffs with other nations as well as among themselves and presenting a common trade front, the European Economic Community would also achieve freedom of movement in matters of services, capital, and labor. In addition, it would harmonize social security, labor standards, and the whole range of fiscal, economic, and social policies among the member nations; encourage freer competition and eliminate discrimination along national lines; integrate transportation to reduce costs; and encourage basic industrial development within the common market and in the overseas territories of its members. Finally, it would set up a "readaptation" fund to help industries that have been hurt by competition and to retrain workers displaced by technology. It is expected that once freed from the confines of national markets, industry among these six member nations will broaden into mass production and distribution, especially in consumer and other finished goods, for which there is a mounting demand. Finally, although Euratom was created by a separate treaty, its signatories are the same as those of the common market and the two institutions are expected to work closely together.

With the establishment of the European Economic Community, Great Britain sought to revive her plan for a free-trade area and revised it to take in the common-market nations along with others, but again France objected. A compromise was an agreement among seven nations (the so-called Outer Seven) setting up the European Free Trade Association. The Scandinavian nations gave up their own plans for a common market and joined the new undertaking. The signatories are Norway, Sweden, Denmark, Great Britain, Portugal, Switzerland, and Austria. The plan became official in January 1960.

Unfortunately, a rivalry immediately appeared between these two European trade groups, and the United States, with Canada as an ally, took the initiative in trying to stop it. Working through the OEEC, the United States proposed that the OEEC itself be revised, expanded, and transformed into an over-all organization for economic cooperation in which the United States, subject to Congressional approval, would assume full and active membership. The object was to stimulate economic growth in western Europe, avoid political rancor, expand American exports, and encourage economic prosperity in Europe to the point where those countries might share in the cost of aid to underdeveloped nations.[7] What this amounts to is a new involvement for the United States in the internal economic affairs of Europe and a new involvement for those nations in the problem of economic aid to countries that need it.

LATIN AMERICA AND THE FAR EAST

Communism does not offer the same degree of military threat in Latin America that it does in other areas but its agents there are nonetheless active, the situation in Cuba being but one example. For some time the Latin American policy of the United States has been one of cooperation and in recent years this has been extended through the Inter-American Treaty of Reciprocal Assistance of 1947 and the charter of the Organization of American States of 1948. As a result, measures to strengthen internal security have been worked out, and defense planning and military cooperation have been intensified. In addition, economic cooperation among Latin American nations is being developed, partly with the assistance of the United Nations Economic Commission for Latin America, on the model of the common-market and free-trade agreements in Europe.

In Asia and the Pacific also, mutual security programs have been developed. The Japanese Peace Treaty was signed in 1951, and was followed by a security pact between the United States and Japan recognizing that for the time being the Japanese cannot defend themselves and granting the United States the right to maintain land, sea, and air forces "in and about Japan." In addition, also in 1951, the United States signed a mutual defense treaty with the Philippines which binds the two republics, separately and jointly, to develop their individual and collective capacity to resist attacks from outside. And finally, again in the same year, a treaty was signed between the United States, Australia, and New Zealand (the so-called ANZUS treaty) pledging them to a program of collective security.

To extend these arrangements, in 1954 the representatives of eight nations (Great Britain, France, Australia, New Zealand, the Philippines, Thailand, Pakistan, and the United States) met at Manila and drew up and signed the Southeast Asia Collective Defense Treaty establishing

[7] Edwin L. Dale, Jr., *The New York Times*, Jan. 17, 1960.

what has come to be called SEATO. This agreement pledges the signatories to recognize that an attack by an aggressor against any one of them endangers the "peace and safety" of all, and "to meet the common danger in accordance with its constitutional processes." This is a far cry from NATO and the alliance is far looser, but it does constitute a kind of common front against aggression. SEATO headquarters were set up at Bangkok in 1955 and include units dealing with military matters, economic matters, and subversion.

On the economic front in Asia, the so-called Colombo Plan was organized in 1950 "for the cooperative economic development of South and Southeast Asia." Great Britain took the initiative but the United States is the most deeply involved of any donor nation. With 660 million people, the region is economically underdeveloped and politically unstable and hence vulnerable to Communist influence. The recipient nations are Burma, Cambodia, Ceylon, Malaya, India, Indonesia, Laos, Nepal, North Borneo, Pakistan, the Philippines, Sarawak, Singapore, Thailand, and South Vietnam. The donor nations are Australia, Britain, Canada, Japan, New Zealand, and the United States. Under the plan each nation does what it can to further regional development but acts independently. By 1959 the total made available to the recipient nations aggregated $6 billion of which $5.66 billion was from the United States. The plan has twice been extended and is due to expire in 1967.

TECHNICAL ASSISTANCE AND POINT FOUR

The Point Four program of technical assistance to underdeveloped countries was part of President Truman's inaugural address in January 1949. The plan was actually brought into existence a year later when Congress appropriated an initial $35 million to get it going. Of this amount, a third was earmarked for the use of the United Nations and its agencies operating in the same field.

The underdeveloped areas of the world are found largely on the Asian, African, and South American continents and are inhabited by an estimated two thirds of the world's population. At the time that Point Four was started, per capita income in these areas was only $41 a year compared with $461 in developed areas; daily caloric intake was only 2150 (1800 being the minimum usually required to sustain life) compared with 3040; the average number of doctors was 17 per 100,000 compared with 106 in developed areas; life expectancy was 30 years as against 63; the tuberculosis rate was 333 per 100,000 as against 64; illiteracy was 78 percent as against 5 percent; and the number of teachers was 176 per 100,000 of the population as compared with 398 in developed areas.[8] The bare figures are enough to indicate that Point Four was the greatest welfare challenge confronting industrialized nations. Moreover, these popu-

[8] *The New York Times*, Oct. 16, 1949.

lations had become increasingly self-conscious and militant since the end
of World War II and constituted a fertile breeding ground for communism. Point Four was the beginning of a program to help these underdeveloped areas get a start toward high standards of agriculture, industry,
health, education, and government.

In addition to the program's humanitarian appeal, the self-interest of
the United States was also engaged because Point Four opens up a field
for investments and foreign trade and acts as a curb on the spread of
communism. In 1952 President Truman argued that an ongoing Point
Four program could be the means of keeping the American economy on
an even keel for the next twenty-five years and that if the program could
raise the living standards of backward areas by as much as 2 percent, the
resulting demand for American products of all kinds would be enough
to keep productive machinery going at high speed as far ahead as anyone
could foresee. In addition to these potential advantages of Point Four,
an immediate one was that by 1952 the United States was getting raw
materials from aided nations in the amount of 100 percent of our imports
of rubber, 77 percent of our tin, 82 percent of our chrome ore, 85 percent
of our manganese, 79 percent of our copper, and 80 percent of our anti-
mony.

International Cooperation Administration

Administratively, Point Four has been handled by a number of
federal agencies. In 1954 they were consolidated in the Foreign Operations Administration, assisted by a number of advisory bodies on such
matters as international development, labor, health, education, and the
like, and operated in the respective foreign countries by native staffs
headed by an official of the rank of minister who worked closely with the
local American embassy. In 1955, however, FOA was abolished and its
technical assistance functions transferred to a new semi-autonomous unit
in the State Department called the International Cooperation Administration. Then in 1957 the Development Loan Fund was created as part of
the ICA, but later became an independent government corporation. It
provides investment capital for projects and activities in the underdeveloped areas of the world, making loans directly to private enterprisers or
to governments for particular projects that meet certain standards of economic usefulness. Loans are repaid either in dollars or, where arranged,
in local currency.

In content, Point Four consists of grants of funds to certain underdeveloped nations for particular short-term projects approved by the local
administrative unit of the United States government. The projects are
carried out with the help of American technical personnel, and in some
cases with American equipment, in fields as diverse as the construction
of harbor facilities, the improvement of a national highway system, the

management of a railroad or a telephone service, and the building of a hospital.

One problem has been a shortage of technical personnel, who must have not only expert knowledge and experience but also adaptability, enthusiasm, and a sympathetic understanding of local languages, customs, and aspirations. This aspect of the matter is so important that a Senate subcommittee report recommended in 1956, after an extensive survey of Point Four, that in some countries it might be better not to attempt technical assistance programs at all rather than to send out mediocre technicians. Yet another problem, and a delicate one, was alluded to by William O. Douglas, Justice of the Supreme Court, when he remarked that Point Four involves a great deal of basic internal reform in all countries that receive aid if the program is to succeed. Thus,

> If we can go to a region in India where there is an equitable distribution of land, where there is opportunity for the common man, and tie into that program—then we are promoting the American ideal—then we are identifying ourselves with the peoples of the world in their aspirations—then we are making impossible this crude, crass, this dismal thing known as Communism. If we go to a region and make a group of landlords richer, then we are promoting the thing that at home we hate.[9]

By 1959 the United States had spent a total of nearly $25 billion on nonmilitary foreign aid and the current rate of expenditure was nearly $1.9 billion a year, including a small portion paid out through the technical assistance program of the United Nations. Large as these sums are, however, increases up to $5 billion a year have been advocated at various times by economists and others who see in Point Four one of the most constructive programs of today. There is the additional fact that since 1955 the USSR has increasingly occupied the field of foreign aid and by 1960 had made grants and loans to nineteen noncommunist nations to a total value of $2.73 billion, in addition to nearly $800 million in military assistance. During the same period, American credits and loans to the same countries totaled $4.27 billion for economic purposes and another $1.46 billion for military uses.[10] The impact of technical assistance has been dramatic in some areas and even the over-all effect is evident. Thus by 1959, illiteracy had been reduced from 78 percent to 65 percent, life expectancy had risen from 30 to 36 years, and per capita income had gone up from $41 to $120 a year.[11]

Because this was only a beginning, however, and also because of the active presence of a rival donor of a different ideological persuasion, there could be no question of abandoning Point Four in the near future nor

[9] William O. Douglas, "The Power of Righteousness," *The New Republic* (Apr. 28, 1952). See also his book, *Strange Lands and Friendly Peoples* (New York, 1951).

[10] Reported by William J. Jorden, *The New York Times*, Feb. 21, 1960.

[11] Reported by E. W. Kenworthy, *ibid.*, Sept. 6, 1959.

even of tapering it off. On the other hand, it is expensive in terms of immediate dollars, a fact that became especially significant by reason of the fact that for a decade the United States had suffered a fairly continual deficit in its balance of international payments, which by 1959 amounted to $4 billion. In an effort to offset this deficit the administration announced that in the future the Development Loan Fund would give "emphasis" to loans and credits that would be spent in the United States, thus for the first time placing "buy-American" restrictions on foreign aid. Later the Secretary of State announced the extension of this policy to part of the field covered by ICA. It was a controversial policy, within the administration as in Congress and among some economists. Critics held that it would have little effect on the balance of payments, that it would increase the cost of goods bought with foreign-aid money, and that it made the United States vulnerable to Soviet criticisms of "economic imperialism." As some pointed out, the deficit could be wiped out by bringing all military forces home, but this was a matter to be decided on other grounds. William H. Draper, Jr., chairman of the President's Special Committee on Military Aid, commented that the drain on our balance of payments was "part of the price we are paying for security and freedom," and that we had better put first things first and pay it "fully and gladly." [12] In 1960 the "buy-American" policy was still in effect.

An accompanying policy of the federal government was to try to induce other nations to share in the cost of economic assistance. One step was to encourage within the UN the organization of an International Development Association as an affiliate of the International Bank. Another was a proposal in the President's 1960 State-of-the-Union message that the overseas assistance programs of the United States, the British Commonwealth, western Europe, and Japan be made to complement each other. As an economist on the staff of ICA remarked, the plan was to put together a series of "multilateral packages composed of bilateral parts." [13] By 1960 a plan was well under way to reconstitute the OEEC as an Organization for Economic Cooperation and Development, with a membership wider than the OEEC and including both the Inner Six and the Outer Seven, and a mandate to serve as a kind of economic high command for the West in competition with the USSR, to promote economic growth and to rationalize Western development efforts in Africa and Asia.

United Nations Technical Assistance

In the United Nations a modest technical assistance program had been started even before Point Four, and in 1949 it was expanded under a small budget of $24 million. Since then the UN has held an annual conference at which the various member nations pledge contributions to this work. The United States has contributed roughly half of the total each

[12] *The New York Times*, Nov. 22, 1959.   [13] *Ibid.*, Jan. 10, 1960.

year and now employs the matching-of-funds principle to induce other nations to give more generously. Nevertheless, for more than a decade the total for UN technical assistance never exceeded $31 million a year— a paltry sum considering the need—and yet much was done with these limited resources. The reason is that recipient nations provide much for themselves in the way of facilities and personnel, the UN supplying the expert knowledge and the supervision.

As it became clear how much could be done under the technical assistance program, the developing nations of the world began to think in terms of larger schemes and proposed the establishment of a capital fund called the Special United Nations Fund for Economic Development (SUNFED) to make possible larger grants than were available through existing agencies. SUNFED was to be a kind of revolving fund administered by an international development corporation tied closely to the UN and offering managerial and planning advice in addition to financial and technical assistance. The projects were to be of a basic, nonprofit-earning type such as public roads, buildings, schools, hospitals, and the like. The United States vigorously opposed the plan on the ground that world conditions were not stable enough to permit the making of long-range financial commitments. Nevertheless, plans for SUNFED went forward and in an effort to head them off, in 1957 the United States offered a smaller, substitute plan which eventually was approved by the General Assembly and went into effect early in 1959 under the direction of Paul G. Hoffman. Part of the money of this Special Fund is to be used to expand the regular work of the Technical Assistance Board and the rest is for projects that eventually will attract capital investments from other sources. The original SUNFED program is far from dead, however, and if enough money is not forthcoming from other sources, a campaign for it is likely to be revived.

Technical assistance under the UN is planned and coordinated by the Technical Assistance Board composed of the representatives of the various action agencies in the program. These are the Technical Assistance Administration, which is one of the regular departments of the UN secretariat and is responsible for economic surveys and other programs not dealt with by other units; plus the specialized agencies having their own separate charters and programs but related to the UN in a working capacity. They include the Food and Agriculture Organization (FAO), the United Nations Educational, Scientific, and Cultural Organization (UNESCO), the International Labor Organization (ILO), the World Health Organization (WHO), the International Civil Aviation Organization (ICAO), the International Telecommunication Union (ITU), and the World Meteorological Organization (WMO). Although not officially members of the Technical Assistance Board, two other agencies have a close working relationship with it: the International Bank for Reconstruction and Development and the United Nations International Children's Emergency Fund (UNICEF), an agency financed by both private and governmental funds outside the UN and dealing with the health and needs of children all over the world.

When the total amount of funds pledged by member nations is known, it is allocated by shares to the recipient nations. Thereafter the UN resident representative of the Technical Assistance Board in each recipient nation, in cooperation with representatives of that nation's government and of the specialized agencies that may be involved, works out and submits to the Technical Assistance Board in New York a budget for the annual program in that nation. Since the recipient nations contribute a good deal themselves in the way of funds and personnel, the total expenditure for the TA program is considerably larger than the $25 million to $30 million or so raised in pledges. Moreover, unlike Point Four, practically all the outlay is for the cost of experts rather than for materials or equipment.

Technical assistance under the UN includes expert help in establishing factories to make such things as penicillin, DDT, steel, cement, fertilizer, and textiles; in training skilled personnel, developing land and water resources, improving methods for processing meat, fish, and other foods, making studies and plans for enriching the nutrition of great populations, devising programs to wipe out epidemic and chronic diseases including malaria and tuberculosis, and making a direct attack on infant mortality—in short, to quote an editorial in *The New York Times,* the object of UN technical assistance is "to raise human welfare beyond the level dreamed of through countless ages and over millions of square miles of jungle and desert, mountains and prairies" [14]—and in the cities as well,

In its first ten years the United Nations technical assistance program spent only $234 million contributed by 85 governments. During that time a few of its projects were written off as failures, some were "below expectations," and some could not be fully judged as yet, but three quarters of them were judged "fair to excellent." Some 14,000 persons, most of them from underdeveloped nations, had been trained. Nevertheless, a principal reason for the failure of projects that did fail was lack of adequate national administrative and technical services. To help meet this need, in 1959 the Secretary General proposed and the General Assembly approved a new program to supply the governments of underdeveloped nations with qualified operational and executive personnel, a program now called Opex. Instead of a permanent panel of experts as a kind of international civil service, however, the director of the program recruits experts to meet specific requests from underdeveloped nations. When he is appointed, the expert's salary is met partly by the host government and partly by Opex. Initial appointments are for a year to determine whether both sides wish to continue the arrangement. The program had not been in operation very long before a total of more than 8500 experts had been appointed to overseas posts of this nature.

In many nations there is both a Point Four and a UN technical as-

[14] *Ibid.,* Jan. 31, 1956.

sistance program, necessitating the closest kind of coordination in planning and execution. Generally speaking, the UN program emphasizes long-range projects such as research and education and the training of local experts, while the American program, being defense-oriented, emphasizes immediate and measurable results. In most cases, therefore, the two programs have supplemented rather than duplicated each other. The UN projects are usually strongest in the areas of education, health, welfare, and economic survey; the American program, in agricultural and industrial production. In those two areas, however, as in the field of public-utility development, the UN and the United States have divided the field, the latter stressing quick results. The UN program is less well financed by a good deal, unhampered by strings tied on for political reasons, and has experts drawn from many nations instead of only one.

There is no more interesting vantage point from which to observe the changing relations of business and government in the processes of economic growth than to be stationed in one of the recipient nations. It seems as though their fervor for progress and reform is already so great that no obstacle can block their designs. Government plays a large role in the early stages of any nation's development because government is often the only agency with enough credit to provide certain minimum conditions of safety, health, and communication. It is only when these conditions have been established that individual credit becomes available. A large concern of public policy in the United States, therefore, is to see that when the proper stage of growth has occurred in developing nations, adequate private capital, both local and foreign, will become available to ensure private ownership and democracy a chance against other systems that we deplore.

INTERNATIONAL FINANCE INSTITUTIONS

In the field of international lending, the two main problems are, first, balance-of-payment or currency matters and second, economic development. To deal with them, a conference on international monetary and financial affairs was held at Bretton Woods in 1944, before World War II had ended or the UN was established. From this conference there emerged a pair of finance twins: The International Monetary Fund and the International Bank for Reconstruction and Development. They got off to a slow start, however, and for several years after World War II it was the Marshall Plan that largely solved the international finance problems that these two institutions were designed to meet. In recent years, however, both have become active and a number of other agencies have been created to work in the same field. Among those that may be mentioned here are the International Finance Corporation and the International Development Association.[15]

[15] Other agencies in this area in the United States rather than on the international plane are Inter-American Development Institution, just coming into being in 1960 and

The International Monetary Fund, which began business in 1947, is the only institution set up solely to deal with the balance-of-payments problem. Its sixty-eight members include almost all the free nations of the world plus Yugoslavia. It began to be active in 1956 and in the next three years made loans or stand-by credits available to twenty-eight of its member nations, thus helping a strong flow of world trade.

The International Bank for Reconstruction and Development was a more dynamic agency than the Monetary Fund from the outset, and has been much closer to the technical assistance field. It has the same membership as the Monetary Fund and the two institutions work closely together. In addition, both are loosely affiliated as specialized agencies of the United Nations. The three main purposes of the International Bank are (1) to make long-term capital loans for reconstruction and to encourage economic development; (2) to promote private foreign investment in foreign nations; and (3) to promote the long-range growth of world trade. So organized and empowered, the International Bank appeals equally to internationalists and to the conservative private banking fraternity. The original capital of the International Bank was $10 billion but its assets expanded as loans were repaid and as private investment houses came to share the risk. When a $50-million loan was made to Belgium several years ago, for example, it was in cooperation with a Wall Street firm; by 1955 commercial banks and private investors were participating in nearly every loan made by the bank. By 1959, because of the steady growth of the bank's business, its authorized capital amounted to $21 billion and its net income for the year was more than $53 million, or better than the preceding year by more than $10 million. The International Bank has a skilled recruitment and training program and a record for making first-rate economic surveys throughout the world.

Because it must raise much of its money by selling bonds on the New York and other financial markets, the International Bank must be tough about its own loans. They must be repaid in the currency loaned, usually dollars, at bank rates of interest and over a term of years considered appropriate for the type of project involved. Hence the difficulty soon arose that many underdeveloped nations that needed credit most were unable to get it. To meet a part of this need, in 1956 the International Bank secured the establishment of the International Finance Corporation with $100 million of capital. This institution was to stimulate the flow of venture capital from private sources into underdeveloped nations. Where the International Bank concentrates on public projects such as power, transport, and other public utilities in the underdeveloped nations, the IFC was to try to reduce barriers to the flow of private capital in the same areas. Its loans go direct to private companies on a risk basis, not to governments. Its start was slow but by 1959 it had fifty-seven members,

---

designed to offer both "hard" and "soft" loans for development projects in Latin America; The Export-Import Bank with a variety of functions in the lending field; and the Development Loan Fund, discussed above.

had loans outstanding amounting to nearly $20 million, and claimed that for each dollar committed, more than three dollars of private funds were being invested. Administratively, the IFC is financially independent of the International Bank and has its own president, but the two institutions have a common chairman and common governors and directors. The IFC has a small independent staff and uses the personnel of the International Bank wherever possible.

These combined institutions, however, failed to meet the growing need of underdeveloped nations for more money. Despite sound internal policies, by 1959 some of them had reached a point of foreign indebtedness to the International Bank, to the Monetary Fund, and to individual creditor countries where they could not safely borrow any more on "hard" terms. Hence, at the instigation of the United States, the International Bank approved the creation of the International Development Association with a capital of $1 billion subscribed by the member nations, which in general are the same as for the other institutions. Although by 1960 the IDA was not yet in full operation, its purpose was to facilitate the flow of outside capital to underdeveloped nations on terms less "hard" than were otherwise available.

The Future of Technical Assistance

"Ours is an interdependent world," said an Indian statesman recently, "and it is quite clear that a situation in which benefits of science and technology are available to only a few countries while the others continue to live in poverty and want is not tenable for any length of time either from an economic or from a social point of view. . . . Political freedom has little meaning if it does not result in substantial and fairly rapid improvement in the living standards of the mass of the people." [16]

Indeed, so close have all nations become in the past few decades that international affairs, especially on the economic plane, are among the most important determinants and regulators of domestic policy, in this nation as elsewhere. Paul Hoffman has remarked that "All countries, whether their incomes are high, medium, or low, must in their own self-interest accept proportionate responsibility for a rapidly expanding world economy." [17] A good deal is heard about the major aid programs but the fact is that more and more nations are coming to the aid of those that are underdeveloped, and they are the majority. Aside from the large donors, which include the United States, the USSR, Great Britain, France, Australia, and Canada, almost every European nation offers bilateral aid for particular projects. Thus, Sweden has furthered development in Ethiopia and Pakistan; Norway has focused her efforts in India and Korea; Switzerland offers fellowship and scholarship programs; the Netherlands,

[16] Morarji R. Desai, Finance Minister of India, in an address to the twelfth annual Far East Conference, reported in *The New York Times,* Oct. 7, 1959.

[17] Reported in *The New York Times,* Dec. 9, 1959.

Denmark, Belgium, Italy, Spain, Portugal, Austria, and West Germany all offer aid on a bilateral basis.

In 1959 Sir Oliver Franks, former British ambassador in Washington, one of the principal organizers of the European response to the Marshall Plan and now chairman of Lloyds Bank, brought a new dimension to the problem of economic aid when he prepared an analysis of what he called not the East-West problem but the North-South problem; in other words, the relationships of the industrialized nations of the North to the underdeveloped and developing nations of the South. He proposed to the State Department that the United States join as an equal partner with other industrialized nations in an international committee to guide these relationships, to define the magnitude of the problem, to discuss questions of priority and programing, and, if possible, to agree on a general program in which each nation would assume and coordinate its fair share of the burden. "We shall run into real difficulties about the new economic problems which confront us in the broad relationships between Western Europe and the United States," he concluded, "unless we are prepared to look at these issues and resolve them in the light of the wider objectives which we must pursue together." [18]

Supplementary Reading

Elliott, W. Y., *et al., The Political Economy of American Foreign Policy* (New York, 1955). An insider's view.

American Assembly, *International Stability and Progress* (New York, 1957).

Rockefeller Brothers Fund, *The Mid-Century Challenge to U. S. Foreign Policy* (New York, 1959). America at Mid-Century Series.

————, *Foreign Economic Policy for the Twentieth Century* (New York, 1959).

Rostow, E. V., *Stages of Economic Growth* (Cambridge, Eng., 1960).

Staley, Eugene, *The Future of Underdeveloped Countries* (New York, 1954). The economic and political aspects of technical assistance.

Buchanan, Norman S., and Howard S. Ellis, *Approaches to Economic Development* (New York, 1955). A systematic treatment of the subject.

————, and F. A. Lutz, *Rebuilding the World Economy* (New York, Twentieth Century Fund, 1947).

Sharp, Walter R., *International Technical Assistance: Programs and Organization* (Chicago, 1952). Point Four and the UN programs from the standpoint of administration.

Hoselitz, Bert F. (ed.), *The Progress of Underdeveloped Areas* (Chicago, 1952). By sixteen social scientists including Jacob Viner.

Frankel, S. Herbert, *The Economic Impact on Underdeveloped Societies* (Cambridge, Mass., 1953). The techniques of growth.

Williamson, H. F., and J. A. Buttrick (eds.), *Economic Development* (New York, 1954). The problem of raising living standards in underdeveloped areas.

[18] Reported by James Reston, *The New York Times*, Dec. 8, 1959.

Opler, Morris E., *Social Aspects of Technical Assistance in Operation* (Paris, 1954). UNESCO publication, Tensions and Technology Series.

Brown, Harrison, *The Challenge of Man's Future* (New York, 1954). Raising standards for four fifths of mankind.

Steiner, George A., *Government's Role in Economic Life* (New York, 1953). Chapter 8 is entitled "The Impact of National-Security Crises of the 1940s on Public Economic Policy."

Hirschman, A. O., *The Strategy of Economic Development* (New York, 1958).

Kindleberger, C. P., *Economic Development* (New York, 1958).

Gilmore, Donald R., *Developing the "Little" Economies* (New York, Committee for Economic Development, 1960).

Thorp, Willard L., *Trade, Aid, or What?* (Baltimore, Md., 1954). By an outstanding economist.

Commission on Foreign Economic Policy, *Report and Staff Papers* (Washington, D.C., 1954). The report of the Randall Commission.

Myrdal, Gunnar, *An International Economy* (New York, 1956). By the Swedish economist.

Hoskins, Halford L., *The Middle East: Problem Area in World Politics* (New York, 1954). Oil, Point Four, and the people of the Middle East.

International Bank for Reconstruction and Development, *The International Bank for Reconstruction and Development, 1946-1953* (Baltimore, Md., 1954). Chapter 8 deals with technical assistance.

15
THE EFFECT OF
PROLONGED DEFENSE

Post-World War II defense organization; civilian defense; industrial mobilization for defense; issues of policy: inflation, taxation, price and wage controls; world trade and political stability: tariff policy, ITO, GATT, OTC.

The high cost of financing economic rehabilitation in other parts of the world, especially western Europe, following the close of World War II and the strain on the administrative organization of the federal government that accompanied and followed the war, caused Congress and the President to undertake a considerable reorganization of federal agencies, to sweep away administrative debris left over from the war, and to facilitate the formulation and coordination of the continuing defense program.

POSTWAR REORGANIZATION

Among other innovations, the Legislative Reorganization Act of 1946 reduced the number of Congressional committees and in other ways attempted to increase the efficiency of Congress. The Employment Act of 1946, recognizing the need for a stabilized economy, among other things provided for a three-man Council of Economic Advisers to the President and to Congress. An internal reorganization of the State Department extended through the incumbencies of several secretaries. The National Security Acts of 1947 and 1949 combined the Army and Navy departments and added a department for the Air Force. Other parts of the executive branch were simplified, reorganized, or abolished as a result of the Hoover Commission reports of 1949 and 1955. And finally, the Defense Production Act of 1950, with later amendments, laid the foundation for industrial mobilization in case of need. Although there were other and broader objectives, one effect of all these moves was to make it easier for the federal government to convert to a wartime footing if a crisis should arise.

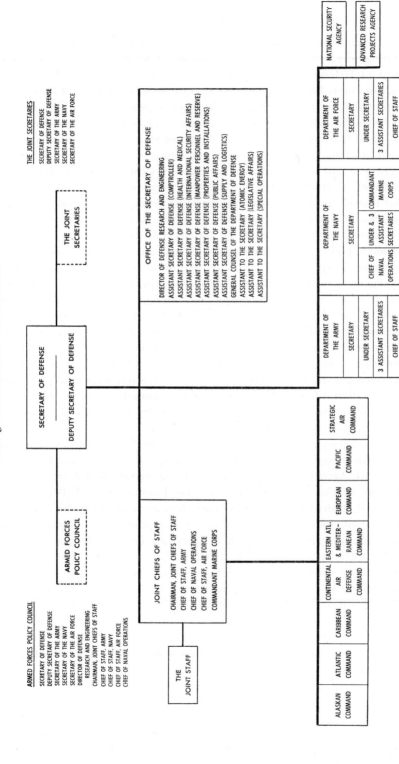

FIG. 9. DEPARTMENT OF DEFENSE

SOURCE: Adapted from *U.S. Government Manual, 1959-1960*.

The Military Establishment

Leaving aside for a moment the industrial mobilization agencies and dealing only with the military establishment, what is now a single Department of Defense includes three subsidiary departments for army, navy, and air force, but each remains separate in some respects. Coordination is provided by membership in the same superdepartment; by common staff agencies which, down to a certain level, handle finance, personnel, and legal matters; and by a Joint Chiefs of Staff which is the nerve center for professional military work. In the Office of the Secretary of Defense, seven assistant secretaries deal respectively with comptrollership; health and medical matters; international security affairs; manpower, personnel, and reserve; properties and installations; public affairs; and supply and logistics. In addition, three assistants to the Secretary are responsible for atomic energy, legislative affairs, and special operations. Finally, there is a general counsel and a director of defense research and engineering.

Some sharp public disputes among the various units in this complex arrangement have caused several major readjustments as to responsibility and relationship—a natural sequel to a merger of agencies that had long been independent and, in a sense, rivals. In addition, the technology of war has been profoundly altered by electronics, nucleonics, and the intercontinental missile, and it is no longer possible to draw a rigid line between air, land, and sea defenses or between tactics and strategy. Thus the management of an enormously tangled institution such as the Pentagon is more than difficult. The general organizational outlines as of 1959 are shown in Figure 9. Charts for the subsidiary departments will be found in the *U. S. Government Manual.*

In addition to the Defense Department, in the Executive Office of the President there is the National Security Council, of which the Central Intelligence Agency and the Operations Coordinating Board are a part, all progeny of the cold-war situation that followed World War II. The National Security Council advises on all matters affecting the integration of domestic, foreign, and military policy, appraising the objectives, commitments, and risks of the United States in relation to its actual and potential military power. The Central Intelligence Agency coordinates all the government's intelligence activities concerned with national security and undertakes certain other intelligence functions on its own account. The Operations Coordinating Board, which was not set up until 1953, acts as an over-all coordinating agency with regard to policies, planning, and operations having to do with national security anywhere within the federal government. The National Aeronautics and Space Council was added in 1958.

Civil Defense

In a literal sense the home front is now a front indeed in case of war, especially atomic war. Although total civilian defense is impossible, industry and government must nevertheless be maintained and civilians protected as much as possible. Many millions of people are required in a civil defense organization, they must be trained and organized, and most of them will have private full-time employment as well.

The Federal Civil Defense Administration, first created as a temporary agency, was put on a permanent legislative footing in 1951. The mandate of this agency was a wide one and included planning, training, the use of resources in time of crisis, a nation-wide warning system, an emergency communications system, the stockpiling and distribution of civil-defense materials and facilities, and the right to invoke extraordinary powers in case of emergency. Chief responsibility lay with the states, with the federal agency acting mainly as coordinator. At the operating level, reliance was almost wholly on volunteers.

As the cold war cooled, however, public apathy, which had always been a problem, became even more pronounced and was reflected in Congress by starvation appropriations to the FCDA. It was estimated in 1956 that some 60 million persons (more than a third of the population) might be killed or wounded in case of attack and that the national warning system was capable of reaching only 15 to 25 percent of the people.[1] A revised civic-defense policy then shifted main reliance at the ground level from volunteers to public agencies—federal, state, and local—at all levels. The FCDA reorganized, concentrated on the most essential of its activities, sheared off some of the minor ones, and finally in 1958 was merged with the Office of Defense Mobilization, which then became the Office of Civil and Defense Mobilization.

Part of the difficulty attending civil defense, in addition to public apathy, is that no one seems to know just what can be done to protect civilian populations in time of nuclear attack. The report of the so-called Gaither Committee, a secret document submitted to the President in 1957, took a pessimistic view of the possibilities. Later the Rand Corporation, a private institution which conducts both classified and unclassified research for government agencies, submitted a report on the same subject that was cautiously optimistic. The problems of blast shelters, fall-out shelters, and the evacuation of large cities in target areas are at the heart of the difficulty.

As presently set up in the Office of Civil and Defense Mobilization, the function of civil defense concentrates on research, planning, assisting, coordinating, and encouraging civil defense at the state and local levels. The agency provides for a nation-wide warning system, for emergency communications, and for the procurement and storage of emergency civil-defense supplies and equipment. It disseminates information, conducts training programs, and may make financial contributions on a matching basis to the states for certain defense personnel and administrative expenses. Its main emphasis, however, is on encouraging the states and localities to take action on their own account. By 1959 every state except

---

[1] Reported by Haldore Hanson, "If the Enemy Did Attack . . . ," *The New Republic* (Jan. 27, 1956).

Pennsylvania, New Mexico, and South Carolina had developed civil-defense plans. The county, however, is considered the basic unit for emergency planning and by 1959 only 572 of the 3047 counties in the country had such plans completed.

Industrial Mobilization for Defense

Wartime industrial mobilization has a long history. The first modern achievement was during World War I when many efforts, later elaborated during World War II, were tried for the first time. These included war-time industrial planning, materials priorities, certain types of production and price controls, the operation by government of a few vital industries, control of industrial relations, and food rationing. Between the two wars a master blueprint for industrial mobilization was worked out in some detail, but when World War II started, the plan was virtually scrapped and "It was only in 1943, after four years of testing and experimentation, that a stable organization was developed to meet the demands of the war emergency. What emerged differed radically from what had been planned in the decade of the 1930's." [2]

The mobilization of war production in World War II centered around the War Production Board, whose duty it was to allocate production between military and civilian needs. But a major difficulty was to discover just what the military needs were, and what the basis of reckoning had been so as to make possible a projection of future needs, and it was not until after Pearl Harbor that such information was forthcoming. Thereafter, however, production totals were analyzed by functions and economic processes such as procurement, raw materials, facilities and construction, distribution, manpower, and the like; they were also analyzed by industries and major commodities. In 1942 WPB had a staff of 18,000, including the best statisticians, planners, industry experts, and economic technicians of all kinds that could be assembled. Difficulties of internal administration in an agency with the entire economy as its field of action, as well as problems of relationship with other agencies, were quick to appear. By the end of the war there were some fifty of these emergency agencies, including especially those dealing with manpower, defense transportation, wage stabilization and labor disputes, price controls and rationing, and, at the top, a kind of supercoordinating organization, the Office of War Mobilization.

But despite the difficulties of administration and coordination, the record of achievement was outstanding to the point of surprising even those who had set the goals, for the United States produced more goods and services in a short time than the world had ever seen before. Thus in terms of 1939 dollars, total output rose from $88.6 billion in 1939 to

[2] Office of Civilian Administration, *Industrial Mobilization for War: History of the War Production Board and Predecessor Agencies, 1940-1945*, Vol. 1 (Washington, D.C., 1947), p. xiii.

$135 billion in 1944, or an increase of 52 percent. The percentage of gross national product going into the war program rose from less than 2 percent in 1939 to 40 percent in 1943 and 1944, but at the same time consumer purchases also rose to a point nearly 12 percent higher than before the war. The nation's total productive capacity rose 50 percent during the war, largely in war materials but also in such civilian items as iron and steel, synthetic rubber, aviation gasoline, aluminum, and magnesium. Employment increased despite the drain occasioned by the armed forces (11 million persons), and so also did labor productivity, which expanded by some 25 percent; although part of this was due to longer hours and around-the-clock shifts, other factors were higher incentives, a pooling of technological know-how, and the development of new products and processes.

When the war ended and WPB went out of business, some continuing attention to industrial mobilization was needed as the cold war began to declare itself, and consequently Congress passed the National Security Act of 1947 which among other things created the *National Security Resources Board* to advise the President with regard to industrial and civilian mobilization, the effective use of resources, the unification and coordination of certain federal activities in time of war, and the strategic relocation of industries, services, government, and economic activities, the continuous operation of which is essential to the national security. Until the outbreak of the Korean war in June 1950 this agency was the chief unit in Washington responsible for industrial mobilization, but its authority was merely advisory. Three months after the new war started, however, Congress passed the Defense Production Act which, with later amendments, accorded large powers to the President and became the foundation for most of the industrial mobilization activities that followed.

These included the *National Production Authority* within the Department of Commerce to see that the requirements for materials needed for arms production, including labor, were met on schedule and the remaining supplies distributed for civilian use; the *Economic Stabilization Agency* to control inflation and help maintain a stable national economy; the *Salary Stabilization Board* to stabilize the salaries of persons not represented by official labor organizations; the *Wage Stabilization Board* with both wage stabilization and labor dispute functions; the *Office of Price Stabilization* (successor to the Office of Price Administration of World War II) to prevent inflation and preserve the value of the national currency by setting price ceilings designed to stabilize the cost of living and costs of production, both civilian and military; and the *Defense Production Administration* to determine policies and programs governing the allocation and use of resources.

As the Korean war continued through 1950, in December of that year President Truman proclaimed the existence of an unlimited national emergency and the following day, by Executive Order, set up the Office of Defense Mobilization in his own executive office, to direct, control, and coordinate all mobilization activities of the executive branch of the government, including but not limited to production, procurement, manpower, stabilization, and transport. The ODM itself was a small organization concerned with policy guidance and control and with the settlement of interagency differences, with its operating activities distributed among the regular government departments. The main areas of jurisdiction were manpower, materials, production, stabilization, telecommunications, plans and readiness, and transportation, plus several advisory boards in these and other functions.

This, then, is the main outline of legislation and organization for the mobilization effort of the federal government as it existed by the end of the Truman administration.[3] By the time President Eisenhower came to office in 1953 the Korean war was coming to an end and the national economy was about to start on an upswing destined to outdo the predictions or even the most optimistic of the experts. All the emergency agencies in the foregoing list except the National Security Council and the Office of Defense Mobilization (which, in fact, was strengthened) were abolished as federal controls were taken off wages, food, all consumer goods, and rents. A fluctuating international situation, however, caused a continuing alertness in Washington as to the need to reimpose controls quickly on wages, salaries, prices, and rents if a sudden attack should occur. Believing that a thousand company plans are better than a single master design, the Commerce Department urged the nation's industries to prepare their own plans for resuming production after an attack. The department also created the Business and Defense Services Administration to promote current defense production and long-range industrial preparedness. The ODM announced a scheme to keep production machinery in readiness. The Industrial College of the Armed Forces began to train civilians in the techniques and requirements of industrial mobilization. Plans were discussed in the administration and in Congress to give the President stand-by powers to impose wartime controls. Provision was made for the training of a ready reserve of from 3000 to 4000 business and labor executives for government service in an emergency. And finally, the Federal Civil Defense Administration was merged with the Office of Defense Mobilization.

From a planning and decision-making standpoint, the international and domestic programs of the federal government are now more closely tied together than they have ever been in the past. Further, the OCDM as the central agency of industrial mobilization is small and relatively streamlined and hence is able to maneuver quickly, un-

---

[3] Other agencies not mentioned here are the Defense Materials Procurement Agency, the Defense Transport Administration, and several units in the Department of the Interior, in addition to many other permanent agencies that contribute in some part to the mobilization program.

burdened by an overload of detailed responsibilities. Nevertheless, the great weakness of federal organization is still largely unsolved: how to secure as much coordination in the execution of a program as there is in its planning. Administrative solutions are, in fact, of a piece with decisions on public policy, for each is essential to the success of the other.

ISSUES OF POLICY AND PRINCIPLE

Important as these structural and administrative matters are, however, they are not usually as interesting as fixing goals and securing agreement on the proper policy to be followed on a number of related economic issues that have to do with the prolonged effect of defense on the national economy: inflation, taxation, price and wage controls, and world trade, to mention the more important ones.

Inflation

Inflation is a serious threat to the economy of a nation that has had to deal with war, even of the cold variety. When full employment has been reached, money is plentiful, consumer goods are becoming scarce, and government spending is on the increase, the usual temptation, for political reasons, is to add to the national debt instead of raising taxes, especially in election years, and the United States is always within at least two years of a Congressional election. Moreover, the majority of the population that benefits from inflation in the form of higher wages, incomes, and profits is lulled into a sense of false security, compared with the minority that must make do on fixed salaries, annuities, pensions, and the like. To this must be added the obvious fact that from a political standpoint, the prosperous majority, represented as it is by powerful pressure groups such as trade associations, labor organizations, and professional groups, is far more influential in the formulation of national policy than the minority that lives on relatively inelastic incomes.

A cycle of higher wages and profits creates a cycle of higher prices, and if this spiraling cannot be stopped, then there are certain consequences: money becomes of less worth, creditors receive relatively less than the sums they loaned, government costs go up, the value of savings declines, people on fixed incomes find their incomes sharply reduced, and nations purchasing from the United States must pay prices for military and civilian goods so high that the stability of their own national economies is threatened. Because it is accompanied by rising costs, our military planners rightly stress inflation as a major peril to a successful defense effort. But in addition, inflation is often followed by depression, which is equally disruptive to a defense program. Although our economic and political system could doubtless survive the ordeal, "the possible weakening of our security efforts . . . carries with it the threat of quick achievement of Communism's global goals." [4]

By the end of 1950 it was estimated that the cost of defense for the next four years would be at the rate of more than $50 billion a year. A little more than a year later defense spending was scheduled soon to reach an annual rate of from $60 billion to $65 billion, as against $35 billion in 1951. Simultaneously, a front-page headline in *The New York Times* announced, "Prosperity Still Rising with Inflation Frozen into Economic Structure." [5] The reciprocating relationship between war and inflation is dramatically illustrated in Figure 10 and by figures on the cost of military equipment. By 1952 the cost of initially equipping a basic infantry division had increased from $19 million to $91 million in seven years, and the cost of an armored division had gone up from $40 million to $293 million. In aircraft procurement, the "fly-away" cost of a B-29 used in World War II (the largest aircraft in that conflict) ran to something like $680,000, compared to $3.5 million for the B-26 of 1952. Even though equipment at the later date included many items not used earlier so that the figures are not strictly comparable, the calculations nevertheless show a basic difference in costs.

Economists generally agree that control of inflation must rest on adequate fiscal and monetary restrictions buttressed by an informed public opinion and an effective governmental mechanism. One group of experts advocates a strict anti-inflation budget policy, the careful timing of military expenditures so as not to concentrate them in a short period, self-acting checks in a more progressive tax system so that when incomes rise through price inflation, an increasingly large percentage is automatically taken in taxes, and finally, greater economy and efficiency in government wherever possible. [6] Another group of economists points to a whole arsenal of controls that *must* be taken in some kind of combination if the evil of inflation is to be avoided, the main remedies being general controls, specific controls, and price and wage controls. Moreover, controls will prove more or less useful according to the stage of a defense or war effort at which they are applied, and hence proper timing is essential. [7] In addition, as pointed out in the 1950 *Mid-Year Economic Report* to the President. "The more prompt and vigorous we are with these general measures (i.e., fiscal and credit measures), the less need there will be for all of the comprehensive controls [such as price controls] which involve the consideration of thou-

[4] G. A. Lincoln, W. S. Stone, and T. H. Harvey, *Economics of National Security* (New York, 1950), p. 537.

[5] *The New York Times*, Jan. 2, 1952.

[6] Twentieth Century Fund, Committee Report, *Financing Defense* (New York, 1951), pp. 149–161.

[7] Jules Backman and others, *War and Defense Economics* (New York, 1952).

sands of individual situations and thus involve infinitely greater administrative difficulties and much greater interference with individual
choice and initiative."

As already noted, wartime federal controls on prices, rents, salaries,
and wages were removed in 1953. Thereafter, average price levels remained fairly stable until 1955 when a sharp rise occurred which has
continued with few interruptions. In contrast to the classic type of inflation which is based on an excess of spending power, this so-called
"new" inflation was said by some economists to stem partly from such

FIG. 10. WARS AS A MAJOR CAUSE OF INFLATION— FROM 1812 TO KOREA

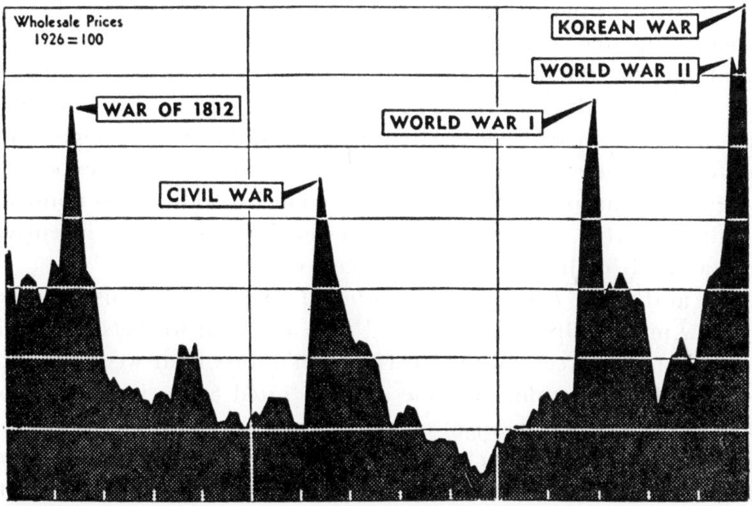

SOURCE: Courtesy of *The New York Times*, May 25, 1952

relatively modern developments as strong labor unions able to secure
high wages and concentrated monopolistic industries able to "administer"
prices irrespective of demand. The nation was at peace, the federal budget
was generally in balance, and a tight-money policy had been in force
for some time. But prices went up anyway. The President appointed two
cabinet committees to study the matter, made several personal appeals
to business and labor to exercise restraint, vetoed bills that would
have increased government spending even though the objectives were
desirable, and asked Congress to increase the interest limit on long-
term government loans, which Congress refused to do. But neither
Congress nor any member of the administration proposed to increase
taxes.

Tax Policy

In 1949 taxes in the United States were 18 percent of the national income; in 1958 they were about 22 percent. What would be the effect on the economy if the figure were to range from 25 percent to 33 percent of the national income? At the end of World War II the national debt was in the vicinity of $272 billion. Thereafter the continuing cost of past wars was an additional security expense, approximating $12 billion a year divided almost equally between interest on the national debt and benefits to veterans. By mid-1950 the cost of major national security, including expenditures for the armed forces, the stockpiling of raw materials, and the atomic energy program, amounted to $20 billion a year for each year since 1945. Then there was a sharp swing upward as the Korean fighting broke out. President Truman requested a total budget for 1953 of $85 billion, of which 76 percent was for the security and international aid programs described in the preceding chapter. By 1958 the total cost of past wars and present major national security aggregated $51.4 billion, or 71 percent of the total federal budget. If we must expect a similar annual expenditure for these two purposes for some years to come, in addition to nondefense expenditures, what will be the effect on new investment, the incentive to save, standards of living, and social services?

The authors of *Economics of National Security* face this issue head-on. "How much will we pay to live?" they ask. Will workers be required to contribute 10 percent of their earnings in a forty-hour week as survival insurance? If the national income of the United States is $400 billion a year (a figure reached in 1959) or better, then we could safely spend $75 billion on government (exclusive of emergency defense needs in case of attack) and be no worse off than we were in the early 1950s. In other words, if the economy continues to expand, the level of income for the individual might be no higher than it has been but it would be adequate. The important point is that expenditures are relative to income; if national income is high, then high taxes hurt less; but if national income is low, then high taxes will certainly be painful.

A more pessimistic prognosis is that of a staff of distinguished economists who, in a book entitled *Making Capitalism Work*,[8] argue that government debt and taxation may prove the undoing of American free enterprise. It is true, of course, that our national debt has risen remarkably since World War II, from about $43 billion in 1940 to about $276.3 in 1958. High taxes, say these experts, seriously hamper industry's ability to invest in new tools and equipment. Government spending reduces private spending in crucial areas of the economy so that eventually the government might take over the economy "lock, stock, and barrel." According to this unpromising view, an increase of as

[8] Dexter M. Keezer and others, *Making Capitalism Work* (New York, 1950), p. 279.

much as $10 billion in government spending might wreck the economy. Actually, of course, the figure for the increase in government spending since 1950 is not $10 billion but over $40 billion, although the ratio of spending to national income has not greatly increased. And as far as the national debt is concerned, the present worry is not so much with the amount of the debt, serious as that may be, as it is with the additional effect of major new borrowings that would be required in case of war or some other national emergency.

After several tax increases, federal revenues reached a peak of $69.1 billion in 1958. The highest mark during World War II was $44.5 billion. By comparison, in 1941 the total was $7.1 billion and .in 1932 it was only $1.9 billion. But the national income also rose, of course, from $40 billion in 1932 to $81 billion in 1940, to $181 billion in 1945, and to $400 billion in 1959.

With these figures in mind it is interesting to note the comment of Colin Clark, an Australian economist who in 1950 posed the question with regard to taxation, "How high is too high?" His answer was that the wise political and economic limit of taxation is somewhere near 25 percent of the national income.[9] If his deductions are correct (and his argument makes interesting reading), then taxation in the United States is still considerably below the danger mark, being only about 20 percent of the national income in 1959. It should not be forgotten, however, that this relatively favorable level of taxation [10] is still accompanied by a certain amount of deficit spending by the federal government each year.

Price and Wage Controls

Price and wage controls, long continued, tend to weaken the self-regulating price system and thus help undermine free enterprise. On the other hand, if such controls are not imposed when needed, then a runaway inflation might prove even more disruptive. The proper decision, therefore, is likely to be a fine one. In practice, of course, the problem is complicated by pressure groups trying to make up Congressmen's minds—and usually doing a pretty effective job of it —and by popular attitudes and prejudices, which also carry much weight in decisions on public policy. The greater is the need, therefore, for statements of economic principle that will stand up when tested and that can be readily understood by the citizen. In case of war, the necessity for controls is indisputable; during peacetime, the presumption against them is equally clear; but in a cold war which

[9] Colin Clark, "The Danger Point in Taxes," *Harper's Magazine* (Dec. 1950), pp. 67-69.

[10] In 1950 taxation in Japan was 30 percent of the national income; at the start of World War II it was 26 percent in Great Britain and in 1949 it was 43.7 percent; in 1950 in the Netherlands it was 30 percent and in Norway it was 40 percent.

is neither one thing nor the other, the decision becomes a hard one.

Most economists believe that in preventing inflation, price controls are only one tool among several and that fiscal, monetary, and wage controls must also be imposed. Because government responds to public demands, however, varying degrees of price and wage controls, rationing, and the like are usually forthcoming when the atmosphere is tight enough to warrant them. Moreover, the government may do much to avoid formal price controls if its purchasing methods are sufficiently skillful. Thus, where government is the principal buyer in a particular market, it can investigate profits and, through its bargaining power, keep prices in line; and even where government is only one of several buyers, because of its size it can usually exert a considerable pressure, if the need is clearly seen.

During World War II when rationing and price controls were essential, the Office of Price Administration was given the job of stabilizing prices, preventing speculation and price increases including rents, eliminating profiteering, hoarding, and manipulation, securing increased production, preventing a postemergency collapse of values, and encouraging cooperation between the government and producers, processors, and others to these ends. This was a very large order indeed, but the public support OPA received helped make it a success. Some 7000 local rationing boards were quickly set up and manned by local citizens, serving without pay, to handle price ceilings and the rationing of scarce items such as tires, sugar, meat, automobiles, fuel, oil, and gasoline.

The problems of decision in such an enterprise are enormous. For example, when and at what level should price ceilings be established, and when should they be changed? The test was to find the point at which inflationary price rises could be curbed without preventing the shift of resources to war production. Another standard was to maintain price ceilings at a point that would yield earnings to an industry equal to its annual average earnings in the 1936-1939 base period, adjusted for changes in investment. But what is meant by "an industry"? An industry, said one legal ruling, is all the firms that make a particular product, but the terms "iron and steel industry" and "cotton textile industry" refer not to single industries but to congeries of industries. Again, how are costs and profits to be determined when they include "inadmissible" or "unrecognizable" costs? And what is the meaning of "net worth"? Nevertheless, though such difficulties were legion, not only in its own work but in its relationships with other wartime agencies (especially the War Production Board), OPA did its job efficiently and democratically, was freer than most wartime agencies from interest-group pressure, and helped to restrain inflation without impeding essential supply.

Price fixing in any form means that the supposedly automatic forces of the market must be superseded by decisions deliberately made by man and often incompatible with those forces; accordingly, the more of man-made decisions there are, the greater are the areas of the economy that must be regulated if opposing forces are to be kept in balance. It is partly for this reason that, in practice, price controls have usually been accompanied by various other kinds of controls including rationing, commodity priorities, subsidies, ceilings on wages and salaries, and the like.

The first control agency in the field of labor during World War II was the Defense Mediation Board created in 1941 to settle labor disputes that threatened to obstruct the production or transportation of equipment and materials essential to the national defense. But in 1942, because of the pressure of inflation, the need had gone beyond the settling of labor disputes to include ceilings on salaries and wages. Consequently the National War Labor Board was set up as final arbiter of wartime labor disputes as well as to control adjustments of wages and salaries under $5000 a year. The board functioned until the end of the war, with the usual difficulties attending controls in this very sensitive area and with organized labor itself in two and sometimes even three separate camps. When the board was terminated in 1945, it was succeeded by the National Wage Stabilization Board set up in the Labor Department to continue the work of stabilizing wages and salaries and settling certain kinds of labor disputes. But this agency also came to an end in 1947. As already noted, the need to renew controls during the Korean war caused the creation of two new units in the wage and price field in 1951, but two years later all federal controls were off everywhere.

World Trade and Political Stability

In any discussion of emergency controls, inflation, national income, national debt, and taxation in a period of defense, the pivotal question is, how long is the tension going to last, which raises the question of what can be done to relieve international tensions. Governments make wars and hence must find the means of preventing them. The economic area is a main one in which to work.

A nation that fears an outbreak of war strives for economic self-sufficiency, reduces its dependence on international trade as much as possible, and tries to build a kind of garrison state with reserves of arms and materials securely stored and ready for use. But economic isolation will not work, says Samuelson, a proposition on which most economists are agreed.[11] The goal of peace means full support for international economic interdependency. Rather than economic self-sufficiency,

[11] Paul A. Samuelson, *Economics: An Introductory Analysis* (New York, 1951), pp. 682–683.

therefore, the better policy is for a nation to specialize in areas where it has a comparative economic advantage and to buy from other nations the things that cannot be as economically produced at home.

Protective tariffs are equally objectionable on other grounds, because in effect they offer a subsidy to marginal units of production, violate the law of intensive production in nations enjoying a relative economic advantage, discourage the international exchange of goods on a mutually profitable basis, raise the cost of living by limiting competition, and prevent the free exportation of surpluses, such as agricultural products from the United States. The tariff issue has always been a thorny one in this country, with the first high tariff enacted soon after the winning of the Revolution. But with our enormous productive capacity and our potential for exports, it has become clear that if we would sell, we must buy, and hence since 1934 there has been a gradual lowering of tariff walls.

In the federal government, the U. S. Tariff Commission was created in 1916 with six commissioners appointed by the President with Senatorial approval for six-year, staggered terms, and the usual bipartisan requirement obtains. The commission's duties are to investigate foreign and domestic tariff regulations, make surveys of domestic and foreign industries, study foreign and domestic manufacturing costs, and report on foreign discriminations and the operation of the customs laws. In other words, the commission is an arm of both Congress and the President in fixing tariff rates but has no administrative powers of its own.

In 1922 the so-called flexible tariff was enacted, providing for rate adjustments (upward, on the average, as it proved) of existing duties by Presidential proclamation in accordance with certain procedures and limitations. In 1930 the Smoot-Hawley Act sent rates to an all-time peak. Finally in 1934 Secretary of State Cordell Hull succeeded in getting Congress to pass the Reciprocal Trade Agreements Act, which since then has periodically been extended and amended. The act authorizes the negotiation of trade agreements with other nations willing to make concessions relative to specific articles; thereafter the President may reduce tariff rates for like concessions from other nations and his freedom to increase rates on the articles covered is circumscribed. There are also certain so-called escape or peril-point clauses that permit raising rates if domestic producers are threatened. Although a trade agreement resembles a treaty in that one of the parties is a foreign power, in reality it is an executive agreement and as such does not require Senatorial approval.

By 1946, reciprocal trade agreements had been signed by the United States with twenty-nine nations and tariff rates were somewhat lowered in consequence, but by that time it had become clear that bilateral arrangements were of only limited use. In 1947-1948, therefore, delegates from fifty-six nations met at Havana to negotiate an International Trade

Organization charter, the purpose being to establish rules of conduct for governing international economic relations and to create an agency to provide information and technical assistance, administer the charter, and settle disputes. But the United States failed to ratify the finished charter and it has not been implemented.

Meanwhile, under United States leadership, the representatives of twenty-one nations (by 1960 the number had increased to thirty-seven) agreed to lower tariffs by multilateral agreement and to maintain these rates in order to stimulate recovery in devastated nations and as a barrier against communism. Built on top of the reciprocal-trade-agreements program as far as this nation is concerned, the General Agreement on Tariffs and Trade (GATT) provides for concessions on about 45,000 items, accounting for more than half the world's imports. The United States reduced its duties on these articles to the floor set by the Reciprocal Trade Agreements Act, which is 50 percent on some 60 percent of our imports.

GATT is an agreement rather than an organization, its weakness being that its members meet only once a year, and there is no permanent secretariat to keep up with current foreign trade developments or to supervise the observance of trade agreements. To supply this lack, it is proposed that an Organization for Trade Cooperation (OTC) be established, but the proposition raised so many smoldering protectionist sentiments that Congress has always withheld approval, and the other nations concerned are waiting until approval is given before setting the plan in action. As presently outlined, OTC would have an assembly of thirty-seven members, an executive committee consisting of five leading trading nations plus twelve others representing different areas and types of economies. There would also be a permanent secretariat to study trade conditions and publish facts and figures on international trade. OTC would not be part of the United Nations but might, of course, have an informal relationship to it.

A formal international agreement on tariffs is a major issue of world economic policy. In the Western bloc, for example, some nations subsidize their merchant marine and their exports and tolerate international cartels that tend to restrict markets and encourage monopoly.[12] In other cases, nations monopolize certain commodities that enter into world competition, making it hard for private enterprisers elsewhere to compete on equal terms. Imperial preference in Great Britain and tariff walls that are still high in the United States are additional problems. Although the total volume of international trade has greatly increased since 1950, these restrictive practices constitute an unnecessary brake on healthy trade among the Western nations, thus lessening their prosperity and their ability to defend themselves as well as driving some nations, in desperation, into trade with the Communist bloc. And finally

---

[12] See Chap. 23, below.

there are those who fear that unless OTC is firmly established, an alternative and much less desirable world trade organization antagonistic to the private-enterprise system will be set up, at the instigation of the USSR, within the United Nations. The stakes in international trade policy are therefore high and the outcome is uncertain.

Supplementary Reading

American Assembly, *International Stability and Progress: United States Interests and Instruments* (New York, 1957).

——, *Representation of the United States Abroad* (New York, 1956).

——, *The U.S. Stake in the U.N.* (New York, 1954).

——, *The United States and Latin America* (New York, 1959).

——, *The United States and the Far East* (New York, 1956).

Rockefeller Brothers Fund, *International Security: The Military Aspect* (New York, 1959). America at Mid-Century Series.

Wallace, Donald H., *Economic Controls and Defense* (New York, Twentieth Century Fund, 1953).

Chandler, Lester V., and D. H. Wallace, *Economic Mobilization and Stabilization* (New York, 1951). Contains a valuable collection of materials.

Lincoln, G. A., W. S. Stone, and T. H. Harvey, *Economics of National Security* (New York, 1950). An informative book on this subject.

Backman, Jules, and others, *War and Defense Economics* (New York, 1952).

——, *The Economics of Armament Inflation* (New York, 1951). The economic policies and principles to be applied.

Abbott, Charles C., *The Federal Debt, Structure, and Impact* (New York, Twentieth Century Fund, 1953).

Hart, A. G., and E. C. Brown, *Financing Defense* (New York, 1951). The fiscal and monetary aspects.

Elliott, W. Y., *Mobilization Planning and the National Security*, Public Affairs Bulletin No. 81, Legislative Reference Service, Library of Congress (Washington, D.C., 1950).

——, and others, *The Political Economy of American Foreign Policy* (New York, 1955). Its concepts, strategy, and limits.

United States Bureau of the Budget, *The United States at War* (Washington, D.C., 1946). The best comprehensive official account.

Nelson, Donald M., *Arsenal of Democracy* (New York, 1946). By the former head of the War Production Board.

Mansfield, Harvey C., and associates, *A Short History of OPA*, Office of Temporary Controls, General Publication No. 15 (Washington, D.C., 1947). Chapters 4 and 5 deal with rent control and rationing.

Baldwin, Hanson W., *The Price of Power* (New York, 1948). Military requirements.

Harris, Seymour E., *The European Recovery Program* (Cambridge, Mass., 1948).

——, *Price and Related Controls in the United States* (New York, 1945).

——, *The Economics of Mobilization and Inflation* (New York, 1951).

Commission on Organization of the Executive Branch of the Government (first

Hoover Commission), *National Security Organization, Appendix G* (Washington, D.C., 1949).

Office of Civilian Administration, *Industrial Mobilization for War: History of the War Production Board and Predecessor Agencies, 1940-1945,* Vol. I, *Program and Administration,* Historical Reports on War Administration, WPB General Study No. 1 (Washington, D.C., 1947). Recommended for this course.

Scitovsky, Tibor, Edward Shaw, and Lorie Tarshis, *Mobilizing Resources for War—The Economic Alternatives* (New York, 1951). Stresses policy issues.

Steiner, George A. (ed.), *Economic Problems of National Defense* (Bloomington, Ind., 1941).

——, *Government's Role in Economic Life* (New York, 1953). Chapter 8, "The National-Security Crises of the 1940's."

Finletter, Thomas K., *Power and Policy: U. S. Foreign Policy and Military Power in the Hydrogen Age* (New York, 1954). By the former civilian head of the Air Force.

Randall, Clarence B., *A Foreign Economic Policy for the United States* (New York, 1954). By an outstanding businessman.

Mason, Edward S., *Controlling World Trade* (New York, 1946). The role of cartels.

Chalmers, Henry, *World Trade Policies* (Berkeley, Calif., 1953). Periodic surveys of trade policies of the principal nations.

Redford, Emmette S., *Administration of National Economic Control* (New York, 1952). The principles applicable.

Mikesell, Raymond F., *United States Economic Policy and International Relations* (New York, 1952). Chapters 13–18 are especially useful.

Hancock, W. K., and M. M. Gowing, *British War Economy* (London, 1949). Experience of a sister democracy.

Committee for Economic Development, *The Uses and Dangers of Direct Controls in Peacetime* (New York, 1949). The dangers of prolonged defense.

16

ATOMIC ENERGY

Potentialities; McMahon Act of 1946; problems and issues; legislation of 1954; atoms for peace; international control; Euratom; testing ban; AEC program; use of contract device.

The discovery of how to release atomic energy has created more interesting problems of business-government relationships than any other major development in modern history. Used carelessly, or deliberately, for destructive purposes, atomic energy could wipe out civilization on this planet; used for constructive purposes in industry, medicine, and agriculture, it could have an equally profound but beneficial effect on the future of mankind. Which of these two alternatives will prevail is not yet settled and thus our stake in the determination of policy in this area is about as basic as any that could be imagined. By its very nature the development of atomic energy in each nation must be controlled by the most responsible segment of society, which is government; and because its possession by any nation makes it of vital interest to the security of all nations, there must be some form of international control as well. At present there is hardly any aspect of life that is not touched in some way by this revolutionary new discovery.

ATOMIC ENERGY LEGISLATION IN THE UNITED STATES

Atomic energy was largely developed in the United States during World War II and was a decisive factor in the ending of that war. Produced and tested in the greatest secrecy, the fact of atomic fission was dramatically made public with the dropping of two bombs on Japan, and thereafter it was imperative that Congress act at once to guard the secrets of the process and the health and safety of the people. The choice was between two basic formulas: a continuation of the essentially military control under which atomic energy had been developed, or a change to civilian control.

McMahon Act of 1946

The McMahon Act of 1946, supported by atomic scientists and eventually by an overwhelming Congressional majority, placed control in civilian hands. It established the Atomic Energy Commission of five members, one to be designated as chairman, all appointed by the President with Senatorial approval for terms of five years, one vacancy occurring each year. The commission appoints a general manager to handle the executive phases of the work. A deputy general manager, five assistant general managers, a number of division and office directors, a general counsel, and a controller are in charge of various aspects of the program. A hearing examiner assists the commissioners at the top level.

The AEC's main activities cover classification, information, intelligence, nuclear-materials management, security, international activities, manufacturing (including raw materials, production, construction, and supply), research and industrial development (including biology, medicine, and isotopes and reactor development), inspection, licensing and regulation, military application, planning, and industrial relations. A General Advisory Committee of nine civilian members is concerned with scientific and technical matters relating to materials, production, and research and development. In addition, there is a Military Liaison Committee of seven members to represent the Defense Department in all matters which the Department deems to relate to the application of atomic weapons or atomic energy. Finally Congressional oversight is provided by a Joint Committee on Atomic Energy consisting of nine members from the House of Representatives and nine from the Senate, which since its creation in 1946 has gained a high reputation for efficiency, expertness, good sense, and leadership.

The stated purposes of the McMahon Act (subject to the overriding necessity at all times of making the maximum contribution to the common defense and security) are to promote world peace, improve the general welfare, increase the standard of living, and strengthen free competition in private enterprise. As might be supposed, the objectives of world peace and free competition have in practice presented the chief difficulties. Another inherent problem is that of security regulations and the consequent shielding of a government activity from public knowledge and hence from constructive criticism. The legislation stipulates that all information concerning the manufacture or utilization of atomic weapons, the production of fissionable materials, and the use of such materials in the production of power shall be classified as restricted. Only if the AEC decides that particular information will not endanger the national security may it be made available. Disclosure without such permission is punishable by fine and imprisonment and, if the intent is to injure the United States, by life imprisonment or death.

Problems and Issues

The atomic energy program soon raised a number of problems such as had never before been encountered in government administration. For example, because of the requirement of secrecy, how were members of the joint Congressional committee to know what was going on within this man-made monopoly with a high security wall thrust up around it? Actually this has been worked out fairly well, in part, at least, because of the high caliber of the committee. Even more important in practice, perhaps, how is the public to be prevented from developing unwarranted assumptions, and how are scientists to make needed contributions in an area shrouded in mystery and to which only a few are admitted? How is an enterprise in which more than $25 billion of the public's funds were invested by 1960 to escape becoming the entering wedge for large-scale government ownership in a free-enterprise system? Alternatively, if the assets, patents, and revolutionary technological developments in atomic energy are turned over to large-scale private enterprise, how can public giveaway and private monopolistic policies be avoided? Allied to this question, the McMahon Act states that competition shall be safeguarded, but how can this be done when the capital costs and the risks of even a part of the atomic energy program are seemingly greater than any one corporation —however enormous the assets of some of them may be—is able to undertake? Up to the final steps in the production of atomic energy for both wartime and peacetime purposes, the method is identical; how therefore can the peacetime uses be fostered without risking the leak of basic military and security information? And finally, how can the production and use of atomic weapons be internationally controlled so as to prevent nations from destroying each other?

On the credit side, however, certain great benefits of atomic energy to mankind were soon appreciated. Because the components of this type of power are easily transported, remote places lacking natural sources of power but having abundant raw materials may become industrial centers, thus advancing standards of living especially in underdeveloped nations; revolutionary new methods in medicine including the treatment of cancer are possible; man-created photosynthesis may provide an increasing food supply for the world's mounting population; radioisotopes may be used in advanced technology and production; sea water may be made available for human and industrial uses; and finally, atomic energy is a source of power far exceeding all others except the rays of the sun, and even those may some day be harnessed.

Indeed, with only one proviso, the beneficial potentialities of atomic energy greatly outweigh the new problems that must be solved before these potentialities are realized. The proviso is that in the meantime there shall be no blundering on the part of statesmen, however accidental, that might cause our civilization to reach a point where it will no longer have any use for potentialities of any kind, beneficial or otherwise. Consequently, the economic and political leaders of nations and of the United Nations have been and will continue to be tested as never before. It is worth noting, furthermore, that in the making of their decisions, the margin for error has been reduced to virtually nothing at all.

Legislation of 1954

Eight years of experience with the McMahon Act showed a general satisfaction with it and even with its administration. Consequently the Atomic Energy Act of 1954 was passed not because of any failure of the original design but because of a desire to instrument two related policies of the Eisenhower administration then in office: to broaden the international control of atomic energy to include our friends and allies as well as other nations in process of choosing sides between the East and the West; and second, to transfer a part of the peacetime development of atomic power from governmental to private operation. The first of these propositions created relatively little controversy but the second raised so many issues of public policy that it became a *cause célèbre* as it passed through Congress attended by filibusters and passionate expositions in the press on the subject of public versus private power.

Of the major provisions of the 1954 legislation, two relate to international control: first, where the secrecy imposed by the 1946 act can safely be relaxed, the United States may share information with its military allies and hence increase the effectiveness of all; and second, there may be an exchange of information with other friendly nations concerning the peaceful uses of atomic energy, subject again, of course, to adequate safeguards. The first of these provisions was of immediate assistance to NATO and especially to our British and Canadian allies who had been restive during the sole-possession period. The second was dramatically inaugurated by the shipment of small peacetime reactor models to distant nations, such as India, in order to demonstrate the possibilities of this new technological development.

With regard to the domestic program, in the 1954 legislation the main steps leading to a relaxation of the government monopoly and the encouragement of private enterprise were these: (1) the Atomic Energy Commission may *license* the private construction, ownership, and operation of atomic power plants, the private possession and use of nuclear fuel, and the private sale of by-produce materials. (2) Government *patents* may be privately used and the companies may acquire their own patents under certain conditions. (3) Licenses, when made available to private corporations, *must be freely granted* to those that are eligible during the first five years (subsequently extended) of the act, thus paying lip service, at least, to the antimonopoly provisions of the McMahon Act. (4) The AEC may not itself enter into the *commercial power business,* but it may sell the power generated at experimental installations; in this connection, public agencies have an equal right with private utility corporations to apply for licenses and the principle of preference to municipal and cooperative undertakings is maintained. These last provisions, of course, were among the most controversial, called forth the deepest-hued periods of oratory, and the solution represented a compromise in Congress between the adherents to different sides in the power question and the pressure groups in each case.

Taken together, the provisions of the 1954 legislation did somewhat relax the drastic secrecy imposed by the McMahon Act, but they did not by any means solve all the special problems created by the development of atomic energy.

INTERNATIONAL CONTROL

Although issues relating to public and private participation in the field of atomic energy are great, those surrounding the international control of atomic weapons are unsurpassed in their possibly fateful effect on the future of mankind. Since the end of World War II there have been several rather distinct periods of negotiation in an effort to avoid this danger. In the initial period, a committee of the United Nations tried to reconcile the opposing positions of the United States and the Soviet Union and to come up with a plan that would effect a compromise, but none was found. Following this, the United States and the Soviet Union, working through friendly or uncommitted nations, tried to secure support for their respective sides. The upshot was that as far as atomic arms were concerned, the tendency was to consider their control as a part of the larger problem of disarmament in general.

As an alternative, the United States led a move to give the UN a more pominent role in the development of atomic energy for peacetime uses in the hope that through this indirect approach a solution might be found to the problem of control on a wider basis. There was also a very practical development called Euratom, a plan by which six western European nations combined for the peacetime development of atomic energy. Then in 1958 a series of talks was started in Geneva looking toward outlawing of atomic testing. And in 1960 a new series of disarmament talks was undertaken.

The original American plan for the control of nuclear development, submitted to the UN in 1946, provided (1) that total control is necessary because the processes in atomic fission for both peacetime and military purposes are similar; (2) that a UN atomic development authority be created with powers resembling those of the AEC; (3) that peacetime uses be promoted by licenses to both public and private undertakings; (4) that the international agency have sole control over the military application of atomic energy; (5) that the international agency also have sole control over the mining, processing, production, and storage of fissionable materials, the manufacture of atomic weapons, and research in the atomic field; (6) that distribution of atomic materials be fair and no nation be allowed more than its share; (7) that the international agency be accorded powers of inspection so as to prevent the secret mining, storing, or conversion of fissionable materials; and (8) that the veto provision in the UN charter be abrogated so as to allow the Security Council to impose military or other sanctions by a simple majority vote.

The Soviet Union rejected this plan on a number of grounds and insisted on the banning of all atomic weapons and stockpiles as a preliminary to any further action toward international control. The Western nations could not agree to this and hence, but for the determined efforts of the smaller nations on the UN atomic energy committee, negotiations would have broken down long before they did. Actually, this phase of the talks lasted a good two years.

The Atoms-for-Peace Plan

At this point, late in 1953 President Eisenhower offered as an alternative his atoms-for-peace plan to the UN, proposing that all nations possessing atomic ores and fissionable materials contribute to a common pool administered by an agency of the UN. This agency would store and safeguard such materials, employ a staff of scientists further to explore the peaceful uses of atomic energy, allocate materials for peaceful uses among nations that lacked them, and act as a clearing-house for information.

The USSR again refused to negotiate until existing stockpiles had been outlawed and accordingly, in 1954 the United States and a number of other Western nations proceeded independently. Two years later, by the summer of 1956 and after long negotiations, the charter of this new agency had been approved by the General Assembly of the UN, signed by more than eighty nations including the USSR and ratified by sixty-seven nations, again including the USSR. A Board of Governors was constituted with thirteen permanent and ten rotating members. Vienna was selected as headquarters city. Sterling Cole, former Republican Congressman from New York State and experienced in the field of atomic energy, was appointed director general. A staff of more than 300 members was appointed, a budget of some $5 million was secured, and by the winter of 1958, with a membership at that time of seventy nations, the International Atomic Energy Agency was operational.

According to its charter, this agency was to act as banker and broker to provide fissionable materials and technical skills to nations seeking nuclear development. It could help in establishing atomic plants for peaceful purposes, inspect the results, establish standards of health and safety, and provide against the diversion of supplies to war-making ends. It was to receive deposits of fissionable materials and nuclear equipment from "have" nations and make them available to "have not" nations for approved atomic energy projects. Inspectors of the agency may enter member nations to examine plants using agency materials or aid and to make sure that none are being misused. President Eisenhower announced that the United States would make available for sale through the agency 11,000 pounds of uranium 235, and would match contributions of other nations until 1960.

This arrangement was a far cry from the original plan of international control proposed by the United States in 1946, and in practice it has worked out usefully but not brilliantly. In the first year or so the agency concentrated on developing a training program for specialists who would return to their countries with some degree of technical knowledge in the application of atomic energy. A number of studies were undertaken, including one on the disposal of atomic wastes. A manual was drawn up on the safe handling of radio-isotopes. Negotiations were begun to secure a supply of enriched uranium for nations that lacked it. Technical assistance to underdeveloped nations was begun. Information was collected and disseminated. A general conference was held each year to discuss the work of the agency and what more it might do. Nevertheless, the major part of the program —the distribution of nuclear fuel for peaceful purposes—was largely frustrated. For one thing, many nations found atomic power to be extremely expensive and lacked the financial resources to develop it. In the first two years, only one distribution transaction was handled by the IAEA, the sale of Canadian uranium to Japan. But the main difficulty was the fact that the United States continued its former policy of supplying materials and know-how on a bilateral basis with individual nations, thus bypassing the IAEA. By 1960 there were more than forty of these agreements in existence and Congress ordered a restudy of the whole atoms-for-peace program as far as the United States' part in it was concerned.

Euratom

The development of the European Atomic Energy Community, a plan known as Euratom, was inspired by the fact that densely populated and highly industrialized as it is, western Europe was faced after World War II with a growing power deficit. More than a quarter of its oil and coal needs were imported, the possibility of uninterrupted importations from the Middle East was uncertain, there was the unhappy prospect of diminished economic independence and lowered standards of living unless some domestic source of power could be developed. Consequently, stimulated by Jean Monnet of France, by 1955 plans were being discussed to set up a nuclear pool among six western European nations. A conference under the auspices of the Action Committee for the United States of Europe early in 1956 brought together delegates from the controlling political parties in France, the Federal Republic of Germany, Italy, Belgium, the Netherlands, and Luxembourg, as well as representatives from trade unions having an aggregate membership of some 10 million west European wage-earners. The result was a declaration urging their respective nations to entrust the development of their atomic resources to a supranational commission. A few months later the proposal had been accepted in principle by each of the six nations. The necessary treaties were duly negotiated along with those that created the European Economic Community (the so-called common market), and both sets of documents were signed early in 1957. The ratifications for the Euratom plan were completed in the following year and the agency became official early in 1959. Headquarters are in Brussels.

Euratom combines the resources of six nations, none of which (with the exception of France) is large or rich enough to create its own atomic energy industry for either peaceful or military uses. The scheme includes atomic research, exchange of information, common production, installations, and investment, and stipulates that the participating nations shall use nuclear energy only for peaceful purposes. Agreements have been negotiated providing for assistance from Great Britain and even more from the United States, which will make available loans, technical know-how, and a twenty-year supply of atomic fuel. Euratom hoped to have a combined generating capacity of a million kilowatts by 1963 and to go considerably beyond that in the years that follow.

A Ban on Atomic Testing

Meanwhile, of course, the control of nuclear energy for military as against peaceful purposes has not been subject to any kind of agreement on a world basis, and the growing assumption has been that none can be reached except as a part of a general agreement to disarm. Short of an abrupt change in international tensions, any such plan is more likely to develop by stages than all at once. It was the growing fear of radioactive fallout from atomic testing that stimulated the next step in the process.

Radioactive fallout occurs faster and more heavily in certain areas —especially the Northern Hemisphere—than was first assumed. The maximum permissible concentration—the amount of radiation believed to be relatively, but not necessarily completely, safe—is unknown. The certain dangers include cancer and genetic disturbances affecting future generations. There is the added possibility, of course, that civilization itself might be destroyed by the irrational use of atomic weapons. For these reasons, a ban on atomic weapons and testing has been urged by atomic scientists and lay groups alike. Albert Schweitzer added his voice to the protest.[1] In 1958 there was a voluntary suspension of testing, and the United States, Great Britain, and the USSR began talks in Geneva to draft a treaty banning testing for other than peaceful purposes. The UN called on the parties to this conference to refrain from further testing while negotiations were in progress and repeated its admonition a year later when France was preparing to explode her first atomic device. France refrained from voting on the UN resolution, made two tests on schedule, and promptly applied for membership in the "club." By early 1960, despite some progress on the treaty, a basic deadlock remained in the talks at Geneva. Nuclear testing is, of course, part of the larger problem of international disarmament and the technical feasibility of a system of inspection and control, and hence was on the agenda of a ten-nation disarmament conference convened in March 1960 and the ill-fated summit meeting that did not take place in May.

DOMESTIC PROGRAM OF THE AEC

Merely to list some of the areas of jurisdiction of the federal Atomic Energy Commission gives some idea of the myriad issues of public policy arising in this revolutionary new field. Some of them, such as monopoly, have already been dealt with and others, including the regulation of utility rates and the question of public ownership, are discussed later. But many issues remain. For example, when "company" towns like Oak Ridge and Hanford are established, there is the matter of who is to run them: the citizens, the contractor who built them, or the AEC itself? Ordinarily the question is not a hard one to settle but because of the need for secrecy and security regulations, the AEC decided to be its own town and school manager, and industrial manager as well, and thus became the victim of every kind of administrative headache that can be imagined. More recently, therefore, this ancillary administrative obligation has been turned over to the contractor, but there too, problems arise because an industrial concern is not necessarily adept at city management.

Other troubles are due to the fact that most of the work of the AEC is done by contractors such as General Electric, Du Pont, or Union Carbide. To show the extent of this arrangement, in a recent year 95 percent of the AEC's $2-billion appropriation went to pay contractors and at the same time the AEC had only 7000 employees as against 200,000 for the contractors. All kinds of problems are complicated by such a dual arrangement, one of them being labor rela-

---

[1] *The New York Times,* Apr. 24, 1957, Apr. 28, 1958; *The Saturday Review* (May 18, 1957).

tions. Suppose, for example, that the unions dislike the policies and practices of a particular contractor; suppose that under ordinary circumstances they would go out on strike; but remember the public-interest considerations in keeping the atomic energy program rolling. Although the AEC has tried as far as possible to hold its contractors responsible for labor relations, it has nevertheless had to give much of its staff and time to the problem.

Statesmanship is equally necessary in the area of relations with other governmental agencies, especially the Departments of State and Defense. To the State Department, for example, the main administrative links of the AEC are with the Office of the Secretary, the Special Assistant to the Secretary for Disarmament and Atomic Energy, the Assistant Secretary for International Organization Affairs, and the U. S. Representative to the UN on Disarmament. In the case of the Defense Department the wheels within wheels are even more intricate: In the AEC itself there is the Military Liaison Committee, already referred to, and a Division of Military Application, while within the Defense Department there are perhaps a dozen assistants, deputy assistants, and directors dealing with atomic energy matters. The result of these weblike arrangements is that the demands on the coordinating abilities of those concerned in any way with atomic energy are about as exacting as any to be found in the federal government.

The six main activities of the AEC are, first, research and development to encourage scientific and industrial progress. Under this program the AEC owns approximately twenty research and development centers in all parts of the nation, some of the best known being Oak Ridge, Argonne, Brookhaven, Los Alamos, Sandia, and the Nevada test site. The second function is the dissemination of unclassified information as well as restricted information as authorized, through an information service and divisions of classification, intelligence, and security.

The third function, and also the largest, is control of the possession, use, and production of atomic energy, both civilian and military. Under this heading the AEC promotes the discovery, mining, and initial processing of uranium and thorium, licenses their production and shipment, arranges for purchase and storage, provides production facilities and storage for military needs as well as plants for the production of fissionable materials. The AEC also supervises the work of contractors, either operates the plants or provides someone to do the job, allocates nonmilitary supplies to those having permission to receive them, stores fissionable materials, and disposes of wastes incident to production.

The fourth function is to encourage the production of atomic energy for peacetime uses. To this end the AEC operates divisions dealing with biology and medicine, reactor development (the generation of power), and the promotion of the international program in these areas. The AEC also licenses private applicants for nuclear fuel, provides the fuel itself, controls the sale by licensees of by-product materials, and protects the health and safety of workers and surrounding communities. The AEC also administers the patent and antimonopoly provisions of the McMahon Act, although in fact little has been done in this area so far.

It was in connection with this fourth function of the AEC that a major problem arose after the 1954 legislation, which sought to encourage private enterprise to develop atomic power for domestic uses, because industry failed to take advantage of the opportunity thus offered. Other nations forged ahead: the USSR gained an early lead; the first major atomic installation for domestic power in the free world was built in England and opened at Calder Hall in 1956 with a generating capacity of 60,000 to 90,000 kilowatts of electric power fed directly into Britain's national grid; the plans of Euratom, the atomic pool of six nations on the continent of Europe, were even more ambitious.

In the United States, on the other hand, the AEC scattered its efforts among all kinds of experimental reactor research while it waited for the power industry to step forward. But the power industry complained that the risk and the cost of atomic plants were too high for private initiative; that the requirements of secrecy created uncertainties and confusion; that insurance protection, potential business, and prospective profits were inadequate; and that competition from and regulation by government would be too great. A major split soon developed between the administration and the AEC on the one hand and the Democratic members of the joint Congressional committee on the other over whether the government itself should construct a number of atomic plants. In 1957, after much bitterness on both sides, Congress approved such a plan and a new era of domestic atomic policy was apparently inaugurated. The chairman of the AEC resigned when his term expired, and a measure of harmony was restored between the AEC and the joint Congressional committee. By early 1960 the AEC was able to present to Congress a ten-year plan for the development and construction of nuclear power reactors designed to achieve economic nuclear electricity by the late 1960s in areas of the country that have high-cost power. In addition, the AEC proposed to concentrate rather than to scatter its efforts among different types of reactor concepts. Henceforth, instead of relying solely on private industry to carry the load of building developmental atomic power plants, the AEC proposed to assume responsibility for building reactors up to the prototype stage, where their economic feasibility could be proved, and to do so either in cooperation with the private power industry or on its own if the industry was unwilling or unable to participate in the program.

Fifth comes the operation of the international cooperation program to make available to cooperating friendly nations the benefits of peaceful applications of atomic energy, in so far as considerations of security will permit. And sixth, there is the internal administration of the AEC itself to carry out these various activities. Within this function the AEC maintains relations with Congress, looks after administrative coordination, personnel, and finance matters, arranges for the administration of "company" towns, and operates several field offices in various parts of the country. Even so brief an outline shows the over-all program of the AEC to be such as to test to the utmost the administrative abilities of its staff.

THE CONTRACT DEVICE

Of all the interesting aspects of the field of atomic energy, however, none is more challenging to business-government relationships than the use of the contract device between government and private enterprise. Combining public ownership with private operation, it is a relatively new device in the history of American industry and suggests, says Tybout, "a 'missing link' between capitalism and socialism," [2] a characterization that seems fully justified by the facts.

The contract method is, of course, widely used by government during wartime for the construction and even the operation of ships, industrial plant, and for many other purposes, with public expenditures during World War II, for example, mounting into the billions of dollars. But never prior to the atomic energy program has there been any instance where 95 percent of a public agency's budget and personnel has been under private management, through contract with a private firm. Said the AEC in its *Fourth Semiannual Report:*

> By carrying forward major operations through private contractors, with deep roots and a firm base in the American economy, the atomic energy program not only benefits from accumulated experience and established resources, but also enlists the interest and support of industries and universities for future private development. Correspondingly, the Government machinery for supervising the enterprise is kept at a minimum.[3]

The contract device may not succeed in combining the best possible aspects of two separate worlds but at the very least it does prevent a complete monopoly at a single point in society.

Generally speaking, when government controls a program and wants to farm out construction or operation, there are three types of contract that may be used. The first, or conventional type, is the *fixed-price* contract. The two varieties here are the *lump-sum* contract stipulating a certain amount of money to be paid to a contractor on completion of a large, integrated project such as an office building; and the *unit-price* contract providing for compensation to a contractor on the basis of a certain price per quantity of product regularly delivered over a period of time, as in the case of uniforms or office equipment. Fixed-price contracts are most

[2] Richard A. Tybout, *Government Contracting in Atomic Energy* (Ann Arbor, Mich., 1956), p. vii.
[3] Washington, D.C. (June 1948). Quoted in *ibid.,* p. 55.

often used where competition and public advertising for bids are possible. AEC has employed them sparingly and has been subject to some criticism for that reason.

The second main type of contract is the *cost-plus-fixed-fee* kind which means just what its name says it does. This type is the backbone of the atomic contractor system, constituting some 80 percent, by value, of all atomic energy contracts and establishing the dominant pattern between government and business at all major atomic installations. The third type, a *variable-price* contract, tries to place the risk for unforeseen changes and contingencies on the government rather than on the contractor, and hence it is a cheaper means of procurement than the other two. Again, two varieties are the *escalator* contract which moves up or down according to stated conditions, and the *price-redetermination* contract in which final calculation and possible renegotiation may take place after the work is completed. The advantages of the contract device as used by government are that it reduces the operating burden on government and at the same time draws on the established business-practice and management skills of going private concerns.

Although the contract device has much to recommend it, however, there are certain issues to be considered before it is adopted as the ideal solution for particular types of business-government relationship. The most trenchant criticism of the method and of the AEC's use of it is by Adams and Gray in their book, *Monopoly in America*.[4] Adams makes these points: (1) Most of the contracting for the AEC has been done by a handful of private firms constituting, in fact, a kind of oligarchy that by now has acquired a degree of experience and know-how giving it a large advantage over other firms that might want to enter the atomic field. (2) If ordinary patent procedures were suddenly instituted in the atomic field in place of the present government-controlled system, this handful of active companies would have a considerable unfair advantage over less fortunate competitors. (3) Most of the research and development now taking place and contemplated for the future in the field of atomic energy will be subsidized, both directly and indirectly, by the federal government.

Other students of the problem have called attention to additional factors that could prove unfortunate from the standpoint of the public interest. In the cost-plus contract, for example, how can the government be sure that the contractor will put his best trained executives and labor force on the job? What incentive is there for close bargaining with the unions when government foots the bill in the end anyhow? How can government stay out of labor relations, even if it would, when everyone knows it is the real employer? Does not the cost-plus contract inevitably substitute administered prices for free-market prices, and what is the effect of this on changes in industrial output?[5]

[4] Walter Adams and Horace M. Gray, *Monopoly in America* (New York, 1955), pp. 148–150.
    [5] Tybout, *op. cit.,* Chap. 8 and p. 140.

Moreover, only a small part of the AEC's contracts (about 15 percent) have been let by means of competitive bidding, which in itself is an encouragement to monopoly. Further, the cost-plus contract offers no incentive to efficiency, promises no penalty when costs are high and no reward when they are low, and costs may actually be padded. The continuing need for AEC supervision creates a serious dilemma: if control is lax, the public interest in safety and economy may suffer, but if it is overstrict, then the advantages of managerial flexibility are lost.[6]

In the face of these criticisms, some of them serious, what is the alternative to the contract device? In the early period of nuclear research in the United States the requirements of a nation at war were such that only government had the financial means to develop an atomic energy program in a condition of the utmost secrecy; consequently, government is now in possession of a giant monopoly capable of changing the desirable balances between private and public enterprise in the nation. Assuming that this balance continues to be important to us as a people, then the contract device is one means by which it may be maintained, and it should be possible to improve its application without diminishing its usefulness. But what will happen if the monopoly, necessary as it is for security reasons, slips from government's hands into those of private groups? This is one of the problems dealt with in the chapters that immediately follow.

Supplementary Reading

Dean, Gordon, *Report on the Atom* (New York, 1953). A general account for laymen.

Newman, James R., and Byron S. Miller, *The Control of Atomic Energy* (New York, 1949). One of the first accounts and still one of the best.

Secretary of State's Committee on Atomic Energy, *A Report on the International Control of Atomic Energy* (Washington, D.C., 1946). The author of the first American plan for the international control of atomic energy.

Wallace, Donald H., *Economic Controls and Defense* (New York, 1953). A Twentieth Century Fund report.

Thomas, Morgan, *Atomic Energy and Congress* (Ann Arbor, Mich., 1956). Policies, legislation, and the effect of secrecy since 1946.

Lapp, Ralph E., *Atoms and People* (New York, 1956). The story of the development of atomic energy.

Finletter, Thomas K., *Power and Policy: U. S. Foreign Policy and Military Power in the Hydrogen Age* (New York, 1954). By a former Secretary of the Air Force.

Bush, Vannevar, *Modern Arms and Free Men* (New York, 1949). By the scientist who headed weapons research during World War II.

Blackett, Patrick M. S., *Fear, War, and the Atom Bomb* (New York, 1949). The military and political consequences of atomic energy.

[6] Clair Wilcox, *Public Policies toward Business* (Chicago, 1955), pp. 796–798.

Dahl, Robert A., and Ralph S. Brown, Jr., *Domestic Control of Atomic Energy,* Social Science Research Council, Pamphlet No. 8 (New York, 1951). Stresses the secrecy problem.

American Academy of Political and Social Science, "The Impact of Atomic Energy," *The Annals* (Philadelphia, Nov. 1953). An excellent series of articles.

Diez, David, *Atomic Science, Bombs and Power* (New York, 1954). What atomic energy holds for mankind.

Tybout, Richard A., *Government Contracting in Atomic Energy* (Ann Arbor, Mich., 1956). Case material as well as a systematic treatment.

Wilcox, Clair, *Public Policies toward Business* (Chicago, 1955). Chapter 28, "The Control of Atomic Energy."

Adams, Walter, and Horace M. Gray, *Monopoly in America* (New York, 1955). Chapter 7, "Legislation and Atomic Energy," discusses the monopoly aspect of the matter.

Atomic Energy Commission, *AEC Contract Policy and Operations* (Washington, D.C., 1951).

United States Congress, Joint Committee on Atomic Energy, *Atomic Power and Private Enterprise* (82d Cong., 2d Sess., Joint Committee Print, 1952).

———, *Investigation into the U. S. Atomic Energy Commission* (81st Cong., 1st Sess., S. Rep. 1169, 1949).

Association of Atomic Scientists, *The Bulletin of the Atomic Scientists* (semi-monthly). A mine of information.

American Assembly, *Atoms for Power: United States Policy in Atomic Energy Development* (New York, 1957).

"Atomic Power Development," *Law and Contemporary Problems* (Durham, N.C., 1956).

PART VI

REGULATION
AND
PUBLIC
OWNERSHIP

17

PUBLIC-UTILITY REGULATION

The issues; the public-utility category; state regulatory commissions; federal regulatory commissions; the "fourth" branch; work of regulatory commissions: service, valuation, rates, profits, hearings; effectiveness of regulation; federal vs. state authority; legislative landmarks: transportation and the ICC, communications and the FCC, electric power, natural gas, and the FPC; holding companies; future of public-utility regulation.

Transportation, communications, power: this is the general area that in any nation is called public utilities. In the United States it is largely occupied by private companies regulated by independent government commissions, whereas in most other countries this large sector of the economy is the principal area of government ownership and operation. A transcendent issue of public policy in the United States, therefore, is whether the utility field is to remain in private hands under government regulation or whether it is to become government-owned and operated.

Considering the conservative temper of our people, the outcome is likely to depend on whether they remain satisfied with public-utility regulation or whether they lose confidence in it, which in turn leads to other concrete issues of public policy. Thus, is it indispensable that public utilities be treated, as they have been for the past eighty or so years, as complete or partial monopolies, or would it be better to introduce competition into this field? The question is especially applicable to transportation which is already partially competitive and tending to become more so, and it is at least equally applicable to radio and television. The implications of competition versus monopoly in public-utility regulation are so vast and so strategic that the decision might well determine whether in the long run the United States will continue to cherish free enterprise or whether it will adopt state socialism.[1]

Some pertinent questions are these: Can independent regulatory commissions satisfy both producers and consumers? Here the chief problem

[1] Walter Adams and Horace Gray, *Monopoly in America* (New York, 1955), Chap. III, "Regulation and Public Utilities."

is that limited appropriations by state legislatures have placed many regulatory commissions in an impossible competitive situation with the utilities, which can charge their own expenses back to the consumer. Again, can the commissions attract and hold good men with qualifications similar to those of a judge, or are the salaries too low, the opportunities too limited, and the temptation to "play ball" with the utilities too great? Further, at what point does regulation go too far, becoming an infringement on the proper freedom of the utility management, causing divided authority, loss of efficiency, and stagnation of enterprise? Do the utilities, knowing they possess a legal monopoly, act as public trustees, or do they take advantage of their situation to earn exorbitant profits? Is it true, as some contend, that public-utility regulation corrupts the rest of the economy by causing other industries to try to escape from the area of competition into a haven where prices and profits are fixed? And is it also true that since public utilities' profits depend on sympathetic regulatory officials and public opinion, the utilities enter politics and spend huge sums in order to create this sympathetic attitude? [2]

The answer to these questions varies with the differences among industries and among the regulatory commissions. The American telephone system, for example, is the most efficiently managed in the world, and yet to the question of whether its regulation is complete and shows the true costs thereof, the answer is much less favorable. Likewise, electrical utilities are generally well managed, but their regulation leaves a good deal to be desired in many ways. Railroad management has greatly improved in recent years but the prestige of the Interstate Commerce Commission is lower than it was in 1920.

Thus we are less interested in the details of utility management than in solutions to problems of public policy. Our search is for trends and the usefulness of particular institutions. Is the regulatory commission device still a valid one? In view of current trends, is it a proper one for the future? Is more competition possible? These are the questions that interest us.

How, then, shall we get at them? The usual treatment of the public-utility subject in a textbook is through a number of technical chapters on such things as valuation, rate bases, allowable profits, and so on. But these important subjects deal largely with accounting, law, engineering, and may therefore properly be reserved for a special course in public utility economics. Our objective here is rather to identify the issues of decision —the issues of public policy—and to evaluate technical subject matter only as it relates to the over-all effectiveness of utility regulation. Those

---

[2] Henry Simons, author of *Economic Policy for a Free Society* (Chicago, 1948), speaks of "an accumulation of governmental regulation which yields in many industries all the afflictions of socialization and none of its possible benefits; the moral disintegration of representative government in the endless contest of innumerable pressure groups for special political favors; and dictatorship."—"The Requisites of Free Competition," *American Economic Review,* Supplement, Vol. XXVI (Mar. 1936), pp. 74–75.

who desire more detailed information will find the necessary references in the bibliography at the end of the chapter.

THE PUBLIC-UTILITY CATEGORY

A public utility is a legal concept that applies to an industry designated as such. In common parlance, however, a public utility is any service to which the public is legally entitled and whose rates, service, and even earnings are regulated by a government body. In the legal sense, for example, the railroads, airlines, and bus companies are not public utilities, but the public, not bothering with such fine distinctions, usually regards them as such. Another legal characteristic of public utilities is the enjoyment of an exclusive franchise, a right to supply a service in a given locality and for a fixed period of time, as when a city, to prevent two rows of utility poles running down the same street or two competing bus lines operating over the same route, grants the right to only one of them. In other words, government grants a franchise, which is a legal monopoly, and in return imposes public controls over rates, service, earnings, and the value of the property so employed. But in the popular sense not all utility services enjoy an exclusive franchise, as when railroads build parallel lines or truck and bus lines compete in the same area with railroads.

For our purposes, therefore, any monopoly or semimonopoly service *subject to control by a regulatory commission* and operating in the fields of transportation, communications, and power, may be considered a public utility *for the purposes of this discussion.*[3]

This treatment of the subject has the advantage of being in line with a recent tendency to deny that public utilities are in a category detached from the rest of the economy. For a long time after the Supreme Court's decision in the case of *Munn* v. *Illinois,*[4] decided in 1877, any business "affected with a public interest" was considered a public utility and in a discrete category by itself. As a legal monopoly it was considered to be outside the competitive system. The change was initiated when the *New York Milk* case [5] was decided in 1934, at which time the Supreme Court held that the milk industry has most of the characteristics of a public utility and may be regulated, but strictly speaking it is not a public utility. This decision broke down the walls of the closed category by admitting that industries differ in the degree to which public control is desirable and applicable; that legislatures and not the courts will decided how much public control is required; that a public utility is not necessarily a monopoly; and that rates and earnings do not inevitably have to be fixed by a government commission.

---

[3] Banks, insurance companies, and stock markets are also subject to administrative regulation but are not commonly considered public utilities; they are dealt with elsewhere in this book.

[4] (94 U.S. 113. 1877).   [5] *Nebbia* v. *New York* (291 U.S. 502. 1934).

Consequently, public control is now subject to an infinite variation, as has long been the case in some other countries, such as Great Britain. And in addition, competition and free enterprise may be strengthened, if we have the wit to do it, by discouraging those who seek the safety of monopoly by hiding behind a legal formula. The *New York Milk* case complicated the problem of public-utility regulation for lawyers who like sharp distinctions and closed classifications, but made it easier for economists and students of government interested in reinforcing the competitive system and preventing monopoly. On social balance, therefore, the *New York Milk* case was a distinct gain.

It is commonly said that the legal concept of public utilities grew out of the transportation category because the first regulated undertakings were the railroads. But this historical concept has long since been outgrown until today public utilities occupy what in some ways is the most strategic area of the economy. In a modern industrial society, for example, what is more important than power, unless it is transportation or communication? The telephone industry alone accounted for something like $5.6 billion of the national income in 1957, electrical power accounted for some $6.7 billion, and the railroads for about $7.4 billion. Furthermore, the categories are constantly expanding so that at the very least the picture today looks like this:

Transportation: railroads, local and highway passenger transportation (most of it by bus), highway freight (the trucking industry), water transportation, and the airways.

Communication: telephones, telegraphs, radio, and television.

Power: electric, hydroelectric, atomic, gas, natural gas, and pipelines.

To show the importance of this vast segment of the economy it is only necessary to call attention to the fact that in so-called underdeveloped nations, power, transportation, and communications lead the list of "musts" in a program of economic growth.

The Pattern of Control

Commissions to regulate public utilities are authorized and located at all three levels of government: local, state, and federal. Local regulation is much less important than state regulation, but as in so many other fields federal control is expanding and will probably outstrip the states. At the state level, regulatory bodies go by various names, the more common being public-service commission, railroad commission, corporation commission, or commerce commission. Their jurisdiction covers local gas and electricity rates, telephone companies, and local and intrastate transportation, especially by motor vehicle. But the federal government controls interstate railroads, atomic energy, radio and television, and the interstate aspects of telephones, electric power, natural gas, and the pipelines. Indeed, divided jurisdictions in certain areas, especially telephones and electric holding companies, is a major obstacle to their effective regulation.

At the federal level, the six major regulatory commissions in the utility field are:

Interstate Commerce Commission, 1887

Eleven members.

Jurisdiction over railroads, motor carriers, inland waterways, pipelines (other than water and gas), express companies, carriers using rail-and-water routes, and sleeping-car companies.

Activities include the maintenance of just, reasonable, and nondiscriminatory rates; establishment of through routes and joint rates; posting of rates and regulations; suspension of proposed rates; determination of mail transportation rates; accounts and records of carriers; valuation of carriers; requirements as to switch connections with other lines; a car service covering every aspect of the handling of cars and locomotives; pooling arrangements among carriers; consolidations, mergers, acquisitions of control and other antitrust activities; competing water carriers owned by railroads; awards of reparation; securities issued by carriers; the form of bills of lading; compilation and publication of statistics; administration of railroad bankruptcy laws; fixing time zones; hours of service for railroad employees; medals of honor; safety appliances; investigation of accidents; automatic train control; locomotive inspection; and the transportation of explosives.

Federal Power Commission, 1920

Five members.

Jurisdiction over interstate electricity and natural gas sales and transportation.

Activities include the licensing and acquisition of power projects; control over rates, services, securities, headwater benefits, and federal lands for power purposes; investigations of water power resources; regional power surveys; coordination of federal programs having to do with water resources; the form of electric-utility accounts; investigations under various flood-control acts; regulation of the natural-gas industry including imports, exports, rates and charges, cost of property, extension of facilities, abandonment of service, certificates covering operation, state compacts, uniform accounts, incidental power, and eminent domain; and finally, special authority over the power industry in case of a wartime or a peacetime emergency affecting the use of electric power.

Federal Communications Commission, 1934

Seven members.

Jurisdiction over telephones, telegraphs, radio, and television.

Activities include regulation of interstate common carriers by wire or radio in all their activities: extension or reduction of service, through routes and charges, accounting, depreciation practices, acquisitions of control over other carriers, rates and charges, discriminations and preferences; it also licenses and classifies radio and television stations and assigns frequencies; requires the use of radio for safety purposes on board certain classes of ships; holds hearings, imposes penalties; and has special duties applying to privacy of communication and to emergency situations including war.

Securities and Exchange Commission, 1934

Five members.

Jurisdiction, so far as utilities are concerned, over electric and natural gas holding companies.

Activities include control over public-utility securities, properties, and other assets, intrasystem transactions, service and management arrangements to prevent abuses; limiting system operations to physically integrated and coordinated properties; simplification of complex corporate and capital structures; adjustment of voting inequities among holders of securities; passing on proposals for reorganization, merger, or consolidation.

Civil Aeronautics Board, 1938

Five members.

Jurisdiction over passenger and commercial aviation including lines, airways, and airports.

Activities include issuance of licenses, regulation of rates and rate practices; mail transportation; relationships between carriers; consolidations, mergers, and acquisitions of control; accident investigation; and agreements relating to the civil aviation operations of foreign governments. Its work is supplemented by the Federal Aviation Agency, created in 1958 to regulate air commerce and control military and civilian air traffic in the interests of safety. This is an independent agency operating under a single administrator.

Federal Maritime Board, 1950 (formerly the U. S. Maritime Commission created in 1936; the present Board is an independent agency within the Commerce Department).

Three members.

Jurisdiction over shipping in foreign commerce and in intercoastal waters.

Activities include regulation of rates, services, practices, and agreements among common carriers by water; setting rules and regulations affecting shipping in foreign commerce; participation in granting subsidies for the construction and operation of ships to secure parity with foreign operators.

These and other regulatory commissions, plus the government corporations, constitute the so-called fourth branch of government, occupying a no-man's land between Congress and the President. Not only does this frustrate those who would periodically reorganize the federal government but it does in fact cause administrative difficulties. Thus, these agencies are not subject to full Presidential control: the President appoints commissioners but may not remove them except for statutory reasons.[6] The duties of commissions are almost wholly quasi-legislative and quasi-judicial rather than promotional, as in the case of the regular departments. A criticism of utility regulation, therefore, is that instead of looking forward to expansion as a business would, the commissions look backward to precedents and hence their attitude is negative. How to solve this problem without sacrificing the independence of the commissions has never been worked out.

The Work of Regulatory Commissions

More judge than policeman, a regulatory commission is supposed to protect the interests of both *consumers and stockholders* in a public-utility enterprise. But the dual function is a hard one, and commissions are sometimes criticized on the ground that consumer interests are not sufficiently emphasized. One proposed solution is to create an office of consumer counsel at the state level or in the larger cities to receive consumer complaints and to represent them before the commissions as a friend at court.

A problem of monopoly is that complacency so often causes a lowering of *standards of service*. A function of commissions, therefore, is to see that consumers receive good, frequent, and regular service. Unfortunately the commissions are usually so understaffed that if anything much is done in this area it is because consumers themselves have lodged complaints. Once stimulated, the commission may investigate and set the matter right.

Privately owned public utilities are legally entitled through *valuation* procedures, to "a fair return on a fair value"; if the return is less than this, they are being deprived of their property without due process of law. But what is the value of utility properties and services? On the answer depend the rate base, the rates themselves, the fairness of profits, and the degree to which rate changes may be granted. What should be the basis of valuation: original cost, reproduction cost, prudent investment, or the balanced judgment of the commission? Operating costs as well as fixed capital costs must be considered in any such reckoning.

It is hard enough to determine the value of millions of dollars' worth of property and even harder to keep such data current under constantly changing prices. Valuation for the commission is done by teams of engineers, accountants, and management experts. The utilities have their own experts in these fields and the commission members must choose between the two sets of estimates. If the commission is wrong or even if the utility only thinks it is wrong, then the case may be taken to court for final settlement.

When valuation has been determined and the rate base established,

---

[6] In the *Rathbun* case, *Humphrey's Executor* v. *United States* (295 U.S. 602. 1935), the Supreme Court held that commission members, being quasi-judicial, are not subject to removal by the President in the manner that other federal appointees are.

then the *rates* themselves must be set for different classes of users (commercial, residential, industrial, and the like) which in the aggregate will yield enough revenue to cover all the costs of operation plus a fair profit. There are many difficult problems of judgment. For example, how high may executive salaries go before they become "unreasonable"? How high may be the fees paid to consultants or for service contracts before they are "exorbitant"? This latter problem becomes even harder where such services are provided by a holding company. To what extent are different rates justified between various classes of users? Is it enough that rate treatment within classes be consistent, no matter how great the spread among different classes? Even more important in its economic effect, how far may the commission go in insisting on so-called promotional rates, that is, a lowering of rates to encourage a greater volume of use? Electrical utilities, to take but one example, for the most part have opposed such experiments, and yet most economists are satisfied that lower rates and greater volume would help correct some of the more persistent problems of regulated enterprises.

Is a public utility a risk enterprise? Usually it is not. Its market is secure, its rates are set, and its earnings are determined by public authority, and it frequently enjoys a monopoly in its own area. The legal rule is that *profits* must be sufficient to attract new sources of capital for purposes of expansion and betterment and to keep the utility's credit position secure. But if a comparison with other forms of enterprise is involved in order to determine a rate of profit, to what is such a comparison appropriate? Surely not to a competitive industry, or to steel, or even to banking. The answer is, "to what will cause investors to invest, in preference to something else." This means, in effect, that for a regulated utility enterprise, profit is what the commission and the courts consider "fair." It is a good deal more, as a rule, than the return on a bond; in some cases it has been as high as on many speculative stocks; generally speaking, it is high enough to make public-utility investments very much in demand. To what extent then is profit the result of good management? Where competition is minimal or lacking, it is pretty hard to say.

The determination of these difficult issues of regulation involves not only extensive field investigations but also lengthy *hearings* before the commission or its administrative staff. And it is here, in the making of decisions, that the work of regulatory commissions most resembles that of courts of law. As a rule, hearings may be formal or informal, with the informal type predominating. Hearings are usually held before a specially trained staff member called an examiner, or, in more important cases, before one or more members of the commission itself. Generally, however, the members of the commission are not brought into a case—even an important rate case—until the record is complete and the case is ready for final review and decision.

This, in brief outline, is what a regulatory commission does. But it is not the whole of the matter. In most jurisdictions, other kinds of decision also are made that affect the economy to its core. For example, regarding competition versus monopoly, to what extent shall financial combinations, interlocking directorates, mergers, and holding companies be tolerated? May a utility enterprise properly do a small volume of business with high prices and profits when clearly lower rates would produce greater volume and improve the profit picture? Then there is the question of labor relations: under the Taft-Hartley law, many utility services, being national necessity industries, are subject to a no-strike rule, and consequently the rights of organized labor must be the responsibility of the commissions as well as of the utility enterprises themselves.

THE EFFECTIVENESS OF COMMISSION REGULATION

From what has been said here it is apparent that if public utility regulation is to succeed, a number of conditions must be present. Here is a suggestion of such a check list:

1. A regulatory commission must have a satisfactory statutory basis granting complete coverage of all utilities within its area and of all important aspects of its trusteeship.

2. The financial resources of a regulatory commission must be roughly comparable to those of the utility, or the consumer will come off second best. Because legislatures are almost universally niggardly in this respect, in some states the cost of regulation is charged to the utilities themselves, thus affording somewhat greater assurance of adequate funds to the commission.

3. The members of regulatory commissions should be the equal of utility executives in training and ability, and the job should be made sufficiently appealing to attract men of high caliber and to hold them a lifetime. Ideally, a commissioner should be trained to some extent in engineering, accounting, law, and economics—admittedly a difficult combination to effect.

4. The commission must have a staff large enough to make thoroughgoing, firsthand investigations as well as spot checks from time to time to determine the quality of the service rendered, without waiting for complaints to be lodged by unhappy consumers.

A number of studies have been made of these issues at both the state and federal levels [7] and the consensus seems to be that considering what the utility companies have at stake (the threat of socialization under government ownership if they do not behave as the public thinks they should), it is surprising that regulation has not progressed more than it has in the past sixty years. The two greatest weaknesses are lack of funds and a shortage of topflight personnel who will make a lifetime career of regulation. Salaries are about the same as for other types of government em-

[7] See the bibliography at the end of this chapter.

ployment, the salary range for commissioners, for example, being around $4000 to $5000 a year in the poorer states to $15,000 to $20,000 a year in the federal government. But no such salary is comparable to that of a public-utility executive. In Vermont, for example, where the author was once a member of the legislature, the governor was paid $8000 a year, the head of the public-utility commission $6000, and the president of the largest electrical utility $25,000. If public-utility regulation is to succeed, one method is to raise the salaries of commissioners a good deal higher than they are at present. If they would, the utilities themselves could bring this about because frequently their political organization is among the strongest in the state and their pressure on the legislature would be decisive.

For many years the ogre of public-utility regulation was judicial review of commission decisions, where years of work, as in valuation, were overturned in a single case or where the legal standard laid down by the court was so confusing that regulators were uncertain how to proceed.[8] Happily, these difficulties have been largely eliminated and hence today if anyone is to be blamed for inadequate regulation it is not the courts but the legislatures. This change for the better in judicial decisions occurred at about the time of the *Hope Natural Gas* case decision in 1944 which will be referred to later.

The politics of public-utility regulation is a fascinating subject, but a disturbing one, too. "While originally the companies were vigorously opposed to regulation," says John Bauer, "they have come not only to accept it but largely to convert it into an instrument of protection for themselves." [9] In a chapter entitled "Causes of Failure," Clair Wilcox calls attention to the diffused nature of the responsibility, saying that the courts, the legislatures, the executives (governors), and the public at large have all been involved.[10] As late as 1948 the Twentieth Century Fund reported that "many state regulated electrical utilities are earning profits which may be regarded as unreasonable," and thus found "a basis for the wide-spread feeling . . . that state regulation in general has failed to achieve its primary purpose." [11] "Practically up to the moment," wrote John Bauer in 1950, "electric rates have remained generally excessive and consumers have not got the benefits of regulation as intended." [12]

[8] An example of the former is the case of *O'Fallon Ry. Co.* v. *United States* (279 U.S. 461. 1929), overturning years of work on railroad valuation, while a good illustration of confusion is the leading case of *Smyth* v. *Ames* (166 U.S. 466. 1898), suggesting a rule of valuation which, in reality, was no rule at all but a number of opposing alternatives.

[9] John Bauer, *Transforming Public Utility Regulation* (New York, 1950), pp. 137–138.

[10] Clair Wilcox, *Public Policies toward Business* (Homewood, Ill., 1955), p. 575.

[11] Twentieth Century Fund, *Electric Power and Government Policy* (New York, 1948), p. 244.

[12] Bauer, *op. cit.*, p. 127.

Divided Jurisdictions

In some ways the most frustrating part of the whole problem of utility regulation is divided jurisdictions. In the case of the railroads the federal government has pre-empted the field so that here the jurisdiction is unified and no problem exists. But in the case of electric power, the Federal Power Commission sets the rates at the point of production but not at the point of distribution to the consumer, and a large producer may have points of distribution throughout several states. In the case of telephones, the Federal Communications Commission limits its attention to the long lines (long distance service), leaving the regulation of local services including those of giant interstate companies to the state commissions. But in both power and telephones, most state commissions lack the staff and the knowledge to cope with the complexities of technology, distributable costs, corporate organization, and interstate relationships. Under such conditions the reasonableness of rates to local consumers is understandably hard to determine.

The position of the federal government in regulation, says Koontz, "must necessarily become more powerful." Possibly also, he adds, the public-utility industry may ask the federal government to assume the leading role in regulation in order to escape dealing with too many commissions and laws. There are those who believe that the cause of regulation has been weakened by the tendency of the federal laws to defer to state control. Such critics see the rapid increase in interstate public-utility business and note that most state regulatory bodies have neither a sufficient tenure of office nor an adequate staff to administer a law as effectively as can a federal commission.[13] Most state commissions fear that the federal regulatory agencies will eventually encroach on state jurisdictions to the point where the state commissions are no better off with regard to power and communications than they are at present with respect to the railroads.

LEGISLATIVE LANDMARKS IN TRANSPORTATION POLICY

The evolution of federal regulatory control over transportation may be briefly summarized according to the following enactments:

1887. *The Act to Regulate Commerce,* among other things, set up the Interstate Commerce Commission. The authority of the commission proved insufficient, however, to eradicate evils such as rebates, discriminations, and exorbitant rates. The first court decisions were generally unfavorable to the ICC and constituted another handicap to early regulation.

1903. *The Elkins Act* put teeth in the section of the act of 1887 that

[13] Harold Koontz and R. W. Gable, *Public Control of Economic Enterprise* (New York, 1956), pp. 241–242.

forbade rebates—that is, concessions to individual shippers from published rate schedules.

1906. *The Hepburn Act* made the commission's orders virtually self-enforcing by imposing heavy penalties without the necessity of a court order. This act also authorized the commission to set reasonable rates for the future where previously, because of adverse court decisions, authority had been limited to rates on shipments already made.

1910. *The Mann-Elkins Act* corrected certain regulatory deficiencies and established a Commerce Court to expedite judicial appeals from the commission's decisions, but three years later this court was abolished.

1912. *The Panama Canal Act* was the first attempt to coordinate federal control over the different forms of transportation. The fixing of joint rail and water rates and through routes was authorized and the railroads were forbidden to enter the field of intercoastal shipping as a means of limiting competition.

1920. *The Transportation Act* introduced the modern phase of railroad regulation in which the ICC exercises controls so extensive and intimate as in some cases to constitute managerial supervision. Among the most important provisions, (1) railroad rates had to be sufficient in the aggregate to produce a fair return on the investment, with the railroads considered on a national rather than on a system basis; (2) jurisdiction covered construction, abandonment of service, security issues, and consolidations; (3) minimum rates might be prescribed; (4) commission-determined valuations were to be the legal foundation of rate making (physical valuations commenced as early as 1913); and earnings, if any, over a certain percentage were to be "recaptured"; (5) extensive managerial controls were provided for; and (6) intrastate rates might be prescribed when necessary to remove discriminations in interstate commerce.

1933. *The Emergency Railroad Transportation Act* repealed the recapture clause of the 1920 law and provided a new rule for rate-making which emphasizes the carriers' need for revenue.

1936. *The Motor Carrier Act* gave the ICC jurisdiction over the transportation of all passengers and property by motor carriers engaged in interstate and foreign commerce.

1938. *The Civil Aeronautics Act* established a five-man Civil Aeronautics Board to exercise the functions of rule-making (including the prescription of rules, regulations, and standards of service), adjudication, and investigation.

1940. *The Transportation Act* of this year, the basis of present policy, extended federal authority over water transportation except foreign shipping and gave the ICC unified jurisdiction over domestic transportation except by plane.

1942. *The Interstate Commerce Act* correlated previous legislation and extended control over freight-forwarder rates and practices.

1948. *The Mahaffie Act* related to railroad financial structures; the

Reed-Bulwinkle Act authorized the ICC, under certain circumstances, to approve agreements between carriers relating to rates, fares, and charges, after which such agreements are exempt from the antitrust laws.

1958. *The Transportation Act* of this year authorized the ICC to act in the discontinuance of train or ferry service between points in different states or within a single state by railroads subject to the Interstate Commerce Act, and authorized the commission for a limited time to guarantee the repayment of certain loans made to railroads by private investors and lending institutions.

1958. *The Federal Aviation Act* created the Federal Aviation Agency out of two preceding aviation agencies to assist in the regulation of air commerce.

Unresolved Issues

The above analysis shows the extent to which all forms of interstate transportation have long been the object of federal concern. Nevertheless, a number of persistent unresolved major policy issues remain, the first of which is the means of survival of the railroads. A member of the Interstate Commerce Commission predicted in 1958,[14] for example, that if railroad traffic continued to decline as it had in the preceding decade, parlor and sleeping-car service would come to an end by 1965 and coach service by 1970; commuter service, he said, would be the last to go.

When they were first organized in the early nineteenth century, railroad companies had a virtual monopoly on public transportation, and as they grew strong, they were regulated accordingly. But today the monopoly of the railroads has disappeared as the passenger car, the trucking industry, and the aviation industry have increasingly been preferred by passengers and freight forwarders. And yet the regulation of the railroads continues with few relaxations. They cannot alter rates, merge, reduce schedules, determine the size of crews, or discontinue service without government permission. In addition, federal subsidies, enjoyed by the railroads in the days of their youth, now go to younger competitors, especially the airlines. Meanwhile, as passenger and freight traffic decline, costs rise and taxes remain heavy; thus the railroads find themselves in an impossible position. Spokesmen for the companies maintain that freedom to compete would save them, but they are not free. And yet they still carry millions of passengers and tons of freight a year and it is unthinkable that the nation could do without them.

Since one of the main factors in this situation is regulation, the President's Special (Cabinet) Committee on Transportation Policy and Organization studied the matter in 1955 and recommended that competition be encouraged, partly through a relaxation of regulation, so as to invite technical innovations and managerial improvement. Economic regulation

[14] Howard Hosmer, reported in *The New York Times*, Sept. 19, 1958.

should be reduced, said the committee, as far as possible consistent with the public interest. There should be an attempt to avoid restrictions, conditions, or limitations on individual modes of transportation. Where rates are concerned, regulatory commissions should have the power to investigate them so as to prevent discriminations, but should not be allowed to fix exact rates.[15] This report was criticized in some quarters as being too favorable to the railroads but its endorsement of increased competition accords with what most economists believe.[16]

Three years later a Senate subcommittee held a series of hearings in which the situation of the railroads was again gone into. A program was offered, including repeal of the excise tax on railroad transportation, guarantees for $700 million in loans to the railroads for a wide range of purposes including operations, and the appointment of a three-man committee to study transportation policy, especially regulation. As an editorial writer in *The New York Times* remarked, "We have a curious situation." We need the railroads and yet government, year after year and hearing after hearing, fails to come up with a positive policy; instead, "it continues a policy of negation through regulation." If the railroads are really doomed by "progress," continued this observer, "then why not try letting them, for once in their long history, have their own way, their last chance to compete as they will in a free-enterprise system? If this took them along the road to suicide, then at least government would not be to blame." [17] By 1959 the Commerce Department was restudying the problem of the railroads and the ICC was studying itself.

A second major policy issue is whether various carriers such as the railroads should be allowed to acquire control of competing forms of transportation such as motor carriers, water carriers, and airplanes. In the name of competition the answer would seem to be a clear No, and yet in recent years there has been a move toward corporate integrations of this kind; there may be more now that all land transport agencies are subject to a common regulatory control. The desirable public policy is probably to discourage financial interlocks while encouraging cooperation on a competitive basis.

A third major issue is whether to establish a federal Department of Transportation, a proposal for which there has been increasing support in recent years. Like most other regulatory agencies, the Interstate Commerce Commission, by its very nature and organization, does not appear capable of fostering and promoting the industry. The commission approach properly emphasizes regulation and control, both of which, however, are negative. A number of suggestions have been made to release some of the ICC's authority, prune off nonessential services, reorganize its

[15] Presidential Advisory Committee on Transportation Policy, *Report* (Washington, D.C., 1955).
[16] A good statement of this position is found in Adams and Gray, *op. cit.*, Chap. 3, "Regulation and Public Utilities."
[17] *The New York Times*, Jan. 16, 1958.

administration, and separate its administrative from its judicial functions as recommended in 1937 by the President's Committee on Administrative Management. The Interstate Commerce Commission, said one of its members in 1960, is an "organizational monstrosity." [18] The remedy, he added, is not to abolish the agency but to improve it. So far, however, none of the suggestions to this end have been favorably received by lawyers and others interested in improving regulation. If Congress were to create a federal Department of Transportation of cabinet rank, as has been done in Great Britain and many other countries, the ICC would be absorbed and its administrative and judicial functions separately provided for in the new framework. There are strong arguments in favor of such a scheme. More than anything, transportation needs bold and imaginative policy planning, a positive stimulation rather than a repressive attitude and rigid rules. Experience seems to show that the positive approach is more likely to come out of a department than a commission. Experience also shows that if one form of transportation is controlled, the need soon arises to treat competing forms in the same manner. Hence the merger for regulatory purposes of rail, motor, and water carriers. And if all these are included in a single agency, why not also include offshore shipping and aviation, which are now treated separately? To this question, the over-all department seems to be the answer. If developments in other nations are a guide, a similar one in this country is not unlikely at some time in the future.

LEGISLATIVE LANDMARKS IN COMMUNICATIONS POLICY

The Federal Communications Act of 1934 is a landmark in public-utility regulation because for the first time in American history all the interstate wire and radio facilities of the nation were placed under a unified jurisdiction. Jurisdiction over telephones, telegraphs, and cables was taken over from the Interstate Commerce Commission and radio (later also including television) was absorbed and the Federal Radio Commission abolished. In the scope and variety of its regulatory tasks, the Federal Communications Commission found itself with a welter of duties next only in magnitude to those of the ICC. Moreover, in its discretionary power to grant or deny radio broadcasting and television licenses solely on the basis of "public interest, convenience, and necessity," the commission exercises a power unsurpassed anywhere in public-utility regulation. A large part of the work of the FCC consists of making investigations, holding hearings, and arriving at decisions in particular cases. From these decisions, appeal may be taken to the federal appellate courts, which are usually willing to regard as conclusive the commission's findings of fact.

Monopoly is greater in wire communications than in any other public

---

[18] Anthony F. Arpaia, reported in *The New York Times*, Jan. 7, 1960.

utility. In 1909 the American Telephone and Telegraph Company acquired control of the Western Union Telegraph Company, but because of the threat of an antitrust action, relinquished control and agreed to stay out of the telegraph field. In the 1940s Western Union, for its part, absorbed Postal Telegraph and now has the field to itself.

Today, to all intents and purposes, AT&T has a monopoly of the telephone industry. The company controls roughly 90 percent of local telephone service, constituting the desirable part of the business; owns and operates 98 percent of the long lines of the nation; owns Western Electric Company which produces 90 percent of the telephone equipment used in the United States; owns the vast wire facilities that provide the circuits for Western Union; through patent control, virtually dominates teletypewriter and telephoto facilities; and occupies a strong position, again through patent rights, in sound recording and reproduction for motion pictures. AT&T has more than 1.6 million stockholders, total assets of better than $17.6 billion, and in financial magnitude is the biggest corporation in the United States. AT&T covers the nation through twenty operating companies, which it controls. In addition to being a holding company in this respect, it also operates all of the long lines in the country.

The regulation of so powerful and ramified a system is a task almost exceeding comprehension. If the state utility commissions are unable to cope with such a degree of integration, even the FCC, with radio regulation alone constituting a herculean task, is hard put to it to supervise the telephone industry as well. For example, license contract fees are fees charged by AT&T to its twenty operating companies, which in turn charge such fees to operating expenses, accounting for 80 percent of the subscriber's dollar. So what is a "reasonable" fee? Prior to a decision of the Supreme Court in 1930,[19] AT&T maintained that "costs incurred by it in rendering the alleged license contract services were immaterial to the validity of the contract fee as an operating expense." The Supreme Court ruled that these costs must be proved, but that also is no easy task. Other thorny issues are the amounts allowable for depreciation reserves, the cost of rendering a long distance service, and the figure for a "fair return" on the investment. In one year, for example, the depreciation reserves of AT&T came to 28 percent of the total investment in properties. How should such vast sums be treated in arriving at valuations and rates? The company and the commissions have frequently taken different sides on this issue as on others.

In the case of so vast and concentrated a utility edifice, it is easier to determine what constitutes a satisfactory standard of service than to discover whether a subscriber is paying a fair amount for what he receives. How much can subscribers reasonably expect a commission to do under such conditions? There are no criteria whereby the value of a telephone service may be determined, a problem in pricing by no means confined to

---

[19] *Smith* v. *Illinois Bell Telephone Co.* (282 U.S. 133. 1930).

the telephone industry. On the other hand, as the result of a comprehensive investigation of AT&T for which Congress appropriated $1.5 million, the FCC claims to have secured reductions that saved the telephone subscribers $30 million during the course of the investigation alone,[20] so the situation is not entirely hopeless.

As for radio, the number of channels being limited by nature, the need for government regulation in this field is axiomatic. Nevertheless, it was seven years after radio broadcasting began that federal control was established by the *Radio Act of 1927*. This jurisdiction is now part of the unified control of the FCC and constitutes one of its chief headaches. Politics, religion, economic interests, pressure groups, every controversial issue in public life seems to involve radio and television in some way or other.

The authority of the FCC over radio and television is extensive. No one may operate without a license; stations must be classified, assigned frequencies, and have the nature of their service prescribed; with minor exceptions, no license may be issued unless a permit for the construction of the station has been obtained; and the standard governing the granting of licenses is "public interest, convenience, or necessity." Most of the trouble comes from trying to give objective content to these exasperatingly elusive words. And as if this were not enough, scores of applicants want licenses for every one that can be granted.

The act also provides that if a legally qualified candidate for public office is permitted to use a broadcasting station, an equal opportunity shall be afforded all other candidates for that office. Further, the broadcasting of information concerning lotteries, gift enterprises, and similar schemes, as well as the use of obscene, indecent, or profane language over the air, is prohibited, involving, of course, matters of judgment similar to those required in policing the moral content of materials passing through the mails. The act specifically stipulates, however, that the FCC shall have no power of censorship over radio communications.

Problems of radio and television control are complicated also by the growth of monopoly in the major networks. As Wilcox points out, three problems of transcendent importance that affect broadcasting are (1) the need for better geographical coverage, which could be taken care of by creating more regional stations with higher power and clearer channels; (2) the need to correct the worst abuses of advertising, for which the FCC itself has the necessary authority if it would use it; and (3) the need for better content and balance in the programs for the sake of discriminating listeners, which might be accomplished by using more municipal and university programs or by establishing FM and television stations supported by popular subscriptions.[21]

A Congressional study of the FCC, started in 1958, revealed the

[20] *Report of the FCC on the Investigation of the Telephone Industry in the United States,* made pursuant to Public Resolution No. 8, 74th Cong. (1939).
[21] Wilcox, *op. cit.,* pp. 675–676.

commission's domination by the industry it was supposed to regulate. The commissioners were said to promote concentration of ownership, and in some cases to accept favors from litigants, to misuse expense accounts, and to be subject to influence peddling. The industry was beset with the scandals of fixed quiz shows and payola. Sherman Adams in the White House Office and two members of the FCC, including its chairman, were forced to resign. In other nations, most radio and television systems are owned and operated by government or by a public corporation tied to government. Presumably for the United States there is a better solution based on improved regulation, but by 1960 none had been offered.[22]

LEGISLATIVE LANDMARKS IN POWER POLICY

The Federal Power Commission is the only federal agency having authority to regulate the rates and service of electric utilities; its jurisdiction now also covers the natural gas industry, a rival of electricity in the power field. The FPC was created under the *Federal Water Power Act* of 1920. Like other independent regulatory agencies, it makes investigations, decides cases, and looks to the courts for judicial enforcement. The act emphasizes hydroelectric power and accordingly the FPC is authorized to license a project for water-power development if the applicant fulfills certain tests laid down in the statute. Thus, the project must include a comprehensive plan to improve or develop a waterway for the benefit of interstate commerce, water power, and "other beneficial uses." If the proposal only partially utilizes the power potentialities of the site or interferes substantially with navigation, conservation, and other national interests, the application may be turned down by the commission.

The jurisdiction of the FPC was enlarged by the *Public Utility Act* of 1935, Title II of which is called the *Federal Power Act*. The original Federal Water Power Act of 1920 with certain amendments was incorporated into the new law, which greatly increased the scope of the commission's work. Specifically, the FPC may now regulate the rates of a licensee (1) part or all of whose power enters into interstate or foreign commerce, (2) where no state authority exists to secure reasonable nondiscriminatory rates, and (3) where the states concerned cannot agree among themselves. Finally, the jurisdiction of the FPC was rounded out by the passage of the *Natural Gas Act* of 1938 which conveyed a wide authority to regulate this industry.

Next to atomic energy, natural gas is called the wonder fuel of modern times, for it can be used for almost any purpose that requires fuel and its cost is low. The supply, however, is limited and nonreplenishable.[23] For

---

[22] Koontz and Gable, *op. cit.*, p. 233.
[23] A good brief study of governmental regulation in this area is that of Frederick F. Blachley and Miriam E. Oatman, *Natural Gas and the Public Interest* (Washington, D.C., 1947).

some years the industry has been a battleground for powerful economic interests, the issues being conservation of the resource, the uses to which gas should be put, integration and holding-company control, and what constitutes fair prices and reasonable profits. One group lobbies for no governmental controls, another for an extension of them; one for pipelines to distant markets, another for using the supply where it originates. Both groups argue, of course, that what they favor coincides with the public interest. In consequence the halls of state legislatures and of Congress, the offices of state public-utility commissions and the Federal Power Commission, and the dockets of state and federal courts have echoed to the natural-gas controversy. It is no accident that one of the most significant cases on public-utility valuation and rate-making should be the *Hope Natural Gas* case.

At the state level, the extent and character of regulation over the industry varies considerably, being more important, of course, in the Southwest where natural gas is produced in large quantity along with petroleum. Generally speaking, state control is not very effective in this area because the interests affected are especially powerful in their home territory.

At the federal level, forerunners of the Natural Gas Act of 1938 were the Code of Fair Competition for the Petroleum Industry of the National Recovery Administration, and the *Connally Act,* popularly known as the Hot Oil Act, passed by Congress in 1935. This latter measure prohibited the shipment in interstate and foreign commerce of petroleum or its products produced in excess of the amount permitted by state law. The Connally Act was not broad enough to cover the situation, however, and after investigations by Congress and the Federal Trade Commission, Congress passed the Natural Gas Act. Under this legislation, the jurisdiction of the FPC extends to the construction, extension, or abandonment of facilities for the transportation or sale of natural gas in interstate commerce; its exportation and importation; rates, charges, and schedules; determination of the cost of production and transmission; ascertainment of the cost of properties; establishment of rates and depreciation; the keeping and rendering of uniform accounts and records; and the prevention of interlocking directorates among the natural-gas companies.

This law ushered in a new pattern of federal regulatory control, its breadth justified by Congress on the ground that natural gas is a diminishing resource. The record of enforcement has been spotty, however: sometimes independent and fairly effective, sometimes subservient to industry control. Generally, regulation continues to be opposed by the industry which in 1956 secured the introduction in Congress of a bill to exempt natural-gas producers from direct federal control at the well head, although retaining controls on the transmission of the gas through pipelines. The debate was long and the activity of pressure groups, representing producers on one side and consumers (for once, organized on a particular issue) on the other, was among the most spectacular in some years. The bill was finally passed and sent to the President, at which point a Senator revealed that he had been the victim of an attempted bribe by one of the gas-producing companies, the implication being that this was only one of several such instances. As a result, the President, who had favored the bill, now vetoed it. A similar measure supported by the administration was lost in Congress in 1957, but by 1960 the matter was far from a dead issue.

A Valuation Landmark

The Natural Gas Act has twice been put to judicial test with results that constituted a source of encouragement to students of utility regulation, because if the line of reasoning followed by the Court is acted on, it might have a wide effect on valuation, rate-making, and the independence of regulatory commissions. In 1942 in the *Natural Gas Pipeline* [24] case decision it was stated that

> The Constitution does not bind rate-making bodies to the service of any single formula or combination of formulas. Agencies to whom this legislative power has been delegated are free within the ambit of their statutory authority, to make the pragmatic adjustments which may be called for by the particular circumstances. Once a fair hearing has been given, proper findings made, and other statutory requirements satisfied, the court cannot intervene in the absence of a clear showing that the limits of due process have been overstepped. If the Commission's order, as applied to the facts before it and viewed in its entirety, produces no arbitrary result, our inquiry is at an end.

Two years later in the *Hope* case [25] the Court reaffirmed this position with the statement that "It is not theory but the impact of the rate order that counts. If the total effect of the rate order cannot be said to be unjust and unreasonable, judicial inquiry is at an end."

In both cases, in giving meaning and effect to the Natural Gas Act the FPC had adopted "actual, legitimate, original cost or prudent investment as the standard for establishing the basis on which rates were to be regulated," [26] and this basis of valuation was upheld. These two decisions, therefore, seem to justify the following conclusions: (1) The tendency apparently favors original cost and prudent investment rather than reproduction cost new. (2) To an even greater extent the commissions are encouraged to use a mixture of methods which they deem best suited to the purpose at hand. (3) The Supreme Court is now apparently willing to respect the independence of regulatory commissions more than at any previous time and to refrain from substituting its own methods and conclusions for those of the commissions so far as the facts of the case are concerned. (4) The judicially contrived rule of "reasonable return on fair

---

[24] (315 U.S. 575. 1942).　　　　　　　　　[25] (320 U.S. 591. 1944).
[26] Blachley and Oatman, *op. cit.*, p. 79.

value" may still be retained by the commissions that choose to do so but it has ceased to be the "law of the land." [27]

Public-Utility Holding Companies

Until 1935, holding companies were a major aspect of the utility field, as in the case, for example, of the great Insull empire that eventually came crashing down around its founder's ears, causing financial ruin in a wide circle around him. The steps in the development of the control of this device are interesting. At the outset, holding companies were used by electrical machinery manufacturers to help small utilities finance new equipment, but later they were employed to create large systems under a single control, thus securing the economies of large-scale operation as well as higher profits flowing from the building and servicing of giant organizations. The next step was financial manipulation, for the holding company enabled investment bankers to provide promotion profits to those who floated holding-company securities. For some time also, the holding company made it possible to evade what state control there then was in the utility field, federal control being virtually nonexistent. And finally, the holding company could be, and in some cases was, used to divert large profits from investors to the centralized management.

During the 1920s and early 1930s the electric power industry was pyramiding through holding companies at such a feverish pace that today the term *holding company,* although applicable to any industry, generally connotes electric utilities. As a result large segments of the industry were placed under banker control. Prices paid for properties were often unduly high, book assets were written up, consumers were then charged higher prices, and inflated securities were unloaded on unsuspecting investors. Meantime, the utilities themselves were milked by the holding companies —which had relatively little money invested in them—through excessively high fees and high salaries paid to holding-company officials. Finally, to keep these transactions from coming to light and to bolster the shaky financial edifice which the big manipulators had created, pressure had to be put on state regulatory commissions, legislatures, and the public itself to keep them in line.

Nevertheless, the attitude of the public became unfriendly, and to counteract it the electrical utility companies undertook an elaborate educational campaign spearheaded by the National Electric Light Association and generously supported by financial contributions from member companies. For a while, on the surface at least, everything seemed to be going along nicely for the industry: the 1920s were boom times, investors were more interested in the size of their dividend checks than in the methods by which profits were made, consumers were generally quiescent

[27] James F. Bonbright, "Utility Rates Reconsidered in the Light of the Hope Natural Gas Case," *American Economic Review, Papers and Proceedings,* Vol. XXVIII (May 1948), p. 465.

and had no real basis for determining the true cost of the service anyway, and state regulatory commissions were relatively feeble. Then suddenly a motion was offered in the Senate ordering the Federal Trade Commission to investigate the financial and public relations practices of electrical utilities in interstate commerce. The utilities companies fought the motion through their pressure groups, but it was passed despite their efforts and the result was one of the most thoroughgoing investigations in the history of Congress.[28]

The investigation was carried out in 1928 and its disclosures afford an amazing insight into the methods and objectives of pressure groups in American life. It was found, for example, that the National Electric Light Association's expenditures amounted to from $25 million to $30 million a year—three or four times the total cost of state regulation at the time— and that these contributions were charged back to consumers in the form of proper operating expenses entering rate determinations. "All the money being spent," said the managing director of the NELA, "is worthwhile— don't be afraid of the expense. The public pays the expense." [29]

Thus with ample financing the campaign had been a bold one to sell the public on the so-called business-managed electric light and power industry and to check any extension of government "interference," especially government ownership. Investors, employees, chambers of commerce, banks and insurance companies, the universities and the public schools— any group that might be used for either long- or short-range advantage— were fitted into the pattern with admirable imagination and initiative. The number of customer stockholders was deliberately increased as "the best kind of public ownership" and the means of "combating the growing tendency for public ownership." In an NELA publication it was said to be "high time we mustered all of our employees, male and female, to demand their right to the rewards of individual initiative and endeavor, which will be theirs under private operation." [30] Special attention was directed to the schools and colleges, the aim being "to fix the truth about the utilities in the young person's mind before incorrect notions become fixed there," [31] the program here consisting of everything from colored picture books for kindergartens to special retainers to university professors. Other drives were directed at the state legislatures and the state public-utility commissions. The industry saw to it that the work of the state commissions was carried out along lines satisfactory to the power companies, a result achieved by launching a vigorous attack on general public opinion, ultimate source of commissions' finances, personnel, and effectiveness.

[28] The committee produced 100 volumes of hearings and reports. For popular summaries, see Hugo Black, "Inside a Senate Investigation," *Harper's Magazine*, Vol. CLXXII (Feb. 1936), p. 275, or Carl D. Thompson, *Confessions of the Power Trust* (New York, 1932).

[29] Speech by M. H. Aylesworth, 13th Annual Convention of the Southeastern Division of the National Electric Light Association, 1925, quoted in Federal Trade Commission, *Utility Corporations* (S. Doc. 92, 70th Cong., 1st Sess.), Part 7, p. 29.

[30] *Ibid.*, pp. 278–279.   [31] *Ibid.*, p. 141.

Unfortunately for the industry, however, the program was oversold. The objectives and methods of the power companies, once brought to light, caused a public revulsion against the industry and, temporarily at least, against high-powered public relations methods in business generally. Congress was studying control legislation when the great depression intervened and many holding companies fell of their own weight. *The Public Utility Holding Company Act* was passed in 1935 (Title I of the Public Utility Act of that year) and applies to gas and electric utility companies engaged in interstate commerce, but its significance is even wider because holding companies are also a problem elsewhere, as in the railroads or banking, for example. This legislation is a landmark also because it attacks the tendency for utility companies to expand their activities beyond state lines, thus eluding state control and occupying an area where only the federal government can act effectively. As a measure primarily aimed at financial transactions, the administration of the act was entrusted to the Securities and Exchange Commission.

The two main objectives of this legislation are first, to regulate the present and future financial transactions of holding companies so as to prevent such abuses as were uncovered in 1928. Under this heading the SEC controls the issuance and sale of all securities and passes on all proposals for merger, reorganization, or structural change of any kind. The second aim is to correct past abuses by unscrambling structural and financial integrations contrary to the public interest and by eliminating financial practices stemming from mere paper or financial combinations. In short, "useless" holding companies are now banned and those that remain must perform a vaild function.

The law also prohibits loans by operating companies to holding companies or by subsidiaries to parent companies; the payment of "excessive" dividends; and political contributions by members of holding-company systems. In addition, lobbying activities, whether before legislatures, commissions, or elsewhere in government, must be reported to the SEC; the accounts and finanical reports of all approved holding companies are supervised by the SEC; and all sales, service, and construction contracts must likewise by approved by the commission. The act gives the Federal Power Commission jurisdiction with the SEC over electric and gas holding companies relative to security issues, mergers, and the sale of property by operating companies transmitting electricity in interstate commerce for resale, and to companies incorporated in one state and operating in another where the issuing company is not subject to the control of any state agency.

Since under the Public Utility Holding Company Act only a registered and approved holding company may exist at all, the act has real teeth. The only question as to its effectiveness, therefore, is the manner of its administration, and so far the results have been encouraging. In 1939, for example, the servicing charges for most of the affiliated companies ran to less than 1 percent of the consolidated gross revenues of the systems concerned, whereas formerly such costs had been 7.5 percent or even 10 percent in some cases. In another instance, 35 large companies had been refinanced and the average interest rate reduced from 5.05 percent to 4.044 percent, representing an annual saving of $40 million for two and a half years. In 1946, 106 public-utility holding companies with assets aggregating some $15 billion were subject to the jurisdiction of the SEC, and as a result either of action directed by the SEC or through voluntary compliance, they had disposed of their interests in 399 electric, gas, and nonutility subsidiary companies with assets of more than $6 billion. By 1950, 751 companies with assets aggregating more than $10 billion had been freed from holding company control and were therefore no longer subject to SEC regulation. In the same year, 46 holding-company systems, whose aggregate consolidated system assets at that time amounted to nearly $13 billion, were still registered with the commission. By 1952, 85 percent of the total job had been done, much of it through voluntary action by the companies themselves.

This experience shows rather conclusively that the problems encountered in divestment and dissolving corporate combinations are by no means insuperable, an encouraging object lesson for critics of the monopoly laws. However, this sweeping reorganization should not be interpreted as meaning that the regulation of rates and services will henceforth, and unaided, become effective; it merely removes a major obstacle to the effective control of electric and gas utility companies. For the future, furthermore, because of the growing size of the interconnected systems and the possibility that a nation-wide grid may someday be established (the FPC has been considering this development) the involvement of the government may be expected still further to expand. The result will inevitably be to restrict the influence and power of the state regulatory commissions in the total situation.

THE FUTURE PROSPECT OF UTILITY REGULATION

Looking at the picture of utility regulation on a broad canvas, as we have tried to do, it would appear that there are three possible lines, or some combination of them, that public-utility regulation may take:

1. In certain areas such as transportation, it may be possible to introduce larger draughts of competition which would be beneficial both to the utilities and to the economy. Wilcox, for example, poses this paradox, "Regulation may be made effective by its very ineffectiveness," meaning that earnings, instead of going up, may go down, bringing a higher degree of self-regulation through the price mechanism.[32]

2. Public-utility regulation could be made more effective in other areas, such as the power industry. The main difficulty is not that students

[32] Wilcox, *op. cit.*, p. 573.

of the problem do not know what to do—the main outlines of a constructive program are contained, for example, in a Twentieth Century Fund study, *The Power Industry and the Public Interest,* as long ago as 1944.[33] Rather, there is a lack of incentive on the part of the vocal public, and especially public-utility managements, to make such a program succeed.

3. Additional government "yardsticks" may be brought into existence, with a resulting increase of public ownership and operation. Two strong defenders of competition and free enterprise. Adams and Gray, have this to say about future policy: "Given the ineffectiveness of regulation, the need for competition, and the natural barriers to entry, the public interest requires freedom for federal, state, municipal, and co-operative bodies to produce and distribute electricity generated by nuclear fission." [34]

Because the powers of government in the United States are divided three ways among the legislative, the executive, and the judicial branches, the problems that confront the nation are ordinarily dealt with in three different areas according to the need. In the regulation of particular segments of the economy, however, the traditional process was thought to be inadequate and the commission type of agency, in which the three processes of government are combined, was favored as having a number of advantages. Thus, (1) a continuing relationship with the industry to be regulated would lead to an understanding of its problems and hence to better regulation; (2) a single agency would be more flexible in procedure, quicker to act, and less bound by outmoded tradition; and (3) such an agency would be independent and hence largely free from political pressures and the temptation to favor a particular interest over the public interest.

With experience, however, disillusionment with the administrative process as exercised by an independent regulatory commission has accumulated. These agencies have become, if anything, even slower than the courts. The Federal Communications Commission, for example, may take up to five years to decide between competing applicants for a television channel, and cases before the Federal Trade Commission have been known to drag on for a decade or more. Procedures before the commissions are often frozen in method, inflexible and bureaucratized to the point where dispatch and innovation are almost impossible. Furthermore, the commissions have shown themselves to be at least as susceptible to political pressures as any other branch of government. And finally, they have generally become so closely identified with the industries they regulate that they have difficulty operating with the public interest in view; instead, they are more often concerned with their own particular segment of the economy and consider themselves responsible to it rather than to the public.

The inadequacy of commission regulation has been studied many

---

[33] Twentieth Century Fund, *1 he Power Industry and the Public Interest* (New York, 1944).

[34] Adams and Gray, *op. cit.,* p. 158.

times by authorities in the field and by Congressional committees. From the level of the commissions themselves the matter was underscored in 1959 when Louis J. Hector, a member of the Civil Aeronautics Board, resigned in protest against what he believed to be an obsolete system, suggesting that the whole concept of regulation had probably gone too far and should be thoroughly overhauled. Large segments of the American economy, he said, were now too important to remain under the control of regulatory commissions. In a memorandum to the White House detailing his criticism, Hector ascribed the failure of commission regulation largely to the fact that such an agency has several incompatible roles, each of which is performed without proper reference to the over-all policy of the administration in office. Commission actions are not coordinated with other governmental actions, nor are they subject to the general policy of the President. For their part, the industries also are badly served because a commission finds it so hard to "give a true judicial hearing to parties who come before it in litigated cases." The agencies, said Hector, "are long on judicial form and short on judicial substance." In addition, some commissions are required not only to regulate a particular industry but also to promote it, and the two functions are often in conflict.[35]

As a solution to the difficulty, Hector proposed that the commissions be disbanded, that adjudication be handled by special administrative courts, and that all other commission functions be transferred to the regular departments of the executive branch. Another critic of commission regulation, Professor Emmette S. Redford, agrees with Hector on the general inadequacy of commission regulation but offers a different solution, which is to give the President the same kind of authority over the commissions as the Secretary of the Treasury exercises over the Comptroller of the Currency who regulates national banks; in this way the President could influence policy without interfering in specific cases.[36]

In the end, of course, the choice of a solution to the problem of commission regulation is in part, at least, up to the pressure groups who represent the industries concerned.

Supplementary Reading

Bauer, John, *Transforming Public Utility Regulation* (New York, 1950). A definite administrative program.

Fesler, James W., *The Independence of State Regulatory Agencies* (Chicago, 1942). Results of a nation-wide survey.

Ruggles, C. O., *Aspects of the Organization, Functioning, and Financing of State Public Utility Commissions* (Cambridge, Mass., 1937). An early survey.

Bernstein, M. H., *Regulating Business by Independent Commission* (Princeton, N.J., 1955).

[35] *The New York Times*, Sept. 17 and 21, 1959.
[36] Emmette S. Redford, *National Regulatory Commissions* (College Park, Md., Bureau of Governmental Research, 1959).

Redford, Emmette S. (ed.), *National Regulatory Commissions* (College Park, Md., Bureau of Governmental Research, 1959).

———, *Administration of National Economic Control* (New York, 1952). Chapter 10.

——— (ed.), *Public Administration and Policy Formation* (Austin, Tex., 1956). Case studies.

Salomon, Leon I. (ed.), *The Independent Federal Regulatory Agencies* (Phildelphia, 1959). Contributions by Louis W. Koenig, Anthony Lewis, and others.

United States Congress, report of House Subcommittee on Legislative Oversight, *Independent Regulatory Commissions* (H. Rep. 2711, 85th Cong., 2d Sess., 1959).

Raver, Paul, *Report of the Committee on Progress in Public Utility Regulation*, Proceedings, 49th Annual Convention of the National Association of Railroad and Utilities Commissions (1937). Another nation-wide survey.

Mosher, William E., *Electrical Utilities* (New York, 1929). The crisis in public control.

Twentieth Century Fund, *The Power Industry and the Public Interest* (New York, 1944). Constructive proposals.

———, *Electric Power and Government Policy* (New York, 1948).

Rostow, E. V., *A National Policy for the Oil Industry* (New Haven, Conn., 1948).

"Regulation of Natural Gas," *Law and Contemporary Problems* (Durham, N.C., summer 1954).

Koontz, Harold, and R. W. Gable, *Public Control of Economic Enterprise* (New York, 1956). Chapters 4–12 deal with many technical aspects.

Adams, Walter, and Horace M. Gray, *Monopoly in America* (New York, 1955). Chapter 3 is entitled, "Regulation and Public Utilities."

Bonbright, James C., and Gardiner C. Means, *The Holding Company* (New York, 1932). Background of the Public Utility Holding Company Act of 1935.

Troxel, Emery, *Economics of Transport* (New York, 1955). Chapters 15–16.

Nelson, James C., *Railroad Transportation and Public Policy* (Washington, D.C., Brookings Institution, 1957). A balanced and up-to-date treatment.

Latham, Earl, *The Politics of Railroad Coordination* (Cambridge, Mass., 1959). A further application of power-group analysis.

Presidential Advisory Committee on Transport Policy and Organization, *Revision of Federal Transportation Policy* (Washington, D.C., 1955).

Gorter, W., *United States Shipping Policy* (New York, Council on Foreign Relations, 1956). A comprehensive postwar survey.

Siepmann, Charles A., *Radio, Television, and Society* (New York, 1950).

White, Llewellyn, *The American Radio* (Chicago, 1947).

Coase, R. H., *British Broadcasting* (Cambridge, Mass., 1950).

Edelman, Jacob M., *The Licensing of Radio Services in the United States, 1927-1947* (Urbana, Ill., 1950). Administrative formulation of policy.

Robinson, T. P., *Radio Networks and the Federal Government* (New York, 1943).

Federal Communications Commission, *Investigation of the Telephone Industry in the United States* (H. Doc. 340, 76th Cong., 1st Sess., 1939).

18
PUBLIC OWNERSHIP
AND OPERATION

---

*Comparisons with other nations; issues of public policy;
varieties of public enterprise; rules of business enterprise;
undertakings of the federal government; of state and local
governments; of municipalities; changes of policy under
the Eisenhower administration; factors in growth and decline of public enterprise; problems of public management;
public corporations; effect on the economy; effect on government; future prospects.*

A major difference in business-government relations between the
United States and other nations is the relatively slight emphasis in this
country on government ownership and operation. Here, state enterprise
is considered an adjunct, or support, to the effective public regulation of
private undertakings, whereas elsewhere—notably in Great Britain,
France, Italy, and Australia—public ownership is an alternative to regulation. There are, of course, exceptions, as in the case of our Post Office
Department, or municipal water-supply systems that were once predominantly private operations, or certain manufacturing activities of
the armed services; but in general, in the United States we have converted private enterprises to public ownership only with the greatest reluctance.

In short, the American people have assumed that society is better off
when as much of the economy as possible is owned and operated by
private individuals or groups, leaving to government its essential functions
of promoting and fostering all legitimate economic interests, regulating
those that are or threaten to become monopolistic, or too powerful, or
constitute a threat to the public welfare, and stabilizing the whole economic edifice in order to keep it in balance. Thus, the public and the
private parts of the economy each play a proper role and it is unwise
public policy to confuse and admix them except in emergencies such as
war, economic depression, or the failure of private enterprise in certain
situations.

Studies of public economic enterprise on a world-wide basis show rather conclusively that its growth is everywhere due to one of two factors or to a combination of them: belief systems on the one hand and practical necessity on the other.[1] In the United States, necessity has predominated because few Americans believe in socialism as a political-economic philosophy. We have sought to strengthen competition and to prevent monopoly either in government or in private governing groups. Although the policy is a sound one, as already shown, it is being severely tested today.

Comparative studies also show that state enterprise grows fastest in public utilities: transportation, power, and communications, to which may be added the category of banking and insurance. This same trend appears in the United States, with the greatest relative growth of public economic enterprise since 1932 occurring in banking and insurance. Public responsibility for manufacturing and retailing, on the other hand, is rare in all nations (save the USSR), but especially rare in the United States.

What encourages or hinders the growth of public ownership and operation? Is there some innate necessity for this development? Can it be rationally controlled and directed? And can it be reversed? What factors favor public regulation as against public ownership? What is the quality of management in public economic enterprises and on what does success or failure depend? Is it possible even to analyze factors such as these? What is the effect of governmental economic undertakings on the economy as a whole, as well as on other programs of government? And finally, what is the future prospect for public ownership and operation in the United States? As in other chapters, our objective here is less to explore technical details than it is to identify reliable guidelines for future policy decision.

THE NATURE AND SCOPE OF PUBLIC ECONOMIC UNDERTAKINGS

We are not much concerned here with services that were once privately owned and operated and are now fully accepted as appropriate public undertakings, such as public education and the postal system. Nor are we concerned with tax-supported enterprises where appropriations and expenditures are so mingled that costs, net earnings, or even break-even points are hard or impossible to calculate and no pretense is made of operating a business service. The manufacturing activities of the armed forces is an example of this kind of enterprise.

Rather, we are interested here in fields of enterprise still predominantly in private hands but in which public ownership and operation exist as in the case of electric power and credit facilities for

[1] See for example, W. Friedmann (ed.), *The Public Corporation: A Comparative Symposium* (Toronto, 1954), p 545.

farmers and home owners. In this debatable area, public opinion is still
undecided as to which way public policy should go. This type of
public business operation offers a service over the counter, as it
were, at an ascertainable price, such as a loan from the Farm Credit
Administration where the interest rate is known and the farmer may go
instead to his local privately owned bank if he prefers. Metered water
supply, gas and electricity services, and local bus transportation are
similar examples.

When government operates an over-the-counter business service,
its methods should be those of a private business enterprise. (1) All
costs must be clearly identifiable to determine whether the service is
paying for itself. (2) All units of service must be sold at unit prices to
permit comparisons with similar or rival services. (3) Costs, both
quantitative and qualitative, must be accurately known in order to
determine the relative efficiency of the undertaking. This is a difficult
task for a monopoly service but no easier under private ownership. (4)
Where a subsidy is included, it should be separately accounted for
and treated as an appropriation and not as a business revenue.

It will be objected, perhaps, that because government often violates
or disregards these basic rules of business enterprise, one set of assumptions applies to private business transactions and a different one
to public enterprise. But this is not a valid argument. When government operates a business activity, then it must observe the same rules
as private business so that citizens, lawmakers, and public officials may
make comparisons with similar undertakings under private management.

Is it essential that a public economic enterprise earn a profit?
Ideally, yes. To make comparisons possible, all costs should be accounted for and covered by earned income. If the decision is to
adopt a break-even policy, the fact should be announced in advance
and fully understood by the public. If these propositions are the
counsel of perfection, they also constitute the policy that the federal
government has been trying to follow since the passage of the Government Corporation Control Act of 1945.

Federal Government Enterprises

The extent of government ownership and operation might be indicated in a number of ways. In an interesting article on "Government Ownership" in the *Encyclopedia of the Social Sciences,* Stacy
May has a long list with scores of entries beginning with "abattoir"
and ending with "woolen mills," and points out that somewhere or
other all these services are provided by government. Such an exercise has a suggestive value but reveals little about trends or weight-
ings. In 1949 the first Hoover Commission reported that the federal government owned or was financially interested in approximately one hundred important business enterprises, but even when
these are divided under the five headings of public lands, lending

and insurance agencies, transportation services, supplying and engaging in manufacturing services, and generating, transmitting, and distributing electricity, the analysis still does not show much (and might even be misleading) until weights are assigned to these various categories and dominant trends are noted.

The growth of public enterprise occurs in response to external or internal stimuli, chief of which are war and depression. During the 1930s, for example, the fastest growth was in power, credit, and housing. In the next decade, however, a Twentieth Century Fund report shows the following percentage changes in the number of work units per 1000 of the population, for certain selected public enterprises for the years 1942-1950:

Percentage Increase

Over 200   Rural electrification miles energized
            Columbia River system kilowatt-hours produced
            Commodity Credit Corporation corn loans

100–200   TVA kilowatt-hours produced
            Federal Home Administration claims paid on property loans
            FHA property improvement loan insurance

50–100   Alaska Railroad ton-miles
            Panama Canal tonnage
            Municipal electric-utility production

Although this is only a partial list, it does indicate that the sharpest increase in public economic activity during the 1940s was in electricity, credit, housing, and transportation in about that order. Some of this activity, such as housing credit, represents a carry-over from the previous decade. Declines were noted in the 1940s in state liquor store sales, certain classes of agricultural credit, inland waterways tonnage, private housing loans outstanding, and public housing starts.[2] Incidentally, this comparison offers a rather good cross-section of federal business enterprise.

Some federal business enterprises are very large. The Reconstruction Finance Corporation, for example, made 640,000 loans and loaned or spent outright nearly $49 billion during its lifetime, 1932 to 1954. Nevertheless, by any test, public enterprise is only a small part of total enterprise in the nation, accounting in 1957 for about 1.2 percent of the national income. Of the $4.2 billion earned by public enterprises, just about two thirds represented the income of federal ventures, one third that of state and local governments. These figures also show how rapidly federal activity has outstripped state and local ownership and operation, dominant prior to 1932. To conclude, however, that the small percentage of national income derived from public enterprise shows public business enterprise to be relatively unimportant would be

[2] J. Frederic Dewhurst and Associates, *America's Needs and Resources* (New York, Twentieth Century Fund, 1955), p. 604.

misleading, because the trend may be a good deal more significant than the dollar volume of business transacted.

State and Local Government Enterprises

In state governments there is a considerable variety of business activity but with a preponderance in the fields that have been mentioned: transportation, power, housing, and insurance. Since the repeal of prohibition the administration of state liquor stores has become a prominent state activity, orginally justified as a method of control but becoming—and by more than coincidence—a substantial source of revenue as well. In transportation, examples are the Port of New York Authority with assets of $920 million and 4400 employees; the operation of harbor facilities in Boston and New Orleans; and the administration of the Erie Canal, 523 miles long. Although for several years state enterprise seemed to have reached a plateau, there is now a considerable expansion because of the increasing number of toll roads, bridges, and throughways. Indeed, the current tendency of state governments to create "authorities" (another name for public corporations) has caused much concern among students of state organization and finance.

Like municipal power projects, state power projects received their principal impetus during the depression of the 1930s. Nebraska, for example, is now served exclusively by publicly owned electrical utilities. Beginning with a number of municipal plants, the system was expanded by the state legislature in 1939 and again in 1946. Another example is the Power Authority of New York State, created in 1931 when Franklin D. Roosevelt was governor. With Congressional authorization of the St. Lawrence seaway and power project and state authorization to build connecting transmission lines, this state public power authority entered a new period of considerable expansion. The power potential of the St. Lawrence is estimated at 750,000 kilowatts and that of the Niagara at more than 1 million kilowatts, making the St. Lawrence project one of the largest in the nation.

The oldest form of state insurance is workmen's compensation. In 1949 it was written in thirty states entirely by private companies. The other eighteen states had established state insurance funds, in eleven of which private companies were allowed to compete with the state, but not in the remaining seven where the state enjoyed a monopoly. With generally lower costs and lower rates, the state funds pose a threat to privately operated insurance systems. The main incursion on private enterprise, however, is in compulsory unemployment insurance established in 1936 as part of the social security system and financed by payroll taxes collected from employers.[3]

---

[3] See Chap. 22 below, on Social Security.

There has been a strong movement toward compulsory automobile liability insurance in some states, causing private insurance companies to fear that should it become widespread it might result in state-monopolized liability insurance funds. Other developments in the insurance field are more or less isolated happenings: state hail insurance in North Dakota, South Dakota, and Oklahoma, and state life insurance in Wisconsin and Massachusetts.

Municipal Activities

Being corporations anyhow, municipal governments have long operated a number of diverse trading activities such as public markets, wharves, docks, ice plants, slaughter houses, laundries, and liquor stores. As in the case of state and federal governments, however, the main concentration is in transportation, electricity, and housing. In addition, three fourths of American cities now own and operate their own water supply systems and New York City has its own municipal radio station. Indeed, the pattern is increasingly variegated and interesting.

The reason, perhaps, is that there has long been a feeling, in Britain as in this country, that municipal "socialism" is less objectionable than other kinds because government is closer to the voters and cities are normally organized and operated for semibusiness purposes such as public works. Municipal trading activities grew rapidly during the New Deal period when the federal government acted as banker to the cities, and municipal electric plants, water plants, and public housing were being encouraged. An additional stimulation today is the increasing difficulty of most municipalities in securing adequate tax revenues in competition with state governments.

A crisis in mass transit, compounded of increasing fares, deteriorating service, and threats of abandonment have brought the problem of local transportation rather painfully to the fore. Partly for this reason, public ownership and operation has increased. In many cities, including several of the largest, the public transportation system is publicly owned and operated, and in at least one it is publicly owned and privately operated. Whether the publicly owned systems succeed in operating on a paying basis seems to depend on whether the city fathers have the courage to fix rates high enough to cover all costs or whether rates are kept low for political reasons. With a 15-cent fare on its transit lines, Chicago has had a good financial record; with 5-cent and 10-cent fares, New York did not. Even with the adoption of the 15-cent fare in New York the prospect was still not bright and there is much pressure to raise the fare still further.

Public ownership in electric power has grown at all levels of government, causing private power companies to be more concerned with public enterprise than any other group in the economy. It may be more than a coincidence that public criticism of utility regulation has been concentrated primarily on the problems of the private electrical companies. After 1937, due largely to the New Deal power policy, more than half of all local electrical systems became municipally owned, although most of these installations were small and the private utilities continued to control the large, interconnected systems. Gas companies also are frequently municipally owned, to the point where by 1958 there were 515 such companies in 34 states, reflecting a gain of 14 percent in the preceding eighteen months. Most of the new companies are located in the South, however, which had lagged somewhat in this field.

Public housing is another municipal activity that was spurred by federal policies during the New Deal era. Most states now have enabling legislation permitting cities to set up public housing and urban renewal authorities. By 1958 the total number of dwelling units in low-rent housing programs was more than 557,000, of which 444,000 were completed. More recently the federal policy has been to encourage private building, to make loans for new private construction and improvements, and to reinsure existing premises for rehabilitation purposes rather than to encourage public housing per se. Nevertheless, the impact of growing populations in the large cities is such that as an extension of the public-housing concept, there is now also a public slum clearance and urban renewal program in more than 300 cities. Progress is slow, however, partly because appropriations are small.

The Eisenhower Administration

The trends described here were interrupted in 1953 by the Eisenhower administration which was pledged in advance to "getting the government out of business" and encouraging the transfer of current public economic responsibilities to private enterprise as far as possible. Consequently there were these developments:

1. Former President Hoover was asked to make a second study of the executive branch of the federal government. The first, which had been published in 1949, stressed internal organization and management; the second one, completed in 1955, emphasized the "proper" functions of government and especially the need to get the government out of business. The most controversial of the commission's reports (there were many volumes) were those dealing with electrical utilities and lending agencies, two areas where public ownership had grown most rapidly during the preceding twenty years.

2. Early in his administration President Eisenhower referred to TVA as an example of "creeping socialism," and the cry was eagerly taken up by the opponents of public power. The Hoover Commission recommended curtailment or, alternatively, liquidation of TVA as a government operation. Its appropriations were reduced and when

it sought to finance its own expansions through the sale of revenue bonds, the plan was vetoed by the Comptroller General on the ground that such bonds would not be included in the public debt. TVA was asked to pay back to the federal Treasury in the 1957 fiscal year $75 million, which was nearly $40 million more than TVA had scheduled in its forty-year repayment on power facilities as required by law. In 1959, however, Congress authorized TVA to issue $750 million in revenue bonds to build new steam-powered generating facilities, the expansion programs to be subject to supervision by the Treasury Department and the Budget Bureau.

3. As already indicated, one of the two main purposes of the Atomic Energy Act of 1954 was to encourage private enterprise in the development of atomic energy for peacetime uses.

4. The government-financed industrial plants left over from World War II were sold to private enterprise (prior to 1953 but also afterwards), sometimes at prices near their cost but often much below. This became a controversial issue because of the pattern of selling to large companies and hence decreasing competition by strengthening their already great power.[4]

5. The Reconstruction Finance Corporation—which had been created during the Hoover administration in 1932 with a capital fund of $500 million, and which for more than twenty years rescued private business during the depression, helped finance public works, carried a large part of wartime industry financing during World War II, assisted with farm subsidy payments, and contributed to peacetime reconversion after 1945—was liquidated in 1954. In its place, however, a Small Business Administration was created with a capital fund of $300 million, $25 million of which could be used to make loans to state and local governments for public-works programs. It was widely remarked by cynics at the time that with the best intentions in the world, the Eisenhower administration was learning that when one lending agency is abolished, another must almost automatically take its place.

6. The number of federal business corporations (like the Reconstruction Finance Corporation and the Commodity Credit Corporation) was sharply reduced from over 100, which was the number immediately after World War II.

7. Private power companies were given preference, especially in the West, over their public competitors. A celebrated case involved the Hell's River Canyon project on the Snake River in Idaho, an issue of great political significance in the Congressional election of 1954 that eventually in 1958 was won by the supporters of private power.

8. The Department of the Interior encouraged the transfer of

---

[4] See Walter Adams and Horace M. Gray, *Monopoly in America* (New York, 1955), Chap. 6, "Disposal of Surplus Property."

certain rights and privileges in public lands, forests, and mineral resources to private interests, causing a storm of protest from those concerned with conservation and leading the Democrats to coin the word "giveaway," which was applied to atomic energy and the war-time industrial plants as well as to the public domain.

9. In 1956 the Director of the Budget reported on the administration's campaign to take the federal government out of competition with private business: in addition to the liquidation of the RFC for a return of more than $1 billion, some 355 activities of the Department of Defense had been eliminated (such enterprises as repair shops for office furniture and automobiles, landscape nurseries, bakeries, laundries, and the like) and 137 installations operated by civilian agencies had been closed or curtailed.

10. And finally, the Dixon-Yates contract would have authorized private utility companies rather than TVA to replace TVA power siphoned off for new atomic energy plants in the Tennessee Valley area. But a boiling up of political controversy, especially among Congressmen from those states and the public-power states of the Middle and Far West resulted in the cancellation of the contract.

Whether the dominant policy of the Eisenhower administration, as reflected in the steps here described, would cause a permanent reversal of the public ownership trend of 1932-1952 could not, by 1960, be clearly foreseen. As in the past, much depends on practical considerations such as national emergency, economic depression, and the trusteeship role of private interests.

FACTORS IN THE GROWTH AND DECLINE OF PUBLIC ECONOMIC ACTIVITY

Until recent years in western Europe and Britain, as well as in the United States, the issue of socialism versus private enterprise was characterized by so much emotion and dogma that few cause-and-effect relationships could be established as a basis for prediction and control. Since 1932, however, the question has been carefully studied and those responsible for public policy may now draw on a considerable body of objective data. Some of the more important reasons for the growth of public ownership are these:

First, as already indicated, the growth of public ownership in a free society depends in part on a combination of *belief systems* plus practical necessity. No nation can, or apparently should, overlook the importance of both. When a belief system is emphasized to the neglect of practical necessity, then a change may be delayed, but it will be more drastic when it does come than if it had been allowed to occur gradually. On the other hand, if concentration on practical necessity emphasizes expediency to the point where philosophical conviction is weakened, then a nation may lose its sense of direction and the values it cherishes.[5]

A second factor is that in a democracy *the national emergency of war* inevitably causes an expansion of state activity, including public ownership, because the modern requirements of total war cause people to forsake their convictions concerning private responsibility and to concentrate on massed power. During such an emergency, government and big business both tend to become bigger and more concentrated. When the war is over, it is possible to turn back toward competition and the private direction of economic affairs, but there seems always to be a residue of expanded government responsibility. The most rapid developments of public ownership in the United States have occurred during World Wars I and II and in neither case has the reconversion to private responsibility been complete.

Major economic dislocations, such as the depression of the 1930s, also tend to stimulate state activity, again leaving a residue of public ownership that takes time and effort to dissipate, if it is ever finally accomplished. The remarkable thing about the great depression (and it is a tribute to the strength of the American people's belief in private enterprise) is that public ownership and operation did not become even more pronounced.

Again, in the *economic growth of a nation,* as in the early history of the United States and in the economic development of underdeveloped nations today, governments are called on to act as banker, assister, or owner of infant industries, and generally to expand its central concern for the economy, thus creating a considerable degree of public ownership at the outset. With wise political leadership, however, this trend can be reversed as a nation acquires the underlying necessities of a modern economic system.

The reverse, of course, is equally true, as when *private undertakings become unprofitable* but the need for their services continues. In that case government may be prevailed upon to acquire and manage such nonprofitable business concerns at a loss. The so-called Shannon Committee report to Congress in 1933, for example, showed that in the early history of the nation this factor of unprofitability was perhaps the chief cause of government entry into business.[6]

Governments are also required to extend the owner-manager relationship when there has been a pronounced *wasting of national resources,* or when the threat to them is great, thus diminishing the nation's ability to defend itself or to preserve the bases of a sound economy. In this area, government manages land, minerals, forests,

---

[5] A good statement of these principles is found in Alexander Leighton, *The Governing of Men* (Princeton, N.J., 1946), "Systems of Belief under Stress," pp. 287ff.

[6] *Report of the Special Committee Appointed to Investigate Government Competition with Private Enterprise* (H. Rept. 1985, 73d Cong., 2d Sess., Washington, D.C., 1933).

and water supply, an outstanding example being the work of TVA, a multipurpose agency created to conserve and develop the resources of an entire region covering several states.

In addition, government ownership may also be extended by the *failure of private management to consider itself a trustee of the public good* and to abuse its power, especially in cases (as in public utilities) where monopoly or semimonopoly is the condition. The effect of the trusteeship factor is slower to be felt than some others and hence more difficult to detect, but it is nevertheless real. The growth of socialism in Great Britain was partly due to unchecked monopoly and the tendency of private utilities to take advantage of their monopolistic position to earn "unreasonably" high profits, neglect standards of service, and become managerially unresponsive to what the people wanted and needed. More than any other, the trusteeship factor is likely to determine whether utilities shall eventually be predominantly in private ownership in the United States or transferred to public ownership. When belief systems and long-established discontents vie with each other, something has to give. Public opinion is notoriously fickle: the public-private dispute is as much a matter of situation and technique as of ideological predisposition.

So much for the factors that encourage the growth of public enterprise. Although more is understood about them than about the factors that *stimulate a reversal to private enterprise,* certain hypotheses may nevertheless be offered:

In free governments, there seems to be a swing of the pendulum from periods of governmental growth in economic activities to the encouragement of the private part of the economy, as in the contrast, for example, between the New Deal and the Eisenhower administrations. What is not so clear is whether public ownership trends are ever wholly reversed over longer periods of time. A number of additional factors enter here, including the influence of technology, the disposition of young people to own and operate their own businesses or to prefer the seeming security of working for someone else, and the orientation of future leaders during their school and college years.

One way of getting the government out of business is through a reorganization of government itself and its functions after periods of national emergency such as war and depression, or when a different political party comes to office. Both Hoover Commission reports are cases in point. It should be noted, however, that this device may be employed to achieve any desired objective, including putting the government into business as well as taking it out.

Businessmen and others attached to the private sector of the economy increase their chances of controlling the growth of public enterprise when they become better informed and more active in public affairs and the formulation of public policy. So much of our top business leadership in the United States has been emotionally rather than rationally opposed to governmental operations, and for so long, that unwittingly they have gambled with a loss of influence in public affairs. Happily, this situation seems to be righting itself. For one thing, businessmen are increasingly being invited to take an active part in the management of government and thus learn at firsthand some of the difficulties involved; for another, government increasingly impinges on business itself—in the matter of taxation, social security regulations, and the like—so that simply to manage a business, private management must know something about government.

Finally, when governments assume temporary responsibility for the operation of a business service, as in time of national emergency, the type of organization chosen for the purpose may affect the ease of conversion to private responsibility. Thus the Hoover Commission has strongly favored the government corporation for new economic services in preference to one of the regular departments on the ground that the temporary program may more easily be pruned off at the end of the emergency if it has not been allowed to put roots down into the fertile ground of regular government activity.[7]

PROBLEMS OF PUBLIC MANAGEMENT AND THE CORPORATE DEVICE

Until a few years ago, socialists also were inclined to advance their cause by emotional appeals to people's altruism and self-interest. With the advent of large-scale government responsibilities for managing utility and other services, however, as occurred in Great Britain after World War II, attention turned to the practical matter of making public ownership and operation a success and to facing up to stubborn problems inherent in the management of government. These problems are of two kinds: those that accompany a particular type of business and those that accompany public administration as such. The first category can be quickly disposed of because the main factors have already been mentioned: the obsolescent business that cannot be made profitable but must be carried on for the sake of an essential service; the new business (such as atomic energy or railroading in the early days) that suffers characteristic growing pains; the business having a regulatory overtone as in the case of state liquor stores; a business where powerful interest groups prefer a subsidy and low rates to a break-even situation and higher rates, as in the case of the U. S. Post Office.[8] There is no easy solution to the problems posed by such kinds of public enterprise except a citizenry and their lawmakers educated in understanding

[7] Commission on Organization of the Executive Branch of the Government, *Lending Agencies*, Appendix R (Washington, D.C., 1949), p. xi.

[8] In Great Britain the Post Office has long been profitable, a source of considerable revenue. In the United States, however, too much mail is carried at below cost, especially that of advertisers, magazine and periodical publishers, and the government.

and tolerance. Most of these problems, however, relate to enterprises that are useful more for the service provided than for the profit involved.

The problems of a public business expected to make a profit are more serious and constitute the headache of businesses in the second category mentioned above. These are the problems of public administration as such. For example, continuity of policy and leadership is a condition of success in any business management, but in public management, politics enters at least to the extent of causing discontinuity of policy and leadership when a different political party comes to office.

In addition, a business enterprise should stand on its own financial feet, borrowing and retiring its own capital investment, reinvesting its earnings, meeting all costs out of earned income, and keeping a strict accounting. Although government *could* do all these things, frequently in the past it has not, due to the necessity of tighter financial controls on a public agency than on a private one—what in Great Britain is called "Treasury control." A successful business must also have complete freedom to recruit, remunerate, and retain employees in the competitive job market and to promote or fire them if it wishes. This, too, is possible in government, as in the case of TVA, but for the most part the record has been far from good due to restrictions imposed by the requirements of civil service.

If government is to operate successfully in a competitive situation (as when a municipally owned electric plant competes with a privately owned gas company), then the public enterprise must be free to advertise and carry on a public relations program in a like manner to its private competitor. Traditionally, this kind of government activity has been opposed as unfair competition and a waste of the taxpayer's money, but in recent years a more understanding attitude is noticeable and government public relations programs are becoming more common.

Finally, there is a kind of inherent constitutional problem of public enterprise. To produce businesslike results, management must have a certain amount of freedom, independence, and flexibility, but government (at least in a democracy) has two responsibilities toward its citizens that also must be met: each of its parts must be integrated into an over-all program to achieve unity, cohesion, and a sense of common direction; and equally, government must hold all its programs to a strict public accountability. Except for the very largest, most private businesses are immune from the first of these requirements, and not even the very largest is expected to measure up *to the same degree* to the requirement of public accountability. Consequently, in government administration, it is usually assumed that authority must be centralized in the legislature and the chief executive, and that uniform requirements as to financial controls, personnel administration under civil service procedures, and the like must apply to all parts of a widespread program. With each new control, necessary as it may be, the effect is to drain off the flexibility of administration that is needed in a well-run business enterprise.

The Corporate Device

To escape from these difficutlies recourse has been had to the very practical device of the government corporation, which is about as close to the method of private business that government can come. A corporation in private enterprise is a separate legal entity with a charter setting forth its powers within the limits of which it is free to finance and run its own affairs under the control of a board of directors. A corporation obtains its own capital funds, retains its earnings, and tries to balance income against expenses, allowing for depreciation and taxes. It can purchase where and what it pleases, maintain a strict accounting system, and recruit its personnel and compensate them according to its own needs. It can sue and be sued, has no "sovereign" immunities as from taxation, and its paid management is free to respond to market demands. In government the corporate device does not quite work this way, but this is the standard by which variations may be judged.

The government corporation is being used in the United States and in several other parts of the world for the operation of business enterprises. Of the three main types of organization, one is wholly government-owned and operated, another is the mixed enterprise owned and operated partly by government and partly by private enterprise, and the third is privately owned but publicly managed in that government selects the board of directors but allows private individuals to purchase limited-interest stock. The first type predominates in the United States, the mixed enterprise was popular in Europe prior to World War II but since then has been losing ground to the wholly public kind, and the third type, found chiefly in Great Britain before the Labor party took office in 1945, is now becoming rare in any nation.

In the United States the trend has been to restrict the government corporation and to shape it more to the model of a regular government department. Thus civil service laws passed during the period 1935 to 1946 were expressly made to apply to government corporations, with the notable exception of TVA which from the outset had achieved a high standard of personnel practice. In another move, some government corporations were organically attached to one or another of the major federal departments—the Commodity Credit Corporation to Agriculture and the Inland Waterways Corporation to Commerce, for example—where there was a natural tendency to restrict their freedom by integrating them into the departmental chain of command and to make them conform to the traditional bureau pattern. Another trend was to abolish boards of directors made up of prominent citizens recruited from outside the government in favor of boards composed of the higher officers of the department, including the Secretary himself. Such nominal directors brought no independent outside viewpoint to the operation of the corporations and thus vitiated the main reason for which boards of directors are used.

In 1945 government corporations were brought under still further control by the *Government Corporation Control Act,* of which the three main provisions were: (1) all corporations of the federal government shall be federally chartered by Congress, including those previously chartered under state laws, and the power of the President and of cabinet officers to create subsidiary corporations (a power frequently used in the past, especially by the RFC) is restricted; (2) the budgets of all government corporations must be shown in the annual budget of the federal government as "annexed" budgets, meaning that they are not subject to the same review as the budgets of regular departments and agencies but are nevertheless available to Congressional scrutiny; and (3) the accounts of all government corporations shall be audited in the General Accounting Office according to commercial-type procedures that emphasize cost accounting.

Compared with government corporations in many other nations, the American variety is so hedged in and modified as to essential characteristics that most of these agencies are hardly recognizable as corporations. What is the reason? Is this the work of interest groups that would limit possible extensions of public enterprise? Are the traditional methods of public management, bureaucratic as they are, nevertheless superior to those of an ordinary corporation? Must there be consistency in the management of government irrespective of the consequences to individual programs? As against such possibilities, it would seem simply common sense that when government sets out to manage a business enterprise, it should be allowed to use the same methods that private business uses with so much success. If a particular policy is wrong, then it should be changed, but a proper device of management should not be emasculated and then criticized as inefficient.

EFFECT OF PUBLIC OWNERSHIP AND OPERATION ON THE ECONOMY

With only 1.2 percent of the business activity of the nation operated by government, references to "creeping socialism" might seem hard to justify. But as already suggested, trends are sometimes more significant than dollars' worth of business, and recent trends show a marked growth of ownership and operation at all three levels of government, especially in electric power and credit. When municipal power plants were multiplying during the 1930s, it was interesting to watch conservative, rather wealthy communities happily establishing such plants, largely in protest against the holding-company abuses of that era, while the citizens were as active as ever inveighing against "creeping socialism" at chamber-of-commerce and business-club luncheons. When a man has pride in his community and confidence in his town officials, he is apt to consider it no more than good business to have a municipally operated utility service instead of buying power from "outsiders." Since Americans are about as inconsistent as most humans, it is fortunate that we also have a sense of humor.

On the serious side, if the American inclination is to look on state ownership and operation as a supplement to regulation, what may be said of *government competition as a yardstick*? The fact is that some very conservative people regard the government yardstick with favor on the ground that monopoly (as in the case of a utility) is always undesirable, that the best way to keep a utility enterprise alert to consumer needs is to threaten it with competition, and that, accordingly, the government should establish a small number of competing plants just to show what can be done. Thus far, the argument is understandable even if the conclusion is rejected; but the test is this: to what extent is a comparison between particular types of private and public enterprise a fair one? Indeed, are the elements of competition in the two cases ever exactly comparable? Many accountants believe that if sound accounting principles are followed, then comparability is as valid between private and public enterprise as it is between two firms in the same line of business. In practice, some rather serious difficulties have been encountered.

In a nation-wide survey in 1939, the Federal Power Commission found that: [9]

1. With one exception, average typical bills for service were higher in the case of privately owned utilities than for public in all communities of 2500 population or more.

2. The exception was in communities of more than 2500 population when only residential service was in question. Lower average bills also prevailed in communities of less than 2500 population when the power facilities were privately operated and the service predominantly residential.

3. For other services, such as commercial light and power or industrial service, in communities of 2500 population or more, publicly owned utilities always offered lower rates.

4. Public systems paid higher taxes or higher contributions in lieu of taxes than the private utilities: 17.3 percent and 13.2 percent of gross revenues, respectively.

5. In addition, publicly owned utilities provided free services equivalent to 8.5 percent of their gross revenues compared with 0.0024 percent in the case of private concerns.

[9] Federal Power Commission, *Annual Report*, 1939, p. 13.

Some writers, considering these findings, have pointed out that since municipal electric services are generally centered in small communities and private power facilities in much larger ones, the conclusions may not be strictly comparable.[10] They have been buttressed, however, in a study by the Twentieth Century Fund which in 1948 compared sixteen large public and nineteen large private systems and found that public rates were usually lower than private rates, that although the public systems had slightly higher costs for generation and transmission, their costs were substantially lower for sales promotion, customer accounting, bill collecting, and general administration, with lower total costs as a result. Moreover, the public systems had adequately provided for depreciation and, unlike the private systems, had devoted large sums to debt retirement.[11]

Comparisons become increasingly difficult in the case of multi-purpose projects such as TVA. Here total costs must be distributed among several purposes—flood control, navigation, and power. In the case of TVA, joint costs are allocated 31 percent to flood control, 27 percent to navigation, and 42 percent to power. By 1959, total gross investment was $2098 million and net earnings had averaged 4 percent since 1933. Also in 1959, of a total net income of $479 million, $10 million was used to pay interest on bonds, $65 million to retire bonds, and $185 million to reimburse the federal government. The remainder, $219 million, was reinvested in new power facilities. But the private power companies correctly argue that the distribution of joint costs makes a wholly comparable yardstick difficult to achieve.

Since comparisons on a cost basis are open to question, recent emphasis has been on the results of public competition—the role of TVA, for example, as *pacesetter* in the region. Here the results are indisputable: utility rates have declined most in areas adjacent to a public power development, and at the same time the private utilities have made more money than ever before. Rates came down about three and a half times as fast in the TVA area as in the New York–New England area where there was no public program. In the TVA region and the Pacific Northwest it has been established that the demand for electric power is far more elastic than an overly cautious industry functioning on a noncompetitive basis had ever imagined. In the sense of pacesetting, therefore, the yardstick has proved itself in practice. "The yardstick in its true sense," says David Lilienthal, "has served and continues to serve a public purpose. It has led all over the country to a realistic re-examination of the financial feasibility of low rates. It has established the fact

[10] Harold Koontz and Richard W. Gable, *Public Control of Economic Enterprise* (New York, 1956), pp. 706–707, and Clair Wilcox, *Public Policies toward Business* (Homewood, Ill., 1955), p. 749.

[11] Twentieth Century Fund, *Electric Power and Government Policy* (New York, 1948), pp. 405–409.

that rates by private utilities far lower than were thought possible ten years ago are profitable." [12]

In addition to providing more or less useful yardsticks, the effects of public enterprise are also felt in a number of other ways. On the question of *taxation,* for example, should a public economic enterprise pay taxes to the same extent as a private enterprise under the same conditions? Clearly it should and can under the distinction in American constitutional law between the sovereign and the proprietary functions of government. The modern tendency is to avoid the shield

FIG. 11. AVERAGE ELECTRIC BILL FOR 100 KWH RESIDENTIAL
SERVICE IN LARGE CITIES * (JANUARY 1952)

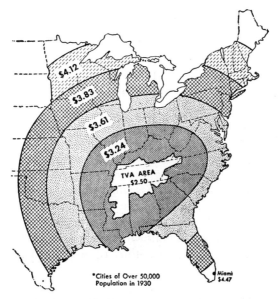

SOURCE: Tennessee Valley Authority

of governmental immunity and for public enterprises to pay their full share of taxes. But in each case the decision is up to the state legislatures or to Congress. TVA pays to surrounding state and local governments an annual sum in lieu of taxes calculated to equal, if it does not exceed (this is controversial), sums that would be paid by private utilities in the same area and under the same circumstances if all of the facilities of TVA were privately owned.

Another area of influence on the economy relates to the position of *organized labor.* A reason given by European Socialist parties for favoring public ownership is that labor fares better under public than

---

[12] David Lilienthal, *TVA: Democracy on the March* (New York, 1944), p. 23.

under private management. But this seems doubtful. In England the labor unions insisted that they be represented on the boards of public corporations on the assumption that their influence would be increased, but once given this right they quickly relinquished it on the ground that it interfered with their independent bargaining position and the use of economic sanctions. Moreover, labor's share in the income of an economic enterprise, like that of any other group, depends a good deal more on managerial and labor efficiency than on the kind of ownership involved be it public, private, or a mixture of the two. Unless a nation is strongly attached to freedom, as Britain is, trade unions may find themselves with less influence and less real power under public ownership than under private ownership.

Another controversial but important issue is whether even small areas of public ownership, as in the United States, cause a widespread unnerving and *anxiety on the part of private business,* thus contributing to a lowered morale. There can be no doubt, of course, about the political sensitivity of the business community as illustrated by the greater reaction of the stock market to political than to economic events. It is also true that the threat of government competition has a beneficial effect on private businesses, especially the very largest, in so far as it keeps them from abusing their power. General Motors has long been aware that domination of more than a certain percentage of the automobile business (it used to be 40 percent) might lead to socialization of the industry, and officials of American Telephone and Telegraph have given the threat of government ownership as reason for emphasizing public policy issues in management to the extent that they have. Somewhere between the two sides of this issue there is a point, not susceptible of precise definition, where too much government ownership transforms a private ownership system into a socialistic one, thus tipping the balance from one side to the other.

EFFECT OF PUBLIC OWNERSHIP AND OPERATION ON GOVERNMENT

A number of subsidiary issues relate to the effect of public ownership on government itself. There is the question of what policy to follow with regard to profit-making. The concern of thoughtful people about the earnings of public ventures is often not that they shall fall short but that they may become unjustifiably large. Advocates of public power argue that well over a hundred municipalities are tax-free because the earnings of the electrical department are enough to pay all municipal costs. Government salt and tobacco monopolies in other nations and the earnings of the Post Office in Great Britain and of state liquor-store monopolies in this country all help defray the expenses of government. But the result is a regressive financial policy causing the burden to fall more heavily than it should on those who are least able to pay. Moreover, such practices adversely affect price levels, and efficiency factors become hard to determine. On all scores, therefore, government should refrain from using public businesses as substitutes for taxation.

The experience of one of the best known and most successful of all public corporations in the United States illustrates another aspect of this problem. In 1921 an interstate compact between New York and New Jersey established the Port of New York Authority, which has had a fabulous growth and record. With the approval

FIG. 12. PORT OF NEW YORK AUTHORITY

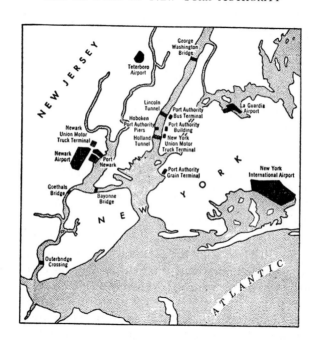

of the federal government, the authority plans, coordinates, builds, and operates the lion's share of all transportation facilities in Greater New York, which includes Manhattan Island, Staten Island, a large part of Long Island, and large surrounding territories in New York State and New Jersey. The authority owns and operates bridges, tunnels, marine facilities, truck terminals, office buildings, a number of industries, a helicopter service, and three big international airports: LaGuardia, New York International, and Newark. Money is lost on some ventures but big profits are made on others, especially through the high tolls charged on tunnels and bridges. In a recent year, revenues came to $105 million, and in the same year the authority made a net profit of $60 million.

The policy of the authority is to finance new undertakings (and to these there is apparently no end) out of the earnings of others. But suppose the tolls charged on a particular tunnel were originally calculated to return all costs and to retire the indebtedness in, say, twenty years. May such a policy then properly be changed? Is it fair to the public, is it good business parctice or an honest policy as to public accountability to allow a money-making property to finance other ventures and to pay the deficits of still others? The authority justifies its financial practices on the ground that it is a single corporation dealing with a single transportation problem. The opposing view (shared by the author) is that every major public enterprise should be separately financed, if necessary by selling bonds to the public. In that case the financial picture is clear and public accountability more straightforward.

On the more favorable side, although public enterprise is exposed to many difficulties, lack of competent personnel is not one of them. A generation ago, President Hoover remarked that in ability and zeal public executives compare favorably with the best in private industry. If government suffers from such maladies as overcentralization, administrative bureaucratic standardization, and too little freedom for experimentation and flexibility, the failure is due more to legislative policy than to administrative incompetence.

In the whole range of policy regarding public enterprise there is no harder problem than the relation of management to the legislature that creates the program to be administered. How shall a public enterprise be held accountable? There are two ways: the legislature itself may exercise close supervision, in which case it is likely to go too far and interfere with the freedom of management; or, in the case of government corporations, supervision may be entrusted to the board of directors. If these are well chosen—men of stature and ability in private life—experience shows such a group to be a safe alternative to supervision by the legislature. But if board members are puppets with no independence of judgment, they are more of a liability than a protection. The boards of public corporations are sometimes called little legislatures, and so they should be. Modern government is required to do so much in so many areas of activity that practical people often wonder if it does not try to do too much. When a public business enterprise is undertaken it should be set up to avoid as much burden as possible on legislatures and chief executives.

Once supervision has been decentralized, additional methods of securing accountability consistent with efficiency from public corporations, are these: (1) limits on profits, borrowing power, and jurisdiction should be written into the charter as a kind of internal control; (2) a separate budget may be annexed to the over-all budget to be considered separately but in conjunction with it; (3) a higher officer of the government (a member of the President's cabinet, if the project is federal) should receive periodic reports and should serve as the chief executive's alter ego in certain areas of control, but his duties should stop short of decision in matters relating to management; (4) legislatures should occasionally set aside time to discuss and review the trusteeship entrusted to major public corporations; (5) audit reports covering managerial efficiency as well as financial practices should periodically be submitted to the legislature and the chief executive; and (6) every individual public enterprise or each segment of a multiple enterprise should relate to a distinct segment of the economy so that its economic effects may be evaluated. With these various safeguards plus boards of directors of stature and independence, the public interest should be adequately protected.

THE FUTURE OF PUBLIC ENTERPRISE

In the words of Chief Justice William Howard Taft in a leading case, a state may engage in "almost any private business if the legislature thinks the state's engagement in it will help the general public and is willing to pay the cost of the plant and incur the expense of operation." [13] In other leading cases the Supreme Court has upheld the establishment of a municipal fuel yard by the city of Portland, Maine,[14] the socialization of banking, grain storing, milling, and other public enterprises by the state of North Dakota,[15] and the creation of a wholesale and retail gasoline business in the city of Lincoln, Nebraska.[16]

Tests of federal business enterprise have been equally positive. Even the public power program of TVA has been upheld under the various express powers invoked, especially the war, navigation, postal, and commerce powers, the Supreme Court holding that it would not interfere with Congress' declaration of national purpose.[17] Consequently, since legal authority is adequate, the future extension of public ownership and operation would seem to depend on such factors as the success or failure of public-utility regulation, the degree to which the economy can be kept competitive, and the avoidance of national emergencies such as war, depression, and the wasteful exploitation of natural resources.

Supplementary Reading

Friedmann, W., *The Public Corporation* (Toronto, 1954). An international symposium on state business institutions.

[13] *Wolff Packing Co. v. Court of Industrial Relations of the State of Kansas* (262 U.S. 522. 1923).

[14] *Jones v. City of Portland* (245 U.S. 217. 1917).

[15] *Green v. Frazier* (253 U.S 233. 1920).

[16] *Standard Oil Co. v. City of Lincoln* (275 U.S. 504. 1927).

[17] The leading cases are *Ashwander v. TVA* (297 U.S. 288. 1936) and *Tennessee Electric Power Co. v. TVA* (306 U.S. 118. 1939).

Musolf, Lloyd D., *Public Ownership and Accountability* (Cambridge, Mass., 1959). The Canadian experience.

Dahl, Robert A., and C. E. Lindblom, *Politics, Economics, and Welfare* (New York, 1953).

Hanson, A. H., *Public Enterprise and Economic Development* (London, 1959). Chapters 11–15.

Twentieth Century Fund, *The Power Industry and the Public Interest* (New York, 1944). Chapters 7–11 deal broadly with public programs.

Commission on Organization of the Executive Branch of the Government (first Hoover Commission): See especially *Federal Business Enterprises; Task Force Report on Revolving Funds and Business Enterprises of the Government; Task Force Report on the Post Office* (all Washington, D.C., 1949). The last-mentioned makes a good case study.

———— (second Hoover Commission): See especially *Business Enterprises,* and *Task Force Report on Business Enterprises* (both Washington, D.C., 1955).

United States House of Representatives, *Special Committee to Investigate Government Competition with Private Enterprise* (H. Rept. 1985, 72d Cong., 2d Sess., 1933).

United States Congress, Joint Committee on the Investigation of the TVA, *Report* (S. Doc. 56, 76th Cong., 1st Sess., pursuant to Pub. Res. 83, 1939).

Robson, William A. (ed.), *Problems of Nationalized Industry* (New York, 2d ed., 1952). Practical problems from British experience.

Lilienthal, David E., and R. H. Marquis, "The Conduct of Business Enterprises by the Federal Government," *Harvard Law Review,* Vol. IV (1941), pp. 545–601. Covers principles of the public corporation.

————, *TVA: Democracy on the March* (New York, 2d ed., 1953).

Pritchett, C. Herman, *The Tennessee Valley Authority* (Chapel Hill, N.C., 1943).

————, "The Government Corporation Control Act of 1945," *American Political Science Review,* Vol. 40 (1946), pp. 495–509.

————, "The Paradox of the Government Corporation," *Public Administration Review,* Vol. 1 (summer 1941), pp. 381–389.

Key, V. O., "Government Corporations," Chapter 11 in F. Morstein Marx (ed.), *Elements of Public Administration* (New York, 1946).

Dimock, Marshall E., "Government Corporations: A Focus of Policy and Administration," *American Political Science Review,* Vol. 43 (Oct.–Dec. 1949), pp. 899–921, 1145–1164.

————, *Government-Operated Enterprises in the Panama Canal Zone* (Chicago, 1934). Case study of the oldest American government-owned corporation.

————, *Developing America's Waterways: Administration of the Inland Waterways Corporation* (Chicago, 1935). Another case study.

Persons, Warren M., *Government Experimentation in Business* (New York, 1934). The unfavorable record during the early period.

Wilcox, Clair, *Public Policies toward Business* (Homewood, Ill., 1955). Chapter 27 is entitled "Policy in Other Countries."

For developments at the state level, see *State Government,* and *Book of the States* (annual); for local governmental enterprises, *Municipal Yearbook* (annual); all published in Chicago.

PART VII

GOVERNMENT
AND
THE
INVESTOR

19

REGULATION OF BANKING, INVESTMENTS, AND INSURANCE

Influence and power of federal finance policy on private enterprise; four types of private financial institution; issues of public policy; characteristics of American banking system; legislative landmarks; branch banking and mergers; state and federal regulation; rise of investment banking; 1929 stock-market crash; abuses in securities transactions; major regulatory legislation; SEC: organization, functions, major criticisms; characteristics and size of insurance business; state regulation and self-regulation; issues of public policy; strengthening insurance regulation; pension funds.

Money, its use, and its management constitute the nerve center of the economic system, and government's role in this complex of relationships has been steadily increasing. Businessmen have long considered the financial policies of government a key factor in the conduct of any private enterprise. Throughout our history, says one group of businessmen, "the greatest obstacles to national financial strength and the most acute dangers of fiscal collapse" have always been the consequences of "weak financial policies." [1]

Under the Constitution, the federal government monopolizes the coining of money and the regulation of its value, and determines the kind of banking system we shall have. The federal government also administers the national debt, now so large as to be a chief means of controlling inflation, deflation, and economic stability, a subject already dealt with in part and to be discussed further. The federal government also spends a large share of the national income, from about 11.5 percent in the years from 1933 to 1940 and 19 percent by 1957. In addition, government profoundly affects economic conditions by its decision on whether to balance or not to balance the budget; helps determine levels of income through its tax policy, especially income-tax policy; discourages and in effect pro-

---

[1] Committee on Public Debt Policy, *Our National Debt after Great Wars* (pamphlet, New York, 1947), p. 12.

hibits such things as the sale of narcotics or commodities produced by substandard labor, and the holding of lotteries; and controls relationships with the states by pre-empting or freeing certain sources of public revenue.

Against this constitutional backdrop the concern of this chapter is with government's regulatory power over private financial institutions and its attempt to protect investors as well as consumers, to safeguard credit, and to facilitate the economic production of goods and services. The purpose is to deal with these relationships in such a way as to show interconnections between institutions and processes; in other words, here again is the familiar story of power and its regulation in the public interest.

The private financial institutions in the United States may be divided according to four main types:

1. *Commercial banks and similar credit institutions.* The growing complexity of the economy has created a need for different kinds of banks including deposit and loan banks (the most common and hence the most familiar), savings banks, building and loan associations, mortgage banks, consumptive credit banks (such as Morris Plan), finance or installment credit unions, and the personal loan departments of commercial banks. There are also trust companies that accept and execute trusts and in many cases also carry on a commercial banking business; similarly, many commercial and savings banks have trust departments as well.

2. *Investment banks.* There are two main types of these, plus a growing number of variations. First, there are investment banks that are not banks at all in the popular sense but are concerned, rather, with the sale and distribution of securities—new stocks and bonds for governments and private businesses needing long-term credit. Then there are investment trusts that sell stocks and sometimes bonds to investors, using the proceeds to invest in the securities of other companies, a $5.5 billion business by 1955.

3. *Securities and commodity exchanges.* Organized stock exchanges offer facilities for buying and selling the securities of business corporations. Some brokers and dealers are members of a national securities exchange and some, called over-the-counter brokers, are not, but both are subject to government regulation. Organized commodity exchanges, as noted in an earlier chapter, offer facilities for trading in commodities such as grain, cotton, eggs, butter, and other food materials capable of being stored. When the trading is in "futures"—that is, a present purchase at present prices for future delivery—the objective is usually to speculate on changed prices rather than to acquire the product.

4. *Insurance companies.* There are many kinds of insurance, including life, fire, casualty, liability, health, and the like, but all insurance companies collect regular payments from policyholders and invest the proceeds, under government standards, to accumulate reserves to pay beneficiaries and make profits. Insurance companies are now among the largest investors in the nation.

Generally speaking, banks and insurance companies come chiefly under state regulation, while securities exchanges and securities sold in interstate commerce are primarily under federal control; but there is a good deal of overlap in the two jurisdictions, especially with regard to banking.

Government financial policy has long been a battleground of American politics. President Jackson fought central banks because he feared monopoly; William Jennings Bryan championed silver because he distrusted the financial power of Wall Street; the Granger movement and men like Henry Ford and Louis Brandeis thought the "money trust" might undermine and finally destroy the independent businessman; and branch banking and banker control of big business have caused sharp political controversies.

From the standpoint of over-all public policy the main issues are these: Should the federal government strengthen its antitrust laws so as to control branch banking, corporate interconnections in banking, and the like? Should private credit institutions be prohibited from owning and managing business enterprises? If the responsible self-government of stock exchanges and other financial institutions were increasingly improved, could government regulation be progressively relaxed? Should one kind of financial institution be prevented from invading the traditional field of another? Should the investments of insurance companies be liberalized as to type or should they be still further restricted? Should federal as against state control of insurance and banking be still further extended? Are a few large banks better or worse for the economy and the public interest than a larger number of banks of the home-town type? To what extent should *caveat emptor* (buyer beware) remain the guiding principle in security investment, and how far should the government go in policing security issues? Moreover (although this is dealt with in a later chapter) to what extent should the government's policy regarding price-and-dollar stability be allowed to influence the decisions of the Federal Reserve System? And finally, as already noted, since the fastest growing classification in the field of public ownership and operation is government credit and government insurance, how far should this trend be allowed to go and what would be its effect on private enterprise?

PUBLIC CONTROL OF BANKING

Banking is more decentralized in the United States than in most other nations. Abroad, the usual pattern is a central bank with powers which the name implies, plus a few major commercial banks with many branches in different parts of the country. In the United States, by contrast, because we have tried to avoid centralization and monopoly, it has always been easy for a few people with a modest amount of capital to charter a state bank, and consequently the foundation of our banking system consists of many small banks organized and regulated by state banking departments that often supervise insurance and securities transactions as well. Above this structure are the so-called national banks, subject to regulatory control by the Comptroller of the Currency in the federal Treasury Department. In addition, the Federal Reserve System controls its own member banks, including all national banks, but its powers are much less than those of the central bank in most other nations.

Legislative Landmarks

The result of our bifurcated banking system is to make its structure appear complicated and illogical in the eyes of most European observers, but behind it is the conviction that only a policy of decentralization can sustain local independence and private ownership. Nevertheless, during the past fifty years or so the role of the federal government has greatly increased, in the field of banking as in others. During the Wilson administration the *Federal Reserve Act of 1913* divided the country into twelve districts with a Federal Reserve bank in each and made them "bankers' banks" rather than institutions the public deals with directly, provided for twenty-four branch banks, required all national banks to join the system and allowed state banks to join under certain conditions, and gave the Board of Governors (the members of which are predominantly private citizens) broad powers over credit policy and banking regulation. Furthermore, the Federal Reserve banks issue Federal Reserve notes which constitute the bulk of money in circulation. As of 1958 there were some 4500 national-bank members and 1700 state-bank members of the Federal Reserve System out of a total of more than 14,000 commercial banking institutions in the country.

During the depression of the 1930s when many banks were closing, Congress created the Deposit Insurance Fund of 1933 which two years later was superseded by the *Federal Deposit Insurance Corporation* organized under the authority of the Federal Reserve Act, but later independently provided for under the Federal Deposit Insurance Act of 1950. This government corporation insures individual bank deposits up to $10,000 for each depositor and may become receiver if a bank fails. All national banks and all state banks belonging to the Federal Reserve System must join the FDIC; all other banks may join if they meet the requirements, and in fact, nearly all have. The FDIC receives no appropriations from Congress and its original capital of $289 million has all been paid back with interest to the federal Treasury. Member banks pay a premium to the corporation to a fund out of which depositors are compensated if a bank fails; by the end of 1958 the corporation's surplus amounted to some $1.96 billion. The FDIC may also help reopen insured banks that have failed, and may make loans to banks taking over the assets of closed banks. Over 127 million deposit accounts are now insured, 254 insured banks have been placed in receivership, and 182 banks in a hazardous condition have been helped over their difficulties. Although this record is no guarantee of the infallibility of the American banking structure if it should be put to a severe test, it is undeniably a considerable improvement over the situation at the onset of the depression in 1929.

In a related undertaking, the Federal Home Loan Bank Board includes within its jurisdiction the Federal Savings and Loan Corporation, which is responsible for deposit insurance operations like those of the FDIC. All federal savings and loan associations, and those state-chartered building and loan, savings and loan, and homestead associations, and cooperative banks, which apply and are approved, are insured up to $10,000 for each investor's account. By 1959 there were 3881 such institutions with total assets of $51.3 billion. The FSLC's capital stock, originally amounting to $100 million and held by the federal Treasury, has been retired. The agency may borrow from the Treasury if necessary, but never has.

Prior to 1935 the authority of commercial banks to invest in bonds was practically unlimited; in that year, the *Federal Banking Act* gave the Comptroller of the Currency greater authority over the security purchases of national banks. A law aimed primarily at trust companies is administered by the SEC: the *Trust Indenture Act of 1939* which defines the obligations of trustees of corporate mortgages, stipulates standards such as reports to bondholders, energetic action in case of default, and the like.

Branch Banking, Holding Companies, and Mergers

Then there is the issue of branch banking and the use of the holding company device to further it. In 1927, largely in response to a branch bank movement in the states, Congress permitted national banks also to do a limited amount of branch banking and after that both federal and state governments took a generally tolerant view of the subject. The real control of branch banking, when any has existed, has been at the state level, supported by independent bankers' associations and fought by the larger banks including Bank of America, a unit in the holding company Transamerica Corporation that in 1955 controlled 43 percent of all bank deposits in California, 44 percent in Oregon, 78 percent in Nevada, and 5 percent in Washington. A growing number of states, mostly in the West but including now also New York, permit state-wide branch banking, and some allow it in restricted areas. Few have taken no legislative notice of it at all. Up until 1956 the bank-holding-company device made it possible in many cases to circumvent what restrictions there were in effect.

Stimulated by the need for more adequate control, therefore, and also by a wave of bank mergers that occurred in the years following World War II, in 1956 Congress passed the *Bank Holding Company Act*. This statute, administered by the Federal Reserve Board, prevents holding companies from mixing banking and nonbanking business and from extending their operations beyond what state and national banks are allowed to do in creating branches. The weakness of the law lies in its divestment provisions, since of the 150 holding companies then owning at least one bank it was expected that the liberal exemptions would reduce actual separations of banking and nonbanking operations to no more than five cases.

After 1950 the bank-merger movement proceeded at the rate of about 150 a year, including three of the largest banks in New York City. The Comptroller of the Currency justified these consolidations on the ground that they resulted "in individual banks and a banking system better able to serve the communities affected and the country as a whole." [2] Opposed to such mergers is the need for competition among banks, the encouragement of local businessmen and the local community, and the avoidance of economic concentrations which, as in the case of public utilities, invite government regulation and eventually government ownership and operation.

Finally in 1960 Congress passed legislation applying to all acquisitions, mergers, and consolidations of banks insured by the Federal Deposit Insurance Corporation, which covers 95 percent of all banks in the country. The administration of the law is divided, according to the type of banks involved, among the Comptroller of the Currency, the Federal Reserve Board, and the FDIC. To assure uniform standards, whichever agency handles a merger must consult with the other two. In addition, in every case except an emergency involving a failing bank, the agency handling it must secure from the Attorney General a report on the competitive factors involved, and there must be a consideration of "the effect of the action on competition, including any tendency toward monopoly." The burden of proof is on the proponents of the merger to show that it is in the public interest.

By 1957 the national banking laws had been amended so often that a committee of Congress studied the situation and offered an omnibus bill to tidy them up, but it was stillborn. In the matter of broader banking policy, the committee recommended that a special commission make a careful study. On the initiative of the Committee for Economic Development, a Commission on Money and Credit was then set up on a grant from the Ford Foundation to work independently under a mandate to "provide a broad, factual and analytical basis to assist the Congress" and all other agencies responsible for monetary policy and legislation.

State and Federal Regulation

The results of state banking regulation, like those of state public-utility regulation, vary from good to poor. Except in times of depression and bank failures, the public does not seem to be much concerned. In the state legislatures, the personnel of banking committees are notoriously

---

[2] Reported in *The New York Times*, May 18, 1955.

drawn from among bankers themselves, resulting in a double-exposure kind of self-regulation. Federal regulation, on the other hand, perhaps because it is more remote and hence more uniform, is generally reputed to be more strict and enforcement is more effective. Federal bank examiners, working out of regional offices, enjoy a reputation for integrity and competence.

The areas of control are these: With regard to *entry into business,* federal requirements for the establishment of a bank are generally stricter than those of the states. Questions that must be satisfied concern the possible duplication of banking facilities, the moral and business qualifications of the sponsors, the honesty and competence of management, and the sufficiency of capital. Once a bank has been set up, *periodic bank examinations* are standard practice in both state and federal jurisdictions, with the Federal Reserve System doing the best job of all. The work is done by a traveling bank examiner who calls anything seriously out of order to the attention of higher authority.

The supervision of *loans and investments* is a phase of control that has grown rapidly in recent years. With the gradual improvement in personnel, bank examiners have learned to do a better job of reviewing loan and investment portfolios. Like insurance companies, banks are constantly looking for more lucrative investments and examiners must decide the highly discretionary question of where reasonable safety for the depositor coincides with reasonable profit to the holder of bank stock. A major issue since World War II has been to determine the percentage of low-yielding government bonds the banks shall be required to hold, as compared with investments having a higher rate of return. The question has been resolved largely in favor of the banks, with the Federal Reserve System winning over the more conservative Treasury Department, illustrating once more how pressure groups meet and vie with one another in the formulation of public policy.

Government laws and regulations also affect the *rate of interest paid* by banks to depositors and the *rate charged* by banks to their borrowers. The elements of public policy that enter here are the prevention of extortionate rates of interest, the provision of credit at reasonable charges, and the assurance of a reasonable profit to the banks in return for the risks involved. Taken together, such decisions do much to shape the kind of society we shall have: whether competitive or monopolistic, advantageous to the strong or protective of the not-so-strong, prosperous on a wide level or only at the top.

Yet another highly discretionary subject is that of *reserve ratios,* the cash on hand or in other banks needed to meet demands for withdrawal. Minimum reserve ratios are fixed by law at both the state and federal levels. Federal regulation of this subject goes back to 1863 and is now vested in the Board of Governors of the Federal Reserve System. To prevent harmful credit expansion, national banks are allowed to raise maximum reserve ratios to not more than twice the legal minimum.

Finally—and here is another analogy to public-utility regulation—banking institutions are limited in their *dividend policies*. In order to increase their financial strength and stability, banks under federal control must carry one tenth of their annual net profits to surplus until the surplus amounts to 20 percent of the capital stock. Consequently, banks are not free to pay dividends to stockholders as desired, even when earnings would seem to justify such action. Such restrictions are also part of the better state regulatory systems.

The main question concerning commercial banking in all its variations is not whether administrative regulation is sufficient, because, except for certain laxities in a few states, it is. The overriding question is, what kind of banking system do we want? A highly integrated one with a few large units or, as in the past, a decentralized system that is easy to get into? If the experience of other countries is a reliable guide, we may expect a growing concentration of economic power in banking and an increasing trend toward socialization to accompany tendencies toward integration in this field. Allied to this issue is the ability of a decentralized banking system to withstand the impact of depression, if a serious one should occur, despite the improvements that have been made since 1933. The fact of numerous units is not in itself evidence of weakness and, if the regulatory policies dealt with here are carefully followed, deconcentration might even constitute the strength of the banking system. In other words, under proper control and with adequate safeguards, the banks themselves might fare better in time of depression as a result of being competitive and decentralized than if they were highly combined in a few major systems.

THE INVESTMENT BUSINESS

Government regulation has come faster to the investment business than to any other in the past generation. Prior to 1933 there was no major regulation at the federal level at all and in the states so-called blue-sky laws were uneven in both coverage and enforcement. The change occurred, of course, after the stock-market collapse of 1929 and later bank failures caused a marked and rather vocal degree of lost confidence in stock markets, banks, and "Wall Street speculators." Almost overnight, therefore, the securities business was changed from one of benighted independence to the most regulated competitive business in the nation.

Investment banks, it will be recalled, today sell stocks and bonds and may not engage in ordinary commercial banking. This separation is partly to prevent monopoly and partly to divorce speculative transactions from fiduciary responsibilities relative to deposit banking. Although the first stock exchanges were organized in 1800 in Philadelphia and in 1817 in New York, investment banking as such was virtually unknown in the United States prior to the Civil War. Investment houses that later were to become famous, such as Drexel and Company, Brown Brothers, and Lee Higginson, confined their activities during this early period to financial counseling and did not sell securities in the market. But when it became necessary to finance the Civil War, Jay Cooke started selling securities for this purpose and thus started the practice that has gone so far in private industry today.

Then in the years around the turn of the century and preceding World War I, a dearth of investment funds in the nation caused the development of modern underwriting, where one or more investment firms agree to furnish a certain sum by a certain date. The present system of offering securities at a uniform price originated during the boom era of investment banking that occurred during the 1920s.

Government regulation was rather slow to catch up with the investment business, beginning at the state level only in 1911, but by 1933 every state except Nevada was regulating security transactions in one way or another. As in the case of most state regulatory legislation, however, the picture was typically spotty. When the federal government entered the field in 1933, state regulation improved and today is primarily concerned with issues of less than $300,000, this being the lower limit of registration authority of the Securities and Exchange Commission. It is still true that state regulation could be strengthened to support federal regulation and even to reduce the need for federal regulation to some extent.

After the collapse of 1929-1932 a number of Congressional investigations brought to light some interesting facts concerning the investment business and especially stock markets. Most serious of all, perhaps, was the stunning blow to public confidence caused by the crash itself. Between 1929 and 1932 stocks dropped in value by $74 billion, bonds by $19 billion, and the investing public lost a total of about $90 billion.[3] These figures alone could well explain the advent of federal intervention. "When the crash came," say the authors of a Brookings study, "there was a widespread demand, as is always the case, for punishment." [4] Nevertheless, the degree to which blame for the disaster should be laid to the faults of the securities business on the one side and to pervading economic and governmental factors on the other is, of course, debatable even today.

Another aspect of the situation was dissatisfaction with the flotation of foreign securities on the American market. There were also complaints of excessive service charges and profits by investment bankers: J. P. Morgan & Company, for example, once received 1,514,200 option warrants on United Corporation stock for which it paid $1 each; within sixty days the company sold these warrants in the market at a minimum price of $40 each, making a profit of some $68 million.[5] In addition to complaints of this kind there was the hardy perennial of fraud in the sale of securities; an underlying fear of bigness and monopoly in the investment banking field; the speculative fever on Wall Street during the 1920s; a dubious

[3] Ganson Purcell, chairman, Securities and Exchange Commission, statement at *Hearings* before the House Committee on Interstate and Foreign Commerce (77th Cong., 1st Sess.), Pt. I, p. 8.

[4] W. E. Atkins, G. W. Edwards, and H. G. Moulton, *The Regulation of the Security Markets* (Washington, D.C., 1936), p. 47.

[5] Report of the Senate Committee on Banking and Currency, *Stock Exchange Practices* (73d Cong., 2d Sess., 1934), p. 125.

alliance between commercial and investment banking institutions; abuses of power in effecting corporate organizations and reorganizations; options to purchase common stock over an unlimited period of time; favoritism to a privileged list of insiders; the abuses of voting trusts; denials of the rights of small stockholders; and, as serious as any, a lack of full information to the potential investor to enable him to know what he was buying.

Major Federal Regulatory Legislation

Once the federal government undertook to regulate the securities market it was as though a log jam had been broken; during the seven years following 1933 eight statutes were enacted by Congress in this field, all of which are now under the jurisdiction of the Securities and Exchange Commission:

The *Securities Act* of 1933 deals mostly with original issues of securities, provides for full disclosure, requires the registration of securities issues, and prohibits fraudulent practices. Responsibility for the administration of this act was placed in the Federal Trade Commission but when the Securities and Exchange Commission was created in the following year, administration was transferred to that agency.

The *Securities Exchange Act* of 1934 created the Securities and Exchange Commission and deals with both investment banking and stock exchanges. There are many parallels between this act and that of 1933 but the later one provides a greater measure of control.

The *Public Utility Holding Company Act* of 1935 covers gas and electricity holding companies, as explained in Chapter 17, and vests jurisdiction in the SEC.

The *Maloney Amendment* of 1938 to the Securities Exchange Act provides for the licensing and self-government of stock and bond salesmen.

The *Chandler Act* of 1938 (Chapter X of the Bankruptcy Act) authorizes the SEC to serve as adviser in connection with reorganization proceedings in which there is a substantial public interest.

The *Trust Indenture Act* of 1939 tightens the solicitude of trustees for the interests of bondholders.

The *Investment Company Act* of 1940 prescribes the methods of securing honest, competent, and independent management in the conduct of investment trusts and investment companies.

The *Investment Advisers Act* of 1940, Title II, subjects investment counselors to public control through registration and licensing, and defines permissible functions.

In essential details, the SEC resembles other federal regulatory agencies, with five members appointed by the President with the consent of the

Senate for five-year terms, one of the five annually elected as chairman, and the usual bipartisan provision obtains. The SEC possesses quasi-judicial authority as well as administrative and investigatory powers, and appeal from its decisions may be had to the federal Circuit Courts of Appeal. The responsibilities of the SEC include:

1. *Registration* with the SEC, with certain exceptions, of all securities offered for sale in interstate commerce or sent through the mails.

2. As full *information* as possible to the investor so as to avoid fraud and misrepresentation. The law is explicit as to the information that must be supplied in the registration statement; full *disclosure* is required and the prospectus explaining the forthcoming issue must conform to the standards set by the SEC.

3. Registration statements are *reviewed* in the SEC and, in addition, the commission carries on extensive *investigations* of securities sold through misrepresentation or other fraudulent devices.

4. The law provides various types of *penalties* for noncompliance or violation. Both civil and criminal prosecutions are possible but civil remedies are more common. All officials taking part in flotation, underwriting, or similar activities are personally liable for using reasonable precautions to see that all statements made are correct.

Approval of a securities issue by the SEC must not be interpreted by a prospective purchaser, however, as a guarantee of the worth of the securities offered. The law expressly prohibits any statement to the effect that registration of a security with the commission is evidence either that the requirements of the act have been met or that the commission has in any way approved the security; the SEC merely controls the procedure under which the security is offered.

At headquarters, the work of the SEC is carried on by three operating divisions, in addition to the usual housekeeping divisions for accounting, personnel, and the like, and its program in the field is carried on through regional offices located in nine of the principal cities of the nation.

Since Congress lacked express powers to regulate securities transactions, it has relied on its commerce and postal powers to justify the assertion of authority in this field. Although the Supreme Court has never directly passed on the question of constitutionality, the lower courts have sustained it and a number of other decisions leave no doubt as to the favorable outcome if the matter should ever come to the Supreme Court.[6]

Stock Markets

Where stock markets are concerned, the only regulatory influence prior to 1934 was that effected by the self-government of the exchanges

---

[6] See, for example, the case of *Champion* v. *Ames* (188 U.S. 321. 1903) wherein the Court upheld the power of Congress to forbid the interstate shipment of lottery tickets, as well as *Furst* v. *Brewster* (282 U.S. 493. 1930) and the *Blue Sky Law* cases (242 U.S. 539. 1916).

themselves. In New York, for example, a governing committee plus a series of subcommittees were chosen by the various interests, rules were promulgated for the operation of the exchange, and violators were tried, fined, and even expelled for cause. Nevertheless, it was not until four years after the passage of the Securities Exchange Act that the system was made really effective by the appointment of a full-time paid executive with real power and by the democratization of control so as to loosen the influence of cliques. In the meantime, chastened by the experience of 1929 and the years immediately following, the representatives of most of the exchanges in the country let it be known in 1934 that "stock exchanges favor regulation which will prevent excessive speculation and which will give to the federal government full power to prevent unfair practices on the stock exchanges."

The unfair practices complained of were varied and some were of long standing. There was the *manipulation* of values by insiders, for example, with speculators forcing quoted prices up and down at will as best suited their prospects for profit. Another was *wash sales* where one broker agreed to buy and another to sell at a higher price than the current market value, although neither had any intention of going through with the transaction, but merely to "wash it out" when the time came. The effect was to create an illusion that the security was in demand and hence artificially to increase its price. In the case of *matched orders,* a party might hire two brokers unknown to each other, one of whom was ordered to buy and the other to sell a certain security at a given price; this also created the illusion of activity and attracted buyers, and when the price rose, the instigator sold his own shares at a profit. *Buying on margin,* a legitimate practice under proper safeguards, may be abused and thus serve to inflate prices in securities or commodities through the down-payment credit system common to the retail trade; when the market is going up, buying on margin makes it possible to earn profits with little capital outlay, but in a receding market, margin operators must cover with additional funds and it is then that the trouble starts. Many who were financially cleaned out during the 1929 crash were speculators trading on margin.

These were the main abuses. But the public also disliked insiders' profiting on confidential information, the use of buying-and-selling pools to force prices up and down, and the conversion of the stock market from a reflector of legitimate values to a center of wholly speculative buying and selling.

The jurisdiction of the SEC over stock markets includes the *registration* of exchanges, of the companies whose securities are listed thereon, and of the securities themselves. Monthly, annual, and other reports are required supplying financial and other data as prescribed by the SEC for the *information* of the investing public. The data contained in these reports are then *reviewed* for compliance with the disclosure requirements prescribed. Then, in order as far as possible to prevent *speculation* that might lead to another stock-market crash, the Federal Reserve Board may set margin requirements and the SEC may limit the borrowings of members, brokers, and dealers. The law also specifically prohibits manipulation, misrepresentation, and other *fraudulent and deceptive* devices in the purchase and sale of securities, in over-the-counter transactions as well as in those occurring on the exchanges themselves.

Finally, the *penalties* are rather fully set forth: (1) In order to avoid manipulative practices by insiders, any stockholder may bring suit against an offender at any time within two years after the profits are realized. (2) Any person injured by the manipulative practices outlawed by the act may bring suit for damages. (3) Willful violation is a crime punishable by a fine of not more than $500,000 in the case of an exchange or more than $10,000, two years in jail, or both, in the case of an individual offender. (4) The SEC may suspend or revoke the registration of securities firms, national securities exchanges, dealers' associations, or members, brokers, and others for noncompliance or violation. And finally, (5) if the SEC is dissatisfied with the rules of a national exchange which refuses to make acceptable changes, the commission may impose trading rules of its own.

Main Criticisms of SEC Regulation

In the early days of its work the chief criticism of the SEC was that its requirements concerning registration and disclosure were needlessly detailed and involved delay and expense to the originating company, but today it is more often heard that the SEC is too close to its clientele, that it is not sufficiently rigorous, and that it is underfinanced and understaffed. In 1949, for example, a task force of the Hoover Commission praised the SEC as "an outstanding example of the independent commission at its best," [7] but in 1952 a committee of the House of Representatives could only say that the SEC had done a "pretty good job" of protecting investors.[8] Two years later a former commissioner charged that new securities offerings were subject to delay, that control over investment companies was shaky, and that the laws controlling the activities of brokers and dealers were widely flouted.[9] This decreasing effectiveness is largely attributable to a drastic reduction in appropriations and consequently in staff, from 1700 employees in 1941 to around 700 in 1954, but there was an increase to 900 in 1959.

On balance, however, what the SEC does it does well, and the question is, does it, or even can it, do more without increased financial support from Congress? Koontz and Gable have remarked that "the securities law has . . . been criticized because it does not really attain its principal objective of building up a group of adequately and accurately informed

[7] Commission on Organization of the Executive Branch of the Government, *Task Force Report on Regulatory Commissions* (Washington, D.C., 1949), p. 144.

[8] *The New York Times,* Dec. 6, 1952.

[9] J. Howard Rossbach, letter in *The New York Times,* Apr. 22, 1954.

investors." [10] Whether this is a fault of the SEC or of the law, of course, or whether the objective is attainable except through voluntary effort, are moot questions.[11]

REGULATION OF INSURANCE COMPANIES

The insurance business in the United States has become so vast that it now exercises a dominant influence in the investment markets of the nation, and yet it has largely avoided government regulation except at the state level. The Temporary National Economic Committee found that the insurance business had become so large as to overshadow the investment field. As early as 1938 life-insurance-company assets exceeded those of the Federal Reserve Banks, were $10 billion greater than the combined assets of all savings banks and building and loan associations, and equaled 70 percent of the total value of all farm property in the nation. Moreover, the insurance companies' rate of growth was faster than that of other financial institutions: between 1929 and 1938, for example, the total assets of all savings institutions (building and loan associations, the savings departments of commercial banks, savings banks, postal savings, baby bonds, and life insurance companies) increased from $58 billion to $70 billion, of which 95 percent was attributable to life insurance and of this, 85 percent was accounted for by the twenty-six largest companies.[12]

The growth of insurance has in no way abated since 1938 and the companies, needing to invest their funds, are now, among other things, the largest landlords in the nation. In 1959, the life insurance companies alone had assets of over $113 billion (an increase of more than $6 billion over the previous year) and some $534 billion worth of life insurance was in force, which was $320 billion more than ten years before.

The insurance business is predominantly privately owned but, as noted in a previous chapter and as will be seen even more forcibly in a later one concerning social security, government has entered the insurance business in the field of old-age and survivors' insurance, unemployment insurance, workmen's compensation, compulsory automobile insurance —even life insurance in some instances; a development that in a few years could tip the balance (in terms of dollar volume of business, due to the size of the social security programs) against the private companies if public confidence in them should deteriorate.

The insurance business is not only big, but, like other economic monsters, tends to become bigger and more concentrated. The TNEC found that the five largest life insurance companies were among the eighteen largest corporations of all kinds in the nation; that one of the five (Metropolitan Life) led all other corporations in size (by 1958 its assets

[10] Harold Koontz and Richard W. Gable, *Public Control of Economic Enterprise* (New York, 1956), p. 462.

[11] See Joseph Livingston, *The American Stockholder* (Philadelphia, 1958).

[12] Temporary National Economic Committee, *Hearings*, Pt. 28, p. 14,725.

had reached $15 billion), that out of the 365 life insurance companies in the country, the 16 largest controlled 81 percent of the assets of the industry (i.e., .5 percent owned 80 percent); and that of the remaining corporations, 40 belonged to the select company of the nation's largest and 20 had assets of more than $100 million each.[13] A single company (again, Metropolitan Life) had to invest or to reinvest something like a billion dollars each year.

State Regulation of Insurance Companies

State regulation of insurance started in the last part of the nineteenth century but did not really get under way until the 1900s. In 1869 the Supreme Court had ruled in the leading case of *Paul* v. *Virginia*[14] that the insurance business was not interstate commerce and thus was not subject to federal control. The National Association of Insurance Commissioners, which seeks uniformity in state legislation and serves as a pressure group in favor of state regulation, was created in the following year. Nevertheless, by 1890 only seventeen states had created any semblance of insurance regulation. There was a much broader activity thereafter but it was not until 1944, when the Supreme Court in the *South-Eastern Underwriters* case[15] expressly overruled its earlier decision, that the regulation of insurance companies became of profound concern to most of the states. Since 1944 there has been no question that Congress may regulate insurance if it wants to; the question is, will Congress want to? How much consumer demand is there for such regulation, if any? What are the problems?

The 1944 decision brought the insurance companies within the orbit of the federal antitrust laws, and in order to provide a period of adjustment, the *McCarran Act of 1945* placed a moratorium on the operation of those laws with regard to insurance for three years. When the three years was up, the Federal Trade Commission began to interest itself in advertising, the promotion of mail-order insurance, and automobile financing, but the National Association of Insurance Commissioners protested the action as an invasion of a field already occupied by the states and the matter rested there. Whether it remains there depends on the degree to which the public is satisfied with state regulation, the avoidance of abuses and scandals on the part of the industry, and whether the public becomes fearful of growing power and concentration among the companies. The immediate effect of the Supreme Court decision of 1944 was to challenge the states to do a better job of regulation.

The degree to which the states now provide for insurance regulation varies widely, with states that are home territory to the major companies —New York, New Jersey, Connecticut, and Massachusetts—going the

---

[13] David Lynch, *The Concentration of Economic Power* (New York, 1946), p. 118.
[14] (8 Wallace [U.S.] 168 1869).
[15] *United States* v. *South-Eastern Underwriters Ass'n.* (322 U.S. 533. 1944).

furthest. Such a state usually has a separate insurance department or commission, but the function may be combined with others including the supervision of banks, building and loan associations, and general corporations. Since 1944 other states have adopted previously prepared model state-insurance laws, in whole or in part as needed, but the record still ranges from very good in a state like New York to perfunctory in some others where funds and staff are limited.

Although wide variations exist, therefore, state regulatory commissions perform at least some of the following functions:

1. Nearly every state requires the *licensing* of a corporation before it may engage in the business of writing insurance policies, an indispensable initial control.

2. The regulation of *financial operations* includes the maintenance of adequate reserves, valuation of the assets of the companies, and control of investment policy, matters that are carefully regulated in states having adequate insurance laws.

3. The *deposit of securities* with state officials discourages fly-by-night operations, makes it possible to check, count, and verify financial holdings, and brings within the jurisdiction of the state assets that may be seized through court action, in case of need, to satisfy the just claims of policyholders.

4. In many states, the *wording of policies* is standardized by law, a type of regulation designed to simplify and clarify policies so as to guard against fraud and misunderstanding.

5. *Rate regulation* is a fairly new development and has not proceeded so far as that of public utilities.

6. The *settlement of claims* was once considered a function of the courts, but more lately it has grown to be a large part of the work of state insurance commissioners.

7. Since state insurance officials must be able to require *reports* and make *periodic investigations,* such powers are frequently accorded.

In the early period of state regulation, the aim was to try to enforce competition as the best way to protect the public interest. Gradually this emphasis has given way to a more detailed type of control over policies and rates, and consequently insurance is now treated more like a public-utility monopoly than as a private competitive business. The turning point occurred around 1914 when the Supreme Court upheld the constitutionality of rate-fixing as applied to insurance.[16]

Rates are fixed in a different manner for insurance than for public utilities, the principal deviation being that there is more self-government in the case of insurance. The technique is to utilize the services of a so-called rating bureau, a private agency supported by a group of insurance companies for this purpose. Patterson found that as early as 1927 it was costing the fire insurance companies of New York alone approximately

---

[16] *German Alliance Insurance Co.* v. *Lewis* (233 U.S. 389. 1914).

$1 million annually to maintain the four rating bureaus serving that state.[17] The rates for all kinds of insurance in all parts of the country are now fixed by these rating bureaus and in some states no other course is legally possible. The function of most state insurance commissioners with regard to rates, therefore, is limited to approving what the rating bureaus have done, and if competition is secured, it is largely on a voluntary basis.

This kind of cooperation, or self-regulation, naturally gives the companies themselves ample opportunity to combine on the subject of rates; state commissioners generally lack authority to prevent collusion. It is partly for this reason that the Temporary National Economic Committee devoted more time and attention to the insurance business (especially fire insurance) in its hearings than to any other subject.

It will have been noted that the regulation of insurance resembles in several ways the regulation of public utilities. Thus the state controls entry into the business, in the case of a public utility through the issuance of a certificate of convenience and public necessity, in the case of insurance by granting a license certifying fitness to engage in the business. Both types of enterprise must submit reports and are liable to investigation, assets are valued, discrimination is prohibited, and rate-making is involved. But there are also some notable differences: The control of insurance rates is usually only nominal on the part of the state commissioners, whereas for the utilities it is extensive; valuation in the case of insurance consists in valuing securities, whereas with the utilities it is actual properties that are chiefly involved; greater reliance is placed by the commissions on reports and investigations in the case of insurance, whereas the utilities companies must usually maintain more direct contacts with the commissions. Areas that are quite different include the deposit of securities, the standardization of policy forms, and the control of investments, requirements that apply only to the insurance companies.

Due largely to the interest aroused by the TNEC hearings, attention in insurance regulation has come to center around certain large issues of public policy and control. Thus, should the functions of the rating bureaus be taken over by the government? Should competition be encouraged or discouraged? Should an attempt be made to curtail the size and power of the giants in the insurance business to encourage the smaller companies? Should the government extend public ownership and operation in the insurance field beyond social security and the various state insurance enterprises that now exist? Do insurance companies earn more than they should? Are there any soft spots in the insurance structure that are likely to give way in another depression? Should federal regulation be established and made largely to supersede state supervision and control? Should insurance companies be allowed more freedom in the investment of their funds? If interest rates decline, will the companies find it hard to

[17] E. W. Patterson, *The Insurance Commissioner in the United States* (Cambridge, Mass., 1927), p. 279.

meet their obligations on policies predicated on a higher rate? And what is the effect of inflation on the benefits ultimately paid out in life insurance?

In the areas of regulation and insurance-company investments, two recent Supreme Court cases seem to lead a little closer to eventual federal regulation, and the first also has to do with investment policies. Thus in 1952 there appeared for the first time in this country the device of the so-called variable annuity, a type of insurance in which payments fluctuate according to the changing market values of the securities on which they are based. Insurance companies are commonly limited by state laws to bonds and other conservative investments, but in connection with a retirement program for teachers, the New York legislature permitted companies in that state to sell contracts based on stocks. Thereupon there arose a controversy as to whether such contracts—since they involved stock transactions as well as insurance—should come under state or federal regulation. The Securities and Exchange Commission claimed jurisdiction, even though under the several acts administered by that agency the regulation of insurance companies, including contracts, was left to the states. In 1959 the case went to the Supreme Court which decided in favor of the SEC.[18] In the following year the Court upheld the right of the federal government to regulate insurance companies doing an interstate business by mail even though they have headquarters in a state with its own insurance laws. The controversy involved a charge by the Federal Trade Commission that a company licensed in Nebraska and in Virginia was not clearly informing its prospective customers of certain provisions in its policies. An order to cease and desist was nullified by a Circuit Court of Appeals on the ground that a state law forbade deceptive practices in that state and "in any other state." But the Supreme Court held that this clause was not enough to exclude the insurance companies from the jurisdiction of the federal regulatory statutes and the cease-and-desist order was upheld.[19]

Yet another issue relating to insurance is how the companies are to meet two recent problems: the insurance of peacetime atomic-energy installations and the insurance against flood damage, which in recent years has constituted an enormous burden on the companies in some states. After a series of disastrous hurricanes the industry studied the situation and reluctantly concluded that some form of government reinsurance was the only solution. In 1956 Congress duly created the Flood Indemnity Administration to carry out a joint reinsurance program with the states, but a year later—the insurance companies having apparently caught their second wind in the meantime—the agency was abolished for lack of appropriations.

Finally, there is the issue of taxation. Since 1921, life insurance companies have been taxed differently from other corporations because of

---

[18] *SEC* v. *Variable Annuity Ins. Co.* (359 U.S. 65. 1959).
[19] *SEC* v. *Travelers Health Assn.* (80 S.Ct. 717. 1960).

the special nature of their business which requires the maintenance of large reserves against payments on the claims of policyholders. Income from profits on premiums was exempt from taxation and so was a portion of the income from investments. The problem was how to determine what portion of income from investments should be taxed. A formula devised in 1942 worked well enough for a few years but by 1947 and 1948 the companies were paying no income taxes at all. Temporary legislation held until 1959 when a permanent formula was worked out, under which the companies were to pay $500 million on their 1958 income instead of the $181 million that would have been due under the former temporary scheme. The new law requires the payment of taxes on a portion of investment income and for the first time extends taxation to underwriting profits as well.

It need hardly be said that after many years of relative quiescence under state control, insurance today is a live field of public policy.

Strengthening Regulation

The insurance business is now so extensive and influential in the national economy that the question of strengthening regulation becomes a matter of some moment, especially since the federal government has not yet entered the field but may be forced to do so. The TNEC concluded its study of the insurance business with a set of interesting recommendations which, if carried out, would greatly strengthen state regulation: raise qualifications for state commissioners, lengthen tenure, increase salaries, separate the supervision of insurance from supervision in other fields such as banking, provide more generous appropriations, increase personnel and place them under a merit system, strengthen investigatory work, pay more attention to the branches and agencies of insurance companies, simplify policy forms, check more closely into top management in the companies, encourage competition, and control abuses relative to low actuarial standards and questionable sale techniques.

The TNEC also recommended that the federal government take steps to restrict the use of the mails and radio by companies not licensed to do business in a particular state; to amend the National Bankruptcy Act to permit state insurance commissions to take advantage of its provisions more readily; to make more explicit the fiduciary requirements of the officers of insurance companies; and to investigate all forms of fire, casualty, and marine insurance.

Some members of the TNEC, however, believed that these recommendations merely scratched the surface of the problem and that since insurance is primarily interstate, it should be directly regulated by the federal government. Accordingly they proposed the establishment of a federal fact-finding and investigatory agency, prohibition of the widespread practice of turning in policies for their surrender value during hard times, the granting of visatorial powers to a designated federal agency enabling it to advise state insurance departments, and the establishment of an Insurance Advisory Council representing all parties of interest, including the companies and the state commissions.[20]

Rising above all these questions is the natural query as to what might be the effect of highly concentrated power on the part of a few companies in a single industry. Clearly when a trusteeship involves insurance companies with assets in the billions of dollars, accountability is hard to enforce. In Wisconsin, for example, the largest insurance company domiciled in that state collected in 1936 premiums amounting to nearly twice as much as the state received in total tax revenue. When economic giants become larger than their supervisors, the supervisors often have their hands full.

Pension Funds: New Power Elite

The latest development toward an indirect banker-type control of economic decisions comes from the development of pension trusts during the last fifteen years. These funds now have assets of $40 billion; they are drawn from 25,000 pension plans covering approximately 15 million employees, or one quarter of the nation's work force. Noninsured corporate pension funds are the larger segment, having more than $22 billion in assets in 1959 as against $15.5 billion for the insured types of plans. Another $1.7 billion are held in the reserves of nonprofit organizations.

"Like those who command any strategic height," says Harbrecht, "the managers of these funds are in a position to dominate the countryside" and to influence decisions affecting the whole economy, especially the issue of centralized power.[21] In 1957, 14 percent of all corporate noninsured pension funds held about 84 percent of all fund assets, and 1.5 percent held 55 percent of all assets in funds of $100 million or over.

Many pension funds held by a few large banks make the degree of control even more impressive. As early as 1954, for example, 60 percent of all noninsured pension funds were held by New York banks and of these, six or seven banks controlled 95 percent of all pension assets, leaving 38 other banks to administer two percent of the remainder. Moreover, as of 1958, liberal state and federal laws allowed the trustees of pension funds to invest 43 percent of pension fund net receipts in common stocks. With voting rights of such magnitude and concentration, the degree of economic power is truly formidable, justifying Harbrecht's analogy to the sudden appearance of a mountain peak on the economic terrain. The principal legislation dealing with this rapidly evolving new area is the Welfare and Pension Plans Disclosure Act of 1958.[22]

[20] Temporary National Economic Committee, *Final Report and Recommendations*, pp. 41–43.

[21] Paul P. Harbrecht, "A New Power Elite?" *Challenge Magazine* (Mar. 1960). See also his book, *Pension Funds and Economic Power* (New York, Twentieth Century Fund, 1959). See also Benson Soffer, "Fringes Are Not Frills," *Challenge Magazine* (Mar. 1960).

[22] Analyzed in Harbrecht, *Pension Funds and Economic Power, op. cit.*, pp. 260–266.

Supplementary Reading

Prochnow, Herbert V. (ed.), *American Financial Institutions* (New York, 1951). Especially Chapters 2, 3, 6, 14–17, 20, and 21.

Guthmann, H. G., and H. E. Dougall, *Corporate Financial Policy* (New York, 1948). Especially good on investment banking, Chapter 14.

Goldenweiser, E. A., *American Monetary Policy* (New York, 1951). By a recognized authority.

Kemmerer, E. W., and D. L. Kemmerer, *The ABC of the Federal Reserve System* (New York, 1950). One of the best books on this subject.

Foster, M. B., R. Rogers, J. L. Bogen, and M. Nadler, *Money and Banking* (New York, 1953). Comprehensive coverage.

Strayer, P. J., *Fiscal Policy and Politics* (New York, 1958).

Bach, G. L., *Federal Reserve Policy-Making* (New York, 1950).

Maxwell, J. A., *Fiscal Policy: Its Techniques and Institutional Setting* (New York, 1955).

Chapman, John M., and R. B. Westerfield, *Branch Banking* (New York, 1942). One of the few books on this controversial subject.

James, Marquis, and Bessie Rowland James, *Biography of a Bank: The Story of the Bank of America* (New York, 1954).

Haven, T. K., *Investment Banking under the Securities and Exchange Commission* (Ann Arbor, Mich., 1940).

McCormick, Edward T., *Understanding the Securities Act and the S.E.C.* (New York, 1948).

Atkins, W. E., G. W. Edwards, and H. G. Moulton, *The Regulation of the Security Markets* (Washington, D.C., 1946).

Blaisdell, Donald C., *Economic Power and Political Pressures,* Temporary National Economic Committee, Monograph No. 26 (Washington, D.C., 1941). Chapter 8 deals with investment bankers as a pressure group.

Stein, E., *Government and the Investor* (New York, 1941). A first-rate study.

Ashby, F. B., *Economic Effects of Blue Sky Laws* (Philadelphia, 1926). Deals with early state regulation.

U. S. Government, *Stock Exchange Practices* (Report of the Senate Banking and Currency Committee, 73d Cong., 2d Sess., 1934). Malpractices leading to legislation.

Dice, C. A., and W. J. Eiteman, *The Stock Market* (New York, rev. ed., 1952).

Cherrington, H. F., *The Investor and the Securities Act* (Washington, D.C., Public Affairs Press, 1942).

Prochnow, H. V. (ed.), *The Federal Reserve System* (New York, 1959).

Livingston, Joseph, *The American Stockholder* (New York, 1958).

National Bureau of Economic Research, *Regularization of Business Investment* (Princeton, N.J., 1954). The conditioning factors, methods, and problems, discussed by twenty-six economists.

Patterson, E. W., *The Insurance Commissioner in the United States* (Cambridge, Mass., 1927). The best treatment of the legal and administrative aspects.

Temporary National Economic Committee, *Study of Legal Reserve Life Insurance Companies,* Monograph No. 28 (Washington, D.C., 1940).

———, *Final Report and Recommendations* (S. Doc. 35, 77th Cong., 1st Sess., 1941). A wealth of information.

Kramer, Robert (ed.), "Regulation of Insurance," *Law and Contemporary Problems,* Vol. 15 (summer 1950), pp. 315–469.

Sawyer, Elmer W., *Insurance as Interstate Commerce* (New York, 1945).

Koontz, Harold, and Richard W. Gable, *Public Control of Economic Enterprise* (New York, 1956). Part V, "Protecting the Investor," is recommended.

Harbrecht, Paul P., *Pension Funds and Economic Power* (New York, Twentieth Century Fund, 1959).

PART VIII

STABILIZING
THE
ECONOMY

20

CONTROLLING DEPRESSIONS

The role of government; issues of public policy; causes of depression; losses in the 1930s; early government measures; characteristics and objectives of the New Deal; NRA and its effect; self-government in industry; public works and work relief; theory and effect of pump-priming; monetary controls; fiscal controls; influence of politics.

There has been no major economic depression in the United States since the great disaster of the 1930s, nor could the nation afford another such experience and retain its democratic-capitalistic system. Fortunately, economists, governmental officials, and the public have learned much about the nature of the economic cycle in the past few decades and certain stabilizers have been built into the economy which make another major disaster unlikely. But depressions have not been eliminated. The post-World War II variety of this phenomenon is shorter, slighter, and more regular—about once in four years—than its predecessors. Some experts believe that recessions should never be wholly eliminated, but others hold that with proper planning, productivity could go forward at a steady pace, would cover a much wider area of goods and especially services such as teaching and medical care, and would never get out of hand in a wild inflation or an equally disastrous deflation.

With a global war following on the heels of depression, the United States endured a period of chronic crisis from 1929 to at least 1945, and with the cold war following the shooting war a return to so-called normalcy was even longer delayed. When a kind of normalcy was attained, it was at a high level beyond the imagination of any prewar businessman. During these years a profound change has occurred in popular attitudes toward government. Businessmen especially now realized that government must inevitably play some part in avoiding depressions, if for no other reason than that government is the only central institution capable of controlling monetary and fiscal policies.

Businessmen also know (but frequently only reluctantly admit) that government spends so much of the national income and administers so large a national debt that public policy must of necessity have much to do with general prosperity and economic stability. There is much less agreement, however, first, on the degree to which counterdepression measures during the New Deal period helped or hindered economic recovery, and second, on the extent to which it is possible to *predict* and hence to control, at least in large part, the ups and downs of economic activity and therefore to take governmental action that will help, along with the built-in stabilizers, to keep the economy in balance. The present chapters deal principally with these two basic issues.

A decision in such matters depends, in turn, on the answer to the question of causation. Are depressions the result of cause-and-effect relationships that can be analyzed and understood so as to guide future action in similar situations? Or are the belief systems of dominant groups all that matter? If it is a cause-and-effect relationship, then the policies of Presidents Hoover and Roosevelt relative to the depression were responses to the course of events, situations for which they were not responsible but had to deal with; but if it is only belief systems that matter, then conservatives and liberals alike will simply "get mad" when things go wrong and both sides will be content merely to vote their prejudices. The modern tendency is to stress the former of these two approaches and to de-emphasize the latter.

There is, however, an additional major factor in the situation: in the free-enterprise system there are certain assumptions and rules of conduct that businessmen and others expect to be honored. If those in control of government are unsympathetic to these attitudes and assumptions, the course of the national economy may be a rocky one. The success of the free-enterprise system depends partly on keeping the entrepreneurial attitudes of economic leaders hopeful and confident. If some government officials directly attack business itself, unduly interfere with property rights and demand for government a degree of economic control heretofore considered beyond what is proper, thus challenging belief systems head-on, then the self-restorative abilities of the economy may be inhibited by government itself. The successful blending of belief systems with the seeming necessities of the situation is most often a difficult feat of public policy decision.

THE GREAT DEPRESSION

How long the depression of the 1930s lasted, or whether it was ever really over before the United States got into the arsenal-of-democracy program of 1938-1941, is still a subject of debate. The stock market crashed in 1929 and the depth of the depression was in 1933 when many banks were closed, mortgages were foreclosed, bread lines formed on city streets, and something like a third of the working population was unemployed. Some economists contend that the depression was over by 1937, some prefer 1939. In the present discussion we have used the convenient designation, the depression decade, 1929 to 1939.

What causes a depression? The simplest answer is that a depression occurs when parts of the economy are badly out of balance. In 1929, for example, there seemed to be no ceiling to stock-market prices and no bottom to farm prices. Most depressions start in the area that includes investment in and production of capital goods, including producers' inventories, because this has always been the least stable sector of the economy. When inventories accumulate, industry slows down and employees must be laid off. Recent recessions have pretty much stopped there. If they go further, then purchasing power declines and people can no longer buy the goods that pile up in warehouses or the services offered by hotels, dry cleaners, barbershops, and the like. When businessmen lose confidence in the distant as well as in the immediate future, they stop investing, building, producing. Just as economic activity may expand at an accelerating pace once the essentials of the system are in order, so also the constrictive forces of the economy may cause an almost complete reversal if the causes of constriction are not recognized and promptly and effectively checked. The problem of public policy, therefore, is to secure stability and steady economic growth without causing overexpansion on one side or stagnation on the other; and to secure across-the-board prosperity without penalizing exceptional ability and effort. The United States learned more about these things during the 1930s than in all its previous history.

No amount of statistics can tell the story of how much the depression cost the American people in heartache or even in material losses. If the levels that prevailed just before 1929 are compared with levels during the following decade, the losses are staggering; but if the higher volumes that have since been attained are compared with the levels of 1929-1939, the losses are incalculable. Here are a few indications of what happened:

At the depth of the depression, 15 million people, or one third of the working force of the nation, were unemployed. National income fell by more than 50 percent in the three years between 1929 and 1932, and wages fell by about 60 percent. In agriculture, by 1935 roughly 20 percent of the entire rural population was on relief rolls. The index for manufacturing production (1935-1939 = 100) fell from 110 in 1929 to 57 in 1932, and in that year also the steel mills were producing at only 20 percent of capacity. The index for wholesale prices dropped from 95.3 in 1929 to 64.8 in 1932; in some commodities, market prices netted less than transportation costs; in 1932 corn sold at 10 cents a bushel, hogs at $2.80 a hundredweight. The exchange value of agricultural commodities for industrial goods fell, by early 1933, to 50 percent of the predepression average. Between 1929 and 1932 the investing public lost a total of around $90 billion in predepression values. Many old people who had thought themselves secure found themselves penniless, and millions of young people ready to enter the labor market discovered there were no jobs to be had.

The depression of the 1930s was different from other depressions because it was world-wide, long-lasting, and all-encompassing. There are some who still contend that if government had not tried to alleviate the situation, the "wringer" would have done its work, the "house-cleaning" period would have eliminated the inefficient and the weak, and recovery would have occurred sooner than it did. But most authorities agree that if government had not done what it did, even allowing for mistakes and wrong policies, it is doubtful if our free-enterprise system could have continued to hold the support of the vast majority of the American people.

Herbert Hoover, whose espousal of individualism and laissez faire has never been surpassed by any President, was nevertheless a practical man and reluctantly took steps that were contrary to his laissez-faire beliefs. Thus, he (1) established the Federal Farm Board in 1929 to peg agricultural prices; (2) created the National Credit Corporation in 1931 and the Reconstruction Finance Corporation in 1932 to support tottering financial institutions; (3) declared a moratorium on international debts and empowered the Home Loan Bank System to discount first mortgages to relieve the strain on building and loan associations; (4) expanded the government's public works program to help create employment; and (5) commenced the federal distribution of unemployment relief. No less an authority than Walter Lippmann has declared that Hoover's program for stopping the depression represented more of a break with the past than did that of the New Deal.[1]

THE NEW DEAL EXPERIENCE

We are now far enough away from the New Deal period to see some things more clearly than was possible only a few years ago. One is that its program was frankly experimental; it used trial-and-error methods in the hope that some would work. Some measures that proved successful have become a permanent part of our institutions, as in the case of social security, TVA, and public-works planning; other measures that worked less well have had to be gradually liquidated.

There is also rather general agreement that the New Deal had no central, consistent, economic policy; it had only a consistent social policy, which was to help the people. George Steiner is right when he says that although the New Deal focused on the right problems—unemployment, insecurity, economic instability, economic concentration, the abuse of private economic power, and the like—it did not attack any of these problems with a rational, consistent, and well-balanced theory.[2] The best explanation, perhaps, is the one suggested by Arthur Millspaugh: that as a middle-of-the-road administration not ideologically attached to either the extreme right or the extreme left, the New Deal could not be expected to have a consistent line of policy. Moreover, and this is at least as important an explanation, when choices must be made in an atmosphere of distress and tension, the results inevitably appear as emergency measures

---

[1] Walter Lippmann, "The Permanent New Deal," in Edwin Rozwenc (ed.), *The New Deal, Revolution or Evolution?* (New York, 1949).

[2] George A. Steiner, *Government's Role in Economic Life* (New York, 1953), p. 188.

and experimental in nature.[3] A main reason for studying depressions, therefore, is to be better prepared, if the occasion should unfortunately recur, to take measures that are adequate, deliberate, and not obnoxiously doctrinaire.

The result of experimentation and lack of a fixed policy during the New Deal was, of course, inconsistency. We now see, for example, that under the National Recovery Administration of 1933-1935, monopoly was encouraged as never before, and immediately afterward antitrust enforcement was stepped up to a point unequaled in American history. Those who lived through this period and took part in some of these programs know that no one ever thought about monopoly when the Blue Eagle was hatched and nurtured; NRA merely seemed like a good way to rally capital and labor in a joint attack on the depression. There were many other inconsistencies in every part of the aggregate program, most of them more easily seen in retrospect than at the time. Our purpose, however, is not to assess or to judge the New Deal, but rather to try to sift from the chaff the factors that may be of value in the future.

The three broad objectives of the New Deal, says Steiner, were recovery, relief, and reform—the three R's. Recovery took the form of stimulating business activity out of the depths of depression; relief went to businessmen, farmers, workers, home owners—a program for everyone; and reform readjusted various institutions, group relationships, and economic factors so as to avoid a recurrence of 1929.[4]

There were also three fairly distinct periods in the New Deal administration. In the first, from 1933 through 1935, an emphasis on recovery and emergency relief measures needed at once was combined with reform measures having a more lasting value. The relief and recovery programs included both direct and work relief for the unemployed, moratoria on mortgages (especially farm mortgages), efforts to reopen the banks, and NRA to stimulate industry. The reform programs for which these two years were the seedbed, were public-works planning to provide employment during slack times, labor relations, and public housing, all of which were generated in the National Industrial Recovery Act of 1933 along with NRA itself. Then there was the creation of the Securities and Exchange Commission and the Federal Deposit Insurance Corporation in the field of finance, the Public Utilities Holding Company Act, TVA, social security, and the beginning of all the farm-relief programs that have since followed.

In the second New Deal period, from 1935 to 1939, these various programs matured and others were added, but most of the human misery had been alleviated and the pressure of a running emergency was off. Finally, in the third period, from 1939 through 1941 when the United States entered World War II, some writers contend that

[3] Arthur Millspaugh, *Democracy, Efficiency, Stability* (Washington, D.C., Brookings Institution, 1942), p. 262.

[4] Steiner, *op. cit.*, p. 161.

the depression was over, even though in 1939 there were still 9 million unemployed and it was not until the United States began to build up its war factories to arm its allies that economic activity went ahead in earnest.

The Range of New Deal Programs

The programs of the New Deal literally affected all parts of the economy, from the writing of state tourist guides, painting murals on post-office walls, and repairing schoolhouses under WPA to the regulation of labor relations, production and marketing assistance to farmers, the correction of abuses in securities transactions, the creation of TVA in the field of conservation and electric power, and the building of factories for defense and armament purposes after 1939. Steiner finds ten major programs: money and banking, socialization of financial risks, regulations of business, promoting labor organization and collective bargaining, relief and public-works programs, social security, promoting agricultural interests, industrial planning, reciprocal trade policy, and deficit financing.[5] A somewhat different classification stresses objectives in this way:

Dollar devaluation to increase the supply of money.

Cheaper credit to businessmen, farmers, home owners, and the like.

Control of security issues to prevent stockmarket excesses.

Insurance of bank deposits to protect small investors from loss in case of bank failures.

Reciprocal trade agreements to stimulate foreign trade.

National Recovery Administration to promote self-government in business, eliminate "destructive" competition, and maintain fair labor standards.

Holding company control to prevent pyramiding, monopoly, and consumer exploitation in the public-utility field.

Antitrust enforcement to put teeth in the Sherman and Clayton acts.

Large public works to stimulate indirect employment.

Work relief programs to provide direct employment instead of a dole.

Insurance programs to provide for the aged, the unemployed, and the handicapped under the social security setup.

Labor relations to increase labor's bargaining power and raise real wages.

Wage and hour control to put a floor under wages and a ceiling over hours, thereby increasing the income of the 19 million families in the two lowest income groups.

Agricultural planning to help bring production and farm prices into line.

[5] *Ibid.*, p. 162.

Conservation of natural resources to prevent floods, soil erosion, and the wasteful use of minerals such as oil and natural gas.

Regional development to show what could be done to balance agriculture and industry through planning, as in the case of TVA.

The National Recovery Administration

Looking back on the early days of the New Deal, the symbol most likely to come to mind is the NRA and its famous, and finally bedraggled, Blue Eagle. If NRA were considered merely in the light of what it contributed to the solution of the depression, of course, there is little reason to accord it special attention because in terms of its announced goal it proved to be merely a stopgap that helped turn public sentiment from despair to a measure of optimism. But NRA was also an interesting and highly significant experiment in group or guild government, it had lasting effects on labor relations, the influence of pressure groups, and the tendency toward monopoly, and in its brief life of less than two years it played one of the most spectacular roles in American history.

The National Industrial Recovery Act, passed in June 1933, provided that the industries and trades of the nation should establish codes of fair competition, in connection with which labor's right to organize and to bargain collectively was recognized. In other words, NRA was a deal wherein both management and labor were offered something they both wanted on the assumption that if they could be induced to work together in a system in which each had a definite responsibility, the economy might eventually recover. Business wanted self-government, the elimination of "destructive" competition, and a relaxation of the antitrust laws. Labor wanted higher wages and assurance that collective bargaining and the right to organize would be universally respected. When these two streams were brought together, NRA was the result.

Although fair competition was nowhere defined in the act, it was provided that trade associations should enter into fair-trade agreements and that action pursuant to properly authorized codes was to be exempt from the antitrust laws—a clue to much that happened then and later—but monopolies were to be avoided. But who was to say where the dividing line lay between business practices that were monopolistic and those that were not? In practice, the antitrust laws went into a state of suspension, monopolistic tendencies grew rapidly, particularly through the device of the trade association, and when NRA came to an end, the Federal Trade Commission and the Antitrust Division of the Justice Department found themselves with a bigger job on their hands than they had ever had before.

In order to speed the drafting of the codes and to demonstrate what the formula could do, the President also called for industry-wide adherence to the President's Re-employment Agreement, a blanket code providing for minimum weekly wages, maximum hours, the prohibition of child labor, agreement not to raise prices beyond a certain level, and refusal to buy from nonsigners. It was an ingenious and effective scheme and assenting firms and stores were given a Blue Eagle emblem to display on their premises. In a relatively short time more than 2 million businessmen employing 16 million workers out of a 25 million potential were signed up. This widespread adherence, which carried with it acceptance of the labor relations provisions of Section 7A, not only caused businessmen not coming under code agreements to draft such codes of their own, if only for patriotic reasons, but it also created a terrific avalanche of work in NRA.

It is doubtful whether many officials realized at the outset how complicated American business life really is. In the NRA organization, the economy was simply divided into major industries, but it was soon found that these had to be subdivided many times. The sellers of bird seed, for example, required a separate code, as did hundreds of other dealers no one would otherwise have thought of. Although NRA was declared unconstitutional and went out of existence long before the proliferation of codes was complete, the major agreements were drafted in the remarkably short space of six months, attesting the feverish desire to ride on the bandwagon. During those days, all through trains to Washington were filled with groups of excited businessmen putting the last touches on what they wanted Washington to sanction, because once these codes were approved and signed by the President their provisions were legally enforceable as standards of fair practice.

Even if the NRA formula had been theoretically a sound one—and some businessmen still think it was—the sheer magnitude of the task of organizing, staffing, and administering the program would have made its continued success exceedingly doubtful. Where, for example, were NRA executives to be secured? They would have to understand business practice and administration and at the same time be sufficiently aloof to be impartial. To the credit of the patriotic instincts of the American people, let it be said that many excellent executives of this kind volunteered, but not all that were needed. Unfortunately, the lack made it necessary to bring in men from industries being codified who at least knew their own field. But they then became chief policy officials, meaning that except for higher review an industry could write its own ticket. In 600 out of 850 codes, the code's secretary and the trade association's secretary were the same man,[6] and it was partly for this reason that the initial approbation of NRA came to be well mixed with adverse comment.

Popular support of NRA had in fact ebbed to a low point even

[6] David Lynch, *The Concentration of Economic Power* (New York, 1946), p. 86.

before the Supreme Court declared the act unconstitutional in 1935. The plan was too big and complex to be workable. Consumers saw in it higher prices and entrenched corporate power, industry began to sicken of what it called regimentation, and labor complained that management had been dealt the better hand. But when the law was voided, it was on the technical ground that legislative authority had been unconstitutionally delegated to the President and that Congress was trying to interfere in matters reserved under the Constitution to the commerce power of the states. Because the *Schechter* case [7] related to the sale of poultry in the metropolitan market of New York, the demise of NRA was symbolized in cartoons by a figure that looked remarkably like a dead chicken.

Effect of NRA

What was the effect of NRA on business recovery? It is hard to assess individual experiments because none taken alone can provide more than part of the solution needed. Nevertheless, NRA did offer a symbol and a program around which all parties could rally in the dark days of 1933-1934. Had it done nothing more, from that standpoint alone NRA accomplished a useful purpose. In addition, the NRA policy of spreading work brought about the re-employment of nearly 2 million men.[8] But for the rest the picture is less clear. It is true that prices rose and there was a short-lived spurt of business activity, but it was not sustained. In its long-range effect NRA proved a stimulant to pressure groups, trade associations, guild tendencies, and monopoly, and also "brought about an industry-by-industry approach to the great range of economic problems," [9] in sharp contrast to the traditional piecemeal view. A tentative price-fixing policy, furthermore, set a precedent for a similar kind of action during World War II.

In the field of business-government relations the long-range effect of NRA "was greatly to diminish the reliance upon private initiative in the allocation of resources, the organization of production, and distribution of income, and greatly to increase the power of government officials and of specially interested groups, the latter to a considerable degree acting in an official capacity." [10] In addition, NRA increased the government's power over prices, the use of productive capacity, the size of that capacity, specialization, the wages and hours of labor, and industrial relations generally.

[7] *Schechter Poultry Corp.* v. *United States* (295 U.S. 495. 1935).

[8] *Message from the President.* (H. Doc. 158, 75th Cong., 1st Sess.), p. 181; see also Leverett S. Lyon and others, *The National Recovery Administration, an Analysis and Appraisal* (Washington, D.C., Brookings Institution, 1935), pp. 837–844.

[9] Leverett S. Lyon and Victor Abramson, *Government and Economic Life* (Washington, D.C., Brookings Institution, 1935), Vol. II, p. 1057.

[10] *Ibid.*, pp. 1042–1052.

Self-Government of Industry

Finally, no discussion of the effect of NRA would be complete without some mention of industrial self-government which that agency sought to stimulate. The main requirement of self-government is that the various parties to a dispute shall try to settle their differences as partners in an enterprise of joint concern, an approach traditionally favored by the U. S. Chamber of Commerce and by most trade associations. Despite the collapse of NRA, a program of industrial self-government still has many adherents and some continue to believe it the best way, in the long run, to avoid major depressions. While some regard it as the alternative to public control, others merely think that it could be developed alongside such other regulations in the public interest as are found necessary.

Testifying at hearings before the Temporary National Economic Committee, the champions of self-government in industry contended that only the representatives of a particular business are qualified to determine the behavior of that business and to make the right decisions, and that they can also be relied on not to put their own interests above those of the public.[11] Some witnesses even suggested that business self-rule might make the antitrust laws unnecessary: the president of the Anaconda Copper Company, for example, advocated the outright repeal of those laws and proposed instead that members of various industries be permitted to get together to "cooperate" in the production, sale, and distribution of their products. Industry, he said, would be "subject to regulation, but not regulated by" government, whose only duty under such a scheme would be "to compel industry to conform" to decisions made by self-governing groups. Similarly, a former president of the National Association of Manufacturers advocated freedom "to get together to discuss costs and price without fear of prosecution" and to determine what constitutes a fair price and the methods by which such a price is to be maintained.[12]

In the relations between business and government the two questions most often asked are, What can business do best? What can government do best? There are many areas where business self-government is clearly indicated, but equally there are limits to what it can accomplish, especially in a complex society such as ours has become. The reason is partly that businessmen necessarily keep their noses so close to the grindstone that they find it hard to see problems in a broad framework. But this is beginning to change. The appeal of the 1930s to trade-association cooperation is now being superseded by a "social-conscience" type of approach, as reflected in the development of govern-

---

[11] Temporary National Economic Committee, *Hearings*, Pt. 2, p. 424; Pt. 10, pp. 4248–4250; Pt. 17, pp. 9503–9505; and Pt. 25, pp. 13,324–13,361.
[12] *Ibid.*, Pt. 20, pp. 10,812–10,816.

mental affairs departments in large corporations and by the appearance of books such as W. T. Gossett, *Corporate Citizenship* (Lexington, Va., 1957), and R. S. F. Eells, *The Meaning of Modern Business* (New York, 1960).

Public Works and Work Relief

When unemployment began to mount after 1929, the states and municipalities at first tried to meet the need, as they had in the past, by the use of local methods and resources including both work and various forms of direct relief. But even before 1932 it became clear that since the crisis was nation-wide, its solution would have to be

TABLE 9

EXPENDITURES ON WPA-OPERATED PROJECTS FROM FEDERAL FUNDS BY TYPES OF PROJECTS, THROUGH JUNE 30, 1940

Type of project	Expenditure
Highways, roads, and streets	$2,931,737,719
Public buildings	767,997,960
Parks and other recreational facilities	743,329,295
Conservation	325,993,909
Sewer systems and other utilities	756,994,825
Airports and airways	150,811,719
Sewing projects	586,745,805
Sanitation	160,707,805
Professional and service projects	1,222,566,929
Miscellaneous	138,077,617
Total	$7,784,963,583

SOURCE: Arthur W. Macmahon, John Millett, and Gladys Ogden, *The Administration of Federal Work Relief* (Chicago, 1941), p. 6.

sought on a similar scale. In addition, private construction had fallen from a high of nearly $11 billion worth in 1926 to a low of about $2 billion worth in 1933, and public construction did no better in that same year. Bringing two needs together, therefore, another New Deal antidepression measure was a public-works and work-relief program to alleviate unemployment and benefit industry, especially the construction industry.

The attack was a double one. On the one hand, a program of heavy construction under the Public Works Administration (PWA) emphasized self-liquidation of projects where possible and sought to stimulate indirect employment as orders for materials and equipment were placed and filled. On the other hand, a light works program under the Works Progress Administration (WPA) stressed a plan in which costs for materials were low, most of the money went into wages, the work was quickly done, and large numbers of persons taken chiefly from the relief rolls were employed.

The differences between these two programs are illustrated by the fact that where PWA never employed more than 171,000 persons on its projects at any one time (and more often it was considerably less than that), WPA never had less than 1.45 million on its rolls and the average was well over 2 million, with a peak of more than 3 million in 1936. And where the total appropriations for the entire works program (including PWA) from 1935 to 1940 amounted to more than $14 billion, WPA spent only a little over half, with the balance going to other federal agencies but largely to PWA. Although WPA was criticized by the supporters of heavy construction as addicted to leaf-rakers and shovel-leaners, its accomplishment in terms of a wide variety of useful public works, as shown in Table 9, was not inconsiderable.

In assessing the usefulness of public works expenditures as an antidepression measure it can hardly be doubted that while greatly adding to the community assets of the nation, they were also effective in offering employment, although authorities disagree as to the extent. Some idea of accomplishment and the great load of unemployment that had to be shouldered is found in Table 10 relating to the operations of WPA.

TABLE 10

OPERATIONS OF WPA, 1936-1940

Calendar year	Average WPA employment	Average unemployment	Ratio of WPA employment to unemployment (percent)
1936	2,545,853	7,599,000	33
1937	1,795,734	6,372,000	28
1938	2,764,365	10,099,000	27
1939	2,414,839	9,067,000	27
1940	2,216,273	9,185,000	24

SOURCE: Arthur W. Macmahon, John Millett, and Gladys Ogden, *The Administration of Federal Work Relief* (Chicago, 1941), p. 182.

Thus, from 1936 through 1940, average unemployment throughout the nation ranged from a low of more than 6 million in 1937 to a high of over 10 million in 1938 when, according to many authorities, the depression was over. And since these figures are those of the National Industrial Conference Board, they are relatively conservative estimates. It is also shown that during this five-year period, including 1939 and 1940 when America had already become arsenal to the democracies and business had picked up, average unemployment was still over 9 million and WPA was continuing to find work for from 24 to 27 percent of the total. It is on the basis of figures such as these that some authorities doubt whether the depression was really over until the full transition to a wartime economy finally took up the slack.

As it turned out, even the heavy public-works program did in some measure stimulate recovery, especially in the construction field, and private construction activities nearly doubled between 1933 and 1936. Prior to the depression, private construction exceeded public construction nearly three and a half times, but during the depression, public construction nearly equaled all private construction including public utilities. It was not until 1937 that public construction was outdistanced by the private variety.

One lesson learned through this public-works experience was that to be effective as an antidepression measure, heavy construction must be judiciously combined with the light variety directed at other quarters of the economy, because a heavy construction program alone is too limited in scope and too expensive to provide jobs for large numbers of people. A public-works program must also be planned and scheduled in advance, adequately financed, capable of starting quickly, and fully coordinated with trends in private business. In addition, of course, a policy of higher taxes during prosperous times would not only help reduce public indebtedness, but would also make it possible to accumulate funds with which to finance public works in times of depression, such a method being infinitely preferable to outright deficit financing; but this is a hard policy to enforce because ordinarily the more prosperous the nation, the more do business and other interests demand tax reductions and the greater is the temptation to divert surpluses to other purposes.

THE PUMP-PRIMING ANALOGY

One of the most interesting concepts stemming from the New Deal experience was that of deficit spending, which means deliberately spending beyond prospective income on the assumption that expenditure—even if it creates debt—increases the volume of economic activity and hence reacts favorably on all parts of the economy. Many conservative businessmen were worried over going into debt to achieve prosperity but others, especially bankers, approved of deficit spending because it increased their business. And government justified the action on the ground that it was needed to prime the pump.

The pump-priming argument runs like this: (1) Depression conditions produce low-level national spending, and what is needed is high-level spending in order to get money circulating. (The well is full of water but the pump needs priming before it will work.) (2) Public spending encourages spending all along the line; money gets into the hands of consumers who then buy more goods and services. (When you pump the handle, no water comes forth until you pour a bucketful of water down the pipe.) (3) Once economic activity begins to flow, the need for priming either ceases or is greatly reduced, and national spending continues to expand because volume begets volume each time the production cycle is completed. (4) Finally, once high-level spending has been restored, the taxes needed to pay off the accumulated debt can easily be extracted from the total national income without pinching anyone. In addition, not only does borrowing increase the national income by putting more dollars into circulation, but to collect taxes achieves the same end by stimulating the expenditure for this purpose of funds that taxpayers would otherwise save.

During the New Deal, this pump-priming theory was applied to all government expenditures, including public works, outside of normal operating activities, and in the end it proved to be at least partially successful, because total national spending did increase by more than the initial government expenditure and in addition, national income almost doubled between 1933 and 1939. Unfortunately, after a good start, the gains failed to sustain themselves. This does not necessarily refute the pump-priming theory; it simply means that apparently not all conditions were right during the 1930s. It is possible, for example, that too little attention was given to durable goods as contrasted with consumer goods, that there was a tendency to push costs up faster than retail prices, to push wage rates up faster than the prospects for profits, and in addition, rising tax rates plus dollar devaluation may have acted as a damper.[13] And finally, a psychological factor may have been as determinative as any in that the New Deal period was one of recovery mixed with reform, and many top business leaders may have felt—and doubtless did—that an overdose of reform was causing an unbalanced kind of recovery.[14]

But perhaps the most revolutionary result of the New Deal experience was the practical lesson that widespread consumer purchasing power equals an expanding economy. This was in contrast with the older view that if investment, spending, and income are concentrated at the top-income levels, these people will be sufficiently wise and patriotic to reinvest their money so as to keep the economy expanding. According to this so-called sieve theory, if business confidence is sustained, then prosperity will trickle down from the top to the lower levels of the economy. Nor has this doctrine been proved false; it is

[13] Alvin Hansen, *Full Recovery or Stagnation?* (Boston, 1938). Chap. 17.
[14] Steiner, *op. cit.*, p. 183.

only that the universal-demand theory has been proved a better one. The pump-priming experiment is one factor (along with compulsory collective bargaining, social security, and the like) that contributed to the enunciation, testing, and final validation of the consumer-demand theory. This is at least part of the reason (a more important one was war, of course) that by 1960 we had a $500 billion economy instead of an $80 billion one.

MONETARY AND FISCAL CONTROLS

Another useful antidepression weapon that was tested during the New Deal period is the combined use of monetary and fiscal controls; it was also given top strategic importance during the Eisenhower administration of 1953-1960. The real difficulty is not so much to know what to do as it is to get Congress to adopt economic policies rather than political ones. The task of administration is then to coordinate economic policies and programs so that their impact will be harmonious and unified. Here the Council of Economic Advisers plays a role. The problem is closely similar to that discussed in Chapter 15 which deals with the inflationary forces loosed by a prolonged cold war. But what are the theories? In nontechnical language, they are these:

Monetary policy controls the volume and value of money in the national economy and the regulation of credit through supervision of the banking system. Such policy is the key to prices, inflation versus deflation, and economic stability. Fiscal policy, which relates to taxation and public expenditure, also helps to control the volume of money in the private part of the economy through government expenditures and the cost of debt service, and it also determines the degree to which this financial load shall fall on different income groups within the economy. Consequently, fiscal policy also has a direct bearing on inflation, deflation, and economic stability. Now if these two policies can be worked together so that, to take a simple illustration, when money is short, taxes will drop off, and when money is plentiful, taxes will go up, the result is an effective method of economic control. But to apply it is harder than it sounds because of the influence of politics, human nature, and problems of administration.

The Board of Governors of the Federal Reserve System is the chief actor in the application of monetary policy, with the Treasury Department standing in the wings hoping to provide a cue at just the right time. The Federal Reserve System controls the volume of money in circulation and its cost to borrowers: if credit expansion is desired, Federal Reserve encourages bank loans to consumers by lowering the rediscount rate of the Federal Reserve banks; and if contraction is sought, such loans are discouraged by higher interest rates. Even more important, the Open Market Committee, composed of FRB plus five Reserve Bank presidents, may undertake open-market operations, buying or selling government securities to expand or contract bank and borrower funds in cash or deposits. Buying in the open market increases the reserves of the member banks and hence expands their power to lend; and selling, of course, has the opposite effect. It is here that a conflict of interest in public policy is likely to occur because as against the policy of the Federal Reserve banks, the Treasury Department generally prefers to keep the cost of financing government bonds as low as possible in order, among other reasons, to help balance the budget. An accord reached in 1951 helped to settle such disputes but the situation is still far from perfect.

This factor of government interest rates is central in the business-government relationship because

> . . . the influence of interest rates is woven into the nation's economic fabric. Interest rates affect not only the national budget and the amount of taxes we must pay to carry the public debt. They also influence, for example, the cost of building and maintaining a house, the rates businessmen and farmers pay for money they borrow and the rates savings banks pay their depositors. They affect the rates life insurance companies earn on their investments and, therefore, the cost of life insurance to the many millions of people who hold policies. . . . In addition, changes in interest rates alter the value of investments, such as the prices of bonds, stocks, and real estate, and play a part in the ups and downs of business.[15]

Are low interest rates desirable or undesirable? It depends on the objectives of economic policy. A low interest rate can stimulate investment in the kind of business where maintenance and depreciation are low, risks are moderate, and interest is really a substantial part of total costs, as in the case of hydroelectric installations, and also housing. But, says Professor John M. Clark, "in the general field of industry and trade, low interest rates cannot accomplish as much as many economic theorists give them credit for. Interest alone is a minor part of the total cost . . . especially in a dynamic industry where equipment gets obsolete long before it is worn out and allowance for obsolescence alone dwarfs the element of interest." [16]

The Federal Reserve System may also regulate stability by determining the reserve requirements of member banks, thus again controlling the amount of money available to borrowers and the ease or difficulty with which it may be had. And finally, as a result of the securities legislation of 1934, Federal Reserve may regulate the percentage of margin (the size of the down payment) on stock purchases and hence exercise a considerable restraining or stimulating influence on the activities of investors, but especially of speculators.

---

[15] Committee on Public Debt Policy, *Our National Debt and Interest Rates* (pamphlet, New York, 1947). p. 1.

[16] In B. M. Anderson, *et al.*, *Financing American Prosperity* (New York, Twentieth Century Fund, 1945), pp. 110–111.

Nevertheless, although these are important powers, they are more effective when the economy is on an even keel and only a light guiding hand is needed, than when it is in a depression and businessmen hesitate to borrow even when the banks have adequate reserves and the interest rate is low. Easy credit does not necessarily make the consumer eager to buy stocks, automobiles, or dishwashers, because other factors than monetary policy are involved. The moral is, of course, that it's easier to stay up if you're already up than to pull yourself up if you're down. In addition, there are many factors that may block the working of Federal Reserve controls even in good times, as, for example, a sudden fever on the stock market, a Secretary of the Treasury more concerned with balancing the budget than with preventing a depression, or a reckless consumer credit policy that, like Caesar's vanity, feeds on itself until the point of no return has been reached.

For its part, fiscal policy also is capable of manipulating the economy up or down or keeping it level. Here, however, the perils of politics, human nature, and public administration play an even more prominent role than in the case of monetary policy. For example: (1) It is not always possible or even desirable to balance the budget, though in general it is. But suppose in a particular year the policy is to balance the budget in order to influence business conditions; if it happens to be an election year (and every second year is election year in the House of Representatives) the decision may be in the negative because of the higher taxes that would be involved. (2) Government expenditures directly affect employment totals. Although these may be satisfactory at a given time, it may be politically expedient to increase them even though it means going further into debt. (3) When government spends more than it takes in, the effect is inflationary; and when government spends less than it takes in, the supply of funds available to the economy is restricted and the effect is deflationary. At some point, therefore, inflation must be curbed, but politically, it is always a temptation to keep on spending.

(4) One of the best potential controls is the so-called automatic stabilizer, formulated by such prominent people as Bernard Baruch, Paul Hoffman, and the late Beardsley Ruml. According to this theory, when incomes rise, taxes also should rise and governmental expenditures should fall, thus curbing inflation while accumulating a Treasury surplus; but when incomes fall, then taxes also should fall and governmental expenditures should rise, thus sustaining purchasing power and checking deflation. In this manner the economy would automatically be kept in balance and the extremes of boom and bust avoided. Unfortunately, political considerations are always weighted against this sound policy because when the economy is booming, the administration enjoys the crest of popularity that accompanies it and rarely has the moral courage to increase taxes as much as they should, and when the economy is depressed, tensions and pressures mount so rapidly that

Congress is forced to lower taxes and there are few who will object. If as a nation we could become economically literate to the point of overcoming this difficulty, it would be a long stride toward avoiding depressions.

And finally, (5) in addition to its use as automatic stabilizer, income tax policy is a potent weapon in other respects as well. Thus consumer purchasing power and private investment may both be increased or restricted by the tax rate fixed on middle and low incomes, by the stiffening or relaxation of tax exemptions, and by altering withholding provision up or down. But again, as in the case of balancing the budget, the test is the feasibility of any such proposals, and more often than not that means political feasibility.

In conclusion, it is to be remembered that the causes of depression are complex and numerous, some of the main ones being monetary policy, innovation, various psychological factors, overinvestment, underconsumption, and random external influences. Consequently, the solutions must also be multiple rather than single, making the problem harder for the scholar because it increases the variables and even more difficult for Congress and the administration because the solution requires a mastery of public policy that only a few possess.

Many groups, both public and private, are constantly studying the problem of economic stability and many useful reports and proposals have been made. Some that appeared during the recession of 1958 include, among others, reports by the Committee for Economic Development, the Conference on Economic Progress, and the Rockefeller Brothers Fund. As things stand, it seems to be fairly well agreed that although the economy remains sensitive to depression and is far from immune from another major economic disaster, the so-called built-in stabilizers that grew out of the experience of the 1930s are likely to operate with some success, as they have in all postwar recessions, to cushion the impact of a slackening economic pace. These stabilizers include unemployment compensation, which helps to maintain the purchasing power of workers after they are laid off although, as in 1958, the program may need emergency strengthening; social security pensions, public assistance, and agricultural support programs which help to maintain purchasing power among the aged, the indigent, and farmers; the regulation of securities issues and of stock markets and their procedures, including margins, which help to control the hazards of investment; and the insurance of bank deposits and mortgages, which helps to prevent personal financial losses in these areas. In addition, measures that may be called managerial, to be invoked by government in case of need, are monetary controls exercised through the Federal Reserve System to reduce interest and discount rates; stepped-up government spending for either current or emergency projects in the areas of defense contracts, housing, highways, and other public works; and finally, reductions in excise, personal income, and corporate taxes.

Here are the factors, but who is going to decide which ones are to be applied in given circumstances? And for that matter, who is going to decide what the circumstances are and do it quickly and accurately enough to be useful? As shown in the following chapter, the Council of Economic Advisers is a start in this direction. But in addition the nation could do with men in key positions who know their economics and who are sufficiently fearless and independent to advise and to carry out programs that will benefit the whole nation and are not dictated merely by expediency. Democracy is a hard system to make work because it involves more people and more voluntary effort than any other; but like the free-enterprise system which is its counterpart, the rewards also are greater than under any other.

Supplementary Reading

Burns, Arthur F., *Prosperity without Inflation* (New York, 1957). By a former chairman of the Council of Economic Advisers.

American Assembly, *Wages, Prices, Profits, and Productivity* (New York, 1958).
———, *U. S. Monetary Policy* (New York, 1959).

Steiner, George A., *Government's Role in Economic Life* (New York, 1953). Chapter 7, "The Depression of the 1930's and Public Policy," by an economist, is an excellent treatment of the factors involved.

Douglas, Paul H., *Controlling Depressions* (New York, 1935). By an economist who later became United States Senator.

Dulles, Eleanor Lansing, *Depression and Reconstruction: A Study of Causes and Controls* (Philadelphia, 1936). Another systematic treatment.

Homan, Paul T., "The Pattern of the New Deal," *Political Science Quarterly,* Vol. 51 (1936). A fair appraisal of the New Deal.

Lippmann, Walter W., "The Permanent New Deal," *Yale Review,* Vol. 24, No. 4 (summer 1935). A broad canvas.

Lawrence, David, *Beyond the New Deal* (New York, 1934). By a journalist with conservative inclinations.

Duesenberry, J. S., *Business Cycles and Economic Growth* (New York, 1958).

Strayer, P. J., *Fiscal Policy and Politics* (New York, 1958). Recent and good.

Mitchell, Broadus, *Depression Decade,* Vol. 9 in *The Economic History of the United States* (New York, 1947). A bold treatment of the subject.

Rauch, Basil, *The History of the New Deal* (New York, 1944). A full exposition.

Ickes, Harold L., *The Secret Diary of Harold L. Ickes* (New York, 1953). Inside story of part of the New Deal.

Haber, William, *Unemployment and Relief* (Chicago, 1956). A Public Administration Service study of relief from the local-government point of view.

Macmahon, Arthur W., John Millett, and Gladys Ogden, *The Administration of Federal Work Relief* (Chicago, 1941). The relief and public-works programs of the New Deal.

Rozwenc, Edwin C. (ed.), *The New Deal, Revolution or Evolution?* (New York, 1949). Primarily an evaluation.

Schlesinger, Arthur M., *The New Deal in Action, 1933-1939* (New York, 1940). By an author sympathetic to the New Deal.

Schlesinger, Arthur M., Jr., *The Age of Roosevelt*. Vol. I, *The Crisis of the Old Order 1919-1933* (Boston, 1957). Vol. II, *The Coming of the New Deal* (Boston, 1958). Vol. III, *The Politics of Upheaval* (Boston, 1960). These three volumes are outstanding for the period they cover.

Galbraith, Kenneth, *The Great Crash—1929* (Boston, 1955). The story in perspective.

Roose, Kenneth D., *The Economics of Recession and Revival* (New Haven, Conn., 1954). The story of the 1937 recession.

Slichter, Sumner H., *Towards Stability* (New York, 1934). By an outstanding economist.

Clark, John M., William H. Davis, George M. Harrison, and George G. Mead, *The National Recovery Administration: Report of the President's Committee of Industrial Analysis* (Washington, D.C., 1937). A semiofficial appraisal.

Dearing, Charles L., Paul T. Homan, Lewis L. Lorwin, and Leverett S. Lyon, *The ABC of the NRA* (Washington, D.C., Brookings Institution, 1934).

Gallagher, Michael F., *Government Rules Industry: A Study of the NRA* (New York, 1934). An early appraisal.

Galloway, George B., and Associates, *Industrial Planning under Codes* (New York, 1935). Stresses governmental problems.

Hellman, Florence S., *The New Deal, A Selected List of References* (Washington, D.C., Library of Congress, 1940).

Koontz, Harold, and Richard W. Gable, *Public Control of Economic Enterprise* (New York, 1956). Chapter 27, "Public Control for Economic Stability and Growth," deals with monetary and fiscal controls.

Committee for Economic Development, *Managing the Federal Debt* (New York, 1954). How the national debt may serve as stabilizer.

———, *Defense against Recession: Policy for Greater Economic Stability* (New York, 1954). A comprehensive program.

———, *Problems in Anti-Recession Policy* (New York, 1954).

Wernette, John P., *Financing Full Employment* (Cambridge, Mass., 1945). The best case for monetary controls.

Bach, G. L., *Federal Reserve Policy-Making* (New York, 1950).

Maxwell, J. A., *Fiscal Policy: Its Techniques and Institutional Setting* (New York, 1955).

Goldenweiser, E. A., *American Monetary Policy* (New York, 1951). A research study for the Committee for Economic Development, tracing the evolution of the Federal Reserve System.

Abbott, Charles Cortez, *The Federal Debt, Structure and Impact* (New York, 1953). A Twentieth Century Fund study.

Chase, Stuart, *Where's the Money Coming From?* (New York, 1943). A liberal view of fiscal policy.

Eccles, M. S. *Curbing Inflation through Taxation* (New York, 1944). By a former governor of the Federal Reserve Board.

Hansen, Alvin H., *Business Cycles and National Income* (New York, 1951). Deals with purchasing power.

Keynes, John Maynard, *The Means to Prosperity* (New York, 1933). By an author sometimes called the philosopher of the New Deal.

Simpson, Herbert D., *Purchasing Power and Prosperity* (Brooklyn, 1936). Stresses high-volume demand.

United States Congress, Joint Congressional Committee on the Economic Report,

Federal Tax Policy for Economic Growth and Stability (Washington, D.C., 1955).

————, *Federal Expenditure Policy for Economic Growth and Development* (Washington, D.C., 1957).

————, Senate Committee on Banking and Currency, *Federal Reserve Policy and Economic Stability, 1951-1957* (S. Rept. 2500, 85th Cong., 2d Sess., Washington, D.C., 1958).

21

THE EMPLOYMENT ACT OF 1946

Concern for economic stabilization; objectives and provisions of Employment Act; coordination; Council of Economic Advisers: organization and functions, assessment; forerunners of the Act; kinds and uses of planning; issues of public policy; improvements in Council of Economic Advisers.

Twenty years hence, perceptive Americans are likely to recognize that the Employment Act of 1946, short as it falls of its original objective,[1] was the outstanding legislative statute of the first half of the twentieth century in so far as the health of the economy is concerned. Contrary to the attitude of an earlier generation, this legislation symbolizes the belief of economic leaders in the role of government relative to business in stabilizing the economy. The intent and purpose of the act were not novel, nor does its virtue lie in the perfection of the mechanisms it created, although it has been a good law, and well administered. Rather, it epitomizes as nothing else quite has, the determination of the American people to maintain a stable economy and to demonstrate that limited economic planning under capitalism is possible and desirable.

The objective of the Employment Act is to prevent depressions by maintaining a high level of employment, production, and purchasing power. The act does not include the term *full employment*, a condition that may be presumed to exist when everybody able and willing to work can find a job. Instead, words are used that accomplish the same purpose but avoid overtones and innuendoes that many people object to: thus, reference is to governmental action "to coordinate and utilize resources for the purpose of creating and maintaining . . . conditions under which there will be afforded useful employment opportunities . . . and to promote maximum employment, maxi-

---

[1] This story is engagingly told by Stephen K. Bailey, *Congress Makes a Law* (New York, 1950).

mum production, and maximum purchasing power." This triad of goals eloquently expresses America's view of a dynamic economy at mid-century.[2]

COUNCIL OF ECONOMIC ADVISERS

To achieve its objective, the Employment Act (1) created a Council of Economic Advisers consisting of a chairman and two members appointed by the President and located in the Executive Office of the President, to keep the operation of the economy under continuous scrutiny and to make policy recommendations to the President; (2) provided the means by which the President can send to Congress his Economic Report each year, giving consistency and coherence to his other legislative recommendations; (3) and established a legislative Joint Committee on the Economic Report with members from both houses and with adequate staff, to enable Congress not only to work with the President but also to make its own independent economic analyses relative to the goals of the statute.

Indirectly, therefore, the Employment Act has also contributed to the solution of what has always been a major problem of government: to get Congress and the executive branch to work together under unified party responsibility. As nothing else has, the act recognizes the indispensable role of economics and of economists in planning the operations of public policy, thus introducing at the highest level what socialists boast is their greatest asset—the ability to look ahead to see if the economy is going to remain in balance—without in any way weakening the free-enterprise system or encouraging the aspects of authoritarian planning that democracies object to.

The Council of Economic Advisers is part of the mechanism for dealing with another problem of American government that has frequently been referred to in these pages, in that at the highest level it helps indirectly, in its capacity as adviser to the President, to coordinate the polices of other strategic public agencies such as the Federal Reserve System and the Treasury Department, so as to settle their conflicts of interest. An example of this kind of coordination is contained in the council's report for January 1955, where it is stated that prompt governmental action including monetary policies, tax reductions, and a shift from hard to easy credit before an anticipated decline had begun, created a new confidence where it was most needed, stopped the 1954 recession, and proved the ability of the Employment Act to achieve its objective.[3]

---

[2] Spelled out in Council of Economic Advisers, *Second Annual Report to the President*, Pt. II, "The Meaning of Maximum Production and Means of Attaining It."

[3] *Economic Report to the President* (Jan. 1955), p. 20; see also P. J. Strayer, "Full Employment—1954 Model," *American Economic Review*, Vol. 44 (Dec. 1944).

Organization and Functions

The Council of Economic Advisers is not a control device in the usual sense because it has no authority to issue orders or to act in behalf of the President. Nor is it a lobbying device in the service of the federal government. Rather, its job is to focus attention on economic stability and growth and to advise the President on how these goals are to be obtained. Any authority for action pursuant to the recommendations of the council is the President's and his alone.

In addition to the chairman and two members of the council itself, plus a small staff, there is an Advisory Board on Economic Growth and Stability headed by the chairman of the council and including representation from the Departments of Treasury, State, Agriculture, Commerce, Labor, and Health, Education, and Welfare; the Bureau of the Budget; the Board of Governors of the Federal Reserve System; the Export-Import Bank of Washington; and the White House Office, with members usually drawn from the undersecretary or assistant-secretary level. This group meets regularly to study and secure policy coordination at the top level of government.

In addition, there is a special staff assistant to the President on economic matters whose role is to help with specific problems that reach the White House from sources other than the CEA, but who works closely with that body. The council and the board are both also occasionally assisted by temporary task forces drawn from other agencies, including some not mentioned above, to study particular aspects of problems that enter into the larger amalgam. With the prestige of the White House behind the council, this kind of cooperation is readily forthcoming. This policy of farming out some of the work and calling on other governmental agencies as needed makes its possible for the council to keep its own staff small and expert, unhampered by the confusions that so often attend large size.

The council is more than a tool to help the President prepare his annual Economic Report to Congress, which, incidentally, is *his* report and need not follow the reasoning or recommendations of the council unless he wishes it. Additional duties of the council spelled out in the act are (1) to appraise the various activities of the federal government and to advise the President as to how they may contribute to the goals of the law, a responsibility that bears especially on the work of the Advisory Board; (2) to gather timely and authoritative information concerning economic developments and trends, both current and prospective; (3) to analyze and interpret these data in the light of the objectives of the law; (4) to submit studies relating to such data to the President; (5) to develop programs for economic growth and stability and recommend them also to the President; and (6) to make such other economic studies and recommendations as the President may request.

The functions of the Congressional Joint Committee on the Economic Report also are clearly stated in the act. The committee consists of seven members from each chamber and has statutory authority (1) to make a continuing study of matters relating to the Economic Report; (2) to study the means of coordinating legislative programs in the interest of economic stability and growth; and (3) to guide the various committees of Congress considering legislation bearing on the problems and recommendations of the Economic Report. It was thought that the CEA might overshadow the Joint Committee, but in fact, due to able leadership and a competent staff, the Joint Committee has become one of the most effective research units anywhere in the government. Drawing on outside experts who write papers and participate in panel discussions on particular topics, the staff prepares reports for Congress that carry some weight. Thus for example, by this means the Joint Committee has helped to forestall tax reductions during periods of prosperity.

Assessment of the CEA

Although the Employment Act has been in effect long enough to make possible an assessment of its effectiveness, the matter may still be approached with some caution. The reports of the council are competent and make good reading. There is no doubt that the law has focused the attention of the public, the business community, Congress, and the executive branch on over-all economic statesmanship in a manner that has never before been possible. The general level of economic activity since 1946 has been good but what part of it is due to the 1946 legislation cannot be measured. Not everyone agrees that the council's work had a direct effect on the recession of 1954.[4] In at least one instance that came to public notice, the council has been divided in its views, which is normal enough, of course, in a government agency and it has even been known to occur among economists outside of government. In addition, it is not always easy to draw a line between research on the one hand and the espousal of a particular program on the other, and this also has led to occasional criticism of the council.[5] Then there is the human and professional problem of a distinguished economist who may wish publicly to defend his ideas being in the position of an adviser pledged to anonymity. Or the President may try to sell his own legislative program to the council and get its backing instead of being content with its advice. In most cases, however, these are merely the normal difficulties incident to public life.

Of far greater significance to the nation is whether the wealth

[4] See, for example, Harold Koontz and Richard W. Gable, *Public Control of Economic Enterprise* (New York, 1956), pp. 784–791.

[5] P. J. Strayer, "The Council of Economic Advisers: Political Economy on Trial," *American Economic Review*, Vol. 40 (May 1950), pp. 144–154.

of statistics developed by the council ever gets translated into projections of economic trends, into specific forecasts of the future for policy control purposes. This clearly is where control over economic peaks and valleys is to be secured if control is to be rational and effective. It is obvious that such forecasts are sometimes made for internal consumption, but they do not frequently enough get into the Economic Reports where they could be used openly and authoritatively by Congress and the executive departments. In time, and with growing confidence in the value of the function, more economic forecasting may be forthcoming.

The Clark-Reuss bill, first introduced in 1959—and irrespective of whether it is eventually passed—indicates that public opinion is veering toward public scrutiny of price and wage changes that have long-run significance. This bill proposes an amendment to the Employment Act of 1946 on the subject of price and wage increases that threaten economic stability. According to the announced purpose of the measure, where price or wage increases affect virtually every American, as in areas where there are concentrated industries and administered prices, the executive branch shall be authorized to hold public hearings in which prices, wages, and productivity shall be fully disclosed and thoroughly discussed. These hearings would be a combination of economic study plus "pitiless publicity" and the education of the public.[6]

Congressional hearings on the Clark-Reuss bill were held by the Subcommittee on Production and Stabilization of the Senate Banking and Currency Committee in 1959 and 1960. Gerhard Colm, representing the National Planning Association, was in favor of the measure; Walter Reuther of the United Automobile Workers approved the price provisions but was skeptical about the wage features; the National Association of Manufacturers took the position that the public airing of wages and prices would have a disruptive effect on orderly marketing and distribution; and the United States Chamber of Commerce was generally antagonistic. Whether the bill would become law was uncertain. Perhaps it was no more than a straw in the wind, but it did seem to mark a deep concern with rigid prices and inflationary forces.[7]

The policy issue raised in the Clark-Reuss bill touched a vital nerve of our free American system. From the conservative standpoint the danger is that any "political" solution of the price-wage issue might lead inexorably, if not at once, to some form of official price fixing which could be the death knell of a market economy. But on the other hand, it cannot be gainsaid that study, publicity, and the accompanying sense of responsibility that informed public opinion brings to a subject are basic to democratic social functioning. As is so often the case, basic public policies are accompanied by some degree of risk.

[6] S. 2382, introduced in the 86th Cong., 1st Sess., July 14, 1959.

[7] *Hearings*, Subcommittee on Production and Stabilization, Senate Banking and Currency Committee (86th Cong., 2d Sess., 1959-1960), committee print.

The Employment Act seems thus far to have assisted the executive branch more than it has helped Congress. This is not meant to reflect on Congress and especially not on the members of the Joint Committee. As one economist remarked of the 1954 hearings, "one cannot help but be impressed by the relatively high level of economic understanding of the members of the Committee. There is still much room for improvement in this regard but in contrast to the behavior of other congressional committees the level of discussion is high." [8] Rather, the difficulties are institutional: Congressmen and their committee chairmen are busy; no specific legislation is being considered; and traditionally, studies emanating from the executive branch are less favorably considered by Congress than those originating in Congress. Former members of the Council of Economic Advisers have shown that both President Truman and President Eisenhower relied heavily on its work. In the case of Congress, the plan will probably not fully pay off until the Congressional Policy Committees of the two major parties pay more attention to the Economic Report; but there has been a good deal of progress in this direction in recent years.

FORERUNNERS OF THE EMPLOYMENT ACT

The macroeconomic approach which deals with the over-all economy and the problems of keeping it growing and in balance is now increasingly stressed as a supplement to the microeconomic approach which studies the behavior of individual firms or particular segments of the macrocosm. The extent to which the United States has pioneered in this area is seldom fully realized, and consequently some of the landmarks in this development may be mentioned, with emphasis on those that were the immediate forerunners of and contributors to the Employment Act of 1946:

Early Mercantilist Doctrines

Alexander Hamilton's *Report on Manufactures* in 1791 and Henry Clay's "American System" of 1820 stressed the over-all development of industry and the close collaboration between business and government that would be necessary in the future growth of the nation.

Aid to Infant Industries

Our national policy has always emphasized assistance to new industries, such as the gift of great tracts of public lands to transcontinental railways immediately following the Civil War and the more

[8] Strayer, "Full Employment—1954 Model," *American Economic Review,* Vol. 44, p. 891.

recent subsidies to airlines, offshore shipping, and the private development of atomic energy.

Scientific Management Movement

American business corporations had been greatly influenced by Taylorism at the turn of the twentieth century, and they have pioneered in the techniques and processes of scientific management, which is a main reason for the pre-eminence of American business during the past few generations.[9] Scientific management stresses business planning and forecasting, beginning with the smallest units of enterprise and thence progressing to the national and even the international economy. Today Soviet Russia also has adopted the precepts of scientific management and acknowledges its debt to Frederick Taylor and his disciples. Since the close of World War II, both political parties in Great Britain have turned increasingly to American scientific management as the key to industrial modernization and efficiency; so also have the underdeveloped nations receiving technical assistance under the United Nations and Point Four programs. In this country, as Peter Drucker points out,[10] the greatest challenge to American corporation executives in the second half of the twentieth century is to institutionalize the processes of long-range planning and forecasting, not for five and ten years ahead but for even longer periods.

Planning Organizations

City planning has long been emphasized in the United States, as in Philadelphia when it was settled, Major L'Enfant's plan for Washington, D.C., and Joseph Smith's plan for "the City of Zion," which is Salt Lake City. Today most major cities and many smaller ones have increasingly active municipal planning boards and commissions. Modern governmental planning began with the work of the Bureau of Municipal Research in New York City in 1906 and was followed by the Taft Commission on Economy and Efficiency in 1912, the Budget and Accounting Act of 1921, the Reorganization Act of 1939, and the more recent Hoover Commission reports of 1949 and 1955, to the point where the term *planning* has almost ceased to be an indecent word in public parlance.

Even more significant in their long-run effect are the associations of professional planners who help prepare both economic and governmental plans, with the former increasingly stressed. Among such organiza-

---

[9] See, for example, Harlow S. Person, "On Planning," *Journal* of the Society for the Advancement of Management (Nov. 1936), pp. 143–149; "Scientific Management and Economic Planning," *Bulletin of the Taylor Society* (Dec. 1932), pp. 204–228; and Harlow S. Person (ed.), *Scientific Management and American Industry* (New York, 1929).

[10] Peter Drucker, *The Practice of Management* (New York, 1954).

tions, the *National Planning Association* is directed by outstanding business, labor, and agricultural leaders, and so is the *Conference on Economic Progress*. The *American Society of Planning Officials* emphasizes governmental planning. The *American Institute of Planners* and the *American Planning and Civic Association* stress city and resource planning. The *National Bureau of Economic Research* studies national income and economic growth.[11] The *Committee for Economic Development*, composed of 150 leading businessmen and educators, studies and reports on all aspects of growth and stability in the American economy.

Planning under the NRA

As explained in the preceding chapter, a trade association type of national planning under the National Recovery Administration, abortive though it proved to be, nevertheless encouraged later planning activities on the part of government to secure a rational control of economic activity.

National Resources Planning Board

Perhaps the most instructive experience, however, was the program of the National Resources Planning Board, created by executive order early in the New Deal in 1934 and extinguished in 1943. Although several times renamed during its nine years of existence, its organization and procedures followed a rather stable pattern. The President designated a small board of three to five members, consisting of engineers, industrialists, and social scientists, and the board itself then appointed a chief executive officer and a small staff. Research and planning projects were farmed out to existing federal agencies, and experts from various professional fields were drawn in on a consulting basis as the occasion required. Since the annual budget was small, by comparison the output was large and the board's program and operations were flexible and dynamic.

At first the NRPB confined itself to the study of physical resources—water, land, forests, minerals, and the like—as well as public-works programing, expenditures, and administration. But later its studies were broadened to include economic, social, and human problems on the assumption that physical, social, and human resources are all related. A study was made of population, for example, and one of the structure of the American economy that is now a classic. The board also investigated the problems of large metropolitan centers and regional areas. In fact, in a remarkably short time the NRPB built up a rather complete inventory of American resources, the

---

[11] See three of their special studies, for example, entitled respectively *Capital Formation and Economic Growth, Policies to Combat Depression,* and *Personal Income during Business Cycles,* all published by the Princeton University Press.

problems involved, and the solutions possible. These reports went to the President, to Congress, to federal and other governmental agencies, and to the interested public. The NRPB also stimulated and guided the development of regional, state, county, and local planning agencies; indeed, the country seemed to be moving rather quickly in the direction of voluntary planning in which all levels of government participated.

In 1940 President Roosevelt made the board a subdivision of the Executive Office of the President and shortly thereafter asked Congress to give it a permanent statutory base, but Congress refused and in 1943, for lack of funds, the agency was allowed to lapse.

The traditional jealousy between the executive and legislative departments of government is one reason for the demise of the NRPB. During Congressional debate on the President's proposal, for example, a member of the opposition party argued that the board "has interfered with the regular-established functions and agencies of this government at every opportunity. It has held back proper legislation by improper and unauthorized methods. It has interfered without any authority whatever with the orderly consideration of legislation by committees of Congress. . . ." [12] Although such charges credited the NRPB with more influence than it ever possessed and attributed to it motives not supported by the record, they do call attention to a major difficulty in any attempt to organize a planning function in a government where cooperation between the legislative and executive branches is not assured.

A member of the President's own party expressed a more favorable view: "No other federal agency," he said, "was equipped to give technical advice and support to state and local public-works planning. We should support a program that has no other object than to bring about economy and reduce waste in city, state, and national programs of public construction and development." [13] As between these two opinions and despite the obvious criticisms that can normally be leveled at a new undertaking, it seems fair to say that the NRPB did in fact discharge a useful, even an indispensable function, that it served the public interest, and that the studies it produced are basic in many professional libraries even twenty years after they were made.

Industrial Mobilization in World War II

The experience from which this nation learned the most about macroeconomic planning, however, occurred during World War II when, as never before in our history, the economy was tightly controlled. The processes of a peacetime economy simply cannot be depended on to meet the needs of a wartime economy. It is an inescapable truth, says Clinton Rossiter, that "No form of govern-

---

[12] Quoted in George B. Galloway (ed.), *Planning for America* (New York, 1941), p. 76.

[13] *Ibid.,* p. 77.

ment can survive that excludes dictatorship when the life of the nation is at stake." [14] And although the degree of centralized control was not so great in this country as in the case of some of our allies, the decisions as to what should be produced, who should produce it, and to whom it could be sold were government decisions; prices and wages also were controlled, and even the movement of labor from plant to plant, from industry to industry, and from region to region was required to fall into a unified pattern. [15]

This four-year experience, got through with maximum voluntary cooperation and minimum regimentation, and with more inconvenience than serious sacrifice and loss of liberty to the American people, [16] created the confidence that economic stability and growth can in fact be democratically controlled and led directly and almost inescapably into the Employment Act of 1946.

THE PLANNING CONTROVERSY AND THE FUTURE

Despite the extent to which the United States has pioneered in private planning and more recently has experimented in some forms of public planning, not much progress was made in rationally resolving the issue until attention had been shifted from the "bad" word, *planning*, to the "good" word, *stabilization*. This is perhaps the chief reason that the Employment Act, emphasizing stabilization and growth, has been so warmly received by all shades of political opinion. In the minds of many people, planning connotes socialism, and especially communism, and hence it is hard to secure dispassionate thinking.

It is apparent, however, that if any of the major economic problems discussed in this book are to be solved, then the substance of what is involved in planning must be mastered, even though we frown on the word itself. Even more must we plan carefully and skillfully to save and strengthen the free-enterprise system, because freedom must be planned at least to the extent that dictatorship is planned. [17]

In any discussion of planning and stabilization, the questions that most intelligent people are concerned with are these: What exactly is entailed in planning? Can there be partial planning or must it be complete? Can planning be democratically pursued and

[14] Clinton L. Rossiter, *Constitutional Dictatorship—Crisis Government in the Modern Democracies* (Princeton, N.J., 1948), p. vii.

[15] See an excellent chapter entitled "The National-security Crisis of the 1940's" in George A. Steiner, *Government's Role in Economic Life* (New York, 1953), pp. 192–210.

[16] Statement of chairman of the War Production Board, final report, *Wartime Production Achievement and the Reconversion Outlook* (Washington, D.C., 1945), p. 1.

[17] No writer has made this point better than Henry Simons in his book, *Economic Policy for a Free Society* (Chicago, 1948), in which he outlines a positive program for laissez faire.

controlled? Does it strengthen or weaken the free-enterprise system?

In its basic sense, planning is what the French call *prévoyance,* or looking ahead; it is the process of devising a course of action. The five steps normally involved are (1) research and analysis to understand the problem; (2) the determination of objectives; (3) the discovery of alternative solutions; (4) decision-making involving the formulation of policies; and finally (5), the execution of the plan, which includes such functions as organization, work scheduling, and procedures. Thus planning is similar to the formulation of public policy and legislation, for both involve the same steps. Planning is the antithesis of improvising; planning is systematic forethought plus corrective hindsight. Entailing decision and action, planning is a dynamic concept.[18]

Planning is also a neutral concept, being a technique or a tool to a particular end and never the end itself. Thus planning may be used for any purpose, good or bad, simple or complex, democratic or authoritarian. "The fundamental nature of planning," says the dictionary, "may range from the most democratic to the most authoritarian." There is nothing intrinsic in planning that requires, or even implies, that it *must* be employed in an authoritarian manner, or that omnipotence is involved, or that it may not be successfully integrated with the free-enterprise system. It all depends on how much planning is undertaken, what kind it is, by whom it is controlled, and to what end.

Economic Planning

Economic planning is the determination of goals, priorities, and solutions either for parts of the economy or for the whole of it. If economic planning involves the whole economy through all five steps outlined above, then it becomes national economic planning of a kind usually identified with socialism. But if only part of the economy is involved, then planning is only partial and of the kind usually practiced in a democracy. Planning may be only partial, furthermore, even when thinking is in macroeconomic terms (as in the case of the Council of Economic Advisers), when only the first three of the five steps outlined above are taken: analysis of problems, suggestion of goals, and identification of alternative solutions.

As early as 1939, John Maurice Clark saw what was involved in planning as Americans envisage it when he remarked that the kind of planning with which we are mainly concerned "has one dominant purpose: to eliminate undesirable fluctuations of industrial activity and to make reasonably full use of our powers of production to support an adequate standard of living, on a sound and enduring basis." Professor Clark calls this kind *social-liberal* planning as contrasted with the socialist

---

[18] Galloway, *op. cit.,* pp. 5–6.

or fascist variety. Planning, he says, "is better than improvisation, and integral designing better than pressure-group politics." [19]

The differences between various types of planning, however, are not so much between limited and comprehensive planning as between comprehensive *production* planning (socialist) on the one hand, and comprehensive *strategic* planning (liberal) on the other, the second of which stresses such elements as fiscal policy, antitrust policy, distribution of income, and the like. When this kind of planning is successful, it strengthens free enterprise because power remains distributed rather than concentrated at one point where all major decisions are made, and in consequence government has less reason to interfere with economic arrangements.

Common experience indicates, furthermore, that it is possible to plan one part of an operation and not another, or one part of the economy and not another. Those who hold to the empirical, middle-of-the-road position on planning would plan what obviously needs to be planned for the present and the foreseeable future, but would put off the question of whether new tensions will require additional planning later on.

The principle involved here is probably as important as any in the whole range of public policy: if a problem can be anticipated sufficiently far in advance to avoid the accumulation of dangerous tensions, and if a workable plan can be evolved and pursued in order to avoid those tensions, then government can more quickly withdraw from the scene when the matter is under control, and interference will be far less and much less permanent than if the tensions had been allowed to backfire, in which case revolutionary measures are often necessary. In 1929, for example, no one could predict what was happening, the havoc was great, and the remedies were experimental and sometimes inconsistent; but in the recessions of 1954 and 1958 it was pretty clearly seen what threatened the economy and preventive measures were taken.

It is true, of course, that what happens in one segment of the economy affects many others, if not all, but it is not for that reason necessary to conclude that to plan one area where there is trouble means that the entire economy must eventually be planned. On the contrary, so long as the makers of public policy are *aware* of these interconnections, they can legislate intelligently concerning any one area without touching others to more than a minimum extent. Thus, strategic planning means understanding interconnections between problem areas as well as the cause-and-effect relationships of preventive measures applicable to a single area.

Democratic Planning and Free Enterprise

Planning is democratic when widespread participation on a voluntary basis is provided for, as contrasted with authoritarian planning where

[19] John M. Clark, *Social Control of Business* (New York, 2d ed., 1939), pp. 455–456, 471.

orders are issued from above, without consultation. However, even in democratic governments, a general framework of organization for planning, sustained by a degree of coercive power, is necessary. The NRA program of the New Deal, designed to cope with a dire emergency and to enlist industry-labor cooperation, resulted in a sort of syndicalist solution: it probably went too far toward pressure-group rule and hence encouraged monopolistic practices. The National Resources Board, also during the New Deal period, laid a solid foundation for planning in its research but was weak in instrumentation. During World War II, although industry and labor representation were central features in the operation of the war-production program, their role was by no means wholly voluntary: conversion by industry to war goods was pushed through under threat of the commandeering powers of the government and monetary power was centralized in the Federal Reserve Board. Goods were rationed and prices in certain areas were controlled. And in the operation of the Employment Act, as we have seen, although much depends on the education of management, labor, and agricultural leadership as to what the economic necessities at the time and in the foreseeable future seem to require, in the final analysis Congress and the President may invoke the legislative and enforcement powers of the Constitution.

Where the free-enterprise system is concerned, planning is useful, even indispensable in many ways, but it is objectionable if it results in price fixing by administrative decree instead of relying on the forces of the market. The importance of prices has been stated many times but the following quotation sets forth the essentials:

> Every decision with regard to the expansion or contraction of production, the adjustment of one factor of production to another, and so forth must be made in terms of prices, of various products and various factors; and since prices are valid guides to sound decisions only insofar as they are genuine prices, genuinely arrived at in the free higgling of the market, it follows that a free market—that is to say, the economy of free private enterprise—is the condition without which industry cannot be administered.[20]

Price fixing by administrative decree may be by government—and usually this is necessary to some extent in time of war—or it may be by private concerns acting in collusion. The more private monopoly is allowed to fix prices in this manner, the more is government called on to interfere, in some form of antitrust action; and every interference involves a degree of planning. Thus, planning aimed at fixing prices in the private area of the economy is doubly harmful: it frustrates the forces of the free market with regard to prices, and it stimulates additional planning and interference on the part of government. The inescapable conclusion, therefore, is that only as government regulation succeeds in avoiding undue

---

[20] C. E. Ayres, "The Significance of Economic Planning," in Seba Eldridge (ed.), *Development of Collective Enterprise* (Lawrence, Kan., 1943), p. 471.

concentrations of private economic power can the nation avoid in the long run a condition in which comprehensive public planning in every area, including prices, becomes necessary. The corollary is that the best planning is preventive planning, deliberate and conscious planning to maintain and strengthen the free-enterprise system.

It may be asked, finally, whether planning increases regimentation. The answer seems to be that it may, and frequently does, but not inevitably so. If the right kind of planning is taken soon enough, the effect may even be to increase freedom rather than to diminish it. No one has explained this more convincingly than Harlow S. Person,[21] a pioneer in the scientific management movement, who argued that planning reduces regimentation when it eleminates some of the uncertainties in a particular situation and removes tensions due to neglect. Moreover, since planning involves getting the facts and analyzing the choice of alternatives, a plan is more likely than lack of plan to promote freedom, because lack of plan often leads to blind and repressive measures based on desperation or the idea of punishment for past mistakes, where in fact such punishment does not fit the crime and there may not even have been a crime in the first place. The New Deal, for example, was not always successful in avoiding this type of planless activity, especially at the outset.

Planning for freedom enables government more intelligently to impose a minimum of proper restraints. "The frequent choice of doing nothing," says one authority on planning, "is one of the important consequences of planning because planning makes possible a degree of *laissez faire* which *laissez faire* alone has never accomplished." [22] In this sense, planning becomes the equivalent of economic intelligence.

Improving Economic Planning in the United States

Although most writers nowadays are optimistic as to the possibility of avoiding major depressions, and although the Employment Act of 1946 is commonly favored, it is pretty generally agreed that due to our system of divided governmental powers, failure to plan adequately and to secure prompt and energetic action from the executive department constitute the greatest weaknesses that can be foreseen.

Until the Council of Economic Advisers can undertake and publish both short-range and long-range economic forecasts that will be understood by those in a position to make decisions and to provide prompt and effective preventive measures, we cannot say that the capstone of defense against depression has been provided. The Employment Act is a good start but ways must be found to strengthen its role by legislation and improved internal procedures. A more sympathetic attitude toward what is involved in economic planning might be the key to such a development. Reliable forecasting is not a luxury we can acquire or get along without

---

[21] Person, "On Planning," *op. cit.*   [22] Galloway, *op. cit.*, pp. 6–7.

as we choose; under modern conditions, such forecasting is imperative.

The second requirement, pacing the first, is that the President should have greater discretion to act in case a recession threatens, because Congress is slow-moving and speed may be of the essence in checking the spread of deflation. Such an expanded discretionary power should cover taxes and government expenditures, public-works programs, and government procurement and could be added to the 1946 law by amendment. The fact that the Employment Act calls for equal cooperation from both the legislative and the executive branches might dispose Congress to grant these additional powers, although it is traditionally reluctant, of course, to do anything of the kind. Another favorable factor is that like economists, business leaders also are far more concerned with stability than they were a generation ago, and the influence of the business community on Congress is always a direct one.

The recession of 1958 caused some further thinking in the matter of top responsibility in the federal government for economic stabilization. At the suggestion of the Secretary of the Treasury, the President began meeting at irregular intervals with a small group composed of the chairman of the Board of Governors of the Federal Reserve System, the Secretary of the Treasury, the chairman of the Council of Economic Advisers, and the special assistant for economic matters in the White House Office. This was a small summit group and its base was correspondingly narrow. As an improvement, it was proposed that the weekly meetings of the CEA's Advisory Board on Economic Growth and Stability be made preparatory sessions for the more widely spaced meetings of the smaller group around the President. One advantage of this arrangement is that both groups include representation from the Federal Reserve System, an agency that traditionally is almost aggressively independent of political direction by the White House. Then in 1959 the report of the Rockefeller Brothers Fund went a step further and suggested that the smaller group be enlarged to include representation from the regular executive departments concerned especially with foreign affairs and the human aspects of the economy on the ground that "the implications of stability are broader than fiscal and monetary considerations and should benefit from the counsel of those who have direct responsibility for such interests." The need, continued this report, is for a broadened group to advise on stabilization policy, either anti-recession or anti-inflationary as seems appropriate.[23]

Supplementary Reading

Burns, Arthur F., *Prosperity without Inflation* (New York, 1957). By a former chairman of the Council of Economic Advisers.

[23] Rockefeller Brothers Fund, Inc., *The Challenge to America: Its Economic and Social Aspects* (New York, Apr. 20, 1958).

————, *The Frontiers of Economic Knowledge* (Princeton, N.J., 1954). The role of government in economic stability.

American Assembly, *Wages, Prices, Profits, and Productivity* (New York, 1958).

————, *U. S. Monetary Policy* (New York, 1959).

United States Congress, Joint Economic Committee Report on *Employment, Growth, and Price Levels,* Joint Committee Print (86th Cong., 1st Sess., Dec. 24, 1959).

Colm, Gerhard (ed.), *The Employment Act, Past and Future* (Washington, D.C., National Planning Association, 1956).

Jacoby, Neil H., *Can Prosperity Be Sustained?* (New York, 1956). By a former member of the Council of Economic Advisers.

National Bureau of Economic Research, *Policies to Combat Depression* (Princeton, N.J., 1956). Fourteen economists examine built-in stabilizers.

Blough, Roy, "Political and Administrative Requisites for Achieving Economic Stability," *American Economic Review,* Vol. 40 (May 1950), pp. 165–178. By another former member of the Council of Economic Advisers.

Bailey, Stephen K., *Congress Makes a Law* (New York, 1950). The full story of the passage of the Employment Act of 1946.

Gross, Bertram M., and J. P. Lewis, "The President's Economic Staff during the Truman Administration," *American Political Science Review,* Vol. 48 (Mar. 1954), pp. 114–130. Participant-observers of the 1946 legislation.

Joint Committee on the Economic Report, *Potential Economic Growth of the United States during the Next Decade* (Washington, D.C., 1954). Prepared by the joint Congressional committee.

Strayer, Paul J., "The Council of Economic Advisers: Political Economy on Trial," *American Economic Review,* Vol. 40 (May 1952), pp. 138–146.

————, "Full Employment—1954 Model," *American Economic Review,* Vol. 44 (Dec. 1954), pp. 884–893. A critical appraisal.

Bach, G. L., "Economic Requisites for Economic Stability," *American Economic Review,* Vol. 40 (May 1950), pp. 155–164. The basic considerations involved.

Hansen, Alvin H., *Economic Policy and Full Employment* (New York, 1947). Emphasizes the role of government.

Conference on Economic Progress, *Toward Full Employment and Full Production* (pamphlet, Washington, 1954). How to end our national economic deficits.

Dahl, Robert A., and Charles E. Lindblom, *Politics, Economics, and Welfare* (New York, 1953). Role of government as stabilizer and planner.

Clark, Colin, *The Conditions of Economic Progress* (London, Macmillan, 2d ed., 1951). A human-welfare approach.

Rosenfarb, Joseph, *Freedom and the Administrative State* (New York, 1948). Planning without violence to the free-enterprise system.

Landauer, Carl, *The Theory of National Economic Planning* (Berkeley, Calif., 1947). Deals with full-scale planning.

Galloway, George B. (ed.), *Planning for America* (New York, 1941). Limited planning is emphasized.

Harris, Seymour E., *Economic Planning* (New York, 1949). By a Harvard economist.

Lewis, W. Arthur, *The Principles of Economic Planning* (Washington, D.C., 1951). Shows an awareness of the governmental difficulties.

Merriam, Charles E., "The National Resources Planning Board," *American Political Science Review,* Vol. 38 (Oct. 1944). The story of the NRPB by one who was long a member of the Board.

Nourse, Edwin G., *Economics in the Public Service* (New York, 1953). By a former member of the Council of Economic Advisers.

Mises, Ludwig von, *Planning for Freedom* (New York, 1945). A view opposed to economic planning.

Hayek, Frederick A., *The Road to Serfdom* (Chicago, 1945). Planning leads to serfdom.

Millett, John D., *The Process and Organization of Government Planning* (New York, 1947). Stresses process.

Baldwin, C. D., *Economic Planning—Its Aims and Implications* (Urbana, Ill., 1942). Stresses economic analysis.

Simons, Henry C., *Economic Policy for a Free Society* (Chicago, 1948). A positive program for laissez faire.

Council of Economic Advisers, *Report to the President* (semiannual).

President of the United States, *Economic Report of the President* (annual).

22

SOCIAL SECURITY

Social security as antidepression measure; public welfare programs; social insurance: issues of public policy, operation and appraisal of old-age and survivors' insurance, operation and appraisal of unemployment compensation; conclusions relative to social insurance; extensions of the welfare state; veterans' programs; national health insurance.

The Social Security Act of 1935, with later extensions, constitutes one of the single most important safeguards against recurring depressions in the business-government relationship.[1] Regular payments made to insured individuals when they become temporarily unemployed, when they reach retirement age, or when they are chronically ill or permanently handicapped help maintain a purchasing power that is a mainstay of economic stability. If extended far enough, of course, the social security philosophy leads into the concept of the welfare state, which in its extreme form means the state taking care of people in an expanding area of human needs instead of people taking care of themselves. This concept is a modern battlefield of public policy, two of the major contestants being organized veterans seeking government benefits and organized doctors seeking to ward off what they refer to as "socialized medicine." In addition to the insurance aspects of social security, therefore, the present chapter also explores these ancilliary implications of the social security program.

As of 1960, the over-all picture of welfare activities looked like this:

1. Social security:

Old-age and survivors' insurance

Public assistance for four groups of needy persons: those sixty-five years old and over (some medical care now included), the blind, dependent children, and disabled persons — In the Department of Health, Education, and Welfare

Maternal and child welfare

Unemployment compensation, in the Department of Labor

---

[1] John M. Clark, with his customary clairvoyance, said as early as 1939 that "this act . . . may take rank as the soundest in principle and the most enduring contribution of the New Deal to our economic structure." *Social Control of Business* (New York, rev. ed., 1939), p. 442.

2. Security for special groups:
   Veterans, under the Veterans Administration
   Railroad workers, under the Railroad Retirement Board
   Federal employees' retirement, under the Civil Service Commission
3. Public health and medical programs, primarily in the Department of Health, Education, and Welfare and in the Veterans Administration
4. Public housing, urban renewal, and distressed-area aid
5. State and local welfare programs too numerous to mention

In this listing, the old-age and survivors' insurance program under the first heading and all of those under the second heading are financed through federal taxes and wholly administered by the federal government. With the exception of state and local programs, most of the other activities are federal aid programs in that the states share in the financing and bear the principal burden of administration under some degree of federal supervision as to standards, procedures, civil service, and the like. Finally, state and local programs are wholly financed and administered at those levels. Thus, most welfare functions are still highly decentralized.

SOCIAL SECURITY PROGRAMS

The Social Security Act of 1935 established a Social Security Board of three members responsible for administering three major programs: old-age and survivors' insurance, unemployment compensation (insurance), and public assistance. At the end of World War II unemployment compensation was transferred to the Department of Labor and combined with the United States Employment Service to form the Bureau of Employment Security in that department. And when the Federal Security Agency became the Department of Health, Education, and Welfare in 1953, the two remaining social security functions plus the Children's Bureau and the Bureau of Federal Credit Unions taken from other departments, were combined under the Commissioner of Social Security so that these four programs are now administered as a coordinated unit within the new department.

It is the insurance programs in this amalgam that are of chief concern in a study of business and government because where all social security programs help to maintain purchasing power at the lower levels, the insurance programs also involve taxation, and in addition, impinge on the private insurance business.

The issues of public policy are these: Do the insurance plans really deserve to be called insurance or are they, in part, at least, a kind of a subsidy or relief payment? Do they offer adequate financial protection to the individual? If overextended, might they not adversely affect the economy? Will they constitute an increasingly heavy financial burden on the business community? Is the insurance business, in effect, being socialized? And finally, should the social security program be broadened in scope and coverage, as is the case in some other nations, or is the traditional American idea of spiritual and individual independence still a valid one? In other words, should government refrain from interfering in areas that concern the independence of the human spirit, and leave the question of individual welfare up to the family and to voluntary groups, as was largely the case prior to 1932, or does the complexity and interdependence of a modern technological society weaken the principle of individual responsibility? The social security program inaugurated in 1935 was predicated on the assumption that it does, and the principle is likely to be still further weakened as medical care, especially in chronic cases and for the aged, becomes more of an economic problem.

Old-age and Survivors' Insurance

Governmental social insurance was first emphasized in Germany: against sickness in 1883, accidents in 1885, and old age in 1889. In England, an Old Age Pension Act was passed in 1908. By 1950, more than forty nations were providing social security benefits of some kind, including in some cases unemployment insurance, and ten years later the number had risen to 78. In the United States, the first permanent old-age pension law was passed in Alaska in 1923; six years later nine states had joined in the movement and by 1938, under the impetus of the Social Security Act of 1935, every state had an old-age pension law as part of a national system of old-age benefits for certain employees and self-employed persons.

Under this insurance scheme, reduced benefits are available to eligible retired women of sixty-two years of age and full benefits if they retire at sixty-five; full benefits are also paid to eligible widows at sixty-two and to all other eligible workers on retirement at sixty-five, to their wives if they are over sixty-five and not otherwise covered, to their dependent children if under eighteen (and beyond that if they are handicapped), to the widows and children of covered workers, and to disabled persons at the age of fifty. To show the size of this part of the program by 1960, some 59 million workers and their families were covered, constituting 87 percent of the total working force; old-age insurance trust funds were more than $22 billion; contributions (taxes) amounted to $9.6 billion and benefits to $10.2 billion; and the whole operation involved the biggest bookkeeping operation in the world.

Old-age benefits are financed by contributions from workers, from employers, and from self-employed persons. Currently, employers and employees each pay a tax on all wages and salaries up to $4,800 a year at a rate scheduled to rise progressively from 3 percent in 1960 to 4.5 percent in 1969. For the self-employed the rate is somewhat higher. Benefits have increased several times since the program commenced, a tendency that disturbs those who are actuarially minded. Currently, the minimum benefit for one individual is $33 a month and the family maximum is $254. In 1950 there were only 3 million persons drawing benefits, by 1956 there were more than 8 million, and in 1960 more than 13.7 million. Highly speculative estimates for the year 2000 place the cost of the program at from $20 billion to $24 billion annually, with as many as 36 million persons drawing benefits in a single year.[2]

These huge funds are collected by the Treasury Department and covered into the Old-Age and Survivors' Trust Fund and the Disability Insurance Trust Fund where they are invested in interest-bearing obligations of the federal government or in securities with interest and principal guaranteed by the federal government.

In each election year since 1950 the law has been amended and invariably broadened as to coverage; it might almost be said that there has been open season on social security in every session of Congress. There was a major revision in 1954, however, when coverage was extended to some 10 million persons not previously eligible for benefits (including farmers, farm and domestic workers, ministers and members of religious orders, and some self-employed persons) and the size of benefit payments also was increased. Legislation in 1956 reduced the eligibility age for women, provided for early benefits for disabled persons, and brought additional groups under the act, including military personnel. The main groups still uncovered are federal civilian employees under a retirement system, doctors of medicine, and employees of state and local governments and nonprofit organizations that have not come into the system voluntarily. The chances are that within a few years the system will have become nearly universal, although certain groups of workers, such as transients, present special problems.

From the standpoint of internal administration, it is generally agreed that in organizing and operating this vastly complicated program the federal government has done a highly commendable job. The program is administered through 580 district offices located throughout the United States and its territories. In Baltimore, separate accounts are largely electronically maintained for the 90 or so million people who are already part of the system or who have wage credits toward eligibility. It may be noted here, furthermore, that in its social insurance and veterans' insurance schemes, the federal government administers the largest insurance programs in the world, and they are constantly becoming larger. At no point in this study, perhaps, is the changing character of government activity more clearly discernible.

Criticisms of the Program

Major criticisms of the old-age and survivors' insurance program center chiefly on policy, some of it administrative and some legislative. For example, maximum payments of $200 a month are now available for

[2] Harold Koontz and Richard W. Gable, *Public Control of Economic Enterprise* (New York, 1956), p. 539.

a retired couple, but with the shrinking value of the dollar this is hardly adequate; in addition few people qualify for maximum benefits. Even after the liberalizing amendments of 1954 and later, average monthly payments for a retired couple in 1957 were only $106, which clearly is too little.

Because the average benefit is so small, corporation, labor union, and private pension plans have multiplied, resulting in a complicated and confused situation for employers, for employees, and for the nation. Thus today it is not unusual for a man to have military, labor union, corporation, individual, government employee, and social security pension rights. In fact, the only way a person in the higher income brackets can hope to retire on a satisfactory basis is to have a number of such strings to his bow, and the question may be asked, is this desirable or even necessary? Furthermore, a person entering the social insurance system late in life, as was possible when it was still new, nevertheless receives maximum benefits at retirement, which constitutes a real bonanza for him. But as time goes on, most people enter the system early in their work experience and may have to contribute from their wages for from forty-five to fifty years with the prospect of no greater returns at the end than those who paid out less because they entered later. And as has been suggested, the political expedient is to make the benefits increasingly attractive, but this only intensifies the financial burden of the program.

Another criticism is that when the federal government puts income from insurance contributions into government securities, it is not really setting up a separate trust fund in the actuarial sense usual in the operations of private insurance companies. In the end, old-age and survivors' insurance must always be paid out of the total revenues of the federal government and they can only be secured out of the earnings of the economy. The inescapable conclusion, therefore, is that the readiness of the government to pay (leaving aside the legal and moral duty to pay, which is incontestable) depends on the soundness of the national economy. Even when the total payroll tax gets up to 9 percent (4.5 percent each for employers and employees), it seems likely that the total take might still be less than the amount needed for annual benefits, and the deficit will have to be made up from general revenues. Although a great deal of mass purchasing power will be generated, there will also be a heavy financial burden on productive enterprise. The proper balance between these two considerations is the most important economic issue in the old-age insurance program.

Also in the financial picture is the fact that although the Social Security Act set up financial reserves modeled on those of private insurance companies, this basis has been altered so that today the arrangement is a compromise between a reserve and a pay-as-you-go program. Furthermore, although the current reserve of $19 billion seems large, it falls short of what a private insurance company would be obliged to provide for a similar undertaking. It is true, of course, that there are many unknowns in the picture, such as how many people will automatically retire at sixty-five, in addition to which, government insurance plans are characteristically less conservative than private plans. Inevitably, therefore, the old-age insurance plan must continue to feel its way for some years to come. Meanwhile, the nation will have to rely on the unremitting attention of economists and financial leaders to prevent outright political decisions that could result in serious financial crises at some time in the future.

Unemployment Compensation

As a bookkeeping transaction extending over a much shorter period than old-age insurance, fewer financial issues are involved in unemployment insurance, although it is an ambitious scheme and not devoid of difficulties. Its great virtue, of course, is that loss of employment to individuals or to large groups of workers, followed by a quick recovery of purchasing power, has an immediate and beneficial effect on the blood stream of the economy. Hence, where old-age insurance promotes long-range economic stability, unemployment insurance reduces short-range economic fluctuations.

Compulsory unemployment insurance as provided for in the Social Security Act of 1935 now covers more than 42 million workers, which means more than two thirds of all nonfarm employees. The central idea is to provide workers with cash payments to tide them over during periods of temporary unemployment irrespective of whether the reason for their unemployment is general, seasonal, technological, or due to some other cause. The one requirement is that the applicant shall satisfy the local Bureau of Employment Security that he has unsuccessfully sought other employment in the skill for which he is trained. A worker on strike is not eligible for benefits but a person unemployed for some other reason is not required to accept a job offered as a result of a strike, lockout, or some other labor dispute; or if a condition of employment is that he join, resign from, or refrain from joining a bona fide labor organization. Thus an outside worker may not be denied benefits for refusing to engage in strike-breaking.

Like old-age insurance, unemployment compensation coverage also was considerably extended in 1954 to include employees of firms having a minimum of four workers during twenty weeks in each year (the original provision was for a minimum of eight workers during twenty weeks), as well as all civilian employees of the federal government. Railroad workers are covered by a special national program. Again like old-age insurance, coverage tends to become wider all the time, the principal exceptions at present being farm workers, local and state government employees, domestic servants, the self-employed, employees working for firms that hire fewer than four workers during twenty weeks in each year, and a few others.

From the administrative standpoint, unemployment compensation is interesting as a study in federalism. First, the law was drawn in such a way that all the states were politely coerced into the system by the provision that a credit of 90 percent of the payroll tax would be allowed to employers in states having unemployment compensation laws following the federal pattern, an offer that brought the states into the system in a hurry. The procedure is interesting: contributions from employers under state law are deposited in special trust funds in the federal Treasury; each state has a separate account like an individual bank account; payments are made from this state account; out of the 10 percent retained by the federal government, grants are made for administrative expenses to the states without any matching requirements, but only as long as they live up to federal standards concerning civil service and the like; unemployment benefits are then paid through public employment offices in the states that meet these minimum standards; and except for these minimum standards the states are free to decide what workers shall be covered, the size of benefit payments, and the rate of the payroll tax beyond a certain point. Thus, the federal government sets the standards, collects the funds, and acts as banker, but the states actually administer the program and carry on all face-to-face relationships with the individual.

At present, employers under the unemployment compensation plan pay a tax of 3 percent of their payrolls on individual wages and salaries up to $3,000 a year, but the rate is reduced if an employer also contributes to an approved state unemployment insurance scheme. All states levy a payroll tax on employers and a few also tax employees, but this practice is apparently on the way out. Benefits vary among states and there is usually a waiting period of about a week during which the applicant must be physically able and willing to work. After that he receives weekly payments for a period of about twenty-six weeks in an amount based on average earnings over a base period, the present weekly average ranging up to $40 in a third of the states.

In 1958, which, it will be recalled, was a recession year, 6 million jobless workers received some $2.8 billion in unemployment insurance benefits. During this period, 1.6 million workers exhausted their regular benefit rights before the recession ended and Congress passed the Temporary Unemployment Compensation Act to provide for emergency benefits. By mid-1959, aggregate reserve funds for unemployment compensation totaled nearly $6.7 billion.

Criticisms of the Plan

Criticisms of unemployment compensation are different from those of old-age insurance but they are none the less definite: First of all, should unemployment compensation be federally or state administered? This was a major issue when the law was being planned and it is still a live one. Those who favor a wholly federal program note the uneven arrangements from state to state, contend that workers moving about the country should find the same benefits everywhere, that some state systems are weak and could be improved under federal responsibility, that spoils politics are sometimes marked, that as long as the states receive administrative expenses from Washington there is less incentive to efficiency than under a unified program, and that a unified system could be made more nearly to conform to a bona-fide insurance plan. But there are equally powerful considerations opposing this viewpoint: Thus, it is contended, the system is reasonably well administered now, state enforcement allows for regional differences in employment standards, diversity encourages experimentation and improvement, the federal government already has enough to do without adding to its administrative burdens, a certain amount of Congressional patronage is preferable to a civil service isolated from the stream of life, and federal aid is a desirable formula that should be encouraged rather than limited. At present the odds seem to favor a continuation of the system as it stands.

A second criticism has to do with the coverage of the plan. Is it as adequate as it should be? In 1955 George Meany, president of the American Federation of Labor, dismissed somewhat increased monthly rates as "insignificant gains" more than offset by changes in other provisions that made it difficult for the individual to attain to the higher benefits.[3] The principal suggestions are that the waiting period should be abolished in order to get payments out more quickly, that additional classes of workers should be brought into the system, and that in order to simplify administration, benefits should be set according to flat rates based on the income of well-defined wage groups in the working population, a common procedure in most other countries.

Third, there is an occasional charge of malingering: that the law is used to encourage vacations on pay, the drawing of unemployment benefits while a person becomes self-employed, and the like. But in most cases these are largely faults of administration rather than flaws in legislation and they are less often heard as administrative procedures improve.

Conclusions Regarding Social Insurance

Turning back to the larger questions of social policy raised at the beginning of this chapter, first, is it possible that social security could be pushed too far? The answer is clearly that it could be, since any good idea is capable of being carried to excess. Social security is not the only way to avoid future depressions and maintain purchasing power. Moreover, if the nation were to spend a disproportionate amount of money on these programs it would have less for other purposes that are equally essential, including capital reserves, investment in new productive enterprise, the provision of essential public works, and the like. As has already

[3] *The New York Times,* Apr. 18, 1955.

been suggested, therefore, the main issue in the social security debate in the future is likely to be not whether or no, but how much.

Will social security become an unbearable financial burden? The verdict depends on the answer to these questions: Will the national income be maintained at a high level? Will people retire earlier or later than now? Will payroll taxes become so high as to depress enterprise and investment? Will adequate reserves be maintained?

Will benefits be determined on an economic or on a political basis? Can overlapping programs be sorted out? Should medical and hospital costs for the aged be provided for under the insurance aspects of the social security program? Should retired people be allowed to earn more than the present limit of $1200 a year without forfeiting OASI benefits? The future of social security depends greatly on how these issues are settled.

Finally, does the long-run prognosis indicate a progressive socialization of the private insurance business? The answer appears to be that it does not. On the contrary, private pension plans through insurance companies have been stimulated by OASI operations. If there is any threat to the insurance business, therefore, it is no different from the threat to other large businesses affected with a public interest. If the insurance companies will preserve competition, reject the temptation to dominate industrial and business concerns through the great investing power they possess, avoid serious scandals and failures that would weaken public confidence, and can survive periods of depression if they should come, then it hardly seems possible that government insurance would greatly weaken private business in the same area.

EXTENSION OF THE WELFARE STATE

Turning again to the larger stage on which these dramas are being enacted, what are the possibilities of extending the social security idea to health insurance, medical services, and the like? Even more than social security insurance, these areas have been battlegrounds of public policy in recent years. The basic question underlying all such issues is whether through private, voluntary agencies, a satisfactory standard of service can be provided without the need to increase governmental responsibilities. Allied to this issue is the question of whether people will remain self-reliant and independent in the American tradition, or whether they will increasingly seek benefits "for free" through some government agency. The policy of the Department of Health, Education, and Welfare, as stated in 1956 by its Secretary, was that government should serve as a mechanism for collective action only when individual or collective private efforts cannot do the job, and second, government welfare activities should not foster dependence but should help people help themselves.[4]

[4] Marion B. Folsom, reported in *The New York Times,* July 28, 1956.

Throwing the light of historical perspective on these issues will help provide a basis for prediction. The common-law tradition that America inherited from England was one of private, family, voluntary assistance to the poor and the needy, a tradition strengthened by our belief in self-reliance and in the United States as a land of opportunity. By the middle of the nineteenth century private organizations had begun to respond to the challenge of industrialization and urbanism, and church groups took up a large part of the responsibility for individual welfare as necessary corollaries to their duties. As state and local governments entered the field it was only to control communicable diseases and to provide minimal sanitary and health services for the very poor under a limited public health program. Thus, until the early 1900s if aid to the needy was required, it was considered a private and local responsibility. Then at the beginning of the twentieth century the social-work profession was established under the influence of pioneers such as Jane Addams and provided a basis for voluntary social work that was generally superior to that of most other countries.

Alongside this development, public-welfare administration began to take place at the state level. Between 1900 and 1930, state aid to local communities advanced in areas such as poor relief, aid to the aged, to the blind, and to orphans. By the beginning of the great depression, twenty states were offering some aid to the blind, forty-five states assisted mothers with dependent children, and twelve states had enacted old-age pension laws.

But the really revolutionary change of emphasis occurred during the depression itself, for it had not been under way for very long before three fourths of all relief funds were being derived from public sources and only one fourth from private welfare agencies such as church and other voluntary groups. In 1932 President Hoover commenced a program of federal aid to the states for welfare purposes, and President Roosevelt after him greatly expanded it, arguing that one third of the nation was ill-housed, ill-fed, and ill-clothed. Then, as state and local funds for relief became exhausted, federal programs more and more filled the breach so that in a short time not only was public welfare an impressive public function but the federal aspect of it was the most impressive of all. It is against this backdrop of events that the full significance of the work of the Committee on Economic Security, which drafted the Social Security Act of 1935, is to be fully understood.

Then came World War II which disclosed the existence of malnutrition and mental disease to an extent the American people had never suspected, and the discovery led to a search for constructive remedies. The budget of the United States Public Health Service, much of which goes for federal aid to the states, was rapidly increased during this period, but the greatest increase of all in federal aid for welfare purposes was funneled into the Veterans Administration for insurance, medical services, and other welfare needs of this large segment of the population and their dependents. The next step was that in the face of a rising cost of living and an apparent shortage of doctors, nurses, and hospital facilties, organized labor and other consumer groups began to press for cheaper and more readily available medical and health services, including some form of health insurance. It was at this point that the socialized medicine issue became so prominent.

Fig. 13. Total Welfare Expenditures * and Percentage Distribution by Type, 1930, 1940, and 1950

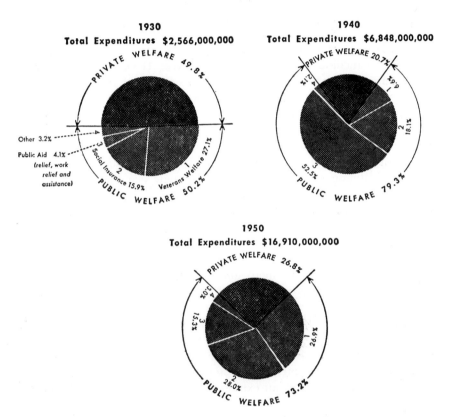

* Excluding public health and medical services.

Source: Adapted from J. Frederic Dewhurst and Associates, *America's Needs and Resources, A New Survey* (New York, Twentieth Century Fund, 1955), p. 432.

Programs for Veterans

Do the activities of the Veterans Administration in the welfare field contribute to the drift toward socialization? The Hoover Commission apparently thought that they do and suggested merging the health and other facilities of the Veterans Administration with a larger unit, the closing of unneeded hospitals, and the tightening up of services provided for veterans and especially for their families.[5] Organized veterans' groups, however, were almost solidly opposed to most of these recommendations, fearing that the Veterans Administration might become less influential and effective if its independent status were sacrificed in a merger.

By 1960 the Veterans Administration, created in 1930, was paying out about $5.5 billion a year, constituting 6.6 percent of the total federal budget, to veterans and their survivors and dependents. Under this program some 23 million veterans were receiving compensation, pensions, retirement pay, vocational and other training, and other benefits at government expense. By 1958, World War I had cost $23 billion in veterans' benefits, World War II had cost $51 billion, and the Korean War $5.3 billion. In 1959 Congress increased the size of payments and broadened coverage to include the widows of World War II veterans and Korean war veterans on the same basis as the widows of World War I veterans, at an estimated cost of $10 billion in the next forty years.

With regard to medical services, the Hoover Commission found that there were 160 veterans' hospitals with an average daily load of 100,000 patients; that nearly half of these patients were cared for in neuropsychiatric hospitals; that more than a third of all veterans suffer from service-connected illnesses or disabilities; that in a single year there is a turnover of half a million patients; that more than 3000 full-time doctors are employed in veterans' hospitals; that approximately 100,000 professional, custodial, and other personnel are needed to maintain veterans' facilities; that the average cost per patient is over $5000 annually; that the Veterans Administration provides outpatient medical and dental care for thousands of additional men and women; and that there are seventeen soldiers' homes in the nation providing housing and care for more than 16,000 men.

Although few people are aware of it, here is socialized medicine for a large sector of the population. But any proposal to reduce such services, of course, is an explosive issue because veterans are well organized and they have performed a patriotic duty for which the nation is grateful. But socialized medicine is also an explosive issue. How will this controversy be resolved, and is it possible that veterans' welfare activities are unwittingly contributing to "creeping" socialism in the medical field?

National Health Insurance

The second Hoover Commission reported that already by 1955 something like 30 million Americans were eligible to receive all or part of their medical care from federal agencies. Federal medical service, said the Task Force report, "is big business," entailing an annual expenditure of

---

[5] This issue was dealt with by both the first and second Hoover Commission reports; see especially *Task Force Report on Federal Medical Services* and *Federal Medical Services* (Washington, D.C., 1955).

over $2 billion, employing about 10 percent of all the nation's physicians, 9 percent of all dentists, and 6 percent of all graduate nurses, and controlling 13 percent of all hospital beds.[6] Moreover, twenty-six federal departments and agencies have some responsibility in the field of health, with three of these—the Department of Health, Education, and Welfare, the Defense Department, and the Veterans Administration—accounting for 90 percent of the total. The oldest federal agency in this area is the United States Public Health Service, created in 1789 and headed by the Surgeon General of the United States. With 85 percent of all federal expenditures for public-health purposes going for direct medical care, one sixth of the total population is now served wholly or in part from this source. The current issue is whether this coverage will be further extended and if so, in what form?

During the latter part of the New Deal administration a number of bills were introduced in Congress looking to some form of national health insurance. In general, the main purpose was to establish a federal-aid program with the states, somewhat on the model of social security programs, under which insured employees and their families would be entitled to medical care from doctors of their own choice, to be paid for from a fund derived from a tax on payrolls and income. The original proposals were to be on a voluntary basis but in 1945 President Truman offered a plan that would be compulsory. Although all schemes were much more limited than the British and other national plans under which medical services are available to everyone, they created a storm of opposition spearheaded by the American Medical Association on the ground that they were "socialized" medicine.

At that time only 30 million people were covered by any kind of hospital or medical insurance and most of that was of a limited sort. But stimulated by the talk of health legislation, the private insurance plans went ahead very quickly to the point where the number of persons covered was nearly doubling each year. This development caused President Truman to urge a plan that would help more people to join in these voluntary private insurance schemes but there was no tangible result.

When President Eisenhower came to the White House, the idea of federal insurance was replaced by a plan for a system of health reinsurance, the "re" in the term supposedly making it more conservative. His recommendation was to establish a federal fund of $25 million to underwrite up to 75 percent of unavoidable losses by voluntary groups (such as Blue Cross) that offer insurance for hospitalization, surgery, and medical and dental care. It was anticipated that such a program would enable private health insurance plans to cover more of the population, including people in low-income groups, farmers, and many who are poor health risks, and that the plan would become self-financing after the initial five-year period.

[6] *Task Force Report on Federal Medical Services* (Washington, D.C., 1955).

The idea was unacceptable not only to the American Medical Association, which did not hesitate to express its surprise and shock that such a proposal should have been made, but to other groups for other reasons. Farmers and organized labor declared that the plan would in no way reduce the cost of medical insurance to low-income families; the private insurance business argued that the impaired health of a large minority of the population (chiefly the indigent) made it unprofitable to insure these people and that, in addition, a federal reinsurance fund would bring the federal government into direct competition with private business.

Rebuffed, in 1955 the President offered a revised proposal along the same lines: that Congress provide incentives for private health-insurance groups to extend coverage to chronic invalids and that it authorize grants to the states to improve medical care for persons on public assistance including the disabled, the blind, and dependent children—in other words, better medical care for some of our neediest citizens. But this plan also was characterized as an entering wedge for state medicine. Consequently, in 1956 the President abandoned the idea of insurance and proposed merely to expand the construction of medical research and teaching facilities over a five-year period. Oliver Garceau's study of *The Political Life of the American Medical Association* leaves little doubt that the average doctor, despite an alleged lack of political sophistication, is an effective lobbyist when part of an organized interest group.[7] Meanwhile, private insurance plans went forward, despite rising medical costs, to the point where by 1960 more than 127 million people were covered to some extent.

By the time of the national party conventions in 1960, medical care for some 15.7 million aged persons had become a top issue of domestic policy. The Forand bill, one of several, offered insurance to the aged under the social security system for hospital care, nursing home care, and some surgical expense. So heavy was the mail in support of this measure that one Senator remarked, "Believe me, the heat is on in full blast, and we are stewing." [8] (This was April, not July.) A Republican alternative measure, supported by eight liberal Republican Senators, relied primarily on federal-aid to the states to provide health-care benefits to the aged, with the federal portion amounting to 75 percent of the limit set by each state, with a maximum allowance of $250 a year for hospitalization. Many Democrats favored the Forand bill. The Republican candidate for President was reported as favoring an alternative to the Forand bill, although the Eisenhower administration had previously decided that the time was not ripe for such legislation. The measure that finally passed in a special session of Congress increased the amount of federal funds available for state medical-care programs for aged persons on the public assistance rolls. The same law also made it possible, on a grant-in-aid basis, for the states to offer aid to medically needy elderly people who were not on relief, the standards of assistance to be set by the states themselves.

[7] Cambridge, Mass., 1941.   [8] Reported in *The New York Times*, Apr. 10, 1960.

There is little question that medical care is a major problem of public policy, especially for low-income groups and the chronically ill; but there is much room for doubt as to the best method of overcoming the difficulties. A prolonged illness can wreck the economy of an individual and a whole family. It has been estimated that 8 million families in the United States are in debt for medical care to hospitals, physicians, dentists, loan companies, and others. With 227,000 physicians as of 1957, the number of doctors available per 100,000 of the civilian population ranged from a low of 4 or 5 in some areas to a national average of 132. Americans are spending $16.4 billion a year on private medical bills, which figures out to an average of some $325 per family, with the top 10 percent spending in excess of $900 a year.

Those who favor the status quo maintain that private insurance programs will eventually take care of the need without pauperizing the population; that the extension of public responsibility would deprive the patient of his freedom of choice; that under a public program the standards and incentives of the medical profession would be eroded; that public medicine would become bureaucratic, inefficient, and extravagant; and that any weakening of resistance to socialized medicine would open the way to a full-fledged socialized system such as is found in many other countries.

On the other hand, the proponents of a national health-insurance plan point to the need to improve the health of the nation as a national resource, especially in wartime; contend that medical care has priced itself out of the average man's pocketbook; deny that a plan for insurance or reinsurance is actually socialistic; state that the present use of medical personnel is uneconomic and inefficient; and argue that the experience of other nations has not justified the dire predictions of the organized medical profession in this country.

That some solution to the problem of prolonged illness will have to be found soon, however, seems clear. Even where the best of medical care is available, the costs are often a serious burden, and the fact is that in many parts of the country the care available is far from the best because of too few doctors and facilities. And there is the additional fact, which few people realize, that the federal government is already in the medical field to the point where, as the Hoover Commission points out, it is "big business." Indeed, says a doctor who has studied this question, "the American system today is a mixture of what may be called limited State Medicine—socialization through government financing and/or control—and private practice," and he adds that of total 1954 medical expenditures amounting to $14 billion, the federal government, from tax funds, supplied some $4.5 billion.[9] The programs on which this money is spent include vocational rehabilitation; hospital, nursing-home, and convales-

[9] Max Seham, M.D., member, Committee for the Nation's Health, "The Tyranny of Labels," *The New Republic* (Feb. 28, 1955). "Unless we get rid of the phrase, 'socialized medicine,'" says Dr. Seham, "or agree upon an exact meaning for it, there will never be a meeting of the minds."

cent-home construction; public assistance grants, public health services; research on air and water pollution; mental-illness control; medical research; and medical care for the 500,000 Indians who are wards of the government. If there should be any suggestion to curtail any of these services, the groups affected would certainly make their protests heard throughout the halls of Congress.

In the whole range of business-government relationships, there is hardly a better illustration of the proposition that public responsibilities decrease with the ability of private groups to offer satisfactory services, and to increase when such services are inadequate. In the case of medical care, it is not quality that is in question, but quantity and cost.

Supplementary Reading

Burns, Eveline M., *The American Social Security System* (Boston, 1949). A textbook.

———, *Toward Social Security* (New York, 1936). An explanation of the Social Security Act and the larger issues involved.

Gagliardo, Domenico, *American Social Insurance* (New York, 1949). Also a textbook.

Kasius, Cora (ed.), *New Directions in Social Work* (New York, 1954). Includes a discussion of the part played by government.

Haber, William, and Wilbur Cohen (eds.), *Readings in Social Insurance* (New York, 1948). A series of essays.

Beveridge, William, *Social Insurance and Allied Service* (Cmd. 6404, London, H. M. Stationery Office, 1942). The famous Beveridge report.

Committee on Economic Security, *Report to the President* (Washington, D.C., 1935). The origins of the Social Security Act of 1935.

Meriam, Lewis, *Relief and Social Security* (Washington, D.C., 1946). A Brookings survey.

Riesenfeld, Stefan A., and Richard C. Maxwell, *Modern Social Legislation* (Brooklyn, N.Y., 1950). A broad review.

Dearing, Charles, *Industrial Pensions* (Washington, D.C., 1954). Private and public schemes.

Millis, H. A., and R. E. Montgomery, *Labor's Risks and Social Insurance* (New York, 1938). Volume II of *The Economics of Labor*.

Perlman, Jacob, "Changing Trends under Old-age and Survivors' Insurance, 1935-1950," *Industrial and Labor Relations Review*, Vol. 4 (Jan. 1951), pp. 173-186.

———, "The Federal Social Security Programs," *Monthly Labor Review*, Vol. 70 (Jan. 1950), pp. 1-8.

Becker, Joseph M., *Problems of Abuse in Employment Benefits* (New York, 1953). A critique of the system.

Epstein, Abraham, *Insecurity—A Challenge to America* (New York, 1936). The American and foreign systems compared.

Reed, Louis S., *Health Insurance: The Next Step in Social Insurance* (New York, 1937).

Ewing, Oscar R., *The Nation's Health: A Ten Year Program* (Washington, D.C., 1948). By an experienced government official.

Mustard, Harry S., *Government in Public Health* (New York, 1945). A Commonwealth Fund study.

Simmons, James S. (ed.), *Public Health in the World Today* (Cambridge, Mass., 1949). A comparative survey.

Eckstein, Harry, *The English Health Service* (Cambridge, Mass., 1958). Its origins, structure, and achievements.

Kelley, S., *Professional Public Relations and Political Power* (Baltimore, 1956). Contains a discussion of the AMA's opposition to the Ewing health-insurance plan.

U. S. Congress, House Committee on Ways and Means, report submitted by the Secretary of Health, Education, and Welfare on *Hospital Insurance for OASDI Beneficiaries,* committee print, April 3, 1959.

———, *Hearings,* "The Aged and the Aging in the United States" (86th Cong., 1st Sess., June 16–18, 1959).

———, *Hearings,* "Hospital, Nursing Home, and Surgical Benefits for OASDI Beneficiaries" (86th Cong., 1st Sess., July 13–17, 1959).

Ross, James S., *The National Health Service in Great Britain* (New York, 1952). How the British system works.

Garceau, Oliver, *The Political Life of the American Medical Association* (Cambridge, Mass., 1941). How pressure groups work.

United States Commission on Intergovernmental Relations, *Federal Aid to Public Health* (Washington, D.C., 1955).

———, *Federal Aid to Welfare* (Washington, D.C., 1955).

Commission on Organization of the Executive Branch of the Government (second Hoover Commission), *Federal Medical Services* (Washington, D.C., 1955).

———, *Task Force Report on Medical Services* (Washington, D.C., 1955).

Commission on Organization of the Executive Branch of the Government (first Hoover Commission), *Social Security, Education, Indian Affairs* (Washington, D.C., 1949).

———, *Task Force Report on Public Welfare* (Washington, D.C., 1949).

PART IX

FUTURE
OF THE
BUSINESS-
GOVERNMENT
RELATIONSHIP

23

TOWARD A SCIENCE OF
PUBLIC POLICY

The need for a science of public policy; principles and good judgment; science and art of public policy; guidelines from comparative experience of other nations: the future of competition, economic planning, public ownership and operation, major regulation, social welfare programs, the labor movement, the farm population, and cooperative associations; basic principles: control, freedom, and the concept of power.

The objective of a study of business and government is to develop a science of public policy in order to establish the kind of economic life people want within a framework of freedom. The need for formulating such a body of instrumental knowledge is greater in the United States than elsewhere because we differ from most other nations in the degree to which private enterprise is possible. An almost miraculous ability to run our own economic affairs without an excess of governmental control makes it unusually necessary that we understand how our decisions as individual enterprisers affect public policy. We must, therefore, master the difficult art and science of cause-and-effect relationships in the area of social control so as to keep and improve what we have and attain more of what we want.

The fact is that in a modern, technological, industrialized society it becomes harder all the time to forecast the effect of decisions that impinge on public policy. A thoughtful economist has recently noted that already in our national economy the pressures working toward unbalance are stronger than those working toward balance, that private economic decision is steadily giving ground to public economic decision, that pressure groups have catapulted us along the road to political centralization, and that the drift of public economic control in the United States seems, in the eyes of many informed observers, to be inevitably toward some sort of administered state.[1]

---

[1] George A. Steiner, *Government's Role in Economic Life* (New York, 1953), p. 386.

Another discerning student of the business-government relationship has told us what we must do to retain our distinctiveness and strengthen the forces of self-determination. Politicians must become statesmen, as they sometimes do under pressure; voters must support statesmanlike policies, as they sometimes do even now; and—hardest of all—men in their everyday dealings must conduct their affairs with an eye to the collective consequences of their deeds. The degree of liberty that we have depends on the degree to which individuals and groups are willing and able to shoulder a broad responsibility for their actions.[2]

Is the knowledge we need a science susceptible of expression in the form of reliable principles making prediction and control possible? Or is it an art compounded partly of principle and partly of philosophy? In fact, it is both. We must develop principles as a method of analysis and classification so as to provide our policymakers and administrators in both the private and public segments of the economy with these indispensable tools; at the same time, in the application of these principles we must recognize that decision-making, in legislation as in administration, involves the art of combining diverse elements in just the right proportions to achieve a desired and proper end. Consequently men of action must be artists as well as scientists in determining the goals of public policy and how to achieve them.

Yet another economist has recognized this truth and states it with his customary skill: The right principle is to respect all principles, to take them all fully into account, and then to use good judgment as to how far to follow one or another in the case at hand. There is always a principle—plausible and, within limits, even sound—to justify any possible line of action and, of course, the opposite of any line that is decided on. The proper course is the one that achieves the best balance among the various sectors of the economy and the role of government relative to them, and the art that distinguishes both individuals and institutions is the degree to which good judgment is brought to bear in the achievement of the necessary balance.[3]

In the present state of human knowledge, science enables us to analyze significant problems, marshal and order the facts, and set forth alternative kinds of action; and, within limits and varying with the subject matter, science also makes it possible to predict probable outcomes if one or another alternative policy is followed in a given case. But by no means is this the whole of the matter: once these steps have been taken, a decision must be made between possible courses of action, the plan chosen must be instrumented, controls must be set up to determine the degree to which predictions are or are not being fulfilled, and corrections and adjustments must be made in the program as it proceeds. This second complex of

[2] John M. Clark, *Guideposts in Time of Change* (New York, 1949), p. 200.
[3] Frank H. Knight, "The Role of Principles in Economics and Politics," *American Economic Review*, Vol. 41, No. 1 (Mar. 1951), p. 6.

responsibilities is not the role for which science is fitted. As Adam Smith would have said (and here he was speaking of economics), this is the art of the legislator and the administrator.

GUIDELINES FROM COMPARATIVE EXPERIENCE

Because of our success in many fields, we have tended to ignore the experience of other nations, even to being contemptuous of the suggestion that a study of their experience could be useful to us. But such an attitude is either a mark of chauvinism or an admission of intellectual immaturity that ill becomes us. To identify and to learn how to use all the cause-and-effect relationships that constitute a science of public policy, we must broaden our laboratories in a search for all relevant experience, combinations of circumstances, and kinds of responses.

A nation that is strikingly like the United States in its business-government relations is Canada, partly because we have influenced one another, the circumstances of pioneering a new continent have produced marked similarities, and the age of our institutions is about the same. But most significant of all, both nations have recognized the importance of enforcing competition and have had antitrust laws on their statute books from early times—Canada since 1889 and the United States since 1890. Until recently, no other nation had recognized competition as a major policy or has provided the basic legislation and enforcement machinery by which to prevent the growth of domestic monopolies and foreign trade cartels.[4]

In Great Britain, failure to control monopoly is a principal reason that socialization came to that nation after World War II, and it was only in 1948, long after the horse had been stolen, that an antimonopoly law was passed and a commission set up to enforce it. In most other countries the approach to monopoly has been either to legalize it or to tolerate it and then try to legislate against the objectionable aspects of it—a method, it goes without saying, that only slightly affects the monopolies themselves. Some nations have had antitrust laws at one time or another and later have either repealed or ignored them. Thus France opened the way for cartels in 1884 and legalized them in 1926; Mexico substituted government approval of monopoly proposals for a former antitrust law

[4] Much of the evidence to support this statement is found in E. H. Chamberlin (ed.), *Monopoly and Competition and Their Regulation* (New York, 1954); Temporary National Economic Committee, *Regulation of Economic Activities in Foreign Countries* (Washington, D.C., 1941); U. S Department of State, *Foreign Legislation Concerning Monopoly and Cartel Practices*, report to the subcommittee on Monopoly of the Select Committee on Small Business of the U. S. Senate (82d Cong., 2d Sess., Subcommittee Print No. 5, 1952); and Social and Economic Council of the United Nations, *Analysis of Governmental Measures Relating to Restrictive Business Practices* (mimeo., Mar. 30, 1953).

in 1931; Argentina abandoned her antitrust legislation in 1946; Brazil has never enforced hers at all; in Australia, New Zealand, and South Africa such laws have long been a dead letter.

The tolerance or active support of domestic monopolies by many countries has been exceeded only by their approval of cartels, which, as mercantilist doctrine used to contend, become instruments of national power. The result is that outside of Canada and the United States, this form of international monopoly dominates industry and trade.[5] Between domestic monopoly and international cartels there is, of course, the closest kind of connection: Unless domestic markets are monopolized, international cartels may be threatened by competition at home; and unless domestic monopoly is protected by tariffs and high shipping costs, they may be undermined by competition from abroad.

Future of Competition

There are, however, some encouraging developments. In 1948, Britain created a Monopolies Commission with a staff of over fifty; progress is slow but what has been done has been done well. The significant thing is that although the Labor government nationalized several industries, it nevertheless thought it in the public interest to try to enforce competition in that part of the economy (the major part of it, in fact) that is still privately owned and operated.

Sweden also has passed an outstanding antitrust law since World War II, stressing advance scrutiny of mergers by a Registration and Investigation Office, followed by full publicity as a means of educating the public and discouraging undesirable concentrations of power. The law seems to be working well and it is possible that we in the United States might learn something useful from that experience.

Although a number of other countries have shown a new interest in the problem, few have done much about it and, in general, socialism has grown faster than the reverse. Wilcox summarizes the results of postwar reconsiderations of monopoly by saying that although the new laws seldom prohibit combinations or cartels as such, they do try to ensure that monopolistic powers shall not be abused by requiring the registration of cartels, the collection of information by a government agency, scrutiny by the national legislature if the report is adverse, and in some cases, *ad hoc* investigations if the public interest is sufficiently involved.[6] But study and report are not sanctions and there are few of these. Except as a trend still in embryo may be developing, therefore, there is no great reason to be optimistic about the future of competition on a world-wide basis.

Against this background, we should be able to make certain deductions and to arrive at some interesting conclusions as to a proper policy

---

[5] Clair Wilcox, *Public Policies toward Business* (Homewood, Ill., 1955), p. 768, and *A Charter for World Trade* (New York, 1949), Chap. 10.

[6] Clair Wilcox, *Public Policies toward Business, op. cit.*, p. 771.

relative to competition in the United States. We have apparently assumed that competition can be neglected without damaging the free-enterprise system with its high profits and widespread private ownership. But experience elsewhere shows conclusively that competition cannot survive without help, and that if it is not enforced, monopoly opens the way for socialism. The logical inference, therefore, is that if we want to retain private enterprise, the one indispensable condition is to enforce the antitrust laws. Though the remedy may seem like an old-fashioned dose of castor oil, such a course is often more effective than some of our modern and more complicated procedures.

If dogmatism is ever justified, it is on the proposition that monopoly leads to socialism. If the trend thesis (domestic as well as international) is a valid one, then the inescapable conclusion is that the United States will eventually eliminate competition and embrace socialism. But if, on the other hand, trends can be controlled by a collective act of free will, which is more in accord with the American tradition, then obviously we must take a good look at the direction in which we are going and then redouble our efforts to strengthen competition.

Future of Economic Planning

A second finding is that everywhere conservatives and socialists alike are deliberately formulating the goals of their economy and the methods of achieving them—in other words, there is increasing emphasis on economic planning. Nor, for reasons that have been noted, is the United States a laggard in this occupation. World tensions today are due largely to differences in economic ideology; technology makes orderly arrangements imperative; we must sometimes choose between defense and civilian requirements; social, economic, and political organization is complex and must be studied to be understood and kept on a proper track; and widespread public control increases the degree of public decision-making on the part of any government.

In a list of five guides to future policy, Professor Steiner accords first place to defining our goals more clearly, arguing that if somehow new guides to the evolution of economic policy are not worked out to replace those that are outgrown, the pressures for rapidly expanding governmental economic controls may well get out of hand.[7]

There is an interesting variety in the methods adopted by democratic countries since World War II to plan their economic policies. Such methods range all the way from a rather complete control as in the case of bombed-out nations to the kind of limited economic study that in the United States is the responsibility of the Council of Economic Advisers. Needless to say, most of the underdeveloped nations also try to plan their

---

[7] Steiner, *op. cit.*, pp. 386–387. The other four guidelines he mentions are balance, a single base for the development of strategic economic actions, determination of the ranges of cost, and delineation of ranges of public action.

economy even when their methods are comparatively crude, because if they fail to set goals, priorities, and balances, the result is likely to be an impossible financial muddle that threatens their entire program. This kind of planning may be more or less complete and fully controlled, or, on the other hand, it may be of a moderate kind based to a considerable degree on voluntary action.[8]

The Netherlands, faced after World War II with the loss of colonies, the ravages of war, and a shortage of capital, set up a planning board with a substantial degree of power to consider the economy as a whole. Denmark created an Office of the Price Directorate with power to regulate prices, wages, interest, and dividends; to specify what goods shall be produced; to determine what new ventures shall be started; and to prepare annual budgets governing investment, employment, production, consumption, and foreign trade. Britain, on the other hand, despite a Labor government pledged to socialization, was content with a small cabinet staff committee on planning with powers and duties that differed little from those of our own Council of Economic Advisers. Although this body might have issued orders to private employers as to production quotas, it concentrated instead on the goals of full employment, an expansion of social services, the reduction of inequality, and the fostering of export trade, and then tried to secure a balance among these various factors. Though they called their program socialism, the methods of the British Labor party were thoroughly democratic.

Now that we in the United States have also decided to chart our course more rationally than prior to the passage of the Employment Act of 1946, future debate in this country is likely to turn less on whether planning should be undertaken at all and more on what and how to plan.

Future of Public Ownership

In western Europe and in Great Britain public enterprise was rapidly extended after World War II. This may be a temporary phenomenon, of course, due to the need to rebuild the economy and to match the centralized methods of competitor nations; it is still too early to be sure but it is not likely that public ownership in those areas will be very much reduced in the years ahead short of an about-face in trends. Professor Friedmann, on the basis of a world-wide survey, concludes that the main reasons, singly or in combination, for the growth of public enterprise are limited private capital, defense and strategic considerations, monopoly services such as public utilities, and socialist philosophy. However, in the majority of cases, he says, "a blend of political and practical factors has been the determining motive" for the creation of public economic enterprises.[9]

---

[8] As a result of heading the United Nations technical assistance program in Turkey in 1953-1954, the author concluded that it is entirely feasible to determine goals, priorities, and balances in many underdeveloped nations with due regard to democratic principles and free enterprise.

[9] W. Friedmann (ed.), *The Public Corporation* (Toronto, 1954), pp. 542-545.

In France, the motivation is at least partly ideological, for the preamble to the constitution directly declares that "Any enterprise, the conduct of which possesses, or acquries, the characteristic features of a public national service or a factual monopoly, shall become the property of the community." The two great categories nationalized were first, electricity, gas, and the exploitation of mineral fuels, all of which are now run by public corporations; and second, certain banks, including the central bank, and insurance companies, that are still run as joint stock companies but with the state as the only shareholder.[10] The reasons for nationalizing in this form are interesting: the corporate device was chosen over the ordinary government department in order not to increase the functions of the state itself, nor to strengthen a system that would subject basic industries to a civil service regime or expose them to a fiscal monopoly. French nationalization is syndicalist in nature in that public enterprises so treated are under the control of producers and consumers who are directly interested in the enterprise in question.

In Italy, also, there was an extensive addition to the public category following World War II, with about half of all productive enterprise now directly or indirectly controlled by the government. Nor is this merely a matter of scattered and unconnected holdings; rather, through its part ownership of some private companies and its outright ownership of others, the state exercises "a decisive influence" in the economy, including such vital industries as shipping, iron and steel, and the exploitation of minerals and fuels.[11]

In the Scandinavian countries, in the British commonwealths of Australia and New Zealand, and in Federal Republic of Germany fresh nationalizations have not been so pronounced since the war as in some other nations, but by American standards public ownership was already substantial prior to the war, the main concentrations being in utilities, transportation, banking, insurance, and housing. In the so-called underdeveloped nations, public ownership has been considerably extended, because as a rule private investors are slow to come forth due to the fear of risk, high taxes, or possibly expropriation. As these nations become economically stronger and more entrepreneurs and business managers become available, it is possible—although not everywhere certain—that the private sector of the economy may expand and public ownership will be progressively abandoned.

The lesson for us is that if we would check the growth of public ownership and operation in this country, we must first, in some way, avoid the catastrophes of war and depression; in addition, private management must assume its full responsibilities for entrepreneurship and risk-taking, resist the temptation to concentrate its power, and be scrupulously fair in its treatment of workers and consumers—in other words, private management needs to be constantly mindful of its role as trustee in the public interest. A belief in private enterprise is an indispensable basic require-

[10] *Ibid.*, pp. 128-129.   [11] *Ibid.*, p. 546.

ment, but in the long run practical power and how it is used are more determinative of the course of a national economy than the belief system of the majority of the people. It lies in the hands of our economic leaders, therefore, to chart the future course for the nation in so far as public or private ownership and operation are concerned.

Future of Major Regulation

It has been noted that the United States is distinctive in the number of independent commissions we have for the regulation of public utilities, transportation, and the like. Other countries have fewer or none at all because elsewhere public utilities are largely publicly owned and hence need no regulation. In Great Britain there were once a Railway and Canal Commission, created ten years earlier than our own Interstate Commerce Commission, and a Railway Rates Tribunal, but they were abolished in the 1930s because their work was not wholly satisfactory. Furthermore, independent regulatory commissions are not consonant with the principles of cabinet government.[12] Later there were electricity commissioners and road-haulage regulators but these also were abolished and for the same reason, plus the additional fact of nationalization. Most other industrial nations have followed the British pattern, preferring the more simple method of operating public utilities and other public services themselves instead of trying to regulate them under a system of private ownership and public supervision.

The implications of this experience are that if we would avoid public ownership and operation to an extent greater than we already have, and would prove that we can continue to be distinctive in relying chiefly on private enterprise in this sector of the economy, then not only must we reconcile ourselves to continued regulation but we must also make a better job of the regulatory process.

Future of Social Welfare Programs

Police-power programs to protect the public's health, safety, and morals, and other social welfare programs, are naturally much older in European nations and in Britain than they are in the United States, but most of them have in common with ours the fact that they have been pushed primarily by organized labor. It is a safe assumption, therefore, that the more influential labor becomes as an organized political force, the more will social legislation be emphasized as an aspect of public policy. Programs such as the Beveridge Plan in Great Britain of social insurance from birth to death are more than a symptom of the aroused conscience of the community; they also show that organized labor is

---

[12] Since the prime minister is responsible for every part of the government, independence is not permissible.

trying to make economic and social gains through government and the taxing power as well as around the bargaining table. During the New Deal period in the United States, for example, the seed bed of most social and economic legislation—the Social Security Act, the Wagner Act, public housing legislation, and wage and hour legislation—was organized labor working in cooperation with the Department of Labor and other groups.

It is not that labor is more socially sensitive than other parts of the population; it is rather that labor has a direct interest in protecting labor markets and working conditions, providing for sickness, old age, and unemployment, improving the educational and health facilities of the nation, and providing adequate housing for families that must depend on wages for their income.

A comparison of protective legislation in the United States with that of other countries seems to justify two conclusions relative to the United States: First, although social legislation appeared in Britain, Germany, and other European nations a full half century before it did here, the United States has made remarkable progress in catching up.[13] And second, if the American labor movement continues to grow in economic and political influence, it will be a perennially difficult problem to decide where economic measures such as wage increases and social measures such as expanded social security benefits should be employed, in what proportions, and what the effect on the economy will be.

The temptation is to adopt political solutions because of their appeal to the wider public as well as to labor, but when such solutions become an undue financial burden on the nation and imperil the incentives of the free-enterprise system, as they may, then of course they should be avoided. And who will make the decisions? Here again is the need for good judgment and a sense of trusteeship in the public interest. Social legislation is not always desirable simply because it is social legislation; before it is wholly or even chiefly beneficial, it must always be squared with considerations that affect other parts of the economic and social fabric of the nation. The future of social welfare programs in this country, therefore, depends on the degree of economic and political insight that can be developed among our national leaders as well as the courage they may possess to say "No" to proposals that in other nations, rightly or wrongly, have been adopted.

Future of the Labor Movement

In other industrial nations, organized labor has become highly political, usually having its own political party which is sometimes also the majority party. The political orientation of labor varies, but in general it may be described as social democratic, or just left of center, favoring a limited amount of economic planning and public ownership, compulsory

[13] In the case of Great Britain, pure food and drugs law, 1860; Health and Morals of Apprentices Act, 1802; unemployment insurance, 1912.

collective bargaining, ample social services, progressive incomes taxes, and the like. In fact, an analysis of the programs of most of these parties when they come to office shows few departures from the programs of our two major political parties in the United States since 1933. Remember that as a new nation, the United States started with what at the time were radical assumptions relative to public education, universal manhood suffrage, prohibitions against titles of nobility, and the like, whereas most European nations, at least, have had to work hard just to reach the point from which we started out on the road to democracy.

Thus the labor movement in this country has had less of a challenge than similar movements in older countries, and it seems safe to say that it will not become political to the same degree. There are, however, a number of provisos: prosperity in this country must be widely distributed; children in lower income groups must be free to rise on the economic ladder; class differences, and especially social differences, must be avoided so that labor may continue to consider itself an equal among peers; free public education must offer the same opportunities as privately financed education; freedom to bargain collectively must not be restricted; discriminatory legislation against labor must not be passed when employers might with equal justice be legislated against; one or both of the two major parties must continue to show the same degree of sympathetic concern for labor's problems as they do for the problems of other economic interests; politics must be relatively aboveboard and free from domination by the "money power"; the media of communication and public education such as press, radio, and television must be available to labor on equal terms with others; and the economy must be kept on a reasonably even keel so as to avoid the extremes of the business cycle.

Our traditions being what they are, most workers in the United States feel that they are middle class and capitalist rather than proletarian, and consequently there is not likely to develop a separate labor party in this country as long as most or all of the conditions mentioned above are achieved and maintained. But equally, as members of the great middle class but with distinctive interests, labor will remain a powerful political force and any political leader who hopes to secure a majority in national elections must take these facts into account.

Future of Agriculture

Many European nations rely on their farming population at least to the same extent that we do, and generally a good deal more because few industrial nations are as self-sufficient as the United States from the standpoint of their food supply. In western Europe the farming population is always among the most stable—with long traditions and emphasis on the family-size farm—and agricultural surpluses are rare. In the United States, by contrast, farming tends to become industrialized, not only in the methods used and the living conditions developed on most commercial farms, but also in financing, as in the case of the agricultural corporation that controls huge tracts of land on which crops are more manufactured than raised. Consequently the economic situation of the farmer himself is more of a problem here than elsewhere: he is increasingly dependent on the industrial sector of the economy for his daily and professional needs, he may easily become unemployed, and he may produce more than he can sell at a profit.

To a far greater extent than most Americans realize, in many Western countries the government is chief exporter and importer of foodstuffs. In the British Commonwealth, for example, shipments of basic commodities are made to the mother country on long-term contracts arranged by state trading companies. Under this arrangement, basic crops such as wool, meat, and butter produced in New Zealand, Australia, or South Africa are handled through a centralized pool; both domestic and export prices are fixed, and producer-farmers share in the returns. Even in Canada, the Wheat Board monopolizes the wheat trade and the Agricultural Prices Support Board may set minimum prices for other food products.

In Scandinavia and in most other western European nations there are various forms of government control over agricultural imports and exports, sometimes accompanied by government subsidies, price fixing pegged to the cost of living, and other measures designed to guarantee parity income to the farm population. Except for export-import controls, much of this is rather similar to the agricultural programs in the United States since 1933, and the result is to hold prices paid to farmers at levels higher than those obtaining in other parts of the world.

For American agricultural policy, the implications are plain: if we would expand our outlet for farm products and thus reduce agricultural surpluses, we must encourage freer trade through international agencies such as the proposed Organization for Trade Cooperation. At the same time we must re-examine our domestic farm policies to see if we are as guilty as others of subsidy payments, price fixing, quotas, and crop restrictions that act as a brake on world trade.

Future of Cooperative Associations

It has been noted in this study that producer and consumer cooperatives play an important role in most nations throughout the world. If their increasing strength elsewhere is a faithful indicator, then we may expect them to gain here also, although perhaps not to the same extent.

Some factors that will stimulate their future expansion are these: the growth of monopoly in food processing, merchandising, and retailing, and a similar trend in areas where the farmer buys; the espousal of cooperatives by labor organizations, which is their chief source of support in countries such as Great Britain and Belgium; the development of a skilled corps of managers for cooperatives on a level comparable to that found in equivalent private businesses; and the development of strong neighborhood allegiances to supply the firm democratic base that cooperatives must have. In other words, if cooperatives continue to gain strength in the United States as they are likely to, it will be due to the conditions that prevail in the economy.

BASIC PRINCIPLES IN THE BUSINESS-GOVERNMENT RELATIONSHIP

Let us turn back now to the matter of a reliable body of principle to guide national decision-making in the business-government relationship.

First, it may be suggested that in the interests of freedom and human welfare, government and the economy should properly be thought of as separate institutions, vying and cooperating with one another but never joining so closely as to become a master, over-all institution as is the case, for example, in the Soviet Union. A single institution controlled by a single group invariably leads to abuses and excesses, as any monopoly sooner or later must, and in addition, stifles dissent, independence, and initiative, which are the conditions of progress. The result is to deprive a nation of its essential freedoms.

On the other hand, there is an equal danger in going too far in the opposite direction, as political reactionaries are prone to do, and assuming that government is something to be put down as much as possible and its functions kept to a minimum. Sometimes, in the net effect of such attitudes, there is little difference between avowed anarchists and stanch reactionaries, because both invite a breakdown of the social order as tensions mount and government is too weak to cope with them. In this connection, the ruminations of a *New York Times* special correspondent, dealing with the economic policy of the Eisenhower administration, bear repeating: [14]

> . . . President Eisenhower's team proved to be "modern." . . . But their very modernity prevented them from doing some of the things they would have liked to do. . . . They found out what government was like, and they decided to live with it. The result was an economy prosperous beyond all previous measures. But it was an economy otherwise not markedly different from the structure that a lot of Republicans had once thought was a Frankenstein monster. Big Government not only proved tough to cut down, but rather useful.

On the question of introducing new economic controls over the economy, Professor Steiner has drawn up a set of nine principles that should govern in the formulation of so important an aspect of public policy: [15] (1) Government economic control should be democratic both in its initiation and its operation. (2) Before individual economic freedom is circumscribed, a convincing showing of advantage to the public interest must be

---

[14] Edwin L. Dale, Jr., *The New York Times*, July 24, 1956.
[15] Steiner, *op. cit.*, pp. 392–401

demonstrated. (3) When the government decides to produce social goods and services there should be a showing that community costs and benefits can be equated.[16] (4) Controls should be consonant with and introduced within the framework of the free-enterprise system. (5) The objectives of the control mechanism should be clearly stated and constantly scrutinized. (6) The attempted solution should be tailored to the need, being neither larger nor less than the problem it is designed to meet; further, it should be part of a rational program. (7) Any control should be strong enough to assure compliance and achieve its objectives. (8) The burden of proof should be on those who advocate new controls, for the assumption of a self-regulating market is that few controls are necessary. (9) Finally, wherever possible, indirect rather than direct controls should be given preference.

As thought-provoking as such formulations are, however, it will be appreciated that they are not meant to constitute a kitful of stereotypes to be automatically applied, like a pattern to a piece of cloth. It is here that the quality of judgment, referred to at the outset of this chapter, comes again into the picture.

A second over-all proposition is that by all odds the most important concept in the business-government relationship is power, which is the means by which group ends are accomplished. So defined, power means money, organization, influence, subservience, manipulation, achievement, and abuse. Properly used, power is a necessary and legitimate tool, but it may also become a monstrosity. The justification for power is found in the principle that to achieve a particular goal, all elements necessary to its accomplishment must be available in the right number and proportions. The same principle applies whether the goal is to plant a garden, construct an apartment building, administer a law, or negotiate a treaty. A companion principle is that if people are to do as they please within the limits of a similar freedom for others, if they are to be free to experiment, to protest, and to remain economically independent if they wish, then power must be widely distributed among many people, groups of people, and segments of the population. How is power to be distributed in this manner? To each according to his need and his ability, and to none too much.

In addition to safeguarding freedom, distributed power also is more efficient than monopolized power because people work better when they are free to draw on their inherent abilities and to grow under increasing responsibility instead of being restricted within a pattern of uniformity by the controls that are needed in any large organization. When many individuals in many medium-sized organizations are thus encouraged, the

[16] He also introduces the concept of marginal utility here: the government should increase the production of social goods (assuming a community demand) no further than the point where the marginal social benefit is the same from all governmental expenditures, per dollar of the expenditure, and is equal to the marginal social cost. *Ibid.*, p. 394.

total achievement surpasses the total achievement of concentrated power operating at a lower level of unit efficiency, but more units. Yet another aspect of the power concept is that progress results from a challenge, a sense of struggle, hard to the point of exhilaration but not to the point of discouragement. Where that point occurs differs with the individual, of course, but in general the challenge is at its optimum if a man has self-determination, as in owning his own business, and is low if he is merely a mechanism automatically responding to signals originating in the front office. Independence, struggle, self-determination, and freedom are the conditions that determine the spirit of a people, and it is spirit on which everything else depends.

Yet another factor relative to power is balance. Each individual must have the degree of power he needs for effective performance; if he has too much or too little, there will be failure or strain at some point or other, the whole arrangement will be thrown out of gear, and the effectiveness of the total operation reduced. A corollary is that since all parts of a system are integrally related, peculiar behavior in one will affect the activity of others, as when depressed conditions in agriculture affect the production and sale of farm machinery. From the functional standpoint alone, this interdependence is enough to justify the trusteeship role of men and women in positions of power, for injury to the public interest winds up as injury to the individual interest.

A final proposition relating to the concept of power grows logically out of those that have been mentioned: if distributed power is to be efficient, those who possess it must learn to act voluntarily and of their own initiative as trustees of the interest of all, because their failure in this respect leads to increased government control and thence to regimentation. Under communism, for example, men act according to orders handed down from the top party and planning officials who assign to each group and to each man within it his appropriate role. Thus the cement of Soviet Russian society is authority. In the United States we do it a little differently: we make use of authority when we must in order to maintain a balance of economic factors, but to a limited degree only, because for the most part we have learned to recognize our duty and to do it of our own free will. Thus voluntarism, a much-used word in this country, is the cement of a free society. If this cement should ever lose its staying qualities, we may look to the appearance of an authoritarian regime to take the place of freedom, both for the individual and for enterprise as well.

These are some of the factors that enter into the formulation of a science of public policy. There are doubtless more yet to be discovered, analyzed, and made applicable. If the present study serves as an aid in that direction, it will have accomplished a part of its purpose. In the end, of course, men and women must formulate their own philosophy of social control to help them become aware of, and sensitive to, the relationships that constitute the business-government complex. It is this awareness and sensitiveness that differentiates the pedestrian from the statesmanlike administrator of a business, a government, or some other group activity.

Supplementary Reading

Hoover, Calvin B., *The Economy, Liberty, and the State* (New York, Twentieth Century Fund, 1959). A balanced evaluation of comparative economic systems.

Heilbroner, Robert, *The Future as History* (New York, 1960). The historical currents of our times and the direction in which they are taking America.

Burns, Arthur F., "Progress Towards Economic Stability," *American Economic Review*, Vol. L, No. 1 (Mar. 1960).

Steiner, George A., *Government's Role in Economic Life* (New York, 1953). The final chapter is entitled "Guides for Evolving Public Economic Policies."

American Economic Association, *Papers and Proceedings, 1945, American Economic Review*, Supplement. The views of professional economists on the economic functions of government and their relative importance under modern conditions.

MacIver, Robert M., *The Web of Government* (New York, 1947). A prize-winning book dealing with the power concept and the role of government.

————, *Democracy and the Economic Challenge* (New York, 1952). Chapter 5 is entitled "The Meaning of America."

Clark, John M., *Social Control of Business* (New York, 2d ed., 1939). Chapter 1, "Introduction and Fundamental Conceptions"; Chapter 29, "Control and Economic Law"; Chapter 30, "Can Democratic Control Succeed?"

————, *Guideposts in Time of Change* (New York, 1949). Chapter 7, "Changing Balances: Uncommon Requirements for the Common Man."

————, *Alternative to Serfdom* (New York, 1948). Chapter 1, "Wanted: A Balanced Society"; Chapter 5, "Toward a Society of Responsible Individuals in Responsible Groups."

————, *Economic Institutions and Human Welfare* (New York, 1957).

Lippmann, Walter, *The Good Society* (New York, 1937). How to reconcile a free-enterprise system and democratic controls by government.

Mannheim, Karl, *Freedom, Power, and Democratic Planning* (New York, 1950). On effecting desirable balances.

Russell, Bertrand, *Authority and the Individual* (New York, 1949). Lecture 6, "Individual and Social Ethics."

Wright, David McCord, *Democracy and Progress* (New York, 1948). Chapter 11, "Three Plans"; Chapter 12, "The Future of Democratic Progress."

Douglas, Paul H., *Ethics in Government* (Cambridge, Mass., 1952). Distillation of the report of the Committee on Ethics in Government, U. S. Senate, 1951.

INDEX OF CASES

INDEX